AT LAS

Rough

The NTS interviews with Francesca Gavin, 2016-2021

Version

Interviews

Introduction

Most books on art and music either focus on the surface or the serious. There are illustrated books bringing together record covers by visual artists and there are academic tomes on the interdisciplinary influence of the different mediums. They are filled with people like John Cage, Arnold Schoenberg, Nam June Paik and Andy Warhol. The focus is often very male, very white and very Western. When I began my radio show on the East London-based online radio station NTS, the aim was to redirect the conversation. To recalibrate the relationship between art and music, effortlessly bringing artists of colour and women into the boy's club.

The name 'Rough Version' originally came from my old blog. It was inspired by 'rough books' – the exercise books used in primary school for practise scribblings that would be written out in more polished final form. The rough version before the final copy. If my writing and interviews in magazines and newspapers was the polished product, Rough Version would be a space for notes, thoughts and something less formal. It was a clear title to use when I began doing the monthly show in 2016.

Talking about art can be boring, elitist, overly academic and obtuse. Art language often takes you further away from an artist rather than can give a sense of who they are and the actual experience of looking at their work. Doing something for NTS shifted that. Artists who would avoid interviews all agreed. Talking about music rather than purely about their work meant people let their barriers down. Music frees.

Wolfgang Tillmans was the first artist to agree to come into the studio for the show. Then on the cusp of releasing his first record, he was open, personal and happy to support the station. Everyone I have on is a fan of NTS, or quickly became one. The hour-long show has a repeated format – an introduction to the artist, some questions of the work interspersed with three or four song choices by the artist to discuss. Sometimes artists bring in things they have made or use in their work. Sometimes they share things they listen to in the studio. Often it is just music that inspires them.

Many students have gone to art school with the hope of following in the footsteps of John Lennon, Chuck D or David Byrne and entering music. The artists in this book all focused on the visual but many had a big toe in the aural. Art and music have overlapping and often different audiences. The sensory connection and language around each subject are different. These conversations exist in the space between.

The show also provided a chance to dive deeper into archival work – something almost all the shows end with. (These extra sections are not collected here but are an excuse alone to look up the archive on NTS online). It was a chance to research and listen to the music that appeared on records with covers created by people like William Eggleston or Robert Longo. An excuse to trainspot and share the tracks at the back of Adrien Piper's iconic film 'Funk Lessons' (1983) or Rineke Dijkstra's 'The Buzz Club' (1996-7) – a process which involved a combination of placing an ear against the screen, Shazam and a lot of internet searching. It was also an opportunity to look at artists that were strongly influential on music – the artist Pedro Bell who invented and drove the entire ethos of Funkadelic or composers like Eduard Nikolayevich Artemyev or Wendy Carlos, whose soundtracks were fundamental to the work of Tarkovsky and Kubrick respectively.

Translating media always has its flaws and benefits. Radio is conversational – and Rough Version less formal than most. A couple of artists chose not to be part of this book and remain as audio – which I totally understand and respect. When creating this book, conversations were slightly edited for legibility. We tweaked the subconscious use of kind of, like, you know and so. The aim was to remain as close as possible to the original audio – while also maintaining respect to the intelligence and originality of the artists' words. In text, clarity is key.

People think the digital archive of the internet is permanent and it is clearly not. (Try looking up articles from before 2005 and you'll be very disappointed). After six years and counting, it was clear that these conversations deserved to be saved. That the relationship these artists have with music was progressive and inspiring. There is a precedent for this archive – Jeanne Seigel's 'Art Talk' which collected her conversations with artists in the early 1980s, often made for her public radio show. I hope that my questions are as insightful and relevant – and that they inspire people to search out the music and artworks discussed here. As Shakespeare put it into the mouth of Cleopatra, "Give me some music; music, moody food/Of us that trade in love."

Wolfgang Tillmans

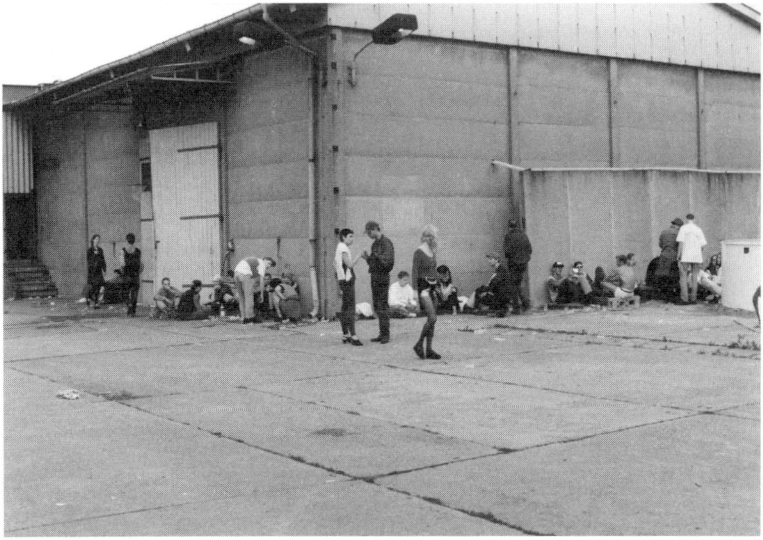

Outside Planet, view, 1992.

15.12.16

Hi. You're listening to Rough Version on NTS. I'm here with Wolfgang Tillmans, who is kindly my first guest on the show. Wolfgang you may know better for his photographic work and artwork, he's done everything from film, to print pieces displayed in exceptionally interesting ways shown at everywhere from the Serpentine to Osaka. He won the Turner Prize in the year 2000. You studied in Bournemouth I read, which made me laugh a lot. And you're here, how are you Wolfgang?

I'm good. I'm a little bit sleepy, but very relieved, because I literally just now released the visual album version of the EP this week. It's always a last-minute rush of getting every detail right. And I've never done such an ambitious video project. This one is 27 minutes, six song film.

I find it really interesting because obviously a lot of your work has been drawn out of club culture or your own experience of music. Do you want to tell me a little bit about how you've been working with the different processes? Now that you're experimenting with other media beyond the photographic, that you're more well known for.

I've been flinging with video and audio for a long time. It's been the love of my life. I was actually making music when I was 17, 18. But then somehow dropped out of it and stayed in touch with music all my life, but not actually making it. I was DJing, of course, for the last 15 years, occasionally. But I've been also very careful about changing mediums. On the one hand, I am experimenting, but I also think sometimes people feel entitled that they can do anything – like how actors suddenly do paintings and this and that. These changes and shifts one often observes slightly critically. And so, I thought if I'm no going back to music, after a 28-year break, it has to be good. It just can't be a vanity project. I've put in a lot of doubt and a lot of questioning, but I must say it did reappear over the last two years. And it became a more and more serious activity and the results, I guess at some point, I had to accept that some people like them.

You had the Frank Ocean seal of approval, obviously! Which was very kind of him. I want to talk a little bit about the content of it. 'Device Control' was the track that was incorporated in 'Endless'. What I found really interesting, was that a lot of the lyrics seemed to be about our relationship with technology. Can you see a connection between that lyrically and your work that you've been doing photographically, visually? I wanted to know if you saw any parallels between those two things.

Technology is usually not the most interesting thing to talk about in a nerdy way. On the other hand, I've also been aware, I guess, all my life, that technological changes are also driving art. And they certainly have driven music. I've followed it, and I'm kind of observing how technology influences our life. A few years ago – like two, three years ago – I realized that mobile phone manufacturers were marketing their phones, completely differently. It was no longer about being a phone, but that there was this possibility of endlessly, constantly streaming your life. Which seems such an incredibly absurd thought. Who is the recipient of everybody streaming everybody's life? At the same time, it's being presented as just matter of fact. That is what you are entitled to. That's the data rate you have and it's not – it is, of course, a kind of critique – but it's not sneering or mocking it, because I'm of course part of it.

We all are. I've been really interested in our relationship to phones and the intimacy we have with it: the screen, we touch it to make sure we exist. We keep it in our pocket. You check it, God knows how many times an hour. It's like an extension of us. I find that it's a really different experience. Certainly, also photographically. Because it's changing, I think, a wider relationship to what image is and how we engage with all of that. I've always wondered how people who work with the photographic medium – I'm not going to call you a photographer, because I think your work is way more than that – but how they view those kinds of changes.

I must say, I am a photographer. I love photography. But of course, the overall term is artist. I don't think there's anything less in photography than other art forms. But you know, what's fascinating is that normally digital has made everything material dissolve, disappear. The VHS, the

LP, was replaced by digital CDs and DVDs. Streaming etc. has made even those digital products disappear. So, there's literally no hard-copy of anything anymore. I changed from analogue to digital about six, seven years ago. I made a transition period of three years until I finally found "Okay, I speak this new language". When I did stand in front of the three-metre size print in the Kunsthalle Zurich exhibition of 'Neue Welt', I suddenly realized: you can only see in front of this print in this place here and now. Because the photograph had such an incredible detail and presence, and physical presence, that cannot be reproduced on any computer screen or in any book, anywhere. So, in my case, digital has actually made the photographs more unique, even. Bearing in mind the exhibition coming up at Tate Modern in February.

Which is a big retrospective.

No, it's not. It's looking at now. It's entitled '2017'. It's not a survey, it's not chronological, but looks at the whole variety of different practices that I do. That was the curatorial guideline by Chris Dercon, which he calls "extended practice".

Good phrase! What a very apt phrase actually. We should probably play 'Device Control' because it's really nice and it seems very relevant. This is 'Device Control'.

—

That was 'Device Control' by Wolfgang Tillmans. Can we talk about part of what your extended practice is? You have Between Bridges, which I think is an interesting project space and something you've used curatorially to expand not only on ideas within your own practice, but also as kind of a political hub. You began Between Bridges in London?

Yeah, ten years ago.

God time flies. What was your aim with the project? And why did you want to keep having this space?

I had this realization, in the mid '90s or mid 2000s, that there was, especially among young artists in London, a kind of amnesia, of knowledge of very recent history. And of any kind of political art. It was certainly not very prevalent amongst the community. I felt I want to make space for art that is missing, that is not represented in the London context. Either artists that died too young, or artists that conceptually, politically made work that doesn't collect well. For example, Charlotte Posenenske. She was a sculptor in the '60s and '70s. She decided to not sign her work, not edition her work and then she died. That sort of erases you from the art market. Or David Wojnarowicz, who was the opening exhibition. He was such a brilliant writer and speaker. He wrote and spoke with such anger about the political situation in America and the AIDS crisis, which was killing himself. He was so outspoken and risked everything and wasn't pleasing any collectors. I thought that is a good reminder to myself, but also to my fellows, to look at and think about the courage of other artists who have spoken out. The program is always somehow interested in political, or art or artists who are engaged in society, because I also wouldn't be calling myself a political artist, but everything I do has an engagement and involvement in society and interest in society.

> *I've also noticed in more recent shows that there's been an increase of imagery of protest. Obviously, you were probably one of the most outspoken artists about the pre-Brexit voting – in terms of the poster project that you were doing. It was amazing. I wish… I don't even know what to say about that, actually. I've also noticed that a lot of the photographic imagery seems to be going more into a clearly political points that you're referencing. The idea of protest itself, which is quite interesting, because it's something that feels really timely. We need to see images because maybe the media edit these things out often.*

I've had a low-level presence of political protest actually in all my books and exhibitions. And at the same time, I don't want to elevate them to commodities. They're usually just there as a presence. I see my exhibitions and books as a space for representation. For a world that I want to live in, or a world that I acknowledge, and things that I find important. For example, in the book 'Truth Study Center', which came out in 2005, there was a photograph – several photographs – of the Iraq War demonstration of 2003. That, of course, for me is the beginning of the now, and the Tate Modern exhibition actually takes its beginning point from that year onwards. Because that's when all the misunderstandings and all the shit we're in properly began. I think there could be so much more done. People have lost their voice, or how to voice their voice, in political terms today. Just liking something on Instagram isn't enough. People who are against the values that we enjoy, and the freedoms that we enjoy. They have nothing else to do other than push against our freedoms. Like the Trumpians and the religious fundamentalists, they are fired with fervour. Whereas we are busy enjoying our life. There is all this hate, and they are pushing and pushing, and we are just not really pushing back. I think there's a lot more work to be done in the new year.

One could argue that 2016 may be the catalyst that will change a lot of that. I think everyone's a bit in shock with a lot of things that have happened. I'm going to play something in contrast to this. We're going to play 'Fast Lane' now, which is from the new EP. This is a reworking of something that you began in 1986. Do you want to tell me where the original material came from, and how and why you decided to rework it?

Yeah, I was in a synth duo singing in the mid '80s – '85, '86. With my late friend, Bert Lessman.

Very Soft Cell, of you. It was the '80s! You're allowed.

They were a huge inspiration, of course. And we were in a small industrial city, near Cologne and Düsseldorf. And recorded and wrote songs. I made one cassette recording of the songs that we did, and I always knew that I kept that tape, and maybe listened to it, every five or 10 years in the last 30 years. I took the tape to Tim, the sound engineer and musician who I work with at Trix studios in Berlin and asked him if we could restore this. He did real wonders. But, of course, there's a limit as to what you can filter and take out and support. But then he had the idea to actually play back the synths that he could recognise, and the drums that he could recognise, and actually lay them underneath the original track. What you're hearing is my voice as a 17-year-old.

Oh my god!

And the original music in the room, played by Burt, but the whole oomph and what makes it like current is Tim playing what he could decipher from the original.

It's a wonderful idea. The idea of an echo of your past and future selves at the same time.

I mean, it's crazy. At the time, I didn't have the confidence. On the first EP there are already three songs from back then and they are actually alright. 'Fastlane' is exciting because Justin Strauss, the New York DJ legend, he's working on a remix of it. He did fantastic remixes that I loved in the '80s and now he's remixing my song.

It's kind of a fantasy come true.

Amazing, yes.

Okay, we'll play that now.

—

That was a new track off Wolfgang's EP called 'Fastlane'. It was part done in 1986.

By the way 'Device Control' and 'Make It Up As You Go Along', they were released under my name. Whereas 'Fastlane' and 'Here We Are' and 'That's Desire', they are released as Fragile.

Where did you come up with a name for Fragile? I mean, it makes me think of packing and packaging, as well as the delicacy of our human existence.

It's really the name that I chose back then also as a teenager in the '80s, as my pseudonym.

Oh my god, it's amazing, so you literally are like reliving that – an extension of an idea of an alternative existence.

Yeah. I was very aware as a teenager of this fragility. I was full of life, in one way, but I was always also humbly aware of my vulnerability and fragility and found people who acknowledged that in themselves always much more attractive than very self-assured people. There was an attraction in this term fragile. And at the same time, I kind of knew and figured out this is written on every bloody box and everywhere and it works in every language, and, at the time, it was more glamorous, of course to say fragile.

How French. Beautiful. Very Les Bains.

Because it's harder maybe to release a love song as Wolfgang Tillmans, the visual artist. But if I was to put all the music projects under Fragile, just gives me more freedom out of context. That even though people hopefully will recognise soon, that Fragile is my work. It's a more open project this way and collaborative in that way, of course.

Going back to you as a teenager, I know, we've spoken about this in the past. About your relationship with astronomy. And I find that really interesting. That one of your early motivations to be looking at things came out of a fascination, a teen fascination, or child fascination with the astronomical. I know that you still follow eclipses around the world and are interested in that kind of phenomenon. I was very interested in that relationship with how you work as a photographer now.

I mean observation is what I think is so important and so valuable. Of course, this has now much more currency than ever because we are now supposedly living in a post truth world.

Allegedly.

I'm not prepared to give into that. The careful study of evidence and the careful study of what we can measure, and what we can see. It must be the basis to all our understanding and actions. So often, of course, we actually follow just fictional productions of our eyes, or our minds. Of course, we are built like this, the brain is built to give us mirages sometimes, but that's why it's so important to question and to observe. And to question one's observation. I learned this as a child in astronomy. Because when you're looking through the telescope you sometimes have to, for example, look a little bit besides the object to see more. Because in the center of your eye, there are the colour receptors, and they are less light sensitive. The side of the black and white sensors which are more light sensitive. Also, other things in telescopes. They appear as something which they are not. I was very accustomed to that early on, and that's something to keep for yourself for life. That things may appear as something else to what they are.

> *Beautifully and poetically put, I might add. A lot of the other work that reminds me of is your approach to abstraction. The medium of the paper and the process of colour, and how you have incorporated something abstract within something very object based. I wanted to know what your interest was in that. Can you tell me more what the draw was?*

The draw was, and is, that my motivation has been – besides making music – really about making pictures. Making contemporary pictures. Because that's what really, really moved me. Seeing art. Art in spaces. It just spoke to me and call it fetish or call it I don't know… but this object means much more than what it is. It's just a piece of cloth on a wooden stretcher but in my mind, I understood this is everything. And so, I wanted to contribute to that. I found that photography in the end was the way to do that, because in itself it is this miraculous process that turns an industrially produced sheet of paper into this charged, beautiful object. That miracle – what is this transformation? To manage that, and to master that, has been something I've been working on all my last 25 years. I observe the mistakes and what happened in dark rooms, and what goes on with chemicals and processing. I've slowly developed tools. How I can manage mistakes. How I can manage chance and control. So, I started creating pictures purely with light on photographic paper. They can only really be talked about in a painting context, but they are so strong because they are not painted with paint on canvas. The eye sees them and recognises that they are photographic. That's where an association machine kicks in, in the brain. You try to associate this with reality and people see skin or underwater or astronomical things or pigments are often evoked. That lets them sort of be free of the predicament of painting. At the same time, they are purely photographic, but they are not representational at all.

I once had an argument, at an exhibition of yours about a similar kind of relationship to skin. In particular, it was the exhibition you did at Maureen Paley's that was focusing on your ex-assistant Karl. There was amazing sense of detail and close up and the variety of taking a single subject and looking at nuance and delicacy. The argument was that how men see other men. I argued that women aren't allowed to look with desire, either – the fact that we have no desire at all. Eventually my argument person agreed with me, but it was quite interesting. But do you see a relationship between that detail and those accents and feelings and nuances with the skin itself? Because that definitely comes across in a lot of work.

There is definitely an interest in the surface and understanding that surface is not superficial in terms of content. Yes, it is superficial, but it's the only thing we have. You can't always open things up and what appears when you open things up is only another surface. I found that the surface of ourselves, the skin, and then the second skin, the clothes, are where sensuality obviously lies. Where we carry our identity and that is not so unrelated to paper, and photographs. Which are this surface and which is actually equally delicate and fragile. I, for example, hang the photographs unframed. This is actually about this delicacy. It's not about a grungy, slacker approach, but it's to do justice and to expose this beauty in the fragility.

I would never say that, looking at the way you hang things which seems so precise. There are different things that aren't framed. Your use of the pin, or fastener, or tape – it's all with incredible precision. It never felt like lazy! I'll put it that way. Your work never felt lazy Wolfgang… I think we're going to play one of our last songs. We're going to talk about some influences on you and you've chosen Mr. Fingers 'Mystery of Love'. Before we talk about the track itself and how you first came across it. Do you want to tell me what your feelings are about club culture I mean and how that impacted on you creatively? I know your work hangs in Berghain. I've danced next to it in Panorama bar.

The track that I've chosen is 'Can You Feel It?' by Mr. Fingers featuring Chuck Roberts.

Oh good!

It's important the 'featuring Chuck Roberts'. It's the vocal version. It just so much represents the feeling that I had in those first house and acid house nights in the late '80s.

Were you in London at the time?

I was in Hamburg, but we were also travelling around Europe on night trains to go to 'i-D' parties. 'i-D' did a party every month in a city around Europe. I went to Amsterdam and Copenhagen, with my friend Lutz, and of course, we went to try to go to London as often as possible. I actually went to the Hacienda once in 1989. The heyday, the end of the heydays. And I took an E with me on an interrail trip for 30 days. 30 days I had travelled through Europe with one E in my luggage.

They probably wouldn't know what it was in the late '80s. It was so early during that period of acid house.

I took it on the last day of the trip in Manchester, at the Hacienda.

And was it worth it?

It was worth it.

Good, good. And do you want to tell me when you first came across, 'Can You Feel It?' which is an amazing record?

Yep. I guess it was on… yes, of course, it was on a compilation 'In the Key of E'. I mean, I wasn't all about E in those days.

I had a smiley face badge I'd wear to school; I remember.

I indulged fully, but only occasionally. That was I guess the trick to keep the mind together. On that record, it was on this kind of compilation together with Bam Bam 'Where's Your Child' and other incredible classics. If you can, get your hands on 'In The Key of E' the compilation.

Which might only be on cassette tape I'm thinking?

And vinyl, of course. The song, what I love so much about it, is this space, that is almost visually bouncing from left to right. It's like super spatial and at the same time, it unashamedly uses the crowd noise. And this anthemic almost Christian – well a lot of the Chicago people actually are Christian and that has often spoken to me. This spiritual side of nightlife. Because it is a communion – coming together a community. For me, nightlife has always been a spiritual experience. An abstract experience just as much as a physical or sexual one. I can sometimes look up and only observe the lights under the ceiling and stare at them forever and let my mind drift. I can think about the world and myself and existence. That simultaneity that you can do that, and then the next moment you want to pull, or you want to dance. That's life.

And three of life's great things at the same time. Well thank you very, very much for coming on. I really appreciate it. We'll now listen to Mr. Fingers 'Can You Feel It?'.

Featuring Chuck Roberts.

Yes. Excuse me Mr. Roberts!

Haroon Mirza

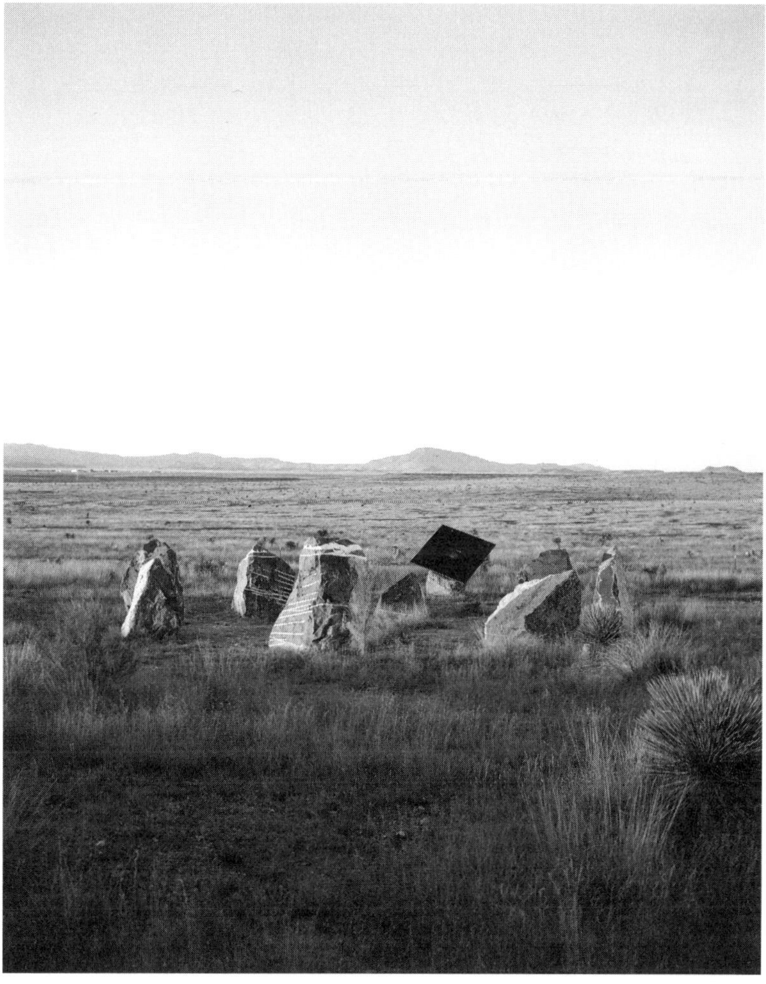

Stone Circle, 2018.

18.01.17

Hi, I'm Francesca Gavin and you're listening to Rough Version on NTS. My guest today is Haroon Mirza. Hi Haroon!

Hi.

Haroon is an amazing artist based in London who studied at Winchester and Goldsmiths and Chelsea – doing two MA's which is very greedy. And then he's won a huge amount of prizes; the Northern Art Prize in 2011, as well as the Silver Lion in Venice, the Nam June Paik Art Center Prize in 2014, the Calder Art Prize in 2015. He's had major shows everywhere from this year in Sao Paulo at Pivô, to probably one of the best exhibitions I've ever seen, which was at the Museum Tinguely in Basel in Switzerland. We're just going to talk about what you're doing, how are you, Haroon?

I'm good. Yeah, I'm well, I'm feeling energetic today.

That's a good way to be! I want to talk to you a little bit about your materials to start with, I'm really fascinated by seeing how that's progressed. Because when I began seeing your work, initially, there was a lot of found objects, kinetic things, weird old turntables, strange things that produced electronic sound or movement in some way. That seemed to progress into things that are more LEDs and sound foam. What is your relationship to material?

I guess I like material, because it's visual – things you can touch and see and have a relationship to immediately. Having a background in painting and art, I always find objects and materials, or just visual material, quite fascinating. I always had a problem with it – why am I attracted to certain materials more than others? Why am I attracted to vintage furniture, mid-century furniture, or turntables, or some things more than other things? That was always a weird concern that I had… I'm concerned about that!

Did you fight that? How did you deal with that?

Yeah, I guess it's something to do with taste. What taste is and where taste comes from and the value systems around that. But at the same time, I was always also interested in – creating systems that are somehow autonomous. And the by-product of that was sound. So, I started working with sound and materials. There was a two-fold thing. One was materials that needed to perform a function to create some kind of sound. Usually that was a sound of interference or electrical signal. And the other one was the materials to support these things somehow physically. That's my relationship with material. It's always a question of value systems – use, value, surplus value, and exchange value of these things.

I love the way you use interference and hiss, and the sound of electricity, and things sometimes embedded in things. What do you like particularly about that effect? And how have you pushed what you're doing with that?

I think the thing for me, with these kinds of sounds, is that they're completely natural sounds, completely chaotic. We forget that electricity is a natural phenomenon. And, although we think we control it, we don't. We just harness it, but we can't control it. It's uncontrollable and quite wild. To create sound from electricity is obviously not a new thing. We've been doing it since the advent of electronic music, which is more than 100 years ago. It just so happened that with recent developments or technological developments with lighting, domestic lighting. LEDs – the processes of controlling LEDs – is the same as some of the processes or electronic processes of early synthesizers and analogue instruments. What that meant was that you could do something visual and auditory based at the same time. So, the medium is electricity.

Do you want to tell me a little bit about how you work with collaboration, because you've obviously got another side your practice, HRM… ?

HRM199.

Ltd! Don't forget the limited! Which has basically been an extension of your practice where you've worked with people like Guy Sherwin, Jeremy Deller, and Channa Horwitz. Do you want to talk a little bit about how you approach collaboration from an art point of view?

I guess it's just about admiring other people's work and being fascinated by other practices… I guess acknowledging that some people do things and that they can do things much better than I can. I can never replicate that. All art is somehow a regurgitation of something else anyway. So rather than trying to do something myself, or push something forward, I'd rather work with someone that's already got to that point and is good at doing it. Then there's just certain synergies and certain types of overlaps between work and practices in aesthetic and sensibility. The main thing is that no collaboration is the same; it's always different. There are always different reasons for collaborating, different ways of collaborating, different sort of methods and solutions that you come to. Sometimes working with, collaborating with artists who aren't even alive anymore, as in the case of Channa Horwitz, for instance. I think it's just about broadening my own work by using other people's work or using other people's work to educate my own work, somehow.

You do it with a lot of respect – it always feels that way. It feels like you're trying to point a finger towards someone's work going, "this is really interesting, how can I have a conversation?"

Yeah, that's what it is. How one practice can infect another somehow. What's the synthesis of this? I have this idea, this feeling, that actually a single person can't be truly creative. You can only really be creative if there's more than one mind working on something.

I also think it's a really great redefinition of what an exhibition is, or what even an artist is. It's not one single individual. In fact, there is so much else going on and taking part in how something works. It's like a film. There is a whole cast, but they are just not credited.

Yeah. So, the whole point of that show, 'HRM199 Ltd', was just saying, "okay, I have a company". The fact is I've had to do it for tax reasons more than anything else, right! So, I have a company, and that's what most artists who are working at a certain level have to do. It's not an individual. It's a group effort. There's two people that permanently work with me. Then loads of people come in and out, at certain times. I collaborate with museums. I collaborate with other artists, technicians, curators, and writers. It's a big effort. It's a big production involving so many different people. That is seldom acknowledged, and somehow the art world at large, has this idea that we need a singular name to credit all this stuff to. And it doesn't make sense, really.

No, it should be more like a film director or something like that.

For sure.

I'm a firm believer. I believe it's nice that you give credit. How did it work when you were collaborating with Factory Floor? Did you do an album together? You created tracks on there?

No. We've done some tracks together and we've recorded a lot of stuff – hours and hours of stuff. I mean, not hours and hours! But a fair few hours, probably. We just can't get it together in terms of finding the time to go through it all and keep recording more and formalizing it. Hopefully, we will do it at some point. We keep on doing stuff together and meeting up and talking about stuff and just playing gigs together, but we haven't actually formalized anything. Hopefully we will at some point, but let's see.

Something to look forward to. You are a great DJ. I've heard you play many times. Music is obviously a huge influence on your approach to sound. Do you want to tell me about how your DJ practice feeds into what you do? And then we can also talk about one of your influences currently at the moment?

Yeah, sure. DJing, I guess is important in the sense that a lot of my practice comes from the methodology or the technique of DJing. Somehow bringing things together. The collaborative aspect, the overlapping and synchronization, beat matching and all these sorts of things… There's lots of references there. And I like music. I love music and love to play music and listen to music. I think I love to play music out loud more than I love to listen to music, which is weird! I used to not be able to sleep without listening to music, which is also weird. I do this thing where I put headphones on, but then I think it will help me fall asleep, but it wouldn't because I'd be listening to it.

I have the same issue with podcasts...

I started doing that as well! Podcasts. But yeah, I just like music!

I'm really interested in the rhythmic nature of a lot of what you do, because there is often a beat, or you're playing with the ideas of syncopation. You feel like music is bleeding into an object or an installation in some way. It ends up being something beyond. I don't know. It just adds another experiential part, as a viewer at least, to how you enter one of your rooms.

Well, I guess, it's because I think about composition, but composition in both an auditory sense and a visual physical sense. Composition – the word composition – is used in painting as much as it is in music. Painters aren't normally known as composers, which is weird, but anyway, I think the medium, whatever it is, it's some kind of perceptive mode. Experiential. I guess I'm trying to link the visual perception with the auditory perception, which are two very different things. Visual perception is electromagnetic because it's a wave. It's light, but on the electromagnetic spectrum. Whereas sound is a physical thing… Which is quite different. But where do those things collide? Because the bandwidths are very different of sound and vision or the wavelengths. What's the collision of these two things? You can only get close to it through experience. I think listening alone isn't somehow enough or seeing alone isn't enough. It's more about the combination of these two things. But you can't either see or hear these wavelengths that are colliding.

Nice image. Do you want to tell us what you've brought in as one of your things?

I've kept it quite concise, so you mentioned the Pivô project earlier. I did this project while I was in Brazil, where I made a large installation, consisting of four videos and eight channels of electrical signal. It's all synchronized together using this device that Ben and I have developed in the studio over the last couple years, called 'emerging paradigm'. I won't go into that. What I'm going to present is two pieces of audio – one is the first part of this installation. The sound of it, obviously, you can't see it. Which is two videos mixed together and overlapped. And the second part is – later on what's happening in this installation – which is four videos playing together an electrical signal. This is all presented in this complex installation with a surround sound centre-piece. The two videos at the beginning are inspirations for the work, but also appear in the work, which is this video of Hermeto Pascoal, the Brazilian avant-garde composer, lying in what looks like a sauna, slapping his chest! He's got a microphone, and he's recording these bodily sounds and it is just quite animalistic. The other one is… I've actually forgotten her name. I don't even know her full name. She's a Peruvian Ikaro singer. She would normally sing an Ikaro – a song or words that are chanted in a melody during ayahuasca rituals. She's a shaman and this is what she would sing during an ayahuasca ritual.

> *Amazing, a belly slapping and ayahuasca ritual chanting combination! Okay, that sounds kind of great!*

Shall we just go ahead and play it.

> *Yes. Press play.*
>
> —
>
> *Wow, that was a pretty random combination of belly sloshing slapping noises and ayahuasca chanting! Do you want to tell me what was the psychedelic aspect of that influence for you? It's obviously close to my heart.*

It became an influence because I was thinking about psychedelics or entheogens in general. When I went to Brazil, I naturally started looking at ayahuasca, but I had no intention of doing ayahuasca. I didn't have any urges or anything like that. But when I started talking about and researching it, I was compelled suddenly compelled to! I did, and it is quite an incredible thing, and it had a profound effect on the project, what I did there, and what came afterwards. I think there's a lot to be said about that experience, just in terms of how it has informed my work since.

Interesting, so what are you working on at the moment?

The next show that I'm doing is a show which presents my research on entheogens, which I've been doing for the last two to three years in Vancouver, the art gallery in Vancouver. It's going to be this piece again, that was shown at Pivô, but in a different configuration, and then other works related to psychedelics such as psilocybin mushrooms, Amanita muscaria, peyote, and such things. There are various types of works that relate to these plants.

Nice. Interesting. When is that opening?

January. The second week of January – 20th or something like that?

I've always been fascinated with how those things influence what we do. I think there is a real relationship between the psychedelic and the electronic or the technological. I think that's an interesting thing to be reiterating in your work – a natural combination.

Especially when you think about Silicon Valley. All those guys are basically the people that were involved in the counterculture at the time LSD was banned. They went on and developed all this technology. There's this thing I read about Steve Jobs where one of his interview questions was "have you ever taken LSD?". That was like a prerequisite for getting a job at Apple!

Wow, I don't know if that would work at Facebook! I imagine it would be more like a neocon direction! But wow, that's fascinating! Do you want to tell me a little bit about how you approach a museum, because I'm really looking at let's say the Tinguely show... Do you say Tan-g-ly or Tin-g-ly?

Ting – Tang. Well, I said Tan-g-ly because that's how they said it. Only in Switzerland I could say Tan-g-ly but everywhere else Tin-g-ly.

I said Tan-g-ly so I feel better now. What was so fascinating seeing how you took your work and approached a museum. I feel like you have a very different approach, where you are inserting your work almost as a layer on top of a collection, in some way. You seem to really want to be pushing the idea of presentation. It seems to be something that's driving how you're presenting things now.

I guess it is, in a way. Also, there's this idea, a leftover idea of a 'readymade', or the 'reverse readymade' as Duchamp would probably call it. As an artist, you want to push everything you can, you know, but it's not always that easy. It was quite difficult doing a show like that, with a museum like that, for many reasons, both political and practical. It was quite stressful and difficult to do – to the point where the whole point of that show was where one practice can overlap with another practice. Within the context of the Tinguely, it became a bone of contention whether I could place a microphone in front of a Tinguely work or not. That was the point of the whole show, and it was happening everywhere else in the rest of the show... It wasn't possible, because of bureaucracy and ideologies... It's always a challenge but it wouldn't be fun if it wasn't, right?

You have to have something a little bit difficult, and then you can feel more satisfaction when it works! Do you want to tell me a little bit about the R&D side of what you do. It's really interesting that you're including solar panels in your sculptures now, and you've created the weird thing that you didn't want to discuss. I just want you to tell me about your research processes and how you're playing around with things?

Before, when I was just doing things myself, I was always playing around with things and experimenting. Now I have Ben, who works with me very closely. The majority of his role is R&D – researching new technologies and developing programs to interface with these technologies or interface with things. We all know, technology develops so quickly – exponentially, according to the technologists! You're always faced with new things, and new political, economic, and ecological things in terms of the biosphere. So, it's nice to try and work with these things. The thing with technology, in terms of art and art history, is that the art always comes afterwards, way after the technology is produced, because it's almost like you have to let it set in, then you can mess around with it somehow and exploit it. Because it's not even understandable. Like, what's inside an iPhone? I don't know.

I think they designed it on purpose so that we don't know.

Exactly. It's like magic, isn't it?

There is something magical about the way you present technology in your installations. Looking at some sound coming out of a rock is an incredibly strange thing!

I think the trick is to hide the technology. It's not about the technology, it's just about the effect. Not just the effect, but also the narratives and the symptoms and the conditions it produces. The work isn't about technology, that's the thing. It's about other things and technology is just the way to get to those things.

What are you most excited about at the moment?

DMT.

Really?!

Yeah.

It's an honest answer!

Just the idea that this molecule – there's a function to it. There's this famous book by Rick Strassman 'DMT: The Spirit Molecule' in which he claims, that DMT is the molecule that's responsible for spirituality, the near-death experience, and dreaming and all these things. But I think there's a certain thing about that sort of behaviour, that sort of state of consciousness that is fundamental to human history and development and evolution. Graham Hancock really describes it best in his book ‘Supernatural’. The history of the relevance of psychedelics throughout the course of human evolution.

> *I think Graham Hancock is a really nice person to recommend that people read in general!*

Yeah. He is totally brilliant.

> *I love people that are that ‘out there’. I’m going to end with you playing your second track, which is... Well, do you want to tell us a little bit about that?*

This is what was presented at Pivô. It is what the slapping chest and Ikaro chanter evolves into but there’s also two other videos. One is based on the political situation in Brazil, which is, right now Dilma (Rousseff) and the impeachment process which has been going on, which is devastating the country. The other one is cosmological and the scientific discoveries that have happened in the last five or so years, maybe a bit longer, in quantum mechanics. In cosmology, specifically gravitational waves, and the development of the idea of the multiverse. These things are all thrown into the ‘pot’ together, to merge and create these weird narratives. The rest of it is electrical signal – live electrical signal.

> *Amazing. Okay. Let’s listen to that now. And thank you very, very much Haroon for coming on.*

That is alright. Thank you for having me!

Martine Syms

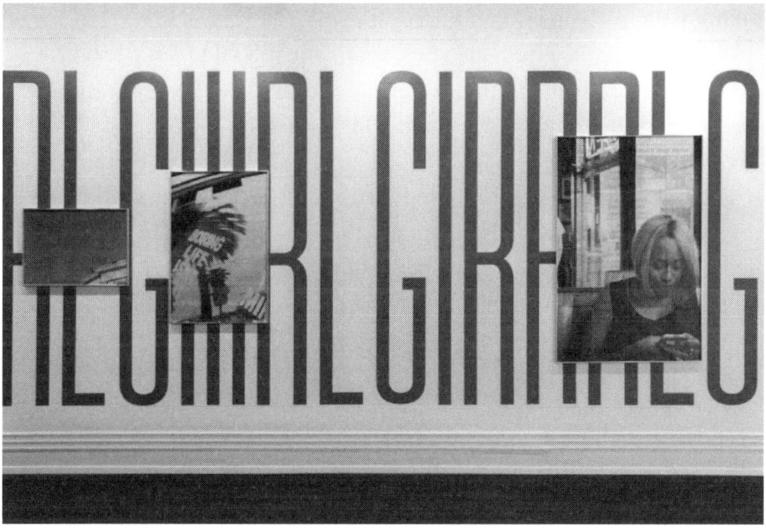

Installation View, Incense Sweaters & Ice, 2018.

22.02.17

Hi, you're listening to Francesca Gavin on Rough Version on NTS. And today's guest is Martine Syms. She's based in Los Angeles. She was a graduate of a great school in Chicago, the School of the Art Institute, and she's exhibited internationally from the ICA in London, to Bridget Donahue, New Museum and the Studio Museum in Harlem, in New York, MOCA Los Angeles, and she's lectured at Yale, South by Southwest and MoMA PS1, with work ranging from everything from video to installation to text to performance to publishing. Thank you for coming in.

Thanks for having me.

Very happy to have you. Let's talk about your work in a broader sense to begin with. Do you want to tell me a little bit about what your process involves? And how you actually start making work? Because you have used such varied media.

Sure. I think for me, a lot of my work originates in techspace, honestly. Or maybe with the idea of recreating something. I'm really interested in repetition, maybe as a generative process… For example, a lot of the moving image work, will start as an essay, or maybe research for an essay, or something like that. Part of my research process is taking images, as well. I guess, gathering or taking people's images and I don't know – I just have an idea for something. For example, the show that's up at Sadie [Coles] right now. The video that's in that is in reference to this one photo from the protests in Ferguson, Missouri. I followed the shooting of Mike Brown, and I had this image stuck in my head that I wanted to recreate as this video. Once I started making the video, I realized that my image, my memory of this photo that I had seen in the news, had changed a lot. I'm always interested in that process. Mediated memories, I guess. How you see these public images, or these public sites where images circulate, and then they get really internalized and it's in my head. I had changed the angle and the lighting and all these little details.

That questions the idea of what history is. That it is such a personal experience and even then, it's relying on something that we can never quite grasp. I always find this a really fascinating concept.

Absolutely. And I'm really interested in those points of the historical colliding with the personal I guess. One's experience, and how to translate that through text or through image making. The cinematography or the quality of the image or the colour in the image. It usually starts with writing. A lot of my ideas are just a note.

Obviously, that is political. I think it's the discussion everyone's having at this moment in time, with the political situation internationally. When you're creating work that references the idea of politics, are you making points about specific things? Or is it about a wider sense, because the danger of making political work is you don't want your things to be dated to a moment, but also reference the importance of that period. I'm curious about your approach to the political.

I think for me, I just have no – when people tell me that they're not political, that seems to be like a response to privilege. So, for me, any visual culture, if it's participating in culture at large inherently is political. As is taste. Whatever typeface you use to the colours you want to use. All those things are influenced by the context that you live in, which is obviously influenced by business, politics, and so on. For me, it's not really this separate thing. It's just things that I'm encountering. With this, with Ferguson, there's nothing really specific, I suppose, about police violence towards Black bodies in the United States! That's an ongoing condition.

Worthy of making an opinion about continuously if you ask me!

That image, specifically, is in reference to these photos of people with milk on their face, because milk mitigates the effects of tear gas. Everyone in protests had been tear gassed, and then they were like pouring milk on their face. Once I made the image, I was sending it around to a few people, just to get some feedback, because, obviously, any liquid dripping on a woman's face can reference porn, too. I wanted to just get people's reads on it. And then another friend brought up these earlier photos from some of the diner sit ins. Civil rights photos where people were – earlier desegregation protests. Just sitting very strictly at counters. I think the one I'm thinking of was in Greensboro, and having milk poured on their head. So, then there was this other kind of echo or resonance with earlier imagery as well. My presentation of it looks very different. I don't think anyone would immediately link between either of those images but it's more those cultural reference. For me, it's in reference to a larger project that's about this Great Migration in the United States – my family's history. Both my parents are from St. Louis. My family is in Ferguson – are very close by Ferguson. So, there's also that reference for me with that…

Can we get to your use of text? Often your work is white on black. It's a very specific typeface. You also have your own publishing house – Dominica, I think it's pronounced. Do you want to tell me a little bit about how you address that and what draws you to particular typefaces and fonts and phrases? It seems quite sloganistic sometimes.

How do I start with that? I would say professionally you just start, I guess, from publishing. Making fanzines and stuff and being really involved in independent music in Los Angeles growing up. I was really involved in the all ages club, The Smell. I played music some but that didn't feel like the place for me. I was really into making jeans and shit like that. And that's how I got started. I guess with publishing and graphic design really, through publishing stuff. Self-publishing. I had always been interested in vernacular typography. It seemed very regional. I liked when you go to another place. I grew up in Southern California but then if you go to another city and the signs and advertising all this seemed to have a different language. And that was something I was always really drawn to. I had a habit as a kid of reading all the ads as I'm driving down the street in the car. Probably really annoying to my parents, I would read every sign that I'd see.

You obviously had language skills; they were probably happy with it!

I guess that's true. I myself, I'd be like, "shut up". I really am interested in that compact form. Whether that be advertising, I really love the language of self-help. These affirmations, mantras, that kind of thing. And then also jokes. They have a similar structure. I like the economy – all are similar to poetry. I guess I got into poetry way later. I was much more interested in, I guess, copy writing. That short economic phrasing and for me how that could really generate a mental picture or that could be this link. In my work, I really like to try, especially with more sculptural work or making that object or the space or install, to generate a specific phrase. And I feel really pleased when people say the phrase that I want, or I was thinking about them worked. I did it. I like text. It produces images and vice versa. So often, I'm going back and forth between them as translation. And I guess that's my interest in that. With typography, I have this background in graphic design and thinking a lot about the use of typography, as this core design function. But that is set, being linked to a more vernacular style, or a high fashion thing. If you change the kerning, or the lettering, the spacing and stuff like that. I guess I just like to play with those because they're another thing everyone's very familiar with, even if they don't know how to necessarily do it. With the typeface, they can recognise when something is set to be high end looking.

These things are so innately built into experience.

Yeah, because they're so familiar. We see them every single day. And you know who is being targeted based on the way it looks. I just like to use that as another tool, because I am able to maybe have a certain command over it. It's just another way for me to shape that information. That led it into whatever I'm installing, and how someone moves through that space.

Another aspect of your work I find really interesting is this deconstruction of our relationship to media. Whether it is gesture within performance, whether it is the process of sitcoms. You seem to be diving into popular culture in a variety of ways and pulling apart what our relationship are to these things that we look at subconsciously. Do you want to tell me about how you've approached that, in those other more performative spaces? Things like sitcoms, etc. I find the idea of looking at representation in sitcoms amazing, because that was also such a basic way of how we experience life.

It was really me thinking about that video, or this video, in particular, the pilot for the show 'I Don't Know', where I was specifically thinking about making a new work in the context of the 2015 Triennial called 'Surround Audience', and it was about some of those relationships. But I had already, when they approached me to do it, I was in the resource room. It had this archival imperative, I suppose. I'd already been working on this film, that started as a traditional documentary about Americans and their national identity being wrapped up in television or television representations. I had started that with a friend, I don't even know God, like, in 2009, or something like that. We were shooting it and doing interviews and research and trying to just get enough to apply to stuff. Then both of us moved from Chicago and it died down and I was still working on it. And I just put it on the back burner for a while… It was generated by experiences both of us had had travelling and in particular, one memory I can think of. I was in Copenhagen. A friend of mine that I grew up with was there. He's half Danish, so he had been there for a while. But we were catching up. And somehow, we started talking about all these shows that we watched when were kids, and then one of his friends was like, "when Americans get together all you talk about is TV. Start remembering episodes". And I was really struck by that.

I grew up in America for elementary school and I was here for the rest of my life. I've got to be honest, actually, I have noticed that too. That seems to be a space where people overlap in a way, that may not happen for a younger generation now not necessarily addicted to TV in the same way…

I think, obviously, in other cultures, similar things happen around TV, but there is particularly the lack of other publics. And it being a really dominant, commercial format. Maybe what I was interested in particularly. I backburner-ed it until I was invited to do the show and it reemerged in a different form. Another thing I was thinking about was some of the ways of being an adult or being a person that I had really internalized from watching sitcoms. There was one character that I was like, "Oh my God" I was re-watching some shows that I watched when I was 12, or whatever. I did things that I saw. I talked to my brother about this. He ended up going to a historically Black college, university, because of watching, God, I'm blanking on the name right now… 'The Cosby Show'…

'A Different World'?

'A Different World'. Yeah, exactly. He went "I wanted to go to a school like that because of 'A Different World'". So, there were things that I had recognised that I did. I was like, "Oh, my God, I actually just did what was in that show". So that made me start thinking about 'A Different World'. It's a quote, unquote, 'positive thing'. But then there's other things – how much of this is seeping in?

How are we influenced by what we consume visually?

Exactly. That's just something that drives me as a general, I guess, interest.

We're going to take a little break now and we're going to play some of the tracks that you brought in. I want to play The Shangri Las and The Shirelles. Can you tell me like why you were drawn to particularly bringing in girl group music?

I love the girl groups. Something I love is that they kind of yell at this one part. That's my favourite. It's just one of my favourite songs… That aggression is like a wail. I really think girl groups are really punk in this way. I don't know…

Maybe The Ramones wanted to be a girl group?

They kind of did, right? But the girl groups did it way better. Some of the first music that I was really into and still listen to all the time.

—

That was The Shirelles 'Dedicated to the One I Love' and The Shangri-las 'Walking in the Sand'. Do you want to tell me about that girl group thing, about feminism? Because I think there is something quite feminist about girl groups. It's this gang idea. Does that influence what you create or is it just a subtext?

I mean, maybe it's more of a subtext, though it has been in other projects. I did a project in 2014 that was really directly about a Black feminist tradition. The show was called 'The Queen's English'. I had found this book called 'Black Lesbians', that had a very broad definition of lesbians that I was really into that was women who want a better world for other women. Yes! Essentially, it was this annotated bibliography that collected texts about Black women by Black women. I used that to structure this show and make images that I made in collaboration with a photographer named Cat Roif. She's a good friend of mine. That were based on, prompted by the blurb, the annotation of the books. I collected a lot of the books that were also on display in the exhibition. And in that case, it was a very direct intergenerational thinking about feminism. The way Cat and I worked together, collectively, and the way that we worked with – not a professional model, but a model that we used. Very much the content of the work was this history of feminism and thinking about what that might mean. In other ways, it's more of a subtext. I would 100% identify as a feminist. No problem saying that. I guess, maybe in some ways, it's always present for me. I'm one of those people who believe that if you're a female artist, we should be discussing your work. The show, and other things I've done, reference a lot of feminist texts, I suppose. In some of my work, it is pretty explicit.

I like the way that you're drawn to things like bibliographies, or the 'Reading Trayvon Martin' piece, where you're literally showing your search history. There's something really interesting about highlighting the process of research. Almost like you're presenting parts to your viewer for them to like, dive in and learn more. That's a nice motivation.

I think I really see myself as a reader in a lot of ways – whether they're sitcoms, certain movies or actual books. I've seen all these things as texts. If it's news photos, these are all like various texts that I'm encountering, and reading and having this process with. Then my work is, when removed from that, in a way or it's the next step of how I've sort of taken in that information. But then in a lot of ways, I like to present the conditions with which I viewed something or encountered it because I do find the, I guess, politics or circumstances around that to be equally important.

> *In a weird way, it's like a postmodern attempt at a sketch? If we're going to think of Renaissance paintings and sketches...*

Yeah, definitely it's like process or your desktop as being your kind of brain.

> *Can we talk a bit about your film work? I love the 'Black Box' piece. You can see excerpts of it on your website online. I haven't seen it as an installation. Do you want to tell me a little bit about the idea behind the work and then maybe what interests you about the fragmentary nature of it? Because it's very much this selection of different clips and text accompaniments that come together. What do you like about those parts?*

'Black Box' was the installation at Human Resources in Los Angeles. The videos that were presented there are actually a series called 'Lessons', which were also at the ICA last April. Maybe some London people saw it there. It was a much different installation at Human Resources. Maybe I started 'Lessons' first. 'Lessons' started, essentially, to be like commercials for a Black radical tradition. In each one, I would take a text. The first five started really from Kevin Yang – a poem he had written as part of his book, a great album. There's a thread of lessons throughout. And his book is really about Black American culture being at the core. Black culture being the core of American culture and art. He's really focusing on music and literature, but really art being the center of that. He has these lessons that are just sort of strewn throughout in the book. I had done this talk at the Walker Art Center in Minneapolis, that was framed around his five lessons that became this, I don't know, manifesto for me in a way. Or a way of thinking about the way that I worked. And they invited me to do a video commission. And I was like, I want to make commercials for each of these lessons. I was doing a lot of more actual commercial video production at the time. I thought I wanted to make these really high budget looking slick commercials for them. I started doing that, but it made no sense whatsoever. Because they don't actually need to be commercials. Then I began working in a much more intimate kind of way. I decided, each one was just going to be 30 seconds. Exactly. The footage comes from a range of sources, a lot of it is original footage, or archival taken from family photos. And then there are other things that are like I'm taking screen grabs or screen captures. Each one is based on a lesson. After I did the first five, I was like, "oh, there's more than five". Then I just decided I wanted to make enough to do a 90-minute feature. So, I've been working on making 180 of them. Right now, I'm at, I don't know, 79 or something? There's no time I have to finish them. So, it's just an ongoing project. But I made this program for them to play because part of what I wanted was that each time they would be presented, the curator, whoever invited me, would program the block of commercials. That's happened once I think, because it wasn't really happening. I was like "I'm going to just make this computer program that'll choose for everyone the order [they are played]". Human Resources was, I think, a cinema space at one point. It's very large scale. A lot of images are something you would typically see on a phone. So, seeing it at that scale is really great. There are three walls that they were projected on. The video would select a video and select a channel to play to so there's this physical moving around. During the openings people would line up on a wall and then that wall would be projected on and then everyone moved to the next wall. The ICA had a similar installation but on monitors. Pieces around, back-to-back monitors. I had to refine this program more at that point. It was a bit more of a thread that would start in a sequence. The block sequences were programmed as well. So, it's something I'm suddenly continuing to work on.

Part of the reason I think it's very powerful is, apart from the speed of this 30-second thing. It's also the fragmentary. The idea that you get a lot of close ups. It seems to be exploring and a lot of things are out of focus, which is really interesting. It's like this element between biography, autobiography, and the archive and how you yourself are inserting yourself into this media landscape in some sense.

Yeah. Part of what I wanted to do is really just challenge all film convention. When I first ever shot him, I thought there would be no hero shots. Where would you put a cut here. Maybe, don't use a voice here. Where you would use this. Take this out here. Like really making conscious, opposite decisions or other ways of trying to make images. I had made similar kind of work actually when I was in school, but I graduated in 2007. People were like, "you can't make a 30-second film". But then now I'm like, "Yes, you can". Just coming back to that way of working. And maybe I was more thinking about it as fragments. But as I've gone on, I think it's not necessarily a fragment, it's about considering all of those things at once as this whole, as simultaneous.

That predates our relationship to social media, and things like Snapchat and Instagram, where we're used to these small segments of moving image. That's how a lot of us absorb image, more than watching a film.

Yeah, absolutely. I was already seeing the threads of that. And a lot of the earlier work that I did was really web-based. But the context, when I was in school, people were like, "Where would you show this? What would you do with this?" It's the world. The context opened up later. That was that relationship, but I already saw commercials already that lend 15 to 30 and so on. It's this way of getting information that we're really, very proficient in. It came from advertising, a lot of television…

Do you want to tell me about another piece of a project you've done, which I know is an older piece: 'The Mundane Afrofuturist Manifesto'. From what I've read, it seemed to be that you were not necessarily criticising that period of work, but how it can be reinterpreted and reconfigured for a contemporary audience. Do you want to tell me why you were drawn to that, and what actually your argument was with the Afrofuturist approach?

With 'The Mundane Afrofuturist Manifesto', I suppose I was working on a record at that time. That is this audio film piece, called 'Most Days', that was released by a label called Mixed Media. It's in New York, and I was working on the sound with Neal Reinalda, he's in LA. The piece is set in 2050, Los Angeles. I had just moved back to LA after living in Chicago for eight years. So much had changed, I guess. I was encountering in a different way. Some things were really bewildering to me and some things was like, "Oh, that's cool. It wasn't like that before. I'm glad we have that". I just structured it, based on this walk that I did every day. Using it as a way to think about what the future in Los Angeles might look like… I was really interested in that every day. Because I think that base is where maybe the most potential is. Because if you think of all these flying cars, or going to space, a lot of that stuff is kind of already happening. But it's our everyday changes that we see what ends up being the most valuable to people to society, to business interests, or whatever. So that's the space that I wanted to look into is. This very specific way of looking at the future, which was really influenced by mundane science fiction, which is a sub-genre of sci-fi. But over the couple months, I was working on this project that previous year. I had kept being invited to all these panels and talks that were about Afrofuturism. Which I didn't really identify with. I never would have called myself an Afrofuturist, but I found that a lot of it was maybe lazy curating, or people were like, "you're Black, you use technology. Afrofuturism". And I guess I was just like, that's not what Afrofuturism is. Also, everybody uses technology. What's so special about me using it? Or that would be to me the thing to talk about. In response, Rhizome asked me to write something. They do a series called 'First Person'. It was people just talking about their work. And they asked me to write about this 'Most Days' project. I was just thinking about ways that I could address Afrofuturism because it seemed like I was directly invoking it. Through this piece, I knew we contextualize as Afrofuturism, that was coming back really full force for any Black artists, who were using technology. It was a way of me just to nip that in the bud. I guess I'm a bit hypocritical in that sense. I guess I'm a bit antagonistic, and I didn't think the way people were using it. I didn't agree with it. And at the time, when mundane science fiction came out, they wrote a manifesto. I just decided to write a manifesto in the style of theirs that was about Afrofuturism. So, the tone and the language is a direct quotation, a lot of it from the original one that came out. And in many ways – it just reenacted the outrage... A lot of people are really upset by my statement, which is fine. That was, I guess, a bit of the point. But another thing for me was it's supposed to be funny. I found it funny. When I was writing it, I was laughing. Friends of mine that I sent it to thought it was funny. There's a something so serious, sometimes the way people talk about it, that I wanted to lighten that up and think about it from a different angle. And for me, my relationship with Afrofuturism, I guess has changed because after I wrote that, I released this record. I also made this documentary for public television in Los Angeles, based on that text and talking with other artists about how they think about speculation as this tool for imagining different futures. What they think the potential of that is, and just using the archival, using technology to really find out or create things. You don't have this past. You don't have this archive to refer to, but how can you use technology to bridge that gap and create continuity? And to me, that way of working in that methodology is more Afrofuturist than any sort of representation of aliens or spaceships obviously. Arthur Jafa. I just had a presentation at Gavin Brown. He quotes me from the documentary saying that we are not aliens. In his talk, he says that he includes that because he completely disagrees with me. That we are aliens and that alien nation, I suppose. My line is that we are not aliens, were alienated but I guess the idea of being alien is something that some have real attachments to…

> *I suppose it's the idea of metaphor and poetry and Utopian ideas are the way to be dealing with real political experiences and the environment we're living in. So, I can understand conflict against those two things.*

I don't think he's productive. To me it's not an end. I'm not saying, I'm definitely not saying "I'm right". Nor was this ever supposed to be like "follow these rules". I don't follow them myself. It was more of a way of thinking through something and using the manifesto language. Using this really strong authoritarian voice was part of the fun of delivering that, to me.

On that note, I'm going to play the last two tracks you brought in. Do you want to tell me a little bit about how you came across them and why you like them? We've got Wendy Rene 'After Laughter" and then the Beatles cover by Charlotte Dada 'Don't Let Me Down'.

I first heard 'After Laughter' when Wendy Yao who does Ooga Booga played that song. I used to work with her at the store, when I was like 17 and I was just like, "what is this?" It's a known Wu-Tang sample and she's like a big Wu-Tang fan. She just played it in the store one day and I was like, "What is the song". Like I said, I was already really into girl group stuff, but I got more into soul, especially sad, soul singers, sad soul music through that song I suppose. And then I think Charlotte Dada and college feels about, right? Because I was really into Afrobeat. Ethiopia was what everybody was playing constantly in their college room.

We're going to play the first track now and I just want to say thank you so much for coming in and talking about your work.

Thanks for having me.

Jeremy Deller

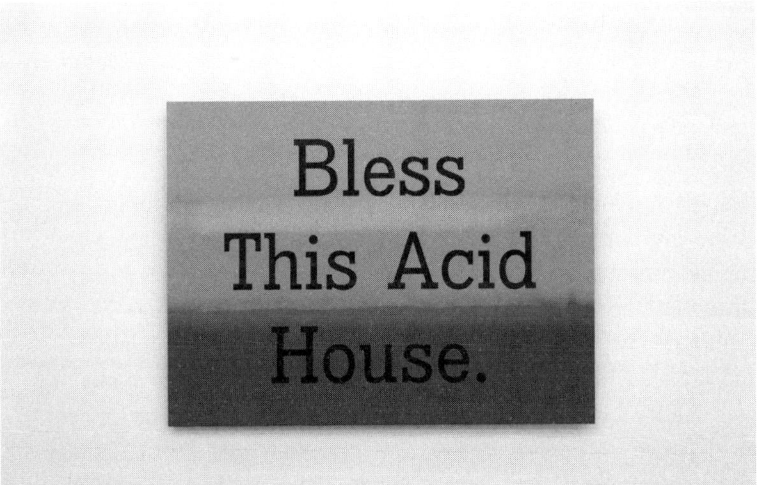

Bless This Acid House, 2022.

13.03.17

Hi, you're listening to Francesca Gavin on Rough Version on NTS. Today's guest is Jeremy Deller, an artist who probably doesn't need an introduction, but is one of the best-known artists that has come out of the UK in recent years. Who has worked in everything from performance to video to installation to print works to objects. He has an exceptionally broad practice! Jeremy is in the studio with me now. Hi, Jeremy, how are you?

Hi Francesca, how are you?

I'm good, thank you for coming in! I want to start talking about your work in a wider way. It's a really funny thing to say, but I think a lot of your references feel notably British. Do you agree with that? Or is that something you struggle with? The context of your Englishness?

Well, I think maybe they're from a British perspective. Yes, obviously, all my formative experiences happened in this country, and I'm interested in what happens here… but obviously, that has an international effect. You can't isolate yourself as a country – even though I know some people would like to… I suppose it's what I know very well, but it doesn't mean I can't work outside the borders of Britain.

Can we talk about one of your most recent projects, I was reading about the Iggy Pop life drawing which happened in 2016. How did that come together? Tell me what the results of it were like.

I approached him about 10 or 11 years ago. I had this idea for him to be the model in life class. It was really a tribute to Mike Kelley, who was alive then, but it was a living tribute to an artist who was still alive. I just thought I wanted to make something that was very 'Mike Kelley'. He was an artist from Detroit, who has worked with music and worked with the avant-garde, and with all sorts of ways of mixing high and low culture. I thought what perfect work it would be for people to draw Iggy Pop's body live, as it were, fully naked. Just as a way of examining, him and his legacy, but also what that body means, what it's done, where it's been.

He's so wiry. It's almost like a Leonardo with the skin stripped off.

His body has changed a lot, actually. If you look at pictures of him, it's not so wiry now, well his arms are but you know, he's 69. I think he might even be nearly 70, so his body has been through a lot. It looks quite different to what it looked like 10 years ago. But interestingly, he'd said no to me initially, for a number of reasons, one of which was that he didn't think he was ready to do it because his career wasn't in the right place. He was still, in a sense, rebuilding his live career 10 years ago, and he wanted to concentrate on that. He felt he was too young to do it at the age of 60. Which is kind of an amazing thing to say. But when he did it last year, he thought it was the right time. That's why it happened very quickly. I approached him again and within a couple of months, we were basically ready to do it.

How did the results turn out? What was the actual experience like?

The experience was incredible really, because if you think about him, and about how important he is, you have to be slightly in awe of him. You can't not be. When he turns out to be a really great person as well, you're more in awe of him. To know that I had him as a subject for just a morning… It was four hours. I had four hours of his undivided attention, basically. And he was naked at the same time. It seemed like a gift really. At first, it was very odd to be in a room with him and him being totally naked, and telling him about poses that I was interested in. And he was basically doing what I told him. That was a very odd thing, to be directing him. Someone who you just don't think could ever be directed, because he has such a wild presence on stage, and I like that. I like the fact that he was very different, sitting down for four hours. He looks different as well. If you look at the drawings, it's a different version of him and his face looks different.

It's also a very different skill, the idea of being still. He is such a physical performer, so used to using and moving his body... Sitting still for four hours is a difficult skill!

It's a huge discipline and he found it quite tough, but he really enjoyed it. It's quite zen. You're concentrating as well, and he was very keen to know about the lighting and where people would be sitting. So, it is still about stagecraft. How and where would he be looking, should he make eye contact – all these sorts of questions and he didn't in the end. We just marked an X on the back wall for him to stare at. And I think he really enjoyed it, because he was saying when he went to New York in the late '60s that really, at the beginning of his career, he did a lot of nude photography as a subject. Then he was coming back to New York almost 50 years later, towards the end of his career. I wouldn't say it IS the end of his career – but it is towards the end of his career, and he does the same thing. He felt it – he actually said – it was very kind… He said it was the other end of the rainbow. It started in New York, in '68 or '69, but it was ending in New York in 2016. Being naked again, but in a very different environment.

What I really liked is that it seems to be an extension of a theme that you've had running throughout your work – this interest in fan culture. The idea of working with your icons. Obviously, you did the Depeche Mode film, which didn't get a full release, which I think is one of the most exceptional films I've ever seen. The work you do with Manic Street Preachers, people draw them, and this idea of fandom in some way. What do you like about that?

Well, it's interesting, because the fan thing, I never really thought about it in that [way]… They are like fan drawings, a lot of them. But having said that, a lot of the class – we had 22 people in the class – about seven or eight of those people didn't know who he was. Either they were old, really quite elderly, i.e. around 80, or they were really young, say 18 or 19… Those age groups probably hadn't been affected by him or knew who he was. So that was interesting. But yes, the fan thing… I don't know, it's probably because I am one myself. I'm always interested when people are almost more into the band than the band are into themselves! Especially with Depeche. They mean so much to people around the world, and especially in certain countries they have a meaning beyond anything that the band could imagine or understand. That was interesting for me.

I really love the fact, looking at Depeche Mode, what you really highlighted in the film you made with Nick Abrahams, was very much this relationship between rebellion, repression or lack of moving beyond some kind of political repression. This reinvention of what being young could be. So there definitely was a political crossover.

Yes, there is and that's what music is great at doing. Often you don't even know. You make a song, and you have an idea for an album and the artist often has no idea how it's going to be used or interpreted or what people are going to think about it. That definitely happened with Depeche Mode. I knew they were big in Eastern Europe, but when they released 'Violator' it just happened to coincide with the end of Communism and in many countries around Europe it became the soundtrack for young people of this new era for them, literally. It's those coincidences which I find very interesting. With Depeche it became bigger. It became bigger than the band. It became a global, political phenomenon.

Looking back at the fan concept. You've made a lot of music as part of your practice and quite collaborative things. Does that fan thing crossover on a personal level with the songs you've chosen, the acts you've chosen to work with?

I think I have an appreciation of music, but I don't really have any formal talent to make it! So, anyone that can make music and especially when groups of people come together and make music, it is a lovely metaphor for how great the world can be. It's quite hopeful really, when you see a group of people play music well. It shows humanity at its best. I'm always amazed by that. For example, a brass band is just, well on the whole it's male and it's a group 28 blokes being blokes and whatever. A couple of football teams together or rugby teams… more like rugby teams actually…

With big instruments!

Yeah, and all that behaviour and banter. All that stuff you might find it quite intimidating, and it can be. Actually, the first time I met the band I just couldn't believe the maleness of it – because at that point the band was all male – it isn't anymore – but then they sit down, and they play this beautiful music. So, from all these individuals, all these guys, you have beauty. And that was something that really appealed to me.

Do you want to take me through one of the tracks you brought in, which is a situation where you have been collaborating with someone else, and tell me about it?

I can. I'll give you the choice. Do you want a steel band or brass band? I mean what would you be interested in?

I would love the steel band because I'm London enough to love the sound of the steelpan!

I love steel bands. The history of them is very interesting, their importation to Britain… I think the first time you probably heard them in Britain was at the Festival of Britain. There's footage of a steel band playing…

So, is that 1955?

Or '50… I should know these things, '53 or something, or '52, close. You can see these Londoners, these people visiting the Festival of Britain watching the steel band and not knowing what to make of it really. They just can't quite believe the sound they're making. But I remember that from my childhood. I just love the adaptability of bands, of big bands. They can play any kind of music and traditionally steel bands, in their repertoire, often play classical music. The way they're set up is like a full orchestra basically. Steel bands can do anything, and they can do it very well. There's great footage online of a steel band playing some Aphex Twin.

Nice.

Yeah, really nice.

This is not a track that you invented or created in any way? It just turned out that way?

I just saw them play online. It's really great, actually. Probably one of the top musical moments of all time in my life, was on Oxford Street. There was a very small steel band with a drummer and percussionist, five, maybe six people, and they were doing this version of 'Hallelujah', the Leonard Cohen song. It was an amazing dance version, with singing. It was just the most incredible cover version I've ever heard. I love the adaptability of it. I like the fact that big bands with groups of people playing together often show social change in a country, just by the makeup of a band. I've always wanted to work with a steel band, and I got to work with one in 2013.

Which track are you going to be playing?

I'm going to play 'The Man Who Sold the World' which is a mysterious track. It's a very unusual song isn't it, with melancholy, the lyrics, and the mystery of it… I just thought a steel band would be a great interpreter of that song.

Wonderful. Here is 'The Man Who Sold the World'.

—

That was 'The Man Who Sold the World' by David Bowie by Jeremy Deller with a steel band.

I should tell you the name of the steel band.

Yes! Tell me the name of the steel band, it's incredibly important.

It's the Melodeon Steel Band from Southwest London.

What a lovely word 'melodeon'.

Yeah.

What I find really interesting, when you work with bands and larger groups, is that you seem to have done that quite often.

This idea of working not with just a single individual in collaboration, but actually working with a city, or multiple groups, or everything from parades to bands to larger sections... I want to know what you like about that scale of collaboration?

I think it's quite interesting to see what's possible, what people can do, what you're capable of achieving as a group of people. And sometimes to have an effect, you need to have numbers. It's a practical thing… but also, it's just a question of, what can we do here? What can we achieve as a group? How far can we take this idea?

The 1814 project, obviously, 'We're Here Because We're Here'.

1914, I don't know what war was on in 1814?

Ha! I don't know... chartism? The 1914 project...

We were probably at war with France in 1814.

Yeah, the Napoleonic wars were still going on at some point... Obviously, that was a huge amount of people and a lot of work and had an enormous global reach as a result of that.

We didn't know what to expect really. We worked with nearly 2000 people to do a performance in public on July 1 last year, which was the anniversary of the first day of the Battle of the Somme, which was the greatest military disaster, in terms of loss of life for the British Army that has ever had. We had, nearly 2000 people in full World War 1 uniform, just appearing in public places all over the country, and then going on walks, going on trains, and buses and just negotiating Britain. Going to contemporary places in Britain and hanging out in shopping centers. They weren't talking to the public, but they had these cards to say who they were representing. Each participant was representing someone who died and had little business cards explaining who they were, like a gravestone effectively. We had no idea if it was going to be successful or not, because we couldn't rehearse it. It just had to happen and once it happened, once it was happening, there's no way you can really control it. You can't control the public, that's for sure. But luckily, people seemed to react to it in a positive way, thankfully.

It seemed like a beautiful concept of how to reinvent the idea of the memorial or monument. Beyond the ways we are used to – classical sculpture and something that represents passing.

Yes, exactly. It was definitely an attempt to go beyond either the big object that everyone goes to make a pilgrimage to venerate, to remember. Or another way of doing it is to have lots and lots of objects in one place, which looks really impressive, because you've got 20,000 pairs of shoes in a big pile or whatever. I didn't want to do that, I wanted something that was human, but also moved around. The memorial went to you really. It found you out. It sought out the public. And that's why I went to busy places, which in Britain now are usually shopping centers and places like that. The memorial moved and found its audience in a way that the audience were not expecting. They had no idea it was going to happen that day; no one knew. It was a secret.

Actually, it was so interesting. It didn't even come out that it was your artwork, until after all the publicity had really emerged from it. There was an amazing media blackout and they collaborated with that in a wider sense without giving it away that it was you.

That was very important, really because as soon as it had been explained as "oh it's by…" you know, "it's by me" or whatever, it loses its mystery or purpose in a sense. It just becomes a thing by an artist. That was very important that a) people didn't know it was going to happen and b) people didn't really know what it was, until it was revealed at the end of the day that this was an artwork and by this person.

Mystery is a really nice thing, and also it makes me think of other wider things, for example, when you were representing Britain for the Venice Biennale, and the concept of 'English Magic'. The idea of the mysterious being somehow intertwined with the process of making art and what artworks can be. Are you interested in those concepts?

Inevitably you're interested in that. Magic is about transformation of an object or something moving around. You're interested in those properties of art that can't really be defined particularly well and affect people in ways they're not expecting. Also in Venice, the whole exhibition was secret as well. People didn't know what was going to be until they got there, and I think that's quite important nowadays… because it seems like nowadays, everyone knows exactly what's going to happen before it happens. And everything's discussed beforehand.

People making an opinion before you even turn up to something.

Exactly. Everything's trialed and everything is revealed and pre-revealed and leaked… I wanted it to be a surprise, at least.

What's also nice about a lot of your work, is you often give away work for free, or exceptionally reasonably. I think it's quite a wonderful thing to do.

Yes, I have quite a weird economy as an artist that I don't sell much work, but I give a lot away! Or it can be quite inexpensive… I don't have that following that some artists have in terms of the collector thing, but that's no surprise really.

Was that an intentional decision? It feels like a decision.

It kind of was. It was almost a reaction to what was going on in the '90s when there was the whole phenomenon of young artists who were becoming known as the YBAs. I was around at that time, and I know, or knew, most of them and we would go to the exhibitions and go to the Saatchi gallery. It became quite clear quite quickly, that however rock and roll they, or we, thought it was, or how anti-establishment, it was still really things that could be bought by people, and then shown in museums and galleries. It wasn't that groundbreaking or innovative. It was quite traditional. It was paintings and sculpture. And that was something I couldn't really make myself, because I don't have those talents. I don't have the interest in it. I was interested in doing something that couldn't really be bought, necessarily… I do think it can be bought. They just aren't though, very often! I wanted to go the other way and so together with a group of friends, we did 'things' rather than 'made things'.

I guess that's why you were never really described as a YBA, so that's a mantle you didn't have to have hanging on top of you.

No. It's interesting because I think I'm not described as them because I never really exhibited with them in group shows. If I'd have been in group shows with them, then you would have just taken on that blanket term. But like I said, a small group of us knew them, and we hung around with them, went to all the shows and that, but we would always be different from them…

Another thing that I find really interesting about a lot of your projects, is that you seem to be drawn to outsiders, for example Bruce Lacey, who you did that amazing film and exhibition with. And wrestlers. What do you like about the idea of the outsider?

I don't know, really. I think we would like to think of ourselves as outsiders as well. That we're different from everyone else. When you see people that really forge their own path against all the odds, against whatever people have told them, it's quite inspiring really. And they're usually very interesting people because they've done these things. They are very single minded often. They're incredibly single minded, and that can be quite difficult. But what they've achieved personally I find very interesting. Adrian Street is a wrestler, who was wrestling for like four or five decades. He left his home at 16 in Wales and came to London in the '50s and worked in Soho and created a world for himself and his look, which is a very effeminate look, almost transvestite. He treated himself like an artwork basically, and became this sort of one-man performance piece, effectively a piece of performance art. He is still like that. He doesn't wrestle anymore – he stopped wrestling two years ago – but he's still into body culture and has an amazing body and works out all the time. He lives in Florida and has a little bit of land and a house with his wife and has a very nice time there, but I just felt it is interesting how someone has redefined themselves through their body in what they've done. It's like a superhero basically. He's his own superhero.

Bruce Lacey was also another character, who also made artworks, who you really felt was also an artwork in their own existence.

Yes. Bruce is an amazing character and I recommend anyone to look him up. He made music as well. He made synth music in the '70s, almost improvised monophonic synth music to accompany exhibitions and soundtracks of films he was making. But he was a punk in the '50s in swinging London – well pre-swinging London – but he was behaving like a punk. A lot of anger there, and he never stopped being, doing that. He had a studio with Genesis… Actually, he was the studio manager for Genesis, and I think there's a lot of cross fertilization between him and maybe early Throbbing Gristle, but definitely Genesis and all his activities. Bruce has a career that cannot be really defined it's so varied. He died about this time last year, but he was working right up to the end in his mid 80s.

He must have been so happy when you brought a big finger and pointed it at his practice while he was alive.

Yes, I made a film about him, and I did an exhibition, and we did a book. He got the whole, full treatment in his lifetime, when he was alive… I was determined to make a film about a great living artist, and very unusual person when they're alive, because then you just talk to them, you don't have to talk to anyone else and we didn't. It was just him. Spending an hour and a half with him, that is basically the film. That's what it was meant to be like.

It's really nostalgic of me, but do you think that those kinds of characters are created anymore? Do you think that they exist?

I think they are; I hear what you are saying, but I think we have to be really careful. You hear people say "oh, there's no decent bands anymore", "no one's doing this and that"… and I think they are actually, we just don't know about it. Because we're getting old! We're not plugged into stuff like that. People say "there's no youth culture" but of course there is but…

Maybe it's just a case that I want more non-commodified art works and individuals working within that and maybe spaces for them to experiment.

I think maybe there is less space for people to do that, to muck about, or places to live even, that's a problem. But maybe outside of London this is happening. Bruce actually just excused himself from London and went to live on a farm. He lived in a caravan on a farm and basically created his own commune of two people.

Easy way to make an organization! Just to have two of you to decide what to do.

Yes, but I think maybe that is a problem. It might be more difficult to find, or to sustain. But yeah, I think there's people out there doing that.

Do you want to tell me another track you've brought in? This one is quite exciting. You haven't played this for 21 years?

This might be a world premiere actually. This is for some reason… I know Jonnie Wilkes, who is one half of Optimo. I know him through friends in Glasgow who went to college with him, and the Glasgow scene is really quite tight knit. A really great scene. I think 21 years ago, I was asked to make, to see if I could make a record with Jonnie in one day… It wasn't a challenge thing, but I just can't believe we thought we could make a record that quickly. But we did! Weirdly we did two records. This is the – I wouldn't call it the 'A-side', but it is a side… So, we came up with one track which I'll tell you what it is after, in terms of what the samples are, but I haven't played it for literally 20 years or so, and it's, I don't know… I quite like it. I'll put it on.

—

Do you want to tell us what that was?

That was samples from a live AC/DC…

Really?

With a drumbeat over.

I'm happy that it didn't sound like AC/DC normally. Do you remember what track it was?

I don't. I think it was a bunch. It was bits between songs almost. I mean the last part is obviously from a song, but it's almost the feedback before and after tracks, by the sounds of it.

Thinking about Optimo, I want to take this in a wider direction. You've done works that reference acid house. The amazing beautiful 'Bless this Acid House' poster which you generously let me use once. Do you want to tell me what your relationship was to that scene? Were you really part of it?

Not massively no. I came into it a little bit later, when it was more what I would call rave. I wasn't part of the whole M25 thing. I'd never pretend I was. But it was probably about two years later, when I was really into that rave moment, if you could call it. With Spiral Tribe and outdoor, more heavier, almost techno stuff.

It was quite dark-core that period.

It was, I remember going to the Roundhouse… They had a four-day party in 1990 or something. And I went on the last day, and that was pretty amazing seeing the state of people on I don't know what day it was, maybe the third of January, or second of January, who had been at a party for four days.

An interesting, different view of what London was. Everything was quite barren and rundown. A very different environment.

Yeah, the Roundhouse was derelict. A lot of places were derelict. It was obviously quite easy to do those, as they were all over Britain. It wasn't just London. Think about post-industrial North of England. It was actually a very helpful time to be post-industrial, because you could just take over old factories and warehouses and have your parties there and no one really cared.

Do you want to talk a little bit about how you started making work after that period? Because I know that you studied art history, and you were working at 'Sign of the Times', a T-shirt shop?

Yes. Well, it goes sort of – art history, leave college in '88, unemployment, work, unemployment, part-time work, unemployment… I would say it was a mixed portfolio of full-time employment, part-time, and then unemployment for about seven or eight years, maybe more. That probably stopped in '97 when I started working, and almost supporting myself as an artist. But in between, I worked in a shop in Covent Garden called 'Sign of the Times' which was this clubbers, trendy club shop… I don't know what the equivalent is now really, it was for young designers to show and sell their work, but also, they had club nights. A lot of people came through the doors. A lot of people who I know now, who I'm still in contact with. It was a brilliant way to meet people. That's where I met Nick Abrahams, who I have made a couple of films with – the Depeche film and also the Bruce Lacey film. It was just this constant stream of people coming to you, rather than you having to find people. It was the first time really that I felt that I was part of a scene in London, because before then I hung out in Bromley, even though I lived closer to the center of London than Bromley, I lived in Dulwich! I lived my social life in the suburbs, which is the opposite of everyone else in the world.

Were you looking for punk? I'm thinking of the Bromley Contingent?!

Weirdly, no, but there was a really good club there called Langtry's. I used to go there every weekend, maybe twice a weekend. On the top floor it was indie, when indie was at its height, I would say, pre-Britpop. And then downstairs, it was rave and dance. So, you had the best of both worlds. And I just thought, well I don't really need to go anywhere else; this is amazing. And it was.

Really good. And I remember one of your early exhibitions that you recreated for your show at the Hayward was an exhibition you created within your family's home when they went away on holiday?

Yeah.

I'm really interested in trying to find unusual spaces to show art and I think that's got to be one of the most out-there places!

But in a way, it's the easiest place, because it is where you live, so there's no transportation. It's where you live and where you make the work, so it's easy to put the work up. You know the space well, and you're at ease with it. My parents went away somewhere for a fortnight, and I just thought well I've got to do this, because I'm never going to show this work otherwise, and it doesn't really make much sense if I take it out of the house. Hence, when I did reshow the room, it was a version. I remade the bedroom…

It was wonderful. There were artworks in drawers. There was an artwork above the toilet. It was like things scrawled on paper. It was pretty much like a representation of you as a youth.

Yes, but basically, I was still a teenager at the age of 27 or 28, because I still lived at home. So, I was a frustrated, teenage 27-year-old. And individually, those works wouldn't really add up too much. But if you show like 100 or 200 artworks in one space, there's strength there between the work.

How did you tell people about the exhibition?

I did these handwritten invitations. I didn't send out that many, because I didn't want loads of people to turn up and trash the house, which I thought might happen. But, of course, it didn't. But people did turn up, because I did tell them, but I reckon maybe in total 20 to 30 people saw that show.

Amazing. How intimate. Great that it has its own ghostly life, beyond existence?

Yes. And it has. And obviously it's a good story, as well. It's fun to explain that.

It is a wider question. What's your process for making work? Do you have ideas and then go find out ways of making it? Or do you get invitations to do things and think, "okay, how can I work within this context?"

It is a mix. You have ideas that are backing up, and you forget, and then they come back. The Iggy Pop one was an idea from over 10 years ago, and then 10 years later it actually happens. You have what I would call standalone ideas, and you try and find someone to host it or to make it happen. And then you do get approached with "would you like to do this?" or do "would you like to work on something here". And sometimes, you can bring the idea you've already had there and just put the two together or you have to think of something new. It's a mixture really. But often the idea is fully formed. Weirdly. Let's say for the Iggy Pop thing. I knew exactly what I wanted when I had the idea. Exactly what it would look like. What the drawings could be, how I would approach the subject and so on. And, in fact, it was absolutely what happened, last year, when the show was up, and it was exactly how I thought about it over 10 years ago.

Do you have a studio? This is a funny question. I imagined you not having a studio? I imagine you working in the cafe in Highbury, where you often go for a cup of tea.

I don't. I work from home, but I have what you would call an office space. A room with a computer in it. I've cleared it out over Christmas, because it's full of too much stuff. It's quite bare at the moment, but it won't be by the end of the year. I accumulate things, but I am trying to keep it under control. I have a space and I use that, and nothing gets made there in terms of objects. That happens outside the space. It's just a place to receive emails basically. It's a safe space.

Maybe we need little cushions and warm cozy places to look at our emails. That's a nicer idea.

Yes, that's how I feel.

Do you want to play one more track?

Yes. I don't think this has ever been played either. It's the massive brass band playing acid house music, which I did in '97. So, it's from quite a long time ago. This is actually a live recording from the Tate Modern, because the band were one of the things that opened the Tate Modern on the opening night. This is a live recording of them, which is actually better than the studio recordings, because it's live and so it has more energy. It's the signature track for them. It's the track that I knew would always sound great being played by a brass band, and it's from a band that I love dearly. It's 'What Time is Love'.

Wow, exciting.

By KLF, of course.

Wonderful, let's play it.

—

That was amazing and really different sounding than the recording in a studio, quite violent.

It's a live recording, so that's always different, isn't it? I think you play quicker as well because of adrenaline. When they were recording it as a record, it was done in a more traditional brass band way, which is actually something I didn't want, but I didn't have the language within me to explain what I wanted properly. I wanted something that sounded more… Steve Albini had produced a brass band. I got a more traditional reverb-ey, polite, respectful brass band sound and actually wanted something really tough like a rock band. Basically, a rock sound.

KLF are reforming. They're doing the children of moo moo, or whatever. They're coming back again.

What are they doing? I don't know. I'm not quite sure what they're doing. I'd be interested to know.

Quite nice that they're doing something…

We need it at this point in our history, I would say that Bill is a great person and I got to know him pretty well. Jimmy less so, but

Bill is a fantastic person. I think whatever he does, I'm sure it's going to be fine.

And totally unusual and unlike anything else we'll hear or see or experience, I would imagine.

I hope so, I hope they do something really surprising, if they are going to do anything. Who knows?

One last thing I want to ask you about is the idea of the use of humour in your work, something that I'm always drawn towards. Your work seems to balance both politics with a baby 'p' and the idea of humour and I love that fusion, and how you use that in different ways.

Thank you. Do you want me to say why that is or?

Just me gushing about you! Yes, why?

Well, it's important, isn't it? You do need it, especially now. Looking at what's going on in America, I don't go to news channels anymore about that. I do, but I don't go to TV news. I just go to the commentators, because they seem to have a better handle on things than anyone else. Also, it gives you a bit of comfort, doesn't it? And humour is so human isn't? It humanizes the situation, and it gives you a bit of hope. And we know why it's good. I mean, I don't even have to explain why, but it's really, it's comforting… Because when situations are absurd as they are now, they can't be explained rationally. I think humour is the best way to explain certain things.

You are laughing but at least you're not crying.

Yes, but also it's actually a more accurate way to look at these problems is through humour and the absurdity and surreal nature of things. Actually, humour is a much better weapon.

Nice. Your last track is a short, weird, strange, sweet thing… Do you want to say what it is and tell me the background of it?

Yes. The background was that I was asked to do a project with a student at a curatorial college called Bard, which is a humanities college in upstate New York. I thought why not make a record about the town that this college is in, and do a compilation album of all the music, or some of the music, that's made in the town. There are all sorts from eight bit to a local teenage rock band, folk singer, bell ringers, pipe band, and all sorts of things… and a children's choir. I forgot about that. One of them is a high school choir and they did these great warm up exercises before they sang. I thought these actually, I wouldn't say they're better, but they were actually really interesting, almost like artworks, like Martin Creed artworks… This one is really like Martin Creed. I'm sure your listeners know Martin Creed's work. So, I'll put this one on.

Amazing and while you do that, I want to say thank you so much for coming in Jeremy, I really appreciate it.

Thank you, it's a pleasure. I don't mind talking about things like this. I really like it.

Good!

Mark Leckey

10.05.17

I'm Francesca Gavin and you're listening to Rough Version on NTS. My guest this month is Mark Leckey, who I'm a huge fan of, who is a British artist, who's worked with everything from performance to film, sculpture to installation. He's represented by Cabinet Gallery in London. He just had a massive retrospective at MoMA PS1 in New York. And you won the Turner prize?

Yeah.

Thank you for coming in.

Hello.

You also have a very good show on NTS, as well. But we're not going to be talking about that.

It's too nepotistic.

Yeah, exactly. Just something else to listen to, if you want a little bit more Mark. Let's start talking about your work in general. Let's talk about your performance pieces. I remember I went to one at a certain time, where a guy next to me actually passed out from the sound he was listening to. Do you want to tell me a little bit about how you've approached performance? I know you used to have a band. And you still create performance works… Do you want to tell me about that whole process?

Yeah, we had a band. I went to art school to be in a band and failed to join a band. And I always carried that on. I always wanted to make music and perform in onstage stage, I guess. I'm not really upfront but just wanted to do live music. So, when I started making art, it afforded me the opportunity to do something like that. I had this band with Edwin Burdis, who was then called Ed Lilique. We were called donAteller. Edward, Ed was an ex-model. Very tall, very skinny. He used to wear little hot pants and fishnet tights, Reeboks – it was a good look. And I'd sort of lurk behind him in an old Aquascutum trench coat with a baseball cap. We just were a bit like a more genteel Sleaford Mods, but not as good.

You did that for like 10 years? Longer?

No. It was more like six years, something like that. It went through different phases, and then it kind of morphed into this other band, Jack to Jack, that I had with Steve Claydon and Kieron Livingston. Some people came in and out of the bands. We tried to keep it going until… I don't know, we got too old.

Do you want to tell me a little bit about how that relationship – where you have a much more straightforward performance to an audience – changed? A lot of the performance you seem to be doing now seem to be about you playing music at sculptures or at art objects? Do you want to tell me how you got from one step to another?

I remembered when me and Ed did our first gig in Brixton and I just remember how terrified we were before we went on and then once after we did it, it kind of broke that fear. It broke through that fear – the smell of grease paint and all the rest of it… I liked performing. I like doing something live in front of a crowd. Just because of that energy. And then, in the midst of doing donAteller, I did this performance at Tate Britain, where this curator Catherine Wood asked me to come in. She said just do a performance. She wanted us to do performance with some of the work there at the Tate. At Tate Britain there is this huge Jacob Epstein – big ugly motherfucker, that's moved around constantly because they don't know what to do with it because it's so hideous really. Hideous and it has… what's the word I'm looking for… an attractive-repulsive energy about it. I'd already made a sound system. And this sculpture, if anyone knows it, is very blocky, very big. Sort of equivalent to a sound system – the sound systems I made anyway, which were just big boxes. I did this thing called 'Big Box Statue Action', where the fantasy, the conceit, was to try and wake the sculpture, or try to re-animate it or bring it to life. Pygmalion-like. There were all these different approaches. I tried to attack it with sound. I tried to seduce it. I tried to sing to it. I tried to revive it with contemporary songs – that were contemporaneous with it. It just evolved into this performance. Originally it was going to be called 'Romancing the Stone'.

Good '80s reference.

Yeah, but I thought that was a bit much. It ended up as 'Big Box Statue Action'. I realized afterwards that it… initially it was just a way of making music. It was an instance to make music from but then I realized afterwards that it was like a more effective form of art appreciation. I often feel overwhelmed by the amount of chat and theory in the art world. This seemed another kind of language in which to address something and appreciate something. I could feel it, you know? Basically, all I wanted to do, the whole aim of the performance, was to know this thing that I found unapproachable, you know what I mean? It's all about trying to experience something. I guess, apprehend something. So, you feel like you are having a moment, an experience with these things. Which I find very hard to do when I go to a gallery and just try and stand in front of a sculpture. Sometimes the magic works. But this was a ritual to make that magic happen.

I always want to touch sculptures. My mum used to go around and touch sculptures. But it's also trying to find a different sensory way of doing things, as opposed to just your eyes. Everything seems to be very eye centered, and maybe we are looking for different ways of accessing work.

Yeah. Yeah. It's both. The sound system is throwing out these very low bass notes, this heavy sort of bottom end. You're getting this big thing, this big sculpture, and the sound is almost equivalent to the mass of the thing. You're creating this form in between some ways. So it is, like you say, on a different sensory level, but it's more about language…. Music is what informed me. Music is my education. I mean, I've learned a lot from art, but music was my initial education.

I think that really comes across in your film work in particular, 'Fiorucci Made Me Hardcore', but also very much in 'Dream English Kid', the most recent film you made, which I love. Which seemed to really be blending you in your environment. A lot of that was references to sound. Whether that's like Joy Division, or raves, or everything else in between.

I mean the thing about music is that it is essentially democratic, I guess – or pop music is at least. And I was particularly fortunate when I was 15, 16 getting into music, it was late '70s, early '80s. I was being I was being schooled by post-punk essentially. I learned through Scritti Politti records what– I've forgotten his name now – who Gramsci was. I learned through Joy Division about Russian Constructivism and stuff. It was a sort of education – a sort of auto-didactic, educational way of disseminating information. That, like I say, basically formed me.

Thinking about that democracy, that also makes me think about sound system culture, which for me, also is a very democratic scene. It's a much more public engagement with art. Do you want to tell me about your approach to the sound system totems? They look quite stylized. They have a really specific aesthetic, that reminds me of things you see in a sound system, but it's also a much more beautified version. Do you want to tell me how you first started working with them, and why you've made them look like that?

I made a record. I used to live in Fitzrovia, used to live off Tottenham Court Road. I was in Soho. I ended up making this record about Soho. I used to go round doing, essentially, field recordings in Soho of drunk people. Of people off their tits. I'd sample stuff that was evocative of certain streets of Soho, and history and Soho. Anyway, I ended up making this record. And I didn't know, how to broadcast. I didn't know how to play it, essentially. I'd already made it into a dubplate – a one-off vinyl pressing. You need a sound system to play the dubplate. So, that was why I made the sound system. They were things that I'd known through raves. Things that I stuck my head into the bass bins of when I was a raver and they were always these totems. They were like very totemic and somehow, I associate them with something – I mean, they are Jamaican, but they've become very British as well. They're almost like standing stones or something. They like these totemic objects.

That we worship.

That we worship and stand in front of and fall to our knees to. They're also very beautiful and they're very rudimentary a lot. I don't like them when they get too sophisticated. It's like going from jungle to intelligent drum and bass. I don't like that. I like jungle. And I like my sound systems quite brutal. They're just big boxes. They're just big, brutal boxes that produce this sound. And they're split into very, again, rudimentary. There's the bottom end, the mids, and there's the tops. How they disperse the sound is – you can see it. It's very visual. You know where it's coming from, and I like that.

You have a very different reaction listening to something like that in a gallery space, than when you're going to outside of it. It definitely is taking things that would have been ignored by 'high culture' – excuse these bland binaries. But the idea of something that would have been essentially something coming out of the West Indian diaspora and coming to Britain and getting incorporated into something. You're bringing attention to it in quite a positive way.

Yeah, maybe. I have more of a problem with that now. I mean, when I did it, it was like 2001 when I made the first one. I still show them. I've just showed them in New York, and they just seemed a bit more… It's like Oasis' third LP or something. They're a bit harder to justify as you get more well received. At the time I just wanted them to be kind of an assault on that white space, on that gallery. I guess there is a historical referencing. They look like big minimalist sculptures; you know what I mean? They've got that kind of reference, but then they do something entirely different.

It seems like a really good point to play one of your tracks. I'm thinking of Acen, because that seems such a natural fit. Do you want to tell me how you first heard the record and why you've chosen to bring that one in?

I went, like I say, I went raving, I was a raver back in from '88 till about '90. Then for a number of reasons, I stopped going. Basically, when I stopped going is when hardcore came onto the scene. And I was a bit snobbish about hardcore when it kicked off, because I'd been into the whole acid Balearic scene, and it just seemed a bit unsophisticated. But now as I've grown more sophisticated, I realized that hardcore was actually this incredible moment of pure creative energy. For about three, four years from early hardcore in '92 through to jungle, drum and bass. That's essentially all I listen to now – hardcore.

Like Two Bad Mice. All that kind of stuff? 'Bomb Scare'. Love that tune.

All of that. You can find shitloads of it, mate. It's essentially like discovering – I remember the 'Nuggets' LP, right? It's like discovering that old '60s garage. It's got a very similar energy, comes from a very similar place. It's just kids then in the garage, kids in a bedroom with an Akai and all the rest of it. Anyway. Acen is just a tune of total inspiring beauty. I fucking love the song so much. It's like my number one.

I'm very very happy to play it. This is 'Trip to the Moon Pt. Two'.

Well, it has to be. There are about eight mixes of this thing. Part two is the best though because it starts off with a nice piano this nicked from the Rolling Stones, 'She's Like a Rainbow' and then it's got a beautiful James Bond drop. This is the best one.

—

That was Acen. Now I want to ask you about a whole, other aspect of your work. I'm really interested about your take on technology. You seem to have been playing ideas around this, in everything from your Felix The Cat work to your talking fridges to perhaps of the underlying narratives of the whole of 'Dream English Kid', the film. Do you want to tell me a little bit about that? I'm trying to think which aspect of that to deconstruct first.

Right.

Let's talk about the film piece, in particular, because you seem to be taking a relationship to technology from the '60s to 1999 and looking at how it has influenced us in some way. I really felt like it was revealing – obviously, you. There was a massive autobiographical element. But it seems to be about the whole context of being British. How it has changed this country. Or maybe it's more universal thing than that. I want to know what your take was on the technological aspect.

Yeah. It's the reason I make any work… or that's the reason to make art rather than music. Because I'm trying to understand why. Why certain things produce an effect on me that is that is so powerful, or so all consuming, or something. It's like pornography. Why is pornography so powerful? It's not just about the act, it's about it's about the way it's broadcast, the way it's constructed, the way it's made, the way it's… the quality of the image. I don't know why I'm picking – It's not just pornography, but pornography is about the most kind of extreme example.

Of something that's made to create desire in the viewer in that sense?

Yeah. As anything is. You can start with pornography and then percolate down. It's like I'll get very excited about pornography from the 1980s, as a particular kind of look. I don't know whether it's just nostalgic, but there's something about the way the image is made up that, I guess arouses me – not just sexually. It's not just erotic but… I shouldn't have started this. Why did I start with pornography?

I have a joy of VHS so I can understand how the material alone also does it too.

Yeah, it's like VHS, but – I guess I'm just talking about the way image production seduces. It's quite basic, what I'm saying but it's so powerful… It's like the only thing that I can know in myself with any certainties are my desires. And yet my desires seemed so much to be dependent on these technologies that produce them. Does that make sense? That is just engaged in that trying to fathom myself and why these things are so effective, and so corrosive, and so enjoyable.

I remember I once heard you talk at the ICA and say that part of your attraction to working with film was the idea of you wanted to be in the films that you enjoyed.

Yeah.

I find that a really interesting idea. The desire to insert yourself into that filmic space. Even to the extent of which, you'll have an aspect where you'll see a little bit of a reflection of your face in something using mirroring. Mirrors have come up in other pieces you've done. Do you want to tell me about where that and how that's manifesting?

It just comes out the same thing. It's just my whole life seems determined by being attracted to things, being seduced by things, to such a degree that I want to interface with them as closely as I possibly can. I want to get as intimate as I can with these things that have such a hold on me. Whether it's films, or whether it's music, or whether it's an image, a picture, whatever it is. I just want to get closer to it. And at the same time as I want to get closer to it, I want to try and understand it, but I never do really understand it. It's that drive to get closer to something is very – I was going to say it's very satisfying. But it's not. It can be very unsatisfying, but it can also be very productive, I guess. And it helps me exorcise some of these frustrations, I guess. Of trying to get close to something can.

Thinking about your works with the Koons balloon dog, which seemed to also be about trying to take an object and pull it apart, look at it, rework it, recreate it.

Yeah. Why are things so good? It's the same with the sound system and the sculptures. It's trying to apprehend something. It's trying to know something and trying to get knowledge of something in the most kind of absolute way you can. Trying to insert yourself inside it. So, you can go "ah, right?" This is what it feels like, or this is how it's produced, or whatever. You know, it's a fantasy, but it's a powerful one. I'm just repeating myself now. It's a productive one. But there's something else I was trying to think about it. It's sort of gnostic.

Nice. There is a connection between the things. Before we play another track, can I ask you about the how you approach the idea of surface? You seem to be interested in things that are reflective or that play around the idea of this distancing between you and another thing? Surface seems to be something there.

Okay. It's not something I think about – surfaces. Mirroring, I guess. It's less mirror, it's more…. Alright there's one very dumb reason why there's a lot of chrome and stuff. Because I use a lot of chrome in CGI, because CGI does chrome very well. It's like the best sell you can do with CGI is chrome. It's the most convincing. It gives the greatest verisimilitude; you know what I mean? That's why there's a lot of chrome.

Just because the medium does it really well.

Just because the medium does it really well. But again, because the medium that is so well and that you're seduced by that artifice – that kind of excites me. Also, I'm toxically narcissistic. So, mirrors have played a great part of my life.

There aren't any in the studio now.

No, I'm lost.

I can hold up my phone.

I need it.

Maybe that's what an artist's job is to be – to be obsessed with their own interests and share them somehow?

Somehow… I guess, it is that narcissistic myth, isn't it? That you're numbed by your own reflection. I've just been reading Marshall McLuhan, and his idea of narcissism which is related to narcosis. He has this great idea, where he basically talks about any technology that comes along, whether it's electricity or the inter-way or TV, in order for us to adapt to this shock to the nervous system, this new reality, we have to – he calls it amputation. We have to cut off part of ourselves.

We have to numb that part of ourselves that we are amputating. And he binds this all up with this narcissistic myth. There's something – I don't know if I'm putting together his ideas, right, but there's something about the internet as the apogee of technology undoubtedly has made us more narcissistic. There is that kind of impulse always there. And, I guess, it's the same thing. It's trying to fathom that. Why would algorithms produce narcissism? How does that happen?

I wish I knew! I'm writing a book about screens so I'm trying to work it out. I'm going to get you to play another track. Is there any one in particular you'd like to, or shall I choose one from the selection?

Go on and ask me about it. I like talking about these records.

Jeremy, Jeremih.

Oh yeah. I like my RnB.

So, do I.

And I like it sparse. I like it when it's really plastic, and that's this one's the most plastic. Plastic I mean in terms of where you're just the production, just really manipulating every possible aspect of the sound. Also, I like the glamour of RnB. It's that it's a mirror effect, isn't it? It's got this very mirrored chrome surface, RnB. It's just a fucking sexy record, a very sexy record.

This is 'All The Time' by Jeremih. I can't say it. I'm really bad with all names.

It's Jeremih.

—

I'm going to ask you about another motif in your work that I have a deep love – because I got a T-shirt when I was five years old, and I used to wake up at six in the morning to watch Felix the Cat cartoons.

Wow.

Tell me about your love about Felix. I remember, I know this is connected here in 'The Long Tail' lecture that you did and this connection to early television. Tell me about Felix.

It all began when I found – I don't know if I found it on the internet or if I found it somewhere else. Anyway, I came across an – what's the word – unremarked image. There was no information with it. It was just a photograph of a doll of Felix the Cat. A three-dimensional doll on a turntable, a gramophone turntable, surrounded by weird machinery. Very unrecognisable technology, and it was an old photograph. I was like what's that? I tracked it down and it was a photograph taken in 1929, documenting the very first image ever broadcast on television. Basically, it was a small radio station in New York, that was doing kind of ham TV, like ham radio, but it was ham TV. So, there be people out in New York in the local borough who had made their own TV sets and they were broadcasting what was called 'mechanical television', like Logie Baird. They were doing this very early test broadcasts to these ham radio, ham TV operators. So, the very first is mechanical scanning. That's what it's called. It just scans the image in this in 32 lines. It's very rudimentary, very weird, pixelated image. And that was it. This was the first electronic image ever broadcast. My life is, as I said before, bound up with the electronic image and trying to understand its effect on me. So, he just became this avatar of electronic image making. He's like the God, the Godhead. He just ended up getting woven into a lot of stuff to the point where I've divorced him essentially.

Ah. Bye bye Felix.

Bye bye Felix. Also, I got a cease and desist from DreamWorks.

What! Steven Spielberg's company?

Felix was pre-Mickey Mouse. The story goes that Disney created Mickey Mouse after seeing the popularity of Felix. And Mickey Mouse, did for Felix, essentially. Now Disney is owned by DreamWorks. They got him in the end. Not only did they kill him, but they've....

Bought his ghost? Taken his corpse?

Yeah. It kind of stinks. The whole idea to Felix, to me, is that it's with that broadcast, with the beginning of broadcasting, then I became the audience. And I received those broadcasts from earliest age. The idea that somehow, then I have to pay copyright – I didn't ask for Felix to be lodged in my head. They never asked me for permission for Felix to become a part of my life. You know what I mean? It's like any child. I talked to him. I can't do anything more with him, essentially.

I remember I've seen him super large, which I think is beautiful. Going back to that ritualistic worship idea. The idea of God being a giant Felix the Cat is something incredible!

There's something a bit disturbing. I mean he was never meant to be like any God. He's beyond good and evil. He's a close associate of Pepe the Frog. This alt-right figure. One of the other reasons he evolved in that way… A friend of mine, Andy Holden, he has this whole idea that cartoons were just paving the way for a new reality. And we now live in this kind of cartoon landscape. There's something. Felix populates that landscape, and it's an irrational one. It doesn't follow Euclidian laws or any particular law. It's like a harbinger of disorder, in some ways. Like any cartoon character. You wouldn't want one living in your house.

No, they're wild essentially.

No. So, he's a dualistic figure, I guess.

I quite like that idea. There are disturbing elements in some of your work and there are quite a few pieces that feel a bit, I'm going to say ideas around the eerie. I'm reading Mark Fisher's latest book.

Yeah, I just read that.

So good. But actually, you would be an interesting fit into that. Where it's not necessarily just about the uncanny – the idea of looking at a robot and feeling it's half human. It's the idea of this strange otherness. It can be more about atmosphere.

Yeah.

I think actually, some of your work fits it really nicely into that trope.

Yeah, definitely. I just read that, Mark Fisher's last book.

Sadly, what a waste.

Yeah. He talks about this idea of 'The Weird and the Eerie' – it's what it's called. As I was reading, I was thinking damn. I've read a lot of Mark and think damn. We were contemporaries, and I think a lot of what he's talking about in the eerie is essentially very British. A lot of it. The whole kind of notion he's talking about is born of children's TV from the late '70s, early '80s.

Alan Garner, that kind of thing.

'Children of the Stones', all that kind of stuff. Even 'Doctor Who'.

My earliest memory.

Yeah, exactly. Delia Darvish's music is essentially eerie. But there's something about the idea of Britain being a haunted isle. I guess I've always, and especially where I'm from the industrial northwest, which is full of ghosts, full of ruins. It's an eerie landscape. But it goes obviously, with the opening of – I was going to say, 'David Copperfield', but it's not 'David Copperfield'. What the Dickens book I'm thinking of… with Magwitch. We're both going to do this now…

Ahh… Oh my god, I'm going to be sitting here on radio going, "which one is that?" I'm immediately going through TV adaptations…

I'm thinking of…

'Great Expectations'?

'Great Expectations'. Thank you. 'Great Expectations' and that beginning in the marsh, in the Kent marshes. It's an eerie place. I've just been reading this stuff about the myth of Albion and the idea that Britain was conquered was conquered by Brutus, who came here. And all it was inhabited by six witches, or seven witches, sorry. Who bred these giant sons and that's all that lived on this weird, wooded island. This is an early Roman story. We're out there in the weird, misty north.

With Brexit, we're out there even more...

We're floating further out.

I'm going to play one more track and then we'll let you go. Do you want to play the The Modern Lovers one? The Jonathan Richman one? Or the other one?

What was the other one?

'Six Secs'.

Yeah, let's play that one because everyone... Alright, can I talk about Jonathan Richman? So, I have two more records left.

We'll play them both – go on.

Great. Well, one is Jonathan Richman 'Roadrunner', which I think he wrote it when he was 17 or something. He's ridiculously precocious when he writes that song. And it's basically a song about driving late at night around Boston, around the suburbs of Boston with the radio on in your car. Which is something I used to do when I was younger. It has that nostalgic familiarity, but more than that ... Before I make any work, there's two songs I listen to. One is the Acen because it got a quality that I want to get to. I don't quite know what that quality is, but I want whatever I make, I want it to be like that record. And in terms of more a thought than a quality, is 'Roadrunner' which is this celebration of the modern. He's in love with the modern world. In love with this modern feeling. Part of the difficulty about making a lot of art is that there's a notion that all contemporary art is a kind of critique. And sometimes, I'm making work as a celebration. It's not a critique. I'm in love with the modern world. There are aspects of the modern world I'm deeply in love with. And sometimes you want to just celebrate them and say, "look at this isn't this incredible"?

I think you've just described the only reason I do anything! I'm an enthusiast.

And that's a quick one on 'Roadrunner'. And 'Six Secs' is just an extraordinary record of pure joy. It's like joy and idiocy, I guess. I don't know how they made this record. I mean, essentially, I make collages with both video and sound. This has this very crude sampling. Again, I aspire to making something like this. I don't know how they did it. It's just about hangs together – but it hangs together really beautifully. I think they were from Berlin. I don't think they're around anymore. They were called Cobra Killer. If Cobra Killer is out there, I'd love you to make some more music. Yeah, anyway 'Six Secs' by Cobra Killer. This is a great, great weird mashup.

Amazing. We're going to play both those and thank you so much for coming in Mark.

Thank you. It was very nice enjoyable. Thank you very much.

Oscar Tuazon & Gardar Eide Einarsson

The Pig Will Eat Its Children, 2012.

22.06.17

I'm Francesca Gavin, and you're listening to Rough Version on NTS. And my guests today are two artists. My first duet, a duo, double, which are Gardar Eide Einarsson, who's a Norwegian artist based in Tokyo, who works with everything from painting to sculpture to neon, and everything in between and Oscar Tuazon his friend and oft collaborator. He's based in LA and works a lot with architectural work, and things that seem to play around ideas of Utopian structures in space and performance. Hello, boys, how are you both?

OT: Great.

Cool. Well, firstly, you both work together, as well as making your own work. Do you want to tell me how you first met?

OT: We met at the Whitney program, which is kind of a strange educational experiment.

Connected to the museum?

OT: Yeah, connected to the museum. We were working together and from the very beginning, I guess.

GEE: Oscar was one of the first people I met in New York. Actually, I think we met like that third day that I was there. I landed on September 10, 2001.

Good timing.

GEE: Actually, the Whitney program was supposed to start September 11. It was postponed one day because, you know, world dread.

OT: Yeah, the first day was the attacks.

Wow. That's pretty surreal beginning to also like a career thing. You both had just come out of art school at the time. Baby yous, basically. Then you both also ended up working with Vito Acconci, is that correct?

OT: That was part of it. We were. We were working in the studio and making.

GEE: Actually, how it happened was Vito asked. Vito was teaching at the Whitney program, and he asked if there wasn't anyone there who can help him put up a bookshelf in his architecture office. We were like, "Sure, yeah, I guess we can do it". We need the money or whatever. We showed up for a one-day bookshelf building job and ended up what…

OT: A year later.

> *What was he like? I would imagine he's pretty mental and quite strange, obviously.*

GEE: He is mental.

OT: He's just hardcore. When we were working there. He was maybe in his late '60s, early '70s but he's still living in his studio. He'd sleep under the desk when he stayed late at night on a dirty mattress on the ground. And then he'd wake up in the morning after two hours of sleep and give himself a sponge bath at the table, because there was no hot water in the studio. He was living in a cold water flat. And he was just so devoted. I was like, "this is really not what I want to do. Time to look for a new career".

> *Did you find any influence of his like practice on both of you at that time as formative baby artists?*

GEE: I mean I think he's an amazing artist. And I thought, he was also one of the reasons why I was interested in the Whitney program in the first place. I think he was one of the best lecturers there actually, because you could tell that he was pretty crazy. I think he's just an amazing artist. And his attitude is great. Also, this idea of that he puts everything on the line all the time. First, he starts off as a poet, and then he totally switches and then he's an artist. Then he totally switches again, and he's an architect. It would have been so much safer and easier for him to stay being an artist and rest on his laurels.

Instead, he starts up this giant, architectural office and does pretty straight architecture. The architecture itself isn't so straight but…

Oscar looking at your work, actually, I could see the connection because of the architectural influence on what you're making now…

OT: Huge. Huge influence in terms of thinking about space, but he started as a poet, and that was always how he worked. Through speaking and through language and asking questions in the studio. I guess it was that freedom that he had, to really do anything in his work. That's inspiring. It's a freedom that seems like he always paid a lot for, because he would self-sabotage. Not self-sabotage… Just when one thing was done, he would move on to something else.

It's difficult. It's a devotion. So, after you left this project, how did you end up deciding that you wanted to make collaborative work together? I first knew about this collaboration when I saw a book that you did. A photographic book that came out of a Tokyo show. I think is that correct? Do you want to tell me a bit like how you work together?

GEE: We started working together really early, I guess. We had studios at the Whitney program. We were working in proximity to each other from very early on. We were hanging out every day and we were talking together a lot. Actually, our first project together we found in Vito's library maybe…

OT: It was that magazine 'Guerrilla War in the USA'. This magazine published this special – it's so relevant now actually – in 1970, covering guerrilla war attacks in the USA. Hundreds of them at that time. Students blowing up the Bank of America building or…

Weather Underground kind of stuff?

OT: Weather Underground or somebody setting a school on fire. And there was this incredible list of all these attacks and a map and everything. I guess a lot of the stuff that we were doing was around like the stuff that we were reading and trying to bring that into the present.

Moving on to more contemporary ways of how that's emerged. Do you still have that subject matter in the collaborations that you've made? Is there still like a political undercurrent in that because obviously knowing your work Gardar in particular there's definitely a political undercurrent in what you do.

GEE: I think that's all that's always there you know. It's for me always there in my work, and when I see Oscar's work, I feel like it's always there in his work, as well. That's ever present.

I'm quite interested also in how that links to ideas around masculinity. Your work both feels quite bloke-ish to me. It feels masculine concepts are in there and that's part of what you're addressing conceptually, in some way. Do you want to tell me about what your feelings, both of your feelings separately, are about that? Do you feel that? Is that intentional or is it accidental?

OT: Yeah. I see what you mean…

GEE: I mean, for me, it's definitely intentional… I'm interested in it, and I want to be critical of it, but I don't want it to be this critique that stands outside of it. I want to address a fascination with it, but I also want to be aware that, that fascination is there somehow. With masculinity in my work and I guess maybe even in my life, I want to be aware that, that fascination is there and to talk about it. For me, there's definitely masculinity in the work. There's also this exaggerated hysteric masculinity that pokes fun at itself. I hope.

That's a nicer way of doing it, as opposed to just being macho without being self-reflective. It makes sense.

GEE: Yeah. That's a little silly, I think.

OT: There's something very fragile about masculinity and the failure of that…

GEE: I think our work actually both embraces failure quite a lot. Both has this pretty amateurish, look to it all. I think it works with failure quite a bit.

It seems like a really good moment to play both of your hip hop tracks that you brought. I don't know why again, because Gucci Mane and Pusha T are quite interesting things to reference. Do you want to tell me a bit, each of you, why you chose those songs and why you like them?

OT: I chose that track. It's the last track off of Pusha T's last album, and it's so great. I mean, the whole album was great. I think the other tracks couldn't be played on the radio. It's interesting because it really is a gangster rap album. It's really about drug dealing – well you think it is in the beginning. Then it starts to like turn or shift and become very introspective and tragic. The last track is just really haunting and sad. I think he's doing something really interesting that was funny. Cause he's also acting the macho guy and then using a lot of other guests to fill that the rest of the space.

Jill Scott who's guesting on 'Sunshine' brings a really different element, creatively.

OT: She plays in the background.

And why did you choose Gucci Mane 'I Can't'?

GEE: I was listening to that album because it's Christmas.

As in a Christmas gift?

GEE: There is a Santa hat on the cover.

OT: Isn't it a little early to be looking forward to Christmas.

GEE: No, no. It was last Christmas. I just think that I don't know the lyrics are so good. It's so funny and it's hard but it's just like really funny at the same time. Smart, I think. I like it a lot.

Okay. We'll play this now. So, we have Gucci Mane 'I Can't' and Pusha T 'Sunshine' featuring Jill Scott.

—

I want to go back and talk about some of the political stuff. I was really interested in the flag piece that you made recently, Gardar. You're Norwegian, but you lived for 10 years in the States and now you're in Tokyo. You're aware of Americana. Do you want to tell me about the ideas behind that work and how that relates to the political situation America? Which for me, I think is so international and relevant at this point in time.

GEE: It's funny, because it's actually not that funny. It's interesting, because I was always using the US as this case study, because I thought a lot of the things that were present elsewhere, were extra obvious in the US. This violence that lurks right below the surface. That is necessary in order to kind of maintain the nation state and all of that. And, of course, now that's just become so present. It's not even under the surface. And the more I'm not only in the US, also more and more in Europe. It's depressing…

It's like your work feels really prescient, accidentally. You could look at the things that you've done – quoting things from police handbooks, or the graphic imagery that plays into an almost regimented political history of America. It really seems different now than it did two years ago.

OT: It looks so relevant right now, even from five or 10 years ago. It's right now. It really seems very present and urgent. Those themes of control are so present. It's funny, also the Flag Waste that piece… In the work that we're doing, there's flags in a lot of it or dysfunctional or blank flags or broken illegible flags.

Is that, again, about this idea of failure of something? Because when I've looked at some of the architectural stuff that you've done, I've been really interested in its references to counter cultural history, which is a moment which I'm personally fascinated in. Really it is more of a Utopian period where we almost felt like there was a possibility to combine the aesthetic with the political to create something else. For me, it's almost like the representation of the flag is the post-utopian failure.

OT: Going to Standing Rock recently, there are a lot of flags there. There's this whole flag road as you enter the main camp. 300 or more flags from indigenous nations all over the US and Canada. That's a completely different version of the flag, they are flags that are recognised only by a small group of people and that function against, I guess, the American flag…

The graphic power within it in some way.

OT: Yeah… It's not that they're extra-national flags. They are national flags. But I guess for me that it was a way of rethinking what a nation would be.

GEE: I think also a flag is like a statement of intent. It doesn't really mean one thing. It's a thing to rally around, that needs to be filled. An idea that needs to be worked on. And I think a lot of the flags that I've used in the past have been these proto versions of the American flag, for example. That were usually really homemade. Stitched in somebody's living room. I think with the flag waste thing it was about – they were all cut offs, things that had to be gotten rid of, in order to make the actual flag. So, sort of the same as with a nation state, right? There are certain things that have to be blocked out. Certain people that are pushed out. There's always this normative idea, that I thought that piece somehow symbolized for me. And of course, those like cut offs are maybe the ones that I have more sympathy for.

Of course.

OT: It's all the material. The flag as just a material and how that gets processed, like an industrial made and remade. I think the handmade banner that you've made, what does it say?

GEE: "This is unlawful assembly disperse at once or we fire".

OT: Yeah. That's also a flag, right? That's also a banner. There's always a flag contesting and marking some territory, one way or another.

GEE: Yeah. In the beginning it follows the physical layout as a painting. These four sides. It's flat… Similar dimensions to a painting.

> *It's the same picture-screen shape – window perspectival arrangement. I never thought about that connection. Do you want to tell me a little bit, in terms of your collaborative work and also your own things about colour or grayscale? Gardar I can't help it. I think about black and white when I think of your work but then also the work that I've seen you make together is often the colour has been removed. Oscar, a lot of the work that I've seen you make seems to focus on concrete materiality, which again has this removal of colour. I wanted to know what was that about for you?*

OT: We're colourblind!

> *Literally? That would be a very a sad experience*

OT: Different shades of concrete.

GEE: '50 Shades of Concrete'.

OT: I think of a lot of my work, and I'm sure some people would agree, as unfinished. It's not quite done yet. I always felt like painting could happen – that could happen after. I try to just build the scaffold or something, the foundation… but we've managed to do a colourful show this time actually.

GEE. That's true.

> *New. Exciting.*

OT: New terrain.

GEE: That's really interesting – what you say about that, because that's very similar to why I feel I don't really use colour. First of all, my work is usually or always found imagery. Wanting to make it a copy of that imagery somehow. I think it's a big part of it. Also, I don't feel like I want to like compete with a lot of other products. It's important for me that it is, unfinished and it's not that nicely made. You don't have to get stuck in "Oh my god, how did he paint that?" That's not what it's about. If you take a few things away, you don't have to compete with a certain level of polish or something.

It's more a concept or meaning or statement behind something.

GEE: Yeah. And it's also maybe about giving somebody the idea that this is a part of thought process. You're not giving them this closed off finished product. It's something that is part of a process, also for the viewer.

Do you want to tell me what you're both inspired by at the moment? I'm really interested that you did go to Dakota for the pipeline protests. Was that to inspire your work in some sense?

OT: No. I really went, because I felt that it was like that, I could do something there. I couldn't do much. I just did what I was able to do in a short period of time. I wanted to go and support that cause. It was inspiring in ways that I didn't even, couldn't even imagine… The only thing I could compare it to like this very intense communal or collective production around an idea that's commonly held. The urgency and the passion of it. The only thing I could relate it to is making art. It felt like making art with a whole bunch of people. It was like everybody's building something, thinking something. The conversations were just wide ranging. It's a really amazing intellectual environment, actually. People coming from all over and it gave me an idea of how an artwork could do things – anywhere, really.

A great starting point. And you Gardar? Anything in particularly you're looking at, at the moment, which is informing what you're doing?

GEE: When we were working on this show, Oscar and I were talking a little bit about how this particular period in time, historically or politically. It's obviously so terrible, but actually not such a terrible time to be making art. It actually feels quite clear why you're doing it. It's nice that you're working with something that you feel actually is in pretty stark opposition to that whole worldview. I think that this whole – Trump and Brexit and all this stuff – obviously has real world effects that are not inspiring, but as somebody who works with culture, I feel like it inspires me to keep working with culture.

If work doesn't reference our current situation, it's feeling increasingly irrelevant, but also at the same time, that doesn't mean the work has to be directly political staying within it. Because maybe the process of creation itself is a political statement, at this point.

OT: I'm always very sceptical of the idea that art can communicate. I've always thought that the communicative potential of an artwork is so complicated, but it can. An artwork can do things very clearly somehow. And it does feel that it is actually a time where actions – that an artwork can act in the world.

It's a type of action, in general.

OT: Yeah. It's funny. I think one thing that it's made me aware of the urgency of the current situation. I don't know. I'm not quite sure how to say it!

I know it's really quick, but I'm going to play some of your next tracks, and they don't go together at all. The last two did, these couldn't be more different. Do you want to tell me about Little Feat 'Willin''? Oscar first?

OT: It's a great song. It's a song about being on the road. He's got a nice line in there. I mean the whole lyrics are great.

When did you first hear it?

OT: Maybe like five or six years ago and it became my fave. I sang it at karaoke once. I thought that it's a nice karaoke song.

GEE: That's what ties our songs together because mine is also a very nice karaoke song. I partly picked it because I sing it a lot at karaoke.

> *Karaoke segue to Gardar's Pet Shop Boys featuring Dusty Springfield 'What Have I Done to Deserves This?' which is a classic and rather camp song. Do you sing this often at karaoke?*

GEE: I do. That is my current favourite karaoke song. I do all the parts. Of course not. I love that song. It also reminded me of London. I think it has this really great like romantic image of London and Oscar and I have a long karaoke history together, so I thought it was appropriate.

OT: The duets. The duets album is coming!

> *I love karaoke. Oh my god, you can harmonize. Amazing. That's amazing. And yes, I think Pet Shop Boys are a very London band, and I support that. So, I'm going to play both those things now and thank you both very, very much for coming in.*

GEE: Thank you very much.

Hannah Perry

14.07.17

I'm Francesca Gavin and you're listening to Rough Version on NTS. My guest this month is Hannah Perry. Originally from Chester, based in London – though with good doses of Los Angeles and New York – she's a Royal Academy graduate who has shown everywhere from the Zabludowicz Collection to The Moving Museum, to CFA in Berlin and Seventeen in London. She was also in a show I'm very proud to have curated called 'E-Vapor-8' about the relationship between rave and artists. She makes everything from video work, to mirror printed pieces, to wobbly silver walls that move with the bass of subwoofers and performance works that often include collaborations with people like Mica Levi and Holly Blakey. So, we have Hannah Perry in the studio! Hi, Hannah, how you doing?

Hello, good.

This is quite funny; I've known your work for a really long time, and I put you in exhibitions. I want to talk about the contrast and how the works changed since you first started making things. I think one of the things that seems to be constant in your work over the past five years, is this interest in layering.

Yeah.

That applies both to your video pieces, but also to your installations. I want you to tell me a little bit about what you like about the layer.

I think with the layering – with video, you always have this opportunity to layer footage. It's not so much layer, but presenting one thing after another, in that sense. I think when you have material-based things, then you can easily mimic that technique just by adding layers.

So, basically, film was where everything grew out of?

Yes, exactly.

It started with moving image. Let's talk about the kind of material you use, because it's really varied. How do you source material?

I used to use found footage a lot and then more and more I was shooting my own footage on my iPhone. That's what I do now… Just shoot a lot of the footage on my iPhone.

Why did you make that change? Because I remember in the early stuff you would have old RnB music videos. There would be teenagers snogging and raves… It had a Mark Leckey-ish vibe.

Yes, exactly, exactly. I think the films are quite autobiographical. Quite a lot of my soul is in that, even though it doesn't seem that way. One way in which I'm trying to talk about, say, autobiography or a biography or an experience is by not making it just my experience. One way that I felt comfortable in doing that was to use footage that wasn't mine. I was telling my perspective and my story through other people's images. So, it was my voice, but it wasn't my life in that sense. It started out in a comfortable place. Then I suppose I started working a lot with fucking up the footage. I was either putting it through old VHS machines – taking it digitally, putting it into VHS, bringing it back out – getting data from the internet, which I uploaded and downloaded and was just processing and processing the material. So, when I started filming my own footage, it felt like that the mediation still had that removal. But at the same time, I was also interested in a candid, difficult position… I wanted it to be very personal, but I also wanted it to not be all about me! Using an iPhone is like a really good way of being able to just shoot experiences as they come.

It is something that has become a very universal thing. We're all playing with our iPhones, we're all shooting footage, whether or not you stick it on like Snapchat or Instagram stories or whatever. Actually, that's just a really normal interaction. It is surprising that a lot of people aren't making work out of that material… It's almost seen as not 'high art'?

Exactly, but… people are using that as a medium more and more now, especially with Instagram stories and that sort of thing… They weren't at all really when I first started using it as a camera. There's something about this handheld, shaky look. I'm not going out to film stuff with this big, expensive camera to look high spec on a tripod because that feels to me not very 'in the moment'. Just using the iPhone – I don't know, it could be seen like that, but then it's also what you do with the material and what material you take. What you're trying to say with that, and how you layer text, music, and then add to, manipulate the footage…

> *Do you want to talk about how you're forming a narrative? I know you've written scripts related to certain film pieces, and I'm interested in what the difference is, as an artist, using the material we take on our phones and then how you make that into something that feels like an artwork. Is it just about the technical processes? Or is there also a narrative element in the stories themselves?*

Yeah. I feel with my videos, it's heavily edit-based. It's a case of filming everything, or filming all these things, and collecting stuff. I think the work begins when I'm editing through it and placing things together. A lot of the time, it's quite nerdy. It's like categorizing things but in a really abstract way. "Okay, this footage says this to me", or "to me this feels like this"… do you know what I mean? It's making these connections, which build narratives. I think you can manipulate video footage quite a lot to say what you want it to say. I think you can build up narratives within the video and within the sound. More recently, I've been writing scripts, and getting people to read them out loud and record them in the studio. But before, rather than use a script, I'd use a line or use a snippet of somebody's conversation instead, that says the same thing. Or I would use a bit in a song that gives you the same sort of feeling. In a way, using music or video footage as a kind of script…

> *Do you want to tell me a little bit about what those kinds of narratives are? What are the stories? What are the issues? Because when you're involving yourself in something, it seems to be very much about self-portraiture and the representation of*

a young woman being creative... Do you want to tell me a little bit about that? I know that other works have touched a lot on 'the mechanical' and our relationship to technology in different ways. I know you're really into cars, so you have a lot of car references. But also, things like tampons and advertising. What kind of things are doing it for you at the moment? What's your focus?

I think probably a focus that I've always had is working with adult conversations, but using children, for example. A lot of the time I'm using teenagers and bits of footage of my family or people that are close to me and I'll use the footage... A lot of the time it will be a girl in her teenage years – looking at that formative' time. Using that footage represents that moment that we can all relate to on that level. It's like the reason for putting that as a trope in the footage all the time, which I keep coming back to, like you are looking back at your own experience or something like that. One of the tropes in there is youth as a formative time. I used to always make work about where I was from, so social class came into it. Coming from a really working-class background in the north of England. That was always really important, being quite celebratory about where I was from and what that means and why that's interesting and why there is something to say. Especially as I am now living all over the place or moving to London. It changed my perspective on looking back at things...

Weirdly, loads of artists have come from where you're from – Jesse Wine, Ryan Gander...

Mark Leckey!

Bloody hell, it's mental. How are you all from Chester?! Isn't that where Hollyoaks is shot at well? A hotbed of creativity... There is something coming out of that place.

I think that was always why I referenced Mark Leckey when I first started making work because I understood a lot of his references, because of coming from Ellesmere Port as well... living on an estate there. Even though he's talking about a different decade in time or a different period of time or whatever, it still has the same cultural relevance. Another couple of artists were like my access point into making art, because I don't come from an art background. I think that's why that was always really important.

Let's start by playing one of your tracks and then we can talk about your relationship with music afterwards, because I know you've incorporated that a lot. Do you want to start by playing the piece, well one of a series of works you've made with OKZharp? Do you want to tell me about how that collaboration began and how you're using that in your work?

Yes. I'd seen some stuff that he'd done. What I tend to do is get a little bit obsessed with certain musicians, or a certain song, or a certain sound. And then I try and contact them. Actually, I just sent him a tweet on Twitter.

I love Twitter friends. I have them too!

I was like "Hey man what's your email?" I sent him an email and proposed some ideas about some sound stuff. There's a lot of London-based musicians and producers that I am really interested in, and he was one of them. We met up and actually we didn't know what we were going to do, so it wasn't like we were going to make a music track even though that's what it's turned out to be. We were going to make some sound things, some installation, maybe some performance. He could do some live stuff. He had some things coming up with Hyperdub at Corsica Studios at some point which we might make an installation for. At that moment, we just bounced back and forth some things. I'd had these samples I had edited a little bit. I sent them over to him, but he doesn't work in samples. He makes all of his own music, so for him it was interesting, I think, because he's using a different technique to what he would usually [use]. But it worked quite well. I like some of the stuff that's come out of it, and I think, he's also asked me if I can sing? I think I can sing… I didn't know if I was going to use it for a video or not, but by mistake they've been turned into tracks, which I think could be really nice. God knows what we'll do with them…

This is one of the tracks you've made.

—

That was one of the yet to be titled collaborations that you've made with OKZharp. Now, do you want to tell me what are you working on at the moment? You've been doing quite a lot of performance work, to activate the installations. Working with, I think, the choreographer Holly Blakey? Who used to be a teacher, she used to teach me stuff!

Wow!

She actually used to teach me ballet barre, it's hilarious. Do you want to tell me what are you working on now, and how performance is becoming more and more part of that?

I guess it's a different type of practice for me. I have a schizophrenic type of practice where you can be in the studio making video or sculpture or screen print or any of those things, but it's very solo. The thing that's really nice about doing performances, or anything live, or music related, is that you get to collaborate with people, and you exchange ideas. It warps and challenges your usual way of working… I've seen a lot of people who I really admire, and I will approach them and ask to work with them and if they say yes, then obviously, there's always a level of respect there. It's very easy to let go of control, because they'll come up with something amazing, because you just know they will. I love collaborating with people. In some of the performances I worked with Holly Blakey, who is a choreographer. I also work with Mica Levi, who is a producer, composer, general amazing person. She's just so talented. She's classically trained. She does soundtracks for Hollywood movies. I think she did 'Under the Skin' and 'Jackie'. Recently, she got nominated for an Oscar. She's just incredibly talented. And the same with Holly. When I approached both of them, they were both doing their own thing but since then we've been working together, they've both done super, super well. The performances and what we have been doing up until now is half between dance and half between an expression of the body or the expression of a feeling or a movement. Trying to play around with different scenes and different performers. Men and women. Women and women. How they communicate or try and represent how they communicate. There will be sound as well. Sometimes I've written scripts for that but somehow, it didn't really work. The latest thing that I'm working on at the moment is actually writing scripts that, hopefully, I'm going to get teenagers to narrate. We'll have young people. Probably from southeast London. There are some organizations there that I've worked with before, who will narrate the scripts… Then there will be a performance, so there will be movement and sound, and narration. That's the next thing after New York that I'm doing.

I'm really interested in the documentation of the performance you did to activate the installation in CFA in Berlin, which was a few months ago. I was really interested in the way that choreography seemed to really say something about the idea of communication. How do we communicate? Maybe again going back to that relationship to the phone. The relationship of two bodies trying to have some connection between them. I think that's quite an interesting metaphor for your work in a wider sense, which is a way of describing your own personal experiences and how that fits into a wider narrative of being young and female and narrating that emotional state… Would you agree?

Yes, exactly. It was two young performers. They are amazing dancers, but so young. They looked like teenagers. We [gave them] this choreography where half girls were mentoring one another. Girls being interested in having some kind of sexual energy as friends, and then also having this difficult competitiveness. One of them is doing the other one's hair and then the next minute, she would be working with dance and movement, trying to express these little connections between young women. It is directly related to the film. There was a section in the film where it had these two little kids. They were spitting out water and they were joking. It was really sweet. We wanted to try and work with these sentiments rather than write a script.

One of the loveliest pieces I saw in that show was the way that you'd arranged for people to watch the video pieces – in a giant bed covered in huge duvets, with wigs to look like your hair. It really felt like we were in Hannah's bed with her watching a film. It really brought it back to the personal. It was disgusting but good disgusting! Is that something you've done before? Would you do it again?

Yes, I'm going to do that again for New York. I haven't even told them this yet! I was supposed to Skype them last week, but I haven't. What I'm going to do is the entire room is going to be covered in duvets and we're going to tint them, so that they're very, very slightly pink… The whole thing, all the walls, the floors will be one big padded strange room. Which would be great for the sound as well, because it would deaden the sound. On the floor, there'll be all this weird, grotesque expanding foam. Things that you want to touch and sit on…

And people can touch!

Yes, you can touch, and you lie on them. Then the whole floor becomes one big, massive bed. With my hair extensions as well.

What do you like about that? They are like 'In Bed With Madonna'? What do you like about the idea of inviting a viewer into a kind of metaphorical, sculptural bed?

That is the thing, right? Because the film. Is more a narrative piece. It's an aggressive text, but also a very sensual text. It's very commanding, and also a bit freaky. Basically, I was trying to create this idea of a crazy woman, or a cliché of a crazy woman?

Glenn Close in a 1980s thriller vibe?

Totally! I watched 'Fatal Attraction'. That was the one thing that I watched, and I thought, this is actually quite interesting at the moment, because there's so many memes and jokes, and it's topical and interesting to talk about. Like mental health, and how society is stigmatizing that. One of the ways in which I feel female representation has been [used] a lot recently is this crazy ex-girlfriend. Beyoncé 'Lemonade' was this entire ex-wife being en vogue. I don't know. There's something in it. I just really wanted to play with that as a theme. Take that on and being quite.

Critical?

But also some of the script is kind of funny. I looked into a lot of old hate mail that I'd written to an ex-boyfriend years ago. When I look back at it now, it's actually really funny – the anger and aggression. So, I thought, "right, I'm going to take bits of that". I'm going to take some memes online, and I'm going to use them as if I was doing a lot of research into the psychological shifts that we've had since we had to negotiate new technology. Stalking online, for example, has become common… Even the word, stalking. I mean if you did that in real life you'd be arrested. But now it's like "oh I've been stalking such and such online". All these psychological shifts that we've had since social media, all mixed together, have created the persona of this aggressive crazy woman. It was a very feminist piece actually, because it was taking that on as a kind of positive anger, as a positive emotion. A way of embracing the female voice and not allowing oneself to be pathologized, which is, I think, is a huge way to make one feel submissive. It's a way of putting somebody in a box. Burn the witch at the stake type of thing. The interesting thing is I've had it even in work scenarios or with friends of mine… A friend of mine who owned a restaurant was having this meeting. The guy she had a meeting with acted appallingly. He was a total dick and was being a bully. He was 20 years older than she was from a very wealthy background, so he had all this capital. She pulled him up on one thing. If it was me, I probably would have gone completely nuts, but she's not that way. She pulled him up on one thing and his immediate response was "let's not be emotional about this".

Ouch!

You know what I mean? That's what I'm talking about. I thought, how can we embrace this stereotype of being emotional, because that's not a negative thing at all. Or being assertive. I'm not even going to say aggressive. It's assertive. I often think that intimidates people, and therefore, the reaction is "Oh, don't be emotional". It's actually turned out to be a real feminist piece with quite a strong voice, which I didn't intend it to be. I was supposed to look into all this. I was just trying to dig into this emotional stuff, then it turned out to be this different thing.

This seems like a really good point to play the live piece that you've done with Mica Levi, because it's two girls working together! Do you want to tell me a bit about the Mica Levi performance work that we're going to listen to now?

This was actually live streamed on the Boiler Room website.

Swallow that!

Exactly – I just burped! We did it in a warehouse in Hackney, and there were six performers dancing, with my video projected in the background. There was a drummer, a cellist, a violin, and then Mica on the electronic vibes. We composed a soundtrack for the performance. It was great because we could go back and forth between what the viewer could see, which was my video, and then switch it to like a live audience. It's just a really small snippet of that.

Okay, let's hear a bit of Mica and Hannah Perry live.

—

That was Mica and Hannah Perry. Do you want to talk a little about another thing that I really love in your work – your use of mirroring and the idea of reflection. I know you've done a lot of print works on metallic, shiny things. Do you want to tell me about those pieces?

For the next show what I'm going to do is create some more of those like 'sub works' that I have been working on.

These are metal pieces that vibrate with subwoofer bass lines.

Yes. Mirrors that vibrate. There are car subs that we take them out of the sub box and then we sort of hang them in these metal frames. It's really hard to explain until you see it…

It makes it magic actually, when you're watching it, because you can't quite work out how it's vibrating, but you feel the bass… Girls love bass.

Exactly. And some of the frequencies are so low that sometimes you can't even hear them. Or you can cross the frequencies across, so they end up being like a sub bass wobble! We take these subs and then hang them in this metal construction and then stretch over this really thin mirror. Once the sound piece goes into it, once the sub goes into it, it literally wobbles. The speaker pushes the air out. So, the vibrations that you can see in the mirror are like rippled vortexes or something of your reflection, that goes with the sound. I'm going to make them in the next show. I've made a couple of different arrangements of those, but that's one of my favourite things.

What do you like about that? I think it's a really interesting idea to make music into an object, and also reflect our own vision of ourselves. What do you like about that kind of midpoint?

I think making sound sculptural. That's one thing that I found really interesting when I was first working with speakers as a sculptural object. It becomes even more visceral because you get a kind of physical warp… I don't know. There's something about warped reality or something about this warped reflection of yourself… I'm quite obsessed with illusions and how we create things in our brain that are not real.

That's a perfect metaphor for our entire experience of the phone, and representation of the self.

Curating ourselves… I think it's all about our perceptions or how we think other people can see us and everybody's become so self-conscious of that. That is just the way it is now, for good or for bad. I don't even feel that critical about it. It's just this is the way it is now. If you were to ever have an anxiety attack, or if you're going to go into a film and then you're watching it and they show a visual representation of a panic attack. I feel a little bit like that's what it is. This warped perspective. This wobbling intensity. There is a noise you can feel it in the air and it's this pressure. I feel there's something in these anxieties – whether it's a social anxiety or some kind of intense experience. I think it's actually quite hard to make people feel that or feel over saturated with that. I did one [work] that was an entire room. So, you go into the middle, and you're just surrounded by these throbbing reflections. It makes you a bit dizzy and sick. The warped reality, I think is quite nice.

Do you still do a lot of print works on top of the mirror pieces? What you like about that combination? Because they're a little bit different than these sculpture works. They feel close to something like paintings. Do you want to tell me what kind of imagery you are using?

Totally. I worked with screen printing and digital printing on mirror or aluminium. I use this vinyl as well. It's just a lot of car products, basically, that I use a lot of the time. But with the mirror stuff, it's all silk screening and a lot of the imagery will come from my archive photographs, but some of it, well most of it, will come from film stills. Everything usually comes out of the film.

I remember once, years ago, you told me the car thing was connected to your dad and your brother. They were really into car stuff and that you were used to being around that material?

Yeah. I think a lot of the material I use would be thought of as masculine material. Working with builders' scaffolding frames, and car paraphernalia, and things like that, is normal for me. The funny thing is I grew up in quite a macho environment. And I don't mean just men, I think a lot of the women that I grew up with were extremely – I mean, macho is probably the wrong word, maybe that's a bit '80s now!

We need a thesaurus! Bolshy? In your face? I don't know.

Yeah, it's an interesting one. I think coming from that background and being familiar… I mean my dad's a welder. My brother's a welder. My dad laughs about it, actually, because, and this is the ironic thing. All of a sudden, I'm working with metal. I work with cars. My dad's obsessed with cars. My dad also builds these machines that crush up things and I make these sculptures of crushed up metal. It's like, "Are you joking?" You're basically just having your dad's career – a spin-off of your dad's career!

But making a kind of feminist…

Yeah, exactly!

Like a sociological statement about that! But maybe that's what everyone does in a way… We're all really drawing on our own personal experience, particularly our parents. It makes sense that your work is reflecting on that.

Yeah. I like working with those materials because they are representative of that and as a female – I did ask my dad, when I was 14 if I could like learn how to weld and he said, "That's not a woman's job". I was like "I'm going to make my career out of this thank you very much". I suppose there is a bit of that, but also this masculine world… It' too normative to say these things, but essentially that's my experience of it. Very simple straight cuts; very overbearing displays of typical gender roles. That's what I grew up with. I don't think it's actually like this anymore for people of a younger generation or people in bigger cities. But I grew up in the middle of nowhere… I don't think it's the same anymore. I don't think it's that black and white, but certainly where I'm from it was a lot more black and white. Anyway, I'm obsessed with using these materials.

They are nice ones to use. I like the idea that maybe they feel more comfortable in a way, because they're familiar to you. They feel familiar, even though you're trying to twist it. As our last thing, I'm going to play your last track, which is Erykah Badu. Do you want to tell me what you like about Ms. Badu and why you chose this track in particular?

I mean she's literally my spirit guide… I missed the first wave… I wasn't really aware of her until maybe 10 years ago…

You are probably a bit young for 'On and On'.

I think so. But now it's my 'go to' in the studio. I just play album after album. Her music is so amazing. You can really feel it and I think it's a really beautiful thing. She also speaks from a feminine energy which I find quite interesting, this mother thing… 'Mother Nature' connected to the earth and this song in particular, it feels quite meditative. I've always been into all different types of music but there's just something about her music that I can just listen to on and on in the studio, forever probably!

I also really like her last mixtape, all about phone relationships. It is exceptional, representing everything in terms of our experience today through the phone.

Exactly.

This track isn't from that album. This is an earlier piece, which is 'Ye Yo'. Let's play 'Ye Yo' by Erykah Badu. Thank you very, very much for coming in!

Thank you for asking me!

Mark Titchner

The world isn’t working (ND), 2017.

18.08.17

This month's guest is Mark Titchner. He was nominated for the 2006 Turner Prize. He has exhibited at Tate Britain, at the AGO in Toronto, South London Gallery. He did an amazing psychedelic project at the Royal Academy. He makes work about politics, the language of self-help, language itself, dissecting our experience in installation, performance, print, work, painting, and pretty much everything. You've done a lot of work that's incorporated music into what you do. Some performance-based stuff, the psychedelic event you did at the Royal Academy that I was part of, and you've done a thing in IMMA. Do you want to tell me a little bit about how you've incorporated music into what you do?

Yeah, sure. I think first of all, I used to sort of use sound in my work and not think about it as music. I have a bit of a weird relationship with my practice and music. I'm an artist. I'm not a musician. Probably for very silly reasons. I got back into working, I guess more, with music through collaborating with a guy called Nicholas Bullen. Nick has done lots of stuff, but he was famously like a founder member of Napalm Death. I work mainly with language – and I was really interested in what he did to language in his songs. They are just turning it into this pure noise. I think that opened the door again, to a bit more of a collaborative approach to it. Then things shifted, again in 2012. I'm really interested in the idea of performing and live music, but I'm absolutely terrified by it in a really quite fundamental way. Whenever I do the sound on the videos, and if I ever kind of make performance stuff, it's generally done in some really obscure setting. I decided that I wanted to make this piece, it was called 'Six Chairs'. It was a really ritualized performance. I did it in private. I just did it, got quite a lot of amplification, set it up in this room. It was a full-on kind of noise thing.

With six chairs?

Yeah. It was part of a bigger project with some other artists and curators, but it was to do with these points, which I was moving around, and the equipment that was placed on them and stuff. It was pretty, quite punitive! My ears were quite badly ringing. It was about, I don't know, releasing. There wasn't a real point to it apart from this release. And then this really weird sort of chain of events, which really changed my life, happened afterwards. I got a text in the morning from an artist called Jess Flood-Paddock who had a studio in the same building. The thing was so loud, that she'd heard everything. I felt really bad, but she was like; "I've got a friend who is interested in that kind of noise you're making, you should text him". It turned out it was a guy called Alexander Tucker. I'd seen Alex playing live a lot, actually. But we didn't have a connection and we got in touch. And we hit it off. We had a very fun! Perfect sort of 'first art date'…

Haha!

We both got lost in a room about this size in a cloud of dry ice. It was really strange. But anyway, that set this whole chain of events off, which has led to a much kind of bigger part of music in what I do. A lot of that has been with Alex and with Daniel O'Sullivan. Daniel and Alex both do all sorts of things, but together they do this band called Grumbling Fur. We've worked together a lot and in particular, they did a surround-sound soundtrack for a video installation I did called 'Rose'. We've done quite a lot and as a live thing we did it at the Roundhouse and Royal Festival Hall. Daniel and I just produced a piece for IMMA in Ireland with Stephen Dunne, who's an artist based in Dublin and is a good friend of us both…

Love Steve.

What I like working with them is they encouraged me to do things. But because it's outside of the art world, the pressures are different. And I know I'm not a musician, so it makes me feel a bit more at ease. Improvisation is a big part of it. I just did my first live visual video set for a band called Lanier Cat which is Daniel Massimo from Zoo and Jessica Moss, who plays with Silver Milk Zion. I did a live set for them at Supersonic Festival, which was again it was like going through my fear barrier a bit but I really enjoyed actually.

Actually, should we play the Grumbling Fuir track that you brought in?

Yeah, yeah, I should probably just say…

It seems like an apt thing to play…

Yeah. This track is like from their first album, and it was very much about a place in Tottenham called Tower Gardens, which was the home of an artist called Ian Johnson. Ian sadly passed away, but it was a real hub for people. I don't know. Wastes and strays. Everyone used to kind of end up living there. If you needed a home, artists would just, musicians would just be passing through there. Daniel and Alex – particularly Daniel – made so much music there. I think it was a really extraordinary influence. This is a song which was, for me, the beginning of that period. So, it's an older track from them, but it's a kind of important one.

Cool. So, this is Grumbling Fur 'The Ballad of Roy Batty'.

—

That's quite an uplifting, emotional thing.

Very uplifting, I think definitely. It makes me feel happy-sad when I hear it.

I like that combination! Coming back to what you were talking about earlier, when I think about your work, when a lot of people think about your work, language and text is obviously really very much part of it. And I've always liked the twisted take you have on language. Where it's on this borderline. Where it feels, again, happy-sad, or sort of manipulative-positive. Do you want to tell me a little bit about what draws you to the language you use and how you started working with that?

I started working with it, because I'm an idiot really!

Haha!

It took me years and years. I always wrote stuff down in notebooks, put little pieces in books, and just had all this text. I thought it was just a way of remembering stuff. I didn't really ever think about it, going into the work. And then I just had one of those moments of thinking, "how do I stop this work being kind of ambient? How do I kind of really affect the viewer?" And I thought, "well, you know, this really simple thing. If you write a word on a wall, people read it". And when you read something, you internalize it, and then this whole chain of relationships that we have to the world, and language just kind of explodes. It's a very simple impulse. It's morphed a lot over the year. I think, at the beginning, I was interested in – I use a lot of found text. And I was interested in this hierarchy of what if you find something which sounds deeply philosophical in a pop song, and then you write it on the wall out of context. Do you respond to it in a different way? So, it became about this. The importance of the speaker rather than what's said. But it's really moved into I suppose the relationship between the individual and the State or the ideology. So, quite often this voice is a kind of disembodied patriarchal, authoritarian voice. I quite like the idea of this tension of saying something which seems positive, but if it's said, in a way, which is sort of demonstrative then it becomes threatening. So, I think, you're right. That borderline between self-help and…

Big Brother!

Big Brother, yeah! But it's funny, because people do say, "I like that text. That's a positive thing to say". And for me, that's half the story.

I've seen around recently, 'The World isn't Working'. That seemed to be very much part of that post-Brexit strangeness of everything happening around the elections. That seems definitely a borderline statement.

That one came back because I made it originally in 2008. It was for a show, after the crash, and there was this tiny window before Barack Obama became president, where everyone was like, "He'll fix it. It'll be fine". There was a weird optimism around, that and I felt quite cynical about that. So 'The World isn't Working' was a take on the 'Labor isn't Working' posters from the '79 election. But it's come back. The anxiety of Brexit and the markets. I think it's been interesting times, because I feel a little bit like my work has sort of come back into step with the world today a little bit. There was definitely a time where I felt, having a political agenda within your practice, was sort of seen as being slightly passé. For me, I just do believe that's important.

> *I'm thinking about even the first shows I saw of yours, which were almost referencing the subtext of advertising and this brainwashing onslaught was very political. And now, I definitely think if you make work that isn't about politics, it seems irrelevant.*

Well, this is it.

> *I've said this before.*

I've tried to shift again, recently. I've been mainly working on stuff in what we call the 'public realm', outside, for the last five years. That's really been the focus of it. That last group of those projects has really been much more about collaborating with groups of people. The kind of outcomes, whether it's, banners or billboards or whatever…

> *Bus stops.*

Anywhere I can find that I can put something up outside. That's the end result of a longer work in practice.

> *What do you like about public space and the different audience because it's really different from putting things on in the gallery. You just can't help it?*

I know. I just want to communicate with people who aren't necessarily that comfortable going into. I don't want it to be about specialized knowledge. And I think it's important to try and have that debate about our identity in our society in a shared space. Also just knowing that those spaces are so contested. The project I've been working on, for 18 months in the North of England, with young people in Burnley, Wigan and Hull, actually a lot of that has been focused on libraries, as these really contested, threatened, crucial public spaces. And I never intended that when we started, but as I talked more to the group and also looked at what was happening in those towns, it seemed really important to focus on those sites. Because it's not a given…

No. I've written about libraries. I think it's one of the most important things. Everyone thinks people have access to information through their phones, or through computers, but people actually don't have that access. I think libraries – and the freedom of knowledge – are an innately political thing of now...

Somewhere to go! When I was painting a wall in the in Hull Central Library, which is an amazing place, for three or four days, it was so busy. There are pensioners coming to do clubs. There are like toddler groups. People coming who don't have access to computers doing job searching. It is so critical for so many different and diverse groups of people. The idea that you can just say, "Oh, well, people can access stuff on their smartphones", it's really disingenuous.

And it's not true! Marx wrote a lot of things in Manchester City Library. I think that says it all. There's a reason I think it comes out of that kind of communal space. Even seeing other people around you. I think is also really important with the library.

Absolutely. And also, just the sense of the architecture and being in a room… It's not about it being quiet. It's just being in a room where you're surrounded by this mass of information. It is the physicality of it. That still means something.

The British Library is my favourite place to go actually, and definitely my favourite place to work. You feel knowledge is floating in the sky above your head...

You feel yourself getting smarter just by being there.

Yeah, we hope! It makes me a better writer if I write in the British Library!

I think for me, it just reminds me of how much I have forgotten!

Yeah! Another aspect I think is very interesting about your work, and I know that you've done a lot of research about, is Austin Osman Spare. There is almost an occult-ish angle to, or at least definitely an interest or personal interest, in that. Do you want to tell me about how you think that manifests in the work and why you're interested in occult references?

I think part of that is just because it's something I've always been interested in. I remember being taken to Boscastle, to the witchcraft museum, as a pretty young child and being scared and drawn to it at the same time. My grandfather was a vicar so when I was a kid in the summers, I would get dumped in empty churches. I spent quite a lot of time in that space. I think that had a big effect. There were elements of occult artefacts in my proximity as a child as well. I think those things – there is nothing more attractive to a child than something you shouldn't look at. But I think with Spare and my interest in the occult is a lot to do with language and the way that language is critical and the encryption and coding of words into rituals. The idea that languages is space, and it is time and it can be bent and folded. These days maybe I believe in it in a more abstract way, rather than a practice way. But again, it's been something which I continue to be interested in. The Spare thing – maybe less so when I was living in Tower Gardens for a while.

Which is where?

Which is Ian Johnson's place I mentioned in Tottenham. Which has sadly been dismantled now. Ian was the partner of John Balance from Coil, and he inherited a lot of the Coil art collection and a huge amount of Austin Spare work. Some of the best ones and I spent a few months living in a room with some of those paintings, which is quite an experience!

For those people who don't know Spare was like a follower, a painter follower of Aleister Crowley...

He wasn't really a follower... Spare was very much kind of his own person. They came into contact... He was a contemporary in a way, but he was very much, he was a South Londoner with a studio on the Walworth Road. It's a very long, complicated story, but he basically developed his own occult system, which was really based on working with language and writing sigils. What I was really interested in was he was an amazing draftsman. He used to do a lot of automatic drawing – literally trying to draw the spirits. And I think they're beautiful. I live with some of these drawings still. I disengage a little bit from the occult side of it and I think of them as just being these beautiful things. Some of the best drawings that anyone's made.

> *I'm always really interested in that. How you disassociate the individual from the work and if it's possible, in some way. Do we need to know about who an artist is? I know, it's quite interesting as someone who interviews artists...*

I think Spare has been the subject of – there's a lot of mythology around him and part of that is himself. The story was that he was this sort of childhood genius, who was one of the youngest people to ever to exhibit at the Royal Academy. And then he falls in with a local witch as a teenager and she leads him down this road, which destroys his art career, I suppose, but makes him this visionary.

> *Very Adam and Eve! Here is an apple!*

Kenneth Grant, I suppose, took him on and told the story in another way... It's such an amazing fantastical story of London, as well. There's another side to it, which I think is slightly overlooked. Which is that he was a war artist as well and he made a series of drawings of ordinary working people in the Walworth, Elephant and Castle area. The Cockney people who were 40, who looked like they were 90 because they've had such tough lives. Unfortunately, most of those are destroyed. His studio got bombed during the Second World War. I think if those had survived, we would have had this amazing social aspect to his work as well. That he was a working-class person working amongst them. It's a much more interesting story to a kind of occultist working in an obscure cellar with cats in Brixton and dying unknown in poverty. It's a bit of a cliché, isn't it really?

A cliché myth. We're going to play another track now. We're going to play Oxbow 'Ecce Homo'. Do you want to tell me a bit about why you chose this?

Well, I did procrastinate a little about this… Oxbow is a band that I've been quite obsessed by for quite a long time, and they just brought out a record. It's their first record for 10 years. And it's amazing. They come from a noise rock background, but they've pulled everything together. I almost didn't want to share it. It makes me really… It has a very powerful effect on me. I've probably been driving my partner crazy by listening to this album over and over again for several months now. But I think they're a really unique band. And in particular, on this song, you hear Eugene Robinson, who is the rather amazing front man using all kinds of vocal techniques that you might find on extreme music in this incredibly emotional kind of way. There are really tiny, little guttural sounds barely there in his throat and then these huge kind of roars and it's all placed within this really beautifully raw structure.

Mmm nice. Okay, Oxbow 'Ecce Homo'.

—

That was Oxbow 'Ecce Homo'. Another really interesting use of language in all of that. Your work is so much about communication, and you're really drawn towards sound and music and noise that puts barriers or plays or twists or pulls apart communication in some way?

Like with Eugene, it's that range. I like the idea of something you can just – it's in deep in the throat and it's almost, I don't know, like Beckett or something. The idea that language is a spectrum, all loaded with meaning. That idea of using your voice in a way which isn't the normal prescribed way and that being more affecting. I guess that's kind of what I'm – I don't know why but I just seem really drawn to this. How do you make people feel a certain way? Or why is it that I am made to feel a certain way? I'm just trying to understand that.

Do you want to tell me a little bit about some of your other work. You've done things involving video works as well as sculptural things and using LEDs and screens. Do you want to tell me what your feelings are around the use of something technological? At this point, is that an interest still?

I have been working quite a lot with things like video editions… I guess it's a mirror of that stuff in the public realm. Where it's not for sale, you just have it. I've been trying to think a little bit about that. How to make low cost works that people can have. That can be consumed on a phone or on your screens or whatever. It's this slightly compromised relationship, because it then becomes something which is quite throw-away, and actually art needs to be special. I think I'm more interested now in how social networks operate. How we're able to share, share art, and what happens to the meaning of art through those social networks? It's not something that I've completely resolved or even nearly resolved. The other thing seems to be, people have been talking to me a little bit about doing VR-type works, because there's that aspect within some of the video works… I suppose it is meant to be immersive. And again, I just don't know. I think, "yeah, that would be great" and another part of me thinks, "are we there yet?" I don't want to necessarily just do something because it's there and it's cool. You know, a gimmicky kind of…

New media. Like "oooo new media". I saw a Paul McCarthy VR piece recently that was so flat, and actually deeply misogynistic, but also just didn't work. I felt like it was a bit like someone who was playing with the media, and they didn't get the opportunities... It failed. And maybe because it felt like "it's a new medium, you can be inside Paul McCarthy's world". But it didn't work.

I think also for me. Like I said, I think I've been trying to get more of a, take it down to a bit more of a personal relationship with making. Trying to end up with situations where the works are produced through interactions with people. We'd be doing a lot of stuff – workshop based or play based, or conversation based and seeing what comes out of that. And it's a bit of an antithesis really. Because you do become aware that actually, a lot of people don't have access to these things that we maybe in the art world think are kind of 'given'. It's like going into a kind of TV shop where there's all these 75-inch TVs just playing anything, and they all look amazing. It's not art, it's just completely shiny kind of visual candy.

Art should be more than shiny visual candy!

Well, sometimes it should!

Maybe that's a reflection of living in a moment when everybody's becoming so insular. There is a real desire to know that other people exist.

I think bringing it back to an analogy to do with music as well. It is about improvisation a little bit, and not knowing about what outcomes you're going to get. The project that I was telling you about earlier – in the network narrative project up in the north of England, that was a really strange project in a way because there was no site. The content could be anything. This was the commission – it could be anything. So, the only way it was ever going to work, or be resolved, was through this nearly 18-month process of exploring the towns. Exploring what people were interested in, and their relationship to the town, the problems, aspirations, all of these things. It could only ever work like that… Sometimes I long for just going into the studio these days, and just being like, "right, I'm going to do this, and it's on the wall". And at the end of the day, it will be done. Everything feels very complicated, because we have now these projects where… The process of thinking them through and making them is one thing and then there's the next bit which is making them a reality. I suppose part of working in the public realm is actually getting permission to do stuff. Getting involved in the mechanism of how you actually put something out there? How you get permission? Who tells you "You can't have permission"? This whole stuff which no one really sees, and it's quite frustrating in a way because it does become a power game. Sometimes I just felt like, "Oh, well, if we had 10 times the budget, this would be easy" but we have to do it with the resources that are available. So…

It's also quite interesting with work that seems to be critical – having an inbuilt critical space – where you're criticizing the political aspect of things in the government. And at the same time working with public commissions, which often come from a more government or stat- based funding. That's quite a weird, interesting space to be in.

It's complicated. I do permanent public works and, in a way, that's how I manage to subsidize other things. Like making weird noises! A lot of that is to do with building… private investment and all that. It is complicated. Morally it doesn't necessarily all completely kind of add up. But I think of it as being a way of accessing those spaces, as well being an opportunity to do other things as well. Just buying myself a bit of time.

We're going to play your last track, because I'm obsessed with it. And it's really long so I'm going to play as much as I can of it. This is Nurse with Wound. Do you want to tell me about why you chose this? It's just great.

I mainly chose this because I listen to it a lot when I'm working. It's a very long drone piece. It's from an album called 'Soliloquy for Lilith', which I think came out in 1988, which is a treble album. It's extremely long. The tracks are about 17, 18 minutes long. It's basically a recording of a bunch of pedals looped up. It was going to be a recording of the feedback from the pedals but there was some – I guess the legend of it is that there's an electrical fault somewhere in the setup. Steven Stapleton who is Nurse with Wound, he found that by moving his hands in the air around the pedals that he could get these soundscapes emerging… What I really like about them is this idea that Steven Stapleton, still after probably nearly 40 years of making music, still says "I can't play anything". It's still really free. It still anything goes. It's still pulling stuff out of the air and trying to see what sticks and I think that to me, that's really inspiring. But this is just a great. It's a great track. If you can listen to this in the dark with your eyes closed late at night it will take you somewhere else.

Amazing. Thank you very much Mark. And this is Nurse With Wound.

Steve Claydon

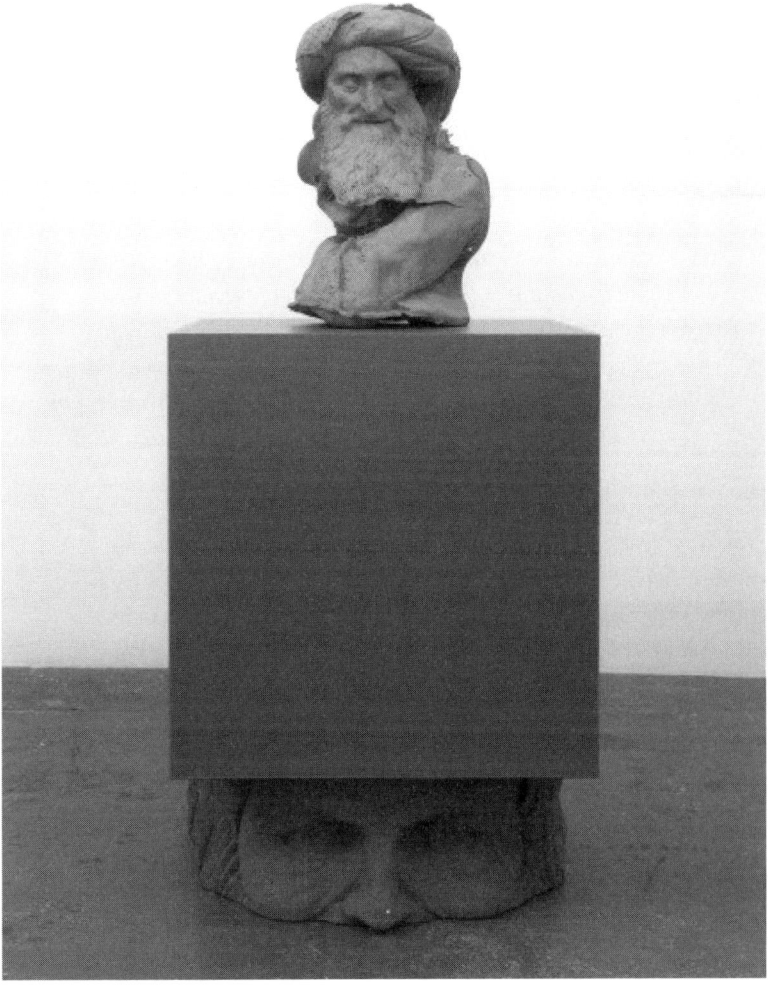

The Graven in Tandem, 2012.

14.09.17

Hi, I'm Francesca Gavin and this is Rough Version on NTS and my guest this month is Steven Claydon. I don't know – are you a Steve or Steven?

Whatever you like, Francesca.

He's a great artist who is represented by Sadie Coles in London. He was a nominee for the Hepworth prize and the Jarman award. He was featured in Manifesta11. You've shown everywhere from Glasgow to Berlin to Los Angeles. You were once in a band called Add N to (X) and do a lot of performance work alongside everything, from sculpture to wall pieces to video. Thank you very much for coming in! Dalston local.

Yeah, it's a pleasure, thanks for inviting me. Also, it's nice just to get out of bed and walk down the road.

Let's start talking a little bit about your work. Part of what I really like about it is that you have a lot of breadth to what you do in terms of materials, because you've worked with everything from video to sculpture. I want to know, what do you like about such a broad approach to what you do? What do you feel holds that together? Do you have a similar approach?

It's just that breadth of materials I think I try to access it in this very even way. Not because I'm trying to democratize things, but purely because I understand sound and stuff as background noise or background material that everyone has around them that you an individual would just access. I don't see, in my practice, at least why specialization would preclude me from being able to work with things that I've hitherto not worked with, or I've kept at bay for a while. So, for me, it's important to be thinking about things, maybe from that molecular level up. That sound, if you think about it in that respect, is made up of waves and air particles being moved. It's about stuff all the way through, and lights even carry a particle. I do work with light, and I work with sound, and I suppose they're the end points. Everything else in between, if you like, is either viscous or solid, or mutable or transformative in terms of what it is. It's all about stuff – that's really it.

Do you want to tell me a little bit how that works that process because obviously, you have been a musician alongside making art in a more physical form... Do you have a similar process when you're making tracks or performing live as you do when you're making artworks?

A similar thought process, for sure. And that usually involves circling an idea or the germ of an idea and then fleshing it out through this sort of orbit. That becomes gradually this closing in on a thing or at least working on it so much that the original germ of the idea has been wrapped in the work itself. And perhaps it's not revealing itself in an illustrative way. The idea is kind of locked into the work encrypted into it. But the act of just like a shark preying upon this object creates a sort of climate or a shell around it. That's how usually most of the works come into being. If I'm making it by hand, or if I'm using fabricators, if I'm using instruments it really doesn't matter. It all comes to the same thing. I have used some really arcane things like old analogue synthesizers and replicas of medieval instruments. I sometimes just use apps and stuff to make the music. Likewise, I will spend hours working on something in the studio that is part of a sculpture. But at the same time, I'm quite happy to use a found object or to get a fabricator to make something for me that I can't do. So, it's quite generous in that respect. I allow a lot of stuff in it. I don't have a closed practice.

Going back to like some of those works, that you've put in a gallery context, that reference instruments. I always find them really interesting. There's a really good one at Manifesta that I curated, because sometimes they're almost functionless in a way. They're things that can't be played but they reference the form or the concept of something that can be played. What do you like about that tension of function or lack of function?

It's exactly that. It's about agency and utility, and how a thing changes when it's either in storage, or it's been locked into a museum cabinet, or it's just been replicated to make something that they've seen in a drawing to try and replicate a medieval instrument or something. It's that changing status of a thing. This equipment will be turned off in a minute and will be performing a totally different function. It'll just be sitting there dormant, if you like, but maybe just being a different kind of version of itself. It's not on or off, really. It's just a slight transformation or modification, modulation in the way that we understand our relationship to things. I think for me, there's something quite reciprocal about that. It's not just us projecting these ideas onto things. I think they have an equal kind of effect on us, which is something that I try to bring out in the work and certainly in the musical work. I would say, since we're talking about music, as part of my practice. I think that the years really, really informed that side of the practice that animistic side. That there's these things that are unreliable – certainly analogue keyboards are very much like that. They just sit there squelching away and sometimes they refuse to cooperate. And it's really strange, that relationship. You had to coax them. A lot of analogue synthesizers – there's lots of stories in the music industry about these things. You open them up, and they've got like mandalas in them and spells and stuff. Because they're being made by hippies in the '60s originally. There was this alchemical, this magical animistic evocatory thing to working with analogue synthesis that you don't necessarily get. It's a different species of interaction that you get with digital stuff. I do like that just as much. But I think it was that that really got me thinking about objects and machines and utility and agency. What happens to them when they're switched off? When they're in storage. Artworks are the same thing, really.

> *Let's play one of the tracks that you've brought in. Shall we play the Cabaret Voltaire 'Big Funk'? Do you want to tell why you chose this and how that fits in? Because it seems to be an interesting follow on.*

Yeah, for sure. That song is sort of on the cusp of when Cabaret Voltaire were using a lot of analogue stuff, and then going into the digital realm and accessing maybe a lot of things that they might have gleaned from the very, very early beginnings of house music and dance music. But at the same time, that their journey from this very avant-garde band into a band that was making things that were still incredibly challenging, but using formats in an appropriative way, was something that mirrored my interest in music I got into it early on. Maybe by accidentally going with my granny to see Sunsplash when it used to be in Bishop's Park in Fulham, when I was a kid. Then hearing these sounds, and maybe hearing a bagpipe, or something and all these sounds coalescing. And I suddenly managed to formulate something like taste, and ultimately through things like two tone and reggae and even indie bands.

I'd say you're probably the first person I've ever heard say, "going out with my granny helped form my music taste". That's definitely an unusual one.

For sure. I think you're going to see Yellowman and Eek-A-Mouse not knowing who they were. Yellowman scaring the living daylights out of me, because he's such a weird looking guy. And just thinking "what was that?" But ultimately, through those little journeys, finding my way through to music that fused some of the scarier aspects, although avant-garde aspects and experimental aspects with more souly or dancey thing that I was interested in. Gogo and stuff and ESG and then Factory Records was a real mixture of that. Very briefly, Cabaret Voltaire were on Factory, but they were one of the bands that really set my mind racing when I started to think about what music might be and so this track for me is pivotal.

Amazing. This is 'Big Funk' by Cabaret Voltaire.

—

That was 'Big Funk'. Looking at your work, another aspect I find really interesting about it is your references to histories and futures. Almost alternative histories and futures. What do you like about that temporal aspect of time?

I think that art is a form of time travel. I think that making music or art you step into this other place. Whatever it is that you're trying to access – if you're trying to push your finger through that meniscus that allows us into a parallel reality – it's very akin, I think, to thinking about yourself as atemporal. Somehow, when you're in that state, none of that really matters. This isn't a conceptual idea. This is the most meat and potatoes painters sitting there a day and a half can go, and they haven't realized they haven't eaten for hours. You're just going into the zone. And I guess athletes and artists and martial artists access that kind of area – certainly in religion and things like that. There was this astronaut called Rusty Schweickart, who tried to describe that otherness as being a sensing element. He got kind of stuck in orbit around the Earth for five minutes. I mean it doesn't sound long. But for him, it was this total life changing thing where he was in his little spacesuit completely relying on no one and just watching the earth go around. He just decided that it wasn't special. Nothing had happened. He was just part of the human organism that had been sort of stuck out on the edge on the periphery. I think it's that para-dynamic way of looking at things. The way that things can be suddenly thrown into the juxtaposition. To chiaroscuro something like that. That is a bit like science fiction. It's a bit like time travel. It's a bit like history in the future. The present is always shifting. We're always either in thinking about things historically, or in a projective way like forecasting. For me objects again do that. They live in the past because they're material and their genesis can go right back to the beginning of the formation of the planet or of the universe. Yet there are constantly modifying in their context, so that they endure and that weird endurance that's the life that's just sitting there silvery strobing under the surface is really what I'm interested in. If you think about time future past – for me it's a kind of time travel.

> *Of all the And N to (X) tracks you brought in you brought 'Buckminster Fuller'. That's really interesting because he's obviously creating architecture that is very Utopian, but also has real sci-fi references, or at least help define an aesthetic of what science fiction emerges in the '60s. Do you want to tell me about how those ideas fit in? Why you chose that track?*

He's a totally fascinating character and adopted by several generations of people and equally jettisoned by them. The hippies were astonished that he would make deals with the people at the American military for the geodesic domes. At the same time, he just thought that was a very short-term perspective. What I really like about Buckminster Fuller is that he chose to disregard received information. He realized that it was so flawed, and he advocates people using their own experience in order to build new ideas around. It's very much like the Ezra Pound saying that whatever you're doing, make it new, make it your own. Even if you're using historical fragments, or projecting into the future, or even relying on things like found objects or appropriation – you make it something that hasn't had a voice or been in the world before. So, he decided, in a very sort of dark moment, where he was about to end his life to start up again, as this project guinea pig B. Again, it's not a formula like that – Add N to (X). It's a kind of command more than a title. This is an affirmative action. This is something that can catalyse or generate some rereading of the world. Add N to (X) were really interested in people like Archigram, but specifically Buckminster Fuller. It's something that's influenced me for years since discovering the crazy guy. Also because of that polymathic way of approaching things. Think globally, act locally. He'd make a skiff for himself to get from one place to another thinking very directly, but at the same time he was making like very low-cost geodesic housing, that he was hoping might change the world. You've got to be thinking in both those realms simultaneously.

Have you ever seen the footage of Ornette Coleman playing in Buckminster Fuller domes?

I've seen stills of it. I've not seen footage.

It's great. It was included in a really good 1986 documentary on Ornette Coleman, which I recommend forever. This is Add N + (X) and 'Buckminster Fuller'.

—

Now one of the tracks you brought in, I really liked because it's got a real rave reference, which is the amazing Blackman remix. Were you intertwined with that history? Was that an influence of you at some point? I mean, you're British and are of a certain age.

Yeah, very much so. I mean, because of what I'd said about being interested in Factory Records that sort of developed through a group of people that I knew into an interest in Chicago house and clubbing, basically. People like Andy Weatherall setting up Boys Own. That was a big part of my youth. From there, I got quite heavily into that. But at the time, I'd sort of stopped collecting records in a way. I wasn't the DJ. I was just receiving.

A happy punter!

I was a totally happy punter, but it changed the way I thought about music for a while. Of course, it was very linked to a lifestyle and to various drugs and it really did seem like this mad new beginning. People really were serious when they were talking about the second summer of love and stuff like that. But it all started to turn into something a little bit uglier, but that's fine. I was going to places like the Mud Club and Shoom and originally the Electric Ballroom when there was very little house music that was accessible in Camden. Then from that, a scene started to develop in Britain, and more specifically, a scene that had very much a British identity. I really hate the term drum and bass. I really liked the original idea of the junglist, which was the urban jungle sprouting this really amazing and very spontaneous music that suddenly got a name. I suppose for want of anything 'junglism' is a better word for it. I was really interested in that. I used to go to, latterly to Metalheadz but before, just dark warehouse raves and stuff, and really, really enjoyed this music that was indigenous London music. But the artist we're talking about now is actually from Manchester, I think. It was one of the tracks that really stood out for me at the time. I didn't hear it a lot. I actually got it on a compilation at the time, and it's always stayed with me. It's an amazing track. One of the other tracks that I selected is 'Living in a Land' by Gene Hunt. That was much more experimental, at the end of acid house. It almost sounds like Steve Reich. It's just got this really amazing feel to it. Then, for me, it was just a revelation when British people started to make their own voice because I had been living in west London and part of a house scene there, but it got very garage-y and speed garage. I quite liked [it] but it was getting a bit lost and disenfranchised. It didn't seem as avant-garde as the music I'd been used to listening to like Future. The jungle stuff and to a lesser extent the intelligent drum and bass was really important.

This is 'Bastards (remix)' by Blackman and it is one hell of a tune.

—

What I really liked about this record by Blackman is it also has the dark core thing, for me, really referenced this architectural urbanness. This real sense of the city. I think in a weird way, it's quite ritualistic in that way. It got almost occultist, that dark stuff coming out at that time. I think that's a really interesting connect to some of the work that you've made. Where there is a sense of ritualistic objects. Totemic things that you're not quite sure what their purpose are. Material found objects that you insert into things, and I think there is some kind of connection there. Would you agree?

Yeah, very much so. People do ascribe rituals to their daily routine and certainly in the city in an urban environment these things just spontaneously grow. I think some of the language of that is always dark. It's like finding out about what a serial killer was doing. Like Jeffrey Dahmer's fish tank and stuff like that. That was very much around when that kind of music was being made. Or Dennis Nielsen up in Muswell Hill, shoving bits of body in pipes. I don't know why that suddenly springs to mind. But there are curious evolutions of things that follow almost a ritualistic pattern. And for me, that's the sort of alchemy of the street. At the time, I made a show called 'The Third of the Third' which was sort of pushing the idea of cargo cults and night buses and people cleaning. I'd be coming home from these club nights at six in the morning and watching people getting on the bus to go and clean Canary Wharf. There's this undercurrent of really – I wouldn't call it tragic, but this infrastructure that was unknown within the city. That is always blanked out in terms of, in lieu of a more glamorous kind of idea of the metropolis. Everything that I access lives within that. I often use a reference to the museum or historical objects as a framework, but then built into that are a lot of other things from my experience, which are some of these more esoteric views about the city.

I think that also really emerges in your video pieces or at least the video work I've seen, which is quite broad. But that seems to have that kind of reference, even the way you edit things. Do you want to tell me a bit about how you've approached video? Because it is a large part of what you do alongside the objects. You work in many, many things.

Video is another timeline way of working. In the same way that you use to Logic or Cubase Pro Tools to make tracks and I think that my interest in film was just as influenced by probably MTV and music videos. Certainly, the kind of imagery that would go alongside going to see like – I was lucky enough to go and see Cabaret Voltaire in the in the '80s even when I was a little whippersnapper and just staring at these incredible video montage work that was the backdrop to the performances. Those kinds of things always struck me as being way more interesting than some of the experimental video that I'd seen latterly. And it was interesting to be involved in Art Sheffield last year, and to see a lot of that scratch video being given its proper place in the lineage of filmmaking and meet some of the people who made it. I very much make my films somewhere between something experimental – something between using didactic language, found footage from quite mundane sources. And then try to treat some of that almost like a kind of piece of music, or movie to go with music.

> *One last thing I want to ask you about in terms of your work which is quite a present thing, is your interest in modes of display, and how we look at things. And whether that's something that draws on the way things are put in museums or in public. I think your work really seems to deconstruct how things are presented to us. How did that interest start? Why were you drawn towards that?*

That's a really good question. Actually, pathologizing it might be a little bit less easy than it was to formulate, because I think it probably goes back a long way. I would quite easily say it was "Oh influenced by rather than going to do an MA I went to work at the Natural History Museum and was fascinated by all of the stuff in storage". But really, I think it goes back further than that. The idea of something being dormant and, in a cupboard, or something like that, has always been playing on my mind. Maybe it was this fear of things being under my bed and grabbing me by the ankles. There's something about that otherness. Like kids getting totally tormented by what's in the cupboard, a scary clown or something like that. So, it may go back to something psychically damaged like that…

And quite universal. I think people have those weird thoughts. I used to have nightmares about big giant rectangles and squares bouncing around my crib when I was baby.

They shouldn't have got you that mobile, should they?

I didn't have a mobile! I just imagined giant rectangles bouncing around me, which was very, very weird. But yeah, that makes sense. That's an interesting thing. Thinking about the hidden.

Very much so and that idea of the revealed in the concealed has remained there for me. You can have objects that are extrovert, and you can have introvert objects, but you can also have things that refute any kind of reading that are just not knowable to us. Somehow things revert to that when they're when they're out of sight. And maybe they're not. Maybe they're coexisting with each other in a different sort of way. I got to see things in storage. I worked, moving art around. I worked in a warehouse where all this art was wrapped and stuck on shelving, and it was all very codified and amazing. And used to think this is way better than the thing that's wrapped up in it. It was a lot of that really. Just trying to get to the bottom of what it is this object that has such cultural potency and can spend most of its life in storage in the Bahamas, for somebody's tax break. So politically there's a dimension, but really, it's a fundamental kind of spooky understanding of what we are as material as well. When you're dead, when you're asleep, or all of these different states of being are at the root of that. Modes of display can really confer activity and authority on two things. Like the way studios are set up with all of this soundproofing has a very particular language in the same way as a museum does and a commercial space, the white cube, or an artist run space or just crap on the street. All of these things are just, again, species of the same thing.

Well, let's finish with your last track, which is 2UP 'Microcosmos' which you mentioned a little bit before? Is there anything you want to say about this? If not, I'll just happily play it.

I listen to a lot more of this house and acid house now. At the time, just afterwards, I think I had just done too much acid and I was more or less having flash backs.

You took acid house literally.

I definitely did and so I did actually have sort of semi-flashbacks every time I heard 303 warping. So now it's nice to be able to listen to it again.

Wonderful. Thank you very much, that's Steve Clayton and this is 2UP 'Microcosmos'.

Georgina Starr

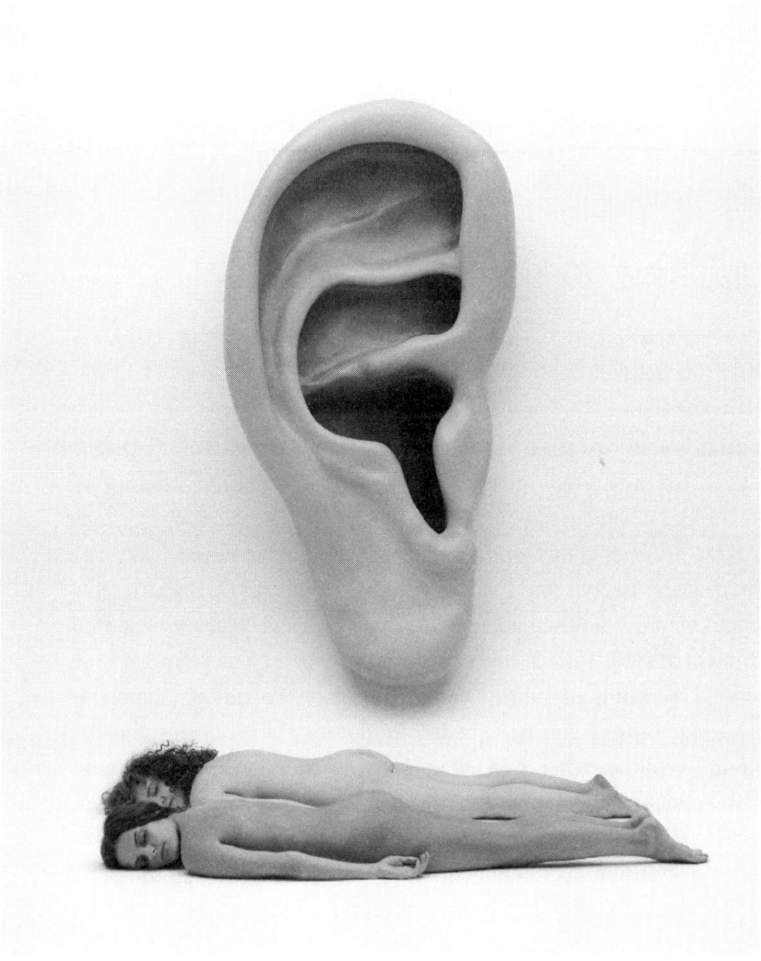

Quarantaine, 2020.

17.10.17

Hi, I'm Francesca Gavin and you're listening to Rough Version and my guest today is Georgina Starr. Hi, Georgina.

Hello.

Thanks for coming. Georgina is a London-based artist. She studied at Middlesex – ceramics – before doing an MA at the Slade and then went on to the Rijksakadmie in Amsterdam. You've shown everywhere from the Tate to MoMA, to the Kunsthalle Zurich and the Venice Biennale. You make a huge breadth of work, which ranges from performance to installation, to sound pieces to objects to drawings, and I want to discuss all of it. So, thank you for coming in! The first thing I would like to talk about, since we're on the radio, is your relationship to sound, because you've made an incredible amount of sound works. A lot of them are archived on Soundcloud under grrrrrrradio. How many Rs are there?

I think there are seven Rs.

Do you want to say what attracted you to sound in the first place?

I think sound was the first thing that interested me as a child, that was outside of my normal interest of just playing around. My dad was a scaffolder when I was young, then he became a scaffolding manager. All his life he had this tape recorder that he used to have to take on site to measure the jobs and I was fascinated by this thing. Because you could record your own voice on it. Even as a four-year-old. I started doing that stuff. I made lots of recordings when I was younger. I started recording my family and then friends. We did fake radio shows a bit like this one but in the bedroom. So, it's always been something I've done. When I ended up going to art college, I didn't really think about it as something that was in any way connected to my artwork until later on, when I started getting interested again in sound. I also have this another connection. When I was a kid, I had this strange thing happen to me when I was about seven. I started to have these sound hallucinations. I think that is something that ended up filtering into my work. It lasted for about a year. I started to hear voices. I think it happens to a lot of kids.

My sisters had the same thing.

I looked into it when I was older and it's quite a big thing with children. It can be anything. Nothing particularly bad happened to me, but it became a big issue. We went to the doctor in Liverpool, and he called it "auditory hallucinations". I really loved the sound of that. For a while we tried to work out what it was and eventually it went away. When I started recording sound later on in my twenties, I was at the Slade at the time, I almost thought I was looking for sounds that were similar to those voices, because they were voices that were talking all at the same time. But I could never decipher what they were saying. It was just this babble of noise. There was a recording I made in a radiator at the Slade. I thought I could hear those voices. It was beginning of me getting into sound and it's just something that has continued for the last 25 years.

I love the autobiographical background of that. You wouldn't expect that. What's so interesting about a lot of the sound pieces – obviously you have a huge breadth – is that some of them seem to be very much about the occult, the disembodied, ideas around seances or voices that appear on telephones. The idea of a lack of physicality to sound is really interesting. What do you like about that idea of the occult and mysterious?

I suppose again it goes back to where were these voices come from. It has a connection with the spiritual. Who were the people that tried to communicate with me? I've always been interested in the idea that there might be something else out there, whether you believe it or not. There is something interests me and people who do believe in it and also people who say they have the power to contact the spirit world. So early on, around the early '90s, I started looking at ways of using that in the work. I started to go and see palm readers and numerologists and dream analysts. Then I started to see a few mediums and that became a big work I made called 'Getting to Know You' where I tried to get to know a guy without meeting him, but just through his palm readings and his handwriting and things like that. Then much later around 2009, I started again working with mediums. That was something that I thought. Was it possible to make an artwork that was predicted? The work would be predicted through the people who said that they could predict the future. So, every month, I went to see a different medium and I recorded what they said. I wanted to try and make the connections between the idea of being able to predict the future but also know things about me without knowing me. It was the invisible voices they could hear that I was interested in.

> *A lot of pieces aren't necessarily music-led. Actually, on an earlier show, I played your whistling piece! But this idea of sound being something beyond music. Being more about, I don't know, the voice?*

Even with the music I like listening to, it's nearly always things with vocals. I like the idea of storytelling within songs and music. I've always been interested in the idea of the voice, especially the female voice, although I've actually not chosen any female voices today. But there's something about the idea of the female voice and the maternal. I did a lot of research into the idea that you can hear your mother's voice when you're in the womb. This idea that the maternal voice is somehow instructive. I've made works about the idea of a female voice, which is instructional, which is giving you direction. Which is something that ended up in a lot of works that I've made.

> *Let's start by playing one of the tracks. I think it would be nice to play one of the pieces that you made for a work. Should we start with 'Theda'? Can you describe the work a bit and how sound played into it?*

'Theda' was a film that I made about 10 years ago, in 2007. It was a silent film. I'd seen a photograph of Theda Bara. At the time, I didn't know who she was, but I was interested in her because she reminded me of my mother. She looked very similar to her. I did a bit of research into her and discovered that nearly all her films had been destroyed over the years, she was in the silent day. She made movies from 1915 to 1925 or something. She had made something like 40 movies, and only one or two still exist. That in itself was quite fascinating to me. Most of the works I make, the research is a big part of it. I started researching things about her, trying to get scripts, as many photos as I could of her work, descriptions of the films. Then I decided to try and remake a scene from all of her films, but with myself playing Theda Bara.

You look quite different from her. She's the ultimate vamp.

I didn't look anything like her, but in the film that I made, I do. I transformed myself. For a year, I made my studio into a set. She was amazing. She played Cleopatra, Madame de Berry, and Sappho. She played all these iconic female roles. I metamorphosed into all these characters throughout the year. I built the set and made the costumes, so it was really huge work. I never knew what it was going to be. So often with works at the beginning, I don't know what they're going to turn into. I edited hours and hours of footage, and it ended up being a 14-minute film. I always knew that I wanted it to be silent. But I also knew that I wanted to have a soundtrack. I invited the London Improvisers Orchestra, who at the time were a 17-piece proper orchestra, who only improvised. I knew I didn't want the classic movie piano player. I wanted people to respond to the film. That's how I imagined it would be and actually looking into the history of silent movies, that's what it was at the beginning. People came and they responded. It wasn't a prewritten or composed work. That's the first one I did in 2007. Then over the last 10 years, each time I've shown the film, I've invited a different musical group to come in and play to the film. Some are improvised. Some people like to compose a little before. But the piece that I'm going to play…

CCMC.

That was when I showed in Toronto. It was a group of three guys. There was Paul Dutton. There was Michael Snow, who's an artist and a big pioneer of video art. He's in his eighties now. He was on piano. Paul Dutton was a vocal artist. And there was John Oswald, who was on saxophone. They've worked together as its improvising group but saw the film once before and then just played it live on the evening.

The scene that we're going to hear is an extract from it. It's a scene that is actually a séance. So, it's perfect.

Seamless!

It's the scene in the film where Theda is channelling the characters.

Amazing. So, this is CCMC doing the soundtrack from 'Theda'.

—

Let's talk about another aspect of your work, beyond the sound things. Ceramics being your very early background, but more recently, I've seen you do installation and performance works. How did you make that move from something so transitory and ephemeral as sound into something that's about presentness?

The sound stuff I did when I was a kid was something separate. Then, after my Foundation, at Middlesex, I did my first degree in ceramics. There were lots of things I wanted to do, and I remember someone saying, "Do you make work for yourself? Or do you make work for other people?" I was thinking what was I supposed to say? I make work for other people, and he said, "you should do design". That was a ridiculous thing. One of those stupid decisions. I loved making things. It was clear in I was going to do something sculptural at the time, but I was good at ceramics. I did a ceramics degree and pretty much in the first year I realized it was the wrong thing. I didn't think like anybody else on the course. They were really interested in design, and I was much more interested in the ideas, the concepts and building crazy big sculptures. But it actually worked really well for me, because everybody was doing their own thing and I was left to my own devices, and it was a great course. It's a real shame that a lot of the ceramic courses are closing in London.

Just as that becomes a medium that the art world is obsessed with.

Exactly. I left ceramics in 1990 and got into the Slade. I was just so happy to leave it behind. I didn't have to use that material anymore. That's when I started working with more ephemeral things – sound, video. It was almost a rejection of anything physical. Of anything that could be left behind. I was much more interested in sound and film. Things that were fleeting.

Your installations – are they always temporary, site specific, things that don't last?

The early ones were. My degree show at the Slade was just a record of me whistling. It was as simple as that, and I loved the simplicity and the minimal. I wish I could have stayed like that. But as the years went on, I got much more into making again. In my installations now, it's rarely sound and video. It's objects, rooms, environments, lights, lots of sculpture. They got bigger and bigger. I couldn't hold myself back because when I work, I really like making things. I couldn't just be minimal! I've always admired people who can, I just I like making things too much.

I'm thinking about some motifs that come through in your work. I've been reading a lot about brains and bubbles. Do you want to tell me what those motifs are for you?

The recent work that I made was a piece called 'Le Cerveau Affamé'. That was made a couple years ago. It was a new body of work. 'Le Cerveau Affamé' means 'the hungry brain' in French. It was a body of work that I began years before, in '95, called 'The Hungry Brain'. It was a performance work, and it became part of bigger work of mine called 'Hypnodreamdruff', which I showed at the Tate in '96. 'The Hungry Brain' element was a nightclub, which was a dream. It was a dream that was set in a nightclub, and it had all these characters. I had left that behind and gone on to make other things. There was a scene in that particular performance, that had become interesting to me again. I started exploring it and the idea of the brain. The bubble element is a very sculptural thing. It's made from breath – the childish, playful thing that all kids do. But I became interested in it as a way to communicate. Then I started working with performers. I imagined a space was like an educational facility for women and they'd be instructed to communicate through movement, sound, gesture, and the bubble. Those were the limits that they had. I started imagining the space and it grew from there. So, the bubble became a sculpture and a word and lots of different things. But it wasn't just this playful thing anymore, it was really serious. It was hard to make it like that in the work. But actually, as in the videos and performances, it became quite a powerful object.

Well, since we're talking about French references, it makes sense for me to play your 'Je t'aime Je t'aime' track by Krzysztof Penderecki. Tell me why you chose this.

I chose the Penderecki track because the most recent work that I've made is a piece called 'Moment Memory Monument'. It was partly inspired by 'Je t'aime Je t'aime', which is a movie by Alain Renais, that was made in the '60s. A lot of my work has to do with time travel and shifting temporal zones and temporary time. 'Je t'aime Je t'aime' has a time machine in it. There's a guy who's suicidal. When he's leaving the clinic, after one of his suicide attempts, he gets accosted by a group of scientists and they take him to this institute where they tell him if he goes inside this object, they can take him back in time and he can relive one minute from his past, and then he might be cured. So, he tries to go back to the time when he was in love with this woman. 'Je t'aime Je t'aime' is what he wants to say to her. The film is all about that. But I'd remembered this object from the film. Recently, I got the chance to make a big sculptural work and I remade this object from the film, which is called 'The Sphere'. It has connections to the bubble, but it's a giant brain that you can get inside. This is my fascination with the idea of time travelling…

Wow. Immediately I'm thinking about what that one minute would be.

In 'Moment Memory Monument', I did the performance last week in France, because this object you can get into it. I've never made an interactive work before. I was always against the idea of interacting with the public in an artwork. I made this object so you can get inside and it's really comfortable. Inside there's a voice with a narration I made. It's almost like a meditative voice that takes you back. I should have brought that to play, but it's in French and it takes you back through corridors and inside doorways, and then inside your own brain. It leaves you with a minute of silence. The visitors to the exhibition lie inside it and get to have one minute of silence, then a bell rings and they have to come out. I didn't think anybody would do it but actually everybody that comes out is slightly transformed. One woman came out and was crying, because she'd been revisiting her wedding day. People actually took it seriously and it worked like a time machine. But the track is very beautiful. It's Penderecki, who makes a lot of movie soundtracks. I think, for David Lynch and people like that. I think he did something for 'The Shining'. He did a lot of amazing tracks, but this is very beautiful because it's vocal.

> *A little less horror. This is 'Je t'aime Je t'aime' by Krzysztof Penderecki.*
>
> —
>
> *That was Krzysztof Penderecki doing 'Je t'aime Je t'aime'. I want to talk about another aspect then we touched on it a bit, the idea of the feminine, the female, the female character, feminism. Generally, 'the woman' which is not something I like to ask female artists, because it often doesn't relate to what they're doing, but I think the idea of women-ness is something that you're exploring in your work. I wanted to know what your feelings are about that and how that's manifested in recent work.*

You mean what it means to be a woman making work?

> *Less so. Your work is so narrative led to me. You seem to be creating environments that are about women, the use of women, women as action or just characters. The female character seems very strong in your work, whether it's a mother or Theda Bara.*

It's something I'm instinctively drawn to being a female! I have also worked with male voices. The idea of the female body, the idea of the maternal. Like I said before, the maternal voice is something that I'm fascinated with. I did a lot of recordings with my mother. My mother hates to be recorded. A lot of my family have ended up being in my work, especially my mother's voice. I made a recording of her singing down the telephone. Singing 'Hello' – a Lionel Richie song.

Great song!

It was something I asked her to do years ago for no particular reason. I just wanted to capture it on cassette. Over the years, something has happened with the voice. Every year I taped it from tape to tape and it ended up disintegrating and decaying. Then the voice changes from not quite being a living voice anymore but becomes quite alien. The voice loses any sense of being human… 'Hello' is a love song. A mother singing that to a daughter has got this sort of tenderness. But then it sounds almost like a demand at the end. "Hello, is it me you're looking for?" The voice is completely transformed. I have been playing with the idea of the female voice throughout the work. Apart from being interested in women writers and women artists, I would only say that's what I'm interested in. It's more interesting to me here.

What do you like about the idea of characters? A lot of your work seems to emerge out of autobiography but then manifests as something which is more about the fictional.

Yes, it's a bit of a misinterpretation, because my work is always seen as totally autobiographical. I'd say, out of all the work I've ever made, that maybe 20 per cent, max 30, that is autobiographical. I'm just quite good at storytelling and making it seem as if it is real. I'm interested in it starting from that really real point. Something has really happened. Then it quickly it gets fictionalized, even works that seem completely autobiographical. I really like playing with this idea of who are you as the character in the work. From very early on, I was in my videos. There was the idea that it was just me. I played people. In the 'Hypnodreamdruff' I played a character who was obsessed with the film 'Grease'. She was a very lonely woman whose highlight of her life had been to play, in a high school musical. She was locked in her bedroom, re-enacting the scene from 'Grease'.

How depressing.

It was a nightmare. She played all the roles. In the video I ended up playing all these roles. People thought I loved this film. I was interested in, and it was a character within the work. It's very difficult because I think if you were making a movie people wouldn't think that. But within art, especially as a woman making art, if you're in it and you're playing a role it seems it's always somehow, it's got to be you. That was always a frustration I had early on about using myself in my work. I always thought would that happen if it was a man?

It doesn't. I've had this conversation with many female artists who work with video or performance. There's something about the objectification of the woman's body or you as something to look at that just messes with people's head, and they just fall in some weird cliché.

It used to really frustrate me when I was younger, but I got over it. I felt I had to be clear and have it more defined that it wasn't real. Then, at a certain point, I did not even mention the autobiographical side of it, in case people just thought the whole thing was… There was a work that I call the 'Bunny Lake' series which was spanned about five years. The project was huge. There was a really, really important autobiographical side to it, but I never mentioned it. It was about my relationship with my sister. And in the end maybe I didn't need to mention it, because it didn't need to be explored. But actually, I realized then that maybe it would have been better not to even mention that there was a real side to it. But I loved playing with that when I was younger – what was real and what wasn't. Playing with roles, especially at the time when not a lot of people were using video in their work. A lot of women were using video in the late '80s and early '90s. Before YouTube and people were exploring the handheld camera and lo-fi techniques. It was an exciting time.

I also gave you a lot of freedom. I remember that Turner Prize where it was Gillian Wearing and everyone coming out of that moment. Everyone was like "oh my god video as a medium exists", which is hilarious, but I think it transformed. I think it's changed so much since then. We're all so used to walking around with portable cameras.

It's completely changed now.

Let's talk about another one of your pieces 'Le Cerveau Affarmé'.

That's the one the brain and the bubble.

Do you want to tell me about the track – the vinyl poetry piece you've brought in?

This idea of this educational facility would be instructional somehow. I imagined it a cross between a dance studio and a sculpture studio, and this is the installation that I created. But as a live performance, I wanted a voice that would be the director of the piece. Originally, I was going to get someone to do it live. I thought it could be really nice as a record. I've made a lot of records over the years. This was one of the latest ones. I had been writing a lot of poetry in English, but I knew I wanted the poetry to be read in French. I don't speak French, but I knew I wanted to hear a certain voice and a certain style of reading. I had all the poems that I'd written translated into French. I think I'd also been listening to a lot of French spoken word. I've got like lots of vinyl records by Folkways. They're 19th, 20th century poetry records. People reading Rimbaud, Verlaine…

Baudelaire?

It's amazing. I used to just love listening to them with the translation. The piece we're going to play now is an extract from the record that was the instructional part of the performance. The needle was placed on the record and the series of poems were read. That set off a series of actions and the performance.

Let's hear some of that now.

—

That was 'Le Cerveau Affarmé'. I know that you're influenced by films and literature. What excites you at this moment in time? I know you've been working on a big project for Frieze.

Film and literature are the biggest influences. It's often films I've seen a long time ago that kind of creep up on me again – films from the

‘50s, ‘60s and ‘70s. I made a lot of work early on about Jerry Lewis and Dean Martin films.

Not going to say they are my favourite films. I’d go back to the Alain Renais!

Jerry Lewis just died, so he’s on my mind anyway. I made the work about him and Dean Martin. It’s called ‘Visit to a Small Planet’. The year that I showed it, Dean Martin died. There’s this odd resonance between them both dying because I’ve revisited the Jerry Lewis thing recently with the ‘Moment Memory Monument’ work. A lot of people have this idea of the slapstick element, but what happened in a lot of those early films – there is a film called ‘Artists and Models’ that he made. It’s a masterpiece. It’s got the most incredible, ridiculous, surreal storyline. If you can take yourself away from the screechy character of Jerry Lewis, and just take apart the idea of the film and the narrative its fascinating. What made me feel much better about my love of Jerry Lewis was I was reading. Jacques Rivette is my favourite film director. I was reading about Jacques Rivette and one of his most amazing films is ‘Celine and Julie Go Boating’. I’ve watched that film a million times and I was reading an interview with him. It said that one of the influences for a scene from ‘Celine and Julie Go Boating’ was Jerry Lewis’ ‘Artists and Models’. Yes! It’s not just me. That’s what I love about Jacques Rivette is that he mixes high and low culture. He can be just as much influenced by slapstick, soundstage musicals from the ‘50s at the same time as loving Artaud or whatever. That’s something I’ve done myself in my work. Nothings untouchable. It can be the most trivial stupid thing, but nothing is out of bounds. It’s how you use it. I really like that interplay between high and low things. A filmmaker like Jacques Rivette speaks volumes. What was really amazing at the weekend I got to introduce ‘Celine and Julie Go Boating’ in France, with Jacques Rivette’s wife. She was there and he died last year. She came to the to the screening and we got to chat a bit about his films, which was really amazing.

It seems like a dream situation.

It was.

There are not that many people that are left.

Yeah, it was really fantastic.

To finish off, we're going to play your last track, which is Scott Walker. This is middle period Scott Walker 'Farmer in the City'. Do you want to tell me why you chose it?

Like most people, I'm a huge Scott Walker fan. I really like those big orchestral songs. I've always loved Dean Martin, Frank Sinatra and Jacques Brel.

Scott Walker was a version of all. 'The Old Man's Back in Town'. Almost Cold War, huge epic.

It was epic, his voice, very filmic and theatrical. When I first heard Scott Walker, I thought he was their age. I started listening to him in the early '90s. I had 'Scott 3' and 'Scott 4', and all those albums. I thought that he was over fifty. When you're young, when you're in your twenties, everyone over fifty is old. I thought they all from the same era. Then I remember moving back from Amsterdam in the mid '90s and I saw that he had a new album out and it was 'Tilt'. I just was like, I've got to hear this, thinking it was going to be very similar to his old stuff. Of course, his voice was the same, but the album was incredible, experimental. It had noise, electronics, he was playing with poetry. This particular track is the first track on the album, and later I found out that it's got a subtitle, which is 'Remembering Pasolini'. A lot of the words he took from a poem that Pasolini wrote to his lover, who was actually really young actor in some of his films. He'd written this kind of poem to him. I think the track was about that poem. He stole a few words from it. It was also about trying to retrace the murderer of Pasolini. You can hear that force and the tragedy. It's just an epic song. It's just amazing. And Scott Walker, I think his voice can make your bones tingle.

That's a beautiful way to end thank you so much for coming in Georgina and this is Scott Walker, doing 'Farmer in the City' inspired by Pasolini, which is amazing.

Jeremy Shaw

07.11.17

Hi, you're listening to Rough Version on NTS with Francesca Gavin and my guest this month is Jeremy Shaw. Jeremy, how are you?

Great.

Good, wonderful. Jeremy is an incredible artist. He's based in Berlin, but he's originally from Vancouver. He's shown at MoMA PS1, and the Schinkel Pavillon and KW in Berlin and you have a massive show in London at the moment at 180 The Strand, which is running for two months. You also have a big show coming up next year in Hamburg? In the Hamburg Kunstverein. And of course, the Venice Biennale, where Hans Ulrich Obrist said you were one of the most exciting pieces to emerge from that and I have to agree. So, Jeremy. I know your work really well. I've curated you in a lot of things. I think one of the fundamental things about your work is this idea around transcendence. Do you want to tell me where that came from, and what interests you about it?

I'm not sure exactly where it came from. But I think probably from a very young age, I was interested in somehow getting out of the present moment. Even as a really young child I would do these games with my friends where we would knock each other out – these blackout games, and that evolved into…

Was that your gateway drug?!

I don't know! It was really early, like six, seven years old! And then, I was always looking for something a little more. I was raised Catholic and got into experimenting with drugs when I was in high school and that evolved into gaining an interest in other people's ideas around transcendental behaviour, attempts to escape the present moment. That's been an evolutionary process within my work, where it started with me experimenting mostly with drugs… and then leading more to a general investigation of other people's practices and other aspects of a similar type of behaviour – from religion, to dancing to meditation, or however people choose. It's this universal notion of attempting to leave or escape the present moment. I say that all the time. That's how I put it rather than talking about a full transcendental experience. There are these universal notions of skewing time…

What's so interesting about the film works – and we will talk about 'Liminals', but also the film works you've made before this – they are these very sci-fi influenced. I know 'Altered States' is one of your favourite films.

It is!

It's a great film! And if we look at the film pieces you've done, what's really amazing is they seem to be having some midpoint between almost retro 1930s or 1960s, or some kind of 20th century idea of spiritual transcendent practices, mixed with the concept of technology and a futuristic post-human thing. I find that contrast really fascinating. What did you like about fusing these two things and the narratives for what you do?

I think it was just a full circle. I'm working within the classic science fiction short story format of being able to aggressively confront a viewer with tons of information. Within that format I'm able to bring a lot of these interests together – like the '60s and '70s notions of these utopian ideals of experimental somatic techniques and dabbling in multiple spiritual traditions that might not be your own, mixed with a current interest in evolution and 'the singularity' and things like this… Sorry I can't remember what you just asked!

Why do you like that? It's such an interesting combination.

Yeah. I don't know, it just gradually evolved. I made this film 'Quickeners' in… It's been a slow process. I think it started with these outmoded mediums – like using 16 mm VHS – in a way to almost disarm the viewer… When you propose something, or when you present something in VHS or 16 mm or any of these outmoded mediums, I think the audience isn't really expecting to be surprised. People are familiar with these mediums, and they come in and I think it builds this familiarity, this sort of comfort with the work and from there you can really, I think subvert it. So, when you start combining a really succinct 1960s aesthetic with perhaps post-human theory, placing it 500 years in the future (which is what 'Quickeners did) I think there's a real cognitive dissonance that happens, which is something that I've always aspired to and is what I always really enjoyed with art and with music, which I'll talk about actually with one of my selections…

> *Why don't we go into that? Which tune do you want to start by playing, because you brought in some amazing things!*

Well, I wanted to play something that seems very out of character. It's a song called 'What a Wonderful World' by Louis Armstrong. Which I'm pretty sure everyone on the face of the earth knows by now. It's one of these songs. It's a perfect song and it belongs to the world. It's like air. But I have a really strong memory of this song because when I was a child, quite young, 5 to 10, I had a babysitter named Charles van Sandwyk, who is actually a really incredible Illustrator. And he was 11 years older than me, and he would babysit me. He was very unique in that he was into jazz, and this is in the mid '80s. He was a teenager and he liked jazz and he had an etching press in his basement, and he was very into 'The Wind in the Willows' and very twee things. He was South African, and he loved Louis Armstrong. He would always play it for me when we were hanging out when he was babysitting me and so I had this great connection to Louis Armstrong, and this really great connection to him, Louis Armstrong and the song 'What a Wonderful World' which was this perfect, beautiful thing. Then I went to a film with my dad in 1987 called 'Good Morning, Vietnam', which is a film with Robin Williams where he plays a radio DJ who was broadcasting to the troops in Vietnam. This song 'What a Wonderful World' was used in a scene in the film, but it was used in this horrific bombing scene where there's a montage of the village, he's stationed in being bombed as I recall, which had really violent implications. I just remember being so confused by this song that was so idyllic placed against these images that were so horrific, and it did something so… It was really… I just remember being totally aware of it and at 10 years old, really trying to critically dissect what was happening here and why I was feeling horrified by it, but also somehow excited and deeply moved.

It's almost a first breakthrough adult experience.

I could feel the manipulation too. I was aware that I was being manipulated. And yet, I was excited by it in a way, too. And it happened again, maybe we'll have time to play the song later, from a film I saw that same year called 'La Bamba'.

Classy movie!!

Remember that? Oh, no, it's great! It's about Ritchie Valens skyrocketing to the top of the charts as a 16-year-old, but he keeps having this recurring dream and it's beautiful. I mean it's a little different, because this one climaxes in something that is the opposite of the song but it uses 'Sleepwalk' by Santo and Johnny – which is easily in my top 10 songs of all time – but it posits it against this dreamy dream sequence of him as a child playing in the schoolyard, playing basketball, and then at the climax of the song, these two airplanes collide overhead, and the debris falls and he's looking through the debris… So, it's very similar but I think 'Good Morning Vietnam' was more explicitly this beautiful, idyllic song with this horrific imagery. That was something that has kind of permeated my practice, often this juxtaposition of somewhat antithetical image and sound.

I'm a Robin Williams fan. I'll probably play both tracks, but I'm going to start by playing the Santo and Johnny 'Sleepwalk' because it's incredible and it makes me feel good things. This is the 1959 Santo and Johnny track 'Sleepwalk'.

—

That was 'Sleepwalk' by Santo and Johnny. Now obviously we were talking about…

I was just telling Fran that it was weird to open the show with that song, because it is a real closer!

I'm opening with a closer! Before you were doing art stuff you were also doing music stuff. Obviously, music has been really fundamental to what you do. You worked as Circlesquare. You were signed to Trevor Jackson's label Output but you still DJ.

Do you want to tell me a little bit about how the processes change and how you've moved and how making music has influenced what you do in terms of making art?

Well, I played the bassoon when I was very young! For real! Which is called a faggot in German, which is funny.

Wow!

Foreshadowing.

That's a great piece of knowledge for everyone.

And my father played the bagpipes which are called the doodlesacks.

I feel so much more informed!

But I stopped that when I was 14 or 15 and I started playing guitar, just messing around quite casually in high school. But then when I went into art school, I got actually really deep into it. I bought a sampler and got deep into making electronic music. I was still using guitars and singing etc. During my early art school days, which were straight out of high school, I actually got more into music than I did in making art. I wasted a lot of time in art school I think, because I wasn't that interested… I actually tried to keep them separate for quite a long time, especially when I was working with Trevor on the Output label and had this Circlesquare project. I didn't ever want it to present it in the art gallery as an artwork. I was really making art as art and making music as music and that was really important to me at the time.

A split personality so to speak?

Yeah, I was always suspect of music in the gallery. I mean, that's changed now, of course, but at the time, I thought "Oh, that's like, when you're not good enough to make it in the music world, you put it in an art gallery", which is totally untrue. But that's how I was feeling at the time. I wanted to have these parallel careers that were equally as rigorous, and I tried for a while. It's rare that they would crossover…

Smoothly…

Should we go into it?

Yeah, yeah. Maybe one is enough?

Anyway, I tried to keep it separate. But there was this moment in 2002, where I wrote a song, that's going to take me a minute to explain… It had been a really hard partying summer and so I wrote this song that's directly in reference to this summer and I had this material from when I was a teenager. We used to film ourselves skateboarding all the time. Another thing where this cognitive dissonance thing came in was skate videos and watching what song people were going to select to skateboard to. I think Rodney Mullen actually skated to 'What a Wonderful World' at one point. I had this material that I used in art school a lot and it was this footage – This was a moment in the mid '90s when consumer cameras came into play and people were skateboarding – filming the antics around skateboarding had become almost more important than the skateboarding itself. We were always filming ourselves partying and doing stupid stuff like jumping off bridges. I had this material of these two girls getting into this nasty fistfight at a party and its girls that I knew. Really bad girls, and they start a fight with this one girl and it's this really ruthless catfight. I used this material in art school and got into a lot of trouble for it a bunch of times, actually. I was really not in favour in art school.

With the girls or the faculty?

The teacher. I remember the teacher telling me "Jeremy there's a difference between home video and video art".

Wow!

Suggesting that I repeat my foundation year. I wrote the song and for some reason it just reminded – this footage came back to mind. It's the only time I really fuse the two and it's a film that I have, a video, that I have shown lots of times called 'Seven Minutes' and it's this Circlesquare song, but with this slow-motion footage. So, it's this romanticized moment of my youth reworked to a song from another moment of reflection in my 20s.

> *Ok I'm going to play this. This is 'Seven Minutes' by Circlesquare. This is the moment where you fused both sides of your personalities, so to speak, your music and art personalities. So, this is 'Seven Minutes'.*
>
> —
>
> *That was 'Seven Minutes' by Circlesquare, and very shoegazey.*

Definitely. I got into that. I grew up in Vancouver, so sometimes things just didn't make it to you… I got interested in shoegaze really quite late, I guess. By the time I was into it, it was very uncool over here. You guys were totally into Blur and Oasis by then, that Brit, nasty lad revival thing that absolutely repelled me as a teenager. Anyway, I got deep into Slowdive, My Bloody Valentine and these bands and they remain a solid influence in a lot of what I do. As well as Cocteau Twins and the more gothic side of that stuff. It's always been really influential. This dissonance that those bands were…

> *I like the idea of, that meeting point between being a fan of something and how that feeds into you as an influence. You are the biggest David Bowie fan, but not everyone knows this. Literally the biggest David Bowie fan I've probably ever met. And it's amazing we're not playing one of his tracks, but you've made work that references it quite acutely, especially the 'Christiane F' project that you did in the streets of Berlin, which was incredible. Do you want to describe what the project was a little bit?*

That one? That's a piece where I found 11 of the international posters for 'Christiane F', all languages except German, basically, and reprinted them. Then we plastered the city. Berlin has a really incredible amount of hoardings for posters – legal and illegal. At one point, we had something like three thousand in the city for weeks on end. Three thousand of these things, advertising the release of the 1981 film, but with no new information or anything. It was an acknowledgement of my moving to Berlin and, and coming there… When I grew up, I rented 'Christiane F' because Bowie was in it and because he had done the soundtrack.

Probably my favourite Bowie album is 'Christiane F'.

Is it? My only vision of Berlin as a kid was 'Christiane F', which is this totally bleak portrait of a 13-year-old junkie. And yet, I was totally drawn to it. When I arrived it was amazing to meet so many expats that had had a similar experience. Almost everyone had had this early vision of Berlin via that film. It wasn't until I think 'Wings of Desire' that we had another vision of the city on screen. You didn't see a lot of Berlin back then, and the wall coming down… I reprinted these. Posted them up with no new information. And again, another side of that is that Germans weren't aware. That book was something they read in high school, but they weren't aware of the cultural impact it had outside of Germany, which is quite huge, I think, as a cult film. We reprinted these posters and had them all over the city without any new information. It was something I'd done before. I did it in Vancouver. I reprinted posters for the Expo – the 1986 World's Fair – during the lead up to the 2010 Olympics. We were promoting this 1986 fair again with no website. No tip off that this is a setup and again, it creates this kind of slippage of time, even for a moment. You do a double take. Why is that being promoted? Are they reissuing this? Are these really from 1986? What's happening? Especially the one in Vancouver was super effective, because people would come across these walls of posters from 1986 and be so confused by what they were. It was great to watch it on Instagram and see people's reaction to them. It's been a lot of fun to engage the public this way.

I would agree. I can see the relationship between that and your film work where you've got this idea of two elements of time being formed, disintegrated.

Like physical. Weirdly, my work is always about altered states and transcendental behaviour. I mean you might not think it seeing a 'Christiane F' poster but actually it is a physical version of that, in a sense. It's inciting this time slippage, even if momentary, with the viewer and their understanding…

I think we should play another one of your amazing track selections. Since we're talking about the '80s, I think we should play 'Doot Doot'! Do you want to tell me why you chose this by, is it Freur?

I don't even know how to pronounce it… Because it was the first song I thought of for some reason. I had this moment with this song… I can't remember. It was related to the 'Seven Minutes' one. It was that same summer I was talking about. We had been out all night. I was just with Todd and Tyler and Nicole, three friends, and we came back to her house, and she had this cassette that her friend had made. It was 2002 so cassettes were still a viable option before the revival. We were in a pretty good place I'm sure and this song came on and I was so totally confused and enamoured by it. I couldn't understand… This is 2002, so it was the height of electroclash and '80s revival. Tons of people were aping an '80s sound production. Then this song came on and I could not tell if it was older or newer, it was just so confounding to me. I probably played it 20 times in a row much to the dismay of these guys. I couldn't stop listening to it over and over. That was that moment post 9/11, The Strokes era, when all of a sudden it became okay to be completely referential. You used to get criticized for sounding too much like something else or too much like the past. Anyway, this song had me up in arms. I was like totally enamored with it. I thought it was the most beautiful thing I had ever heard. And it had this really, not naïve, but casual production. It was really compelling. We didn't know what it was, because there was no track list, so it took me a while to figure it out!

The old days of crate digging was crazy!

It was really frustrating. Then I found out what it was and also learnt that they had gone on to form Underworld, which is totally bizarre. Actually, I have a good Underworld story.

Tell me your Underworld story!

I was here in '99. I went to New Year's Eve at Alexandra Palace and New Order was playing and Underworld as well, who I never really cared about at all. But they went on and I think I had just taken some drugs and they were doing this big rambling, dubby spoken word intro that went on and on. Then when the bass drum dropped the first kick I vomited, a really hard puke and was so stoked. I was like "oh my god, the music just made me barf!"

Well, that's a very strong reaction! I think we have to play their earlier version of 'Doot Doot' which is from 1983 from Freur.

—

That was 'Doot Doot' by Freur. Now another trope in your work and something that you've been revisiting is dancing and the representation of dancing. Most notably, the film you made with Leiomy Maldonado, one of the best-known Voguers in the world, and you're currently working on another project, I believe, involving dance. Can you tell me a little bit about what the attraction to dance is, and how that emerges? The representation, the depiction of it? Because I think that's a lot of what makes it very interesting. You're not just showing people dancing. It's more about something else going on there at the same time.

I think it's, again, back to the universal notion of altered states or of transcendental behaviour. And dancing is to me one of the most common. Drugs, dancing, prayer – they're really root forms of human expression.

How did you end up deciding to work with Leiomy? This was before the voguing revival thing. You're definitely ahead of that moment in terms of an underground awareness, let's say.

I think, like so many people of our generation, you grow up watching 'Heavy Metal Parking Lot' and 'Faces of Death' and then you see 'Streetwise' and 'Paris is Burning' and you get enamoured with subcultures and these things that you're not a part of but look so alive. With Leiomy and voguing in general – I saw 'Paris is Burning' like everyone, probably when I was 18 or 19. But then I never really saw anything after that. I had no connection. Then Eli Sudbrack – Assume Vivid Astro Focus Eli – we were once on this farm in Portland. Stuart

Comer was doing film programmes on this farm. And Eli – this is right on the edge of YouTube, what he was doing was not usual – he was doing these eight-hour programmes that were just mash-ups of a Kraftwerk video and then a B52 performance and then these super raw voguing clips and I hadn't seen anything like it really since 'Paris is Burning', or 'The Queen'… I just couldn't believe it. I was shocked because they were these really low-fi mobile phone videos of kids voguing in what looked like cafeterias, youth centers etc. I was shocked by how it had evolved into this more aggressive form. That was the initial reintroduction. Then via YouTube I discovered more and more of these clips and Leiomy caught my attention like so many others, I was totally enamored with her balance of power and elegance. She has this way of dancing like she's existing simultaneously in multiple planes of time. I was living in New York in 2011 on a residency for the year, and I just wrote her and said "Hey, I have this idea, I really want to make this film" and she was like "Sure". So, we got together and talked a bunch and then we shot it. That film specifically co-opts the aesthetics of a 1967 Norman McLaren film called 'Pas de Deux', which is Canadian. McLaren was a Canadian animator, who invented the step and repeat technique, an optical printing technique, which animated the Muybridge effect of multiple exposure photography. High speed multiple exposure…

> *It also ended up being something used a lot in the '70s in music videos – Michael Jackson for instance…*

Exactly, it became totally tacky. It became a real cliché. It was even included on a lot of video cameras. There was a strobe effect, that did a similar thing, like echoing. I had seen the film when I was 10 or so, at school. They once played this 'Pas de Deux' film, which is a man and a woman dancing the 'Pas de Deux'. It's this starkly lit black and white thing, eventually the effect, this trailing ghost tracer effect, really consumes the film, and to me, as a kid, it really haunted me. The film was capturing images of someone in multiple planes of time on screen, it really was. And it leads into this, I don't know, the matrix. It was almost a really early version of being able to capture multiple realities, or multiple temporalities on one frame or on a linear timeline. That's what the work evolved into. Leiomy set against the same backdrop

– exactly the same as ‘Pas de Deux’ – but doing what she does. Then adding these effects and using them as a way to embellish what I see. Where she hits these transcendental moments. A way to expand these cathartic movements that she was engaged in. To answer your question… I use a lot of slow-motion effects and repetition and it’s a way to really scrutinize the movement and the catharsis I see happening. To zero in and in my own special scientific way of, zero in, amplify it and then stretching it out. It’s like scrutinizing these people who are having this cathartic moment, and then attempting to have a similar effect on the viewer. It’s kind of a loop of scrutinizing to hypnotize.

I think there is a really interesting relationship between how you’re approaching that filmically and your sculptural pieces. You’re almost doing it with photographs. You make these Perspex – they’re also showing at the 180 The Strand show – where you are creating something that seems to make a straight photographic image pull apart and be stretched and widened. It almost looks like it’s like a 2D version of strobing.

It’s a physical manifestation of these ideas. These documentary photos of people in states of religious or technological rapture…

Technological rapture! That is a great phrase!

Straight out of a press release!

Actually, I’d argue that is what a lot of technologies are trying to position themselves as.

With the acrylic, I’m usually zeroing in on a part of the body where I see this happening and then exploding it. It’s like a kaleidoscopic effect. It’s a very explicit illustration that these people are having some kind of experience that is skewing their reality or presenting multiple realities. It’s like a physical manifestation of the film work.

It is a nice midpoint. I think we should play another track because you have so many good ones with us. Shall we play a little bit of ‘There in Spirit’?

Yeah, sure.

Do you want to tell me what this is?

There in Spirit is a project between myself and Todd Shillington aka Konrad Black, who I've known for over 20 years. We've collaborated multiple times. We started working together again. I ended Circlesquare around 2009 and that's when I started to focus on art but bringing the music into the art practice more. Then Todd and I subsequently started working on music for music's sake again, but it's been a super slow process, because it's really tricky. We're both busy. We're really terrible. You get the two of us together and it's never ending. We haven't released a lot, but we have now started to score the films I'm making. We did the soundtrack for the 'Quickeners' film and 'Liminals', the one that's at 180 The Strand. Actually, the soundtrack is coming out with The Vinyl Factory this week. That's our first physical release as There in Spirit, the soundtrack to 'Liminals'. But this is a song that we started eight years ago. It's never ending, we've never finished it, so we should probably just play a clip of it, or he'll kill me.

It's quite an interesting concept anyway – in progress…

It really is. I don't know if it'll ever be finished, but this is called 'Dipsomania', and it's long.

Okay, well, let's play with it. 'Dipsomania' by There in Spirit, which is yet to be released.

—

That was an excerpt of a work in progress 'Dipsomania' by There in Spirit, which is Konrad Black and Jeremy Shaw. I think what's so interesting about that, and your collaboration, is how music is used in your films. It's incredibly central, more than a lot of people who are making film work with a soundtrack. You spend a lot of effort on how the sound is presented, almost to have a physical reaction – hopefully not making us vomit! – while watching it. In 'Liminals' for example, the bass creates this hypnotic relationship. You're in these waves of music and there's an incredible shift in the film. There's a shift in the music and the sound as well. I've never quite heard something like that – or at least it felt like that. Why is it so important for you?

It's back to when I was talking about using 16mm and luring the viewer, by being really meticulous in trying to make something feel authentically from another time, making the beginning of that film feel like it's from sometime in the '70s. Then you have the potential with both the visual and the audio. The audio in the beginning of 'Liminals' is just mono 16mm – really narrow band EQ. And from that, you have all this range to expand, all the way to 5.1. Again, it's playing with this element of surprise in the viewer, of luring them in and then rinsing them out. I don't know if I'm answering your question…

I quite like how abusive that sounds!

It is! It's manipulation, back to how I felt I was being manipulated by that 'Good Morning Vietnam' sequence and how I actually loved it. I love being tricked by things and I love feeling like I've been had. Like an M. Night Shyamalan movie. I love that twist.

I think we all do. Hence the success of Hitchcock.

Exactly. So, audio just plays a huge element in this, because it's something you can do so slowly, and so you can really creep in and before you know it, you're consumed by something completely different than what you had initially started with. The audio is a largely important part of the work.

I know that you're really interested in 'Future Shock', the Alvin Toffler book. It's another thing you've referenced a lot. Can you describe the book? I've always wanted to read it. Do you think your work is dystopic in a way? Or Utopic? Are you interested in this idea of a positive or negative future?

I think it's nebulous. I think I really propose a lot of different things I wouldn't see as – I mean you could call it dystopic, because often the premise is that humanity is on its way to extinction because we've lost the ability to have faith and faith has become an evolutionary aspect of our makeup. So, these people are out there attempting to reignite the faith gene and I guess that is dystopian by design, or on paper. But I don't think I present them that way. I have a lot of… 'fun' is not the right word, but I love this stuff that I'm doing. I think it's presented in a way that there's a lot of hope. It's a dystopian setup but these people, I'm speaking of 'Liminals' specifically, are under this banner of periphery, altruist culture and attempting to ignite or incite a new evolution within the body, to resurrect these faith cells that have become dormant. It's never ending. It's because science quantified spirituality and we learned that all spiritual experience came from the exact same place in the brain and thus, people then discounted it. Because they felt it wasn't an honest experience after this part of the brain atrophied. Then we realized that it had actually become necessary for human survival, so people are out there looking for a way to incite a new evolutionary advancement in humanity so that we can continue to live and exist. There's a Utopian idealism to these people who are now engaging in these antiquated types of spiritual behaviour…

But based in a dystopic context?

Yes, they're going back and trying to regain their faith by basically mimicking what they saw their ancestors do, from whirling to headbanging.

Whirling to headbanging is a good thing to end on. I'm going to get you to play one more track and then we'll finish with, of course, 'What a Wonderful World', because for me, that is always the conclusion. Do you want to tell me about the last track you brought in, 'Demon Seed'?

'Demon Seed' is a song from 1997 by an artist named Exocet, who I think, from what I know, only put out a couple of 12-inches. I was really deep into drum and bass at this moment and again, a little late. This is '97. It was definitely not cool anymore in England, but I lived in Vancouver and got these things secondhand. I was really deep into it, and this was that moment in drum and bass where it had gotten stripped back to a minimal thing by Doc Scott, I think really with a song called ‘Shadowboxing’. They were down to this two-step drum and bass break and the baseline, and these really aggressive sounds and this song came out of nowhere for me. It really borderlines on trance. It’s super melodic with lots of delay but it was just perfect timing for me, because this is my art school era and I was getting into Steve Reich and Philip Glass and things you do in art school, as well as into shoegaze music and ethereal ambient things. This track really clicked in all ways for me, and it sticks out as this anomaly within the world of drum and bass. It’s a beautiful song.

Thank you very much Jeremy. This is ‘Demon Seed’ by Exocet followed by Louis Armstrong ‘What a Wonderful World’. You’ve been listening to Jeremy Shaw on Rough Version on NTS.

Alex Da Corte

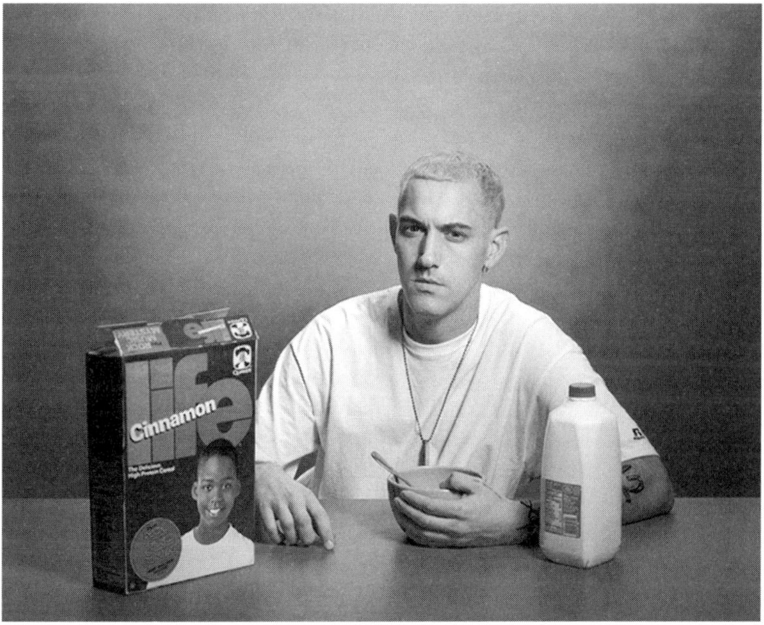

TRUE LIFE, 2013.

07.12.17

Hi. You're listening to Francesca Gavin on Rough Version, and my guest this month is Alex Da Corte. Alex is an artist originally from Philadelphia. He studied at the School of Visual Arts in New York, and then did an MFA at Yale. He has done big shows at the Secession in Vienna, ICA Philadelphia and the Louisiana in Denmark. He shows with Maccarone in New York and Josh Lilley in London. Hello, Alex. How are you?

Hello, Francesca.

Thank you for coming in.

Thank you for having me.

I read a really interesting thing about your work that I think you called it suburban, which I find hilarious when you see it. Would you call your work suburban?

Yes, yes. I would absolutely call my work suburban insofar as I buy all of my materials in the suburbs. And I think about the way that – I think about like the materials or the textures that I grew up with carpet, artificial flooring. I think it has a certain warmth or familiarity to me that is suburban – not from the city.

That's quite interesting, because for me as an urban girl, suburban always feels slightly on the edges of something, a little bit shoddy, which is quite interesting looking at your installations, let's say. Which are incredibly vibrant, incredibly colourful, full of weird objects. Definitely some weird everyday suburbanite things.

Yeah, I think that the colour – the colour is electric. The colour is probably in the club, but if you like remember the suburbs, or if you think about the suburbs, and you're not in the suburbs, then the colours change. The texture of it changes it's icier, or it's colder, or it's a version of the suburbs. But it's not a place you'd live. Like, no one would live in my installation but it's about a place that someone did live in, maybe.

Do you want to tell me what you like about the installation? That immersiveness I almost feel like there's a language going on there, that's in your head. As a viewer, we are trying to work out the narrative, to decipher it in some way.

I started thinking about installation because it was a resistance to photographs. It was a resistance to images. In order to take a piece of it, you had to go there. You had to go and see art and get out of your house or get off your phone and go there. I still think that an installation is a call to a space, to say be a participant and go somewhere, to walk down the street or travel to see art. I think that that's like a really urgent thing to do, especially in a moment where all we see are images. There's textures and sounds and scents and things that you couldn't experience if you weren't there.

I agree that something super important, when we're used to such a surface engagement with something, it feels really different when you're in a space. It makes galleries, museums, important as locations for bringing people together in some way, or even just being there on your own.

100%. I mean, I think that's the reason I want to make a space because I also want to be engaged with like a physical space for a long time. Even in making an installation, you're there so, so long. It's like being in a pressure cooker. You're in the space and you get to know the strangeness of every space. Every space is built in such a way that in order to understand it you'd have to be there a long time, and I don't think we do that much. There's no time. It seems like there's no time, but there is.

Loads, obviously. It's infinite, allegedly. Do you want to tell me how you use sound and what kind of sound elements you've used in past installations? Since we're on the radio.

Let me think. I remember when I was in graduate school, I made this piece of this man sitting in a big pool of blood. I wanted there to be a sound in the headphones that this person was listening to – say imagining what song he was listening to right before he got stabbed. It was a vague portrait of Elliott Smith, or an imagined portrait of Elliott Smith, but done after Caravaggio's 'The Deposition of Christ'. So, he was this fallen figure, and I imagined this emo kid listening to headphones and getting stabbed or something, and just sitting in this big pool of blood. And so, I made a bit of music with a friend of mine that would chink and kind of tink and make little noises that you can vaguely hear through the headphones in this person's ears. And something about that gives it a sense of time. Adding sound to something makes it more like a film and less like a still sculpture, or less like a painting. Because I studied film and video and animation, I always want things to move or exist in time. So, adding sound for me is like a way to move those things forward.

> *You think that film background also makes – sometimes your things feel a bit like a set. Do you think there's a relationship with between those two things in some sense?*

I think so. Because I don't think of cartoons as having sets. But I think of them more as cells, in the sense that it's a backdrop painting. So, it is like a flattened space. If you're in a dream or if I imagine my dreams, I don't think of them as sets, but they are vaguely familiar rooms, that have no specific point to plug in your phone or eat a sandwich. The flattening of the space becomes like a set. It's a prompt for an action, but it's not going to fulfil you completely because its only purpose is to hold up the action that exists in that space, I guess.

> *Let's play one of your tracks because you've got really good ones. I think we should start with Janet Jackson, because I love Janet Jackson. 'Velvet Rope's been coming up a lot, weirdly, recently. Do you want to tell me why you chose this track and what your feelings are?*

'Velvet Rope' is one of my favourite albums, period. I think it's great. We play it in the studio – me and my crew play in the studio front to back. It's a special album for me. When I heard it the first time I was in high school, and I'd just learned to drive. I don't think I knew… it was eye opening in so many ways. I mean the subject matter is progressive, or for my ears at the time was really progressive. Thinking about sexual fluidity and this freedom of speech, and just a kind of vulnerability that she offers in the album was something that I hadn't been exposed to before. And I distinctly remember this interview that she did with 'The View', the conservative group of women that sat around the table. They were asking her about the album, and she was just being free and cute and kind of coy about the taboos that she was addressing. Everyone was blushing, I think, at the fact that this like album ripped her clothes off in a way – before her clothes were physically ripped off like in the Superbowl wardrobe malfunction, let's say. I just remember thinking that's like a beautiful place to be in terms of creatively thinking. Just to be in a place where you can just exist outside of the standard.

> *How lovely. We are going to be playing Janet Jackson 'You' from 'Velvet Rope'.*
>
> —
>
> *Can we talk about your approach to collaboration. You've worked with people like Jayson Musson, Dev Hynes, and the painter Sam McKinniss, I think. Do you want to tell me a bit about how that collaborative process works, why you've been drawn to it and how it's influenced what you make?*

Well, ever since I started working as an animator, many years ago, I always knew that whatever work I was going to do, would hinge on the work of so many other people. All of my uncles and cousins are contractors, and my family was house painters for many years. My brother still is. You're a participant. You're like a part of a bigger machine to build a house or make a home or finish a film. I've always wanted and been attracted to collaboration and understood that that's a necessary part of making anything. There is no singular you, in fact. Working with people like Jayson Musson, or Sam McKinniss, or Dev Hynes, or Annie Clark has been so exhilarating because they are so strong in what they do. Whatever their opinions are, or their talents are, they just throw them at you, and you have to – I don't know, you have to ricochet within their ideas or their world. And that brings out a maybe a better version of yourself, or a different version of yourself, that you might not put forward if you're just working singularly.

What's also interesting is they come from – some of them – come from quite a performance-based background. Has that manifested in the installations, or in your work in some way? It's almost like I can imagine performance taking place in a lot of your spaces, but I've never seen that happen actually.

Right, yeah, I don't think I'll ever do performance. But I think I always wanted to be a musician. I fetishize music and I love music so much. But I have no musical talent, it's not in my bones at all. Working with people that are musicians has been exciting for me. It is the performative yin to my yang. I think it completes the work in some ways or completes this part of me that I maybe don't fulfil in my every day.

I'm really interested in that. I'm quite interested in the idea of the fan and like how that influenced you. Can we talk about Eminem? I read that you researched him for years as part of influencing specific works or was it a wider influence on your practice? What was the Eminem thing?

The Eminem thing… I was living in Paris at the time that I started this, or that I had this awakening about Eminem, a reawakening. A friend of mine sent me this image of a man in front of the 'Mona Lisa'. I remember looking at the image and I think he said like, "Oh, I saw you. This is a picture of you at the Louvre", and I looked at the image and thought yeah, that is a picture of me. But I don't remember taking this picture. This was like around 2011, and then maybe like a day or two later I realised that it wasn't me. It was Eminem. He had brown hair and a hat on but like in the face it looked like me and I like was shocked that I didn't know my own face. That that face could be similar to this guy that I had never really identified with, or even thought much about, besides that he was the super important musician from my youth, and that his politics were like intrinsically opposite of mine, it seemed. He was a misogynist and a homophobe and things that I was turned off by. And the message of his music was something I didn't quite understand. So, I thought, well if your face can be similar and your face is mutable, or can change, or you can swap faces, can you swap politics? Can you swap like perception of the world? Could I have empathy for Eminem and try to see what it is he is speaking to, and where his like rage and his point of view comes from. For years I went about working on a costume, essentially, of this Slim Shady character, which resembled Eminem quite a bit, and tried to understand him better. To see what it would be like, to be in his shoes.

How did that conclude? Were you just eventually realising "No, I couldn't" or was it just the questioning that was the interesting process?

I don't like being blonde. I'm a dark-haired guy. I think it was a challenge. For me like dyeing my hair really changed how I saw the world, and that seems silly to say, but when you look in the mirror, and you're not seeing yourself or you're seeing another character, you do start to lose yourself a bit and feel as though you are in a different skin. There are some things that maybe I benefited from. Maybe I was a little bit more confident or cocksure, and I felt like I could do things that maybe I might not do if I wasn't this way. But I think I tried hard to understand what it would be like to have all eyes on him, or all eyes on me, and just tried to soften my feelings towards him, which I thought were, at a time, pretty resistant to his message.

Interesting. We're going to play another track. Since we're on a you theme, let's play Erykah Badu's 'I Want You'. Do you want to tell me why you chose this specific Badu? We've had quite a lot of Badu on the show.

She is just the queen.

That's it.

That's it.

That's a good enough reason. Here's Erykah Badu 'I Want You'.

—

Can we talk about some of your objects, and how you source them and why you pick them? Everything from like basketball shoes to donuts to cats, China cats to neon signs to weird kinetic swans to Kleenex. Where do you get your things? Why do you choose your things? How does that work?

That's a tough question always. I guess it's like why do you choose the thing you're wearing today? Why do I choose the T-shirt that I'm wearing? Today I'm wearing a blue t-shirt.

And a blue hat.

They're different colour blues though.

I mean, actually, there's quite an amazing sense of colour in what you're wearing. It's quite subtle, but brilliant.

So, I wonder why, what was my mood when I picked this blue shirt, and I thought I don't want to pick the shirt that has True Blood cast on it today, because maybe that's my fancy shirt, and I'm not doing anything fancy today. I thought, today is a day for being mellow, because it's the day before this show. So maybe I just need to have blue because that feels like the sky, or something. And in the same sense, I think when I go to a thrift store or shop, and I see an object – like a lemon zester with a particular green handle on it. It's this beautifully designed lemon zester. I don't really have lemons to zest, but I want the thing because I appreciate the maker, the person who made it and who designed it. And just want to think about, what it would be like to zest the lemon. I then buy the thing, but I don't ever zest a lemon. I just let it sit on my desk because I appreciate the time that went into making the thing. I think maybe this lemon zester will yield some kind of say lemonade, conceptual lemonade, just like the blue shirt will yield some kind of serenity.

The objects that you find, they seem to be more of an accidental discovery in a sense. Do you often leave them to marinate, in a way, in your space?

A hundred percent. I think the studio is that – I spoke about a pressure cooker. I do think of the studio as this big crock pot of stuff. They stay there for a while. Because the making for me happens in this really like chaotic moment, that's quite fast, but it doesn't happen 'til the end. For most shows, a lot of the making happens the day before. But it's been sitting there in my presence for a while, I just don't know what to do with it yet. Maybe that's because I procrastinate a lot, but also, I just have to think about it. The work has to be urgent. The work has to be bombastic and explode in a way, without being sloppy. It needs to have the urgency of "I need this thing to give me electricity right now, or else".

> *It's really interesting also that you're based in Philly, a city I've been to quite a few times. I used to write about new Philly soul back in the day. Philadelphia is quite a strange – I mean it's a proper city, used in a lot of films, such as 'Mannequin' – great '80s reference.*

Love that.

> *It's quite sleepy place sometimes too. Do you want to tell me about how the quietness, and I suppose the space that you get in Philadelphia is influencing that process?*

Well, my studio is in northeast, in a place called Juniata. There's not much happening there besides just families and blue-collar work. That's what's happening. It's like a neighbourhood. It's very electric. For me, I go in and out of the studios, unbothered. They just think of me as some guy carrying big stuff all the time, but that's about it, and that's nice for me. I can kind of just be in the studio and think, and not feel the rush of a city. It just feels really quiet where I am. And it's completely important, because I do work rather slow. It takes me time to figure these things out. It takes me time to discover the things I'm looking at every day, even though I see them every day. It takes me time to understand them.

> *Before we play another one of your tracks – we're going to play the Breeders track next because it's really different I felt – The Breeders makes me feel like a punk urge. It also made me think about your Ivanka Trump experience, which I think is quite a strange combination. Do you want to summarise*

your feelings about what happened or what actually did happen with the Ivanka Trump thing? She posted a picture of your work, you went "fuck this" bluntly. How did you feel about that whole process?

I thought… that process was complicated I think. Because your work, when it leaves your hands, is out of your hands. The objects that I put into my work were someone else's and they're not ringing me up and saying take it off your studio walls. They just let it be. I think maybe for me, I don't take back what I said, but I also have to understand that the politics that are in my work are in my work, and they're not leaving. If she chooses to live with my politics, then the message will come across.

Nice. Let's talk about The Breeders. Why did you choose The Breeders?

Because I fucking love The Breeders so much. There's something about this song, it's kind of a funny album title 'TK' because it isn't necessarily like 'the' hit album. But the message, the words of the song, the title 'Too Alive' is something I either aspire to be or want from my life.

Actually, that comes across in the work. It feels like experience but heightened. Everything feels very heightened in it. So that is apt phrasing for what your installations are like.

And there's a beautiful line that shouts out to girls who haunt you, and I think that's something that I can relate to.

Nice. This is Breeders 'Too Alive'.

—

Okay, that was The Breeders 'Too Alive'. I want to talk a little bit about this idea of narrative. Do you have a clear narrative through the space, or is it just the implication? Are you interested in ideas of narrative? Obviously, if you're coming from a film background that definitely is something that you'd imagine would feed into what you do.

Yeah. I mean I like telling stories, it's something my family did a lot. They were telling stories, whether they were bullshit or not, I believed them to be true, and I love that. Because I think that, especially for, coming from my mom or my grandfather, their stories were about probably some banal things that just needed a little bit of electricity to feel like a tall tale or to feel legendary. Because they came from a sleepy, sleepy town. The stories that I tell, or propose – it's not about telling necessarily, but it's a proposition – are less linear. They ricochet the way they do in dreams, but they're prompts to kind of tie together a whole set of icons that exist in the world, that maybe I don't quite understand but are available to us. In the same way that, all notes are there to collect and turn into song, what do you make of a world where there is a character named Eminem? And the Wicked Witch of the West? And shoes that say superstar on them and flashing neon lights. What world is that? On paper, it sounds like a cartoon world, but it's our world. And why do we live in a world where these icons are proposed, and these idols are celebrated in the way they are?

> *I'm quite interested also in that dichotomy – a word I don't use often obviously – between fiction and reality in your work, because it feels like it's grounded in some kind of realness, but it is definitely otherworldly. It's very interesting that you use words like dreams and memory and things like that. Is there something about that connection between the fictional and the real in your work for you?*

It's funny that slippage because when I find that when people visit these shows, or visit these installations, they say "wow, this is like so crazy". And I'm like no, that's just a chair from IKEA. Why is it so crazy? It's just a chair from IKEA, but without the chair part. We're balancing or like teetering on a line between the very real and raw, and the very surreal and strange. And where is that slippage? For some people, it's just when they sleep, but my proposition, can you walk on your head all the time?

> *We're going to play your last track, which is an incredible track, but it is also the most disco song ever. Is disco an influence into your approach to spaces? Because it's been used*

before by critics, but also like it does feel a bit nightclubby as well. There's a lot of neon lights. There's this intensity of colour.

When I was growing up and like first listening to music, there was a lot of talk – because my mom and dad met in a club, they met in a disco club.

Amazing.

There was a lot of talk of disco, and I listened to a lot of disco. I actually should have played this song 'I Got A Date With The Rain' because it's really beautiful. It was one of my parents' songs. But I did think a lot about disco. I had an afro and fetishized the '70s, for sure. But I think when I'm making work I'm not thinking necessarily about the club, but I do like the warmth of the colours that came out of the '70s. Ovens that were avocado green or cupboards that were a warm yellow.

I have much worse words for those colours.

I think for me the warmth of those colours and the softness of them, they remind me of a kind of love or tenderness that I see in objects now.

Why did you choose Donna Summer 'I Feel Love'? We're going to be playing the extended mix, which is incredible.

I think, this song in particular, the extended mix 'I Feel Mega Love' is such a funny proposition, because you know, what is love? Sam McKinniss wrote this really great essay called 'Justify My Love' for this book that I just put out called '50 Wigs'. He wrote, "what if love was like a bird that landed on the tree in front of you", or something like that, I'm paraphrasing. The idea of love or Donna Summer singing about love at the club late at night, is so silly and strange but also really beautiful. And I can relate to that.

Thank you so much for coming in Alex, and this is the extended mix of Donna Summer 'I Feel love'.

Rhys Coren

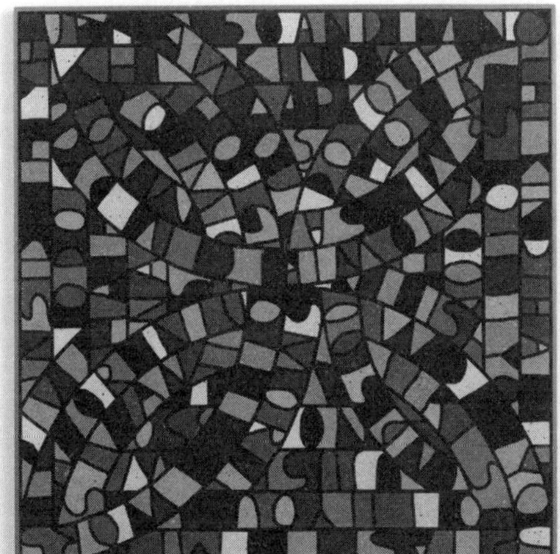

A Stella, 2021.

03.01.18

Hi, you're listening to Rough Version on NTS. And my guest this month is Rhys Coren. He's a British artist who's a graduate of the Royal Academy. He's represented by Seventeen Gallery, and he was one of the founders of online space bubblebyte and now Opening Times, and he has shown everywhere from New York to Stockholm, soon to be in Germany, a variety of international exhibitions. How are you, Rhys?

I'm very well, thank you.

Wonderful. Thank you for coming in. Now, I think you and a lot of exhibitions I've done, particularly about the relationship with music. I want to talk initially about the relationship music has with your animation works, because you've done pieces that I think play around ideas of syncopation and rhythm and actually draw on music quite directly. Do you want to tell me a little bit about that element of your moving image stuff?

The connection that the two have? Well, I guess both have real time rhythm in them. I guess I was working a lot around trying to create abstract animations or groups of different animations, where the thing they had in common was a frame rate. If you were to think about BPM and frame rate together. I was thinking about heart pace, like a heart rate, a 60 BPM. Thinking about loops of music and loops of animation. As long as the animation, something happens every twelfth frame, every twenty-fourth frame, every sixth. That in some way will sync up with a 60 BPM track. They were quite basically abstract forms that had something in common, which was like a definable BPM, or frame rate, or pace and literal duration.

So, the sync kind of came first in a way? Or is just an element outside?

I don't know. I mean, you've known me for a while, and I quite like the numbers, and the idea of these algorithms and these patterns in the durational element of animation. Abstract animation and music just seem to – there was like a logical connection between the two. I guess there was a crossroads where I needed, I wanted to start making work about things I found interesting anyway. Because work, your practice, shouldn't feel like work. And this revelation I had in my mid-twenties. That I could really just focus on something. I really enjoyed and animation and music were two of those things. And then as you sort of obsess over them, and go down these tangents, as you work with it over and over and over, that you start to see weird things like the patterns, and the maths, and the rhythm, and the duration.

Do you want to tell me about some of the tracks that you've used specifically? Obviously, I know you've done 'Roobarb & Custard', the rave track from the early '90s. Do want to tell me about some of the song choices you've had in those works?

The first song that I was going to play today.

Beautiful segue.

Yeah, we didn't even rehearse that. 'Evil Smokestacking Baby' by Haircut 100 is a track that I've used in an animated work. I think quite often – I've listened to so much music. Especially dance music or music that doesn't have… Music that's quite mechanical, repetitive. It conjures up images, and not in a kind of synaesthetic way, as a lot of people would maybe try and understand it. But actually, have more memories or something. So, a lot of the music is usually giving me a really quiet, visceral response. I respond to it quite viscerally, or it gives me really vivid images. Then I just seem to keep listening to some songs over and over. I'll draw and maybe vice versa as well. Certain images make me think of certain songs. I mean I have a certain taste. So, I guess all the music comes from that taste.

Do you want to describe your tastes a little bit?

How dare you?

How the Haircut 100 track relates to that taste?

I don't know. I'm just thinking about music as a way of becoming more self-aware and understanding yourself. And growing up and really liking my uncles and mum's disco and soul, and just feeling euphoric and almost chasing it. Chasing that feeling or something. But then, as a musical genre, dance, if you think about it, you go back through the history of it. I really like anything that can make you dance from the '60s onwards, until even quite modern dance music sometimes. But most specifically, I guess it's '70s or '80s disco. The pop tunes I get remixed by someone until they get played in clubs. Haircut 100 is one of those, I think.

Let's play the Haircut one.

Oh yeah. Great.

Which is from 1984. While you were alive. It's a great tune. It's got actually a quite slow rhythm to it.

I actually used it in an animation I made 2015, where I slowed it. I think it's about 80 to 90 BPM, and I slowed it down to 60, and looped it back on itself. It feels more like a heart rate pace, but I thought I'd play the original today.

Wonderful. This is Haircut 100 'Evil Smokestacking Baby' from 1984.

—

That was Haircut 100. Now, another aspect I think that's really interesting about your relationship with music, it seems to be really embedded in studio practice. Your process of working. Do you want to tell me what music you listen to in the studio and how it influences your process? Not necessarily in the animation work, but actually in your work in a wider sense.

Well, the music I've already talked about, but it just depends what mood I'm in. Sometimes you can go down a Steve Reich or Philip Glass thing. And you're trying to tease out some sort of sadness. It depends what sort of cycle of mood I'm in really. Obviously by the end of the week, it gets quite party-ish.

As you near Friday.

Yeah. It gets louder and more… I guess I'm trying to reflect upon a certain emotion that's already there. And I quite like coaxing out. If I'm feeling a bit anxious or sad, I'll listen to something that's quite sad. Coax out certain emotions and stuff. By the end of the week, I tend to go into a slightly different state, altered state of consciousness.

Maybe you could describe and start talking about, the framed pieces. They are laser cut, abstract shaped works. Do you want to tell me if there's a rhythmic element within those and how you bring those together?

Rhythm is something that's a constant in the work I've been making the last five or six years. It has [developed] into being, potentially, the content. But then you've got durational rhythm, the real time rhythm of moving image and sound. And you've got an imaginary space where rhythm doesn't adhere to a more literal duration or idea. It's a difference, basically, between watching a film and reading, I think. Within the painted works, the marquetry works, it's about the rhythm. The way your eye maybe goes over it, flitters over it, but also about any mental imagery or any imaginative space that you enter. You day-dream. You can look at stuff. It's like Narnia-time or something, and you come out the wardrobe and you think you've been gone for ages, but you only snapped out for three or four seconds or something. And weirdly, when you make animation work, time can just – I think when it's really good – create this kind of spell in a way. Time can just fly by and actually, you've been sat there for 30, 40 minutes or something. Does that answer that?

That answers it beautifully. There's another aspect to what you do which I find very interesting, and also relates directly to some of the music things. You also wrote poetry or text pieces. They're amazing. They're really accessible and short.

Well, they've gone underground, Fran.

Oh, have they? It's an underground element of what you make?

They've become private. They've become a way of disseminating anything I encounter really. Basically, the writing – I think maybe you even employed me to write at some point. You definitely guided me or helped me get employment through writing. I think doing it as a job killed the…

Sadly, I think I have to agree as a journalist.

When I first moved to London, I was writing for different magazines and online people, and copy-writing and copy-editing. It just sucked the pleasure out of writing for me. Also, I don't even think I was very good at it. I'm already doing one thing. I'm already trying to communicate and connect with people through an artist practice, which is nerve wrecking enough, that the fear and the anxiety I get for trying to show any writing was just too much. So, it's gone underground. It's just for me now. I very rarely show anyone the writing.

Wow. I feel privileged that I've seen some of the poetry works.

Also, everyone was going through a phase of writing, weren't they for a bit?

Poetry was hot about a year and a half ago.

You couldn't go to an exhibition without some appallingly written script. Scripts were the thing. I was just like I don't want to be contributing to that. Really. There's enough. Sometimes I just don't finish stuff. I have folders and folders and folders, and books and books and books, and things full of half-finished writing. And it's fine to stay like that. And it evolves. I'll go back to it and edit it, but it's for me really. It fuels a lot of the work. A lot of the new marquetry painted works; they stem from pieces of writing. So, in the same way, an almost abstract visual language has developed through cropping, editing and manipulating, or embellishing found images, found material, and slowly adding visual components that I've authored myself into an abstract practice. I do that with the writing. Some of the paintings can be a single letter. I mean there's even one I had in my degree show called 'The Fundament Wonderment of Fun'. I even took the last letter out. It was like a zigzag of the shadow of an F, which had stemmed from a much longer bit of writing. I was treating the text like a found image and putting it through different processes until I had something quite abstract, I think.

What's also really interesting is that it also has like an autobiographical, emotional route.

Yeah.

Which I find quite interesting because when you look at your work, you wouldn't necessarily know that that's in there, but it definitely seems to be part of it.

Everything is connected in some way to something really real. So that's why I don't actually feel comfortable with thinking about my work as totally abstract. Luckily, there's people like Jonathan Lasker out there, who were really good at describing their work as, it's not entirely non-objective, because of really basic things. There can be a figure and a background. And that's enough to take it out of like a more like traditional, not even traditional, a more straightforward, abstract work. But everything starts somewhere, from something really quite personal. And I slowly objectify that thing until you're left with something more universal, something that can maybe feel familiar without really being able to pinpoint it. That's actually been a really slow evolution of my practice over about seven or eight years. Of pointing at stuff that I find interesting, to editing that source material to find the essence of it or something.

I think we should play another track.

Yes.

I think we should play the Sylvester track, actually, because I think even though we won't be saying what the poem is, you actually have written about this track.

Yeah. I did.

Do you want to tell me which Sylvester you chose and why?

'Over and Over' which I first heard on the Larry Levan documentary 'Maestro', which at the risk of advertising East London's other cool online music company, Boiler Room, is streaming for free on their website at the moment, so you can go and look at that. It's incredible. And it's about the history of dance music in New York. Do you want to play it?

I will. I'm a massive fan of Sylvester. I mean it's a really specific kind of disco. I didn't know this track, and this is Sylvester 'Over and Over'.

—

And that was the full seven-minute version of Sylvester.

Oh, do you know what? There's a nine-minute version, there's a twelve-minute version. I think I even saw a thirty-minute version.

I recently heard an extended fifteen-minute version of 'I Feel Love' by Donna Summer. You know what? It was so good.

The 12-inch.

Just make it longer and longer and longer. We need longer songs.

When you start, pulling threads and you find yourself, think about sort of a guy from Plymouth, born in early '80s. To get really obsessed about a time and a place in history and the kind of music, you start to learn all this amazing stuff about why these dance records started to get longer. DJs were producing them, and taking three-minute radio specific tracks, and looping and looping them and adding breaks to it. It's quite amazing actually to get lost in that history.

A history I enjoy. Can we talk about the influence of the digital in what you do? Because it's not necessarily obvious looking at a lot of your work now. You curated and worked with a lot of works online. Currently Opening Times and then before that at bubblebyte. Do you want to tell me a little bit about how that's influenced you, what you found interesting about that and how that's changed?

Just being a bit of a nerd, I guess. I don't know. The thing that really, that drew me to working with computers at first, and then maybe online, is the idea of like the free culture, and the fact that, in a sort of anti-capitalist way, there's no ownership. And if anyone invents something, or they've done something, they will go out of their way to give you a comprehensive guide of how you can do it yourself. So, all the little techniques and some edits and different things you could do, for example, Paper Rad, who Cory Arcangel and Paul Davis work with, doing all this sort of data moshing and stuff like that. They designed a program and some freeware and made it downloadable with a guide on how to do it yourself. So, they weren't trying to own something. They weren't trying to have something as their signature, look or style. Their first instinct was to share it and get it out there, make it public knowledge. And it just meant that, I could teach myself to do so much stuff, which I maybe couldn't have done. I'm more in tune with learning something digitally, I guess. But then weirdly, by doing, starting bubblebyte, which is an online gallery, which we did, with Atiilia [Fattori Franchini] from 2011 to 2013, and then became more like a collective that were doing takeovers on other people's websites. We initially had our own online platform. And then we wanted to integrate the work of others onto other existing websites. We would animate other people's websites at the click of a button.

They were amazing. You would take over often institutional websites.

Paul Flannery. I just basically helped facilitate him really. But you know that sort of, that took care of whatever that drive, or need was to work in that medium, which then freed me up to make loads of other stuff. Well, I thought I was getting a look from the outside.

No one's looking at you.

(Now closer, closer to the mic.) Yeah, that freed me up really. I was compartmentalized slightly. I was able to do the digital stuff on a completely different platform in a collaborative way, or a curatorial way. And then that just allowed me to do other stuff in my own work.

> *Can I ask you about the takeover as a concept? Because not a lot of people do it. It's really interesting that you're keeping the structure.*

Still, no one does, yeah.

> *You are basically taking the structure, often of something that's quite straightforward and linear, maybe a bit bland. And what makes it interesting is that you end up transforming that into a creative space.*

Because there's only one Paul Flannery. I've got to stress this. The guy really is the brains. We were just caught, conceived of this idea of an institution – we did one on the Royal Academy's website – if an institution gives you access to their backend, which sounds a bit rude – technical term, Fran – then Paul can root around in there and we can sort of, well, we can conceive of an idea that he implements to alter the JavaScript and code of a website, so it literally comes to life. You can have a button there, and every element of it, every image, every piece of text, everything could start to spin around in a big well I think the first proper one we did was Trade Gallery, Nottingham, did their website. Then I think we did one for Cell Projects where there was no explanation, and the website exploded. They were inundated with complaints or warnings that their website had been hacked.

> *Oh, amazing.*

We did a few different institutions, and the really big one was last year for the Royal Academy. It's for my degree show. We've got every one of the seventeen students to create sound and images. We implemented some code, which allowed for seventeen different buttons. And when you clicked on it, the website would ultimately become or reflect whatever that student or artist chose. We changed the name from the Royal Academy to the name of the artist, and we did one for New Contemporaries on Spike Island's website. I remember Dominic

Watson, who was part of it said, 'Dominic Watson Island' instead of Spike Island everywhere. We replaced certain words with their name.

> *I find it a really exciting format. I'm always looking for new models on how you can show artwork. I think that you were really influential – presenting a new model, basically.*

I guess it's so rare to find an artist like Paul with a practice, who can implement the ideas that he has. I guess most coders are so literal. That the idea that you will misuse the technology to make something completely inefficient, and almost blow phones up and computers up. I mean, it would break computers sometimes. It's like everything that they stand for, it goes against. But that's what artists do, isn't it? They misuse everything, I guess.

> *We're going to play another track. We should play Love International.*

Yes, please.

> *Tell me about this track and why you chose it.*

It's a 1981 track, but I didn't say the first one the Haircut 100 song, I heard it first here at NTS, on the Bahamian Moor radio show. Will and Ollie, I guess they've been music gurus for me. They've taught me a lot about music. But Love International, I heard it for the first time at a World Unknown party, which is Andy Blake and Joe Hart's parties. It's their eighth birthday coming up. It would have passed actually by the time this show comes out. But I can't really explain it as a clubbing experience. It's just truly insane. I mean, there's so much smoking you can't see the person next to you, you just have to know they're there by touch. So, you can completely lose your inhibitions and they played this song.

> *Well, I love a warehouse party so anything that connects to that works for me.*

Let's have a dance, shall we?

This is Love International, 'Airport Of Love' from 1981.

—

And that was Love International 'Airport Of Love'. I've been thinking, you also teach, and I find that quite interesting in terms of how you come up with ideas.

What, for teaching?

Well, for teaching. I remember because I've taught recently, and it was a real eye-opener. What the hell do you say to students? But I was looking at some of the ideas you have around music, and what really amazed me was how much a lot of it came down to emotion. I find emotion a really interesting thing in art at the moment. At one point it was deeply unfashionable to have things that were about feeling.

I think it probably still is, isn't it?

Yeah, maybe it is. Why do you think music is interesting as an influence on art to break through something conceptual that seems dry and unemotional-less?

How music helps?

Yeah. Within the basis of your own work, obviously.

Music obviously started off as inspiration and then slowly became content of the work. But it also helped as a metaphor for understanding picture making, especially when I was studying, and to have something that's so simple. Just raw, abstract rhythm at times, or vocals, or whatever the component parts are, and it just have such a profound effect on your emotion or, not even. It can affect your emotion, but it can like really coax out, really raw, visceral sort of emotion. And I think that really helps. Because it sets the goalposts, very high, in terms of what you can potentially achieve with something. The economy of means there. That you can get something so massive from something quite simple. Even some colour combinations and simple compositional elements can have something quite like, almost like an emotive reaction as well.

That also really applies to your use of scale. A lot of your marquetry and painted pieces are really small and intimate. But then on the other hand, you're doing something like Royal Academy where you're doing joint projection over the entire building. There's a real, breadth of scale within that. Do you feel like that changes your visceral reaction, that physical...

I think the scale relates to what I said earlier, whether it's an imaginative space or there's real time, literal, durational component parts, like music or moving image. So, with the painted works, I guess my thinking about growing up watching so much TV, as long as your face is that far away from the little squares, that you will have grown up with. You could lose yourself in that world – like scale, time almost didn't seem relevant. But I just thought, as long as these paintings were bigger than your face, then you could lose yourself in them. And then the techniques that I use, the sort of chopping up all the component parts of the image, so every graphic, every part of every component in the image is individually cut and sits side by side. The in itself is just a fussy, fiddly technique. And then the way I texture the work, slowly trickling paint on it, everything about it seem to want to draw you in. So, it all seemed to just sort of wrap up quite nicely in this idea of intimacy. Work that draws you in. And if I do something, say, two metres tall, it'll only be sixty centimetres wide. Like only one dimension can ever be quite big. This idea that my good friend, Neill Kidgell would often say if big work pushes you back, small work can pull you in. And to think about work that can push you back, this massive, large kind of macho work. I like the intimacy of being drawn into something and being able to lose yourself in something in your imagination.

Just really beautiful. Yeah. Can you tell me a little bit about the Royal A.

Creaky chair, sorry. It's moving a little bit. Can you edit that out?

It's your cheeky bum. Do you want to tell me a little bit about the Royal Academy thing that you're working on? Are you allowed to tell us, give us a hint of how that's going to be?

In January, the Royal Academy are part of a festival of light that's happening in the Piccadilly area. I'm going to be projecting a new animated film on the Royal Academy itself with outdoor speakers. It is amazing because the relationship I have to that place is… I studied there between 2013 and 2016. It was just one of the most incredible experiences I've ever had. And the first Royal Academy president was from Plymouth, same as me – Joshua Reynolds, Sir Joshua Reynolds.

I never knew Reynolds was from Plymouth.

Yeah, and there's a thing called the Plymouth nod, which is, imagine you're driving your Nova around the city centre, and you see someone, and you just give a little flick of that. It's almost, just an eyelid flick. I would give Reynolds the Plymouth nod every morning as I walked in. Every day without fail, and on the way out. It really did have a really profound effect on me.

What's also amazing about the Royal Academy is they pay you to be there, rather than you having to pay to be there.

That sounds like you wouldn't want to be there.

No, but it's such a flip on what our education is, where they want their students. It's a much smaller number but it's a really different model of how you can actually study.

They joke there that they were out of fashion for a hundred years and in the last sort of ten years they've come back into fashion because they never changed their model. They never adapted to a business like a university institution. And now they're privately managed. It's an artist-led art school, which is insane. There are no fees, and you get a bursary, a small bursary.

What's also wonderful is it's obviously an incredibly beautiful space and really connected to what the history of art is. What do you like about layering what you do, which is really abstract and modern, on what is essentially a late 18th century, early 19th century building? How do you feel about that?

The building is about 300 hundred years old. The institution is 250 – they moved. That was an old house at Burlington House. They used to be at Somerset House, the Royal Academy… It was finding the Royal Academy's edition of Albers' 'Interaction of Colours', the full set of all the screenprinted plates, of all the colour games, or colour lessons. It was discovering things like that in their library and archive that really influenced my work and use of colour and stuff. I don't think my works have got more in common with the past, which kind of makes sense in an institution like that. They had a second edition of 'Disasters of War', and things like that. And this full set of Albers' prints and things. The librarians are some of my favourite people there.

I love a librarian.

Lovely Linda, shout out to lovely Linda.

How nice for Linda. We're going to play your last track. It's gone so quickly. We're going to play Queen 'Cool Cat', and I'm not a giant Queen fan but this track rocks. Why did you choose that?

It's the track before 'Under Pressure' on the, what's the album? 'Hot Space' from 1982, but weirdly, I think probably Will and Ollie from Bahamian Moor probably played it to me first. We've gone with like a slower song, two euphoric dance-y songs, so this could be like the wind down.

Now we're just going to mellow out as we leave. Thank you very much for coming.

Thank you.

And this is Queen 'Cool Cat'.

Celia Hempton

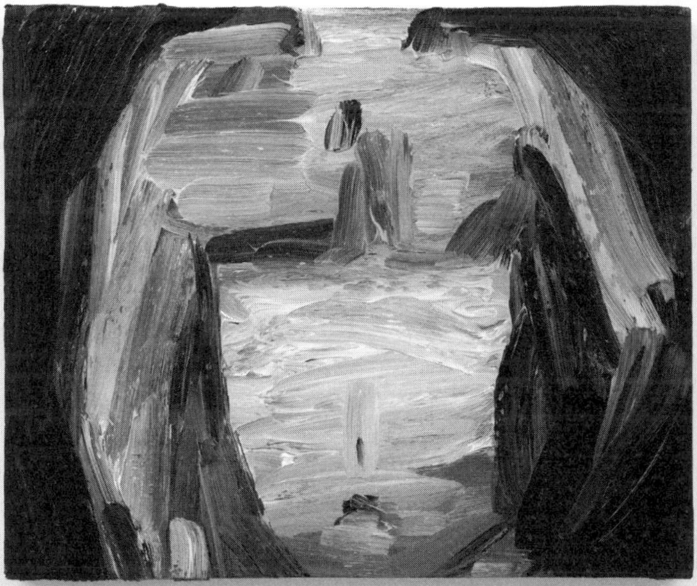

Quebec, Canada, 29th September 2015, 2015.

09.02.18

Hi. You're listening to Rough Version on NTS, and my guest this month is Celia Hempton. Celia is largely a painter, but she does other mediums. She's based in London. She is represented by Southard Reid, and she's worked around the world and Celia is here. Hi, Celia. How are you?

Hi Fran. I'm good thanks

Well, firstly, let's talk about music. Do you want to tell me about your relationship with music. Is it an influence on what you do?

I kind of grew up with music a bit, because both my brother and my dad play music a lot. I've played guitar since I was 14. So, it's been part of my life, really, since I was quite young. Then I was in bands and stuff through art school.

Playing guitar?

Yeah.

Do you listen to music in your studio? I'm always really interested in how that influences like what people make.

Yeah, I do. The thing is, when I'm in my studio, I just need stuff that's upbeat and keeps me confident. I tend to listen to just like Rihanna, Drake, Beyoncé or just Thelonious Monk, or folk music, or something. That's tends to have a melody and nothing too repetitive or complicated.

That's completely different from the tracks you brought in, which I find fascinating.

Yeah, I know. I get distracted otherwise and start listening to music.

So, it's a case of something that kind of gives you a palette in the process of making?

Not to undermine pop music or anything, but it does give me that sort of energy.

I want to talk about, like some of your work. I'm a big fan of a lot of the chat random work... Do you want to describe it, basically, to someone who wouldn't know the pieces and what that relationship to technology is with it?

There's different series of work that I make in painting. And two of them involve basically making a work from a screen from being online. The Chat Random paintings are made on Chat Random, the video chat website. I just log on and scroll through people. It sounds really – I just scroll through. Each person that you're connected to... I don't know if I need to sort of describe what that is exactly? But...

I mean, it's like Chat Roulette.

Yeah, most people know what that is.

Yeah. It's almost in a weird way, almost a dated thing that doesn't quite exist as much anymore. It's amazing, that you have that connection to it still out there.

Yeah. It's interesting how it changes over the years and different people get, or different countries seem to be online more. Because I remember when I sort of started going on it, there weren't so many people, you know. You have a little box that says how many people are online. It was like 50 and now it's like 37,000.

Wow. So basically, you're often largely drawing or painting live directly from those conversations that you're having on screen?

Yeah.

Or what you're seeing?

I scroll through it until I find an image that I want to make a work from. That might be anything from the way the image is – already quite painterly. It might be quite a poor-quality image. Or something as simple as the colours seem interesting to me in some way. Or it might be a person that's compelling. Sometimes it's the banality of it even. I've thought "Oh, that's a really boring image maybe that'd be quite an interesting thing to paint cause it's so typical, in a way, of the medium". There's often a typical stance of the way people sort of frame themselves with their camera – chopping their head off, and then from their head down to their thighs.

A cock shot essentially.

Yeah, but it's never – well, sometimes people frame themselves in a way that's attractive, but quite often people are just sort of slumped in a really unselfconscious seeming way. Which I think is quite interesting compared, if you compare the way people normally sort of present themselves online.

Yeah. It's true when you actually – if you think about whenever you're looking at a computer, we're totally unaware of our bodies. Actually, it is usually like a potato sitting on a sofa or a bed or something.

Yeah. The food, the tracksuit bottoms.

I quite like that, it's almost like the anti-Instagram, the total un-idealization of the body. It's quite an interesting flip to that. And I think that's probably quite good moment to bring in one of the tracks you brought in, which is the Ryoji Ikeda. For me he's an artist who also is really interested in looking at the relationship with tech in a different way. Why did you choose the track? And which one have you chosen?

I think they're all called like 'Hypercomplex'. Or not all of them but on that particular album. I can't remember which this one is actually…

It's 'Data'.

'Data Microhelix'. OK. I think what I'm interested in with him is the way he makes like these really everyday kinds of sounds that you might hear – like a photocopier, or what even sounds to a certain extent retro now. He structures them and makes them into rhythms and sound really obvious. But also, the way the sound seems almost hyper-real. Like you can touch them. There's something quite intimate about listening to something that is what we might think of as something very cold, he makes sort of tactile in a way.

This is Ryoji Ikeda 'Data.Microhelix'.

—

Do you want to tell me a little bit about – I know that we were talking about one series – but do you want to tell me a little bit about the variety of series and also the scale of what you do? Because that's quite dramatically different. Some of your works are really intimate, and almost computer screen size, and other pieces are huge.

I think, if I'm really honest, it comes from just the enjoyment of making and thinking "What would it be like to do this on a really large scale? What would that look like if I did that?" So, I make small paintings that, as you say, are screen size, like laptop size. And then some of the nudes that I've made have been, say, two metres by one and a half metres or something. It will be like a blown up, larger than life image maybe like a large vagina or a large penis. Then the wall paintings, obviously, are even bigger than that and fill a space. I think, as I say, it's a lot to do with just enjoying making things in different scales. But also, I was interested to see what happens when you blow up something that you might think of as really intimate… I assumed it would maybe make it kind of threatening or confrontational in a way, but some people have said "Oh, these huge penises look suddenly kind of really vulnerable, when they're much larger".

I want to talk about two things. Firstly, let's talk about the wall paintings, because the way you present these beautiful washes of abstraction, essentially that you scrawl on the wall. Often, you'll hang the paintings on top of the wall painting. What do you like about that approach to installation?

I think each wall is really different, but it provides a context in which to hang a group of paintings. So, it might be like, a temperature or a sort of atmosphere that I want to kind of gel all of these different elements together with. But I see them – I do actually see a link between those wall paintings and my sound works. I think of both of them as abstract landscapes, particularly the sound works. I relate to how I think about the internet or online space as a literal space, as a landscape that you could traverse almost like an old-fashioned landscape painter that's searching for the sublime or something. I love how in online space you can stumble across strange websites that are like on the fringes of what we normally might sort of interact with online.

Do you want to tell me about your sound works? Do you make them all yourself or are they collaborative? I've heard the one you brought in. It's really open and abstract. It's really beautiful.

It's quite long and meditative, but I wrote that with my brother. He's an actual, proper musician not like me. He is an amazing guitarist and me and him wrote that together hoping that it wouldn't – although we were using guitars and pedals – that it wouldn't actually sound like that. And we could make something where we were using the guitars as a way to mimic somehow, think about online space in that way. So, there's also little recordings I did of guys off Chat Random in there as well.

How did you show it? Did you show it as part of an exhibition installation wise or more as a performance work?

The first time we performed something similar to that together was at Volcano Extravaganza, the Fiorucci Art Trust thing they do on Stromboli, the volcano every year. Actually, NTS do something with them.

It's the most amazing thing on the face of the earth. I mean, the idea of a performance music festival on a volcano. It's sort of a fantasy.

Yeah, the Italians know how to do like drama don't they?

So, you performed it in some amazing old palazzo or outside?

No. It was actually on the volcano. We did it on the volcano, just underneath it. That atmosphere definitely. I mean, one of the things about I guess being on a volcano, as well, is that you can't really do irony so much. You can do the most earnest thing and you can kind of pull it off because you've got like a volcano going off in the background and stuff. Then we did a performance at the Serpentine. And we're about to do another one in France at Le Confort Moderne in Poitiers.

OK. Let's play the track or as much as we can. Is it just called 'Rehearsal'?

It's an excerpt that was a recording of a rehearsal for the Serpentine performance. So, this is just a little excerpt from it.

Wonderful. Here we go.

—

Coming back to your work, one of the most obvious things about it is the body. It is often figurative even though sometimes – I mean I have a lovely edition of yours that sometimes people think is an aubergine rather than a penis, which I love. Do you want to tell me what interests you about the body and the figure?

I think it's interesting to think about because for me what I'm interested in is looking really. And when I think about the body, the main thing I'm interested in is looking at things that I don't get to look at often. Whilst I might see a penis or a vagina or an asshole, occasionally, it's definitely not something that I study for like eight hours solidly to make a painting. You're really staring at and investigating something in a way. I think that's probably the main thing that connects all my work because if you think about it, it's all quite kind of different visually.

Yeah. Stylistically, it's really different. Sometimes it's super clear. And sometimes it's almost muddied in a way. Sometimes your work is really, the muddier work let's say, is much more impasto. It's really thickly painted. You feel the oil differently. Whereas the other pieces almost feel like washes or something.

There are two sides to how you're approaching something, but the process is the same for you in a way? Or do you make some slower rather than quicker?

Yeah, I do. I think I'm just interested in what excites me as being in a situation that I might find uncomfortable. Whether it's like being on the edge of a volcano, making a painting of something when it's cold, and there's like ash flying in your face. Or someone's genitalia where there's just me and them in a room and I maybe don't know them so well. Or like the Chat Random works. And then sort of forcing myself to confront situations that perhaps I might otherwise try to get out of or find uncomfortable in a way.

Interesting. I feel like we should play The Slits now. Because aside from the fact that just the title goes so well, The Slits are really interesting. It's like a feminist female punk band. How did you get into them and why this track?

I was looking through, actually, all the different tracks and couldn't decide, but because some of them are just virtually unlistenable. They're such a jumble of sounds, that just sound like being kind of thrown together. And then some of them have this quite poppy sort of sound. They all have a discordant melodic sense that I find quite compelling, and I think that really struck a chord – no pun intended – with me when I was at art school. Me and my friends were in a band that sounded a little bit like them in a way, I guess. We were called I Love Lucy and the singer Jo, she could do a good sort of scream a bit like Ari Up and we played a gig with them once as well actually.

Wow amazing. Where?

It was in Glasgow. Not with The Slits, with Ari Up's band at that time. I just really relate to that idea. Because with music, I'm not academically trained or anything. I liked how they were making music at a time when there were a lot of like male bands who were doing these big, long guitar solos and really technical sounding things and then they – I mean, obviously there's punk as well happening – but they had this determination to play even though they didn't really feel necessary. They'd never picked up a guitar before or something…

Amazing. Let's play The Slits.

—

Can I ask you what you're working on now?

I'm working on a show in Rome that opens in February.

You lived out there for a while, didn't you?

Yeah. I did. I've got a strong connection to Italy now. It's a show in Rome, with my gallery that I work with there called Lorcan O'Neill. Then I'm going to New York to do a group show at PS1, which is a performance space that's just reopened from being closed for a while where they've been refurbishing it.

What are you going to do performance wise? Something sound based?

No well, it's actually a show that centres around a Kathy Acker film. They've got a couple of artists doing different things and I'm actually showing paintings. But the film's kind of amazing. It's her filming her and this guy that she's met having sex quite graphically, but also psychoanalyzing as they're doing it. She's like, "I don't like that"; "That's not, it's not doing it for me". It's really quite uncomfortable, but kind of amazing.

I love the idea of your paintings, which also have a sense of graphicness, but also not completely about that. That's a really interesting contrast. I'm going to get you to play your last tune.

Okay.

Which is Pantera, which is heavy compared to the other things. Why Pantera? Were you like a rock girl when you were young?

I think yeah, but also just how can you not love the song? I just think it's just so joyous and amazing. Gets me in the mood. This is the kind of music I listen to I guess when I'm making wall paintings quite often.

I suppose it's a really physical process making the wall paintings because they're much larger and you're virtually crawling around the wall. So, you need really energetic music. This is Pantera 'Mouth for War'.

—

I just have a couple more questions. Do you want to tell me a little bit about your approach to colour? Because I think you have a really specific palette. It's not all – I mean it feels like it comes off nature, but it's not always. How do you approach colour?

Colour's definitely, probably the first thing I think about with work. I don't know. I think it is probably quite intuitive, but I tend to veer towards tropical ice creamy colours. I think I'm just yearning for warmer climes.

We all are at this time of year.

I don't know. I mean some of them are really muddy, and dirty looking. The paintings are sticky and slimy. And then others have a really slick clean colour palette and approach. I think there's quite a lot of variety actually in there. I tend to avoid, for some reason – they seem to be quite toned down rather than like high contrast. I don't tend to do like bright green and black or something.

No. There's a muteness sometimes to it, and some of them feel more parrot like. They have accents of stronger [colour] but other things are subtler basically.

Yeah. I think they're quite I think of it in quite a food-like way. Like something that's quite visceral. Maybe because paint is like an oil-based product, and it's got its own sort of viscous-ness and slipperiness. It's hard not to want to treat it with a tactile or bodily approach.

And that makes a lot more sense with your subjects. If you're having these bodily, almost slippery subjects, particularly when you're dealing with things like genitalia. That it is an interesting reflection of your medium. I like that. Thank you very much Celia for coming in and see you soon.

Paul Noble

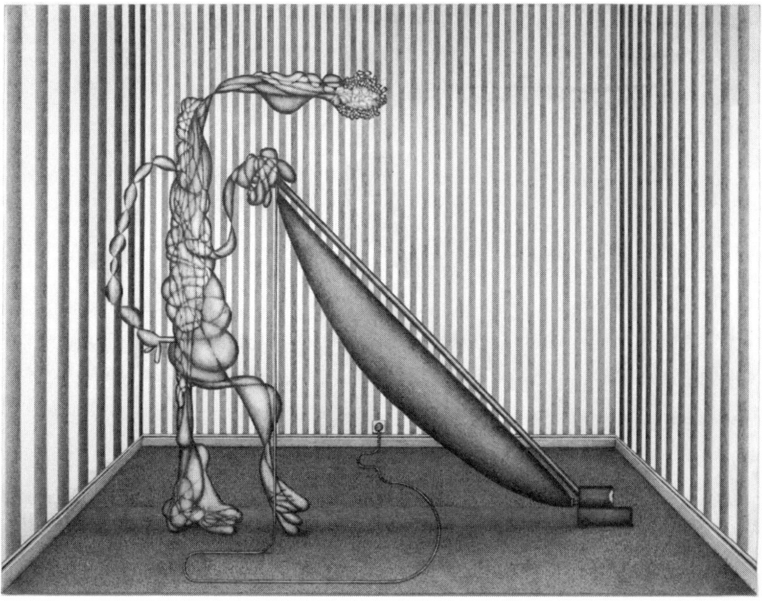

The Cleaner, 2022.

06.03.18

Hi. You're listening to Rough Version on NTS and my guest this month is Paul Noble. Paul is a British artist. He's exhibited everywhere, from Tate to Whitechapel to MOCA in LA, the Migros in Zurich. He's represented by Gagosian. He makes good things. How are you, Paul?

Very well, thank you.

Thank you for coming. So, let's begin, I want to talk about the most obvious thing for people who've seen your work, which is 'Nobson'. Do you mind having a little chat about 'Nobson'. It's never ending...

I'll join some words together whether it will make sense of the thing that I'm doing… You know I'll try my best.

You've been doing it for quite a long time. What, 20 years working on an expanding project.

It was meant to be a finite project. It was never meant to be a drawing project. It was a text, a story that I wrote. When I used to run a gallery with some friends, City Racing, in a squat in South London from 1989 to '99. There was five of us and not many people came, and we used to do all the invigilating. We had a very old computer that I think took floppy disks. I think its maximum capacity was about a megabyte or something. So, during invigilation time, we used to occupy ourselves on this computer, and most of it was actually really Matt Hale saying, "you do this" because he were really willing to do stuff, "but do so during invigilation". I started designing my own font, which was going to be the shape. That story led me to creating. 'Nobson' was a story that somehow had something to do with my time in Leytonstone, where I had been involved in an anti-motorway early environmentalist thing trying to stop motorways. Stopping houses being knocked down.

Before Reclaim the Streets and all of that?

Actually, our action led to Reclaim the Streets because the people from Newbury, which was a similar sort of action, came to join us.

They were called the Dongas Tribe. And the actions from Newbury first, and then in Leytonstone with people at the Dongas Tribe, then led forward into being Reclaim the Streets.

Wow.

You know, a footnote in a…

British activist history!

An interesting part of British history. Yeah. Trying to stop the banks. It was pre-internet, pre-mobile phones. Living in Leytonstone. The best way of stopping houses been knocked down was to have someone to occupy them, like a squatter. We had to have a list of people ready to be able to move into an empty house, but we also had to have people on the lookout for people vacating their houses. We could break in really quickly and occupy them and then have someone else to move in. I remember my mom and dad coming to visit me once in my house, 121 Philibert Road. And we actually had a South American family ready and waiting to be moved into a house that I think we knew was coming up any minute… So, we all became very adapted, source, friendly, sliding up, climbing up lamp posts, and changing locks and everything really quickly.

And this led to 'Nobson'?

Because I'm here. Because the nature of protecting houses, similar houses, being knocked down in two seconds, or the way of occupying a building. It led you to have a very fluid idea about architecture and the place where you lived. Thinking about place, belonging – things like that. And so, I wrote this story, but I had an idea that the way I wanted people to read a story was in a font that looked like buildings. I had this idea of somehow using that in the beginning of 'Star Wars', where the title rolls, and the text comes up like 'Ben Hur' or some sort of epic presentation. So, to do this, I needed to design my own font. Now the letter shapes, I wanted to be vaguely modernist. A bit crap but architectural. So that you'd have a sense of the letters themselves being somehow buildings, that you'd navigate around. And the program I used on this early computer was called 'Fontographer 4.1', which is probably the worst, most terrible program that you could ever use to design your font. I think now it's really easy...

It's a gorgeous name 'Fontographer'.

'Fontographer 4.1'. But an accident of the design of 'Fontographer 4.1' is that as you've achieved designing their full set of the alphabet characters and commas and so on. Whatever it provides a presentation of everything you've done, it's called a key map. And I had a sort of revelatory moment. Where just the accident of this thing, which was like a presentation of the characters called a map, took me to this kind of geographical place. Because I thought, "Oh, it's like cartography", and its words in space. It took me a few years later to realize actually. All I was dealing with was illumination. That's something that's been around forever. That slippage between the pictorial and the textual. But it really excited me and because I'm not dyslexic, but I am sort of a bit hyper visual. So, everything that I look at or even if it's like letters, I'm off thinking visually. So, this was the origin of what I called 'Nobson New Town' but the fact that I call it 'Nobson New Town' was an accident because Fontographer 4.1 is also really crap. Because it only allowed for the use of a six-letter title. I was going to call it something about Mexican sunsets and wherever. I can't remember. I don't know why I think that was to do the idea of the film. I was getting the text scrolling but then I was going to have a light source going over anyway, blah blah. To have a sense of what. I had to think quite quickly, and I just call it 'Nobson', because it's like my name but it's a place. So 'Nobson' is me. It's the place that is me. That's how that's it.

A play on Noble. Would you believe that it never even occurred to me?

Because people go "your work is all about willies and stuff". And I'm like, what are you on about and they have really awful imaginations?

I would say it's more turd-like often than penis, but it depends on the form.

It's a place for everything. Yeah, shit is a big part of our lives.

It is. What I also really like about looking at your work. I saw an amazing exhibition once in Paris, which was called 'An Image in Another Image'. It was basically looking at how, when you look at something, how it's not just one thing. In your work, you can look at a single object that you've represented – let's say a fence or a hospital or whatever, anything. It's not just it. There's so many layers into the representation of the thing. The object of what you're representing a letter. It's blurred.

In music you have the idea of hard listening, don't you? No deep, deep listening. And I suppose you also developed that ability for deep looking, where you see, you see through, and you see beyond. You see the thing that's presented, but then also it's both a plane, a surface, but it's a metaphysical window. This is the nature of the visual arts.

I really like that seamless move into music. I'm going to get you to play one of your first songs. Now we go from deep looking to deep listening. Let's start with the Denim track. Do you want to tell me why you chose this one?

Denim is Lawrence's band, and he used to be Felt when I was a teenage sort of angsty annoying person. Felt was the kind of music that I listened to. It's an introspective guitar jangling, but then he developed as I developed. I didn't know that he'd done this. Made Denim which is a genius pop band. And he always writes fantastic songs, about either taking drugs or having no money. So, this song is called 'Job Centre' and it's about trying to get a job and I picked it because it goes nicely with a board game I made a long time ago, called 'Bolly' which is about ideas of redundancy being useful or not useful, or where do you fit in society?

This is 'Job Centre' by Denim.

—

That was Denim doing 'Job Centre'. Now, Paul, you've made board games but you've also you've been working on a long computer game project. Firstly, tell me what interests you about the idea of playing general games.

It's really a long computer game, because I've known what it should have been. It could have been a really quick thing. But I'm still trying to get to the end point. The game. One of my favourite artists for a long time has been Öyvind Fahlström. I love his layering of image, his use of sub-cultural references rather than high culture. And even though there was, I think he was there as early possibility… I think I'm quite demanding of people who want to look at my work or I make work that demands a lot of the viewer-participant. I thought how can I really hold people in a piece of work? Well, a game is brilliant because it's a time-based thing and it evolves. It's also social. And so, they will, I suppose, their thoughts around it. It's not, again, it's not a high cultural medium. It doesn't problematize the content for people who aren't used to going to galleries. I'm not from a family that ever used to go to a gallery, ever. We didn't have pictures on the wall. I think we had a cuckoo clock and God knows where that came from. There was no music.

It sounds like you come from like the Puritan 17th century.

Yeah, no. We had Shadows in the car. Shadows 'Greatest Hits' whatever but yeah. Awesome. Terrible.

Painful. I was never a Shadows fan. Going back to games. Even looking at a big installation of 'Nobson', you're surrounded by these giant drawings. It's almost like you're in a narrative platform computer game. As a viewer, you're almost in that narrative.

Yeah, I guess. I was brought up in Whitley Bay, a seaside town, which is like the holiday town for Newcastle. If you can imagine that. That's where Glaswegians come on what used to be called Scotch Week. They'd come and beat up the people who really pay for a laugh and then go back home back to Glasgow. We'd all hide. But Whitney Bay is great. Beautiful seaside resort, lots of amusement arcades. And when we were like teenagers, my friends would hang out in the arcades, playing all the computer games. At that time, it was 'Asteroid', 'Space Invaders'. That's what we'd play. That's what we did. My friend Nigel, he was a bingo caller. And my friend, Jelly Nelly, somehow got hold of some gelatine dye and took it to school. And that's why he was called Jelly Nelly. His parents had something to do with amusement arcades. He used to give us free money to play the machines. We just sat there all the time. And my favourite game was 'Carnival', because I've actually got really rubbish coordination. It was the easiest one. So, the computer game that I've been working on, is a revisiting of this kind of nostalgic moment. This early '80s thrill of the noise. And I didn't think too much about it. But I think this is probably my first cultural experience. Because the house – there wasn't culture in the house. I'm not saying that we lived really without culture completely. Because my dad was also obsessed with TV sets and was very proud of the first colour TV set in the street. Anyway, my game is called 'Daddy Hole'. And it probably it's hard to completely invent a game without having some sort of clicks. It's most closely connected to 'Mr. Do' and 'Dig Dug' probably. The content is about the loss. It's about choosing not to have children. It's about the end of family. The game's called 'Daddy Hole', and the hole is the hole that the father digs for himself by choosing to have a family or having a baby. It's the loss of self.

And you also created music for it sort of 8-bit style?

8-bit style. I first approached Nick Curry from Momus. He put me on to a guy called Adam Bruno. Who was in an 8-bit band. He wrote a theme for me, but actually it was completely unusable because it was like a complete piece of music. I've since had it reworked by a neighbour who's a really talented sound film soundtrack composer… Actually, the amazing thing about composing computer sound is that they're micro compositions that are triggered by how you play. So, the composite sound is conducted by the player. It's not like a piece of music that plays. You choose to bring in different aspects by going like attack or left right. There's a thing coming from the top right-hand corner. And the sound collage is always different. So that's quite a thrill.

We're going to play the outro or the intro or both.

Do both because they are really short.

> *Wonderful. Here's the intro and outro to 'Daddy Hole'.*
>
> —
>
> *That was music from 'Daddy Hole'. Looking at like a lot of your work, what also interests me is there is almost a sense of something like neoclassical about it. I've seen elements from 'Nobson' made in marble, which feels very classic and that vibe, but even the idea of architectural drawings. Something we're used to seeing in Palladio and 18th century architecture. Is that something that's playing into things for you?*

No. The marble that you're talking about? The giant ships, sculptures, yes. I did have this idea in my mind. I was imagining if Canova, the most gorgeous of neoclassical sculptors, could imagine the tripartite deity like a shed. Like a shed Sphinx. That's part human, part excrement and part worm thing – that's what they were. I use marble because we acknowledge it as an elevating material that has a history. I went to the V&A to look at what I thought of were large sculptures and most large sculptures aren't necessarily that large. It's just they are higher, if you look up to them. So, it's about reference. It's about vantage point and so on. In 'Nobson New Town' I used lots of technical drawing devices and techniques because again, it's like a low art aspect, not a high art. It's a way of making work that's contrary in a way. Most people think of an artist as a man – as someone who has a signature style… I know that we're not all really the same, but I think actually there's more that makes us the same than makes us different. So, an art for me has to reflect that. Not be somehow expressing difference or individuation. That's where some of the technique, the technical aspects of how I chose to use 'Nobson New Town'. It's more working class. It's a language of the builder, the person who's making things but not necessarily the architect.

> *Your work is very hands on. We're very aware you make things with your own fingers.*

I have tried to get assistance and they all drop by the wayside it's terrible. Terrible.

Tell me about your studio. I've been to your studio. It's huge. Do you listen to a lot of music when you're in it?

I listened to sound. It's not necessarily music. I wouldn't listen to Denim. Unless it's a special treat. I tend to try and find sounds that don't really – they're substantial but they don't occupy my mind, or they let my mind go with the work. Because if I don't have a sound at all, it's impossible to have a vacuum, an aural vacuum. But that's weird because then you have a sense of pressure, but I don't want the arbitrariness of the number three bus or the airplane you think is going to crash at any minute over…

So, what are your weird…?

What do I actually listen to?

What are the actual sounds? Are you just listening to the sound of rain or noise?

I have got an excellent recording of the foghorns of northeast American coast which is very nostalgic for me because Whitley Bay used to have great foghorns. I listen to all sorts. There's a great piano piece. It's about a 15-minute riff, a classical improv piece based on "the people united will never be divided". It's absolutely brilliant. It's Frederick somebody, but it's well worth checking out. Or Dennis Johnson. Actually, love solo piano. Dennis Johnson, November, proto minimalist five-hour epic but completely gorgeous, amazing pacing. So quite broad.

You've also made music yourself…

'Dot to Dot'.

'Dot the Dot' which is a game. You want to tell me, and this was to go with an exhibition that you made?

It was just a sound piece that I made. It's a portrait of Whitley Bay. As teenagers, we'd basically live on the beach. We'd have all our parties on the beach. We'd have fires every night and just get drunk and do whatever and mess about it was brilliant. We were also angsty youth listening to Joy Division, The Doors, The Fall and whoever. Looking at this gray, this gray seascape. 'Dot to Dot' is a verbal description of experiencing the collapse in horizon. The space is like there, then it's not there. And maybe you've gone into the space of the horizon, or it's come to you. It asserts descriptive words, that kind of collapse. And I chose a good friend, who's got the most fantastic voice, Laetitia Sadier, who used to be the singer and in Stereolab. Who now does a lot of her own stuff. I like the authority of her voice. But also, the fact that English isn't their first language. So, she sees words perhaps a bit more crisp, clean. We're too familiar with the things that come out of our mouths that shape our ideas. So anyway, that's 'Dot to Dot'.

> *This is 'Dot to Dot' by Paul Noble.*
>
> —
>
> *That was 'Dot to Dot'. Since we were talking about language, let's talk a bit about words. Your interest in words and the word. What are your feelings about words? Because it is something that comes out in your imagery.*

I have loads of notebooks. When I'm working on a drawing, I have bits of paper that I use as a kind of mask to stop me getting dirt on the drawing. And I'm always making notes. Thoughts come to me, usually, like word thoughts. And I make a note. But I wouldn't say I'm a writer. The visual dominant dominates me. I think I'm just more excited by images. I don't know what to say about that, actually.

> *It's quite interesting, because language is there. But at the same time, it's almost accidental or something we're looking at it from like a side view, or something.*

The very first drawings I made, which was a shift during the time when I was doing the motorway campaigning stuff. I was making a kind of abstract art that was a bit arte povera meets Richard Tuttle. It was very material based. It related most to abstraction, but it did reference the language of other things in the world. And after we all got kicked out of our houses in Leytonstone, I felt a huge not oppression, but I just thought, "My God, what on earth was the use of my visual training in, that I wasn't able to in some way propagandise on behalf of this campaign that we struggled?" I just thought, "What am I doing? Who is this art for?" So, I threw away pretty much everything I've done before, and then started afresh as a as an artist. I started making pencil drawings and I made horrible frames. The drawings were of people basically, shagging books and shitting on books and stuff in libraries. It was as transgressive as I could politely be and drawn as well as I could, but really badly because I wasn't very good at drawing. And it wasn't my aim to be good at drawing. A drawing was something that you did as an adolescent., I always thought that The Fall's first album 'Live at the Witch Trials' was the best cover ever, because the pencil drawing is really cool on it. So, in the library, people were like, shagging and shitting on books. What are the books? What are the books in this slide, because I imagined it was an artist's library. At that time, I just thought artists are really stupid. But I was only talking about myself, because of the failure of my art my superpower to stop the motorway. I started making up joke authors. Like Neil Down and Ben Dover, and so on. I made about 300 or 400 of these books, that exist. I show them in porticoes and Cubitt and other places. They weren't meant to be so funny, but that wordplay... You're right I forgot about that.

I also love that there's so much humour in what you do, which is also really accessible for someone who doesn't come from an art background which I'm a great believer in. It's okay that art can make you laugh.

I've just given you a catalogue you haven't had a chance to look at it, but it's of work I've just shown in San Francisco. They can light interior spaces with doors, but I made one door and it's really, really big. I was thinking what should I call it and I call it 'Large Door' and I thought, my god that's such a fantastic pun and I couldn't believe no one else had done this before. I went on the internet and it's all mine! It's this large door that's also the age of gold. I was thrilled for ages.

That's wonderful. Well since we're talking about words we're going to finish with your last song, it went really quickly.

Which is Charles Dodge, his third 'Speech Song' seamlessly connected there. Do you want to tell me about this record?

Charles Dodge is a genius. He made this recording with I think Bell Laboratories, who were experimenting with computerized voices. This was at the very beginning of what we now take for granted when we make a phone call and have a computer answering us. So, it wasn't like a processed voice. It was a program which led to voice. Charles Dodge, I think is the first composer to have access to the programs. So, you could probably imagine some massive hanger full of whirling stuff just to make a sound that goes "hello". That's what this record is. The text is a Canadian poet, Miles Strand. I would have given more time if this was a longer program, I would have picked something from side B, which is the story of our lives. The story of two computers talking to each other, thinking that they are autonomous beings. Somehow realizing that actually everything that they've done has already been programmed. It's quite a cool pre-Matrix.

Sentient computer moment, that's 'Speech Song 3'. I'm a big fan of Bell Labs they did some amazing work. Super underrated I think really. They're like really cool. Thank you so much. We're going to finish with Charles Dodge and that was Paul Noble.

Florence Peake

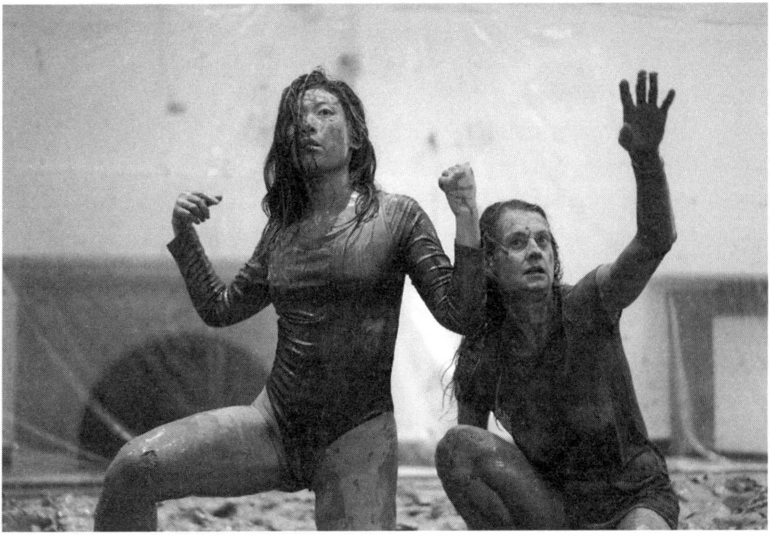

Rite, 2018.

02.04.18

Hi, you're listening to Francesca Gavin on Rough Version on NTS. My guest this month is Florence Peake. Florence is an artist working across a breadth of media but coming out of a dance background – basically everything from installation to drawing to choreography and performance. She's shown at Studio Leigh. She's done projects with Wysing in Cambridge, and lots of stuff in London. And hello, Florence.

Hi.

Firstly, do you want to tell me a bit about your background? You were trained as a dancer? Did you work as a dancer for a long time? How did you make that transition from a dance context to an art context?

I actually still work as a dancer and performer. I feel very privileged to be able to still be doing that 25 years on from when I came out of dance training. Which was quite militant dance training. But I always have had a painting practice that ran alongside the dancing thing. I came out of dance school, and I got scholarships to The Place, but actually rejected it. Because I knew that I'd probably end up with an eating disorder, or some kind of mental health problem, which maybe I still have. I ended up excitingly working with amazing choreographers and performance art makers and filmmakers. I went on to do that and that was very influential on my practice. Collaborating with people before starting to make my own work. The two practices of painting and making sculptures and things, and dancing, they've always been there, running alongside each other. They've just started recently, in the last 10 years, colliding and making sense of how they complement each other. Or how they can work with each other.

How would you describe the aesthetics of what you do from an art point of view? Because it seems quite varied. You use some drawing, but it seems a lot of stuff seems to be instigated by movement in a way. The installations are quite full in contrast. Do you have an aesthetic approach to what you're doing?

I think that it's very clear to me a certain kind of atmosphere and world and things that I want to create. A certain colour and viscerality is probably something that runs through a lot of my projects and work. It always comes from the body in some way to do with movement and the placement of movement and how things are choreographed through space. Even though at the moment when my work seems to be getting a bit more well known, it seems to be very gestural and expressive. Even quite cathartic ways of exploring sculpture installation. I do have quite a formal relationship to the body and objects. There's a hell of a lot of methodology and rigour in my practice. There's a lot of thinking about how these improvisations or these durational performances, or how these things get expressed. A lot of thinking behind them and a lot of methodology…

Tell me a bit about your process, because you have a studio practice. What comes first – the idea of something or does it come out of movement? How does your process begin?

I'm thinking I might have a big sense of something that I want to explore but then I'm pretty promiscuous across media and across art forms. I'm quite unfaithful to a particular thing. So, it will be what happens, where that idea feels it needs to be expressed. Whether it's through drawing or through rolling around on the floor in the studio with ten dancers. They all feedback to each other the whole time. There's definitely a reciprocality to between working with clay or with drawing or with movement. There's always this bouncing back and forth.

Can I ask you how music and sound come into this? Obviously when we think of dance, we think of that being very strongly related to everything musical.

I think this is a big issue in some ways. It's quite a patriarchal issue. The idea that dance needs to be wedded to music in some way.

Are you telling me music is the patriarchy? Which I find shocking. Damn, no. I don't want to give it to boys.

Just in terms of classical dance. You had the male patriarchal composer and then the choreographer who is often a man. Then you'd have the dancers, the ornamentation, or the decoration to the music. It's had this difficult role in relationship to music sometimes. In some ways, there can be this experience of liberating dance from sound or from music. Often, I haven't worked with music in terms of what's been presented, but it has been very key to my practice… I teach a particular technique called Skinner Releasing Technique, which uses sound environments. We craft soundscapes in relationship to the images and visualizations that we teach the participants. There's a world that's creating that in that way. I've worked very much with music in that way, but more as a environmental holding for the movement to take place in. But now, with Stravinsky's 'Rite of Spring' score, it's a big challenge for me and a big ambitious project.

In art circles, at least, Stravinsky's 'Rite of Spring' is known for being so intertwined with the birth of modernism. So intertwined with visual arts. What are you working on what's your connection to it?

Yeah, absolutely. There's this huge canon of choreographers that have taken on the 'Rite of Spring'. Jerome Bell, the iconic Pina Bausch's version. I've been wanting to sidestep that choreographic canon and think of it as a sculptural interpretation of Stravinsky's 'Rite of Spring'. I'm very much excited by this engagement with modernism. I'm thinking of it almost as quite a camp exercise in a way. We've called it 'camp paganism' – me and Martin Hargreaves the dramaturg on the piece. I really started to become curious about the big heroes in modernist choreographers, like Martha Graham, Mary Wigman, Isadora Duncan, and their conviction and their complete faith in – I don't know – conviction to believe in that what they were doing could change something. What their performances could do could change, could really bring some kind of philosophical idea through. I feel that maybe now in more of a cynical age, you don't… I was at a place where I felt, does performance actually do anything? Can art actually change anything? I was looking at these monuments in modernism like Stravinsky's 'Rite of Spring' or James Joyce's 'Ulysses'. Those moments that really felt that they had these huge, powerful impacts on things and those choreographers. It is a play with that scope of history in a way.

> *Let's play a little bit. You've brought in two little segments from 'Rite of Spring'. Why specifically these bits? Just because you like them, or is there any reason?*

I love them. I mean the whole score is… You hear it again and again and it changes every time but especially these two. One of them is very impactful and ambushes. A bit like being punched in the face. And the other one is where it just feels like it's this deep groove, carving a rhythm out. I quite like this very sculptural feeling that the 'Rite of Spring' has in terms of its sound.

> *Great. This is two excerpts from Stravinsky's 'The Rite of Spring'.*
>
> —
>
> *That was Stravinsky. I'm going to take you back a bit. You were talking about the Skinner Release Technique, which I've never heard of. SRT.*

Yeah.

> *Do you want to describe what that is? Because I think a lot of people haven't heard of it. I found it quite fascinating thinking about the relationship between the body and something oral.*

It was developed in the 1960s and '70s by someone called Joan Skinner. That was a particularly interesting time in relationship to contemporary dance, which had come out of modernist dance movements. Graham developed her own technique. Cunningham developed his own technique. I think there was quite a few different body practices that came out of those movements that were rebelling against technique. The Skinner Releasing Technique uses poetic guided imagery, body work, hands on, tactile hands-on studies, sound, and different kinds of movement studies. It's quite closely related to Alexander technique. Relates to different alignment principles in the body to make way to releasing tension and extraneous effort in the body. To allow for freedom of movement. And it's a completely inclusive technique. You don't have to be a dancer to do it.

> *Very interesting, and you use that as a starting point for coming up with ideas or developing ideas? Is that right?*

It's been very influential. I don't know. I use it more if I'm rehearsing with dancers as a way of preparing in the warm ups. I've used it in quite a lot of different ways. But I don't think it's to do with coming up with ideas. It's more a practical tool for preparation and things.

> *Can we talk about in your work? Let's take a look at some examples. I've seen some amazing installations. Do you want to tell me about what your feeling is both as someone coming from visual background, but also physical background, with space? How you are working with putting things in space?*

I've got a few pieces that purely were about that. There's a piece called 'Remake', that was using these long, coloured sticks. It was very minimalist and formal, and working with dancers. The performances were up to six hours long, where we would continuously be reconfiguring and framing the space in our bodies in geometrical shapes with these sticks. This was all to do with this idea of how permeable space is. How we mould and can stretch space through objects being in them. I think sculpture is very – sometimes I find it very tyrannical, in terms of how you place a shape in a space, or an object in the space. Automatically it becomes a director and choreographer that your body is being offered to. Some minimalist sculptors, some Richard Serras – I feel almost subjugated. My body is in relationship to it… Moving sculpture into this space means that there is a kind of flexibility or there is a kind of moulding of space, which I really need and enjoy. Also, that space can be emptied, as well as filled. There are other projects where I'm thinking of how space penetrates our bodies, and how we could penetrate space. Bodies can penetrate objects.

> *They become transparent, or we can physically go through things?*

I like to think that there is that possibility, or how we might psychically merge with an object or how an object can penetrate us… This is where I relate to sound as well. Whereas I think sound has that process of osmosis or can penetrate through one's body. I've used quite a lot of sounding techniques in terms of working with dancers and had practices around different sounding into the body. How that penetrates our psyches. With a dancer I work with. How we think about blending energies and things. I think that then relates to space and how space can fill our bodies, as well. It's quite hard. I usually demonstrate this.

Not easy on the radio. I'm going to play another one of your tracks. Should we play The Internet? Why this Internet track?

I was just talking about the dancer. The dancer is called Eve Stainton and we're making a work together. We're actually in a romantic relationship and we want to explore what this idea of performing intimacy is like. Performing elements of your relationship, where the public, private blur and how to bring the audiences into your relationship. How that audience could penetrate your relationship and how this intimate intimacy can be affecting in some way. She introduced me to this song – I suppose this song is a bit for her.

Aw, that's really cute.

Oh god, no…

Well, I love The Internet. The Internet are wicked, and this is 'Girl'.

—

When you create performance works, are you working with the floor or is it much more about something like a lump of clay? How does it manifest?

The floor in terms of my dance practice has been really important. I think it's a huge resource. Almost thinking of the Earth, the floor rises up to meet you. Thinking a lot about this idea in that in life, we're always touching. We touch things. We think it's very human to be reaching for a cup, reaching out to things and, in a way, forgetting that as I'm touching this table, the table is touching me. As I'm touching the floor, the floor is also touching me. There is a kind of reciprocality and there's an exchange there of support and balance, of tactility. I think lying on the floor – this place of repose as a way of starting to listen to where the body is at. This idea of falling or surrendering into an object. A lot of my work is around the sensual and the sensate and tactility. And the erotic and the arousal being part of that. That it actually opens up for a huge way of experiencing the world and experiencing objects through touch. This idea of being on the floor is also to do with this relationship to touch and skin and flesh. How that softens and how the floor supports that process – an unravelling of flesh in a way. The drawings that I have done in relationship to that have been very much about this falling into the floor. To then make marks that I draw around myself. Then how you place those onto the vertical and changing that relationship from the horizontal to the vertical. This kind of pivot that happens. And with that, how to start transferring that object from the gesture that happened in movement. This ephemeral act of the performance into an autonomous object that can re-perform back to that experience. I'm quite interested in this next step on from the gesture and how things start to re-perform or performed back to each other.

You've also made sound works. Do you want to tell me about your approach to that and how you've worked with your own sound?

Quite a few of my projects have been using my own voice. I've got a horrendous singing voice, but for some reason I can make some good sounds. I quite like working with that real range of sounds. The channelling work that I did with 'VOICINGS' would be very much about entering a kind of trance state. Not trance but a kind of channelling, altered state where then I would sound from. It would be very much like not knowing what's going to come out my mouth and allowing that to happen. There have been other monologue pieces, where I've implanted monologues and voice work into sculptures. The sculptures then speak to each other and things.

What was this piece you did with Maxwell Sterling that you brought in? 'Andromeda Sadgirl'?

That's in the exhibition at Wysing that I did in collaboration with Tai Shani, who's an incredible artist and thinker and incredible intellect and imaginative way of speaking about things. That was a huge inspiration for me, working with her. I did al fresco wall painting, and she did the sculptural work, and we created this kind of archaeological site from a lost civilisation, pre or post-patriarchy. This athletic feat of the imagination, to try to think and embody a reality that would be post-patriarchal or pre-patriarchal, and that was a really exciting challenge. To imagine that I had to almost go into kind of pre-verbal language. Sound before it becomes words, was what I was thinking about. The track that you'll hear was I think a 40-minute track that gets looped, and it's all from my voice. It's all Maxwell, playing with effects and playing around with my voice. I went into the studio with him and we did I think about three takes of "waaa, eeee". That stuff.

It doesn't sound like that in the result.

Then we sort of played with it.

Cool. This is an excerpt of 'Andromeda Sadgirl'.

—

I want to ask you; are you do other things? Do you read a lot of books? Do you watch films? What are the things feeding into you as an influence?

At different times, different things. Very much big influences on me are working with movement practitioners. People like Helen Poynor, who I worked with on the Jurassic Coast. Who's an amazing practitioner who does these movement meditations in caves. That's a really special experience. And Eva Kazakh, who's another Trisha Brown dancer from the 1960s. She's incredible, working anatomically with these great visualizations on the body. I think that a lot of film and different spiritual practices have been big influences on me. Conversations, mainly conversations with friends. I have a lot of really interesting friends – that sounds dreadful. But Joe Moran, Gaby Agis, lots of different people that I hugely respect. I do read but I really love a good, meaty discussion with people.

It is something that's quite underrated I think. I don't think people really give credit to conversation enough.

Hugely influential.

In terms of how things come out. Who you spend time with really does influence whatever you make.

I really find my fellow peers very exciting. My friend Mercedes Grower. She's just had a feature film come out with Noel Fielding. They're all people that we know, and that's been great. Conversations with her. Conversations with Beatrice Dillon, I find very inspiring as well.

We're going to finish with her track. What's your relationship with Beatrice?

We did the Wysing residency together. I find the way she thinks about sound, the sculptural way she approaches sound – I just find so thrilling and exciting. It makes me think about the body and how space and how movement can operate in relationship to sound in a very autonomous spacious way. We did a film collaboration with her girlfriend Anne Tetslaff, who's an amazing photographer and film-maker. She's going to be doing the sound installation for my 'Rite of Spring' project.

Nice.

I'm going to depart from the music completely in terms of using it in the performance and Beatrice is going to work with it.

Wonderful. Thank you very much for coming in Florence and to finish this is Beatrice Dillon with 'Curl'.

Eric N. Mack

11.05.18

Hi. You're listening to Rough Version on NTS. And my guest this month is Eric N. Mack. He's a great artist who recently showed at Simon Lee in London. He studied at Cooper Union and Yale. You were in two of my favourite shows in recent years, 'Ungestalt' at the Kunsthalle Basel – which was one of the best curated shows ever – and Duro Olowu's show at the Camden Art Centre, which was really fascinating about the intersection of contemporary art and textiles. You received the Baltic artist award from Lorna Simpson, and residency at Studio Museum Harlem. And here you are, Eric. Thank you for coming in.

Thank you.

Let's talk in general about your work to start. The first thing that obviously hits is your materials. Like you use a lot of fabrics and textiles and found rags and things like that. Do you want to tell me how you first started using that? Why and what was the attraction?

Well, a lot of my concerns comes from painting – questioning the givens and being kind of bored by them. I mean the usual standard surface that you would paint on would be, traditionally, especially learning in school, would be cotton canvas.

A big giant rectangle.

Right. But also, it's just something about the micro aspect of it. It's the weave. And if you had a little bit more money that month, you maybe would buy some Belgian linen. I'd never saw the real need to have that discernible preciousness, within such a narrow history. There's a lot of people who could probably talk about what's the most important thing about those specific materials, but I found it to be like an opportunity to find some replacements, basically, that would maybe speak a little bit more loudly or have a different point of reference to an experience that I wanted to bring forth. So, it really started there. Even when I was an undergrad, especially, the most successful piece that I felt I made… I was living in Baltimore, and I went to MICA for a year, but I basically stretched a large, white t-shirt on a canvas. There was a real epiphany there and like trying to place the hole of the neck of a T-shirt, so it ends up looking like what it is, but then transform that to the dimensionality… I cut open the sleeve, so that laying it allowed it to be a flat form. And then the sleeves are just below, over the stretcher bar. Then there was exposure, of course, at the top of the stretcher bar with the neck of the T-shirt. I don't know, but that was a kind of breakthrough for me because it ended up speaking about authorship in, I think, a really complex way, that I've allowed to lead a little bit more.

Where do you find your materials? Because what's so interesting when you look at the textiles you're using, either in let's say, a wall piece where you're using drop cloths, almost quilted materials which have such an embedded meaning. Or you're making these sculptural sandwiches which seem to billow, which has everything from a Made in China bandana to like a random old rag. How do you source that? And are you considering where things are coming from a lot when you're choosing the things you're putting together?

Definitely. I mean the most important thing I think, is also that they don't come from just one place. Because things can end up feeling like it's really heavily sourced in one way or the other. Things could feel a little bit too purchased and vacant of any kind of personal relationships. So, I usually have a fragment of something that I've used or things that end up being transformed at the studio for like a year or so. Where I'm trying to figure out how it can be used best. That ends up being a good way of processing material – either through the fact that I wouldn't be so precious with it. So, it would have maybe a little bit of paint splatter or maybe it's already starting to be sun-bleached or something like that, but I also do a lot of my own processing using bleach and dye and paint, in some cases. But I also like the idea of really of going shopping for your life. You go to the grocery store, but you find something weird, or you find something that you thought you could use, and you might try… The challenge would be to throw it in the context of the studio rather than a bathmat, a really cheap bathmat.

Do you like sew everything yourself? Is it all done by you?

Sometimes it's done by like hand. Sometimes I'm becoming more equipped to use a sewing machine.

This makes me think of Ru Paul's 'Drag Race' where people are on it and they're learning how to use the sewing machine.

Yeah. Oh my god, yes. It's true. Yeah, cause they have a Mood Fabrics corner or whatever.

I'm obviously giving you a more of an intellectual approach to your use of fabrics.

Yes, totally. Mood Fabrics is one of my favourite places too so… It's just really well organised.

Let's take a moment and play one of your tracks because you brought in brilliant tracks. You brought a lot of women with oomph. I'm going to have to start with Notorious KIM, Lil Kim because I can't stop listening to this record. Why did you choose this Lil Kim?

Okay, it's really good. I feel like I've definitely grown up with Lil Kim in my consciousness. Which is the benefit of the millennial. We have that. You can recite a Lil Kim lyric and I could definitely finish it or just like any of my friends. It just is really quite innate at this point. Also, she has so much style, attitude, and I love the materialist poetics that she brings. That she's not afraid to just name brands, almost like she's creating her own kind of advertising campaign. And these days, people would take that very seriously, as a point of signalling a lifestyle but for her, it was really about pointing to, or subsuming value and beauty, and decadence, and maximalism. So, 'Queen Bitch'. Really great. I like it in conversation with a Bowie moment too. So, we can do the British juxtaposition.

I love the combination of David Bowie and Lil Kim in any conversation. That's great.

Right? You know, orange hair and go-go boots and everything else.

Well, this is 'Queen Bitch Pt. 2', by Lil Kim with an amazing little bit of Biggie in there, which makes me happy.

—

That was Lil Kim. Since we were talking about how amazing Lil Kim looks, can we talk about your relationship to fashion? You did an amazing collaboration, or made an installation for, Grace Wales Bonner and your dad ran a max-clothing shop or random bargain clothing thing. Do you want to tell me what your relationship is with fashion? Your latest show in London was named after a '90s hip hop stylist. Tell me about what you find interesting about fashion and how you're drawing on it.

I always liked fashion because everybody can have an opinion on it. There's something a little bit more open and about collectivity in this way, that someone on the street can tell you that you look like shit, basically.

I mean hopefully not.

Hopefully not or like say you look amazing. But that point of judgment… It's like whether or not they can picture themselves in what you're wearing, or whether what you're wearing tells a story that resonates to them, or whether it's appalling to them that you would dare walk out – I love that openness. That's an openness that people don't have to fine art. To go to a gallery and just be like, "What are you trying to tell me really?". There are some artists that don't even have the – that don't feel like they could approach a space like that. So, there's something about that signalling that has been really important. I talk about it more like a tangible abstraction. Just fragmentation and the fact that with a fragment, you're forced to kind of deal with how the surface reads. And through that you can possibly tell where something has been, where something will go or where it should belong.

How did the project work with Grace? Because Grace is a really interesting choice of designer because she's someone who's bringing loads of politics and literature and art into her work as a fashion designer. It is always coming. You were meeting in a middle space between the two mediums in a way.

It's amazing. I met her at the Camden Art Centre show that Duro curated. He curated us both in and I was just really taken aback by her work, having seen it on like Instagram or something like that. I think her MA show. But the art, it was a really natural conversation, and it's very rare to have a fashion designer that is an intellectual, that covets language. She has a bibliography that she presents at every collection – at least the last few that I've seen.

Yeah, reading lists. I love the idea of educating your audience, and also the idea of taking something beyond the moment, which I think is really interesting in general.

But that's also something. That these ideas keep going and that there's the point of access, but also the fact that the conversations will potentially keep moving forward.

You made, essentially, sculptural installations around her show?

Yeah.

Was that like a conversation between the two of you?

It was. It was. We talked about that mood board, what we were both interested in creating for the collection. I saw a few images of the collection, and kind of went forth with my own interpretations of thinking about the… Autumn/Winter 19 is what just happened. We talked a lot about sailors. French sailors off the coast of the Caribbean, and movement and nationality. Thinking about the flags, and also this strange relationship between the flag and the sail, which I never put together before. Both are contingent on the weather. That was really, really productive conversations. We started talking about warmth and that being really, really special. I did this backdrop with an idea that the models would walk with the backdrop in a clear sightline, which I think really affected the way that the clothes were seen. Some of the fabrics I used were fabrics that – there's a few. There's like one or two like pieces that ended up being from her collection directly, and just used in a really different way.

What I really liked about when I saw it, and actually looking at your other work, what's really interesting about a lot of your hanging sculptural pieces is the translucency in the materials you're using. This idea of some kind of layering. That you can half see-through things. What do you like about the fact that it's not completely opaque. It's not about necessarily something being completely hidden, things are like revealed in some way?

Exactly. I love a really great complication. It's like the surface ends up communicating but also the translucency allowed for the space that it's in, or the depth that it exists in, to also be taken on. It ends up being kind of like a lens – a flexible lens or a variable lens – that when you walk by it moves because it's like suspended, in a way. And that contingency really jives with what I've been thinking about for a long time. It solves some problems and also adds some, as well.

I like the idea of liking a problem. "Yeah I like a good problem".

Definitely. I think that's what I think. Painting is totally all about that too.

Constantly solving problems and then creating new ones to solve.

Right, exactly like fixing something you know, through coverage or colour-matching in order for a surface to feel more continuous, like an added index.

Let's play another tune. Shall we play the Patti Smith record you brought in?

Yeah.

What's your feeling about Patti Smith and why her? I love her writing. I think she's a great writer.

She is a great writer. She's really interesting. She's been interesting to me because I think, I needed to understand more about like her cultural importance, in order to unlock a certain aspect of, especially New

York. Not just your New York but New York culture, New York style, New York emotion. Thinking about 'Just Kids' and the mystique of the Chelsea Hotel – she's wrapped up in that. And she's a real romantic. She also carries a lot of power, in how her sound is created. The song 'Easter' is on her third album by the same name and it's a kind of breakthrough album for her. But the strange part has to do with the fact that there's so much overt religious content, which is a little goth. A little bit melodramatic. But I think that the real intentionality in the poetry, is it can win you over. The song was just haunting to me. There's repetition in it. And church bells.

Let's play a bit of a religious moment from Patti Smith. This is 'Easter'.

I used the song actually to title some of the pieces in the show.

Oh, interesting.

There's a point where she – the breakdown… There's a slippage between her describing herself and also Jesus Christ. I feel like that power connection is…

I mean, no ego there...

Yeah. I was like "wow, is she doing this?" But also talking about, just referring to a return and transference and this could be a beginning, a new beginning. I like that as a point of thinking about tattered clothes.

Okay, Patti Smith, 'Easter'.

—

And that was 'Easter' by Patti Smith. Another thing when I look to a lot of your work, I'm really interested in the assemblage aspect. I am a magazine whore, and you have copies of the New York Post and Rolling Stone and Mary J. Blige, and amazing newspaper bits with Janet Jackson interviews. Do you want to tell me where that material comes from and why you've chosen specifically, often, images of the African Diaspora and African American icons to be included, or like commentary about some kind of political narrative within it. Do you want to tell me about the magazine and newspaper things?

You know what, I think I'm also a magazine whore.

I mean I can't help it.

I think that was totally my childhood, adolescence – 'XXL', 'Vibe', 'The Source'. It was a complete freak out when I could actually get my hands on 'The Fader'. The first few issues of 'The Fader'. I religiously went to Barnes and Noble to buy it you know. I loved 'The Fader' because it was this cross section between rock music and indie rock and rap or Kanye West on the cover. And then Fiona Apple was on the cover. I think they would do like multiple covers or something for the same issue. Like the Fiery Furnaces… I learned so much. The first time I learned about Chris Ofili was in 'The Fader' magazine. I'm a kid in DC, like 16 or something, reading about him with the trouble that he had with the 'Sensation' show, freaking out. A lot of those images were really beautifully shot and super iconic. I just would keep them for as long as I could. Or maybe until I lost them. I used to also work at McNally Jackson.

My favourite bookshop in New York.

They have a banging magazine section that I used to have to organise and put the new magazines out and also read them in the back – the good ones… When I would return some of the magazines I would collect the images. But some of the older magazines are more like archives, like Interview magazine. That 'Interview' magazine with Janet Jackson that was from '87, but I was born in '87. I don't know. I just like that moment of what was happening that year, other than me being born…

When you're putting the pieces on top of the fabric and creating these collages, is there a sense of narrative relevance? Do you see it as some kind of form of visual poetry or language or communication?

Yeah. There's definitely a visual poetry. I also like an image game, a pictures game – almost a way of playing dominoes or something like that. And they're almost always contingent. They're almost always relative or either the contrast. You either affirm or deny the previous image or something but the fact that it sits next to each other is like really, really interesting. It's almost like curating a little mini show in this frame. What gets seen and how does the gaze connect? Or if there's this denial, just in the body, the stance of the body, which ends up grounding some of the relationships that the fabric could have or have had just wrapped up in fashion editorial. Where they're faking it in some kind of way. The thinking and an abandoned building, and they're on an old couch.

When you're adding elements of what's interesting also sometimes the material is obscured by dye or paint or bleach. Things are covered often. Recently I've seen the things have been quite bloody almost. It almost feels like that.

Yeah.

Why in particular, are you going for that tonally, colour-wise?

Well, the basis of a lot of those things… The dye is great, because it intervenes with the material, and it doesn't overpower the paper too much. Because it ends up being kind equivalent to its own printing process I feel, so there's that. I think there's times when the dye becomes really representational when it is liquid or acknowledged fluid-like material. I like to think about creating a representation in which the work would be outside. And rain fell on it for the first time and then, I guess, they have to have been removed really quickly. That kind of touch is really both representational and also just about a process. A trace of a process.

I'm going to play another track from you.

Sure.

We're going to play Junkyard Band. Great tune. How did you come across this band?

They're a DC band – that's where I grew up. That's where I'm from. I don't know it's another song that I grew up hearing and listening to… Go-go music is such a beautiful genre. Super percussive, and it somehow has been pretty contained to the DC area for some time. That song 'Sardines' was produced by Rick Rubin. I think at that point, when the song was recorded, most of the band was under the age of 17.

Wow, really?

They're kids.

That's shocking. It really doesn't sound like that. It almost sounds like something done in the '70s by grown up men. The idea of them being kids is really shocking.

I think they're mostly kids. I think that they used to perform outdoors in their neighbourhood and stuff, like in the '80s. But I think that they're still together and they still perform.

It's a really fun tune. This is 'Sardines' by Junkyard Band.

—

Let's talk a little bit about New York. You live in Harlem?

Yes.

And your studio is still in the South Bronx?

Yeah.

Do you want to tell me a little bit about how such specific areas in New York – areas in New York where there are actually still New Yorkers. How is the city influencing what you're making and what you're doing?

I mean Harlem changes so much. It's changed so much.

You've been there for 10 years?

Yeah. I've been in Harlem for maybe seven or eight. It's a really special place. I walk up to 135th and I catch the bus and it goes straight to the South Bronx, where my studio is across. I don't know. I just see so much. There's so much energy. The people have a very different temperament than Brooklyn, completely. I think there's a lot of pride to arrogance. Rich people or just anybody would walk with their heads up, you know? That's, like really significant to me, of course, being a historically African American neighbourhood or African diasporic, I would say. I mean, it's elevated. It's uptown. So, there's a little bit of privacy that I think you feel where it's not as rowdy as downtown.

I love that you get the bus because I think you're the only person I've ever heard in New York, who has ever gotten the bus.

That's the only bus I take. Just because literally, I'm not walking to the 6 train cause I live central. At this point, that's the best way for me to get to back and forth.

It's a good route.

Yeah, it's just a good route. But there is something about that location that really offers me a lot to think about. Where I feel like there are times where… you can just exist alongside all these people, and you feel like it's equalising. If the bus is in traffic, we're all late, and we're all struggling. To me like there's something about that, that is really interesting.

We're going to finish with a girl from the area. This is your last track, Azealia Banks. Why this one, 'Anna Wintour'? Very fashion reference heavy.

I love the fashion reference. It's just so funny because my show is called 'Misa Hylton-Brim' and thinking about embodiment and thinking about the glamour, the excitement, the exuberance of fashion. She's Azealia Banks. She's definitely thinking about herself and these ideals. I'm sure she should be at every great runway show or something like that, you know? I like her mix of arrogance and aspiration. She's really something.

That's a really nice phrase. And we're going to finish with that. This is 'Anna Wintour' by Azealia Banks. Thank you very much Eric N. Mack, and you've been listening to NTS.

Awesome. Thank you.

Katharina Grosse

12.06.18

This month's guest on Rough Version is Katharina Grosse and she's a German artist based in Berlin. She studied in Düsseldorf. She's exhibited everywhere from MoMA PS1 to the Venice Biennale, and currently has a massive show on. I think your biggest installation to date. Is that true? At Gagosian in London.

Yes, it's the first time I'm showing canvas paintings and a very large painting, which is an installation piece in the UK.

Cool. Okay, well, that's a good first question, because you're really known for doing these incredible, immersive very large installation works with layers of things. I haven't seen you do things on canvas outside of that. How do those two things balance for you? How do you feel these two things connect?

I've almost done both at the same time. But you're right, these big installations are very spectacular. I like to do those because they help me to bring a painted image into our world, into our life and I can embed the images that I paint into others that already exist, or use trees or soil or existing architecture, to paint over them and make them part of my work. This helps me to expand and go further than I think in terms of space and scale. The scale issue is really interesting in these installed works. But in the studio, I go back to my canvases, sometimes over a long period of time. I can actually cram a lot of different thoughts into a small surface and make many layers.

Yes, you can see the layers and I am really aware that there's a lot more textural section in it. You really feel the drips. It feels like you've ripped away tape or paper or something in that process?

That's right. There's a lot of texture to it, a lot of different… It is sometimes even multi-dimensional. It does not really feel on a flat surface. Also, the way I use colour. I can be specific about many different layers of colours showing different moments in time on a canvas, that is very different. Whereas in an installation, or piece, sometimes I have to make a model. I have to decide on certain things beforehand.

A lot of elements come into my work that I don't make myself, so that is very much what it is about to work with a given situation where you make your work actually exist but at the same time something that is very contrary to it. It's more a paradox when you have an outdoor work or a large installation of work in an institution.

It's really interesting for me as well. Let's talk about one of the first obvious parts of your installations, which is colour. I find it mental to think that you create maquettes for these giant installations, because there feels like so much spontaneity and improvisation in terms of your use of material and colour. I have two questions – process and colour. How does that process work? And how do you approach colour within it?

Well, if you are talking about the installations, I use the models because I want to show other people what I have in mind. They are like sketches, nothing else. They help me to quantify material I might use. They might help me to understand the size of it in relationship to other things existing next to it. I have to define certain things beforehand. Then making the work on site, which is actually painting over the situation that I have manipulated towards my interests. The painting itself I do on site within a certain amount of time. And very often I make a decision about the colour's spectrum when I work on site. That is all developed while I work. So, it is not spontaneous, because I do think through things while I work. What I'm thinking comes from what I've painted before, what my relationship to other existing paintings is, and what I also draw from the experiences I make right on the spot. It's very much working, painting and thinking. It is very much one thing.

How long does it take for you to create those things? Because they can be so big.

That's an interesting question. How time matters in these processes that are outside the studio, because there are deciding factors like the material, my team, the size of my team... Often it's 10 days, or 7 to 10 days. It's a little bit like in a Greek tragedy. It's the coincidence of time, action and location... That makes it very theatrical as well.

I really like that idea because I've heard you talk about the idea of your work within this theatrical context. The work feels very activated by individuals stepping into it, then it comes to life. Do you want to tell me a bit about the idea of painting as something theatrical? I find that a really fascinating concept.

I think that actually looking at something makes the work active. If there's nobody who looks at it, it's just dead material. It has to be activated. But I think an outdoor piece or an installation or a piece of large size is more like putting something on stage. It's more like staging the idea of painting or the activity of painting, rather than a canvas is. I think, it is also compressing emotions into a certain spotlight, so that you access them more easily. You access them without telling a story, which is fascinating to me, and which is why I use painting and the way I paint, because I don't use images that refer to anything else. I don't quote and I don't use language. Colour is struck bear in a sense that it does not tell a story or stand for certain emotions that you could specifically name…

Green means envy or something…

It doesn't mean anything. It's not about meaning. It's about a totally different visceral process that your body feels engaged in when you see the work.

Nice. I'm going to start talking about one of your first songs. Let's begin with the Steve Reich. Do you want to tell me a bit about what you like about Steve Reich in particular, and 'The Mallet Quartet'?

What I love about this particular one is the instruments. It's the marimbaphones, which are so soft, and have such a great depth in their vibrant tonality. He uses them so rhythmically, and the way that these different players engage and pass by one another, as if they misunderstand one another. Then they lock into one another again. That is something that I find very fascinating. The drive it has. The velocity it has. The energy it has, and the structure that seems to undo itself, and then it appears again clear, and then it loses clarity.

I think that we are really made to understand contradictory systems. This need to say, "this makes sense" and "this doesn't", I think is a real misunderstanding of how we look at the world. I think it is really fascinating that we can actually flip the coin any second and make no sense out of every newly occurring coincidence. I think the Reich piece triggers that in me.

Wow, that's an amazing way of looking at music. Do you listen to music in your studio?

I don't listen to music while I work. But I like sound. So, I have a really great studio in the centre of the city, which only has a skylight and a little window [opening] onto a balcony. So, I don't see things other than my work, but I hear a lot of noises. I hear birds and there's a police station next door that has sirens going and I'm aware of what's going on around me, but what I hear around me has nothing to do with my work and I find that very interesting. You know the sounds don't illustrate what I do. And I love to listen to music in the car. I love to listen to all sorts of different radio stations. I have another studio which is a bit of a drive away. I have to drive every day about 30 minutes to an hour according to where I am going – sometimes one and a half hours. I use that to listen to a lot of different music.

Okay, well let's play Steve Reich. Let's play two bits from the three parts from Reich's 'Mallet Quartet'.

—

That was Steve Reich. When I was looking at your paintings, I became really interested in the use of stencils within them. This idea of creating some sense of limitation. Do you use stencils within your work?

Yes, I do. I use materials to cover the areas in my work. Sometimes they're cut out forms that look very specific and sometimes they are just leftover things from other paintings. I have a big pile of cardboard and foam of different thickness, that have different abilities to create contour lines, that are hanging out in the studio. That are maybe two years old and used for a lot of different paintings. What I like is that I can cover certain areas while I work on the painting, so I do not actually see the painting as a defined area that is going to be a picture on a wall later on. I envision what I do like a very large process, so I have a lot of different paintings on my studio walls, and even on the floor. As I paint over them in one very long process, sometimes I can't tell where this is ending and that starts. Covering certain surfaces is part of the notion that I'm actually always dealing with something hidden and something obvious, which is how I perceive the world as well. There's a lot of things that I can't see, but they contribute to my understanding of the world. That's why I started to hide certain things within my process, from my perception and also from my control.

It's really interesting, because it's very much looking at painting as something beyond any of the restrictions people normally think about painting the canvas, for example. It's much closer to something that veers towards the sculptural or architectural. It's almost like you've taken painting and covered all the space around you!

Yes, I've been very much interested in this question of how does painting relate to space and to architecture or to containers that are multi-dimensional. And I've come to understand, after living in Italy for a little while, where on an everyday basis, you're always encountering frescoes or little bits here and there. I was thinking, why is a painting so restricted to a size and to the wall. Then the wall is part of the architecture… I think a painting is very independent of location… It's not like a sculpture that has also three dimensions, and then is very close to architectural thinking, and very much bound to the idea of the material world. I think painting is very much on the threshold of imagination and becoming something that could be a material and that volatile, mobile, vibrant surface. I think painting is like a colour film or something. It can actually end anywhere; it is without topos. It could be anywhere. It could be on your shoulder, on your knee, on your design chair. It could be on a church wall. It could be on a canvas. There is no limit really to where it appears.

You've also worked on exteriors. I find that really interesting. Thinking about how you would approach what you do in that expansive space. Was it different for you working outside?

Yes, it's very different. The conditions are different… It's a bit like swimming in a pool, or swimming in the sea. You swim, but your swimming changes completely, and so does your experience. The outdoor work is very ephemeral. If you paint on a bush, on shrubs, on plants, on a lawn, it goes after maybe ten days, because the plants are pushing back. Also, the surroundings are defining your scale in such a different way.

Can we talk a bit about the album you made with Stefan Schneider, because I find it really interesting. That's when I first became aware of your interest in music. Do you want to tell me about how the project came together and how you work together?

We've been friends for such a long time. He studied at the Art Academy in Düsseldorf where I was a student. He was studying with the Becher's as a photographer and then he very soon became very famous with Kreidler and To Rococo Rot and then he was working with the Kraftwerk people. So very early he found his way into electronic music, actually playing the bass very often. I did a lecture with him, and we were looking at how could we make it different. Rather than having an audience and us speak, we started to sit on ladders, and we played a little piece by La Monte Young, but we didn't play it with the synthesizer. We played it with a band of Oriental musicians. And that's how I started to be part of this. When I was young, I played in an orchestra. I was a flautist and I liked it and I played a lot of classical music. Then I stopped and encountered the synthesizer through Stefan, which was really amazing. Very much like a spray gun. It's this infinity of sound. You can model, modulate it. You can manipulate it in so many ways that I wasn't aware of. I didn't have to play according to something decided beforehand. We started to play together after this lecture and since then, we've done little things in my installations. We played in my installations, we invited people, and we started to do lectures and play. Then we would only do music and then we recorded it, so it's just an ongoing process!

Which track would you like to play from the album?

Let's play number eight.

Okay, this is number eight from the album... what's the name of the album actually?

It's called 'Tiergarten', which is a place in Berlin, where the animals were kept in earlier times, earlier days.

Okay, this is track number eight from Katharina Grosse and Stefan Schneider.

—

Coming back to looking at the work itself. Do you want to tell me a bit about that experience of Düsseldorf. Do you still teach in Düsseldorf? Did you teach as well as study there?

Yeah, I did teach in Berlin for a little while in the former Eastern school. Then I went to Düsseldorf for about five years, and I just gave my tenure back this year in February.

Did you find that had an influence on your work? I was a visiting lecturer for the first time this year in Vienna and I really enjoyed it. Well, Linz, in particular. I just wanted to know how do you find that to impact your process? Is the idea of learning or teaching in some way in your work?

Yeah. I had to learn a lot of things for teaching. I really learned while doing it to be more patient, be more open to juxtaposing ideas, and really listen to what the new generation has to say. At the same time, I really enjoyed passing on what I learned from painting. How I use the things that are in museums; how you can actually be very creative and fantastically inventive understanding art historic information; how you do it not in a linear way. How you actually cut through from cave painting to now and back and forth according to your needs. See a relation between the way that a soccer team or football team divides their space and make that part of how you understand a vivant painting. There are a lot of ways to look at work, and I really liked travelling a lot with my students to Italy, the United States, London, Essen, Warsaw – to see things, shows and so on.

I like that collaborative nature. One of the things that's often brought up in connection to your work is the idea of seeing it within a psychedelic context. Maybe it is the excessive, overwhelming nature of the colour in it. Is that something that you connect to the work or is that something that's not really where you're coming from? Is it an accidental by-product that people are reading into it?

I think there are a lot of different ways you can read the work. I think that is something that I want – that you have a lot of ways to lock onto the work. The work is very open and that's how I understand a canvas painting, as well. It has to be very open and connect to the surrounding factors which are people that are bringing their thoughts to it. If you come from a background that is dealing with psychedelic issues, why not? If you come from a background that's interested in modernist painting, you come from there. Or if you come from just being curious and looking at something without really giving it a label, you come from there. I don't know. I do see that I have a certain addiction to an exuberant manifestation of raw colour and energy that transports. I also think emotions come with it. I think it's great that in an art piece, you can amalgamate everything into it, so you can't really say it's only that or only that, and it's not only colour that I'm interested in. You can't just cut out one aspect of it. I think it is a very complex system and according to where you are with your thoughts, you just hop on.

Let's talk about the spray gun, because I love the idea of seeing you working with a big giant spray gun creating this. Why did you first use that? It's such a huge gun. Do you want to tell me how you started working with it? And how you've changed your relationship with that as a material?

I came to using a spray gun when I was invited to do a work for a smaller place in the Kunsthalle Bern in Switzerland. I had 'carte blanche' they said – you can do whatever you like. My gaze was travelling up on the ceiling, the corner and I thought "oh, that would be a good place for a painting". The way I was looking, my eyes were travelling into the space far away from where I was standing on the floor, and it was kind of mesmerizing. That was when I thought a painting is not dependent on a wall, it can float and it lands because you see it there, not because you manufacture a frame and put it someplace. That's when I did it for the first time. Then over the time, I developed another spray – or I found another spray system with a really long extension, so that you can reach much further. What the spray does is it makes you work faster. It makes you reach further. It is much easier to cover large surfaces. If you do a little scribble, you are able to develop a larger scale right away and it gives you different power over the surface.

Do you feel there's a physicality in that? It makes me think of Gutai painting – the idea of literally using your whole body to make something, as opposed to just your hand. It becomes very embodied.

Yes. You have the possibility to go from the hand to a larger scale. You run, you walk and then you have this next step, which is the scissor lift or the boom lift, the scaffolding… These are all tools that give you, that make you the scale of your body adapt to a larger system. And the body is very important for me to connect to my understanding of the world. I think that a painted painting has the ability to trigger all your body intelligence, as we have so many images in our world that come from homogeneous surfaces – like cell phone screens. I think they are all amazing, but they don't trigger your body intelligence like a painting does. As you said in the beginning, it's very visceral. There are lots of layers. It's even multi-dimensional in a certain sense. I think that there's a certain danger with a homogeneous image, that it reduces the part that is being activated by your system. Whereas I think the painted image, for example, can bring us the desire to use all we know.

I think this is also the appeal of your work. The idea of entering into those spaces is very different than seeing them purely on a digital screen. I think you've got the record for the highest attendance at South London Gallery for your installation there. I think the idea of being within a space… Do you think your work has grown concurrently with that desire to enter space?

I think that's a great thought. I think it is fascinating that you walk into something and before you know it, you're already engaged at looking at a painting. And you're actually disturbing yourself, in a sense, because you walk on the painting. You even cover it a little bit with your feet, so you cover what you want to see actually. I think that's a great metaphor for how we move in the world in a way… And I want to know how a painting can be part of our everyday life. So, not only do we function and have a job, but we also imagine things differently. I think a painting shows that we can enter. It shows us alternatives to our status quo, right?

That's really lovely. I feel like that's a very good moment to end on. Let's finish with your last track, which is Jimi Hendrix. Do you want to tell me about your first memories of Jimi Hendrix?

I think the electricity, of course, that he brings to the musical complexity. There is also that feeling of a never-ending source of streaming thoughts and decisions in his music. It's super… My body vibrates right away when I hear it. It's a little bit like I put my fingers in a socket, I think.

And to finish Katharina's choices we're going to play 'If Six Was Nine' by the Jimi Hendrix Experience, and you've been listening to Rough Version on NTS with Katharina Grosse.

Seb Patane

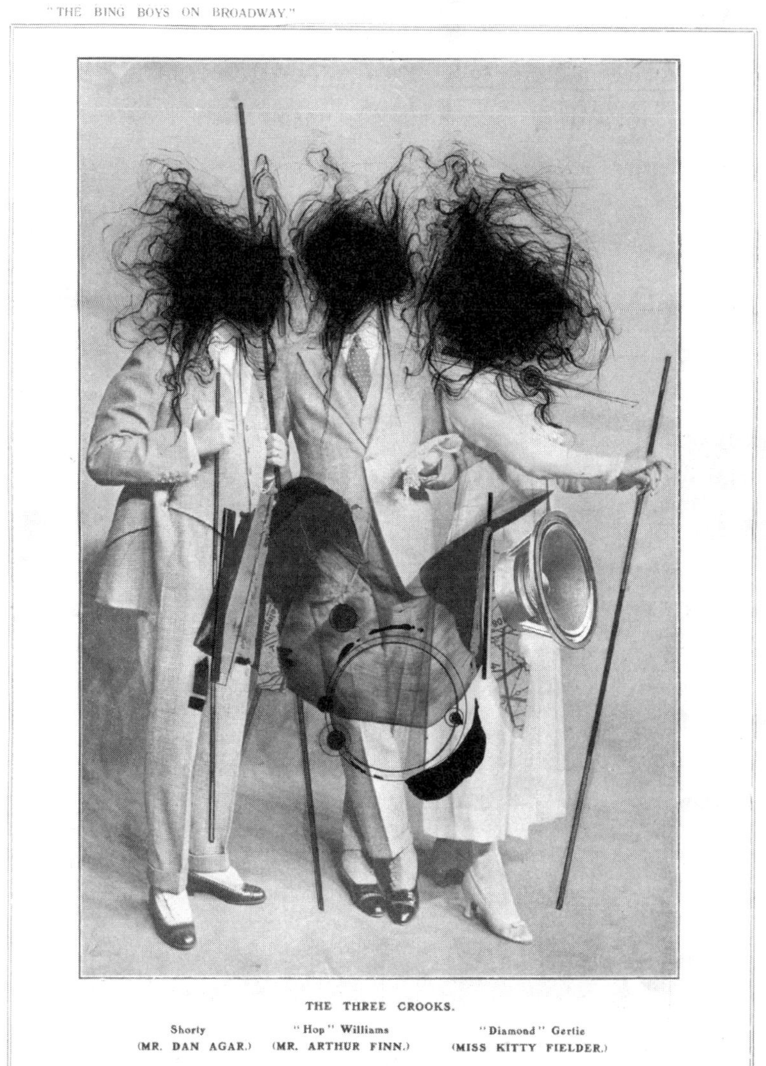

The Three Crooks, 2019.

13.07.18

Hi, you're listening to Rough Version on NTS. And this month's guests is Seb Patane. He's an amazing artist originally from Italy, but he trained and is based in London. He went to Goldsmith's and Central St. Martin's. He shows with China Art Objects in LA and Gallery Fonti in Naples. His work is super varied and includes everything from amazing drawings, often reworking on photographic material, installation pieces, some incredible performance work, incorporating electronic music. He's also done a dose of writing, which I really recommend looking at on his website sebpatane.com. Seb, thank you very, very much for coming in.

Thank you for inviting me.

My pleasure. Well, it's such an obvious choice to me, because music seems to be such a strong influence in your practice. Socially, you create music. Should we look firstly at how music has influenced the work you make and how you've incorporated that into what you do?

As you say, music is major for me. It's really a big part of my life. I shouldn't say this maybe, but I'm a bit of a failed musician, like a lot of artists seem to be sometimes. You do art because what you really wanted to do was music. But art seems to be more accessible to you somehow. I introduced music into my work from the start actually. I think the way I see art making is always starting from a point of dissatisfaction. I just see things that I make, and I always think they lack in terms of movement, or rhythm, or a sense of performance, which I'm always very interested in. But because I'm lazy and I just can't be really bothered to orchestrate real performances, then sound and music seem to be like an obvious choice in terms of creating work, which has an element that makes it transported into a performative state.

I've seen performances you've done and they've been amazing…

Thank you for saying that. They sort of destroy me to be honest. I find them incredibly embarrassing, even though I'm not in them. When I see these people performing for me, I have a very, very difficult relationship with the performers in my work. I've done them. I probably will do them again, but mostly I like to work on my own in my own little room. To work on sound, which has this performative element seems, at the moment, to be more convenient for me. I have a different kind of control, maybe I'm a control freak, at the end of the day, but introducing sound into my work is always a way of making me more anarchic and intangible somehow. Even if I'm doing a collage or a drawing, I always think in terms of rhythm and I need to see how things are moving around the paper, the two-dimensional surface. It's always about movement and music and sound allows me to do that.

Do you incorporate that within installations? When working on sculptural installations. Have you incorporated sound into that?

Yes, I have. I see it usually as an element of the installation. And this has been really hard in the past to convince people that it is an element and it's not a soundtrack. Because we're just programmed to listen to music, when connected to images as a soundtrack. I think slowly, people are understanding a sound can be an element on its own. For me, it's a part of an assemblage, it's a part of a collage. The way I use foreign materials or prints or ink, sound is another element of that.

Do you always create the music you're incorporating into your work? Is it your own compositions or do you work with other people? Or use found pieces?

Mostly original compositions. I mean, I've used samples. I've collaborated with people. One of my main collaborators, Giancarlo Trimarchi, is a musician based in Italy. I've been working with him for many, many years. Recently, I finally managed to get my head around Ableton Live and so I'm doing most of the stuff on my own. But I sometimes get people to have a look at it or to remix it. One of the pieces I suggested we should listen to today has actually been reworked by a musician called Black To Comm, who's somebody that I really admire and loved his music for ages.

The 'Abdomen' piece.

The 'Abdomen' piece, exactly. So that can also happen. I start something and then I give it into the hands of someone else to completely restructure it.

Let's play that track. What did you make this piece for and why 'Abdomen', a very bodily reference?

God, this is such a complex piece for me. I actually made this piece quite a few years ago for a solo show in my gallery in Naples, Fonti. As a sound piece. It's a 12 minute piece with millions of references. We probably don't have time to talk about it all. But it has Gustav Metzger's voice in it, who I met at the time of making the piece and recorded him reading from an Erwin Piscator text. Then it has got a song that I wrote and sing at the end, which is about my hypochondria. It's a mixture between ideas of conflicts and clashes because it has reference to war but also the fear of transformation. And I guess the fears of bodily transformation not only as mental and psychological transformations. 'Abdomen' because the word abdomen in Greek is something like *hypochondros*. It's related to ideas of hypochondria. There's a song which I sing at the end which my friend Andy and I wrote, and it basically talks about dying and it was just dictated by a dark moment in my life. Anyway, I shall say no more.

Bit of death, darkness. This is Seb Patane with an excerpt from 'Abdomen'.

—

That was Seb Patane's own work 'Abdomen', going back to the idea of the insertion of something performative and the idea of that as a layer. Often the imagery that you've been using as source material is either directly from theatre, Victorian theatre bills, or portrait imagery of actors and performers. Or even when you're using like imagery of war, it still has this staged feeling about it. What do you like about that sense of theatricality?

I think it's the relation to performance and the efforts of performing. The faded imagery, the aged imagery from Victorian theatre. I'm interested in them, because they are the first examples of photography. There were very clumsy poses, and the models and actresses were sort of forced to put themselves into these poses that were a little bit unnatural, a little bit silly. I like the failure of that performative effort. And although I am interested in theatre performance, I'm mostly interested in the difficulties of doing it. The stress of setting up a performance. In terms of the war images, that is my interest in scene performance out of context. Contexts that you wouldn't necessarily associate with an art form. Although obviously, we are talking about very delicate material like war. At the same time, there is something about it that can be seen as a setup scenario. So those are the moments when you catch a glimpse of an image of soldiers hanging out in a park in between conflicts. Those are the moments that interest me the most. They are charged with a narrative of performance, but at the same time, they're a bit static. There's a contrast that interests me there.

A lot of your work was often quite monochrome. But the more recent pieces really seem to incorporate more and more colour. Also, more and more different kinds of materials, like enamel and acrylic. And not only these geometric shapes, as well as the found objects. Do you want to tell me about where the colour is coming from and how you're approaching it?

I think it's just coming from my state of mind, to be honest. I spent many years as you said working monochrome and there was a lot of black which I obviously like. But also, one of my interests is ideas about psychedelia, and to suggest that I think the use of colour was something that I needed to try. It's probably a bit too much of a direct way of talking about psychedelia, but visually I tried it and I enjoyed it. It's a real challenge for me. I'm not really used to colour, but it creates a sense of rhythm that I'm interested in. And juxtapositions which, again, challenged me. I don't find it easy. I'm not born a painter or somebody who draws. Not at all. I just set myself those tasks to see whether I can put a collage together. It's a piece of the puzzle. Colours can really help you to articulate that I suppose.

Going back to blackness. You wrote an amazing piece recently talking about baby goth you, entitled 'We Are The Boys From Giarre', which is basically you in Sicily as youth. Tell us a little bit about the piece.

I've been getting into writing a bit more recently. And this is something I wanted to write for a while because our experience was very specific. In general, when I say I'm from Sicily, people have an understanding of my background as something very removed from a typical European way of being. It was and it wasn't. There were connections to a classic European adolescence, but at the same time, if you were a goth during the summer in Sicily, you would die of the heat and layers of back-combed hair falling on your face with sweat was quite a thing. I wanted to talk about that. I wanted to talk about the relationship between the village where I was from and the nearest city to me, which was Catania, and the desire to go there. I think it was almost like the step before coming to live in London when I was 21. I think there's a lot of misunderstandings about what being a goth in the '80s was. And I just thought let's put the record straight a little, because there were so many layers to it.

I remember you being from an area of Sicily that has Aleister Crowley connections, is that right?

I'm actually from the other side, from the East Coast. He had this Abbey of Thelema near Palermo which is on the other side. I actually went to see it a few years ago.

A goth pilgrimage.

I think once a goth, always a goth. I went when I was living in London already. All my friends used to go there all the time, but I only made it like 10 years ago. Yeah, there's a connection for sure. There's a connection to Sicily with a lot of sense of the occult and mysticism and darkness. I'm from near the volcano Etna and that influences you a lot. This black thing sort of hovering around us in a way and sometimes it rains black ashes. It's pretty Gothic.

Let's play another one of your tracks. Let's talk about Fog School. That was a collaborative project, you were working with Pablo Bronstein on the choreography.

That was just for one track. We made the video with Pablo Bronstein and Tim Knight the filmmaker. It's the track actually you're going to play, Fog School. It's kind of a collaborative project. It's like a little gang of people. But it's really me in the end. I mean, I'm the master. Let's call it you know 'the mastermind'.

The puppet master.

The puppet master. I'm quite a bossy one at that. I actually started Fog School about three years ago. I took a retreat. I went to Sicily for three months, during the winter months. I rented a house by the sea, and I went there working. It was the total cliché of the artist going away from the city, but it was amazing. I was isolated enough to be able to basically get drunk at night and to start singing to myself and recording myself. Then from those experiments, I started gathering material to create music and then Fog School started. It's a bit of a part-time occupation. We're not releasing them, but they might be released soon at some point.

How would you describe the sound of what you've been making and the difference between the other works? Because you're not using this within an art context necessarily...

That was the idea not to do it, but then one track had been the sound for a video I made for a show. This track we're going to play was with the video it's almost like an art collaboration with Pablo and Tim. So, there is a little bit of contamination. I want it to be not removed from the art thing. For a new track, we just finished the video with someone in Italy and I actually did that for a project at Artissima, the art fair in Turin. In a way there is a connection. But it's about electronic music and I want it to be about dance music. Although my influences are bit more other stuff we can talk about later. It's my way of making the music I like.

Wonderful. This is Fog School 'The Fog'.

—

That was Fog School's 'The Fog' created by Seb. Let's talk a little bit about your studio practice. Do you listen to music in your studio and what kind of stuff is feeding into your practice when you're doing this? I know you DJ'ed for a long period. It was at The George and the Dragon?

Yes, at The George and the Dragon. I had my own night at the beginning of the noughties called Nerd at Electricity Showrooms. It was connected to electroclash at the time. Really, really fun. I listen to music from the moment I get up to literally the moment when I go to bed. I am very specific with what I listen to, it has to be the right thing and sometimes it takes me about half an hour to decide before I start the day. What dictates those choices? I love the idea of going "No, that's not right for this day". "I'm in the mood for that". "Not quite there yet". Mood. Yeah, literally mood. When I used to have my studio at Gasworks, the studios were like partitions. I was so conscious of what I would hear. In a way, sometimes that dictated it. I'm going back now with your question a little bit in time there. Sometimes I feel like my neighbours would listen to, why I want to project this kind of personality today. Why I'm listening to like Broadcast as opposed to Depeche Mode. I'm really full of it in a way.

You're creating your own filmic narrative.

Yeah. Completely. Well, why not? Also, sometimes I set myself a bit of a concept. Like today, I need to listen to drone music. Because that has to influence me. I force myself. Not that I force myself, I love that kind of stuff. But sometimes I set myself a task. Like today, I won't listen to 'this' because I want to know more about this genre. It's a form of research.

Let's talk about another one of the regular things you look at in your work. This idea of the facelessness stuff. Defacing. Even in the performance work, I remember I saw you do once, the performers had no faces. They were wearing big beekeepers' hats over their heads. And a lot of your drawings, you're purposely not seeing the faces. Where did that come from?

I have an interest in portraiture, but at the same time, as I said, in composition. Once you have faces in an image, all the attention goes to that face. Because there are ideas about physiognomy and the theory that faces to tell a story. I'm not interested in those stories. So, I'm contradicting myself. I am interested in portraits but maybe in a sort of non-portrait. It's more like the overall narrative offered by the bodily gesture, or what's going on around. Things like eyes and face, expression – they just tell too much, and they distract. As I said, in my work, I always want the viewer – hopefully, ideally – to look at a bit of everything and go around and have the eyes going round the gallery space or the paper surface. And I think once you've got faces, that comes to a halt. Because you're looking at the face now.

I want to ask you also about ideas of masculinity and gender within that. Because what's quite interesting, is that it almost removes gender. Apart from the implication sometimes of whether it's male or female clothes. But even then, sometimes, you seem to be doing androgynous clothes in your choices. What interests you in that lack of clarity?

At the beginning, I'm making the drawings of people I'm mostly familiar with. People were saying to me, "You're working a lot with women, female figures". I didn't really see that. I mean, naively, because of course, they were female actresses that I was defacing. I was conscious of moving away from that and I am completely interested in the genderless figure. At the same time, I have worked with ideas of masculinity to sort of question that. To have a look at that. I did a series of works but actually removed the masks. I don't know whether they were quite successful. I think people were a bit taken aback. You know that all of a sudden there are faces. There were lots of beards. I was working with the idea of the archetype and ideas of a certain iconography that is created at some point in time but then comes back. Cycles in history. I was working with images of soldiers from the Victorian era, but if you looked at them, they could have been kids having a beer down the road. I'm interested in that sense of confusion.

Temporal confusion.

Exactly. And historical, I suppose.

Let's play another one your tracks because they're good. Should we play the Taye. DJ Taye. Why did you choose this and when did you first hear it?

I chose this one as it's mostly because of the genre, footwork, rather than the actual track. It's something that I've been listening to for quite a few years, and it really interests me. It's a hysterical, incredibly complex, syncopated rhythmic music. That uses a lot of sampling, but at the same time refers to pop music. A lot of the footwork DJs use sampling from classic pop music and distort the vocal samples to a point of like in credibly repetitive minimalism. This is something that interests me, I think, in terms of music and sound. The distorted voice and some chopping up.

It's a different kind of song-making basically. I can totally see that relating to your work. Okay, this DJ Taye 'Thru'.

—

That was DJ Taye 'Thru'. Let's talk about some of the other things you do. You've started an art class – you're teaching at the moment. How's that working out?

I just found this space that was available to rent basically in this part of an osteopathic clinic. Kennington osteopaths. I enjoy teaching and I just thought instead of going round, chasing applications and all that kind of stuff, I just do my own thing. I just started it. It has a focus on mixed media, collage and drawing. We listen to music, which I select, obviously. We have a cup of herbal tea, complimentary and we go for it. We have a model each time, which I dress up with weird stuff. It has a real relation to my work and it's the only way I could do it, to be honest. Because I've questioned myself a lot doing this. Thinking whether I am able to teach drawing, but I can only offer my experience. And people seem to like it. What we came up with in the end – it bears resemblances to my work somehow because I give my own material. Students are welcome to use my material. It's a two-hour long session. Not too long, but it's been interesting. It's definitely been interesting.

I also love one of your other projects which is 'Queens with Tambourines'. Can you tell me a bit about how that came about. I remember the image that it grew out of... Did it come out of a photograph from a protest saying, "never trust a queen with a tambourine"?

"Never trust a faggot with a tambourine". I always wanted to participate in the Pride parade. But I never knew which group to join, because you have to join a group if you want to be in the good bit of the parade. So last year, I thought, "You know what, I'm just going to create my own". I've been going to a lot of protests – anti-Trump, anti-Brexit – in the last few years and I always thought they were very quiet. And one of them, I saw this group of people with tambourines, and I thought that's genius. It's what I need to buy for myself next time, to go somewhere and protest, to make some noise. That night, I just saw some friends in a pub. We got a little bit drunk, and we were talking about what to do in terms of Pride and it just came out of that. The day after, there was a Facebook page. There was a group made. I did the application. And so, we did it. And it was absolutely fantastic. A real blast. It's a very dry, independent group. Our idea is to make noise. To make a kind of joyous racket and be heard. It's just an excuse to also group different kinds of people. Everybody can come with their own agenda. Their own sexuality. Their own gender identity or non-identity and be part of it. Just as long as you have a tambourine.

Increasingly, with the polarisation of politics, that experience of going to protests a lot. Do you feel like that's feeding into what you're making in some way?

I made one drawing recently. I looked at it after finishing it, I thought this looks like a bunch of people shaking a tambourine and a parade. It's my life. It's fine to mix much things. I think artists are doing that more and more. It's impossible to divide. Not that they haven't done it in history, but I think it's becoming essential to have a tiny bit of say in the current climate. Even if it's a little bit simpler, naive, like maybe 'Queens with Tambourines'. I didn't want to do something too overtly political, which is what I do with my work. I think my work has been seen as political in the past and I am happy with that. I'm aware of that, but I don't want it to be overtly making a political statement. It's more marginal. More on a tangent, where I'm trying to be.

We're going to end with your last song. It goes so quick. Do you want to tell us about this tune? 'Sooper Kosmos' Ecstasy of St. Teresa.

They were a band from Prague in the early '90s. And they made this amazing album, which I'm obsessed with Free D original soundtrack. This track that we are going to play today is actually a remix by this other band called Disco Inferno, that were very prolific in the '90s. The album is an astounding piece of work that has been very underrated. I think it's again very psychedelic. It deals with a lot of ideas of an altered states of consciousness. It uses electronics in a way that refers mostly to things like shoegaze as opposed to contemporary electronica. It's a fantastic piece of work. The voice in this particular remix, it's treated ever so slightly in a way that interests me. The whole track blew me away when I first heard it. It's very cyclic. It has a minimal, minimalist, repetitive structure that I think, to me, manages to somehow still suggest a sense of narrative. It's just a great track that I've been obsessed with forever. It's got all the elements I'm interested in – scattered rhythms all over the place, voices that seem to float out of space, cycles and repetition and bit a little bit of madness. It's the perfect track. The perfect track. How else can we end?

This is the Ecstasy of St. Teresa 'Sooper Kosmos', the Love Stepping Disco Inferno remix. And you've been listening to Seb Patane. Thank you so much for coming in.

Thank you for inviting me, Francesca.

Franziska Lantz

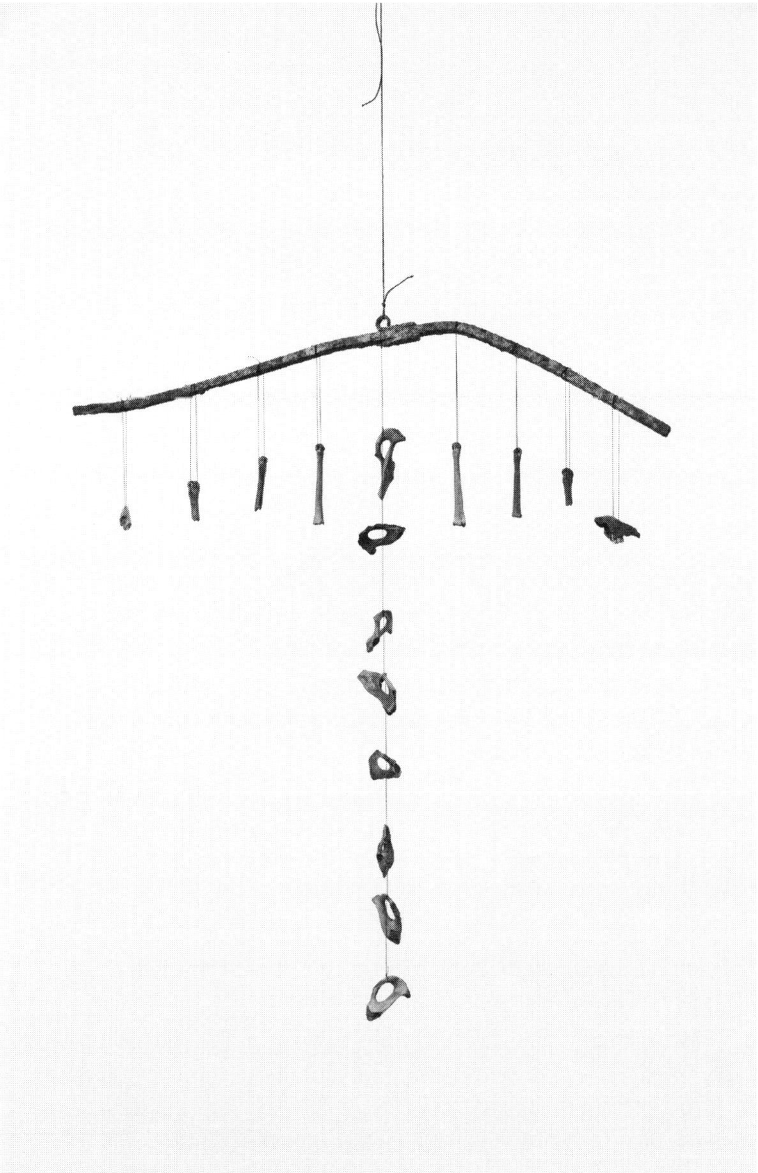

gateway (THAMES), 2016.

16.08.18

Hi, I'm Francesca Gavin and you're listening to Rough Version on NTS. My guest this month is another Fran – Franziska Lantz. Who is a Swiss artist based in London who's represented by Supportico Lopez in Berlin and has shown everywhere from Rodeo Gallery to doing performances at the Zabludowicz Collection – and also produces music. How are you? Thank you for coming in.

Hello, Francesca. I'm very well, thank you.

Good, wonderful.

Happy to be here.

Let's talk a little bit about your work. I got really excited when I first saw your work, partly because of the materials. You source your materials often in the Thames itself. Generally, you are using a lot of defunct materials. Do you want to tell me about where you source your things from?

Yes. In London, definitely the Thames has become my raw material place, search-place. On the shores there is always like a high tide and the low tide. I know when to go, when the tide is very low. The Thames exposes lots of historical materials, but also just industrial trash from metal, building materials, nails, but also you find handbags and shoes and glasses frames…

Why did you first start working with that breadth of stuff? It's literally everything from worn out pieces of clothing that have been eroded by water to like bits of flint and bones.

The bones I think they totally caught my attraction. I was first quite disgusted, because they are from the butchers, thrown out in the old days. But then they are such beautiful sculptures in themselves. Like every single piece, I find extremely beautiful. As I got to know them a bit better, if I had the same kind of bones, the shapes they have inherent strength or power. I totally got enthused by these shapes, and I started with the bones. Now I'm also collecting all sorts of plastic trash and colours because I guess the driftwood and the metal and the bones they are all these kinds of brownish or rusty dark colours. And suddenly I was like, "Oh my God. I need some trash plastic". Which of course is super easy as well – in all the colours, orange, pink, yellow, blue.

When you started coming across this material – which I assume began by accident just from stumbling along it – or did you go with like the intention of "I know weird things are there"?

No, I think stumbling across it. Also, in London I guess. I grew up in Switzerland, in the countryside. I'm a total outdoors kid. I was always outdoors in the forest or just in the streets, in the meadows. So, in London, sometimes I found it quite horrifying. All of these people and the city and this hectic mess. Going around the canals and the river was for me just another way of finding some sort of peace and nature within the city.

A lot of the way you've been using that material – it's often these hanging assemblages. Do you want to tell me about what you like about presenting in that way, and how you combine the things?

The hanging has started early on with the idea, I guess, there is no front and no back. They are maybe characters, proper beings, whole things which need to be able to kind of turn. The movement is very important… How they turn towards each other. They turn away from each other and towards each other. And it is our relationship and interconnection that is important to me, between the different pieces of the installation. And the connections of the singular object, which also consists of many different objects is quite a – I guess I have a studio full of these objects. They are lying around me for a long time, until I know what they are and what I need for this next piece. I know I need a piece of this and a piece of that, too. It's kind of from the gods. I can't quite explain.

They feel very like a puzzle-like thing – even though there's a lot of space between the way you hang things. You drill holes into things I'm assuming?

I drill hole holes into things, yes, but I also collect a lot of things which are easy hangable already. I see "Oh yeah, this could be a base for this". Things with holes and hooks and nooks also, I guess.

When I first saw them also, I think you were presenting the idea, with that kind of personification. The idea of them as almost characters. They almost seem to be almost like the remnants of war. Was that actually something that was part of the title? Was that a reference within it for you? This almost war-like referencing...

Yes, definitely. I think it was called 'Expanding Arid Zones'. The exhibition as well as the record I played as the soundtrack, which is a certification or the apocalypse. This idea of surviving, after wars and devastation.

AKA the future.

The future.

Our future.

Yes. The military clothes, I actually sourced in the army shops, in the army supplies. They are not from the Thames. I just kind of massacred them myself. I burned them and spray-painted and ripped them. And they, for me at this moment, became a natural combination with the bones and the metal. To give this feeling of, I guess, a wild forest. Between mystical forest and a site of burial was also in my head. Where things get worked at, objects that are left over, remnants.

Let's talk about one of the records – one of the tracks you brought on – which is from the record you made. Do you want to talk about the record you made full stop, this specific one? Something arid zones?

Yes, right, 'Expanding Arid Zones'.

'Expanding Arid Zones'. Do you want to tell me about the concept behind the record?

The concept behind the record, I guess it is a collection of improvisations, which I started in the beginning of my very first drum machine experiences. Where it's a very basic simple approach to using the drum machines through effects. Instead of just using the drum machines, they have a very clean sound. And I guess the same as with my artwork, I like the sound to be crushed, dirty, old – sound-texture has to be a similarly weather-beaten object. I'm using sound effects and distortion to get the beats really dirty and raw and lots of noise happening. And I guess the bones had a lot to do with this 'Expanding Arid Zones' idea of marching through the desert was kind of in my head. Like a ritual in the dry lands. This was my storyline for choosing the tracks to this 'Expanding Arid Zones' album.

Let's play two of them. Let's play both of them, actually. You brought in 'Es Go' and 'Salute'. Do you want to tell me a little bit about those two pieces, particularly?

Yes, the 'Es Go' is the dirtiest track, I would say, on the album. It's very full-on, just going for it, I would say.

Full-on!

What can I say it's pretty full-on, I'm playing it – I'm improvising on the machines and it's, I don't know, sometimes you just find new sounds which you didn't even know they exist if you start playing with all the button series.

And it was alone?

Not always but yeah, most of the time. I work in a duo also, DPM357X with Howard Jacques. And we produced the very first record, which was released on Global Warming Records, my label.

We'll talk about that afterwards. Let's play a couple of tracks from Expanding Arid Zones. This is 'Salute' and 'Es Go' by

Franziska Lantz.

—

Those were two tracks from 'Expanding Arid Zones'. Do you want to tell me a little bit about your label and how that relates to your art practice? Because it's really interesting seeing what those crossovers are as a creator. Let's say, between the making of art and the making of music and producing – the production of music.

Global Warming Records became a focus point, I guess, for my outlet in the music and in the art… I'm not an ambassador of global warming, but it helps me really to focus on materials, and also political ideas of where I want my work and the music to go. I started it in 2014, when I did the Supportico show, which is called heat waves, droughts and heavy rainfall. I did it under Global Warming. And because I didn't want to give my label another name, related to music, the pitch, whatever. I just wanted it to be more like a political message, or something which I really felt needs speaking and hearing and thinking about and talking about.

It's really interesting, because the manifestation of that is also not literal. It's not like you're making tracks where the lyrics are talking about... a lot of the work is very electronic and abstract.

No, it shouldn't be a limitation. That's important to me, because lots of people are so "What about you and global warming?", and they tried to challenge me, which is totally fine. But yeah, it's never a limitation, because as an artist, I need to be absolutely free. I need to use also materials which are totally anti-green, or I try to be let's say a point of focus. For content, it helps me to channel my energies into the sort of zone.

As a concept, there's an interesting relationship, maybe with a sense of anxiety. The tracks that you've released are also very intense. Have you been working with other artists under the label, or is it always under your name?

So far, only under my name, under my own. It was basically the idea to release my music because I've been producing so much music in my bedroom. And no one has ever heard it – except for my radio show on Driftshift or on Resonance. I play my music. I really knew I needed to get this stuff out. It was not enough satisfaction to do it all by myself. I used to work a lot on software until I found out – till I had kind of courage to finally use drum machines, which totally set me free. Now I feel okay. Now I can do what I need to do. And then it needs to get the sound out and it's coming from the same point as the visual artwork. It's hitting the same spot, or it comes from the same motivation. For me, it's one of the same things. I don't do the music for the artwork or the artwork for the music. It's both independent, but it's both totally connected.

And you've exhibited them together as well. You've had a soundtrack in a sense to your exhibitions, when you first started doing it.

Yes, I think I always basically combine music, [there] always has to be music with the work. It's important to me to give maybe like a storyline or exhibitions have a theme. For me, it has to be a strong storyline for my motivation. To do it, it has to be an idea, a scene, a scenario with the music.

Can we talk about one of the central contrasts between those two things. Obviously, the music you're making feels – even though you're messing around with things with a very hands-on way – it's still very electronic. You're very aware of the implication of the mechanical, let's say, in it. Whereas a lot of the stuff that you're making within your sculptural work feels very, very organic. You're very aware of how natures battled away at something. It's almost like nature, in a way, is part of your methodology. What do you find interesting about that contrast between organic things and more mechanical electronic things?

I guess in the organic, I'm really interested my work is in terms of growing. I'm thinking it has to grow naturally. I don't want to make massive decisions. I let it happen and grow, and so it works toward existing as they are. In the music, in a similar way the machines, they are on, so I can just make. For me, the way I used them is also a very organic way with the effect pedals. It's quite a spontaneous, improvised way of using machines as instruments. I am not sequencing very tight selections. I'm improvising on it, which brings it in a similar sphere for me. But also, the music maybe is going off in this fantasy space. It's totally limitless. It's all maybe in your head. While then sometimes to go back to the studio and touch materials and really work with the kind of physical. It's a total relief. I think both are totally important.

How does your studio function? Where's your studio? In London?

Yes. It's the garden house. I'm very lucky. I've got the house in the garden – a bigger shed – which I can use. It's full of materials from the Thames.

Sexy shed. We all love a good shed.

Yes, exactly.

Do you listen to music while you're making work?

Yes, I listen heavily to music, loads of Memphis hip-hop. I've been going through that for a few years. It's total darkness. For me, I guess, it's like homemade sounds and samples very simply put together of the mood from this world. It's been a soundtrack, definitely to make a lot of work.

Interesting. Let's talk about one of the tracks you brought in. Let's talk about Drexciya because I love Drexciya. Firstly, when did you first hear this music and him? Why did you choose this specific track, which is 'Lake Haze'?

When I came to London. I was only introduced to this electronic music when I came to London, which was in '98. I was a bit behind of everything happening in the early '90s. It was such a blow to me, basically, when I got introduced to Drexciya. Just that whole idea of the full concept of the mystical scenery. It's a whole world that goes with it and the political tightness with the sounds. It makes so much sense to me. There was just a massive influence on everything I ever did, probably, in art, music.

For me, what I love about it, is also the slight kind of Afro futurist sensation. It always felt like there was almost something political inbuilt in this sound.

Yes. It's about this Drexciyan underwater world. I guess that's their myth which they build of the unborn babies from slave mothers who have been thrown overboard on the slave boats, which adapted to the underwater conditions. They became the Drexciyan warriors, a Drexciyan colony. It's definitely got a very serious political background to it…

And very good basslines.

Yes, basslines. 'Lake Haze' I chose, it's this bassline, which it starts with and goes all the way through with the organs on top. Its heart.

That's a whole other thing. Talking about the attraction to bass and where that comes from, and what that does to you on a physiological level is something that's always really interested me. Why that has such a different effect than other types of music.

I guess it trembles through you. There is no way you can stop it like when you're in front of a big speaker and the bass shakes you.

It's just the most, this most raw experience. Well, this is 'Lake Haze' by Drexciya.
—
I was really happy with that choice.

Yes yes yes.

That was Drexciya. Do you want to tell me, what you're working on at the moment. Are you doing performance works?

I'm doing performance works.

Do you want to tell me about how they manifest? Is it always music-based performances? Or are there other elements to it?

Yes, it's music based. I like to bring in installations of found materials, if I have a possibility to do it on site. That's my favourite way of working. In the beginning of the year. I was in Longyearbyen in the Arctic. I was invited to a residency for 10 days, which is short to accumulate materials, which I found. Then I was just there with all of my music equipment. I kept playing, playing, playing and then played with the landscape and the environment. In the end, it accumulated into a performance, which was playing music with all of the sculptures, or assemblages, which I collected.

What kind of stuff? Because it's so responding to the context of somewhere. The stuff you're getting in the Arctic is very different to the stuff that you're getting in the Thames.

Yes, very different. I found. Basically, I found nothing on the sea because it's totally over-frozen. Totally over-frozen. So, I went to their recycling station, which is a totally new way of going about it. I thought, "there is no way", but I kind of got into it. The Norwegians are very good recyclers, I guess…

Tidy country.

Yeah, I guess I was a bit shocked to be there, because it's full of cars and snowmobiles. It's quite horrible. There are everywhere engines. And there is a lot of industry – the coal mining industry. I found loads of car bits, lamps and coal mining headphones. I found lots of Telenor, which is the telecommunication, cables, I guess, connected and internetted. And so, the works are mostly cables in all sorts of colours, and car bits, and headphones, which are just tangled together in lots of different formations.

Was the concept of that idea of recycling interesting to you as well? Do you feel that opened up different stuff in terms of making things?

Yes, totally. I'm into like recycling, even though I don't want to recycle works in the typical sense of like, "Oh, let's build decent art out of all of these". But I really hate this idea of all this waste. It drives me kind of crazy to see all of these things. And of course, often there is a beauty in rotten, dirty, broken things left in the street. It's quite a poetical site, sometimes. My relationship to these objects, I guess, is quite an intimate relationship…

What else are you working on at the moment. You were saying, you're going to Florence?

I'm going to Florence, where I can also stay for a week. There is the river Arno, so I'm hoping to find some stuff on the river. There are also the forests around… The idea of being [there] very short, so I have to just dive in, and if everything works, whatever is there will be good. I didn't prepare yet. I don't know what I will find. But I'm looking forward just to be there in the moment. To spontaneously do something really in the moment, makes it urgent, and it has to work somehow. I like this way of working, rather than bringing everything which I pre-constructed. Just say, what I do here, I'm going to show it.

I guess it's spontaneity, and maybe life. Maybe an energy that's really different.

Exactly, the energy is I guess it's quite spontaneous and real, which, with all my artwork and music, I'm interested in. I guess real life. It has to be worn and beaten by life.

When you were growing up, did you always know that you want to be doing artwork? Did you study in Switzerland before coming out here?

Yeah, I came to study here while I made a foundation course in Switzerland, which was quite last minute, I was always very much into music. But in the end, I don't know. This whole school way of music didn't quite appeal to me. The same with the art. I was quite unsure what I was going to do or doing. I got to apply to the foundation course, which was a total life change for me. And then as soon as I started there, I knew we had this. This is the way I'm going to go. And the music came only back out of the art education in London where everything is possible. Just everything is art, it just depends on your approach. Whatever you want to do, if you are in it and enthusiastic and put all of your energy into it.

> *I've been looking at, thinking about that a lot recently. The idea of the difference that artists have, coming to making music rather than people from a classically trained background, or even coming from a music background. I think method is one of the biggest things. How do you approach a thing to make a sound?*

I need to lose fear, because there is so much respect because I loved music so much. It was such a big part of my life for so long. But the idea of actually making anything as good as the stuff I like would have been impossible and only after some kind of time, and gaining courage, and hearing certain pieces of music which felt so close to what I feel I'm doing. Yeah, they got me started.

> *Play your last track, which is very intense.*

Very intense.

> *We're going to end on the most intense note, which is basically Caustic Window, aka Aphex Twin. How did you first hear this song?*

I was also introduced to everything Aphex or Reflex when I came to London. This is not maybe my favourite one, but the most influential because it's so hardcore. It's just so relentless. It's so vile. It's so mad, like machines coming. It's industrial, I guess. These sounds, the energies which are kind of waiting. It opened a lot of – I've never heard probably anything like that before. I didn't know what I was listening to, but it was opening up many, many different ways I guess. It's the fearlessness. It's the total one-way energy that is just no compromise about it. It's totally go or die. I guess that's why I chose this track as one of the most influential tracks.

> *'The Garden of Linmiri', did I pronounce it?*

I think so.

> *I always mispronounce everything, by Caustic Window, aka Aphex Twin.*
>
> —
>
> *That was Caustic Window. A nice hardcore track by Aphex Twin. We're just going to finish off talking a little bit about your approach to installation, because I find that really interesting. How the objects speak to each other. Because they feel like parts. They feel like separate things, but at the same time very much of a whole, like a single object or a single installation. Do you want to tell me how you put that together? Is it always improvised in a space?*

Yes, it is improvised in a space. Often, also, it will hang in the studio that way. It's just full of hooks in my ceiling. I arrange things all the time and I rearrange. I know quite well what goes together or what I want to have close to each other. What it does to the whole installation. But, as you say, the singular pieces I don't do with the idea of installation. It just happens this way that it becomes interlaced to bring it all together. I guess almost for the strength or the force of it to be more powerful. To bring more. In the beginning, I was like "I'll bring my whole studio to this show". I didn't want that, somehow, I didn't want anything left back. And I guess I like this idea of the, of the forest, of wading through things, of touching things, of not being afraid to touch things, to make it move to, to be quite physical about it.

> *There's also a delicateness to these hanging structure things. You're almost worried to touch them. It's really interesting that you're so physically engaged, and we feel afraid to touch. Do you know what I mean?*

Yes. I can imagine. I have to, I guess, put myself in there.

> *Because they feel delicate at the same time... Maybe it's just the hanging process makes things feel delicate.*

Exactly. Because they're turning. Usually, they're not that delicate. They might look more delicate than they are. The way they're turning on quite thin thread sometimes.

> *Have you ever made things that come up from the floor? Because it's very different from a lot of sculpture. It's almost like turning sculpture on its head, which is traditionally on a plinth from the base of something. You're really coming from the top down, as opposed to from the bottom up.*

I guess movement was always the best. Constant movement was always my idea. And to be honest, when somebody came to my studio and was talking about gravity, that everything is actually totally hanging in. It's like, wait, I haven't even thought of gravity. For me, it was all about the constant moving. It's the way I approach it, I guess. It's totally different from what you actually will go and experience it yourself.

> *Well, I look forward to your next show, Franziska. Thank you very, very much coming in. Another Fran, a different Fran. Thank you.*

Thank you very much Francesca.

Scott King

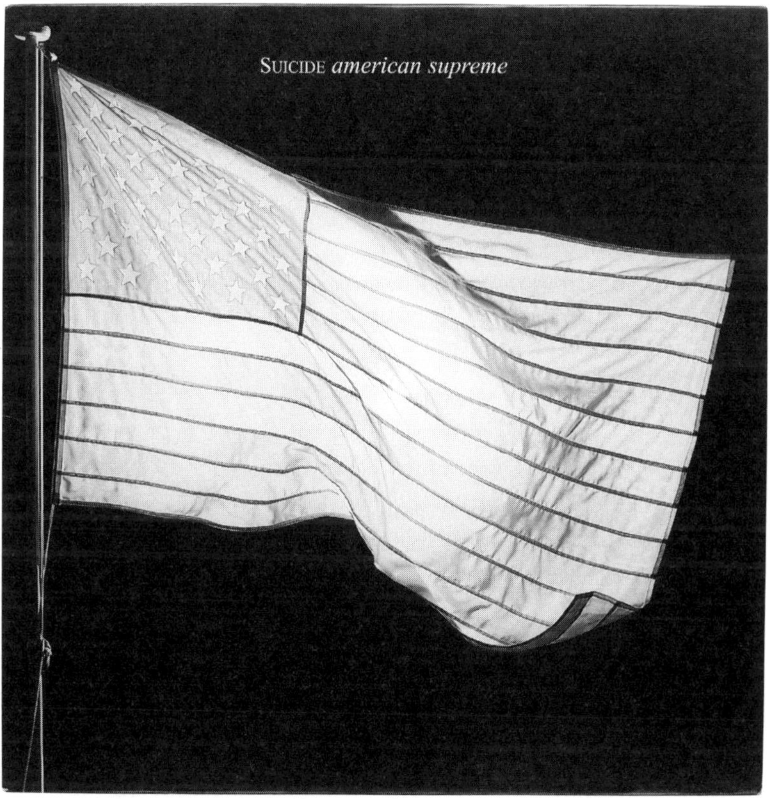

Suicide - American Supreme, 2002.

14.09.18

Hi, this is Francesca Gavin and you're listening to Rough Version on NTS. My guest this month is Scott King who's an incredible artist and graphic designer. He's a former art director of 'i-D' magazine and 'Sleazenation'. He's worked with everyone from the Pet Shop Boys to Suicide to Michael Clark to Malcolm McLaren. He's also an amazing artist whose exhibited, currently at the Haus de Kulturen Der Welt in Berlin and shown at places like Studio Voltaire. And he's great! So, Scott, thank you very, very much for coming in. How are you?

I'm very well. Thank you, Francoise. It's my pleasure to be here.

Good. Wonderful. Okay. Well, listen, let's talk a little bit about your most recent work 'Saxnot, Bread Wins'. Do you want to tell me about how the project developed and what your thinking was?

I had the idea quite a few years ago. For a while I was a chair UAL for three years, and I can't remember why but we had to do some kind of talk. Some kind of group discussion project. I had this idea, it'd been floating around for a while, about a proposal for an Imaginist Butlin's, after the situationist idea for an imaginist Bauhaus. There are many reasons. One is a very long-term fascination with the situationists but also this great love I have of 1970s Butlins, particularly Filey Butlin's which was in the North, just below Scarborough.

Did you used to go there?

Yeah. I went there in 1977 when I was seven, and again in 1983, when I was thirteen. And they were the only two holidays then. We used to go there on day trips. You could pay a small fee to go in there for the day and we all have these very crucial and fundamental childhood memories. The trip in 1977 – I don't know how old you are when you start to remember things, I think you're four or five, but my clearest and most evocative memories are really from that week in Filey in 1977. It's one of those things, when you're falling asleep, if I reminisce – I find it very easy to fall asleep – if I'm trying to think about what I've got to do tomorrow I never can. As I was saying, I've always drifted back to this summer of 1977. I should probably explain Butlin's to people who might not know it. It still exists as a holiday camp but in those days… It started in the 1930s. They were used as army bases and RAF bases in the Second World War. They were already made for that because they're all these cheap chalets, everything was doubly painted. If anything was falling to pieces they'd put more paint on it to hold it together. It was basically crap. It stank of bleach – this very cheap bleach I can still smell now. I don't know what brand it is – I'd like to get it as a men's perfume – but if I smell that I'm immediately transported back to this summer of 1977. I have this very, very strong connection to that holiday. A lot of it is to do this I think: I have these very real memories, very real smells. I can even see the young waitress on roller-skates. It was the time of 'Grease' and everything like that, in 1950s uniform buzzing around serving us and stuff. I have very clear memories of the people we met there from Hartlepool and going to see Zulu and maybe 'Zulu Dawn' or some kind of crappy exploitative film with my dad one evening in the cinema. And none of this now exists. It only exists as memory for me and others because in 1983, we didn't know it when we went there, but was the last season for Filey Butlins. In 1986, after somebody tried to buy and rescue it, it was actually bulldozed. Between '86 and '89 it was totally wiped off the face of Yorkshire and now there stands this new build estate. A kind of barracks-cum-holiday estate on there. I always find that deeply sad that I have these memories and these smells that are very, very clear and yet there's no trace of this place whatsoever. I've gone on about it a bit too long perhaps. I've got a bit of a weakness!

> *I was enjoying the reminiscing. It's wonderful because the way memory forms and the way that influences what you do creatively, it's such a specific thing. I know as a curator that half the shows I do connect to the fact I grew up in Woodstock when I was seven. When you're there I keep referencing the leftovers of counterculture. The idea that you keep being drawn to you age seven going on holiday to a crappy Yorkshire Butlin's is amazing.*

I think that's true, isn't it? I didn't know that you were from Woodstock but that whole thing of counterculture there and that being the kind of Valhalla, if you like, of counterculture.

But also, a faded memory of something that never doesn't exactly exist. It's very much about how does space and memory connect? Because it never really is how you remember it.

No, of course not and that's what nostalgia is, isn't it? Nostalgia is a rereading of memory. I mean nostalgia originates; it was a Swiss concept, originally it was a Swiss doctor and it's the bringing together two words, which I forget, one of which is Greek. In its most literal sense, it means pining for home. But it's a home that never really existed because it's the home of memory. This doctor, he first looked at soldiers. And soldiers, of course, in those days were battling away for years, and he analysed their feelings, and it was about that. Nostalgia is really a kind of misunderstanding or a wilful misinterpretation of something past that you've reread. I think nostalgia is what got me to the 'Britlin's Sexnot' thing because it was my own nostalgia for Filey Butlin's in the '70s and early '80s. When this Britlin's project came to fruition, it was really when Brexit was brewing and before the referendum and everything like that. The two things seem to fit very neatly because I had this kind of guilt about my nostalgia because, I know it's a harmless thing, but obviously, it can be used as a weapon. It was used as a weapon within Brexit. I put these two things together, really. The idea of a Britlin's or Sexnot. It's this imaginary political party that build these imaginary seaside towns, which are essentially 1970s holiday camps. There's a lot of stuff, I think, that went on from the right in Brexit. A lot of people, like my parents will say, my dad, who hated Butlins, by the way. But I think there's a lot of people where I grew up who had this very, very white, Yorkshire working-class areas, Northern areas, lots of people, have this great nostalgia for how this imaginary Britain used to be. And that was a resold to them, I think through Brexit. It's an amalgamation of this initial idea – a proposal for an imaginist Butlin's and then Brexit happening and then my own nostalgia for my own childhood in Filey Butlins.

Looking at your work and I've looked at your work for many years since back when you were doing magazine work, and which when I first interviewed you a long time ago when you were at 'Sleazenation' – can we talk about the role of like satirical humour, because it's so part of what you do. Your work is funny. Your Saxnot work is really hilarious. You're definitely poking fun at social beliefs in some way.

Yeah, when I was at college in Hull, and I graduated 1992. At the end of 1991/92, I sort of found a voice I think, through a couple of things that I did. I always spent my adult life trying to make some kind of art and really failing, I think, in the same way I did graphic design, I was trying to make graphic design and failed. I couldn't do it because I didn't believe in that level of craft or men in check shirts and Red Wings, sort of masturbating over some typefaces. Similarly with art, there's a level of art, a type of art, that I could never do. I wish I could. I could be rich, be invited to things but I can't because everything I do is driven by ideas. I suppose whether I like it or not, often my most successful things are satirical. So anyway, I did two pieces of work in 1992 when I was 22 at college. One of which was called, it might sound rather futile, but it was a breakthrough for me! One of which was called 'No Posters Allowed On These Doors'. I was in the graphic design building which was next to Hull station a very beautiful old almost Macintosh-like building. The fine artists who – there were many more of them and they really ruled the roost. They were in Queens' Garden building, which is a brutal, modernist single-story thing, a mile across town. There's a large set of glass doors and windows at the front of their building and they used it – this is before the internet of course. They used it as a kind of information-exchange, system, place. On these windows were adverts for gigs, adverts for DIY shows, performances, somebody looking for a room etc. It was their space, and it was very much their way of communicating as a community. I went one morning with these posters I'd designed which said 'No posters allowed on these doors'. And then 'This is not a poster' in very small type with the college logo at the bottom. I pulled down all their information, all their posters and gig adverts, and I plastered it with these posters seemingly from the college authorities. And they went absolutely berserk. They went mad. There was many, many meetings over hummus and chamomile tea in the canteen and roll ups and they were outraged, and they complained to the college authorities and the college authorities had no idea what we're talking about. Eventually the students got together, and they pulled down these posters. So about two days later I went back and put up another set of posters which said in small type, 'For the attention of students' in small type, 'no information allowed on these doors' and in very small type underneath, 'this is not information', or 'this is not student information'. I think, again with the college logo on, which I think was so confusing to them that they just left them there. There was no revolution. That was one thing. And then also another thing, which was very much when I first started reading Guy Debord and the situationist stuff. The title is quite pompous, but I think it's a very good idea. When I used to walk home from college to my house in Hull, and obviously Hull is in Humber. It's lots and lots of rows of very straight streets, some of which are just terraced houses, some of which are quite grand. And it was always cold, even in summer. But I remember walking past all these rows and rows of houses at 6:30, 7, and all these families were sitting in their front rooms watching television. So, I picked one of these houses as a site for a performance and advertised it. I made all these posters and put them around Hull and advertise it as a site for performance where people could go and watch this family watching television. It's an invitation to stand in their front garden or yard and look through their window.

But you didn't actually ask the family?

I don't suppose anybody ever went there really! But it was an idea. And it was quite a pompous title, but I was very young. It was called 'Spectacle of the Society of the Spectacle', because of course, the 'Society of The Spectacle' thing is about the passing or watching Guy Debord. My idea was to make a second removal from that. You could watch others watch something else. So, it's things like that which are really not about the design. The design was as it needed to be. At the time everybody used a lot of tracing paper overlays or trying to copy Peter Saville's New Order or whatever it was, or David Carson. And it really wasn't about that. It was just this very, very simple design, which is all about the idea and I think I'd already then started looking at American '60s conceptual art. People like Joseph Kosuth and things like that. That kind of design: really no design was very much what I started to do because it all become about what I had to say really. I only use graphic design as the tools of communication for what I was trying to say.

I want to play a song. Let's play the Alan Vega. Do you want to tell me about why you chose 'Love Cry'?

Well to be honest, I haven't known it for that long. I designed the last Suicide album cover, not their last one. It was 2003. It happened to be the very last studio album, which is – I'm sort of dropping the hint aren't I? – which was a great honour of course because I didn't know it was going to be the last album. But it was a great honour, and it came out very well and it was brilliant to meet them and everything. Ever since I heard the first Suicide album, which when I first heard it… I actually thought it must be illegal, this can't be allowed somehow this is too abrasive and too wrong and too exciting. Like many people of my age, I loved Suicide, but that song 'Love Cry' from Alan Vega's first solo album which was 1980 I think. When I first heard it, I started listening to it in the dark a lot and it is such a listening-to-by-yourself-in-the-dark sort of song. It is that kind of – it's not plastic rock and roll, although a lot of what he did I think was very much about that bubble gum version of rock and roll in many ways. I can only say I just think it's brilliant and that's why I chose it.

Wonderful. This is Alan Vega 'Love Cry'.

—

That was Alan Vega. Let's talk about your interest in situationism – partly because I love talking about that – how did you first come across those ideas and what was your attraction to them?

Again, it would have been when I was at college, so I would have been 20, 21, 22. I suspect it was through punk, through being a fan of Sex Pistols and Matt Worley who I did the Crash stuff with who's a great friend of mine. Matt's a professor of history now at Reading University it seems like in those days, again before the internet when I first got interested in the early '90s and then certainly being in Hull with a limited library and certainly limited culture compared to what people would have got in London. It seemed like the most exciting thing. I was totally confused by trying to read 'Society of the Spectacle'. I got the headlines you know, because all the headlines are really great and really simple and really in many ways you could just read the headline and you would get the idea. Then I read the text and I tried to read more and more. What I could find – it's quite hard to find stuff – I suppose it ultimately is satirical in many ways. Jon Savage is very eloquent on Guy Debord and really just says it's one big piss take. Just a joke about Marxism and communism. And in many ways, I think it is. Especially when you think of Guy Debord's films, which are often virtually blank films. The idea of actually getting an audience to sit in a cinema or even if it's a small Parisian art booth cinema and watch this film, which is essentially nothing, it's very similar to John Cage, it gets to 4 minutes and 33 seconds and what Yves Klein did as well. I suppose what I liked about it really was that it was absolutely about society. It was about the public, and about control systems, yet it was still some kind of art. What I always love is that is never really what one would call full-on gallery art or real commercial design. It's this bit in between. It is something that is neither one nor the other. You could call it grey area but it's actually a very neon pink area where design and art could match up and they never do actually. I very much like pop that's been influenced too much by art or possibly the other way around, maybe art that has been influenced too much by pop or social things. So that was the attraction really. It was the excitement of feeling that. Of course, I wasn't the first young man to discover the situationists.

Or young woman.

I said young man on purpose because it's such a blokey thing sometimes, I think. I'm not being sexist at all. I'm joking about it. Because I think the idea of situationism to me ties straight into the Can fan. The serious bloke with his fringe, and his tatty bag. These kinds of men. They used to be called 'indie' at one point!

The ones drinking pints at the back of a gig.

That's it. They drink pints of bitter and discuss The Fall. It's very, I think there's an element of having an interest in situationism that there was a bit of that. There was very much that kind of angry college technician. It's often frustrated people and I think maybe I was one of them. It made a lot of sense to me at the time.

Coming from that kind of interest. How did you flip it? Because obviously, you worked at 'i-D', you were the Art Director of 'Sleazenation', you did some really memorable – and you've also worked with record sleeves, and graphic design, still, alongside your art practice. What do you find interesting, coming from that situationist influence and then working in the medium you're critiquing? Even though these were all very independent publications.

They were, I suppose if you look at the broader picture, and compare it to working for Tatler or someone. Working for 'i-D', because it was my first job. I actually moved to London in September '92 and I had a place to do an MA in graphic design at St. Martin's as it was then. I went to look at the course and it just looked really crap. I got a place immediately, this guy gave me a place before he even looked at my portfolio, which made me suspicious. I thought, this can't be right. I went down, came down to London one day and I looked and there was nobody in the studio. There's one guy there who was a bit dim. I spoke to him. I thought there's no point in doing this because it is going to cost quite a lot of money. I wasn't prepared to get a job in McDonalds. I was just going to do that. My dad was prepared to pay for it, but I thought it's unfair to take money from him for this. So anyway, I came down to London and I signed on. I lived in a bedsit in Islington. And what people used to do in those days, graphic design graduates. You got a large A1 portfolio, which was life threatening in strong winds. You could easily be blown under a bus in a strong wind and die with your portfolio. And what you had to do then, because, of course, there was no email, was ring people up, which I was terrified of doing. I rang people. I got very lucky that Stephen Male, who was the art director of 'i-D' was this brilliant graphic designer. Him and a few other people really liked me. They passed me from one to the other, because they liked this stuff. I just described these posters and the fact that I wasn't really trying to do graphic design. I was doing something else. They really liked that. Eventually I went to see Terry Jones, who of course owned 'i-D' and he gave me a job on the spot. They'd been looking for an art editor, a designer. In magazines, the designer was the lowest sort of design level. Then after that you had an art editor then, of course, the art director. They were looking for a designer-cum-art editor at the time and they had been for quite a long time. Anyway, I went to see Terry at his house in West Hampstead and he gave me a job straight away, which I was shocked by, and I didn't expect it at all I was completely… I didn't really want a job that day. I wanted to go and celebrate or something. I wanted to have a job and then start in a few weeks. But he started me off. He had his studio in his loft at the house and all he asked me to do is cut some proofs and he asked me to cut them out and I made a real mess of it. They were all bent and stuff like that, which he used to remind me of all the time. I started there immediately and to be honest, it was a real dilemma, because I was very much interested in – I didn't dare think that what I wanted to do was some kind of art, but I was very much interested in the situationist thing, and they were very much trying to do some kind of art. I really wanted to go to the Royal College, I suppose. I wanted some gaps where I could actually just carry on doing what I had started doing on my degree course, but I knew I could never do that for a living, as a job. I wanted some kind of gap.

But when you graduated from Hull College of Art, and you moved to London, and you're offered a job at 'i-D' magazine…

It's kind of the story of my life, really! If I was stronger, or more independent or less seeking some kind of acceptance or claim I would have just said no and carried on and gone to the photocopy shop, but I didn't. I said yes. And there it all began. Even though 'i-D' is very much an independent publication you can look back, certainly at it in those years, and it was. I mean, there still is lots of stuff about rave culture, rioting and protest because Matthew Collins is the editor and he's very much into that. It was much closer in that respect to a counterculture magazine of the '60s. Then what it became essentially was a small version of 'Vogue', really.

It's really interesting because I obviously remember that period and London was very different then. You've got Reclaim the Streets and Spiral Tribe and a whole massive scene in Camden, and it was much more grittier.

I guess looking back London was nearer to what Berlin is now than what London is now. London has become something completely different. And I think particularly – I don't want to get too distracted here – but this whole thing of actually knocking down the [historium] and gutting Soho to build Crossrail, more Nando's, more Pret a Mangers and more crappy chain restaurants can appear. That's the sort of sanitization, well Mumfordisation.

Mumfordisation. I love that. I saw you wrote that on Instagram.

Well, it's a bit out of date now, the idea of Mumfordisation. We can talk about that in a second. But London definitely was a grubby place. It was filthy. Even if you look at King's Cross station, I think it's a great example of what London has become because it was this kind of piss hole. It was terrible. I had a studio there in the '90s and it was so rough which is alright, but pubs used to close at half 10, 11 o'clock. I suppose, because there wasn't this freedom within a mass culture there was more of a countercultural thing. You're saying, and maybe people have changed, of course. There is that. There's a deep politicisation I think as well. So anyway, although I sat there at 'i-D', I was miserable from the day I got there really to the day I left. I was there for three and a half years, and I used to sit there dreaming about the kind of artwork I wasn't making. 'i-D' was an apprenticeship for me, and I did learn an awful lot from Terry particularly. I'm very grateful for that. But I think I also became the art director very quickly. I was art director by the time I was 24 years old, which sounds a bit like a Peter Cook joke. I was too young, but it was my own fault because I nagged Terry to be the art director and I wanted to be. Of course, he was still in charge, but he was away a lot doing freelance work, so I did have quite a lot of autonomy. It was a huge experience learning in retrospect. Of course, I mean the other thing with 'i-D' was that Terry used to say, "you're allowed to make mistakes". At that point, it was still a platform for people who were graduates, often who had moved to London, but not always. Edward Enninful was obviously from London. It was still this experimental platform where you could do it wrong and wouldn't get fired which is amazing in retrospect.

Let's play another one of your songs. Can we play the William Byrd because I think it's a wonderful contrast. Tell me about your interest in English choral music?

I bet you say that to all the boys! It's quite recent really. You know, I'm 48 and I work from home. I have a room, a studio in our house, and there's only so many Fall records a 48-year-old man with an art leaning can listen to, you know what I mean? I can't listen to Joy Division anymore. All this stuff that I kind of obsessed about. I can't even hear it anymore. There's no kind of reverse snobbery where it's become messy. It's just I don't hear it and I'm terrible at finding new music because musicians to me are always hero-ish. They're always older, so I find it very hard to get into some band that's played by some 27-year-olds because I feel a bit of a prat. My relationship to music was very much about hero worshipping. Hero worship sounds a bit much, but it was that to a degree, it was very much a template for how I thought things should be: the bands I liked. Because I've only ever liked particular bands, not many and obsessively, usually for a few years in blocks although I like them all, I went through different phases. For example, when I was 18. So, 1988. Everybody else was dancing in fields and doing ecstasy I was into Dr. Feelgood, this archaic Canvey Island R&B. I was sitting in my room listening to that when everybody else was enjoying themselves. It's always been a bit against the grain, I think, what I like. I'm a bit like an amateur archaeologist really. So, Willian Byrd makes sense now. What I found, and again I know I keep saying I'm old, but I have a real problem with noise. I can't concentrate. There's a bloke in some flats behind our house that plays endless disco music. He drives me mad. I can't even listen to the radio when I'm trying to write something or do some work or whatever it is. William Byrd, I really love it. And I think it's very beautiful. But also – I hope he's not listening to this.

I mean its 15th century, so I think you're OK.

It can be background as well. Not quite choral music, but you can just play it and it's there you know?

This is 'Agnus Dei' and its song for five voices. And it's really beautiful. So totally different, a bit of Willian Byrd.

—

Post-'i-D' you ended up at Sleazenation and at the same time you're starting to exhibit more. Was that happening? I mean obviously you made this iconic cover that was everywhere of Cher's Che Guevara.

Oh that, yeah.

Very of a moment. But you also really made your name. I mean also that magazine was super irreverent.

Well, I left or was sacked, I'm never sure if I was sacked or if I left 'i-D', whichever in summer of '96. And I wanted to start my own publication, something much closer to 'Oz' or 'International Times'. Something much more countercultural or at least a critical voice rather than – I saw 'i-D' as being increasingly like a mainstream thing. This is where Matt Worley comes in. Matt, as I mentioned before, worked at the BBC, but he'd studied history and I think at the time he was also doing a PhD in history. We had a mutual friend from college called Pete. Pete and Matt had grown up together in Norwich and I went round to see Pete one day and I went into Matt's room. It was like a treasure trove to me. It was all these German Joy Division bootleg records and odd Sex Pistols things, Situationist books – the usual stuff. I just thought I must meet him. We met and I told him about the magazine, and I'd asked a few people about writing for it but what they were doing wasn't right, because it wasn't harsh enough. Matt just wrote – after we had met in the pub a few times – he just wrote this great rant about the new lad, because, of course 'Loaded' was massive at that point. It was ultimately this deeply idiotic tabloid, moronic, middle-class graduate, sexist, wannabe football hooligan thing. We just thought it was rubbish. So, Matt wrote this anti new lad rant which became the first 'Crash', which became 'Death to the New' meaning death to the new lad. So, before 'Sleazenation' Matt and I were doing Crash and we did quite a lot of stuff. Anyway, I ended up doing 'Sleazenation' because the editor at the time had been an assistant to Wolfgang Tillmans and Wolfgang's a good friend. It was very immaturely done and that's no disrespect to anybody there, but it wasn't being done like a good magazine. It was not organised properly. Magazines are all about pacing and construction and stuff like that, and even if they don't look like they are they have got to be planned like that in order to work. They asked me to go in and redesign it, which was I think, at the end of 2000. The Cher Guevara cover. I was so pleased with what I'd done, and I enjoyed doing it so much, I thought it was a really good opportunity for me to really try and have a voice with the magazine somehow, or I don't know. It just seemed a good thing to do that I carried on doing it for very, very little money. It was an unspoken agreement between – well, I thought it was an agreement anyway – there was an unspoken agreement between me and the publisher I think. That they paid me virtually nothing for doing it and I didn't work there. I didn't have to be there unless I wanted to or had things to do. I had basically control over it as far as what everything looked like and to a large degree over what went in it, although there were obviously various editors and stuff, and they would determine the written content. Everything visual was – without being an arse – I think I could control mostly, especially the covers. I felt when I was at 'i-D' that with a really great magazine, nobody ever remembers anything much about it. They remember the cover and a fashion story. If you look at the great Judy Blame stuff from 'i-D' or look at some of the best issues of 'The Face', you remember the cover and you remember this one brilliant fashion story. I thought if I have a really great cover, and a great visual story, not necessarily fashion story, that's enough, and everything else will work. That was my rule to myself.

How did that kind of influence you increasingly making art and showing?

Well, because I ultimately didn't care about 'Sleazenation' as a business or the people or anything like that, because they paid me so little money, and I had some more money from somewhere else at the time. I started to think "I'll just do what I want". Really, I saw myself as – I hate to use the word artist for me or anybody else, I could talk more about that – but I saw myself nearer to being what one imagines an artist to be doing at a magazine than an art director or certainly a graphic designer. In that I would try and override them to get what I wanted and use it as a platform to do what I wanted. One of the things I did there, which I was really pleased with, and I think still stands up well is the football hooligan story, which is called 'Epidemic Fashion Story'. In which I just took press pictures of English football hooligans abroad and represented them with fashion credits. Things like that. That kind of came about through necessity really, because often with Sleaze because it was so badly organised, you'd find that you suddenly had eight blank pages. I had to think of something. It wasn't just me forcing myself onto them, I was improvising to fill in the gaps sometimes. Similarly, with the covers, you'd get a photo shoot back, and it was really crap and you had to get rid of it. Therefore, I had to improvise, or it just hadn't been planned or whatever it was. Magazines, as you probably know, advertising can fall out. Therefore, the pagination changes completely. Things like that. It was very good for me for that. I enjoyed that. One of the great influential artworks to me when I was at college, and still, I think was Dan Graham's 'Figurative' where he put a till receipt into, I think it was, 'Harper's Bazaar'. That level of intervention in a mass media magazine, as big as 'Harper's Bazaar', to me that was very exciting. I still get very excited about it. That again was an influence for me with 'Sleazenation'. I was thinking it's just a minor style magazine, but it's also been printed 80,000 times, whatever it was. It's going around the world so if I think of it more like how you imagine an artist or a conceptual artist, rather than an art director, who's responsible for the business of it, and everything else. There's a possibility to use it as a platform to make work.

Let's play another song. Let's play The Deviants, because this was quite a great track. Do you want to tell me about the band?

The Deviants were originally The Social Deviants, and they're led by a man called Mick Farren who was this sort of lunatic. I forget his name. I think he's called Danny. In 'Withnail and I', the guy who makes the Camberwell carrot is called Danny, who's this kind of drop out hippie, with a white man version of afro and leather trousers. That's essentially Mick Farren. I don't think the character was modelled on Mick Farren but that's what he was like. He was also a writer. He wrote for International Times and various underground publications in the '60s and he was a bit of a knob really to be fair! But he was also so brilliant. He wrote this very, very unintentionally funny book called 'Give the Anarchist a Cigarette', which is about his life and times in the '60s and through the '70s. Things like trying to treat Germaine Greer as a groupie and being punched in the face, I think.

Things like that. He did everything a bit wrong. He also led the White Panthers who were the British wing. The White Panthers in America were kind of based around the MC5, and they were in support of the Black Panthers. McFadden was in charge of the British wing of the White Panthers who were based around Notting Hill and that all Hawkwind, pre-Hawkwind scene. He was a kind of anarchist, and he was a kind of clown. He had a great high opinion of himself and how cool he was, which I think is what makes him really funny and what I think makes him very much like Danny in 'Withnail and I', but he's a very interesting figure. He actually died on stage at the Borderline in London a few years ago. But he was an admirable character. Really, he just did what he wanted to do. He wrote a lot about sci-fi. But anyway, this song 'You Got to Hold On', again it's very much a middle-aged man in the pub debate, but I always think this could be one of the first ever punk records.

Amazing. This is The Deviants 'You've Got to Hold On' and it is quite punk.

—

Can we talk a little bit about politics? Because I feel like that's something that emerges in what you do. Is it intentionally political? Or is it just like the desire to just say fuck you to everything?

Nah. I avoid getting involved in party politics. I guess the opposite to Wolfgang Tillmans, for example, who has been very vocal about the EU and lots of other issues in recent years. I'm very uncomfortable with that. I suppose that could be me being a coward in a way. Or it could be that I don't really know what I think, and I'm much happier with things like 'Anish and Antony Take Afghanistan'. A satirical thing, I think maybe it's the English way, you know. Not to be too overt. We didn't really have a revolution, did we?

We're very institutionalized, aren't we? Also, maybe the best way to discredit everything is just to…

I guess that's kind of a Sex Pistols thing as well isn't it? That idea that everything is wrong. It's very easy, and of course, it's not true. But

I'm not very comfortable talking about party politics at all, really. If I was really honest, a lot of that, I guess, is this interest from a very young age, not very young, early '20s, in Situationist ideas. Also, I read a book which really, really affected me too much, which is called 'Bigger Cages, Longer Chains', which you may know. It's a very small pamphlet book. And it had this one image in it – which I can never get out of my head – it was done in a sort of Xerox way, and it was a picture of some anti-nuclear protesters in the '60s or early '70s and they're all holding hands and singing. And the caption – the speech bubble – says, "if we sing louder, will they stop?" I think that sums up my attitude, really. I'm very nervous, really, saying too much about what I think because I think I could be hung! But I'm not sure if I believe in the idea of being told we can start marching on Regent Street and stop at Trafalgar Square. I'm not really sure I believe that.

> *It's very restrictive, you can put it that way. Can we talk about another aspect of your artwork, which I love, which is the ephemeral objects: tea towels, mugs? Do you want to tell me what you like about it? Obviously, it's such a natural fit with like, graphic material.*

Well, there's many reasons with a tea towel thing but the real thing I guess is I have a deep love and sort of horror at the Tate Modern shop and at the MoMA shop and all this crap you know. I think it's absolutely brilliant that you can actually go and see a Rothko at MoMA and then on the way out you can buy a Rothko fridge magnet. The tea-towel particularly I think, because it's such an innocuous and sort of old-fashioned parlour object… and harmless. It's so seaside, as well, I guess. My grandma always had towels. She went to Canada once. She had a Canada – I don't know if it was Toronto or Quebec – tea towel you know and also a Skegness one. In old fashioned English chip shops, there are tea towels as decoration. I like that and of course it's very close to a painting. In reality, it's a piece of canvas really. I like that. But it's really this memento souvenir aspect, and that – because it's just crap – aspect that I really like. The idea of taking these great masters paintings and putting them on a tea towel. I really love that. That fascination with that is really what got me interested in tea towels, because they're shit you know! It's the whole kind of political and cultural and financial divide between the tea towel and the canvas in a frame. It's a very, very thin line in many ways. I like all of that. The first time I did any tea towels was actually at a gallery. It was a gallery I used to be represented by. It was Gregorian Maniani's gallery. It was about 2001 and I did a set of tea towels which are called 'Anarchist Tea Towels', and they were [communications] from the Anger Brigade, the British weak equivalent of the Baader-Meinhof from the early '70s and late '60s who were actually based just up there in Stoke Newington. I took all their communication: the things they'd said to the press, and I just reprinted them onto tea towels. I really liked that idea; I still like that idea actually. It was this idea of an alternative British history and the alternative to Westminster or Big Ben or what you usually might get on a London tea towel. It was this other history. And it was, of course, theoretically at least, it was a mass-produced tea towel. I liked that. And I liked that it would be this edition and things like that. It certainly wasn't me aligning myself with the Anger Brigade and that kind of politics. It was just offering it really…

> *The idea of anarchism on a tea towel is absolutely hilarious. The contrast of something to playful, so heartfelt and so earnest is just amazing.*

They were incredibly earnest, the Anger Brigade. They were pretty crap. Their greatest crime was doing a drive by shooting on the Spanish embassy. Well, one of their great crimes. They killed a Yucca plant in the drive-by. They shot dead a Yucca plant. They did other things that were a bit more horrible, but they weren't the Baader-Meinhof. It was very much an English British version.

> *Kind of frumpy. Let's play your last track, which is The Supremes 'Back in my Arms Again'. What do you like about The Supremes?*

Well, as I keep going on about, over the years – I grew up in Goole, a small town, a port town in East Yorkshire.

> *I knew a scaffolder from Goole when I was younger.*

Did you? I probably know him. I will ask. Northern Soul was a huge thing up North and so was scooter culture. I was too young for Northern Soul, but I had scooters. And at the Vikings pub in Goole, on the edge of Goole, there's a big dance floor, where Ultravox played once. They used to have a Northern Soul disco. It was just that, it wasn't real Northern Soul. It was Motown. A man with a moustache and his mobile disco and his slightly tinted, bifocal glasses playing Motown. It's very much a childhood thing. It connects to the whole scooter culture that I was very into from the early teens, and I just love The Supremes. I think the Supremes are just so joyous, particularly that song. It's nothing but joy is it and that's all right sometimes.

Well on a joyous note, amazing thank you very much for coming in. This is the Supremes 'Back in My Arms Again'.

Aria Dean

19.10.18

Hi. You're listening to Francesca Gavin on Rough Version on NTS, and my guest this week is Aria Dean. Aria Dean is an incredibly accomplished artist, writer, critic and curator. She's the Assistant Curator of net art and digital culture at Rhizome. You've done some amazing shows there, but you've also shown a variety of places. You've done a residency at Hammer and thank you – literally off a flight from Los Angeles, so I'm feeling very privileged. Thank you for coming in.

Thank you for having me.

Wonderful. Okay, listen you do like a huge breadth of stuff. And I kind of want to know how it interacts. Did you begin – I mean, I knew you first as a critic and curator and coming out of that. Did the art come out of that process, or was the art there first?

The art was there first. I majored in art in school in the States, in undergrad. I always did, make art in high school, and whatever. And I definitely entered the art world primarily with the hopes of showing, making and showing work. But I always wrote, and writing was always the centre of my practice, even when I was in school. For a long time, I think I was worried that I would have to be a writer or an artist, and then it kind of has worked out that I've been able to kind of be both, wear both hats. But yeah, the art definitely came first.

And in terms of, I don't know, I'm trying to think about like the content of what you're doing. A lot of the stuff I knew you as critically and obviously curating is definitely coming out of, let's say, more of a digital sphere. And the work that I've seen you make is actually much closer to something sculptural. I'm quite interested in this kind of two veins of yourself.

Yeah, I think it's funny. I think the writing that I've done, and the curatorial work is so directly related to digital culture and the internet. I think that with the work that I make, I think that it's always been informed… I think I like initially in school was very interested in like net art and new media. And I think that's sort of the logics and ethos of what I'm interested in, the way that I approach it, I think definitely is informed by that research interest and by that being, I guess, like a native territory for me. But I do think increasingly, so much of it has increasingly become about sculpture and about like that format of working. But I think at the same time, so much of it increasingly veered towards the digital. I've been doing more video stuff lately, that's more involved in thinking through the things I've written about images and image circulation online. And then also, I think a lot of times, in my work, the titles that I give the work, I think often draw on things from the internet, or from digital technologies and stuff like that.

I want to talk a little bit about one of the shows that you did, which was the 'New Black Portraiture', which I loved.

Thank you.

Do you want to tell a little bit about the concept of the show. It still lives online?

Yes. It's still available online. 'New Black Portraitures' was an exhibition, online exhibition, that I curated for Rhizome. It's the first show, first and only show, that I've curated so far – myself and for Rhizome. Basically, it grew out of my research and writing interests about Blackness in digital spaces. How Black communities form and sustain themselves online, as well as sort of the history of image making in relationship to the internet, but also in a longer, in terms of a longer relationship between Blackness, images, and cinema and TV. And how media and particularly portraiture and the photograph has been used to craft our understandings of Blackness in the Western world, as well as I guess, enforce and reinforce that party line on what the Blackness might be. So, the exhibition featured a number – I think it was seven or eight young artists – including Sondra Perry, Hamishi Farah, N-Prolenta, Manuel Arturo Abreu, Redeem Pettaway and I'm forgetting…

It's all online.

Yes it's all online. So, we basically commissioned – oh Rindon Johnson was also in it. We commissioned some new works and showed some existing works. A lot of them are video but some others were more sound oriented, and we also commissioned a week long performance piece from this artist-musician N-Prolenta who was in the exhibition that was called 'Banana Island'. Which was this really insane Twitch live stream thing where they locked themselves in this studio in Brooklyn for a week and were sustained by. On Twitch you can give – you can donate money to the gamers or whatever. Basically, they were sustained by the donations. It was a really intense…

Oh my god.

Yeah. Then it culminated in a performance at the New Museum. So, it was just trying to think through ways of approaching portraiture and the question of the portrait and not purely through making portraits, but sort of interrogating, what does the portrait mean? What is a portrait? How does a portrait live online now, and also interrogating is it positive or negative. Does the portrait do violence or does it – is it a space for positive representation and things like that.

Do you feel like that online space, and I'm seeing this more as coming from a Rhizome background, do you think that's reinventing some of those, say limitations of representation that have come around? Or is it just reinforcing them in a different space? I've spoken about this with artists like Mandy Harris Williams. Where you're looking at, let's say, the racism inbuilt into algorithms, or inbuilt into the design, or how we end up consuming imagery. I wondered; do you feel like that? That show for me felt quite interesting, because it seemed very much like artists taking control of their own representation, in some sense.

Yeah. With the way that I curated it, the process was that I knew who I wanted to have in the show. The provocation basically is portraiture, and they all were people who I, in one way or another, had been in conversation with previously. A lot of this actually started with Juliana Huxtable who was in the show. A lot of the conversation actually started with this conversation that I moderated between her and Lorraine O'Grady, a cross-generational dialogue about Black woman and art, and stuff like that. A lot of it grew out of this longer conversation. We all entered I think with the understanding that like the portrait was a tricky territory. I think that some people took it up in the sense of trying to give voice to their own stories and take control of the means of producing portraiture or whatever, other people I think came at it from "no I'm not interested in the portrait. How can I like evade it? How can I like shut it down, entirely?" Refuse it I suppose. I think that the show left me with more questions than it left me with answers about that particular question.

Well before we end up talking about your work, I think we should play a tune. I would like to play 'Me or Us', the Young Thug tune, because this was so unexpected from what I think is Young Thug. Do you want to tell me why you chose this?

I chose it… It was the last song that I chose of the songs that I sent you. It samples 'First Day Of My Life' by Bright Eyes, which is a favourite of mine from middle school. And I think that for me, I chose it in part because I think it gathers together the two threads of my musical interest. Not only two threads of my conceptual interest, in terms of working and writing, but I think the sort of indie sincerity, but also like hip hop bravado and post-millennium hip hop kind attitudes. I think like the fact that it does both of those at the same time. It's really fun, and I think that the 'Me or Us' title and "who are you loyal to me or us" line, I think also gets at the questions of community and individuality versus collective, that I'm interested in or something.

I love seeing this in Young Thug. OK, this is Young Thug 'Me or Us'.

—

So that was Young Thug. Let's talk about your own work. I want to talk about your approach to materials, because it seems very specific in terms of what you're choosing. How you're working with materials. Do you want to tell me about how you started choosing the things you work with?

Yeah.

Not a small question.

I know, and I'm also just so long winded, so please stop me if I'm going on for far too long. I think the whole shebang is about materials, in a big way. When I was in school, I recently was looking back at old notes on. How I was describing what I was trying to do from years ago. I was interested in, was trying to deconstruct and defamiliarize the material apparatus of identity. I think that holds true. "Oh yeah that's a really good way of like saying that". And maybe not totally deconstructing now, but I think toggling the levels of familiarity, the levels of signification, de-contextualizing, re-contextualizing. I guess, I hate the word remixing. I think so cheesy to talk about in terms of art…

Quite '90s.

So '90s, but I guess it's kind of accurate. I think that right now, the way that has taken shape is that I've become really interested in trying to take materials that relate to, quote unquote, "Blackness", in some like very, broad sense. I was doing stuff with cotton, which I identified as this like extremely cliched signifier for the history of slavery in the United States, and the New World overall. And trying to toy with that, and put it use it in different forms to hypercharge its signifying abilities, and then evacuate it of those abilities. Because cotton is such a ubiquitous and banal material, in its various substantiations. But then that's taking other materials. I've been doing this stuff with this clay from this part of Mississippi where my grandfather's from. We're making these minimalist sculptures out of that and trying to use various materials that I identify as having a relationship to my own history, or a larger set of racial histories. To try and get at a question about, and this is the part that I'm still trying to figure out how to totally talk about, but using that to work through a set of questions about like objects and perception. And how materials and narrative can and can't be reconfigured in relationship to a given artist, based on identity. How do these minimalist sculptures made of this clay for my grandfather's region of Mississippi, perform in relationship to me as the artist? How would they perform, if I wasn't standing anywhere near them? And then also, forget me, but just how do they perform in space. What is the relationship between the viewer and the object. Really approaching it – I've been like a broken record quoting Robert Morris' 'Notes

On Sculpture' – really approaching it as, what are the conditions under which the object is seen and the condition that's being taken up being Blackness? And so, trying to grapple with objects in that sense.

> *That's really interesting as a viewer coming in and looking at those materials. I read an interview with you, where you're talking a little bit about how your own history and autobiography, in particular the Yazoo River, which for me is really fascinating only because it's like an element of history that I don't know about. Not being from Mississippi. I'm interested in how much you're giving us of you in the work, and how much you're totally removing the entire concept of an artist's identity being part of the work at all?*

Right, right. I think that it's hard. I just did this show in LA at Chateau Shatto. This is where those clay sculptures are that are dealing with those questions. It's really hard, because on the one hand, the history and the context is important to the object, and what the object is doing, let's say. But I guess with this work, with the Yazoo stuff, I've never been there. My dad went there once when he was five. My father's father was from there. We don't know any of our family who's there, if they're still there. It's kind of this weird cross section. OK, it has something to do with me in some way, but I have no sensuous or emotional, affective, real relationship to it. In the process of initially trying to make work around the river, when I did the show in London, actually at Arcadia Missa, God, almost two years ago now, someone had messaged me. I was basically looking for someone to take footage of this river, and someone messaged me on Facebook. They were like, "you should really consider whether or not it's okay for you to make work about this place that you aren't from, and it's appropriating like Southern histories and blah, blah, blah". Well, in theory, there's something to that, but at the same time, it helped me in the sense that it made me realize what I am interested in is the simultaneous proximity and distance. That I am, inevitably, so close to it, and have some sort of conceptual relationship to this place. But I have no actual relationship to it. That's to say that I think that for me, I don't think that I… I'm not really interested in putting myself in the work. I am in it in so far as it's originated with me in some sense. But I also feel like it's – I definitely think I've started to really view all these works as like interrogations into a problem, rather than displays of my own subjectivity, or something. And I think that, that also is a problem. I'm very, really interested in terms of artists and the objects that they make, or the practices or performances, whatever interventions they do. How much of a work is required to be some display of an artist subjectivity, and how do we like really… Is that the sort of only relationship we can have between artist, object, audience. Is it, artist tells you they did this thing.

> *I studied History of Art and that was one of the most frustrating bits. Because actually, I don't care about someone's biography. Even though you can't help but make anything and it reflect your biography, I understand that. But isn't the whole good, yummy, juicy bit about art, as a medium, is that you can see so much else in it. Whatever the politics are, the situation, the time that you're living in. The social structures, attitudes. There's such a variety of how materials are formed. Where did you get it from? What does that say about capitalism and consumption? Art is probably one of the very few mediums that can have so much breadth beyond just the individual. So, I think it's kind of lazy, even though obviously, this show is talking to artists! But actually, it's lazy criticism to just be looking at something just through the veil of autobiography.*

I agree and I think that it's something that, I have a real bone to pick about it overall. I think that it's something that is increasingly popular to… It's become very hard to lean on that in a way that I think is even more aggressive than… I don't know, I've only been in the art world now for less than half a decade but like it seems that historically there's a trend towards really, really aggressively reviewing artworks. If you look at wall texts in most institutions, at least in the US. And that might also be an American problem in some capacity, but it seems like everything is like "this person is hashtag this identity, hashtag that identity". Not using the actual hashtag but essentially you could read those wall texts as metadata list of like this is how this person [is]. They're from this place. I was talking to a curator about this the other day. It's fine on some level, but it becomes a problem when it draws you away from the work. Pay attention to all these facts about this person, and not necessarily in a relationship to what's on the wall but because that's who they are.

People read the text more than they look at the object, basically.

Yeah.

I hate wall texts. Unless it's like super plain. Except for like the guy who did Massimilliano Gioni, is it Chris Wiley – he's damn good. I'm going to play another tune. Let's play The Birthday Party because this is a totally different angle. What do you like about 'Release The Bats'?

That one, I chose that because I took the title of my show that I had at American Medium in New York last year from that song. So "Baby is a cool machine" is like the line they had in the chorus, I believe. That song – I'd liked it at one point. I kind of forgot about it, and then I was rereading I don't even remember which Mark Fisher text it was, but it was like this thing about goth and post punk. And he was talking about the song and goth and like artificiality. I returned to the song, and I just love the line "baby is a cool machine". I think it's like so good and connects to a lot of the things that I feel like I've been trying to do in making work. And it's just a great song.

Any reference to Mark Fisher is always a good thing in my opinion. Okay, so this is The Birthday Party 'Release The Bats'.

—

Um, let's talk about, I've heard you talk about repetition. I'm quite interested in how you see this and actually, in reference to jazz. Maybe because I come from a jazz background I find that really interesting. The idea of how do you use repetition in your work? How do you feel like also that's something that extends in a wider way to work that you find interesting? Let's say in both a gallery space and a digital space.

I think in my work, repetition, I have a bit of an obsessive relationship to it, I suppose. I overall hate and often will refuse to make anything just as a unique object. Everything always has to come in a set for me. I mean I have done some singular works, but usually those are like things that are more like annotative to an exhibition or me breaking form with the slicker, ready-made objects and things. That comes from a series of theoretical propositions that I became very obsessed with. A cluster of them, I guess. One sort of element of it, comes from Eduoard Glissant's 'Poetics of Relation', which is this idea of a torqued seriality which is Fred Moten's way of describing Glissant's relation, I believe. This idea of things existing in a serial relationship to one another, but not quite in a collection. Not quite '12345', but rather – it's so hard to describe verbally...

I'm enjoying the process!

Like they're the same, but different. This goes back, I wrote this essay about memes, which is the object lesson that I can use, I think, to get at this idea. But a meme being a given. If you're on Instagram, a given post that you see that's, whatever joke, but then the ecology of all the images that use the same image or the same format of this and then that kind of joke. Being one and all the same time. So, that's torqued seriality is that relationship between these individual objects, that isn't quite individual but torqued along the way. And then it runs into François Laruelle's idea of the generic, which he sort of frames as this non-philosophy thing. He frames the generic as – he calls it an aesthetic, but in Caribbean ethics, it could be a lot of different things. But a sort of state that finds a middle ground between the continuous and the discrete, the one and the many. It's way out there. For me, repetition is interesting when it does that. I wrote this essay about that, as well, in terms of like Black portraiture and Lorna Simpson's use of repetition. Having generic figures. They don't have any identifying facial features. They're often refusing the camera's gaze, but they're often repeated across the frames and end up forming this set together. But it's not really a set of individual moments, but rather just this weird, repetitive thing. So, I think that's like my obsession with it, in some sense. Jazz, I feel like is another. I guess not quite the same as memes. It's not the object object object, and repeated. But the repetition with improvisation models a similar concept, which I think is like one that you find in a lot of different like Black cultural formations. I had read some of it before, but I'm finally reading all of Kodwo Eshun's 'More Brilliant Than The Sun', so I'm really vibing with thinking about hip hop and house music. Anyway, that's a tangent.

My favourite jazz album I have at home is eight different versions of the same song. So, I totally understand that. Because there's something amazing about this idea. You always know, it's always the same melody. You know what the song is, but how people rework that, but you're right, it's very much something that comes which we don't really get in music. I suppose remix culture does it to an extent but it's not quite the same.

Yeah, it's not. I was thinking because I was saying to the Travis Scott album, 'Astroworld on the Planet', I was reading the Kodwo Eshun book. I was thinking it's really hard to parse through – and this is something that I'm interested in as well in general. All the stuff that Kodwo is like theorising in that book, where are we right now in 2018 with hip hop. Also, because hip hop is just pop music. And even the legal relationship that musicians have to their – it's a different kind of... Even the thing with Frank Ocean recently. I think, there was something where he issued a cease and desist to Travis Scott or something. I might be getting this wrong. I think he, Travis Scott, used a Frank Ocean sample. And then Frank Ocean was like, how dare you or something. I feel that kind of thing is a different landscape.

I think it's time to play a hip hop tune on that note. Let's play New Boys 'FM$'. How do you say that?

It's, oh my god. I think it's called, are you allowed to curse on NTS?

Yeah.

I think it's 'Freak My Shit' is the song. And it's by New Boys. They did that song, oh my god, I forget... 'You're a jerk'.

What do you like about New Boys?

My friend re-introduced me to this song recently, just randomly and she was like, the song is so good. I was like what, this is so random, the 'you're a jerk' guys? And then I listened to it, and I was like, "wow", this is actually a gem of a song. They really, I think got short changed because, I guess they're from LA, they were known, they had this party anthem song. It was kind of like kitschy, I guess. This other song is like really good, and I think it should be like uncovered and listened to.

> *Let us bring more attention to New Boys with 'FM$', whatever you want to pronounce that as. Here you go.*
>
> —
>
> *That was New Boys. Can I ask you – Obviously you read a lot. Is that a major influence? Are you looking at other artworks as an influence on what you're doing? Or are your influences and inspirations really coming from other media?*

I think that, if we were talking a year ago, probably it would be a lot of like reading. I think that most of the artwork inspiration would mostly be me being like I don't want to do that. I'm trying to do something different. But I think that in the last year, part of turning really more aggressively towards sculpture, I think has opened up. I remembered that when I was in school, I was so obsessed with minimalist and conceptual art, and these white guys from like the '60s and '70s hanging out. Which I think took me a long time to get – become okay with that being the stuff that was getting me really excited in terms of actual artworks.

> *Accepting the fact, you like middle class white men basically…*

I mean whenever I would bring up… For instance, in my American Medium show, I did this piece that shouted out to Ad Reinhardt. When I did talk about it, people were like, "yeah, taking on, militating against the history of white men and sculpture". I was like no, I'm not trying to take sculpture back. I mean, sure, someone is out there trying to do that, and that's fine. I'm just more interested in where they – and this is concept-overall in my writing and my art making – I'm not really usually that interested in trying to say like, "No you shouldn't have that. I'm going to take it now and do my thing". It's more I'm interested in where someone like Robert Morris or Ad Reinhardt drifted into a territory that I think actually a lot of like Black radical theory has already possibly trodden and done a lot with. Not saying like "Oh, they got there late" like they're bad. But saying, okay well what happens if you cross pollinate these things? And try to make something. It doesn't have to be something new but just do something different or how those things relate to each other, be it through an object, or be it through writing. So yeah, I usually just like old white guys doing really minimal work.

Isn't it funny that we're really like – I mean I'm not going to say that I only like old white guys, but there are some good old white guys.

Yeah.

And isn't it weird that we feel like I don't know, I find it strange that I almost feel like I have to be apologetic for liking that now. Which is quite funny, I don't know why? I like everyone.

It's frustrating. Because people were like, "Oh, that's cool that you're into that because I bet it's because you hate them". And it's like no. It doesn't mean that I love them either, or that I don't have any issues. I don't know, it's just yeah. I've now gotten to the place where I really spent a lot of time figuring out how to tell myself, I don't have to apologise for being interested in this stuff. The same thing with like theory. I love Heidegger. I really enjoy a lot of Heidegger's writing. I mean his politics, obviously, were bad.

Not good politics…

But there are Heidegger texts that are incredibly useful, and useful in terms of saying, "Hey, this is actually incorrect, and we can amend it in this way", But also, he wrote this thing, 'The Age of the World Picture' that I think if you want to talk about… giving too much credence to autobiography in terms of artworks, this text completely just lays out, you know, how we got here.

I mean, it's quite a fundamental thing. I mean, let's take the poetry of Ezra Pound. I mean, he's a Nazi. So, do I sit there and go damn I got no pleasure from reading that? That's a really interesting position to be in now. How does the artwork differ from the individual? Maybe that's what we love Shakespeare. We know bugger all about him. We don't even know who he is necessarily.

Yeah.

But I find that also very interesting that you feel as an artist and a writer, however, that whatever actions you're making and choices you're making in terms of making an object are still somehow, whether you like it or not, being placed within the context of your own identity or people's perceptions of your identity.

Yeah. I mean I think that I for a long time, the goal was deconstructing the material apparatus of identity for a long time. I was trying to run away from that fact. Not because I didn't hate myself or something. I just I was like, "Wow, wouldn't it be cool to not have to deal with this and do whatever I wanted to do". But then, at some point I'm like, this problem that continues to follow me of people having certain expectations, is actually quite interesting. It is a quite interesting territory to actually try to work in and exploit and play with, I guess, and interrogate. So, I've like recast it in my mind as an interesting thing, that is actually worth like making work, not making work about, but you know making work with, I guess.

Prodding your finger into the viewer. Let's play a last song. So, you have a choice, you can do YG or Modest Mouse.

Modest Mouse.

Okay. So, this is 'Teeth Like God's Shoeshine'. Why Modest Mouse?

It's another title-related thing. My show at Chateau Shatto, that's up right now, is called 'Lonesome Crowded West', which is the title of this album. Which also, I learned is one of very few albums to get a 10 out of 10 on Pitchfork. I was told this by Parker Ito in Los Angeles. The show is called 'Lonesome Crowded West'. I got obsessed, somehow. I must have been listening to this album because I wanted to. I was like "Oh wow, I should totally call my show 'Lonesome Crowded West'" because all this work is about this issue of individual versus collective and Black ontologies. And can an individual stand on her own or is she just like part of the crowd. I was working on all this stuff – like the 'Lonesome Crowded West' is, I am the 'Lonesome Crowded West' in relation to all this stuff with the Yazoo River work and this other crowd video that I was working on…

> *That's beautiful. This is Modest Mouse, 'Teeth Like God's Shoeshine'. And thank you very much Aria Dean.*

Thank you for having me.

Adam Pendleton

05.11.18

My guest this month is Adam Pendleton. Adam is an amazing American conceptual artist who works with everything from silkscreen and mirrors to sculpture, to film. He was in the Forbes 30 under 30, twice, and he has shown everywhere from the Museum of Modern Art to the Whitney. And he's represented by Pace Gallery in London, where he has just had a huge show. So, Adam, thank you very much for coming in.

Thanks for having me.

Wonderful. Can we talk about – we'll talk about your work for a while, and then I'll get you to play some of the music you brought in. Let's talk about 'Black Dada'. Because even as a title alone, it's an amazing concept. Do you want to tell me about what that idea was for you, and putting together 'The Black Dada Reader'? And how that's informed your work?

Well, 'The Black Dada Reader' itself was very consequential because it began as an in-studio publication, in around in 2011. It was just me compiling and putting together different text by writers, artists, choreographers and a really kind of strange brew of people from Gertrude Stein to Jean-Luc Godard, to William Pope.L to Joan Jonas to… gosh, Stan Douglas. So, it was quite the mix. I think that the earliest text that appears in 'The Black Dada Reader' is a text by W. E. B. Du Bois, which was published in the early 1900s. And then you have more contemporary things like a text by June Jordan, I believe it's from the 1980s or 1990s. It's this mix of the historical and the contemporary. Beyond that it's a mix between theoretical and conceptual positions, and how ideas occupy space, and how they interact and rub up against each other.

So, was it more like a scrapbook of your influences and your own reading list, in a weird way?

That would be an accurate way to describe it, yes. It's kind of like a scrapbook, but it's also for me a collage, both in a visual sense, but also in a conceptual sense. Of how these ideas reshape and reform each other by existing in explicit relationship to one another within the space of the Reader. So, it was really, I think, the first time that I had created a kind of academic space in a strange way? Although I would like to look at the underside of that word for this term, Black Dada. That, at first, it was just a conjecture, something that I just pushed out into the world to see what would happen, and that was in 2008.

It's a great hook.

Yeah, it is.

There's something about the entire concept of, let's say, a Black reworking of the concept of Dada, which in itself is like absurdist and revolutionary. That's exciting, even just those two words.

Well, I think there's something inviting about that which is absurd, right? Because of its absurdity, it becomes generous. There's a kind of inherent generosity embedded in that gesture. And I think that's what is all ultimately generative about Black Dada is that it can be many things at once. It plays itself out in the world without claiming or demanding that you understand it as any one thing, but it's rather a very capacious and open space.

I was trying to see what the relationship between that is and your actual work visually, because your work is very often using silk screen, and there's this lovely sense of layering, and a collage of language and imagery. I can see that level of juxtaposition in text come out in your juxtaposition of image. It's almost like there's a methodological connection between those two things, would you agree?

I think so, yes. I think one of the things that the term has done for me is it's made me have to answer a series of questions. One of the most important ones being "What does Black Dada look like?" And that's often times what I'm grappling with, when I'm putting together an exhibition or even working on an individual piece – be it a collage, or a painting or a text that I'm writing about the work. It now has a kind of foundation, but it splinters off. It's something that I can pick up when I need to and let go of when I don't need it. It's in and out of focus.

Can you talk a little bit about how you work. Do you work from source imagery? Do you collect imagery that you incorporate in your work? Or how do the visual influences happen in what you make?

I collect books. Books that are filled with images often. And I'm interested in books as an archiving device, as a kind of archival resource. Also, how libraries function. I have a quite extensive personal library, but it's kind of illogical in a lot of ways. The ways in which I'm sort of organizing the books and subject matters and content, the different periods the books are from. They can be books on architecture, or art, art history, or philosophy or poetry. In the studio, I create these temporary sculptures where I stack these books, physically to look at aesthetic relationships, but also theoretical relationships at the same time. That's a starting point for me, these temporary sculptures, and then you open the book up right, and then another dimension appears, another aspect, another kind of way of dealing with the subject matter presents itself.

Let's play one of your tracks because you've brought some really interesting ones. Let's play the Alicia Hall Moran. How did you come across this and why did you choose it?

Alicia Hall Moran is a New York-based singer, and composer and musician. She's someone that I've been working with, collaborating with for, I think, a little over a decade now. And one of the things that I really enjoy about working with Alicia is we can talk verbally about an idea, a musical idea, and she brings it to life for me with music. So, I'll say "Oh, I want it to sound like this", or "Oh, what if the music did this", and then she can make that happen either by herself, and or engaging with other musicians. The track that I brought in is off of her most recent album. I find it fascinating because it's a mix between gospel, classical, jazz and I would even argue blues. She is trained as a classical singer, but you hear her moving towards and pushing towards a more soulful space, I think, for a classically trained singer. There's something about it. There's a kind of energy that's embedded in the gestures that she's making.

'This is Two Wings' by Alicia Hall Moran

—

That was Alicia Hall Moran. Do you want to tell me a little bit about your performance works and how those collaborations have manifested with Alicia? Or with other people, because you've done stuff as part of Performa, I think, in the past?

Yeah, I did a piece with Performa in 2007. Actually, Alicia Hall Moran and Jason Moran, the pianist and composer, were the musical directors for that piece. The three of us worked very closely developing what became 'The Revival', which had a band that was led by Jason Moran. Then there was also a gospel choir. And then there was me giving a secular sermon that focused on experimental uses of language. A lot of my performances when I do them, and I rarely do them, are language-based or text-based performances.

Why did you choose gospel in particular within a performance like that? Is that something that you particularly connect to in some way? Because some of the other tracks you brought in also have gospel references.

Well, I like to, for example, think about the relationship between gospel music and Gertrude Stein, namely because of repetition. You'll have this incredible sense of urgency that exists within gospel music by repeating the same thing over and over and over again, but slightly differently, right? There's this serial aspect to it, that I find in a lot of literature that I'm drawn to. It's not something that people usually say, "Oh, this relates to Gertrude Stein and gospel music". Although, I think Gertrude Stein would, she did write a libretto. So, I'm sure she would maybe jive with this thought, one could say. I like to sort of just turn things upside down. I also like the emotive or emotional space that gospel music opens up when you listen to it intensely. To look at that in relationship to something like conceptual art or minimalism, which is kind of a cooler temperature. So, what happens when these two things come together? What temperature is that? How hot is that? Or how cold is that?

Let's talk about language and words and linguistics and how you use that in your work. Often, a lot of your painting pieces, for example, include phrases. Do you want to tell me why you chose those phrases, and how do they relate to your choices? You've used Black Lives Matter references, for example, in some of your work. Do you want to tell me about your choice of words?

I like to get people's attention to the level of the language. I like to think about the encounter with the art object, as a site, as an encounter that creates a site of engagement between the viewer and the object. Which is also to say between the viewer and the idea. The idea that is on display or made manifest through the art object. I think language, one, it makes us think in a certain way, on a certain level. I have to read this. I have to understand this in a specific way, but I abstract a lot of the language that I'm using. So, it's not necessarily explicit what is being said. That way, I think is how you get people to actually focus on the language, and what language does, and how it shapes our experience.

I read a really nice thing saying that you resist the relationship of autobiography and interpreting your work, which is something I'm a great believer in actually. I was talking about this the other day. I find it quite frustrating that we have to only see art, or any medium, through the gaze of someone's own history.

Sure, yeah.

Why do you resist it? What are your feelings around it?

I think we as human beings, we appropriate, right? Which is to say we see things, we like them. They become a part of who we are. They become a part of our identity, our texture. So, I think in that way, autobiography matters. But at the same time, there's no logical way for me to explain who I am or why I am or what I am. It's not a conversation, I would argue, that's actually worth having. We should always be existing in a state of becoming. We should be perpetually becoming, which I would argue is an ethical condition of being.

Can we talk about politics for a bit. I remember once, for one Venice Biennale, you were included in the, was it the Belgian Pavilion?

It was the Belgian pavilion, yes.

> *Interesting, Do you have any Belgian connections? That was a very political pavilion.*

It was.

> *It was pretty much about freedom of speech. Do you want to tell me about that in the context of living in America and making work now, and how politics informs what you're doing?*

I think we have to live political lives. Which I think is maybe different than political art, or making, saying your work is about politics. To simply say that you have to live a political life, which is, I think, to say, you have to be engaged with what is going on around you. And you have to be critical of it, but on many different levels – on the level of how are you critical as an artist, but also, how are you critical as a citizen? How are you critical as a lover, or a father, or a sibling? There's so many different ways to think about being a political being in the world, and what kind of social configurations you want to support and give your voice to and give your energy to. I think, too often in art, we say, "Oh, that's political". But what are you standing for, right? You can't just say it's political. You have to know what politics you stand for. I think I'm particularly interested in a politics that embraces that which is complex, a kind of complex realism. I'm not so interested in saying this is wrong, or this is right, because that's no different than saying you have to be like this, or you have to be like that. We should be able to be, again, many things at once. That is a political position that I can embrace. When I say that out loud, you might say, "Oh, that that's pretty simple", or "That's pretty obvious", but I think one of the things that's particularly wrong with politics is this drive to simplify things. I think there should actually be a drive to make things more complex.

> *Nice. Let's play another track. Let's play Albert Ayler, his version of 'Old Man River'. How did you come across him?*

That's a great track, and what an incredible musician. Someone who embraced the avant-garde dimensions of his medium of music, but at the same time, embraced the more traditional or spiritual or folk aspects of what music can do. Which is what that example is. He would also push the boundaries of the saxophone and make it whine, or make it wail, or make it cry. The difference between a voice and a sound, and the space between those two things.

This is 'Old Man River' by Albert Ayler.

—

That was Albert Ayler doing 'Old Man River'. Can we talk about monochrome, because you do work a lot often in monochrome often Blackness, often on reflective materials or grey, not necessarily on white. What draws you to that kind of duality, or lack of nuance?

I use what is necessary. There was, I think in 2008, colour, as people like to call it, started to be less present in the work. I think it was about how I wanted to shape people's attention. And I didn't want people to say, "Oh, what a beautiful blue" or "Oh, what a beautiful red". I wanted them to actually look at what the work was doing. And I have to say, I noticed a real shift, when colour was not a central tenant or component, in how I would go about making something. It was more how far can I push the black and the white, and the tones in between, essentially. You don't miss it, you know. I don't think people look at the work and say, "Oh, where's the red?" I don't think you walk into a show – it actually became very much so beside the point. But I use whatever is necessary. In 2012, I did a video portrait of Lorraine O'Grady, an African-American conceptual artist, and that was in colour because the piece demanded it. Whatever is necessary, but I think that is the question, what is necessary? How do I make a compelling, convincing, honest argument for the work?

Can you tell me a bit about the mirroring as well, and what, in particular, those references have for you? Why did you want to have the idea of the viewer being reflected in your work, at the same time as looking at it?

I think art historically, I've been interested in how people like Robert Smithson or Joan Jonas or Dan Graham have deployed mirrors or mirrored surfaces in their work. It goes back to that notion of creating a site of engagement and the mirrors literally allow the viewer to become implicated within the space of the work. You're looking at yourself literally, and the work is also looking back at you to a certain extent. It's a moment of combustion, one could say, where you can't escape the encounter. You have to contend with the dynamics that are at play.

Let's play another track. Let's play your final tune, this is Silver Harpes, with an 'es', 'I Am Saved'.

That is wrong. It's Silver Harps just with H A R P S. They've been mis-credited!

I am horrified! I found a 1981 vinyl version but it's very, this is a really hard track to get. Do you want to tell me about Silver Harps?

You know, I actually don't know that much about them. I did look them up and there's not – unfortunately, there's not a lot of information about them. But what a great song. I actually used this song in a video portrait I did of Yvonne Rainer, and I paired this song by the Silver Harps with archival footage of Yvonne performing 'Trio A'. Again, an unlikely juxtaposition that I think both makes you listen more intensely to the music, and also makes you pay closer attention to the gestures and what do they communicate, what they say. What kind of space they create?

This is 'I Am Saved' by Silver Harps – without the E.

—

And just to finish off, do you want to tell me a little bit about how you approach video? Are you still doing video works now? Is that something that's ebbed off in your work? Particularly, the idea of you doing portraiture is really interesting to me. Particularly portraits of female artists or creative people. It's not the first thing I think of when I think of your work.

I've been doing a series of video portraits since… I shot the first one about six years ago, in 2012. And well, excuse me, I shot the first one actually in 2011, but I didn't finish editing that piece until 2014. That was a video portrait of David Hilliard, who was the one of the founding members and chief of forum and the Chief of Staff of the Black Panther Party. That was then followed by a portrait of Lorraine O'Grady, which was followed by a portrait of Yvonne Rainer. I just recently shot two additional video portraits that I will edit and work on over the next while. It's an ongoing project for me. It's a way to bring other people, literally, into the space of my work, but also a way to queer the notion of the artist's voice, the voice of the artist. What if the voice of the artist is someone else's voice? What if someone else speaks for you? What if you ask someone else to speak for you? But also, this funny notion of portraiture. How do you accurately represent someone? And what are you representing in that moment? What moment in time, and can you ever actually represent who and what someone is? I think that's one of the things that the video portraits look at.

Can I ask you how you show them because one of the great notable pieces about your work is your approach to installation. You create amazing spaces that almost echo the layering within the work in a really kind of physical sense. How do you approach an install?

Lots of models and site visits.

All the tasty logistical things.

Yes, which I have to say I really enjoy. I think all exhibitions begin with either a site visit or a model being built in the studio. And then slotting ideas, which is to say slotting artworks into those spaces to see how they transform, or condition or recondition them. That's really what I spend a lot of the time in the studio doing. I also typically make subtle tweaks to spaces, building one wall or two walls – nothing too dramatic. There's always a practical element to it. But it's amazing how practical decisions can have these wonderfully rigorous or aesthetically compelling elements, come out of these practical moves.

Do you work alone? What's your studio like? Do you have little team of baby Adams around you?

I have – no there are no baby Adams. I have a team of individuals.

> *Excuse me. I did not mean to denigrate your team. I apologise team!*

That I respect deeply. Who bring wisdom, and expertise, and generosity to a lot of the tasks we take on.

> *Do you listen to music in the studio while you're there? Is it something that feeds in or is it a much more zen-like space?*

It's actually very quiet. I prefer when it's quiet, yes.

> *Better for thinking, maybe.*

Perhaps, I think that's a debate worth having.

> *Well, I want to say thank you very much for coming in Adam that's great.*

Thank you, thanks for having me.

Dozie Kanu

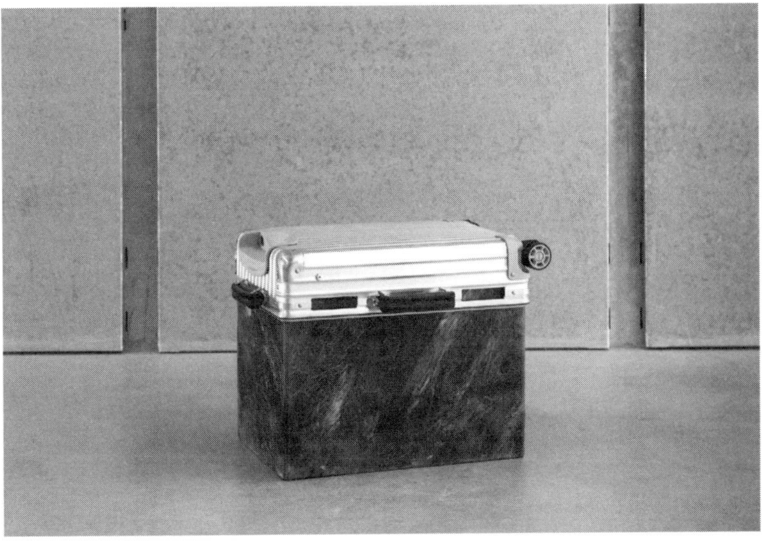

RIMOWA Shell Stool, 2018.

19.12.18

Hi, this is Francesca Gavin and you're listening to Rough Version on NTS. This month's guest is Dozie Kanu. Dozie is born in Texas, and he's trained in New York and now based in Portugal. He's an artist that's working very much at the intersection between design and furniture and art. So very much showing architectural design objects, often reworking something like a chair or a suitcase within an art context. He's exhibited at Soft Opening in Piccadilly Circus, an amazing space I recommend looking at, and Spazio Maiocchi in Milan. Dozie thank you for coming in. Let's talk about how you exhibit your work because even though you're working in let's say more functional objects, often you're showing that in art spaces, or like within an art context. What do you like about flipping things and moving them outside of someone's home and into an art gallery basically?

I just think that the context of the art gallery offers people to look at the object and try to find something else in it. I've seen like a lot of other artists do it really well. Vito Acconci, even Mona Hatoum does a lot of design stuff. I think, with who I am and with my upbringing, it would not be authentic for me to just say that this is something that I made. It's supposed to serve this purpose, and there's nothing else to it. I think to be authentic with myself, it's more beneficial for me to put it in spaces like that. It's to try to give something else to it.

We'll talk about your background because I'm really curious about your background. Do you want to tell me first about your choice of material? If you look at your chairs, benches and whatever, the objects you're creating, often almost feel semi-industrial. But they are also big slabs of marble and stuff, or like tires or steel. How do you choose the materials you're working with?

I really just tried to use whatever I can get my hands on. Cement, for instance, is like $3 a bag. You can still do a lot with it. You can dye it. You can mould it in any shape, as long as you can make the mould for it. I also tried ready-made sculptures but bring ready-made objects into my work, and reconfigure them so that they perform another function.

Not just have them being purposeless. Because that's what a lot of artists are doing now. They're just taking found objects and putting them in the gallery.

Duchamp, 100 years of that.

Exactly. It's not interesting to me anymore. I think it's more interesting to make that object perform in another way, and so that's how I choose things. I don't really work in any – I'm not like meticulous like that. I'm not like trying to use the same materials or trying to work in a confined way. It's just whatever I'm feeling like using at the moment. Next I'm thinking about working with plastics – for my next body of work. And my most recent stuff that I just finished in Portugal, it's all, made out of bent rebar.

A variety. Doing things as one-offs or are they more series of things? Because they feel like one-off objects to me.

A lot of them are one-offs but some of the more simpler works, I'll make in editions. I made these marble cubes, and they're really easy for people to look at and be like, "Oh, that's cool. I want one". So, I'll make a few more. I've made 10 of those thus far. I'll probably make 10 more and stop.

Before we play a track, because I love your music taste, let's talk a bit about your background because I'm really curious. So, you grew up in Houston, but your parents are Nigerian? How the hell did you end up in Texas?

Interesting. My mom grew up in Nigeria. My dad grew up in Nigeria. My mom was a really smart girl growing up, and she got accepted into some program here in London – Hackney, actually. They paid her to go to school and study nursing. Then when the program was done – I don't really know the specifics – she was given three options of places to where she could work. It was like Orlando, New Jersey or Houston. She would be set up. They would have an apartment for her, and she would be working in the hospital. And for some reason, she chose Houston. I don't know. And I guess she was visiting home and there was a connecting flight in New York. My dad was living in New York at the time. So, they met on a plane.

Really cute.

They started talking, and my dad found her again. She had come back to Houston, so he came to visit her and then he never left.

Wow, that's adorable. What was it like growing up there? Turning out to be a furniture designer coming out of Houston. And working in an art context, in itself is a crazy thing...

Actually, I've started noticing that there's actually a very well-respected art community in Houston, and every time I go back, I'm more and more blown away by what's in Houston, like the Rothko Chapel and all of that stuff.

That's pretty, pretty high up there as a good thing!

The Cy Twombly gallery, which is crazy. But growing up in Houston, well, I grew up on the southwest side of Houston. If my mom had not gotten a promotion and a better job, I would have went to the same schools as Beyoncé. I was zoned to that school, that was why the school was famous because Beyoncé went there.

But you went to school with Travis Scott anyway...

In high school, yeah. I like moved to another part of the town and then I met Travis, but it's weird, because all my cousins and stuff, who were like older than me, they were really, really affected by I guess, the city. The way the inner city was configured and structured. So that's where I get a lot of my traditional Houston sort of ratchet influence from because I would always be – they would be picking me up from places and they would have two 15subwoofers in their trunk, just going crazy. And I would just be eight years old. But then, after we moved to another part of the city, and I started going to a predominantly white school, and I think that's where my mind started to open up to a more diverse, eclectic view of things.

I'm going to play one of your tracks. I think that music, just thinking about the subwoofers in a car, makes me... Let's begin the Smerz track. God I love this track, why did you choose it?

I was trying to choose something that's kind of a now feeling. I believe they have a show on NTS. My girlfriend's Norwegian so she introduced me to them, and it's very rare that I listened to a new artist and I'm immediately, like, "Okay, they're good". They just have really good taste, and they blend everything. It's dark and it's light at the same time. I think they are making some of the most interesting stuff right now.

Really love this track. OK, this is Smerz 'Oh My My'.

—

In terms of that hip hop experience of growing up in Houston, I've read that you also credit that as something that influences your approach to design, would you agree? Is there a relationship for you between music and when you're making?

Definitely. I mean, there's a relationship between everything that I'm digesting. I listen to music a lot. And it's inevitable that it ends up in my work. Hip hop, especially. Just how it's almost commanding culture in a way. Black Culture, at least.

Maybe international music culture now. I mean, that is pop music now essentially. I want to talk to you a little bit about the show I saw Milan where you were reworking Rimowa suitcases. That was done with Kaleidoscope magazine, did they commission you to do that?

Yeah, they approached me in February, late February, and the show opened like in April. So, I had to work quickly.

Your approach was really interesting. You basically deconstructed the object and remade it. Remade a suitcase or took it apart and used it as almost the basis to rethink about how to present something in so many different ways. I think there were film elements in there as well?

Yeah, they made a short film with a filmmaker named Sam Hiscox. But my approach was really based on the concept of travel, and what that has awarded me and what like the benefits that it's given me just me having the guts to want to leave Houston at 18 and be like, "I'm going to New York". Then even after New York, being like "I'm going to Tokyo; going to London". No idea what it would be like or who was there. I didn't have any contacts there, but just going and figuring out as I go. I wanted to offer that show as encouragement for other people to do the same. The first object that I made was this – it started as a stepladder. It was supposed to be a stepladder, and then while I was drawing and I was like "Oh, that could also be a bookshelf" and those two things together. The more you read, the more your mind is elevated and elevation with travel. How you learn and how you're exposed to more, which elevates you with travel and sort of how it all tied together. Then I made a miniature version with that too, which everyone loves.

It was also really interesting when you pull apart an object that's really familiar to everyone. Everyone knows what a suitcase looks like. Seeing the inner workings of it, slicing it and seeing the weird foamy sections, seeing how you use this corrugated metal casing. When you're making something are you just experimenting with it, or do you already have an idea? Or do you pull it apart and think, "OK what are my elements? How can I put it together? How does it work?"

I got this big crate from Rimowa, and I had no idea what I was going to make for the show. And I just pulled everything out. I call it knolling. That's the proper word for it, you arrange it all on the ground, neatly. I just started looking at things and trying to figure out, "OK, this could turn into this". I started standing things up and seeing how they stood by themselves. And it sort of just turned into the show.

Really, really interesting work. You've also done a show in London, which was at Soft Opening, which is also reworking the concept of a chair, but it's a sliced electric chair. By the way, it's a really good ad for the show, which is a cartoon about out how to do the Electric Slide. Do you want to tell me what your references are about the electric chair and why you chose to make an object out of that?

Well, it's kind of funny. I met Antonia [Marsh] in December last year, at Art Basel.

This is the curator of Soft Opening, the gallery.

Yeah and then I met her again here in London in February. She said that it would be cool if I did something for the show. I just had that in my mind. OK it's time to start thinking about what it could be. I had these lecture chairs that I had designed. They're like auditorium seating. I had sent them to a friend who is removed from the art world. I like to get their opinion on things because it's sort of uninformed. Right after I sent it, they called me 30 minutes later. I thought they were calling because they saw the drawings, but they were just calling to say hi. I was like, "So I'm guessing you saw the drawings of the lecture chair?" And they're like, "Woah, you're making an electric chair. That's next level". They were really excited, and I was like, "No! No! No! I said lecture chair". And they were like "oh". It was a sort of dead. After that conversation, I was like I guess I've got to make one now. I started thinking about how it could relate. I started thinking about where I could show it and I was like; Antonia wants me to make something. The public display of it relates to how people are executed. Because it's a public thing. You could watch through a glass.

Of course. Actually, the gallery's in a window in Piccadilly Circus tube station. That literally replicates what it's like watching [an execution] – I mean, which I only know from films. I'm happy to say I've never seen that in my life, and I hope I never do. It's crazy, I mean. Coming from state where that's still happening. Is that still happening in Houston?

Yeah, it's happening in a few states in the South.

Was it political? Do you feel like there are political elements in what you're doing?

Definitely. Definitely. I think it's kind of inevitable. I'm a Black male, and a lot of Black males are sentenced to death row. It's not solely just Black males, but the majority of male incarceration. I feel like I completely dodged that whole trajectory that I could have easily fell into. A lot of the guys that I still talk to are sort of entangled in that sort of world. I didn't want it to be so shock value and almost obvious. I'm really into the whole idea of displacement, because I'm not actually. I mean, I am American, I was born and raised in Houston, but I would go home and there'd be African culture at home. It's a confusing thing, because I would go out in the streets and people would look at me and assume that I was Black, but I was sort of being fed different things.

> *This is a really good time to play the Fela Kuti you've brought in. I might add, which is an amazing record. Do you want to tell me why you chose this particular Fela Kuti, and when you first heard it?*

I've been listening to a lot of African music lately, and I'm going for the first time.

> *Wow, incredible, to Nigeria?*

Lagos, yeah. My dad was recently sent back home by the government.

> *Really?*

Yeah like three or four years ago.

> *Wow, that's intense.*

I'm not going to go into the details about why, but I'm going there for the first time. I've sort of built up this imagining myself there. The music helps with that scene.

> *And Fela's is, again, an incredibly political artist.*

Yeah and he would play – my dad would play a lot of Fela growing up. So, Saturday morning chores he would be playing loud Fela in the house.

I love that.

I didn't really know what it was or what it meant or anything like that. But it sounded good. And now I'm 25, and I'm like, oh, OK!

Very appropriate. 'Colonial Mentality' is the track. This is Fela Kuti doing 'Colonial Mentality'.

—

How is Lisbon and why did you choose it? It's apparently the new Berlin, as a girl who has a big thing for Berlin.

I mean first of all, I want to say, I'm not in Lisbon. I land at Lisbon. I live an hour and a half north of Lisbon. It's a completely remote area on the countryside.

Incredible.

It's fields all around this warehouse that me and my girlfriend found. We converted it, completely renovated it. It took us like, four and a half months to do it. It's pretty big. It's like 2000 square feet.

That's quite large... When I look at your work, it feels quite urban in some ways. So, it's really interesting that you're working – obviously Portugal having a very well-known manufacturing history. Everything's made out there – certainly in the fashion industry.

That's one of the reasons I went. I met a marble manufacturer when I was in Basel, and he invited me to come for the first time. I visited his factory. The Rimowa project that I did was actually made in that factory, because I didn't have a studio space when I got there. He had this big warehouse thing behind the factory that he let me work in it. And it just started getting weird, because they were really busy and all the workers had stuff to do and I was always like, "Could you come help me with this for a second?" I was like "Alright, I need to get my own space". That's when we found the other warehouse that we've renovated. That's how I got there.

A huge contrast too.

I think it's just another one of my classic instincts to just go somewhere new and like, say, fuck it. You know? Let's try it.

What have you got coming up later in this year? Are you working on specific projects?

Yeah. I got commissioned to do the big holiday commission in Miami during Art Basel. I'm completely transforming the neighbourhood…

The Design District?

The design district yeah. I'm making these large outdoor climbing frames for children.

Amazing. It's a very different kind of space to be working with, and also maybe a very different kind of audience…

The whole neighbourhood will be covered. All the trees will be covered in these weird alien looking bird feeders that I designed. They'll be hanging from all the trees. I don't know how it's going to – I don't want it to feel too decorative. I want it to still be communicating something…

But that's also engaging with the people who are actually from Miami, which I think is something that doesn't happen very often with events during Basel. And Miami is… I have work there quite often. It's quite a strange city.

It is strange.

It's a weird place.

Even the people's tastes in art. It's like, what's going on?

I mean with a few collections. The Rubells are pretty good at what they collect generally. But yeah, it's a strange city when it's not during the fair. I think it's got quite a weird, empty atmosphere… I have issues with the rich/poor divide. The rich/poor divide there is quite horrific, basically. It's very visceral.

I agree.

Was there something you liked about working particularly with an audience from the city? The birds are an audience that are actually from the city in a way.

I just thought it was a great opportunity to do my first public thing and just see how I like working within that.

You studied art, but you moved into furniture design through set design?

Yes.

How did that process work? That's very installation based.

I think the more solo exhibitions that I get to execute, the more that will come out. But I studied – I wanted to be a film director and slowly – me going against the grain – I was like "I like the sets. I want to focus on the scenes". Then I started looking around, trying to figure out because my mom was forcing me to get a job. I don't like working in places that I'm not interested in. I had to find somewhere where I could be learning what I wanted to learn, but also earning money. There was this fashion show production company Bureau Betak. They did like all the big runway shows for like the big luxury brands, and I worked there for a season. I got picked up by an interior designer and started working within that space. And it slowly just trickled down to the individual object as I progressed, and while I was working for the interior designer, I was simultaneously working as an assistant in an art studio. So those two things just bridged. And I was going to classes, all at the same time.

I was going to say were you at college while you were doing this, because you're only 25 now. This is still a stage – this is what people do after they graduate.

It was crazy. I had to schedule my classes after hours, like after six and stuff. Then I would be in interior design studio like three days a week and the art studio like two days a week. It was crazy.

Let's play another track. It's Koopsta Knicca, did I say that correctly?

No!

Tell me how to say it.

Koopsta Knicca.

There you go, didn't say that properly. 'Smoking On A J'. How did you choose this track?

I love this track. It's kind of like a pep talk for me. The energy of it. It feels like a precursor, the foundations of a lot of what became the Houston sound. This is actually not a Houston artist. He was one of the members of the Three 6 Mafia in Memphis but when I listen to like early UGK and early [DJ] Screw tapes, it feels like a lot of what DJ Paul was doing in Memphis. Then they later connected. The two cities became like very close…

Well, let's have a dose of Southern hip hop then. This is 'Smoking On a J'.

—

Let's talk a little bit, just to finish, about the influence of film on you. If you wanted to be a director, what directors were you drawn towards, and how did that influence what you're making? Do you feel it's influenced where you are now?

It has influenced me because there's a lot of narrative aspects to the objects that I'm making. Even later on, when the object is almost complete, I start to think about how it could work and the story – apart from my story. Stuff like that. But I mean, directors that's really, really…

Or even specific films.

Got that notion across, I would say, like Paul Thomas Anderson. Obviously Kubrick.

Kubrick forever. Literally ever and ever. Every single one of them.

Mmm… Luis Buñuel. He was really great with how he placed everything in the space.

That's a really interesting combination of people as well. I love Luis Buñuel. He is all of those things, which maybe for me, that's an interesting connection to what you do, because there's almost this misuse of something. I'm thinking about something like people sitting down to go to the bathroom and going into toilet to eat. That surreal misusing of an object or a situation that twist on our perceptions. I could see how that could come out in how you're misusing things, but they're still functional in a way. What other functional objects do you want to be creating? Are there specific ambitions you have in terms of making things?

I'm always going to make chairs. I don't know, if you noticed but…

I mean, that is every designer's dream, clearly…

Yeah. That is like the Holy Grail of design. There will always be a need for chairs. I knew this early on. Every chair that I make, it's called 'Chair', and then the Roman numeral for the number it is. The chair that's being shown here in London, the electric chair, it's chair five. It's the fifth chair that I've made.

They're very varied, your chairs.

They are all different.

I've seen ones that are almost like two chairs stacked on top of each other in metal.

Those were the first chairs that I made.

Interesting. And then the other ones, which are almost like slabs of concrete marble held together by...

A strap. Yeah.

They're incredibly different in terms of what they're doing.

All different. I used to think that as good artist or a good designer, you would have to be able to look at their work and know who it was on sight. But that's not really what it is now. You don't have to make something that looked like your last thing. A lot of people work within that constraint...

To the freedom of making different objects, then. I'm going to finish with your last track, which is Jay-Z 'Imaginary Players' with a very good Rene & Angela sample.

I actually like this song, mainly because of the sample. If you listen to Jay-Z's verses, he's not really rapping about anything important, but the sample is so good that he could just sort of talk. He's just talking.

It's really funny. He's one of those people that people can forget him almost within a music context. He's become some other thing now, which is quite strange. You think of him as a businessman more than you think of '99 Problems' or whatever.

Yeah. I love '90s Jay, by the way. It's when he was in his early twenties, his mentality. Listening to that, after who he is in his forties then you listen to who he was in his twenties – he sort of prophesies a lot of the stuff that he's doing now. It's something I want to adopt.

You were living in Brooklyn when you were in New York as well.

Yeah.

Which is again, very different from the middle of nowhere of Portugal.

Marcy also – so same neighbourhood.

Well then it's very apt to be choosing this. This is Jay-Z 'Imaginary Players', thank you very much for coming in Dozie.

Thank you so much for having me.

Liz Johnson Artur

25.01.19

Hi, you're listening to Rough Version on NTS, and my guest this month is Liz Johnson Artur, an amazing and highly underrated London-based artist, focusing on the representation of the African diaspora. She was included in the last Berlin Biennale, where she showed photographs of film and work on textiles and she's currently working on a major, yet to be announced, New York solo show, which continues to place her firmly, if belatedly, in an art world context. Liz, thank you very much for coming in.

Thank you for inviting me.

Okay, firstly, I want to begin at the beginning, as you have quite an unusual background, because you were born in Eastern Germany?

Bulgaria.

Excuse me. So, you're born in Bulgaria, to Ghanaian Russian parents, and you end up growing up in what was then East Germany?

West Germany.

Okay, Give me the background. Tell me the story.

Alright, I'll give you the background. I was born in Bulgaria, and my mom is Russian, and my dad is Ghanaian. So, they met in Bulgaria in '69. And then they had, well, they had me. It was a brief affair, I guess. But my dad had to leave, because he came to Bulgaria as a Ghanaian student. At the time, it was a really small group and there was some kind of incident where suddenly the Bulgarians couldn't guarantee any more security for these, I think it was something like 20 students. So, he had to leave, and my mom stayed in Bulgaria. Fast forward, at some point she decided to try to go to Germany, to West Germany, which at the time wasn't easy being a Russian and coming from Bulgaria. But somehow, the way people do if they have to move, they find ways. She found a way to get to West Germany and to start with we had a tourist visa, and then it was, how do you say – it was an interesting time. If you want me to go into it, it was an interesting time, because this was '69. I think in '68, Willy Brandt, who was the Chancellor in Germany, signed these so called 'East Contracts' They were significant because they opened up the Cold War situation in East-West Germany, but also with the Soviet Union. What it actually meant was that people like us had Soviet passports that could be used abroad. Because officially Soviet citizens were allowed to live abroad. You just had a specific passport, which was very hard to get. Anyway, one thing leads to another, and I got ill. Because I got ill, and my mum, she's a radiologist… The guy who treated me, the doctor, he found out about our situation, because at that point we were illegal, and he offered her a job and through that she got a visa. And that's how we ended up in Germany.

Coming from that German background, you've been in London since around 1990?

I arrived in '91.

How did you end up here and how did that intersect with you starting to take photographs?

Things kind of came together. I never planned to come to London as such, because I wasn't really attracted to… I didn't know much about British culture. Music wise I wasn't into the Beatles. I had a very basic knowledge of England, of the UK. But a friend of mine, he said "Oh, I'm going to London, if I find a place, do you want to come?" And at that time, I still had a Soviet passport, which meant I couldn't really travel anywhere without visas. I was like "yeah, if you find a place in three months, I come" and he did. I had to keep my promise and I came over… the way you have to do things in order to move from one place to the other. I had some friends helping me. I got a tourist visa to come to London. I saved and also, because at the time I was thinking of maybe getting a German passport, because it was really difficult for me to move around. I applied to the Royal College and because of that I could get a grant in Germany, which I applied for. That was connected to applying for German citizenship… All that happened in London. So, suddenly I was in London. I was actually free to travel once I had a German passport. And I kept London as a base because it was a place that I didn't know much about and I think in a certain way, that's a good place to arrive to… I wanted to go to New York, because I went there a couple of years before. That's where I actually started taking photographs.

Why New York? What was it about New York that sparked the urge to do that?

Again, things happen. My mum met this guy, this Russian guy, a Russian Jewish guy. She used to do a lot of trips to try to make business. She went on this trip to the Soviet Union, but they got stopped in Romania and because they had similar passports. They had to spend, I don't think it was in prison, but they couldn't move on. They got to know each other and a year later, I was like "Oh, yeah, I want to go to New York" and she was like "Oh I know someone". She hooked me up. I went to New York and stayed with him. It was funny, because he knew only my mum, so when I arrived, he was like – when you have this desk, where they look for people, and he was looking for me. I came up to him and said "Hello" and he was like "Damn!". Then we took his car, and we drove to Brooklyn. I'd never been to America, so for me America was something I only knew from the movies. He lived on this street and from what I remember it was just Black people. I hadn't actually experienced anything like this, because I've usually travelled to Eastern Bloc countries. Anyway, here I was, and they lived in this house, which was Jewish. That was funny, because we got on because I speak Russian and, on that level, you get to know people. But they had some car, some expensive car outside, so one of the family members was always close to the window, checking if anyone was too close to the car…

New York was wild then.

It was. I think it was. It was interesting to be introduced through this Jewish Russian perspective. I grew up with a Russian mum, so I felt very Russian. They took me to this restaurant, which was in Brighton Beach, and I think, and I've probably said it before, but it's these kinds of moments when you realize… Obviously, I wanted to go out and take pictures and they were like, but you can't go to Harlem or when you go here you go straight to the underground. They had all this advice for me. Then they took me to this restaurant and Brighton Beach is an interesting place… At the time it was the Soviet Union. It was the Ukraine. There's a lot of immigration that happened from that part of Russia to Brighton Beach.

My grandparents.

There you go. For me, being in this restaurant was almost like being in Russia. The party I was with was all like this and then suddenly, they had this sort of performance. I remember four Black women dressed in Ukrainian dresses, singing Ukrainian songs.

Wow.

That was weird. I can only describe it like this. For me, it was a weird moment. I remember a few days later, I also had enough of staying with them, because it was just getting too much. So, I moved to Manhattan. And slowly, I guess it's relevant for my work, because I think there I overcame the idea of can I approach people? In New York, after about two months, or two weeks of not being able to take my camera out, I started taking pictures. In my book, I put a few of those in, because I kind of start there. Then coming to London, I just continued, I guess.

Looking at the work, and your work is amazing, can we talk first about what attracted you in particular to doing individuals? Because it seems to be somehow intertwined with the idea of discovering something, people. It seems very people focused?

Yes. I guess I have to go back again to when I was a kid, and we lived in Bulgaria and then Germany. We always took these trips to Russia to see our relatives. You get on a train and then spend three days on a train. You know you never travel just a few hours, so people come on the trip. You share whoever shares with you the cabin. You meet strangers in a very small space. I've got a lot of memories, when people can just be open and be themselves because there's nowhere else to go for like 24 hours. You meet people, you hear stories, and I think as a kid, it was something that really fascinated me. Also, I think, for me, the thing is the exchange of one to one, which you can have when you take someone's photograph. It is something that really still drives me, I think. I'm an artist, I'm not a politician. I don't need to collect numbers, I do sort of collect people, one by one and I find that quite interesting. Because one by one you meet all kinds. At the same time, I also tried to, in the context of my work, to put it into one. I want to create one big thing out of one plus one plus one.

> *1 + 1 + 1 = a huge thing!*

Yeah, why not?

> *Let's begin with one of your songs. Let's do the Shut Up and Dance track because that also makes me think very much about early '90s in the UK and what was happening then. Why did you choose this track?*

I think it's for two reasons. Because I love Nicolette and I chose tracks that somehow relate to either people I photographed or people I just about got to photograph. I didn't catch Nicolette, but we talked on the phone. Actually, I discovered her music afterwards. I've always loved 'Shut Up and Dance'. I lived just around the corner from here when I arrived in '91, I had a place here, and they were from Hackney as well. It's very much London and because music is a big part of my work. I do like the idea of music that comes from London and Shut Up and Dance and Nicolette definitely does.

> *This is Shut Up and Dance featuring Nicolette, 'Single Minded People'.*
>
> —
>
> *That was 'Single Minded People' by Shut Up and Dance and Nicolette. Let's talk about your relationship to music. You've done more commercial-based work, which to be honest I was again unaware of. How does music influence your private practice, your artwork, in terms of what you do?*

I think I've always had music around me. I've never considered myself a musician. I never played any instruments; I don't dare sing in public. I'm very much a consumer of music. I guess it's always been part of all the places I've been. As a kid, I was really into a Russian version of K-pop, I would say. They're singers, they're not so much rappers. A lot of times it's just a guitar. It's a kind of gangster slang and I really love them, because my cousin used to have them. I really was into that. Then I remember I used to be really mad about Queen. It's hard to think of, but yes. So, for me, music has always been part of something I engaged with. I've always loved it. I think when I started taking photographs, one of the things I love is to be around people playing music. It's just the best setup – having some music and being able to move around with my camera. Music is very important to me. I think it's also something through my commercial work. Working for M.I.A. was the thing where it was both. I photographed her, but also what she involved in her music and her videos are something that I can easily relate to in my archives.

We should probably talk about the concept of what your archive is. Before we do that, can we talk about the amazing images you have done of dancehall clubs, which I assume are in London. How did that come about? What attracted you, because they're amazing images, they were in the Berlin Biennale.

I think most of the things in my archive really come about because I either happen to be somewhere or I heard about something. I think nowadays, it might get easier. Really my approach is, if I hear something about something, I try to find a way of getting in. The dancehall thing – a lot of it came out of doing pirate stations. I was working with a journalist, Sarah Bentley, and she did the research, which for me is really nice, because I'm not good with research. There was someone to research it and I think it was a night, there were a few nights where I just got in somehow…

What year was it?

I think between '95 and '98/99 I did a lot of going to dancehalls through meeting girls at the carnival. Then I hooked up with them later on and they just took me around. I think a lot of it is word of mouth, because in a way what I do is not planned. I don't know where it's going to end up. I definitely don't want any agenda. I wanted it to be just things that I encounter.

If we're talking about late nineties, turning up to a dance club with your camera, what was that interaction like? Because it's not like now, where everything is photographed, and everyone's very used to the idea of performance. It was a very closed world.

It was, but when I look at pictures I think "shit, how did I do that? How did I get it?" But really, the basis of most of what I do has to do with respect and people trusting me. It's not always the thing that you do verbally. When you get into places, there is this thing. Because I work with flash a lot. In dark places… a lot of clubs have other lighting. Once I'm in, I go as far, as close as possible, and see what happens. If someone doesn't like it, they let me know. I move on. But a lot of times in clubs, people are there to enjoy themselves and not be suspicious. They are usually places where people come together for something. It's not something where I get constantly attacked. I can go with the rhythm. It's something that interacts with each other. I just did PDA.

My sister was there on the weekend!

Getting in takes a certain kind of people respecting what you do. Once you're in they let you. I think I have to treat people with respect and that's usually what I get back.

Before we talk about your archive and the concept of the archive, I want to play another track. Shall we play the live version of Gregory Isaacs' 'Night Nurse', which I think is amazing. In a similar way, like London dancehall scene, you really feel like the crowd is really very much part of this. This is at Brixton Academy. How did you come across this version?

I found the record; I've got a bit of a record collection. When I had to move, one of the things I had to do is uncover the things I hadn't seen for years and years. That's one of the records. One of the reasons why

I took this one is because it's a recording in Brixton Academy. I hadn't seen Gregory Isaacs there. I saw some other people there, but it's home ground on a certain level. It's a time before I came to London, but I've been to places where that feeling was there. I have this story with Gregory Isaacs. I didn't know who he was, but someone told me "Oh, yeah, Gregory Isaacs is playing in Burgess Park, you have to go" and so I went. But I didn't really know who Gregory Isaacs was, so when they came off stage I wasn't really sure who to photograph. Anyway, I found out later and I got a picture of him, just from the back really. Then about a week later I was at Carnival, just standing somewhere with my camera and someone taps me on the shoulder. I turned around and it's literally Gregory Isaacs in front of me, and I had my camera. They just wanted to know how to get to a certain stage. I had to take the picture first, but he didn't mind, and I told him how to get there. I got a picture of Gregory. So, I had to put him in the mix.

Here is 'Night Nurse' live at the Brixton Academy by Gregory Isaacs.

—

Let's talk about the concept of Black Balloon Archive. How did you come up with the name? What did you find interesting about your approach to what an archive is?

Just that this name, 'Black Balloon Archive', is really a working title. There was a point where, I don't actually know why. It's something I've been doing for 15 to 20 years without thinking about a name – just accumulated pictures. But I think there was a point where I thought that I needed to focus, because my archive is physical. It's making sense of not just negatives, but I also like to print things. I like to get them out and work a lot in what I call work books. It's like having a framework, so I thought I need a title for it. I was listening to, I think it was Syl Johnson, and he's got a song called 'Black Balloons' and I just liked the first line. It's a blue sky you go out and you are bound to find a black balloon. I felt like that's exactly how I moved. That's where I took the name, and the archive. I am intrigued by archives. I love going to, I wouldn't say archival museums… I find the British Museum too much I have to say, but it plays into it. I think this thing of who collects, who makes the decision, what is important, what isn't – all these things I find quite intriguing… I guess one reason I take pictures is so I can get close to people, but also I get a lot of stories. I collect things and I find them important. I find them important in relation to living in London, photographing people. I did a story in Russia, where I just wanted to find other African Russians. All these things, I think are worth collecting. I'm really intrigued by my own archive. I'm intrigued by what the things are that I feel I need to keep. I don't know if the framework of an archive means I can always contribute to it, but then I also look back on it. I like that play. I guess now I'm showing my work more, because for a very long time I didn't.

It's shocking to me that I found your work through the Berlin Biennale, and you are a London-based artist. Believe me, I'm looking at work. I was actually quite shocked…

I worked in the '90s for magazines like 'i-D', 'The Face' and all these things. I've always done my thing. I must say, I'm glad I did it, the way I did, because I never really got distracted. I could always follow whatever I wanted. When you do jobs, you do get directed, because there's other interests involved. Also, I never looked at my work as art. I'm a photographer, that's where I'm coming from. It's an exploration of the photography that I like, and to see if I can push it a bit further. I think that drives my archive as much as who I want to represent in the archive.

Something interesting, when I see your works in an exhibition context, is your approach to material. You're not just showing photographs straight, though you do that too. You're also working on textiles, almost like a layered collage. How did you start experimenting with that? Because it's really successful.

I think again, this is a natural process. It's part of digesting photographs. It is part of making sense of them, because you know every photographer has an archive. That's the nature of what you do. But the question is what you do with it, whether you just accumulate, which photography, especially today, can lead to. I think also it's how I look at things, how I try to investigate things. I use the camera, so the result is a picture. I think, the things that I do, where I put things on material or anything… I love printing, I love black and white printing. I never really liked colour printing.

Well, your colour things have a monochrome vibe. They've got colour in them, but they're not actually colour, if that makes sense.

When people ask me, I say "first of all, I am by heart, a black and white photographer", that's where I come from. I think when I say that I think it has a lot to do with how I compose pictures and how I like to think about light. I usually see a picture in black and white. And then the colour surprises me when I see the negative or I see it in colour. Where was I going?

Materiality?

I say it's a natural process, because I started at some point, I use a little bit of digital, but I've always worked analogue simply because it makes sense to me. I really discovered photography through the darkroom. That's the process that I really enjoy. To give it up wouldn't have made sense and I think out of this printing in the darkroom, sometimes you print beautiful prints, sometimes you do funny prints, all these kinds of things. I guess I wanted to materialize photographs because that's how I deal with them. I have touched a lot of photographs. I don't just look at them. I suppose now that I show my work, I feel like I want to show how I think photography plays a part in people's lives. Really, they have a physical presence. I think I like to play on that physical presence simply because there's so many things you can do if you think of something – how it feels and how it looks and trying to put those two together. I think it's interesting.

Let's play another track. This is a really good version of Sun Ra 'Space is the Place' from a specific album, which I'm going to look up… Tell me about your how you first heard about Sun Ra? I mean it's such a good version.

I have to tell this story because Sun Ra is special to me because I discovered him, or the first time I heard the word Sun Ra, was as

I said, when I lived with my mum next to the hospital in what you call nurses' homes. One night, I think I was 12 or 13, I wake up at one o'clock at night and there's this big noise and my mum is going crazy… She's says, "I'm going down there" and there was a guy who lived underneath. So, she's going down and I think I better go with her because she can really make a drama. We go down and we get to the door and it's really loud and my mom knocks on the door and this guy opens up. I think he was a nurse in the hospital, I'd seen him before, and my mum goes "What do you think you are doing?!" And he said, "but it's Sun Ra!" What I remember is his face. The way he said, "but it's Sun Ra!" and I thought "damn, Sun Ra!" and all I could hear was this noise. I couldn't make anything out of it. Fast forward to the first time I went to New York, and I was staying with these people, and I just remember Sun Ra was this guy being so happy. Looking so happy. This girl I was staying with, she's says "There's a gig in this place, do you want to come?" And it was Sun Ra.

Wow.

They played in this… I can't remember the name of the place, but I researched it and they had a residency there. It was a place where the band was all over, and I've never experienced something like this. I was like damn, Sun Ra. I remember Sun Ra. When I came to London, I saw Sun Ra. It was one of his last gigs in London, and I got a picture, so I'm quite chuffed I've got a picture of Sun Ra, as well.

Another good one for your archive. This is a version from the album 'The Antique Black'. This is Sun Ra and his Archestra and 'Space is the Place'.

—

That was 'Space is the Place'. What a good version. You are also working with video work. The video piece that you shared in Berlin really captured a lot of the feelings around politics at that time, but in a really intimate, personal way. Do you want to tell me about it? Why do you want to make video, and what was your aim with the piece?

Video or film in general is funny because I've always been very attached to the still image. I've never really had this urge that I need to make a film, or I need to make videos. But when Berlin asked me if I wanted to do a new piece – that was in March – I said yeah, I'll do something. Off the top of my head, I said "yeah, I'll make a video". I was a bit under pressure, because technically I'm so focused on stills that for me video just doesn't come…

It is such a learning process.

It is and I think it's also a thing where I have to learn to work with other people. I'm so used to working on my own from start to finish… I have a really good friend and we've worked together before, just playing around with videos. I had this thing to do a video and I'd combine because I still like to bring stills in. The video just came about. There was a point last year, I think around March, where I moved from my old studio to my new studio… I just thought I'd do a stretch of three months and see what happens. See who I meet. The characters in the video are really – I met the person who showed me my flat. She was really nice, and we had a chat and then she picked up her phone and said "Oh look. We have this boy, my aunt is fostering him, but he is so good at drawing". She showed it on the iPhone. I was like "Damn, I want to meet him". I think just to sum it up, I wanted to have voices from London, because since Brexit. Grenfell. There are so many things. The Windrush. These are all things that I think, for someone who has been in London for 25 years, is shocking. I mean, never mind the people who it actually happened to. It's a lot of the people that I've met. Windrush, when I heard about that, I have a friend who has been thinking for years whether to get a passport because he's been living here without a passport. You would never question "is he Londoner?" Suddenly, I was like "they could deport you?".

Wow.

I think those kinds of things played into it. I tried to find born and bred [Londoners] and bumped into them. I thought, I need some voices from Peckham, but I also wanted them to be real. There's the sequence of the man getting arrested. I just happened to be there with my camera, because I don't run around with my camera all the time. But if you walk around South London, Brixton, you bump into situations like this. Simple as that. I think it was a collection of those voices. I have to say also, because at the time, I sometimes take pictures for Paul Bradshaw, who does the 'Straight No Chaser' magazine. He asked me to photograph Keshi Kanoshi, who is a saxophone player and composer. That was when I was finishing the video. I asked her if she could compose the music, which I think was what made the video really work, because she connected all these things. I think that's what hooked me on to working with video – that I can use music. That's a very nice thing.

Will you make another film?

I will. Because I have a show coming up in New York next year. I will make a video. I will make one that I've actually started and then kind of left. I did it in 2010 when I went to Moscow and shot Afro-Russians. Then it's something that I had to leave and couldn't work on and now I'm going to work on this. That's going to be in the show. I'm going to do another piece which is photographs and sound. The thing about showing for me, I try things out that I used to try out in my workbooks. Sound and video is something that is actually nice to do. I think I'm more interested in it because I can approach it as a photographer.

Where's the exhibition?

In the Brooklyn Museum.

Wow, good. That's a nice level of exhibition. We like this.

I've never been there. But when they asked me, I thought I better Google what it is like, and it looks impressive from the pictures!

Well, just to finish off, because that was it. It goes so fast. Let's put on your Larry B track. How did you come across Larry B?

That's my new obsession, Larry B. It happened this summer through someone I met in Berlin. I met Larry, Jason, Misha… I just bumped into them. I started taking pictures – it's been really nice, because I got to know them. A lot of times when I photograph people, it's a moment. I guess, in a certain way, that's the only way I can do it. But sometimes you get to know people. I think when Brexit happened, I was very angry and pissed off, but I think what it did was make me look at London in a different way. One of the things about London is people, and there's always something happening, and discovering PDA, discovering people that could be my kids in a way. To see their energy. I think it's very hard for that generation as well. When I came to London, you could find a place. I never had to kill myself to pay rent. Now it's very hard to find a room and not kill yourself. I think Larry B because I think it's where it's at.

It's amazing. This is 'I Gotta Pick Myself Up' by Larry B, and thank you very much Liz Johnson Artur for coming in.

You are welcome.

Michael Landy

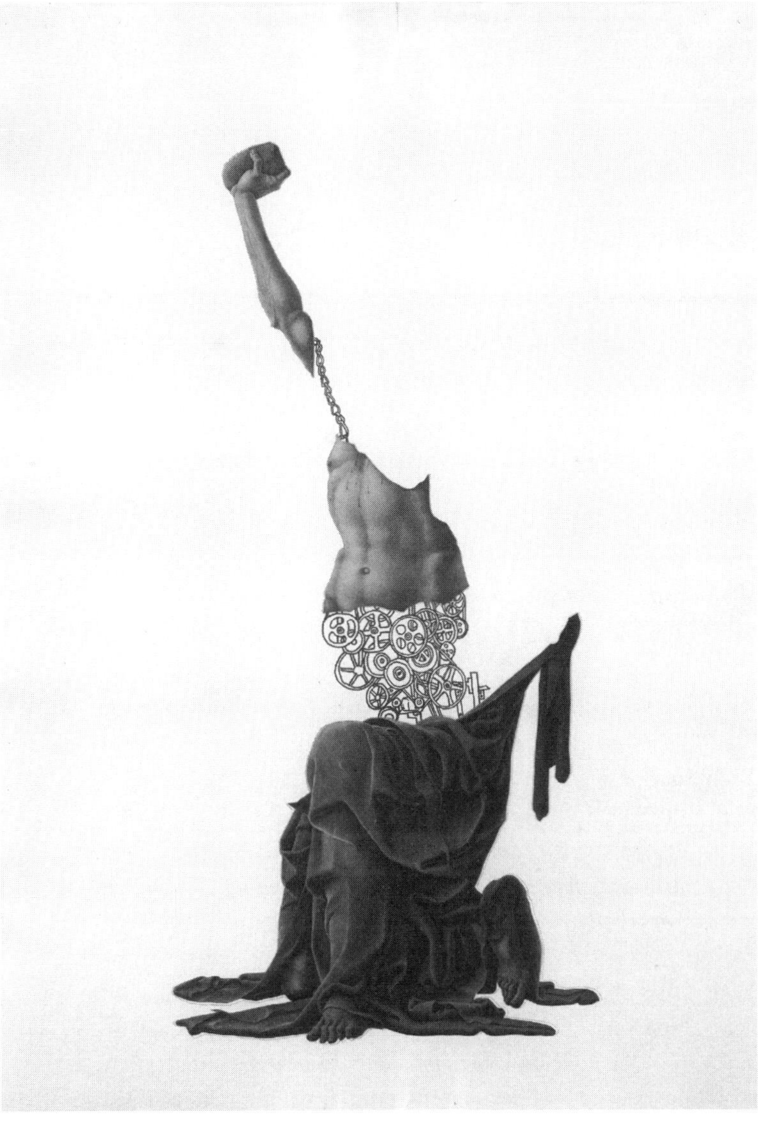

Saint Jerome Beats His Breast, 2012.

22.02.19

Hi, you're listening to Rough Version on NTS, and this month's guest is Michael Landy. He's a British artist best known for an enormous piece he did in 2001, called 'Break Down', where he destroyed all his things. He's also exhibited at South London Gallery, the National Gallery and many international places. Lastly, the Baltic Triennial. And he is a member of the Royal Academy of Arts, an actual RA. Michael, thank you very much for coming in.

Not at all.

In this post-Christmas, post New Year revival moment.

Yeah, we're both saying it's taken a while just to get everything in its gear.

I find in winter my brain is slow like a clock that's kind of losing its battery.

It's winding down. Well, now we're about to wind back up again.

We'll manage! Which is actually quite a nice segue into talking about some of your work in particular. I want to start by talking about your 'Saints Alive' project. I loved it so much. I'm such a fan of what you did that I just think that's a project that we should discuss more. You were doing a residency at the National Gallery in London. This is four years ago?

Yeah, four or five years ago.

It's an amazing combination between animatronics, collage, drawing and art history. How did you end up approaching it? Was it all drawing on the collection of National Gallery?

Yeah. I was an artist in residence at a national gallery for like three years. First year I didn't actually do anything at all. I just had to go and look at the collection because I didn't know the collection wasn't something I would – I just didn't know. First thing I did was just spend all my time looking at all the paintings at National Gallery. And there was one room by… oh my god, my bright mind. Sorry, if it was the fifth or sixth of January be working much better than the fourth of January, but by a Renaissance… Carlo Crivelli. I knew I'd get there eventually. There's a whole room of Carlo Crivelli and I thought who is Carlo Crivelli and then subsequently two years later I actually made a lot of sculptures based on some of his paintings. Basically, they're saints, iconography of saints. That's what really pulled me in really. Signs and symbols of particular saints.

Is that because like you come from – I remember reading that your mum's Catholic?

Yeah, Mum and Dad are Catholic.

Was that part of the draw?

Not really. I was intrigued by Christian iconography – sign, symbols, what they mean and then there was a whole book called 'The Golden Legend'. It's the legend of all the saints and all their stories. I became really intrigued by that really and that's what really pulled me in. Obviously, I don't paint so and obviously the vast majority of National Gallery is 99.9% is painting. I had to come at it a different way. I've wanted to make them come alive and that's why I called it 'Saints Alive', because I wanted to make these saints come alive again for a whole new audience. Because we've lost our faith in a sense. I had a show in Mexico and in Mexican Catholicism saints are still very much alive. They have like drug dealers' saints. They create their own saints. I really liked the idea of just making the saints come back alive for a whole new audience. I had like Saint Jerome, he'd like beat his chest with a rock and he'd like take his mind off the dancing girls of Rome. Because he had sexual hallucination he had to beat himself. His best mate was a lion, and they lived in a cave together. He would read the Bible. You find out all these amazing facts about all these people – men and women because you have virgin martyrs like Saint Apollonia. It's always some Roman chap falls in love with them, and they say "no, I'm not interested in you" and ends up with them having their heads chopped off.

The work was quite violent but so was the stories.

They're really violent. People being tortured. Saint Apollonia, she's the patron saint of dentists and she has her teeth extracted. That's how you can tell who Apollonia is because she holds a pair of pliers with a tooth. Saint Catherine. She was tortured on a wheel. You can always tell Saint Catherine cause she's holding a wheel or there's a heel in the background. I mean becoming an artist in residence and it's Velasquez, Titian – all the great and the good. And you're sort of judged in that context, which is also quite frightening.

It's hard competition!

It's a tough gig.

Did that also lead to you having a retrospective in Switzerland at the time?

Yeah. Tingley, Tangley, Tingauly. He's called all sorts, at the Tinguely Museum. It's all based on Jean Tinguely, the Swiss kinetic artist, died in the mid '90s I think. I saw an exhibition of his when I was a textile student at Loughborough at the Tate back in 1982 and I just absolutely loved it. People were throwing balls into this machine and would pop out and stuff was made out of junk, and it would fall apart. It was my epiphany moment of what art could be. As I said I was studying textiles and suddenly just all this junk coming alive. You put your foot in the foot pedal and it would come alive or not because sometimes they didn't work as well. Then 30 years later as a middle-aged man, that's the kind of feeling I wanted to recreate. The feeling I had then but for a whole new audience at the National Gallery. That's the connection in a sense in a way.

His stuff is almost like musical instruments as well. That also came across in your work. There would be a rhythm of the banging and clanging...

Yeah, sounds like Saint Jerome would beat his chest with fiberglass rock. There are lots of sounds. Some parts of the sculpture were made out of junk and the rest of it was cast fiberglass, but all based on saints from the National Gallery collection.

Is sound something that you've incorporated in your work before?

Not really. When I did 'Closing Down Sale' back in 1992, there was audio like "step inside look around place, everything must go and is reduced. Don't be shy cause I was shy when I was a little girl".

Was that a voiceover?

Voiceover, yeah. "Too late, too late will be the cry. The bargains you wanted will have passed you by. Don't be shy because I was shy when I was little girl". What else was there? "Too late, too late will be the cry for 515 or 616 or 66 we said we treat you and by golly by George treat you we jolly will do. For today we're going to clear the right way. Yes, we're mad. No, we're not joking. Crazy! Crazy! Crazy! Crazy! Crazy! Crazy! Crazy! Do yourselves a favour, and everyone gets a bargain here today. Bargains! Bargains! Bargains! They will not be repeated, and they will never be seen again". You've got to give it a bit of oomph.

How on earth do you remember that?

I destroyed all that in 2001. I destroyed all the audio tapes. So, I had to patch it all back together via memory.

Was it you doing the audio of that in that original piece?

Yeah, it was. Because that was on a tape cassette recorder. It would drive the gallery staff mad. They told me afterwards, they would switch it off when I left the gallery.

Rebellious!

It would just drive them insane.

I want to play one of your tracks, and I'm going to play the Purcell because for me, that seems like a nice segue from the Renaissance work. Do you want to tell me why you chose this specific Purcell piece?

Because I created a Brexit kiosk in Latvia, Riga Biennale during the summertime, and I played 45 hours of British music. And I didn't know the Purcell. It was one of the tracks from my Brexit kiosk.

How did you put the music together?

It was all sorts. Classical, Welsh miners singing, 'When I'm Cleaning Windows', all sorts of bitter punk. I mean not all strictly British, but predominantly British music. Marching music. A plethora of music. 'I'm Back in Britain' by Bruce Forsyth. All sorts of slightly jingoistic because that's the idea of the kiosk. It looked like a leave campaign thing that just landed from outer space and ended up in Latvia. I customized an ex-Soviet kiosk, and I had this sign going around it saying open for business, because that's what Theresa May says. "Britain's still open for business" and I painted in Union Jack colours and sold British products. Marmite. All sorts of British stuff that mostly I connected from the '70s. I sold merchandise – hard Brexit condoms, tote bags, fridge magnets – all anti EU rhetoric taken from British tabloid press over the last 30 years. Also, I had British newspapers and some foreign newspapers, centered around when we, when we first voted to leave and then other stuff dating back 30 years. Like 'Up Yours the Laws' and things like that.

It's not even a metaphor for what this country is. It is actually just exactly it. That's Britain, isn't it? Britain is a little kiosk.

It's an idea of ourselves in a situation of the world. Napoleon allegedly said we were all shopkeepers. It's like this nation somehow has a bigger sense of itself than he really has. That kind of pomposity, I guess.

Well to honour your Brexit kiosk. This is Henry Purcell? It is Henry Purcell, 'King Arthur' by the English Baroque soloists and John Elliot Gardiner. Here you go.

—

That was Purcell doing 'King Arthur'. Let's talk about your idea of destruction. I'm thinking of your recent show at Thomas Dane, where you crushed your things, and the 'Art Bin' at South London Gallery where you throw away things. We can talk about 'Breakdown' later. Do you want to tell me about what you like about the destructive element of those things?

I think like we were talking about Tinguely and he has this auto destructive analysis, in a sense. So partly, I'm responsible for it and I'm partly not responsible for it. I think it's about order. Ultimately, I like to order things. Like my most recent show, Thomas Dane gallery, I use the gallery inventory, a lot of particular bodies of work and some of them were from 'Saints Alive'. But that also is all the things that remains unsold. The stuff that remains on the galleries inventory.

Stuff in storage, basically?

Stuff in storage and there is an awful lot of art in storage. I'm interested in leftovers and what we value and the worth we give to things. So, I decided to make each body of work into a cube. I put all these drawings, particular drawings, into a hydraulic press and kind of glued them and pressed them all together with 50 tons of pressure. I'd make all these minimalist cubes. I think I had about 17, all in told. The Saint Catherine wheel that I showed at the National Gallery all those years ago, that you could actually spin the wheel. This big ginormous two-and-a-half-meter diameter wheel with the legend of Saint Catherine…

You crushed it! No!

I crushed it. I crushed it and made it into a cube.

That's quite heartbreaking. I really liked the work.

I think 'Art Bin', which I did at South London Art Gallery, was a celebration of – I called it a kind of monument to failure. I think all artists understand failure because that's part of the creative process. It wasn't strictly failures because artists were intrigued because failure is an odd idea. Obviously, it could be a technical failure. It could be all sorts of different failures. I wanted to celebrate failure, creative failure, so created this huge 900 square cubic meter transparent bin and I asked artists, both well-known artists and unknown artists, to throw their art into the bin. That's what we did!

And then you just took it to like the dump?

Then it all went to landfills.

Were there any dump searches going through there looking?

Half my artistic career is in a landfill site somewhere.

In all these cases and I'm going mourn your Catherine wheel piece just for myself. You put all this effort into the creation of these things, what do you find interesting about removing them? Is it a recycling of energy? Do they just become material to you in some way then?

Probably all those things, actually. I guess with my exhibition 'Scaled Down', where I cubed all my works, I mean you're literally turning them into another work in a sense. I'm not really getting rid of them. Obviously in 'Art Bin', most artists threw works in because they didn't want them anymore for whatever reason. They didn't want to have them around and it was a collective celebration of failure. I think it's all dependent on which project really, we talk about… I did 'Scrapheap Services' a fictitious cleaning company that got rid of people no longer playing a useful role in life back in '95. That was destructive but putting people onto the scrap heap and then forgetting about them for thirty years until they vote for Brexit. I mean that's also a very destructive thing. I think that's why I've always been caught up with whether it's a detail in a face or detail on a plant or detail on side my parents' house. I think they're all things worth – whether we're getting rid of a human being or a human being that has had an accident and what value we give to them. I think that's all the things I've always been interested in. Even Christian iconography, Brexit. That's obviously an ongoing thing. All those issues.

I like the idea in a way of you being haunted by the people that you threw on the scrap heap in the mid '90s.

Yeah. I mean, at that juncture, you know, we were coming from a post-industrial to more service led industry and we have basically shut all those towns down. And then we forgot about them for thirty years.

Your father was a miner.

Yeah, my father was a tunnel miner. He came over cause the studios where we're talking are near Ridley Road. My mum used to take us there as kids because I was born in Hackney. My dad came over here in the late '50s and built bits of the underground. He had an industrial accident in the probably mid '70s. So, I made a piece of work about that years later at Tate Britain, where I basically showed the intersection of my parents' house. We'd moved to Essex by this time. I showed the front and back of their house and then some videos I made of my father. Basically, was like scaled copy of our family house, the one on Kingswood Road in Ilford, Essex.

Do you feel that experience has informed some of the politics of what you're doing? I'm thinking of your next track, The Wolfe Tones. Which is very political.

Well, I'm Irish, Catholic. I think this song might have been banned in the 1970s. My parents, they came here to make – that's Brexit as well. They came here to make a better life for themselves really. They came here because Ireland at that juncture had nothing to offer them. So, they came here to send money back home, but also to make better lives for themselves. That has a value unto itself. In Brexit, in my Brexit kiosk, I mean Latvia is also an EU member now. People come to this country to make better lives for themselves. So, when it came to the vote, I thought, I can't stop the free movement of people. You can't stop people and it's a ridiculous idea in the first place anyway, and who am I to stop because my parents benefited from that.

It's also the song you've chosen it's a really strange song, because it's quite happy and cheerful and talking about the troubles in Northern Ireland.

It's dragging children from their beds. My grandmother refused to come over to his country because her husband came to work here back in the '50s I guess, but she refused to come because she hated the British so much for what they'd done to Ireland. So, this is a sort of taster of that.

This is 'The Men Behind the Wire', from The Wolfe Tones album 'Let the People Sing'.

—

That was The Wolfe Tones 'The Men Behind The Wire'. Let's talk about the biggie, which you're best known for. The Artangel project. At C&A – that underrated shop which dies. That is so much of a moment. Obviously, you destroyed all your belongings. You had nothing. It was all done in front of 50,000 people. What was the aftermath of that like actually? I mean the process itself is obviously weird and disturbing and strange. Like you become a little lone person with nothing around you. How did that feel? What was the emotional aspect to that, once you remove yourself from the conceptual idea of making it?

Liberating actually. I mean it partly took me four years to get to that juncture where I could destroy my worldly belongings in front of complete strangers. But I find it really liberating. I was very euphoric for quite a long time you know. I didn't make art for about a year afterwards. I felt a real sense of liberation. It wasn't like I was going to change my life. I didn't change my name. It wasn't like I was going to go to a desert island and exist there. In no time at all I had to buy a toothbrush and all those kinds of tedious things that I would have to do. I rationalized the whole thing for the two weeks because I mean that was the artwork in a sense. People came along and they witnessed it and they brought their own feelings of ownership and worth. I destroyed my whole record collection there. I made an inventory of everything I owned at the same time. I played all my music throughout the whole two weeks. I had vinyl music and we have a record player, and we had a resident DJ who would play all my records. And then one by one, we would destroy them but it really helped the whole work a day, structure of the day. It lifted the whole mood really…

Do you remember any particular songs that you were playing?

We were playing 'Breaking Glass' by David Bowie in the morning, and I think 'Love Will Tear Us Apart' by Joy Division as the last song. That became a kind of ritual. Dave who was destroying my Saab – a mechanic destroying my Saab 900. He would shout "Is there life on Mars?" I made a whole inventory of everything I own. Some of those were my record collection.

Do you ever miss any of the things? Was there any loss? Or did it just disappear, and you felt nothing about it?

It's hard to feel at that point. Because you're also curating the whole thing in a sense as the two weeks go. It unravelled as we did it. I thought it was just the idea of trying to destroy all 7227 items. I didn't realize that's what we would set out to do. So, the first week was actually quite slow and methodical. Then we had to speed up because it was based on a recycling facility. So, everything was done in great care. But we were falling behind, which sounds ridiculous, so we had to speed it, ratchet it all up. Because I thought it was just the idea that we were trying to do. But it became a thing that the public wanted to see or done in time.

So, you were pressured to destroy everything! You were just going to attempt it.

"We want to see the whole thing". People wanted to see all the stuff, all the remains, all the stuff that had been taken apart in front of the shop windows. C&A on Oxford Street, which is now a Primark. It's a really wonderful place to put on something like that. Oxford Street is where people go to shop. They go to consume. They come to watch some bloke take all this stuff apart. And that was what made it. Also, it's not in a gallery. People would just come. They would try and steal things. They did steal things. They'd offer me money for things. I destroyed holy water. I don't even know how we did that. I had old love letters. I had like things of like material value, like my car, but then we had bits of moldy plastic that had fallen off my VCR that also had to be given an inventory number, as well. It's a whole myriad, whether it's financial, family pictures. Like I was saying earlier on, people talked about if they run into a fire, what do they save? It's not normally the VCR. It's normally family pictures, things of sentimental value.

Afterwards, I remember, let's say 10 years later...

Did you go to see it at the time?

No, I didn't. I used to go to C&A and I had a snood bought from me by my mum there. If you remember the days of snoods. My grandfather lived near there. I lived around the corner when I was like 10. I was probably too little.

Do you still have the snood?

I do not have the snood anymore. A snood is not a useful item. Most people don't even know what a snood is.

I'm saying I'm struggling to recollect what it is.

A snood is like a scarf hood combo. It was a scarf that would be like a thing around your neck that you could put over your head.

That's what I thought it was. But I wasn't completely sure.

It's a terrible thing. It's a very unattractive item. But when you're little it works. I remember 10 years later; someone burned all their stuff maybe inspired by The KLF and there was a really angry public response to it. London was really different in the early '90s. It wasn't the conspicuous affluence. No, it wasn't all about designer stuff. It was pretty shabby. There were lots of abandoned buildings. It was a different city in some way. Do you think the reactions you had then were different than, say, if you did something like that today?

I'm not sure. No, I think that'd be pretty similar. I think people on the whole, cause I can't wait as you thinking British people were actually alright, on the whole. Because people came to it quite openly.

Obviously, some people were angry about what I was doing, destroying all this stuff, when I could have given it to charity, or whatever. But I think on the whole people honestly wanted to get to understand it a bit more. And people were very generous, because like I said, we could have spent a whole time just talking about it for two weeks and not actually done anything, because people really wanted to talk about it. And as an artist, you fantasize about doing those projects where people really respond or want to talk about it. I've done exhibitions where no one talks about it. Where it may not even get reviewed. It may not even exist. And then you think "why have I done that? What was the point?" So having something where people really respond to, it is always what I dreamt about. I've been wanting to be an artist, probably since I was a kid. And I didn't even know what that was. I used to draw people in pubs. Put anything in front of me and I would draw it, and that's the beginning part before I could even know what it was. I just like copying stuff.

After this project and in general throughout your practice drawing is still a really big part of what you do.

Yeah, I didn't do it at Goldsmiths. I went to college at Goldsmiths. But I think afterwards, I started to draw again, but not whilst I was at college. Interestingly enough…

You were in a full conceptual context…

It was conceptual.

Goldsmith's didn't like drawing then.

It was actually quite an open school in some respects. But it wasn't, for me – only weirdos did live drawing.

And on that note, we're going play your last song, since we have Bowie references… Why did you choose this Bowie song?

I love David Bowie. When I went on my foundation course, all the young, beautiful people all played David Bowie. I was very dismissive of David Bowie when I was younger, but then between ages 16 and probably 21, that's all I played.

Basically, inspired by the young and beautiful people.

Because I wanted to be young and beautiful. But I was young. It's just the other bit I was still working on…

Yeah, well inspired by beauty. This is 'Space Oddity', the 2015 remastered version by David Bowie, and thank you very much for coming in Michael.

Thank you. I've enjoyed it.

Appau Jnr Boakye-Yiadom

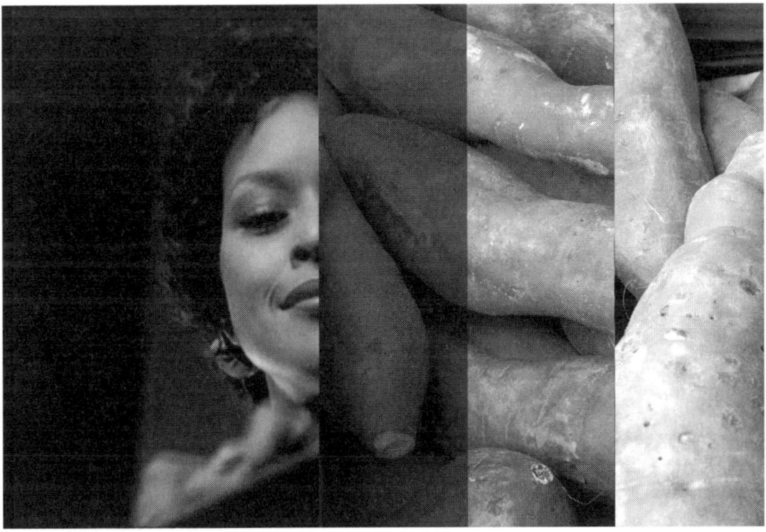

Carmine Lake 2015.

27.03.19

Hi. You are listening to Rough Version on NTS, and my guest this month is Appau Jnr Boakye-Yiadom. Thank you very much for coming in. Appau is a postgrad from the RA he was showing last year in my favourite exhibition, which I talk about all the time, which is 'Michael Jackson: On The Wall'. He was also in the Dakar Biennale, showed as part of V22 Young London and currently, just did a show at Jerwood, in Union Street, in London. Appau, how are you?

I'm good thank you. I'm good.

Cool. Thank you very much for coming in.

Thanks for inviting me.

Let's talk about music, and in particular, drumming seems to be something that's really central to a lot of your work. Do you want to tell me about how you started working with that? What appealed?

Yeah. I guess it was just the fact that with drumming, there's a universal language. I'm just trying to think within my practice of other linguistic, no, sorry – not linguistic but other forms of language. Drumming is one of them. Also, with using drumming, it's the fact that it works on impulse. There's this idea as well, that I'm trying to push things towards a deep rooted affect, in some sort of level of experience in which you're… So, the artwork, hopefully, eventually, becomes an experience rather than just you're a viewer that's come to see something. Something has been performed for you like an immobile cultural viewer. You're actually involved, and it requires time.

I mean, also the thing about rhythm, and actually music, you could argue, full stop, it actually has a physical reaction, not just a cerebral one.

Yes.

It actually makes you have a physical movement in some way or feel things in a different way.

Yeah. I guess you get to work, it pushes some level of intuition with it as well. Especially when you're working with rhythm. You go with your intuition in some respects. And most cultures, I'm thinking about within other works. I'm using drums from other cultures, because I'm quite interested in how most cultures have their versions of a drum. How they are used in a lot of, in many cultures, as a spiritual sign, because it's this extension of the spiritual in some respects, because as I say it requires some level of time in which to go into this transcending flow of it.

The way that you've used it, let's say in your last installation I saw at Jerwood, you activate the installations you make that incorporate rhythm with live elements too. How did that start happening – the idea of pre-recording, and then live, and then reworking an installation with those elements?

With the Jerwood Space, the exhibition that was there, I think, in particular, it's just the fact that you have this link to performance, in some way. Because performance is this thing that… I don't know, in some respects, in cultural respects – I'm coming from it as like a Black performer in that sort of way. This idea of expected performance and creating some level of distance from that. You're never getting the physical performance, it's almost an after effect. Just to not only hint on that level of performance, or expected performance, but also to just, as I say, to try and step away and find ways to experiment and step away from this idea of having, of looking at someone performing. You encounter this level of scrutiny that is added to that.

You're basically removing yourself as a way of removing expectation? Or highlighting the fact that people have preconceptions?

Yeah, highlighting the fact that people have preconceptions. Just trying to move away from this idea of trivializing experience. I think when through expectation and through that level, I think sometimes experiences or what people are trying to convey ends up being trivialized and so it becomes part of – it's compartmentalized into something that people feel comfortable with, or they understand. It fits into those spaces. Whereas the actual sophistication in which it's working on, is sometimes overlooked. That's what I want to connect with almost.

> *I mean, it's quite interesting at the same time, other things that you use element wise, like you'll use images of fruit and vegetables that often again, have cultural references or expectation around them. Like, let's say, okra, that kind of thing. But also, that's not the only fruit and veg I've seen. You like fruit and veg. How did that start and is that something you see as a continuation of those ideas around like how cultural identity is formed through expectation?*

I suppose with the okra, it's the fact that these things are very readily available. I suppose it does have that link to it, that they're available. They have this link it's this interlinking culture in which they embody, in some respects. Okra and black bean, which is there, and there's this rice shelf. These are all obviously things that are from the outside world, from outside the UK, but they're very available. Stepping away from ideas of singular culture, and singular narratives, and just showing how they're interconnective in some respects. Whereas using the drum, particularly the use of the drum kit, is another way of linking those ideas. You have the drum kit, which obviously comes from different, the whole drum kit is parts of single percussions that have been brought together. They have that link to them. And they all, although they've come from different parts of history, or different parts of the world, they have a new use to them now.

> *They become a united one thing in a strange way.*

Yeah, yeah.

> *I mean, this brings me – the first track that we have to play if we're going to be talking about drums is Art Blakey and the Jazz Messengers. And you've chosen 'Caravan', do you want to tell me about this track?*

Yeah, because like I say, I like this idea of versioning, which is often displayed in culture. It's a way of moving away from this singular narrative, which is something that can be quite prevalent, within a Western vocabulary it can be quite a prevalent thing these single narratives. Or where that's not, where things don't seem as relevant, they might not seem as important. And that's the sort of thing I'm thinking about. I just like the fact that 'Caravan', Art Blakey's version, is a version of an original which is done by Duke Ellington and Tito… forgotten his last name.

I'm thinking of all the Titos I've ever heard of – Puente?

So, there's various versions. Where you have different versions, I like the idea that they are drawn upon different narratives. Art Blakey's version of it is very – it's got a lot of energy to it. And it relates to other works I've been working on and other conversations I've been having, so similar to this thing that I've been working on with another artist, or a conversation we've been having, and we've been creating ideas around. It's the artist Ima-Abasi Okon. We've been working on this project where we had Barry White's 'I'm Going To Love You A Little More Baby'. This track's been sampled so many times, and we draw upon the samples as different perspectives of certain experiences maybe or just using that as a foundation to display a new voice in a way, a new version. So that's why I was really drawn to Art Blakey's version. Also 'Caravan' is something that's used quite a lot within drum standards, I think. I'm not sure why.

The joy of jazz. This is Art Blakey and Jazz Messengers and 'Caravan'.

—

Another element you use in a lot of your work is also video, using a lot of archival material. I'm really obsessed with the repeated use of one of my favourite film directors, Russ Meyer. You do this tiny, tiny little clip from the film 'Up', where it's a black screen and a face is revealed of this woman with like a small afro. Do you want to tell me two things, firstly, why Russ Meyer, the man who has a glorious taste in breasts? And also, what particularly you like about like editing and the use of the archival?

Okay. Start with the first question – Russ Meyer. It was the fact that… there's a certain level of cinematography that he uses, obviously. He has to convey the sort of innuendo that goes along with making erotic or sexploitation movies. There's that level in which there's a real focus on close up shots, not necessarily of people, but of objects in relation to each other.

I mean, they're really weird. Because it's self-taught weirdness, in a lot of ways.

Yeah. He's also from a certain generation of directors. He was a veteran from the Second World War, in America.

Totally right, yeah.

You were allowed to go to art school if you were a veteran and convey some sort of practice within university. So, he decided to go into film and directing and all that angle. I assume he wanted to go into like Hollywood and that scene, and then he went into this whole sexploitation thing. I mean, there's certain areas of it that's quite beautiful. I'm not just saying…

No. I mean you didn't show Francesca 'Kitten' Natividad – I know all their names, all the actresses. I'm such a fan. You didn't show that. What you chose was actually just a woman's face. The motif you're going for is also an interesting angle. The way you've installed it in different shows, you've used the same motif. Is that correct?

It's always been used for that particular body of work… He always shows women quite strong.

Oh, yeah. The women are really powerful in Russ Meyer films.

Yeah. They take the centre stage. They're not just a side part to a guy.

Do you always show them like higher up? Because it was quite strange place to see a video screen – two meters off the ground, looking down at us as a viewer. That's a really interesting dynamic. Whereas in other pieces you've done, screens or speakers, where it's on the floor. I'm thinking at V22. It was really vibrating. It was almost like the floor was vibrating when you used that. What do you like about the up and downness of things?

I suppose with that particular piece is the fact that she unzips. She is actually unzipping a guy's trousers. So that angle is just amazing. This would have been shown in the cinema originally, so you can imagine that's quite an overpowering image to just see somebody's face be broken up on the screen from an unzip. I just wanted to try and hint on that position of the viewer. Having it up high, ideally, you come quite close underneath it, and then you become that penis almost!

Oh, it's my first time! What do you like about the editing side of things? Because that's also something you've used. In other pieces, you've used a lot of archival footage. What kind of archival footage are you being drawn to, and what do you like about that?

I don't know if it's necessarily that I particularly like archival footage. I see the archive as being a part of this use of technology. I think that's where I link it in with sound. It has this relationship with technology. I suppose the most obvious and trivial thing is that you get it from the internet, and it's all a part of this technological thing. But there is another aspect, especially when you think about things like Russ Meyer. You think more about that sex or pornography side of things. It's the fact that these things, they're part of a culture which has shaped technology. They have shaped it domestically. Without things like porn, the internet hadn't been shaped.

VHS, the same.

Yeah. Sound has that same thing. Where people are taking something and moving it from its given use. The intentions in which it was designed for has been developed into something else. People have run with it and created something that's really unexpected.

Just those two things together, I think is quite interesting for me to think about actually.

It actually makes me think of one of your other song choices, which is Novelist and is it Mumdance?

Yeah.

'1 sec' and you chose the instrumental version, which hasn't got the lyrics but it's really interesting in terms of a track. Because you're hearing a lot of the way technology works or quite weird electric sounds. How did you come across this track?

I heard the track first. And then I was really interested because the instrumental was part of the track. When you listen to it, you realize it's so much field recordings. There's a bit of cellotape there – he's put rhythm to cellotape. I'm also… that sort of grime genre of music. I particularly like the fact that – I know if you think about things like drum and bass and you think about jungle, they're unapologetic. Which I particularly like. The fact that they have a certain villain sound to it, and it's like it really plays on that sound of things being really rooted, just dark. That's what I mean about its being unapologetic in that sense.

And, so London, too.

Yeah. If you listen to it there's a lift moment, and then this dog barking. You've really accumulated things that create that feel.

And really narrative-led as well. So, this is Novelist and Mumdance from 2015. It's the '1 sec (instrumental)'.

—

Let's talk about Michael Jackson. Because you were in my favourite exhibition. Firstly, how did you get invited to be in it? I mean, you're there alongside David Hammons and Isa Genzken and Paul McCarthy and huge, big artists and you're like a little baby artist coming along. How did that actually come about?

Yeah, I suppose we talked about it for a couple of years. That was the fourth time it was shown. I made that in 2009. It was made the same year that Michael Jackson died, but before he died. It was the result of a residency, which was in a gallery on Hackney Road called Primo Alonso. It was at the end of the residency. I had an exhibition and put that in it as well.

Do you want to describe the piece to people? Tell us what it looked like?

So, it takes Michael Jackson's dance move, not the moonwalk, but where he's on his toes, at the end of the moonwalk on the Motown 25, I think that's the first time he exhibited that move. It's kind of quite similar to Elvis' 'Jailhouse Rock' – sort of on his toes. The shoes are Michael Jackson's penny loafers, and they're tied onto these balloons which are attached to the ceiling. So, they look like they are lifting the shoes up into that position. And obviously, Michael Jackson then uses that thing as his logo for… I don't know what it is.

Just generally his logo.

His logo, his branding, that position. I really like that Michael Jackson was also somebody that used to – he would take things from everywhere. And he was quite open to where he was taking things from. That way of making something unique, and not trying to be, not trying to become an author but trying to make something from things that exist and showing how these things connect. I find that quite interesting about him.

With the balloons, I mean the shoes are held by balloons, do the balloons die? Or is it like a mirage?

They die. They go through transitions. Like most of the works, they go through transitions. So, they do fall. And they are replaced, and it's quite similar too, as it was his logo and his image. I think there's somebody that's very aware of mortality. It takes a lot to continuously maintain that work, as well as it would have done his image, which we have all seen. It was really hard. He's had moments that weren't so desirable in some respects that people might think… You have to replace it to keep this thing going.

What do you like about the idea of, artwork that has that idea of transition, or transformation or change within it? It's quite specific.

I think most things go through that. I think that's what I mean about trying to remove this authorship or this like singular paternal narrative to most things and just having things exist as they come about. They go through interaction with other things. Nothing is singular. Most things are made up of two or more things. I think that's one way of relating to that.

I think this leads on quite well to your MF DOOM choice, which is very sample heavy, and definitely made up of many different parts. Why did you choose this specific MF DOOM, 'One Beer'?

Every aspect of that track is, it's just basically if you were to do a spider diagram of that, it just links it, just continues and continues. From the way he uses his lyrics, the way it starts off one way and it shifts. It's just incredibly creative in that sense. I just find it really exciting when I listen to that track. Even the beginning. You take this whole Frank Sinatra track.

Yeah "I get a kick out of you; I get a kick out of beer".

The samples. He takes things from films, from TV. He's just absorbing it all and finding this new thing within it.

This is MF DOOM 'One Beer'.

—

Can we talk about colour? Because I became really interested in the way that you use colour in your video stuff but also you paint walls, you paint sound spaces. What are you drawn to colour-wise and how does that work?

I think like I'm used to, I'm interested in how colour has another language, so I'm usually using it either referring to pigment. How people might have used certain colours for painting. How pigment is a makeup of interactions, a global interaction to make pigments in many senses. Also, there's a certain language culturally, with colour. I had this piece, this particular surround sound piece, that I've been working on, which makes reference to, the initial reference was to Ghana and Asafo flags. I was, through research, finding out that certain colours sitting next to each other within this particular culture within Ghana. Asafo people are by the coast. It's quite established as a flag. It's quite a well-known thing in the rest of the world. Certain colours sit next to each other. So white with green means something. Yellow and red means something else. It has another form of language. There's another code that it operates on.

You also have referenced Hieronymus Bosch's 'Garden of Earthly Delights', the palette within that. What particularly appealed about Bosch's palette? I mean, you think about Bosch and colour is not the first thing that comes to mind actually. It's almost narratives. It's like a crazy comic book for the 16th century or something, the 15th century. What was the Bosch colouring thing for you?

I think I wanted to have a way of… I was looking at painting… My idea was not to have "I love this Hieronymus Bosch and I want to align myself with this history of artwork".

Hell yeah. We all know a lot of artists do this.

I'm not interested in that sort of thing. I wasn't interested in that. I think what I was interested in was how he was using performance. The painting's very performative. He has these three panels, and there's an orgy of people at the bottom of one. There's just this idea that, he's made this very fantastical image of food, and of people's interactions. Also because of the fact that… it was just this idea, this level of exoticism. I think it's like an early narrative of that way in some respects, in which he is conveyed within painting. Because not only are people of multi ethnicities in the painting. He's living in a culture, Flemish culture, in which they're now connecting to the world. He's depicting images that he's seeing. People depicting from these places. So, you have food that people are depicting. You have animals that people are depicting. What's really interesting for me is whether these things was something that he depicted first hand, or is it something that he made fantastical, in some way. Because people would have gone and drawn. They would have invited artists to go to these places, let's say South America, to go and draw some birds or whatever. Foods that are there, and then he would have been an artist. I don't know how close at hand he would have been to those artists that brought back these images. I don't know if they were like peers, but he would have obviously seen these things, and had some influence. That's what I found interesting.

It was, I suppose, the birth of early modern capitalism. It's that same period but those are the same things. That's how you end up with the idea of colonisation.

Yeah, yeah. If you look at paintings that are a little later, this idea you have a lobster in the painting with symbolism in that sense. Lobster representing travel, as well as wealth. It has this whole thing in there, which is this idea like at one point travel, and the inclusion of an outside world was… There was an importance within that, and which it still does, but it's representation or its visual relevance is something else.

I won't let you leave without playing your fourth track.

Oh, okay.

Oh my god, it's so good. Why did you choose Depths Of Love? It's one of those rare 45s that people put on YouTube that are really hard to get hold of.

Yeah, and I don't even know how I came across it. It's one of those things that I actually don't have on vinyl, which I would quite like to get hold of. So… I just find myself drawn to that track and I've used it for a piece of work, just that beginning bit. It's just the first 10, 15 seconds. I just can't understand what… I just want to get to know what it is. I just want to get in there a bit more with that track. It just lingers. It's one of those things that lingers.

> *Maybe we can all get in there with you. So, this is Depths of Love 'I Just Can't Find a Love' and Appau Junior thank you very much for coming in.*

Thanks for inviting me. Thank you.

Kaye Donachie

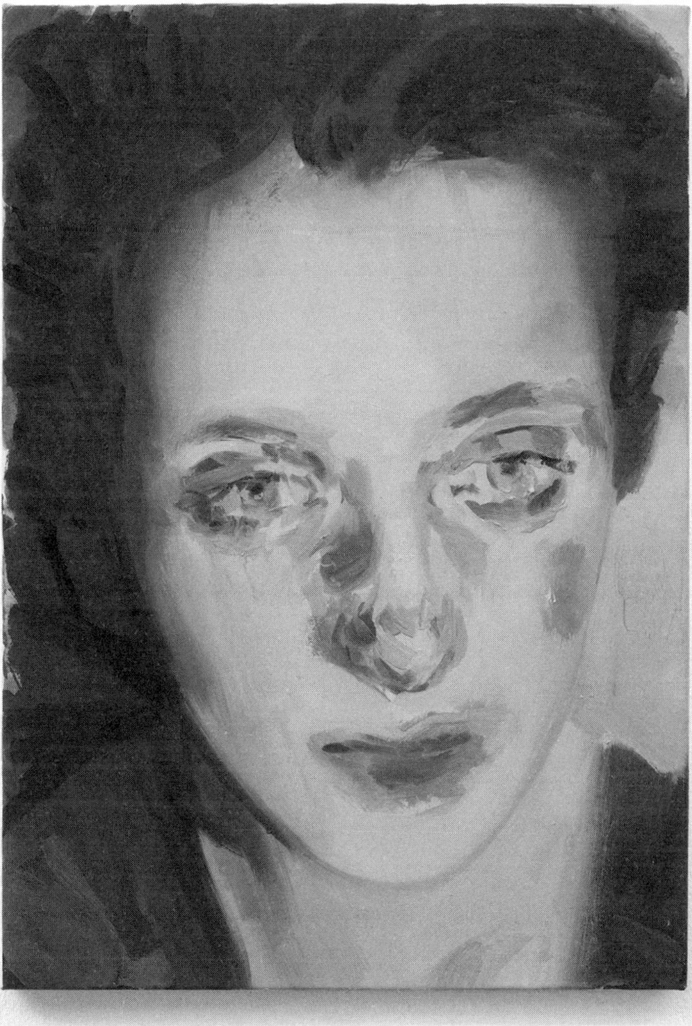

The eclipse that settled, 2018.

06.05.19

Hi, you're listening to Rough Version on NTS. And my guest this month is Kaye Donachie, an incredible painter. She's represented by Maureen Paley in London and has exhibited in places like La Plateau in Paris. Her works are a fascinating combination of looking at countercultural history, drawing on these idealized, fascinating women who are often depicted as muses, and actually discovering their own real histories. The results are just incredible, beautiful paintings. Let's talk about your process. A lot of your work focuses on faces. Do you want to tell me a bit about how you choose the characters that you paint and how you approach the face?

I'm not actually interested in the face so much as the biography or the story behind the person. Usually, I've watched a film, or documentary, and sometimes I read books, read poems by the people, books, fiction, and all of those ideas circulate around. Then I come up with this idea of an image of a person in my head. The paintings can be inspired by the photos I find of them. But usually, it's a strange amalgamation. Then I build on, use the face as a kind of cipher for emotions or thoughts. They're not really portraits and such, a representation of a particular person. They're more like reflections or ideas of particular moments in time, or emotions and feelings or thoughts I've had about that person… So that's how they come about.

Tell me about some of that research. What kind of things specifically are you looking at, or any particular periods or people? Because it seems to be very much looking at bohemian culture?

Yes. I was very interested in these very avant-garde women from the turn of the century, through to the '20s, '30s, and even '40s, and sometimes more recent figures in history. What fascinates me, there's a distance that we have from those stories that allows me to have an interpretation. And what I find really interesting about these women is that they were usually part of that art scene or cultural scene, but always on the periphery. It's only really now as we re-examine them that they are becoming more to the forefront. But I think what fascinates me looking at them at that time, as people in their circle, is how they constructed their own identity. How forward thinking they were as women, and their approach to making art, writing and their lifestyle. That, for me, is a way into seeing a character. They are protagonists. They're not a portrait of a particular person but more like an actor in a play.

Are there particular people that have been inspiring you recently?

I suppose for my recent show at Maureen Paley's, I was very interested in Iris Tree and Katherine Mansfield. In my show in Hove, in Brighton, at Marina de Luna, I was very interested in the writings of Anne Quinn. There's this idea of conversations with these women in their writings and artwork. I suppose these layers of different times and different voices. So that's how it usually starts off. Usually the people I'm interested in, people like Lee Miller, Noush, Frances Henri, so they can be all sorts of different women at different times.

Do you think there's a feminist motivation for you? Bringing attention to these female characters that had a lot of oomph at the period, in which they were sometimes marginalized, or made into the muse rather than a creative individual?

I suppose. Yes, definitely. But I think when I'm painting, I'm really thinking more about our emotional connection to the work. That's the most important thing. The story is the beginning and how I respond to it in terms of painting. The message is in terms of thinking about, not necessarily how my relationship to that person's story, but just using the face as a kind of reflection for all of us. They are just moments in time or thoughts or emotions. That's really how it comes about. I like their stories. It is about rediscovering something. These women's stories are much more written about. At the time, they probably were important, but it's just that over time, we've forgotten, and they are lost in history. It's about redeeming those people and those stories again.

Redemption – nice word. Let's play one of your tracks. I think after this, it makes sense to play the Janis Joplin one. Why this Janis Joplin and when did you first hear it?

I grew up in the '70s. My parents had a really eclectic music collection. So, there was everything from Status Quo to punk, Lou Reed, all sorts of things and actually this song would come on the record player, and it instantly arrested me. It's a bit like that when you see a painting. Something about it can stop you in your tracks. It's her voice, this power, this force. The track starts and suddenly it's full energy almost into the second bar of that song. I don't know how she gets that energy. Straight away it's there. It's this war cry, almost. I remember as a child being completely mesmerized by this voice. The whole song has these lulls and ebbs and flows. Suddenly this power comes in, this energy and she's angry, she's sad. It's euphoric. It's all sorts of things at once. Then you have these male voices holding up this force of a voice almost supporting her anger. For me, I think it was the first time I really thought God, this is what really grabbed you and makes you totally feel an emotional response to a soul.

Wow. This is Janis Joplin 'Piece of My Heart'.

—

That was Janis Joplin. Let's talk a bit about your colours. You have a beautiful palette and what you do. There's a lot of washes, even though you're working in oil. It feels muted in some way. Almost like everything has been under gauze. It feels more like watercolour rather than oil. What do you like about the colours you choose and that looseness?

Well, a lot of the images I look at are black and white. I suppose when I almost feel a colour, if that makes sense. I think colour can be indicative of a particular time. You can have a pink that feels quite 1940s. You can have a green that feels like a '20s green. We have this relationship with colour in terms of a particular period. When I'm looking at the images, it's almost like I can see a mood through the colour and then I'll just premix most of my colours before I start. It's never mixing as I go along. I really have a clear idea. I see the black and white image in colour and what mood I want to convey from that. There's a lot of planning before the painting starts, in terms of colour more than anything, because it's so precise and particular. I suppose they are quite muted and soft. It's that quietness that poetic-ness that I want to create in the paintings and use the colours to convey that.

Another thing that makes them feel really intimate is also the scale. Most of your faces are face sized. They're intimate. Have you worked larger and what do you like about focusing on the smaller, that we can relate to as another individual? Almost like looking in a mirror in a weird way.

I mean they are they're made really quickly, so the scale of them helps me with that, because I just want to capture a moment. I want it to contain and energy. The way that the face is painted is really important in terms of this energy. After I finished, I'm exhausted because I just need to get something down quickly. It's about the idea of mood. That's why all the colours are pre-mixed. Then I just execute it. I think in that moment it's to be very intense and for me that's where the scale comes in… I want you to have that intensity when you're looking at the brush mark, or maybe looking at the construction of the face in the painting and you're having that response, that I think is almost innate. It's a bit like a Manet painting. You see the brush; you feel it and it's spontaneous and instantaneous. I have worked larger but the scale in terms of doing a portrait or head works for me, because it does have that intimacy.

I love Manet. Great reference.

I think most painters love Manet! His lemons are the best.

He did really good asparagus too.

The still lives are the best.

'The Execution of Maximilian' in the National Gallery is probably my favourite painting.

There's something – the touch goes beyond time.

The work you make feels like it… It is contemporary, but it also feels very timeless. It doesn't necessarily feel rooted in the now in a lot of ways. I feel you're searching for? Something that lives outside of a moment in time.

I take that as a really big compliment, because that's exactly what I hope for. I think there's something about painting that is very different to other art forms. I think for me the paintings are much more closely related to the cinema and film, because when you see a film you see many images. When you leave the film it's all condensed into one single image that may not even be in the film. It's a way that our memory works when we recall something. I think in a painting you have this one single image, but it triggers off so many, so that's it's like there's no need for a narrative because the person's making it. When you see a painting. For me that's the interest in it.

I really like the cinematic. I never even thought of that in your work.

How does memory work and how do we construct images? Photography is interesting. I use photography, but when I think about making a painting, I think it's about the association we have with one particular image and what that triggers off. We see so many images, but what a painting does is it slow it all down and then speed it all up, in terms of how we approach it and can understand in terms of their own memories, their own images.

I want to play the most emotional of the three songs you brought, which is by Prince. Do you want to tell me about this specific Prince song?

It's so sad. Maybe because I used to listen to it so much on my headphones on my Walkman in the '80s over and over again. It's a song I think is totally poetic. Those first opening keys on the piano. I don't know, it's something so personal. The way he almost speaks the song, it's almost like he's walking into a slow jog. It never really gets there. Every time I hear it, it has the same effect. You're not hearing the song; you're hearing it inside of yourself. It's like a personal thought. I think for him to achieve that, to make you feel like it's your song, that only you're hearing. That internal feeling is really clever. I don't think I've ever heard a song quite like that before.

It's very unlike a lot of Prince's best known.

The key changes, everything about it really hits the right notes – I feel I have a lot of empathy for it.

This is 'Sometimes It Snows in April' by Prince.

—

That was Prince 'Sometimes It Snows in April'. I want to talk about erotics, because I think there is something about desire in what you do. Is that something intentional? Or is that me projecting something onto female faces? I just want to know what your feelings are about that. Do you think that's an element that plays in there somehow?

I think the erotic is in the application of the material itself. I think the way that a painting has a particular energy. I think we respond to those energies in different ways. When I'm painting, I do think it's a kind of erotic experience. But I think you are dealing with this construct, this physicality, this manipulation of a medium. It's not necessarily the image. I think it's about how we look at something – the surface and connection that you have your eyes to really understand something from a surface. Looking at the material. There is this physicality. How does that make us feel… I think it has its own eroticism. Not necessarily eroticism in terms of sex, but in terms of making us feel alive or waking up…

I'm interested in the way that your body of work seems to be playing on the idea of beauty, or the concept of beauty. Not the most fashionable of subjects. What are your feelings around that? Is that something you're also trying to unpick? Our perception of what beauty is?

Beauty is so complicated, and it is unfashionable. Because when we think about beauty, in terms of something fashionable or of the aesthetics of what is in fashion, how someone looks – it's such a complicated area. If you even take a selfie. We can manipulate and put cat faces on ourselves. Our idea of what is beautiful: big eyes, small lips, big noses, small noses, whatever it is, is such a personal thing. At the same time, it's quite a generic thing. I think beauty is different in fashion, than in terms of art. Take the Mona Lisa, everyone says that painting is beautiful. Then you can have a de Kooning and have completely different extremes of approaching what is beauty. One is about the aesthetics and about how we respond in terms of aesthetics. And the other one, is in terms of fashion. It is very complex. I think I see beauty in my work in terms of history, in terms of art, not necessarily in terms of where we are here now.

When you did that show in Paris at Le Plateau, you were contextualizing your work. Do you want to talk a bit about how you placed your work alongside other pieces?

I really, really enjoyed that show. It was a huge space. There were so many rooms and so many different areas to play with. I came up with this idea that it would be really nice, rather than just rooms and rooms of my own work, I could actually have a conversation with all the other women that I looked at or were influenced by. I didn't want it to be a historic thing. I wanted to work out how we could bridge it all together in a moment of time. To make the show work like a poem. There were echoes backwards and forwards between our works or our ideas. I wanted that space to work or the show to work like a painting, so it was multi layered. It had these echoes and different references, so it was like a continuous poem. For me, it such a nice opportunity to be able to do that. It just created a completely different sense and context for how I make my images.

Can I ask you where you feel and if you feel, 'you' are within your work? Does that make sense? I'm not going to do the thing that so many female artists get about the 'representation of woman'. But I'm trying to work out where you sit with what you're making.

It's that cliché, isn't it. People say when you make a portrait, that you always paint yourself. I'm not sure if I really believe that. I think what I see the paintings as, are reflections of my inner self. My interpretation is a response. I am there in the paintings. I don't know these people. It's a revision. They are spectral figures. For me, they are like ciphers of different thoughts, moments in time. I'm not interested in them as women – I'm interested in them just in terms of painting, actually. The image is one thing. I actually think a lot more about how it's going to be painted more than anything. I think that's where I am in the work in terms of my house, the touch, the drawing in the painting, the colour – all of those decisions.

As a segue into your last track, I want to talk about the melancholic, because sometimes there is melancholia in your work, a tearfulness or that atmospheric vibe. Would you agree?

Definitely. I think this is to do with self-reflection and a space. Even though they're made really fast there's a lot of contemplation there. I don't think in contemplation, you ever really feel euphoric or really happy. I want them to be silent, like a space of quietness. So, the sadness… it's very hard to explain. The sadness is more of a silence. I want there to be a space for the viewer to interpret something in the image, so there needs to be this void. And I think in that void, it becomes melancholic. They're not shouting. They're not telling you what to think. There's no narrative for you. That's what I don't want. It's almost like filling in the gap. You need it to be quiet.

We're going to end with Justin Timberlake, a delightfully pop choice. Why did you choose Justin?

It's this track. I really like this track of Justin Timberlake. I could have it on again and again. I could listen to over and over. For me it's like breathing. There's something about the beat and the melodies like it feels so bodily. The beat of it is like a heartbeat, like a pulse. When I'm listening, I feel like I'm breathing. What I really love about this song is how cinematic it is. It's like a prophetic fantasy, probably to do with the video, but it's got the best opening and ending of a pop song. I think it's a perfect pop song. The rain starts at the beginning and at the end a man's voice goes off into this strange echo into the distance. It's really an odd way to end a pop song. You can hear the rain throughout the song. You can hear the muted beat almost like he's creeping along, mimicking how you feel someone's moving and then you have these strange echoes of his voice in the background as well…

Brilliant. Do you listen to music in your studio when you paint?

I listen to the radio. To sports.

Really? Any particular sport?

I really love football. The news and football.

I didn't see that coming!

I do listen to music. Whenever I get tired, I put music on to get me going. But sometimes it's a bit of a distraction, because I start thinking of a quick dance or something. Having the sports or news on is really a "no". Having a football match to listen to is brilliant.

We're going to finish now with Justin Timberlake's 'Cry me a River' Thank you very much for coming in.

Thank you. I really enjoyed it.

Lawrence Lek

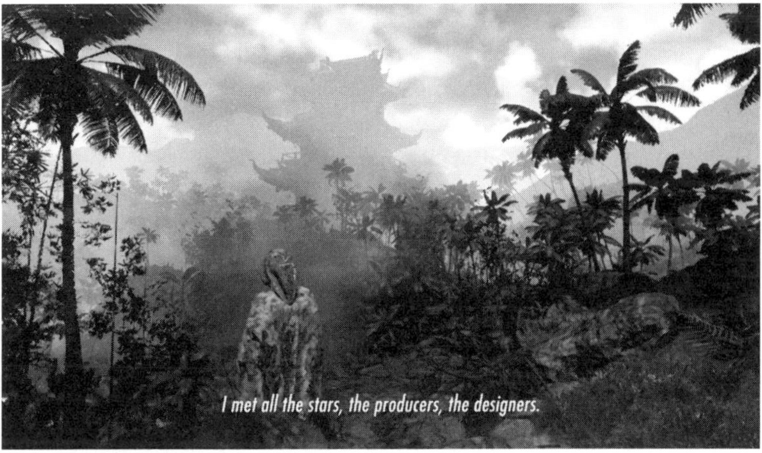

AIDOL, 2019.

31.05.19

Hi. You are listening to Rough Version on NTS and my guest this month is Lawrence Lek. He's a London based artist, filmmaker, musician. He shows for Sadie Coles, and he makes amazing site-specific virtual worlds using game software and 3D animation, installation, and performance. He even made a virtual reality version of the NTS Studio. He often renders real places but within fictional scenarios and was the winner of the 2015 Dazed emerging artist award and has exhibited at Glasgow International, Art Night, Wyising, Cubitt, and the Julia Stoschek collection. Lawrence, thank you very much for coming in.

Thanks, Fran.

You come from a music background. Should we talk a bit about that? Because that's always been something that's fed into your work, in general?

Yeah, sure. I've always been making music, but I studied architecture, worked as an architect for a long time. But on the side, I was always making music. While I was working, I was doing a lot of electronic music, really DIY. This was around 2008, 2009. Actually, the whole method of circulation was totally different. This was the peak of Myspace. It seems like a distant memory in a way, which is great. Starting to make videos and films and installations, gradually, I wanted to feed soundtrack stuff back into my work. Actually, for the Dazed award at the Royal Academy, nearly four years ago exactly, I worked with Oliver Coates who did the soundtrack for my film 'Unreal Estate'. That was an amazing collaboration and we worked together on something for Glasgow [International], as well. Then I worked on a project called 'The Nøtel' with Kode9. Initially, an album launch of his last album 'Nothing' that evolved into an audio-visual-performance and that spawned some installations last year. The collaborative aspect has always been really important. And I'm just so happy that, especially with the newest films, 'Aidol' and 'Geomancer', I was able to make the soundtrack one of the main focuses of the work.

We will talk about your latest film, and I really want to, because it's very much about music. When you're using music within your film pieces it's quite open. I mean, the aesthetic of what you do is often quite tech/game influenced. VR. You feel the use of technology and what you're creating visually, and there is this openness to a lot of the spaces you're describing. When you're making music that goes into the soundtracks, how are you reflecting that? Because the sound you're making also has quite an openness.

Yeah. Initially, with some of the first self-released albums, I guess the 'concept album' idea was soundtracks for films that didn't really exist. The idea for the music is a travelogue-type thing. It's always about a journey. Even if the song didn't exactly have lyrics or doesn't have words to go with it. It's essentially about taking you through this sonic landscape. One of my first collaborators was a sound artist and now he runs a record label called Quantum Natives. He goes by the name Yearning Kru for his productions. I would always send him stuff and he would just comment on it and help me figure out what exactly it was I was doing. He mentioned this term to me 'Nomadalgia' which is basically another way of saying travel sickness. It was coined by the writer and theorist, Mark Fisher, as a counterpoint to the idea of hauntology. So, if hauntology is the sickness of things that are absent, then momadalgia is being a nomad and missing it. Like nostalgia, except it's not nostalgia for a place, but a nostalgia for being in motion. And that was what he likened my music to, which was really nice because that's something that I had always been going for subconsciously.

Wow. An amazing word. I feel like I know that feeling, as a girl who travels way too much! Often your films are not populated by individuals. You're almost left with the residue of the human. We feel spaces, but, even in your latest film, you've got a simulacrum of an AI performer, but it's not actually a person. What do you like about that absence?

I think some people who use CGI really focus on it as a technological medium, it's about simulation and so on, but for me, coming from architecture, 3D rendering is what you do to advertise things before they exist in real life. I guess my use of simulation is really to do with the space that is created. This world building aspect, or basically set design, where it can be much more expansive than might be possible with a real-life film. When I use voice in the music… The image in a film, or even in VR, is confined to the 180 degrees that you can see in front of yourself. Sound and the voice go beyond the frame. It envelops you really within it. So, when I don't have human figures… People often ask me, why aren't there people in my work and I sometimes say, actually, there are people but just because there aren't digital avatars of human beings – which are just obviously, placeholder sprites anyway – doesn't mean that it's not populated by voices. Because with all my work even back to 5 or 6 years ago, was always populated by whispers, voiceovers, people singing in the background, that you would hear in the air. But you would turn your head and they're not there. I think related to that nomadic aspect. The absence of a film body doesn't necessarily mean that the voice of the human is missing, because it's definitely still there.

Let's talk about the latest film 'Aidol'. AI-Idol. I really like the name. Why don't you tell me about the story within it?

'Aidol' is one of the latest in a series of interrelated works – 'Geomancer' from 2017, and one called 'PlayStation' and one called '2065' that are related to this video essay I did called 'Sinofuturism'. I had the idea for 'Sinofuturism' when I was researching AI and technology. I noticed that there was a huge parallel between what was being said about China and industrialization, everything from labour practices at Foxconn to the fear of an emerging aggressive superpower. Seeing that dialogue was a mirror image of what was being said about automation and AI. If the Chinese workforce is going to take away our jobs, that's exactly what they're saying, essentially the algorithm taking away human knowledge or work. Out of that video essay, these works that look at AI, not from the conventional science fiction human versus machine standpoint but looking at it from a much more subjective point of view. So, in a sense, they are thinking about AI as a kind of creative consciousness. Not as fantasist thinking "it's going to overcome the human" in this post-human way. But really thinking how do we, or how do I as an artist, try and think about what I'm doing, when even being creative is no longer so special, or this whole romantic idea of genius is no longer there. So back to 'Aidol'. The tagline for it is that a fading superstar enlists the help of an AI songwriter to make a comeback at the e-Sports Olympics. Like Beyoncé or Prince doing the halftime Super Bowl performance, but in this case it's in 2065 and instead the real physical Olympics. It's all about e-Sports and a new kind of entertainment economy that's built up around game culture and new forms of entertainment. Basically, mass art that is just beginning to emerge today.

I want to play the track from it because it's beautiful. Do you want to tell me where this takes place within the narrative of the film?

I think that the song I gave is called 'In My Prime'. It actually happens in the end scene of the film. It's the epilogue. The whole film is about the making of this album, which is between this human superstar and this AI. The film is bookended by two songs, which are actually folk songs. The first is just a snippet of a Joni Mitchell song called, I think, 'All I Want'. And the last song which is 'In My Prime', which is the one that's going to be played. A traditional English folk song that was recorded in the '60s by a band called Pentangle, who are a classic English folk band. I did a Vocaloid version, which is this Yamaha vocal synthesizer version of it.

This is 'In My Prime' by Lawrence Lek from 2019.

—

That was 'In My Prime' by Lawrence Lek from his latest film 'Aidol'. Let's talk a little bit about the architectural influence in what you do. I'm particularly interested in looking at a lot of your films that have touched on ideas around gentrification, and let's say, a changing – local landscape, while we are in Dalston – but also a British one. But then also extending that to an Asian one. What do you find interesting about examining that? How has architecture, apart from what we said earlier, influenced what you're doing?

I think when I was studying architecture, and I really still am in a way… It's not a very popular reading of it, but there's this Walter Benjamin quote: "architecture is always experienced in a state of distraction". In a way that's quite similar to how music is today. There's always music in the air, it's in the background, or I think, in his interpretation, it was really related to this rootless wandering traveller in the early 20th century who didn't have a home and would go around Europe and see all these symbols of modernity. The arcades, the shops. Before there was a shopping mall there was the shopping arcade. I guess he was thinking about the parallels between his experience of wandering and these products of experience wandering around, and all the while that's framed by architecture. These buildings, or new styles that were popping up around him. I think if you fast forward to the early 21st century, one of the things I am against with architecture is this idea that it has any form of permanence. I did this project called 'Dalston, Mon Amour' – which is literally set in Gillett square outside – that looked at the Alain Resnais film 'Hiroshima, Mon Amour'. Which looks at how memory gets fragmented through the experience of war. There are two characters in the film who speak to each other – a Japanese man and a French woman, and they have this strange inability to communicate verbally. Most of the communication is done through flashbacks or through touch, or through things that are actually quite hard to communicate through film. I tried to collage this very strange form of memory onto a video game and that gave form to 'Dalston, Mon Amour', which had a sequel the next year called the 'Europa, Mon Amour' which was actually done, I think, a week or two before the Brexit vote. I scattered around some of the Wolfgang [Tillmans] anti-Brexit posters and various symbols of the square. Really simple things that I was seeing and putting them into the work.

> *What's amazing looking at that film, it also had such sadness to it. I would have thought it was made post-Brexit rather than pre-Brexit. It's very much that apocalyptic, empty landscape of memories of something that's passed... It felt totally afterwards, not before! How prescient of you.*

Yeah, it was meant to be a thought experiment. "Oh, wouldn't it be stupid if this actually happened?" Because it had snippets of Fox News and news reporters telling both sides of the story. I didn't expect that it would actually happen.

That's got a lot of that lovely whisper thing that you mentioned before, which I really liked in a lot of your films. Almost like a Janet Cardiff work where you feel like someone's whispering in your ear. The idea of voices that aren't quite heard or they're saying things that are like inner experience. How did you start working with the whisper?

The thing about the whisper is that it can be this very intimate thing, but it's also used as a device in horror films to build a sense of suspense and mystery and intimacy. Because the thing with a whisper, even from a recording point of view, is that it's quite hard to capture, which is why you have to go up close to someone's ear to hear it. There are various things with samples that were taken – sometimes used in music and often samples from film which obviously you get all the time in electronic music. This idea of film sampling, which goes back to a lot of electronic music production in general, is really something I was looking at. For example, in 'Europa'… no in 'Dalston, Mon Amour', I think I used 'Not Over Yet'. I did this half-time, half-speed version of it, where all the voices are chopped and screwed. In 'Europa, Mon Amour' we actually go up close to the NTS radio booth… I think there is 'Don't You Want Me' by Felix, another classic rave tune. In both of those, there's really a sense of loss. What I think is fascinating about it and in some of those greatest rave tunes, and also dance and disco tunes, they're incredibly joyous and really sad at the same time. They're dancing to forget, forget their troubles.

I've got to say it's a perfect segue into the second one of your tracks which is Liquid 'Sweet Harmony', which for me completely embodies what you've just said. It is sad and internal and intimate and emotional, but is also a huge, iconic, liberating, ecstatic track. Is that why you chose it?

Yeah, exactly. There are two things. I'm pretty much a night person and when I'm working on things I either need to listen to something to get me motivated, but motivated in a way that's also quite thoughtful. It's an amazing tune. Another thing that's interesting about it is that I thought it sampled a female vocalist but it's actually CeCe Rogers, who is a guy… It's been sped up so much it really has that you know like shrill rave sample thing which is incredible too.

> *Okay, this is Liquid 'Sweet Harmony'.*
>
> —
>
> *That was Liquid 'Sweet Harmony'. I want to talk to you about your process. A lot of your work feels very contemporary, playing into the technicalities of game design and the technologies of rendering and that approach to aesthetics. How did you first start working with that? How do you take an idea and work it through those materials?*

I think, like I said, for architecture, because 3D rendering is a very commercial tool that you see with renderings of property development and so on. Actually, with video game engines, the difference is like the difference between composing something in your studio and playing it live. With the early video game stuff, I would build a video game and screen capture it to a soundtrack. For example, in 'Unreal Estate' for the Royal Academy, I actually did a whole like voiceover with the music. I played it on my phone and then screen captured the game live with an Xbox controller. When the voiceover said, oh, you know, "welcome to your house of many servants" and so on, I knew that by that point, I would have to be inside Burlington House, the Royal Academy's place – in the virtual version. There's this live aspect of the performance within the video game version, in traditional CGI animation, where you click the button once you've done all your modelling, you wait to see what it looks like. With a game engine the difference is that it's 'real time' and of course there's many different technicalities related to that. I like that it gives me the opportunity to actually deal with it in a very live way. That's not necessarily a good thing. For 'Aidol' which is actually a feature length CGI film, we were messing around with it, right to the end, which is great creatively, but quite stressful in terms of time pressure. The other thing I would say, is what's fascinating in terms of this subculture – it's not even subculture anymore. I was saying to a friend, Daniel Swan, who is also an amazing video artist, that now that CGI has become the new normal. We see its digital influence, like Lil Miquela and so on. It makes me rethink, what does it mean to create? Clifford Sage is also a musician, and a computer graphic genius, he worked with me to do most of the 3D rendering for 'Aidol'. All the while we were just listening to tracks like 'Sweet Harmony' or whatever – random stuff – and just thinking about that bridge between performance, which is often hidden, you're creating a digital work, and the labour that goes into it, but also the liveness that people don't see when they see the finished film. It's a nice thing with video game engines, that it gives the scope to actually create a performance at a later stage, which is kind of what I did with 'The Nøtel' with Kode9. Sometimes it's a gallery installation and sometimes it's an AV performance at Sonar or something. It's great to have that flexibility.

From the viewers point of view, there is something about the aesthetics of gaming, which does feel different from a lot of other forms of electronic environmental creation. We're used to having an element of interactiveness. So, even when we're not holding the controller, we somehow feel we are in the place of the protagonist when we're watching it and I think that really comes across in your latest feature.

Totally. I think it's just this funny thing that I'm literally playing a video game on stage and that's what the performance is. But also, this idea of the first person. There's the first-person narrative in literature. There's a first-person point of view in a video game where you really, you're embodying the character. I think that's what makes many video games either very addictive but also quite engaging. That's the whole premise of the idea of a role-playing game. You are another. You can fully become immersed in the body of an alien, of another being, of some other creature, that's completely unlike your own physical body. And I think it's very problematic in some ways, but also, it's quite liberating in others. In terms of this empathetic point of view.

I want to play another one of your tracks. Another one that you brought in that you've created yourself. Do you want to tell me a little bit more about it? This is the one from 2017, 'Heart Sutra'.

This is from the 'Geomancer' soundtrack. 'Geomancer' is the direct prequel to 'Aidol' and it's about this satellite AI who comes down to

Singapore in 2065 on the eve of the Singapore Centennial. The idea with 'Geomancer' is that I wanted to create a 'Portrait of the Artist', but portrait of the artist as an AI… It's this coming-of-age narrative – not from a teenager but from this technological teenager. They're basically really emo and they're grappling with the conditions of their existence. In the story, the manufacturers of the AI, this fictional company called Farsight, has built in this self-help AI – like we have Siri or Headspace, but for an AI. It's a Buddhist self-help AI who just recites the heart sutra. The Heart Sutra is basically one of the canonical sutras of Buddhism and it's about accepting the illusion that you are your body. This track is setting that to music.

Amazing. So, this is 'Dive (Heart Sutra)' by Lawrence Lek.

—

That was 'Dive' by Lawrence Lek. I want to talk a little bit about how you display your work and the complexities within that and how often you do things within installation. You've also deconstructed our awareness of the fact that things are on screens. I think the latest film is a projection work. Is that correct?

Yeah.

Do you want to tell me about some of your feelings about displaying, the screen and installation and presentation of what you do?

I think the fantasy with any screen-based work or any work in general is that the viewer or the reader or the listener becomes immersed in it. In the latest one, 'Aidol', I knew that it would be a huge challenge just to make a CGI feature length film. To really focus on it being a film, the sound is really important. I worked on the sound and some of the underscore with Seth Scott, who's a composer and sound designer, to make it an immersive thing, and the sound in 'Aidol' is really the most important thing. That comes across a little bit in the installation just through sheer volume and the viewing conditions but the other thing with 'Aidol' – and you get this with many of my works – there's a hall of mirrors, or screens within screens. For example, in the film 'Aidol' there are I think 3 or 4 sequences where it's actually a music video within the film. At some point there's also the video game within the film. Sometimes it's literally like zooming in and zooming out of the screen that the characters are watching inside the film. There are people watching people on their screens and outside their screens. In a way, it's easy to think of the screen as this device for distraction and addiction and all these things. For me, at least with 'Aidol' and with 'Geomancer', because they're really about non-human vision or this different idea of seeing and looking at things, that becomes a portal into another world. I think that's what film has always been. If it's a good film, you don't think about the screen after 3 minutes.

I want to play your last track; this has all gone very quickly. Why did you choose This Mortal Coil?

This song, which is 'Song to the Siren' by This Mortal Coil, in contrast to Liquid 'Sweet Harmony' is, from this era of studio experimentation. It's sung by Liz Fraser and it's This Mortal Coil, but it's basically a Cocteau Twins song from a compilation. Even more than the tracks themselves, I'm fascinated by the stories behind them. 'In My Prime' is a Pentangle traditional English song that was acapella, and this song, which is primarily a beautiful song, was a Tim Buckley song. As a weird strange anecdotal aside, when Liz Fraser sung it, I think she was going out with Tim Buckley's son Jeff, who tragically died, who knows why, while swimming… Sometimes they say that the work should stand on its own two feet. You shouldn't know anything about the author or the creator, but for me it's the opposite. When I was studying architecture, it was completely cold and mechanical until I read more about the life and times of the people who actually made these works. Then it's no longer this pure artwork or music or anything. It actually came from a certain experience which I think, at least for me, enriches the song or the building or the work itself. When you start to understand the world that it was created within and draw parallels between what you can use from your own every day, lived experience, in order to create something new out of that. Of course, I don't think it should be necessary that people know the backstory, but for me personally, the backstory is great, because it moves things forward and makes you reassess your memory.

Everything is context. This is This Mortal Coil 'Song to the Siren' and you've been listening to Lawrence Lek on NTS.

Paul Maheke

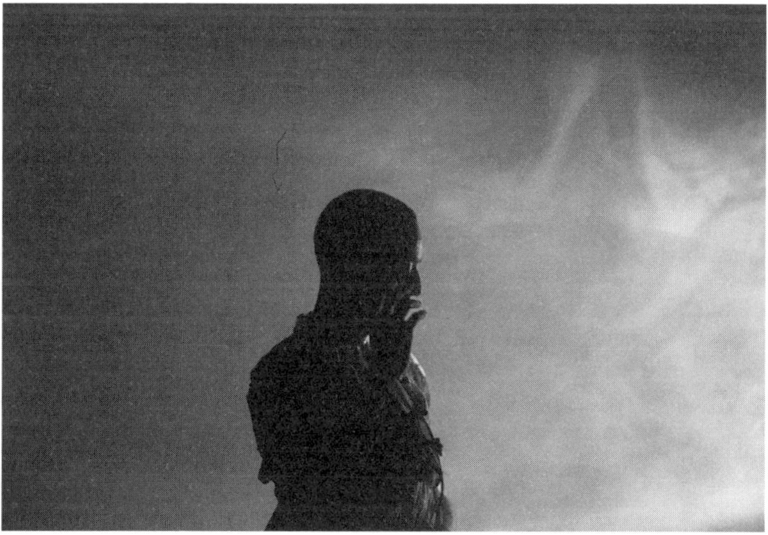

Sènsa, 2019.

28.06.19

You're listening to Rough Version on NTS and my guest this month is Paul Maheke, who is a French artist based in London. He was trained in Paris and then attended the Open School East, which is an open university project. He's just back from the Venice Biennale. He's exhibited everywhere from Chisenhale to my favourite project space in Vienna, Kevin Space, and a variety of other places with work that goes between video to performance to installation to sculptural objects. And thank you very much for coming in Paul.

Thank you for inviting me.

Let's talk about that for a start. Your practice seems to be very grounded in performance, even though the first thing I ever saw by you was actually a video work. Do you want to tell me about how you started working with the body in that way?

Actually, surprisingly enough, I only started working with performance or performing for an audience about four years ago, which actually coincides with me arriving to London. Dance was always important in my life, as a teenager, I wanted to become a choreographer. I'm not professionally trained. I think dance was always around. I think, after my graduation from my MA in France, it must be eight years ago, I got really bored of my practice at the time. I was mainly working with drawing and installations. And although the work was already concerned with body issues, I felt like I needed something else. That's when I started to work outside in public space. The first action or performance that I did was with my little brother. I just asked him to wear a T-shirt that I had embroidered with sequins and then we would just walk around in the countryside. I think that's when I started to understand that movement was very important to me. And that was mainly the way in which I was relating to the world, through sound and movement. That's when it started off, I think. Then, when I arrived in London for Open School East, I started to devise a series of programs and events that were looking at dance and music as a means of emancipation. I mainly invited women or female-identifying people to talk about the practice: music producers, activists, DJs. There I met with the choreographer Jameelah Johnson Small. Jameelah was the first one who asked me to perform for an audience as part of her festival that she was co-organizing at Guest Space. So that must be 2016.

So, it's been a very natural process? Looking at your approach to performance, is how you seem to think about the use of the body in quite a different way from let's say, straight choreography. It's not 'dance' necessarily, it's much more focused on things like gesture, or pose, or even facial expressions. What do you find interesting about a more minimalist take on what the body means and how you can describe narrative in some way by using the body?

I think, again, at first and maybe even now, I've drifted a bit away from that idea. But movement versus choreography, I think that was something that was always at the back of my mind. How to think of movement as something other than an illustration of something. Something that would be more of an internal process, that would impact my surroundings. I was fascinated with dancers that were talking about dance as this vibration that would set the space in motion. And I think that really stuck with me.

Since you mentioned your brother, I think we should play the track that he was part of. Do you want to tell me a little bit about why you chose this specific one? And if you've used it within your work and what your relationship is to it?

My little brother is working in digital archives, but he's also a musician on the side. And he has this project called Mihasu and I thought that it would be nice to play one of his tracks. It's one of his latest releases. I think he's very talented, so I wanted him to be included.

I'm all about family. Family works for me. Literally everything I do is probably because of my sister, Seana. This is Mihasu 'Walking Hand in Hand in The Rain'.

—

That was Mihasu 'Walking Hand in Hand in The Rain'. I like that idea you were talking about, the energy that comes with movement. When I've read about exhibitions you've done, you talk about activating the space with performances, and then the space has resonance when you're not there. Do you want to talk a little about the idea of activation?

It's actually very fundamental to how I intend my exhibitions to be experienced. For example, at the Chisenhale Gallery I was really interested in producing a show that could be experienced on different terms. There were moments when the space was occupied by a group of three performers and moments when the exhibition was in a deflated state.

Like a balloon?

Almost yes. Put at rest. I think I like the idea of using the performance as a way not only to activate, but to occupy a space in a different way, and maybe produce a different experience, just by putting bodies in an environment. I guess activation, although it's an overused term, I think it's still really relevant to how I think of art. Because for me, it's very important to think about the environment that I'm creating as a place where people can gather together, meet and maybe think about art as a pretext, an excuse to discuss. I think that's why I'm also interested in live format.

Getting people in the room is such a different experience. Isn't that the point of exhibitions? Why we should look at not just a reproduction or documentation. I totally understand that. Do you want to tell me about the process? How you come up with the ideas of what you do? What are the sparks?

It's usually very organic. I'm trying to let it flow somehow. It mostly comes from readings or things that I'm seeing. And usually, the shows are feeding off each other, so one thing is leading to another, and so on. I'm always working with faces, it's never very logical or rational. Or maybe it can come across as logical because there is thinking behind it, but in the way it manifests in my brain, it's not at all. It's like a layering of info and different references. And then at some point, there's a huge amount of work put into editing, putting things together and working with associations. I like to think of my exhibitions as a space of coexistence. How to make those various elements live together in a way that would be interesting and meaningful.

I was also really interested in the idea of thinking about the body as an archive, and ideas of history or ignored histories, whether they're queer, Brown and Black or colonialist histories that have been ignored. How do you feel that emerges in your work? How are you touching on those topics?

It's interesting because for me, they may be less topics than they are modes of production. They are things that I'm using to produce. They are concepts or even just experiences, because they are also my experiences but using queerness and Blackness as a way to produce a work, rather than a work about Blackness and queerness, is something that really interests me. And similarly, this idea of looking at the body as an archive. I think I was interested in looking at the idea of archiving in a way that didn't feel too rational, and this system of archiving, is not necessarily the thing that I'm interested in. Just looking at the body as a receptacle of histories, experiences, that may or may not belong to you, that you may or may not be aware of. I think using dance in its improvised form was a way for me to unpack this archive and look at it from a more sensitive emotional perspective.

Let's play another one of your songs. Let's play your Nina Simone, because it's interesting in terms of the idea of the historical. Why did you choose a specific Nina Simone?

I think I'm a bit of a torch singer inside! I think the voice of Nina Simone is always the one that kills me. And that song, I like the balance between this joyful feeling and the extreme sadness of mourning somebody.

The lyrics are really dark in this. This is 'Alone Again Naturally' sung by Nina Simone.

—

That was Nina Simone. Let's talk about installation. What do your installations look like? What is the breadth of them, because some of them seem quite minimal, or more mood orientated, rather than filled with objects. You're not an altarpieces installer. How do you approach installation?

Space is very important for me, as well as context. I guess, if we go back to this idea of using queerness as a way to produce art, often the installations are trying to convey this kind of queer experience of a space. What would be a queer experience of an exhibition space, for example? And using this idea of fluidity of things being transient, a space together – I think that's important. Thinking of the space as, for example, a welcoming environment is important. That's when I started to use light, specific colours, sound… because sound is also very effective on the body, and I'm interested in that. Sitting situations or situations that will enable the audience to stay a little bit longer, or to experience the work again on a different temporality. Some of my works are for example, an hour and a half long and I know that it's most likely that most of the people who would visit the space will only stay for a maximum of 15 to 30 minutes. But I like this idea of something that you only traverse, that you only go through and that you can embrace on a different level. Although there are many stories and layers in what I'm doing, I think it's also important for me to have a very sensitive aspect to it, and a formal excitement that you can experience in the space. I'm often thinking of what my parents would do or how they would receive the work, because they're not from the art world at all. They don't have an art background. I'm always thinking of that. It's always at the back of my mind.

When you've incorporated sound, often music is collaborative. Do you want to tell me about some of the people you've worked with? And how that functions?

Yes, I think I'm quite a faithful collaborator. There are a few friends of mine that I have worked with on several occasions. One of them is Sophie Mallette. I met Sophie back in 2015, when she was an associate of the program at Open School East. The latest collaboration we had was for the Chisenhale show where it was basically a carte blanche, I commissioned her a soundtrack and gave her a brief, but it was completely open. Then there was Casey Medicago, a music producer and DJ. With Melaka, we worked on different terms, but now, we are working on a collaborative performance, commissioned by a performer and Block Universe which will be presented at the end of May in London, at Hoxton Hall and then in New York in November.

As part of the performance itself? How does that function? Nkisi has made a specific track for you and you're creating movements together? It is really interesting, because a lot of her work is also interested in ideas of Congolese cosmology, and alternative forms of communication beyond, let's say, the visual. I'm curious to see how the sound element works with what you're doing as a performer.

For that specific work, from the very beginning, Nkisi and I really worked together on the content, as well as the structure of the work and what we wanted. Melaka is not only producing the music. We completely devised and produced the work together. It's been an ongoing conversation between the two of us for the last year or so, around the idea of exploring the realm of the invisible and going beyond the representational. That's something that we are super interested in ghostly presences, as well as crazy, geeky stuff about frequencies and resonances, because Maleka is a huge geek, and she's incredibly knowledgeable.

She's a very glamorous geek.

Oh yes, she is.

Let's play her track. So, this is 'Can You See Me?' by Nkisi as chosen by Paul.

—

That was Nkisi 'Can You See Me?' Let's talk about the ghost thing. I think the ghost's thing is really fascinating because obviously there's a more metaphorical take on what that is in your work. And then there's a much more literal explanation about your fascination with ghosts. Tell me about your feelings about the ghostly.

The ghostly is everywhere and has been present in my work for a long, long time. Because I think I was always fascinated in forms of appearance and disappearance and what's left and told and seen. But it's also tied into my upbringing in a family, where witchcraft was part of the narrative that we would hear or listen to through tales that my father would tell us from the Congo. Even my mother was from this area in France where witchcraft is still very present. I guess that influenced me. But, more recently, I think the ghost is a figure that is of interest for me because it speaks to the idea of the future, the past and the present, as well as somehow a less rational thinking around embodiment and life. The ghost is also very selective! It may or may not appear to you. Some people believe in them, some others do not. The ghost is also very material. For me, the ghost is also the sound. For example, one of the inspirations of the work with Nkisi is this idea that we are still living in the sonic remainders of the big bang. We incorporate these sonic elements into our environment, to the point that we are completely oblivious to them. We don't hear them. But the ghost is also a figure, a very resilient figure. I often think of this French artist called Robert Malaval, who often referred to the ghost as a kind of political figure of resistance. I think that's something that's also stuck with me.

> *So many good ghostly things in that. I was also really interested in another aspect of what you do about the idea of looking at club culture, in particular, vogue culture, as an alternative to the white cube, a different space for a cultural engagement. Do you want to talk more about that, and how that has emerged in what you do?*

It brings me back to my first solo show, actually. That was at the South London Gallery, after this residency that I'd done there. My proposal was based on this idea of creating a brown space. The idea of the brown space was to queer the white cube and how to approach or dismantle or disrupt the aura of the white cube. I still think about that. I'm still interested in the ways in which the club is gathering people together. It's an intimate setting, yet it's still public. Also, given the queer legacies around club culture. The fact that the dance floor became, at some point, a political space. I always want or dream of my performances, or my exhibitions, as momentum that would be similar to a night in a club somehow, with that same sense of empowerment as well as just celebration. Although the celebration can also be a little bit melancholic and dark. But I think the club is a good way to look at Utopia. A Utopia that would acknowledge its difficulties or its impossibility. I like that.

A Utopian club world. I'm going to end with your last track, which seems like a quite apt thing, which is 'Party Girl' by Michelle Gurevich. Which is quite a weird narrative about a party girl. It's a more melancholic take on it. Why did you choose this song?

It's a song that I actually used in the show at Chisenhale, and the song was re-performed by Carrie Topley who was one of my performers. I love the song. I love the feel of the song and this very melancholic figure of a party girl who is extremely glamorous, yet very mundane as well. Who lives in the dark and occupies those darkened spaces and the space of thc night. I think that's something that is of interest to me as well.

Amazing. Thank you very much for coming in Paul. That was Paul Maheke, and this is Michelle Gurevich, 'Party Girl'.

Graham Little

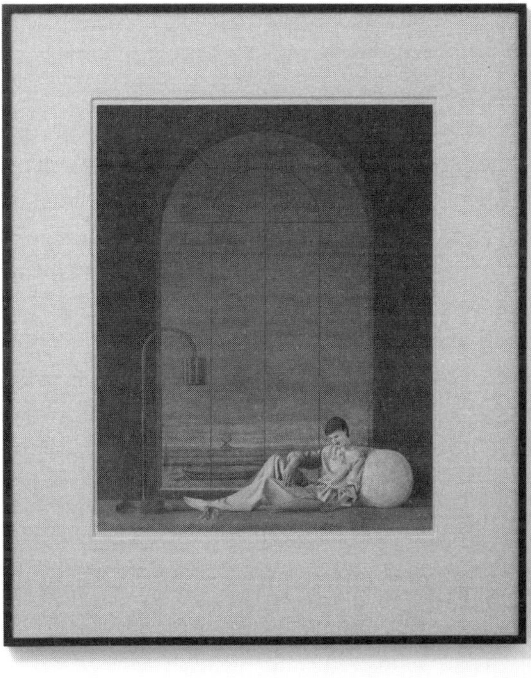

Untitled (Drawing Room), 2017.

29.08.19

Hi, you're listening to Rough Version on NTS. And my guest, this month, I'm very excited to say, is Graham Little. Graham Little is an artist based in London, but originally from Scotland. And he's shown everywhere from Camden Art Centre and Manifesta11 to MoMA PS1. He's just coming out of a great show at Alison Jacques gallery, accompanied by a book, which I really recommend getting, with an essay by Martin Herbert, and thank you for coming in Graham! Hello, how are you?

Very well.

Let's talk about figures and the characters you have within your work, because I'm really interested in how you come up with those characters that you create within your work?

I find them in various places, a lot of the time in a German fashion magazine that I really like that has patterns in it, where you can make the clothes. It's from the '80s and I particularly like that one, because there's no sense of sexual allure in the images, which I find really boring about current fashion photography, as it seems to be all about that. And obviously, the fantasy is then to pull you to buy something which I just find distasteful in lots of ways. These images are really quite mundane, in the sense that they're doing quite normal things. They're having a cup of tea or making something, and I love that. I really just wait until there's an image that just feels very special. Then usually after quite a few years actually thinking about it, I'll then sit in front of it for a long time just staring at the image and trying to listen to what the person in that photograph seems to be saying, or requiring, or worrying about, or trying to tell me. Then I change what she wears, or he wears, and change the environment, what's next to them, according to that. Just so they have more power, I suppose. It feels really important for me to do that.

It's amazing, because there's such a sense of stillness in the works that you do. It's interesting to me that they come from photographic sources at all, or some elements of it do, because they feel visually, aesthetically, to live in this very soft focused otherworld in a way. They seem very of a single unit somehow, a single place?

I'm so enjoying what you're saying that I don't have an answer to it! Say it again!

> *Let's talk about the settings for a minute, because really a lot of the works are put in domestic settings, but they also feel like they are referencing Renaissance art history... You definitely feel this historical sense of things. When you are taking the original source image and putting it in this fantasy space, how are you creating those spaces? What's drawing you to that background?*

I suppose I still have this odd feeling that… I think because I don't watch TV, I just spend an evening looking through an art book. I've spent so long looking at painting, that the world of the Renaissance actually feels so real to me and so thoroughly described, that I'm certain that if I travelled to Italy, some part of Italy, I'd actually find the Renaissance still there. I'm absolutely convinced. That's why that's a very real part of my paintings, I suppose. And I also have this feeling, it's not based on any writing that I've read, but I have the sense that femininity somehow was designed or began in the Renaissance. I don't know if there's any basis to that, I really don't, but I always have that feeling. I think that maybe there was a different attitude in the Middle Ages to feminine sexuality, I think there must have been…

> *Obviously, you have started to do images of men now and we'll talk about that in a bit but looking at these idealized female icons of beauty – we can give you a whole Beatrice/Dante reference there! Let's talk a little bit about what interests you about beauty in a wider sense?*

I think it's funny. I actually find it very hard to process beauty. I find it very tricky and I'm aware that I don't find it necessarily pleasurable – female beauty. Of course, I do, but what I mean by that is, I experience it as a massive stabbing pain. Actually, I find it very very painful, and I don't know if anyone else… I've never really talked about that before but, it's very difficult. The work somehow allows me to legitimately have some kind of femininity, that's okay. Instead of sexualizing the pain or turning it into an addiction. I think that the drawing started off by me immersing myself in femininity, when I felt really more and more uncomfortable being masculine. The sculptures that I made before the drawings were definitely about that. Especially the initial drawings, that were a way of bathing myself in not being a man, because that's all you were looking at and you could forget about all the crimes committed by men and the prisons being full of men. The fact that a man's body seems to have so much muscle which suggests violence, whereas a woman's body has softness, and it has a layer of fat which causes it to be beautiful actually. That there is the potential of producing another being inside, which is a ridiculous thing, and for breastfeeding…The fact that a women's body can produce a food substance feels absolutely ridiculous – which is maybe not necessarily true, but it seems an opposition that one sex is for nurture and one sex is for something else… I struggle with that a lot. The works always feel like I have to make them. They feel very therapeutic actually, and increasingly so. They are specifically therapeutic rather than being generally so. And I'm very grateful that I'm able to do that…

> *The new pictures you have done of men are very feminized images of men, that almost look like Fra Angelico or something like this. Why did you after all this period of time of focusing on female figures did you decide that you wanted to do male figures?*

I think for such a long time I just did not want to, and then it starts to catch your attention and you think; "Well, I don't really want to, but it would be quite interesting…" Then you get to another stage where you think; "Actually, I really would love to see just what would happen" but I still don't act on that. I just wait until that moment – I generally do this in my work – I wait until that moment where the next day after breakfast, when I simply have to draw my first ever man. I wait until that feeling. And I always find, if you do wait until that moment where it's simply "I have to now!", then it works. When I painted my first man, it certainly seemed to bring up so many issues relating to my upbringing, which wasn't awful, but it made sense of the fact that I never did paint men before that time. The first man I painted was actually a man in a pair of pyjamas that were fairly feminized – with three bows in different places, one bow over his ankle and apiece of trouser actually went right over his foot, a bit like a onesie for a child. I was just trying to quietly make the point, which Grayson Perry made a while ago, which is that surely men are actually the hysterical gender of the two! In the sense that if a man is driving along and someone cuts them off, they can get out of the car and actually be ready to assault that person, to terribly injury or destroy their car or even kill them. They'd be prepared to do that. And I've felt those feelings too. I mean, that is a complete overreaction! That's something that women might do occasionally, but I think less so than men, and that feels quite frightening. Sorry, what I was trying to say is that I was trying to save that first man. I always feel that maybe man is the less secure emotionally of the two. If you watch two men meeting together, they will make jokes, and they won't be brave enough to talk about really difficult emotional things. Whereas women will sit down and generally they seem to, from what I can see, talk about really quite difficult things…

> *We've been trained to allow ourselves to have those conversations. It's more a norm, right? It's the idea of being more emotionally open. Women are, arguably, put in a position where that seems normal. I totally agree with that. I feel like it's a good time to play your first track. To play the Sparks track, which I find really interesting. This idea of the fluidity of gender and representation of gender. When did you first listen to Sparks and why this Sparks tune?*

Could we play the A-ha one first?

> *Yeah. Go on.*

Is that OK?

> *No, please! We'll start with A-ha.*

I suppose the A-ha I was listening to in the '80s. I was listening to it through the wall of my bedroom… My sister was listening to that, and I was listening to Metallica at that time. I think I remember Frank Zappa saying that a lot of love songs in the '60s and in the '50s are men talking about how they want to hold their baby very tight and make her feel secure and he pointed out, quite interestingly, and quite rightly, that actually it's that men who want to be comforted in that moment. They want to have sex and actually it's about their gratification and their needs. This A-ha track – I could not work it out. It seems to somehow reverse that. It doesn't seem to be doing that. I only read a few days ago that it was actually written by one of the singers to console someone who just lost somebody. Someone had died, and so it makes sense as to why it didn't quite fit into what I thought it was. It's about the only piece of music that will get me singing in the studio.

This is A-ha 'There's Never a Forever Thing'.

—

That was A-ha, which I remember quite well from my youth! Let's talk about your studio practice for a bit. What's your studio like and how does that context influence what you're making? Because there's such a stillness looking at the images you make, I almost expect you to have a monk-like environment or space…

I work at home. I just find that lovely, because all the things that you need as emotional support or physical props, visual props, books that you love – they're all there. I used to work in a sort of industrial studio for about 10 years and I found it so bleak! Instead, I have the distraction of children, coming up to say hello, or sometimes crying or arguing. I find that preferable to the bleakness of other studios, which just feel so empty and human-less. My studio is as nice as I can possibly make it. I tidy it a lot. There's no equipment around. It feels similar to my bedroom when I was 16, where I used to actually make fashion drawings from fashion magazines.

Where did you grow up?

In Scotland, in Dundee. We used to be taken up lots and lots of mountains and I'd come back and just draw in my room. I like pretending that my work is just a hobby, that I'm not a professional artist at all. It was just what I liked to do. It does feel a great luxury to be able to do that. It feels very nice…

Why drawing in particular? Because if you look at your work, it's so detailed and there's such a fine line in what you do, you can almost think it was painting actually, when you look at it. What draws you to pencil? I'm assuming you're using pencil?

It's not a pencil, it's a drawing material; gouache. Sort of a poster paint, water based.

My god, you're skilled! That's the basic material that most of us use when we're younger! I can't believe you can do that level of detail!

It doesn't really want to do what you tell it to do. But I like the fact it just feels intimate, which coloured pencil used to feel as well, which is what I used to work in. It feels quiet and it feels manageable and oil paint feels too pressured. Similar to having a big studio – that feels pressured too. Gouache feels a bit hopeless somehow. It's a bit of a low-down material. I like that. And I do like its connection to design, that it's not necessarily so much of a fine art material.

In your last show you actually had a few pieces that are almost unfinished. That seem to be referencing Arts and Crafts design or some kind of graphic interior elements.

There are some pieces I want to make, and I've been making them since my last solo show, where they feel like they're heading towards my version of constructed textiles. I think one of the things I always like about making the sculptures and the drawings is that they really allow me to do so many different things. In a sense the drawings allow me to design my own clothes, have my own fashion set up, and interior design, and jewellery, and portraiture, and decoration, and abstraction… I suppose the constructed textiles remind me of when I was doing my BA. We were asked to choose which subject to do, and I really struggled to choose. I wanted to be in the fashion department partly because there were lovely, friendly girls there who were very smiley, and you had lots of radio music playing and the fine art department always had quite a lot of depression and staring.

I love the idea of this being like the fundamental difference between two mediums – fashion; smiley and plays music. Fine art; grumpy and they stare. It's beautiful. I love that.

I used to travel around from different departments in BA and ask questions and talk to the head of design and ask which material scissors I should buy and ask perspective problems of the architect department. I think I essentially still do that now, and I really love that. Anyway, nice question.

I think it's time for another record. If you want to play the Kai Althoff. This is an incredibly beautiful object.

Kai Althoff works under lots of different aliases in his music. This particular alias is called Orla, which I think produced one album. It was made as a gift for a museum in 2015. There are very few copies of it… I just dreamed of what it might sound like. The cover opens up into this almost octopus-type shape with arms and it's ornately drawn over the top. It is just incredible. Kai Althoff actually sent me a copy with lots of other stuff in a big parcel, which was just one of the loveliest things. He has encouraged me so much throughout my solo show, it was so, so nice. Then I did finally get to hear the music. It just has the feeling of Bowie from the '80s. Not his music, but all the influences being funnelled back through a metal tube and the noises that would be made through that metal tube. Which makes sense, because Kai Althoff was brought up in Cologne and has his family there, but lives in New York now. And Bowie in the '80s, and in the late '70s, is shuttling back and forth between New York and Germany. It makes sense that it would have that feel to it. This piece is mostly glockenspiel or xylophone, I don't know which. I always had a fantasy that I would be in an '80s thrash metal or speed metal band but their music would suddenly stop and then I'd be able to do a glockenspiel solo in the midst of that… This is the closest I come to that.

This is Kai Althoff's Orla, and the track is called 'Stork'.

—

That was Orla and the track was 'Stork'. Can you talk a bit about how you present your work because I find it really interesting – the framing of your pieces and the scale. They are a really intimate scale, but also you frame them in these hessian textural, jute frames that feel like '70s museums. What draws you both to the intimacy of the scale and that way of presenting things?

I think Rothko is typically thought of as being immersive, but actually, when I go to the Sainsbury's wing of the National Gallery and you're up close to a painting, and it's 30 centimetres away, it's actually more immersive, because no one's going to walk in front of you, because you're so close to it. There are no air particles there either. There's no sense of you being in front of another object. You're in that world. So, if intimacy is my goal – which it is with the work, one of the goals, one of the motives – then that gets more realized with a small piece, than anything larger. Also going back to just making it manageable, because I don't want it to be something that's ever even slightly a nightmare, because the sculptures became so technically impossible. They became a nightmare…

What were your sculptural works like? Because I've never seen your sculpture.

They were an Ikea version of Baroque! The idea is a painting you can walk around and then they unravel like a piece of music through time, instead of a painting which you have the feeling you see at once. They defy categorization. They are painting and sculpture. They're masculine and feminine. I think I always quite like that the drawings are equal, as you said. They could be paintings, they could be drawings, and I don't define them either way. They can be both. The hessian surround – I think it's linen – is just to give a greater feeling of warmth. It also allows the painting part of the work to be given a textured surface, but it's not underneath the illusion. It's outside of the illusion… It is of a bit of a joke on that too, in some way…

What paintings are you going to see at the National Gallery? What are the ones that you keep revisiting? Because that's a very amazing collection.

I just love it. I love London because I can cycle up there from my house, get there in 30 minutes, lock my bike up right outside the door, run up the stairs and instantly I can see a painting which is priceless and has been around for centuries. I will look definitely at Piero della Francesca.

I mean the background and detail, the little weeds…

I know and they're just peculiar paintings and they're very tonally, very strange because tonally they're very shallow and as a result the colours sing in an odd way. It's odd because they are designed so geometrically and carefully, but if you look at the background of the 'The Baptism of Christ' with the dove above his head. If you look at the landscape there, it's so casually painted. It's not at all careful. It's just splashy. Then I will look at Vermeer… I love the movement of Rubens. It feels like the only painter, along with Bridget Riley, who can actually create any kind of visual movement… I will look at Uccello, Lippi, Sassetta, and sometimes Van Eyck.

Glorious collection.

And definitely every time, the Raphael 'Madonna of the Pinks', which is just such an amazing painting.

I love the idea of the repetition of seeing these paintings. We are going to play another one of your tracks. György Ligeti – how do you say his name?

György Ligeti.

Thank you. Tell me about Ligeti.

I found this record in a skip in Peckham, so it suggests that the pub might have played it one day, which is hilarious. I've never found a compilation of his work on CD, but for some reason it's on this record. It's from 1957 and it's an electronic composition and I feel very understood by this piece of music. I often have days where I play A-ha backed with Ligeti – back and forth between the two – and they create the most lovely balance. It makes sense of the world.

Amazing. This is a György Ligeti 'Glissandi' from 1957.

—

That was Ligeti. Let's talk a little bit about material, the representation of textile. There's such a fluidity in your materials. They often feel translucent. Basically, you're really good with a piece of cloth! One of my favourite things I saw you do was a drawing where you did a big sleeve. Tell me about what you find interesting about textile.

I think it's a peculiar thing. I really love it. It's very hard to put into words. That's a really tricky question to answer, I don't know why that's so difficult.

How interesting that it's an emotional thing for you…

It almost feels very expressive and allows… I remember going with my mum to various shops, even if it was just Marks and Spencer, and she was very careful about the way she spent money. I generally would have to beg her to let me buy something. She would go up to pieces of fabric and she would just feel it in her fingers, and she would always talk about the quality or the lack of quality of a certain garment. That always stayed with me. Also, my dad actually studied at textile college in the borders. He worked with the most coarse version of fabric, which is jute, which was a large part of the industry of Dundee. I don't know if that has influenced me, but I always look at paintings from the past and I'm aware that when you see a painting which depicts a certain moment in history, that the painter is not actually depicting the clothing of that moment but depicting their own contemporary clothing. That feels fascinating! Also, certain films – I'm talking about certain films of the historical period. Say Joan of Arc that's made in the '50s and then a film made in the '80s. You'll learn more about the '80s and the '50s, than you will about Joan of Arc, just by looking at those two films. They are very different films. I think fabric is so specific and pattern is so specific. I play this game with my children, where we pick up the cover of a book, and we have to guess the year that it was made. They are getting better at it! Just from picking up small visual clues. I love that. The specific nature of design – how it's so particular.

Often when I'm looking at material within paintings, I often feel that it's representative of the history of art in some way. It's almost a summation of the idea of replicating life. Can I do sequins? How much can I work with silk? That seems to be the pinnacle of art, skilful trompe l'oeil in some sense. Your work seems to play in that.

Yeah, right.

Do you want to tell me a little bit about composition? Looking at some of your works this year you're cutting things off in an interesting way. You are playing around with architectural elements within the compositions more. How do you work with composition?

I think that different artists have different favourite things. I think probably perspective is my least favourite thing and I find it really tricky. Probably my favourite three things are maybe composition, tone, and colour. The list goes on… pattern as well. But I think I just absolutely love being able to make composition. I do spend an awful long time making really small adjustments a bit like Richard Tuttle who seems to have another very fetishized [approach]. The movement of objects until things feel right. I love trying to get things right and I always feel that you can get things better. I remember talking about this in BA and they would say to me "Oh Graham, there's no such thing as getting it right you know, all those solutions are good". I'm still not sure about that. I do think that great paintings are great because they've been composed. Incredibly great pieces of music are so moving because they have been thought through so carefully and there's different feelings in different segments of the music, where you go from a quiet area, and a predictable area, to a very discordant area. That has to be decided! I think contemporary art at the moment – well for a long time it has been denied, and it's been very odd. You have not been able to talk about these issues, and I think they're starting to come back… I think actually a lot of women painters are actually bringing that back, you know. I think Donna Huddleston is doing that… The names are going out of my head… Ella Kruglyanskaya is doing that. Jonathan Gardner as well. I find it very exciting…

We are going to finish by playing the song I tried to make you play at the beginning, which is the Sparks and Giorgio Moroder track. Which in itself as a combination of two people is amazing. When did you first hear Sparks?

I studied with David Thorpe, who was so lovely to study with. We just laughed most of the time actually. I think you know him Francesca… I partly chose this one because of your amazing ability to dance… Which is the opposite of me! I think dancing is such a beautiful thing, and I love it so much in its various forms from contemporary to disco, but I have this brain that doesn't allow me to dance. I will dance for about a minute and it's all going really well and then my brain will start talking to my body and saying why are we doing this? What is this for? Why? Why are we celebrating at this particular moment when we weren't celebrating for the last three weeks? But this is about the only piece of music that will actually get me dancing in the studio. Giorgio Moroder has an incredible power to do that. It's very well composed too…

This is 'My Other Voice' by Sparks with Georgio Moroder and you've been listening to Graham Little. Thank you very much for coming!

Thank you.

Mike Nelson

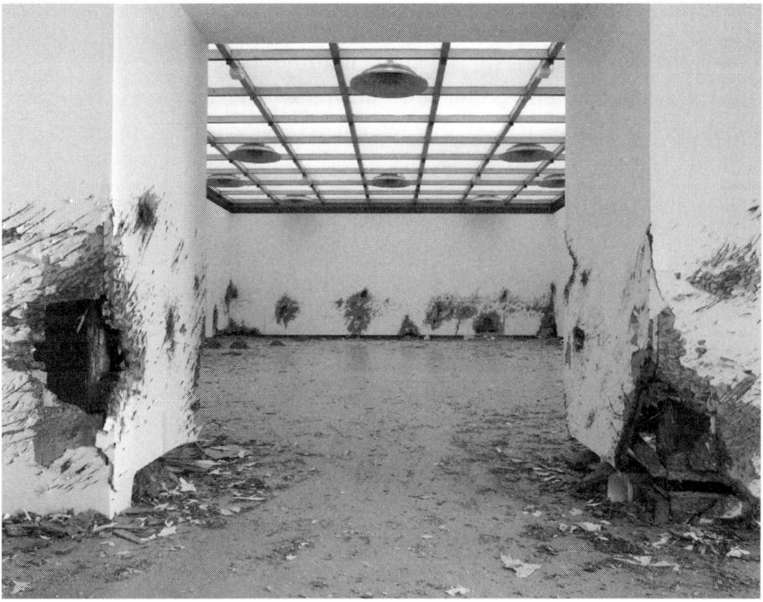

To the Memory of H.P. Lovecraft, 1999-2008.

25.09.19

Hi. You're listening to NTS, and this is Francesca Gavin with Rough Version. And I'm very happy to say my guest this month is Mike Nelson. Mike is a British artist, based around London, on the edges of London, who represented Britain in the Venice Biennale in 2011, and had an enormous show at the Duveen Galleries at the Tate Britain this year, and is represented by Matt's Gallery. Mike, thank you for coming in.

Thank you, for letting me come in, a man from the provinces – suburban Crystal Palace.

Suburbia, you've made it in from suburbia. Actually, is there a direct train to Dalston?

It's not so far away.

Let's talk about your work in a wider sense. I've just come from the Tate, which is on for a little bit longer. One of the things that I look at whenever I've seen any of your work is your interest in rooms and the separation of spaces. What do you like about the idea of the room?

I think there's an intimacy, I suppose, I think. To try and have an intimacy with a work of art is quite a difficult thing, in many ways. The room is a device in many ways to allow that to happen. Very much with the Duveen. I mean, it's an awkward space. It's a big corridor. An incredibly fantastic, large corridor. But the thing that struck me was that I wanted to close it off and make it into its own space, because it's a huge space. It's 10 meters wide and about 100 meters long. That was one of my first impulses but it's one which allowed me to indulge one of my greatest likings for hanging doors.

Do you like hanging doors?!

Well, yes, strangely. I think it's a slight, obsessive compulsive aspect to me. I like physical activities and construction making. I think it allows a certain meditative space in terms of working in both in terms of the process of thought, but also just general wellbeing. But if my body starts to groan under it after too many years of it, I might be addressing that in the near future.

Thinking about that installation, there's a lot of swinging doors and actually in your installations. I've seen these doors that swing open.

It's a double swing hinge, I suppose.

Thank you, for the professional explanation.

A lot of those and a double swing which seemed appropriate, I thought, for the Tate Gallery in that it was like a saloon door slight joke on a salon door. As it swings back and forth, you get a glimpse of what lies beyond – the head of a Henry Moore or an old master painting in the distance. Hence why they were like that.

When you first started making installation-based work, let's talk about that. We can talk about more of the Tate work later. How did that grow? Was that something that you were working on at the very, very beginning? Obviously, 'The Coral Reef' in 2000 is your best known installation.

Within Britain anyway. I suppose, as a potted history, I was making quite dogmatic, political work when I was at college. Less fluid, less narrative. I found that the reception of the audience's was a little limited compared to when I started making more work, which tapped into a narrative or fiction, which rediscovered when I left college after my BA. That really led through a succession of more, chaotic and a sculpture installation. Probably the best known body of which were 'The Amnesiacs', this kind of biker gang that was somehow built out of the debris washed up by the seas, which somehow tapped into the novels of Stanisław Lem and the Strugatsky brothers. 'Solaris', the film made by Tarkovsky, being an example of it. Then I suppose 'The Coral Reef' was the first work that really addressed an architectural space. And that was very much an equation of a literary structure into a spatial structure. The reference point for that was 'A Perfect Vacuum' by Stanislav Lem. I suppose it's a generic type of novel, that perhaps

Calvino or Borges would have used as well. But particularly this novel called 'A Perfect Vacuum', a review of non-existent books, where the first chapter reviewed itself, but also argued as part of the anthology of short stories at the same time. In many ways, I've been sort of flipping between these more spatial architectural constructions and sculpture, but at the same time, not really considering them as being any different to one another. In many ways, the objects and the scenarios or the tableau within the architectural constructions, were just as much a sculpture as a free-standing object that's in the Tate now. I think my desire to make those special structures say in the Tate was very multifaceted in a way. I was both looking to somehow translate literary space into the spatial, structural space. But I was also very much reacting to a period in the '90s, where everything seemed to be video installation, and you would walk from one video station to the next, pass the sculpture without even looking at it. This idea of entrapment, which was both in the concept or the idea of the work, in terms of this idea becoming lost in the world of lost people was also sort of physical in your entrapment. There was a double room. I don't know how much listeners know of the work, but it was a series of, the idea of the review was translated into the idea of a reception. And based roughly on the generic minicab office in London, where they'd be very haphazardly built. One object or two objects would perhaps suggest the identity of the people that run the mini cab. In many ways, the idea of these different spaces that you walk one to the next – sorry I've lost the thread…

> *It's really interesting to talk about the mini cab thing. Once I went into a mini cab office, I felt like I was going into your work, which was incredible. But it's also, there was something when you went through those spaces, wandering through the structures that you create, they're quite eerie. They're quite unsettling. You get the hint of something being there, the remnants of like a story.*

I was very much interested in the idea that an artwork didn't have to exist in a constant existence, but more in the idea of it being fragmented into the memories of many different people. Disseminated somehow. The work wasn't read at that moment in time, but was going to read somehow, perhaps sometime in the future. Maybe 10 years in the future, three months in the future. Perhaps when you buy a newspaper, or reading a book, or something that might make sense. It was a way to fracture looking at a piece of art. Also, it was a way of perhaps denying an immediate consumption and perhaps an economic consumption on some level, as a way of somehow avoiding the marketplace of art. I think, in terms of the trajectory of what I've done over the years, I think that work and that idea has had less traction a bit as I've become more successful, and exhibitions have been more occupied by more people. The idea of the construction of these types of spaces being appropriated by people and people's outside perhaps, firstly, in immersive theatre.

They bit your style, bluntly.

Certain age groups have actually approached me to work with them. Very nice, very kind and respectful of what they do but it's not really what I do. But at the same time, I think over this period of time, has changed the reading of that genre of work that I made. The pop-up restaurants pop-up cinemas, all sorts of things. Obviously, to me, they don't look the same and function the same, but I think it actually stopped people looking at them in the same way that they looked at them when I first made them. They don't understand them in the same way because of its absorption into popular life, I suppose, of everyday people. Even to the point where now, if you go to Frieze Masters, one particular gallery is constructing whole environments rather like mine, but by an art direction company. I suppose it's a very subtle difference but to me, there is a difference. The difference is what your motivation to do it is. I think the motivation to make a work of art can also often be felt. This is something that's very hard to quantify in looking at the work. You can't always be – and especially with this clutter, with too many people…

I love the idea of people as clutter, by the way, beautiful. The city is so cluttered.

You can see why I wasn't so much into immersive theatre and I'm more into sculpture sort of… I like the absence.

Actually, I really saw that come across. I remember on one piece, which was at the Hayward where it was almost like a minimalist version of one of your spaces. Was it inspired by Lovecraft?

It was inspired by Borges in fact. It was a short story called 'More Things'. In brackets it said: (To the memory of HP Lovecraft), which is where I took the title for the work from… There are two quite pure versions of the idea of the equation of literary structure to spatial structure. That work and another work called 'After Kerouac'. But with that work where it was the white space just ripped as if a beast had eaten it, from the height it could reach. Then there were piles of dung, which we're just consumed and digested remnants of the walls. In a way, it wasn't minimal, but ultimately very much the same as 'The Coral Reef', so in some respects, but visually different.

Before you talk about this, I think we should play a song because you've got some great songs. Let's start with the Dave Crosby because that's an equally important song to me. When did you first hear this Dave Crosby track?

I probably would have heard it in my teenage years, but it wasn't until probably my mid 20s that it became one of those staple songs that I could have listened to. I think it might have been actually my friend, Robert, that reintroduced me to it. I always refer to it as being David Crosby, I suspect it is Crosby, Stills and Nash, and maybe even Young. I'm not sure what it's from. It's from 'Déjà Vu', isn't it? So, 1970. To me, the lyrics are painfully almost trite in many ways. And yet, the delivery of it is so sublime. It almost moves me to tears when I listen to it, somehow. There's an essence I think around the idea, I think for many people around the years they were born. I was born in 67. I think that period of the late '60s, both in terms of art references, but also in terms of music, that just constantly stays with me. I think embedded in is this contradiction to many people's ideas. That actually making art or making music or being a musician or being an artist, a poet is just a bit of a waste as job and a bit easy. And actually, embedded in it, that actually there is a sacrifice to being this thing because it is a burden in some ways. And I feel that when I hear this song.

This is 'Almost Cut My Hair' by Dave Crosby from 'Déjà Vu' in 1970.

—

That was 'Almost Cut My Hair'. I'm going to use that also as a lyrical segue into the political undercurrent in your work. That song is very much about let's say the representation of rebellion. The idea of longer hair being that late '60s concept of not conforming in some sense. Do you want to tell me about how you feel about politics? You're saying, at the very early stage, that was more evident. I still feel like there's a very strong political element in your work. But it's in no way didactic. The current things that you've made using dysfunctional, disused factory machines...

I'll just say that I could have chosen that as well, because there is a reference in one work from 2004, called 'Triple Bluff Canyon', which was a reconstruction of 'Partially Buried Woodshed' by Robert Smithson in 1970. In that work, I reconstructed this work which was the woodshed on the Ohio State campus in 1969, '70. Robert Smithson, land artist, was invited to make a work on the campus. He turned up in a bad cold. It was at his liking, for burying a building. So heaped a load of Earth on top of this old woodshed until the central beam cracked. I reconstructed this but built it somehow into a desert landscape in the upper galleries of Modern Art Oxford. It was a response for me. The work was posthumous criticism of that. Because 'Four Dead in Ohio' by Neil Young is a reference to the shootings that happened later that year, on the Ohio State campus and the demonstrations against the war in Vietnam and Cambodia. Later on, that year, somebody scrawled on the front of the woodshed in its buried state, the date May... I can't remember, the 4th or something, 1970. This work became indecipherable to political event of the time. After his death, Robert Smithson, he fell out of a plane, I think, the next year, the work was posthumously politicized by Nancy Holt – an artist and his wife. Where she talked about this idea of things being buried. I mean, in a way, I think there's a subconscious aspect where I could understand that. But I thought it was slightly fanciful, but I decided to purposefully republicize that work by burying it in a desert, in reference to the second

Gulf War that had just happened somehow. Almost like it was a displacement by Smithson, where I am reflecting two wars and one, Vietnam and one in the Gulf and this idea of foreign wars. So, I just wanted to say that just because there was some reference…

Beautiful but there even is a political element within your use of materials.

Even the structure of acquiring the materials. I mean, with the work in the Tate, the Duveen galleries were made into this sculpture caught in 1937 and opened by King George VI. And if you go to the exhibition, there's some big wooden Union Jack hoardings with the initials G E these are actually from the coronation of Georgia VI in 1937, which I fortuitously found in a junk shop next to me in Crystal Palace.

How convenient!

It was quite astounding. I was in the midst of building, and I was like, "Oh my God. Look at these". When they first approached me, and I questioned the formality of the space. Of closing off, giving an intimacy, making it its own space. I was very much thinking about the idea of a sculpture court. Thinking over to the British Museum, and to the Victoria and Albert Museum. Thinking about the things that existed in these spaces, and the fact that they were these objects, which came from our empire, or from our foreign interests throughout history. Thinking about how they came to be, who paid for these spaces to be constructed. Predominantly, they are industrialists. This was our winnings from the Industrial Revolution in many ways, and Imperial expansion into other countries. Exhibiting of these objects that we somehow procured for ourselves through our power and wealth. I thought: "What could you share? What would a monumental sculpture court look like now in our current state?" It occurred to me that the remnants of the end of that Industrial Revolution, on that point of obsolescence, were very interesting. I've always thought in relation to 20th century sculpture. Because they both allowed the construction of sculpture that appeared in such a way that it did in that post-war period. It also dictated, to some degree, to sort of aesthetics of the sculptures. The sculptures then spoke back to the design of the machines that made them. I thought this could be interesting. It started to become a certain idea. How do I get hold of these things? Now, I mean, I've been hanging around strange markets and salvage yards all my working life, all over the world, but they're getting far fewer. They're getting hard to access. But it struck me that, there's a way to access these things, which I don't normally use, which is the internet. These, liquidation sites. These online auctions where they liquidate companies. I think ideologically and politically, this made a lot of sense, because it's the epoch that superseded itself, the Industrial Revolution. But also, a sense of consumption through it, somehow. I went about going onto the sites, viewing these different companies that were being liquidated. All you have are these small, grainy pictures. It is a very complicated, and really quite an unpleasant process on these objects. Obviously looking for certain objects that represent certain types of industry that seemed important – not just industry but agriculture. Then, structurally, I had to build certain aspects of it. The wood that you see, that constructs the large walls, the octagon and the North Duveen and south Duveen gates – that all came from a barracks in Shropshire, in Shrewsbury.

Nice dose of military reference accidentally thrown in, or intentionally thrown in.

Intentionally, yeah, because the 1870s barracks – beautiful construction, been demolished and sold off and liquidated by the MOD. There's not just the private companies liquidating but also the state. The doors within the octagon and the North Duveen are from an old bone hospital in Bolsover Street I ripped out years ago. Even a work in the very far end, is constructed out of all the steel sheets from a low-rise social housing block, which was welded on to sort of keep the squatters out.

It's really interesting idea like liquidation of history and like a wider sense. A lot of your work seems to be like looking at ideas of archaeology, or looking backwards or rethinking what history is, in some way. The liquidation of British history says something about our moment in time. Quite depressing metaphor bluntly.

You couldn't really avoid trying to make sense of the time we're in. In many ways, I was quite pleased with the result, because I don't think the work is didactic in terms of a certain position in regard to what we're doing to this country at a certain point. But actually, is more talking about what underpins the division in this country, ultimately. When I spoke to a guy delivering this. He came in from Essex, and he was delivering the stuff. He was chatting to me about what do you want this stuff for? He says, "it's going to the Tate", and obviously he's chatting away to me, but obviously thinking, "I'm just some guy unloading a lorry". I start chatting to him, and we can have a chat for quite long. It's quite a lot of stuff to unload because a big article. He starts getting suspicious about how I know so much about this, what's happening with that. I own up as to that I'm meant to be making it myself. But his kind of politics in regard to our current situation was very much at odds with mine. Yet, his understanding of the matter in the material, and what I was talking about, was exactly the same. It was a different conclusion. But ultimately, I felt as though there was something in this that spoke to the majority, as opposed to a certain Metropolitan, perhaps elite – as we might be seen.

> *Let's not do that! That seems a very appropriate moment to play your Fall track. Which is definitely not a London elitist band. When did you first hear this track? And why did you choose it?*

I was actually, if I really was honest, I would have chosen 'Kicker Conspiracy' because that is the first track I ever heard by The Fall. But this one I like because it's an interesting bit in it, where there's a shout out for a taxi for Mr. Nelson, which of course in regards to 'The Coral Reef' is perfect and always intrigued me. When I went to Australia to do a couple of shows, I realized why. I was in a television show from the '60s that it's very popular, called 'Mike Nelson', about a scuba diver.

> *Really?!*

I do like a bit of snorkeling as well. So, I was particularly taken by this and apparently it's a reference to a Jethro Tull concert where a ringing phone on stage is answered by a man in a wetsuit and he shouts out to the audience 'Taxi! Taxi for Mr. Mike Nelson'.

Wow, that's amazing. Thanks for Jethro Tull referencing. Well, this is 'Rebellious Jukebox' by The Fall from 'Live at the Witch Trials'.

—

That was The Fall.

I would say that I think he is one of – he was one of our national treasures. The man was a genius.

Yes, may he rest in peace. I want to talk a little bit about the aesthetics of what you do because looking at your sculptural work, your objects are quite beautiful and often quite anthropomorphic. There is a human-ness in them, even if they're made from found wood to industrial objects to everything.

The anthropomorphism in the work in the Tate is twofold, because again, I was thinking about, a wing, the bull, a Syrian bull in the British Museum. Thinking about that in relation to a machine. A machine somehow having anthropomorphic aspects or looking like a beast, an animal or a figure. But at the same time, when you look at something like a winged bone in the British Museum, who made this? Who were these people? What were these people that made this thing? What culture did they come from? I thought that it was possible that that was something which was still actually in existence within workshops, factories, now even though on the point of obsolescence. That there's a certain generation that might look at it. And even not a generational thing. It might even just be that you're not familiar with such things.

I mean, I'm not great on Sumerian sculpture.

But even with these machines, where they would look so out of kilter with our life now, because I think the acceleration of technology has made us so distant somehow to that kind of physicality. That there is the sense of, who are these people that work these machines? I think there's an absence, when you look at the object. There are these objects of the people that have worked them and probably worked them for decades of their life. So of course, the patina or the presence of these people are still there with these objects ultimately.

When it comes to how you work, you have a studio?

A small studio, yeah.

And mostly you don't make your things there?

That whole show at the Tate was made within the Tate. I could have collated the material. And I obviously looked for objects, which I could make into different things, but I didn't know particularly what was going to go where. I mean, a lot of the material that allow me to stack things up came from a factory in my hometown of Loughborough, where my cousin worked and many of my friend's parents worked.

So, you're always working site specifically in some way then making the things?

Pretty much. I mean most of the shows I've made it's been pretty nomadic. In Brazil, I collect the stuff in Brazil. I turn up and I can drive around and pick it up and find it and build it. Melbourne, Sydney, New York all these places over the years. Obviously, London's a bit easier because I'm here. It's a bit of a moment in time perhaps for me because I'm of a certain age now where I'm not as fast as I was. This practice is getting more difficult. Over the years, I've tried to keep it very light. In fact, I didn't have a studio till four years ago at all. I had two big metal toolboxes. Then, I made an exhibition with the tools. My old tools that are on the edge of their own obsolescence and the toolbox – that was an exhibition itself. I suppose that marked a certain moment as well. It was quite psychological, quite emotional. Because it was the giving away these tools was perhaps an acknowledgement that time is limited to some degree. So now I just took on a studio in Crystal Palace, a small old shop. You can't really get anything any bigger than six foot by three foot in and out the door. So, I can't really construct anything of any scale. It's more of a space just to think and be surrounded by interesting objects and go through the emails and do some drawing or whatever.

You make drawings?

I do drawings in my notebooks. People say have you got architects drawings and engineers drawings. I said, "No, I just have these". Even when in Venice, when we started building it, the Venetian authorities came around and said "you can't do this. It's illegal, we're going to close you down. Who's your architect? Who's your engineer?" I haven't got one. We're just building it. We had mezzanines with concrete floors…

They're Italian, surely this is normal…

No, no. They weren't happy at all but luckily, I'd worked with a very nice Italian architect in 2001 on the first Venice project I did. I did a huge Venice project in 2001 as well. So, I rang Cecio and he's great. He just said nice okay, we will do it this way. I'll give him a number of my engineer. Every time I came to build something, and it could be a little problematic in terms of structure or weight, I do a drawing of how it's going to be build, in my notebook and then I take a photograph, send it to him and he'd say, "I know bring the timbers in the structure in by 10cm" or "add an extra cm of concrete" or "make sure we put the steel in at this height". It was kind of nice actually. It was a nice process.

I'm going to play another song I want to play your Love song. It's a good Love song. Why this Love song?

I chose this one because it was not an obvious one. It was probably one that a lot of people would never have heard. It comes from the album 'Out There' which is still 1970 when the line-up of Love has changed. It's not the classic line-up. It's not 'Forever Changes' or 'Da Capo'. I think it's probably not thought of as good, but I think this has got huge power. I think it's again, that's why the idea of the late '60s, the idea of the counterculture, the idea of the hippie culture or whatever. It sums up sort of like that moment of change, that moment of shift by the very name of it. 'I'm Down'.

This is 'I'm Down' by Love.

—

That was Love. I just want to cover a little bit more before I let you go. Do you feel like there's something British in what you do? Do you think there's a Britishness about your approach?

In the '90s, I was very un-British, I would imagine. The climate of art, the culture of art then was very much at odds with what I was doing. I think it's hard to avoid the fact that I am British. That's what I've been brought up as. I think my interest in other cultures, which have always been…

Turkey is something that's hugely recurrent.

The whole Islamic Muslim world. I travelled there and it was the first place I'd been to really. I'd been on a French exchange. And then the next trip was out to the east of Turkey with my old girlfriend. I really only went there because she was there. And yet, it was like a sensory sort of trip. I look back on it now and the heat and the sounds, the smells of like the mosque, the different sort of like visual information everywhere. I found it was quite an incredible overload. I think it's something you realize that certain people are affected far more by such things than others. I think it took me years to actually unravel that experience. But of course, after that, I travelled hugely, especially in the Middle East through to Pakistan, up into Xinjiang province of China, and all across Morocco, Egypt, into Syria and all around back east Turkey again, and then down through China, into Mongolia, into Tibet. I did all these trips, just looking out, but predominately in the Muslim world. It was an area that seemed so much of an antithesis of the culture in which I've grown up within… That interest fed into the work and perhaps the insight I got from that travelling gave it a certain sort of essence that was beneficial in terms of its vision of history at that point in time. But it was a darkness as well sort of in terms of my understanding of it, I suppose. I think when you talk about Britishness, I think when I was at college, I was interested in the idea of the exotic. The idea that the West views the other as exotic. I was very aware of the complications of that equation, and my complication within it, but also interested in that, because ultimately, that is our history. I don't want to perpetuate it, but I'm interested to look at it, and to make some sort of sense of it.

I'm going to ask you one more thing. I want to talk a little bit about, like ideas around reality in fiction and what you do. I've got some amazing books of yours. I've got a really good book, which is loads of different books cut up forming a novel. Amazing book. But in a wider sense, that idea of the fiction, because even when you're using real things where they have the remnants of realness, but they're used in an unreal space.

I think it's that attempt to try and unravel itself and ability to project into an imaginative space, which I think is increasingly difficult in a world that's so crowded with matter. I grew up for half of my life without the internet, or the most formative time without the internet. And I do find that the presence of information quite disconcerting. I almost feel as though it's tangible in the air. I'm aware of it wherever I go. It's like matter. I mean, that probably sounds quite mad…

It's probably true. I mean, it's stuff in the air.

I think it's allowed us to be very knowledgeable. But it's actually stopped us from having that space in which to project into. With the works often now, perhaps they're becoming more like a slowing down process where there's a way, again, to find that imaginative space where you can project into. Especially with sculpture, I like the idea of things that appear to represent something or suggest something. But then you walk around it from another angle, and it falls back down. It's back to what it actually is – the matter it's made from. I think in many ways that you could equate that to an understanding of the world. I think when it becomes more illusory. I suppose that is what fiction does as well, because it creates images or pictures in your mind.

On that note, we're going to play your last track, because we're running out of time. Why did you choose this? It's also the shortest of your tracks, by Shirley Collins and Davey Graham.

It's probably quite a good one to end on in relation to fiction. This is very much in the British folk tradition. But also taps in very nicely in regard to my interest in the other and other countries. Davey Graham, where I bought an album by him in a jumble sale years ago. 50p.

Great price.

Great label, Folkways, I thought can't be bad. Never heard of him, back in the '90s. Put it on, I was absolutely blown away by his guitar playing. And then found out that actually this is the guy that underpins all the guitar players from the '60s Jimmy Page, Eric Clapton, John Renbourn. All of them pay homage to Davey Graham. I think he was born of Scottish and Nigerian parents. When he was a young man, he went to North Africa and the Middle East, and he travelled, picking up different guitar licks. Back in the early, mid '60s. And brought it back and played guitar like no one else ever had done. I don't think he was a particularly nice man. He was a heroin addict, most of his life. I think through the '60s and '70s. But on the NHS. I don't think Shirley Collins enjoyed making this album with him. But the teaming of him with her, whose voice is probably the best folk voice ever. I'm a great fan of Sandy Denny and Fairport Convention, as well, but I think probably Shirley Collins just about pips it. She's actually still about it, Shirley Collins and in fact, she played at a festival that we were at with Mark last year.

This is 'Hares on the Mountain' by Shirley Collins and Davey Graham. Mike Nelson thank you very much for coming in.

Imran Perretta

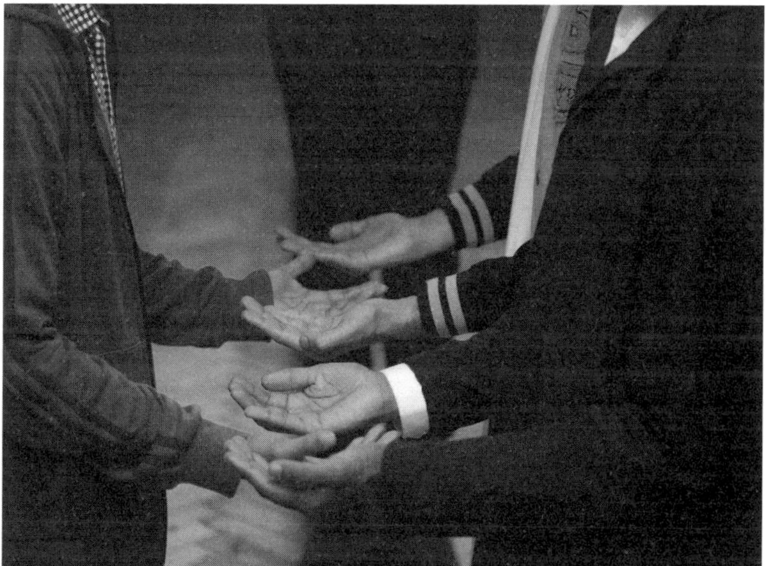

The Destructors, 2019.

30.10.19

Hi, you're listening to Rough Version on NTS. And my guest this month is Imran Perretta. Imran is a young British artist who was a recipient of the Jerwood FVU award last year and was shortlisted for the Jarman award, he also makes film work and he's been given a big show at Spike Island in Bristol, which is going to move to Chisenhale in London next year. And he's really good. Hi!

How are you doing? Alright?

I'm doing really, really well. Let's start by looking at your work in like a wider sense. Would you like to tell me a little bit about your process, because it seems that a lot of your stuff is based on either workshops or conversations and is drawing off documentary to lead to a narrative.

Often yeah…

Turning that into something else… How does that start?

I think it depends on the project, really. I can speak for the project that I'm on at the moment, which is – what you were talking about just now. The show that's going to start at Spike then go on to Chisenhale along with the Whitworth and Baltic.

Wow. You are doing all four corners of the country!

I know, all four corners, man! The work is called 'The Destructors' and a lot of the narrative of the film comes from personal stories. I think that's what led to find the language to write the words that became the script for the film… A lot of work came from these workshops that we're doing with young people in Mile End – community projects and a social justice organization called JAWAB. It was just an amazing, fruitful and extremely open discussion amongst a lot of young Muslim boys, who live in and round Mile End, about some of the issues affecting us. Just shooting the breeze and being able to create a safe environment where people could just say what they wanted without fear of judgment. I think for me, those conversations were,

I don't know… They allowed me to sort of find the language within my own narrative to begin to piece together this long form poem, that eventually became the script for 'The Destructors'.

This isn't the first time you've addressed ideas about Islamophobia, and colonialism and the experience of being a young Muslim man in this country. All the negativity that comes with that, or the positivity that comes with it…

Yeah. I think for me, I'm always trying to aim upwards and think about how the state is responsible for concretizing a lot of legislation around policing marginal communities, including Muslim communities. But also, other adjacent communities that are not necessarily faith-based. Thinking about how – for me anyway – I feel my responsibility as an artist is to always be looking upwards at the ruling class and at the powers that be. Using my energy in that way, I see it as positive. I'm drawing on Audre Lorde and thinking about directing my eye upwards. I think that, as soon as that energy goes, I don't know what I'll do… I'll probably do something else. But I think that's my momentum, my motivation… the well from which I draw my energy to be making art in this political way and with this particular language.

I want to start with your first song, because I want to get them all in and all four of them are really good. Why did you choose this one – the Raga Bhairav?

This is a tune that's really beloved by me and a friend of mine, Paul Purgas, who I share a studio with, who's a brilliant artist, and also an incredible musician. We have a sort of collaboration together called AMRA. This is one of the tunes that we came together on, where we were just blown away by it. It's this proto acid-house…

I mean, it's incredible I can't believe it's made, when is it made – in the '60s? '70s? It's insanely contemporary.

'70s yeah. It is crazy. This guy Charanjit Singh, was just a composer and a session musician in India, playing on a lot of Bollywood soundtracks. He went over to Singapore and bought a Roland 303, which is a Japanese monophonic synth. Almost unwittingly, and I certainly don't think he would ever claim this and no one else would, it's like a proto acid-house vibe written in Indian scales and Indian melodic modes. Each track on this album, which is called '10 Ragas to a Disco Beat', is based around a different Indian scale. I'm simplifying a bit, and it's just insane. I don't want to talk about it too much, you just have to listen. It's quite nuts.

OK. This is Charanjit Singh 'Raga Bhairav'.

—

I want to talk about the way you're saying you are drawing on your autobiography and you're working from your own personal experience. How do you balance your own experience as an individual? Being a south London boy. You're drawing on those things, the interviews you do, that kind of experience? How have you united those two things?

I think all those things are inseparable. I think that the only responsible thing for me to do is to reflect on my own experience and if I reflect on someone else's then it's with their consent and with their collaboration. So invariably, I'm writing or making music from, or creating visual material from, my own archive, or from my own experience. Because somehow to me, that seems like the only ethical thing to do. I think that my existence is multifarious. I'm a Bangladeshi Italian kid who grew up in a Muslim household, but with Roman Catholic grandparents on the Italian side, and I'm from Streatham. It's not unusual, actually, in South London, to have this kind of syncretic background. But I think for me, I'd be remiss to not try and reflect on it publicly. Because I think that those things are important for people to hear and to reflect on. This idea that there's not a myopic narrative around multiculturalism and that actually you can have a broader discussion that not only engages with and celebrates this syncretic culture. But like I said, that also can aim upwards at the ruling class and say, "these are the ways in which the powers that be can create a social death amongst marginal communities, some of which I'm part of". I am part of more than one you see, and we all are.

Do you want to tell me about how aesthetics come into your film work? How does the visual connect to what you're doing, which is narrative-led and very much about internal dialogues within people?

Sure. I like to use a lot of green screens and VFX and stuff like that. For me, it is very much about the magic-real aesthetic. I think it's about being able to superimpose otherworldly phenomena, like a plume of smoke on top of a blurred-out image of a Bangladeshi village or something. There are obviously leading interpretations there. I think for me, what's interesting about working with visual effects and the limitations of visual effects, is how they can begin to disrupt real life imagery, and in some ways, create these dreamlike and often, quite sinister frictions or abrasions between dissonant imageries. I think that's key because I think we're so used to images of black and brown death in the media and violence against gendered bodies and racialized bodies. Sometimes re-engaging with that trauma in a very direct way actually becomes counterproductive. When you begin to take it to this world, it becomes almost supernatural, slightly magic-real. It [becomes] very clear that this image, this layered image, is artificial or constructed in some way you can engage with. And you talk about that trauma without having to show real life images of it. For me, that's very important. How do you show violence without showing violence? Do you see what I mean?

Very much so. It's also that you become very aware of the construction of media imagery. Highlighting the fact that image is mediated.

One hundred percent. All the time, right? So, it's better to lean into it and try and do something else with it. Try and try again to create a sort of productive dissonance, as opposed to reinforce imagery that we've seen that can be dehumanizing or in some way appropriative or whatever else.

Do you want to talk a bit about the music collaboration you do, before we play your next track?

Yeah, shameless plug!

Tell me about AMRA and how that came about?

Paul and I have just been mates for a while, and we have similar music taste. There's many things we've diverge on, but we've been able to educate each other on each other's musical background.

He's in Emptyset as well.

Yeah. Paul is in Emptyset which is a pioneering, brilliant avant-garde electronic music band with Ginz (James Ginzburg) which is really just brilliant. A brilliant act – really boundary pushing in a lot of ways in terms of digital, analogue, and also in terms of conceptually driven music. For me and Paul, I think both being brown men, the thing that was interesting to us was the engagement with our own musical histories and to try and score our own existence, using a South Asian aesthetic, that is rooted in bass music and some of the subcultures that we've come from. In Paul's instance, coming from a more techno scene, and from my influence, which was more like a garage grime scene that I was part of when I was a teenager, and at school. The collaboration was born out of a mutual geekery, if you see what I mean, and the last track you heard was something that we really bonded over a few years ago. We've continued to complete each other's musical knowledge in a way and bounce off each other creatively, which has been super cool.

This is 'Heema' by AMRA

—

Have you incorporated any of that sound within your film work – your own art stuff? How's that manifesting?

I do all the soundtracks to my films.

Because you want to do everything?

It has control freak vibes in it! But I think one of the things about learning to make things when you are at art school is that you've got to do it yourself. You can't go and employ someone to do the VFX, you've got to learn how to 3D model. You can't go and get someone to mix and master your soundtrack, you got to learn to do it – or at least I did. And actually, I'm just a massive YouTube geek. I just love to do endless tutorials on YouTube about shit like that. I've weirdly trained myself up over many years to be half decent at lots of things, which I guess is some kind of career, isn't it?

Well, that's a good side of YouTube! There are many bad sides…

Indeed! We stick to the tutorials. Autoplay is turned straight off. Sound has become a really big part of the films, I guess. Because there's a symbiosis between the writing, the sound and the images. Well, at least I hope it's quite a tight relationship. I guess it's given me quite a specific visual and sonic language to the films, which is still growing and changing and evolving. But my background really is music, so it's always going to be a big part of any of the art stuff I do. I always say I've got this art career, I don't really know how, because to be honest, if I was a better musician, I would have just bunged this all off a long time ago! If I was a better guitarist, I would not be here! It's one of those funny things…

Do you want to tell me a bit about the Calais film?

Yeah, sure.

Describe what that was. You went out to Calais – I hate using the word jungle – but you were hanging out with a lot of displaced people who were in the camps before they got removed. I don't even know if they are still there. It's such a complex situation.

Yeah. Extremely complex. That film is called '15 days', and that was 2019. That was last year. That was a film I made in collaboration with a friend of mine, who at the time was living rough in the woods just by the motorway in Dunkirk. In one sense it is the Calais film, but it is also the Dunkirk film, which is a small detail, but an important one.

Particularly within the context of people thinking about British history and things like war. The first thing you think about is the beaches of Dunkirk...

Right, and what you find in that landscape is loads of bunkers. There's actually a bit of footage in that film. '15 days' is the name of the character in the film – my friend whose testimony we made the film around. He had a camera, and I had a camera, and we were filming in various places. I filmed at this ridiculous bunker in Dunkirk, at the site of the old jungle, which at that point had been raised and turned into – or was at the beginning of being turned – into a nature reserve. The border police were there very quickly, but I had this trump card, which was this British passport that let me get off scot free, but they had pepper spray at the ready. Actually, in the film, there are snippets of that encounter, because I kept recording while they stopped and searched me. We were collecting footage from inside the camps, from outside the camps. Trying to get vignettes of details within the camp that would give a sense of the scale of the occupation of the woods at that time, but also the humanity within it. The solidarity and all that stuff. But then you acknowledge the police violence and the brutality and the very cruel dehumanization that people were facing in those camps… All while trying to preserve everyone's identity. In the whole film, you never see anyone's face. '15 days' is obviously not his real name, but that was the name that he came up with when we first met each other. That became this alter ego around which the narrative begins to unfold. He told me that he came up with this name, because that was the amount of time that had elapsed between the day that I met him, and the last time that the police had come to take all his things away from him from the camp. He was just counting the days and it just so happened that I met him on the 15th day. We created this relationship and made this film.

It seems quite an apt moment to play your third track, which is 'Ghosts' by Japan. It has a haunting element to it, and the film has a haunting element. Do you want to tell me why you chose that song?

Firstly, Japan are all from Catford. I'm from Streatham, but my dad's from around there and so I just thought you need to put a bit of South

London in there! I gotta keep on brand. I think that tune is part of this era of avant-garde pop in the '80s that has really influenced me. I think of bands like XTC and A Certain Ratio and a lot of people that came out of the post-punk era but were not necessarily making post-punk. Japan is in some ways quite problematic, because there's a lot of conversation around appropriating Eastern aesthetics in their work and it's totally legit. But I think musically, they're a very fascinating band. The bassist is this guy called Mick Karn who used to play this fretless bass and he's just a genius. David Sylvian, who is the singer, then went on to work with people like Ryuichi Sakamoto, and a lot of avant-garde Japanese musicians, so there's this really interesting mythology around that band. I think this track was the only track they ever did that was in the top 10 or top 5? Something like that. It's one of those tunes that my dad's been playing to me, indoctrinating me with ever since I was little, because he used to be a music journalist. I just think rhythmically and melodically it's just all over the place and it's just so interesting. It's just a really brilliantly written piece of music and I just had to play it.

> *I really liked it, too. Thanks for that. This is 'Ghosts' by Japan*
>
> —
>
> *Can we talk a bit about narrative and what interests you about narrative? And how you structure your work? Are you thinking of the beginning, middle and end? Are you interested the idea of storytelling within what you do? Or is it much more about something, let's say, atmospheric and poetic and open?*

I like to think it's all of those things. I like to have my cake and eat it! I didn't grow up going to galleries or really engaging with artistic moving image. My interest in narrative comes from basically watching narrative feature film, that was what I grew up with. That and music videos and stuff. I mean, music video is the big one that I always go on about, but ultimately, I'm led by narrative because it's all I know. I think maybe I work with narratives that are slightly fractured or fragmented in some way. Ultimately, there's a sense of – 'a to b' is the wrong way to describe it – but I'm not trying to be purposefully obtuse in the way that I tell stories, because I think it's just not me. I'd rather just tell a story, because maybe I could spin some yarn about oral histories. I think that's also part of it, but for me, I think it's quite an art to be able to tie something up but leave it ambiguous as well. That's a real challenge. And I'm not convinced that I'm able to do it, but like I try to. Or at least be able to give something like a circularity, but then also leave something open at the end… All the storytellers that I admire, like Michael Haneke, for example – in his films there are these big, purposeful narrative moments, but then at the end, you're kind of like, what the fuck… Or Abbas Kiarostami or someone like that. Where you're always left at the end with more questions. Actually, I think for me, that's the only thing that art does well. It makes complex things more complex, and it allows something to end with a question. It's a trite way of describing something really multi-layered and complex, but for me, that's the only thing that's interesting about it. Once that's gone, I'll just do something else.

The thing that you're doing at Spike Island in Bristol is a two-screen piece. Do you feel you're getting something different from being in the art context? If only on a physical level rather than within a cinema context?

Oh, yeah, for sure. I'm able to do or be facilitated in making mad decisions – like attempting to make an animated lung or putting plumes of smoke in a kitchen. The sort of dissonant images that wouldn't fit in the cinematic context, unless it was very loose and avant-garde. I think moving image in the art world allows us this fluidity of images and sounds. My soundtracks are a bit nuts. I don't think they would fit a slick, cinematic image so much as something that people engage with knowingly in a slightly different way, which is the art context. That said, I'm not beholden to it. I want to make a feature film that would be cool!

I hope so! We're going to play your last track.

Cool, cool.

Your last track is by Trimbal?

Trim, yeah. Trim has got loads of different names…

I found Trimbal when I was looking up the track.

Trim, Osama Trim Laden, Trimbal, Trimothy, Trimski… He's my favourite MC. He's vastly underrated. He's the geeks favourite MC, because he's quite a jokes guy. He's got lots of different monikers and he's been in and out of Roll Deep and is the only person brave enough to have a beef with Wiley… He's just quite a nuts guy.

This track is crazy.

It's insane, isn't it? This is James Blake at his best for me. I mean James Blake is sick. I'm not shading James Blake, but it's at a particular time where he hadn't started singing yet and I think this track is an amazing collaboration. The video is really cool, as well. But Trim – doesn't need any help from me. Trim is the ultimate grime MC, a total one-off. He has the most unique flow, and he switches it up, just as much as he switches his name's – Trimble, Trimski, all that stuff. For me, he's the most underrated grime MC out there.

This is 'Confidence Boost (the James Blake harmonimix)' by Trim. And thank you very much for coming in Imran.

Thank you.

Liam Gillick

Cadence!

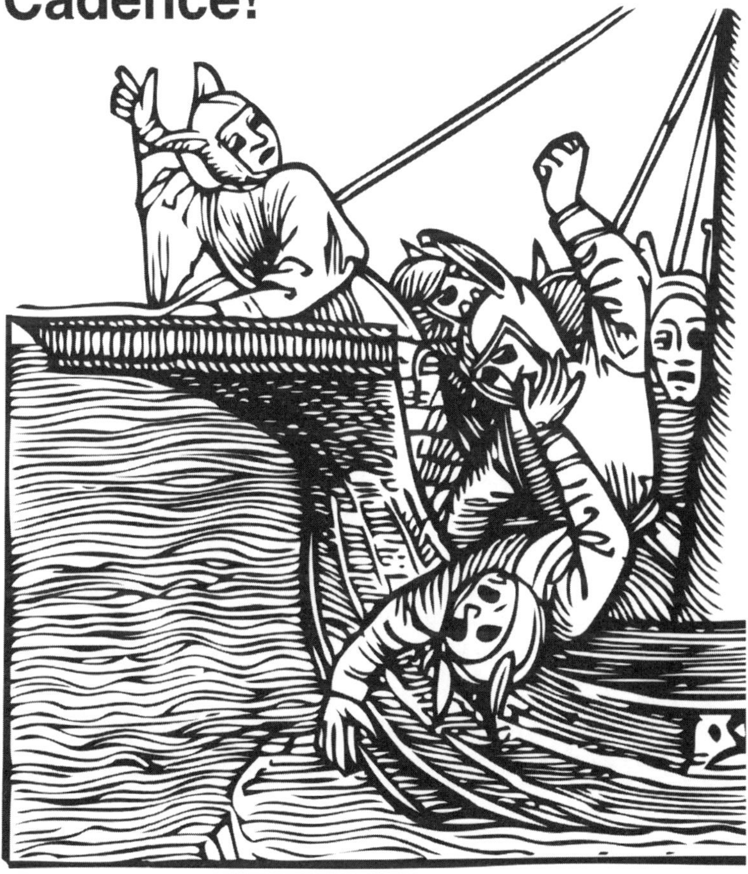

Cadence!, 2021.

29.11.19

Hi, you're listening to Rough Version and my guest this month I'm happy to say is Liam Gillick. He's done everything – you've done everything Liam. Venice representing Germany, Documenta. You've curated. You've written. You've exhibited everywhere around the world from New York, MOCA, MoMA, Tate, everything. You're here. How are you?

I'm okay.

Good, wonderful. You have such a varied practice. But I actually want to start with music, because it's a really interesting part of what you do. Firstly, how have you incorporated music into your installations or other projects you've done? Or your films and the use of music within that?

I mean, you start with music. If you're a suburban person born when I was, music is the beginning of everything. I've never really seen a separation from anything else. I don't see any kind of barrier or border between the music side and anything else, except the one that I imposed myself. For a long time, I never used any music in any artwork, because I felt that the emotive potential, the effective potential of music was too strong. And in a way it's almost like cheating. Powerful. It wasn't until '98, that I used music in any artwork. It was 10 years after my first show. That's quite a long time. Then I started doing it in earnest as it were, for other people, not for me. It was a parallel activity. Rather than something integrated, and I still use it. I still deploy music very carefully. And I'm weary of it. I'm a bit frightened of it.

But you also released an album. Did you see that, as you say, in parallel to your artwork, and something a side thing, rather than something that was integrated within it?

Yeah. I've done a few different records, mainly with German friends and German record labels.

Germans love to release a record, don't they?

I've done it with a sense of melancholy and loss, because, of course, I didn't do anything like that till I was older. It was like a task, like taking out the rubbish! Now, that sounds bad. I remember being of an age where the idea to do a record was something incredibly difficult, because it was expensive and complicated, and kind of hard. So, I'm still slightly ashamed of myself, because I know my 18-year-old self, who was so tribal and so knowledgeable, and so acute – I'm still troubled by that person. I remember a few years ago, someone said, "What advice would you give to your 18-year-old self?" and I said, "I think it's the other way around". I'm still being watched over by my 18-year-old self to check that I don't disappear into the biggest crime of all. There are many kinds of international crimes artists can do as they get older, and one of them is being in a band and the other one is DJing. These are two things I avoided even if I would like to do them.

It seems like an appropriate moment to play one of the songs you brought. I'm thinking Neu. Which I assume you were into in that earlier period of your life? Do you want to tell me why you chose this specific Neu track?

It's a classic example of inner suburban, acute self-consciousness. Right at the point when people were listening to Kraftwerk, I decided I was much more interested in Neu who were more difficult to get hold off and slightly more opaque. There was no way you could look them up. And it has that driving rhetoric thing, that beat and it sits in between things. I'm always attracted to things that sit in between certain languages, certain musical artistic languages.

Okay. This is 'Hallogallo' by Neu.

—

That was Neu. Can we talk a little about your approach to collaboration? Let's start with the most recent one, which was with Gelitin in Vienna, who I love. They're amazing. I want to get them on one day. Do you want to tell me how that came together? Because again, there was an improvised, mental music element to that, at least for the opening side. Do you want to tell me what you find interesting about the collaborative process?

I've known them a long time, since the time they were in New York. They had their studio at the World Trade Center, which is an amazing artwork. If people don't know about it they should look it up. They built a balcony out of one of the windows on the 100th floor of the World Trade Center. There's a whole conspiracy theory around that to do with what on earth these people were doing there in the year before 911, and what was going on, which is definitely worth looking up.

> *I love the idea that Gelitin caused 911. If you saw them, it's just insane, but hilarious.*

On a serious level, I think that there's often an assumption that natural collaborations or working together – they're natural when the work seems to be visibly similar, or there seems to be a visual language, which is similar. The thing with them is actually, that we have a shared politics to a certain extent, rather than a shared aesthetic. We've always talked. We share some galleries together. We talk about ideas, about politics, about difficulty. We've always wanted to do something together. The trouble was finding a frame to work against, because, for me, they definitely work best when they encounter a structure. I'm a much more devious, entryist person, but they need a clear thing. They did a famous sculpture, either in Salzburg, or maybe Linz or Graz. They were going to do a public artwork, which was going to be a statue, and they kept it all under cover. It was all very secretive what was going on. When they finally unveiled it, it turned out to be the figure of a lanky skinny man, peeing in his own mouth. It caused a genuine scandal. A genuine upsetting of conservative, bourgeois sensibility. Now, the problem is, when we work together, when I work with them, we can't really do that. It doesn't make any sense. We have to do something else. That's the way a lot of working together works. You need to find a new way to reframe something, create a new frame for it. And in this case, we decided cinema would be the frame that we're working against. Although the exhibition is in the Kunsthalle in Vienna, and normally, if they were working there, they'd be against the institution. In this case, because they're working with me, it doesn't make sense to be against the institution. As I have a more slippery relationship to institutions, it would be a false consciousness. We ended up using cinema as a frame and to become indifferent to the institution. That was the key. That gives you an idea about that collaboration. And all the collaborative work I do have some structural reframing of relationships, more than art.

Coming back to what you said earlier about that idea of the political, when you look at your work, let's say the more abstract pieces, politics isn't necessarily the most obvious element. But I'm really interested in how the political is inbuilt in what you're making. Is that motivating to you and how does that emerge in what you're producing?

There's an unresolvable dichotomy in the work. Which has always been the case, but it's been expressed differently at different moments. Meaning that there's an understanding that art starts with disappointment. Meaning that you're not satisfied with the way things are. And I am still committed to the idea that art is a problem or a difficulty that needs to be played with. Meaning a vocabulary that's primarily non-didactic, which in my case, a kind of abstraction. It's something that is still difficult and evasive and hard to pin down. However, I've used this analogy before, if I'm dealing with this kind of abstraction, it's a bit like the scene at the beginning of 'Sexy Beast' where there's a large boulder in a swimming pool. I'm trying to keep afloat, a concrete, minimalistic cube that's sunk in a neoliberal development of beautiful apartments and I can't keep it above the water. It's being taunted, the activity of doing that is being taunted, or marked or spoken to, by the side of the pool. That is what is always happening. On another level, the abstraction that I do use is really clearly based on our vocabulary, which is very precise. It's to do with the built world. It's to do with the interface. It's to do with the way buildings breathe, it's to do with the organs of modern development. There is a way to just look at the work and analyse it visually and deconstruct it. We're in a time when criticism does not find that kind of procedure very useful. But it's all in there. It can be described and talked about and looked at and whatnot. What am I saying here? There's this ongoing argument happening in the work, and it took me a long time to accept that. I masked it and hid it for a long time. But now, thanks to years of not doing therapy, I've managed to come to terms with it.

I love that. I want to play another one of your songs, which is a completely different note, which is Augustus Pablo, who I think is one of the most amazing people ever. Why did you choose this specific Augustus Pablo track?

Coming from the suburbs, I got a car when I was 17… because I was going to get a motorbike, I got a car. By having the money to buy a motorbike, I got given a really crappy 1969 Volkswagen fastback type three. And this is what I used to listen to all the time driving around North London in the late '70s. It was heavy 'dub', what we called 'heavy dub reggae'.

This is a perfect example of that. And this is 'King Tubby Meets Rockers Uptown' by Augustus Pablo.

—

Beyond the collaboration, you've also incorporated some of your icons into your work. I love Lawrence Weiner. I saw him last week. He's adorable, love to Lawrence. You've also done work about Richard Hamilton. Do you want to tell me a bit what you find interesting about incorporating references to the influences within your work or addressing that conversational element of art?

I think one of the things that isn't really spoken about very much is, when people think about Goldsmiths, at the time I went there. One of the key elements was not teaching people how to be art business people.

It's such a Post-Thatcherite thing.

In fact, the teachers were mainly '60s people who believed in no divisions between disciplines. No studio walls, open discussion constantly, symposiums, seminars, and treating people like human beings and artists, not like students. At Goldsmiths what was interesting, is when it worked well, the idea was you're already in a discussion with artists who were doing things that were active and involved. It seemed natural to enter into conversation with people that you were interested in. I'd like to include Louise Lawler in there, who I worked with on the show in 2013 in New York. How can I describe it? It's both parallel play. A bit like you can theorize the way children operate. It's never truly collaboration. It always has an element of an encounter. With Richard Hamilton, who was someone I met and talked to, I wanted to just make a tribute to him, because I think he's a very complicated figure. And very important in certain ways, but I can recognise something about my own failings in his work, somehow, whatever that means. With Lawrence, he was the first adult artist I met who treated me as a complete equal and that meant an antagonistic relationship. Because it means you have to deal with him. He's probably been, apart from Philippe Parreno, the artist I've spoken to the most and thought about the most. But again, it's a parallel play. It's not a collaboration, even though we did a whole exhibition together. The work was essentially an absolute embedding of both of our work in one object – the whole floor of the MUHKA in Antwerp in 2011. It was not a collaboration. He always talks about jazz – he did at the time anyway. Meaning improvised jazz, or the idea of being what he called a sideman. Sometimes when you work with someone you just walk in the room, and you can play the bass. You just pick it up as you go along. And this is an interesting way to look at it. And I do think collaboration is not a collectivity. It's not collective, it's not two people merging into one or three people or four people. It's a sort of recognition. It's a way of having a conversation, a bit like this, which has a kind of bounding set of rules or structures around it, that gives you a reason to have a conversation.

The way that you use these people, sometimes they feel more like material. The relationships, or autobiography rather than necessarily collaboration, particularly in the film work.

I think with Richard I wanted to see if you could make a film sitting at home in New York and not leave the house and make a whole documentary about someone. Then it turned out that actually I did have the chance to go to London and get into the ICA and the Tate after dark and wander around and do what I wanted to do. It expanded itself. It's like a dream in the sense of a fever dream. More that you're talking to someone or you're showing back to them something they already know, maybe. It's hard to say what that means. I'll give you a good example. I was sitting outside a restaurant yesterday late afternoon when I got back, and a man came and sat down and announced that he was Charlie Burchill from Simple Minds. Now he looked the right age. He looked way too thin, but he had quite expensive clothes on. He had a certain look and he had lots of shopping bags. He claimed that he was waiting for his daughter who had gone shopping. We ended up having this long conversation about – he ended up doing this long monologue about meeting Nelson Mandela and what Jim Kerr from Simple Minds is like. All these other things, but it was clearly not real. It was clearly a complete, weird, slightly damaged person, who had assumed this other identity.

Wow.

It left me in a state of admiration for this guy, but a feeling that I don't know anything anymore. This guy was as real as Charlie Burchill from Simple Minds, but he was clearly not real as well. And that's what the films are like. It's not easy to describe. You're creating a false reality or something. What Philippe Parreno calls it – who I've worked with a lot. We're going to work together on a big show of early work we did together next year in Holland. He always calls it a holiday away from ideas. Because when you work together on something, you can't really have any ideas. You're in a different sort of engagement.

I'm going to play another song, which is Workshop. Do you want to tell me about this track?

When I first heard the record 'Talent' by Workshop, which included Kyle Toff, the artist and a number of other collaborators around him, various people involved, I was really, really struck by… it's nearly 20 years old… I was really struck by the whole thinking around his artwork and the way it was expressed musically and collectively, it just seemed so perfect at the time. I still find that, in the music of Workshop, there is something that you don't find in his artwork. That's very contemporary in a particular way. I keep coming back to it, so that's why it's here.

Wonderful. This is Workshop, 'The House of Marvick'.

—

Let's talk about your woodcut pieces, because I think they're really interesting. How you're using text and images of labour. How that grew and why specific wood cuts? Why those images and this changing of texts you use. Let's talk about that.

I'm really fascinated by flatness and fear. Also, the propagandistic aspects of woodcuts, I find really fascinating. The way that it's so limited brings you back to when you're a kid and you do linocuts or something. I'm interested in the way that in German-speaking Europe, there was a period where they tried to retain contact with a pre-modern aesthetic but frame it within a Swiss new design. You would find in Germany and Switzerland – less in Austria – the use of graphic design, which incorporates old imagery, medieval imagery and very clear typography. I'm just borrowing that. I did the book jacket to celebrate the 40th anniversary of the Künstlerhaus in Stuttgart, where I did the same thing. I used an old wood cut and typesetting. For me… How can I talk about it? It's really difficult. I think there's something about going to that point, which evades some of the more simple-minded understandings of how we talk about modernism and modernity. These kinds of things. There's something about it that goes back to a kind of resistance. There's a great history in Britain of like a literature and a film and an idea of the Luddites and the whatnots. Going further back to peasant risings. Also, my Catholic background, on my father's side, the idea of the image of people being chopped up and piled on a bonfire. These are very deep inside of me as images and ideas. I always think they complicate any simple-minded reading of the way we deal with aesthetics and fear and ideology. On the other hand, I used it in the past, just to be irritating. In 1994, Angela Bullock and I were in a show Georg Herold organised for the Portikus in Frankfurt that was called 'Karaoke (Fussball VM)', which means World Cup Karaoke. Basically youngish, British artists meet youngish German artists in the Portikus and have a good time and make art. We decided we weren't interested in this bullshit of World Cup. We did a work called 'We Are Medieval', where we basically dug a pit outside the Portikus, and sat in it. Then we made a resistance film that we shot in the garden, where she was wearing a wimple and I was wearing a beard. We made a freedom fighter video to resist this attempt to make art part of a sort of ironic industry of entertainment and leisure. We were going to refuse.

We were going to remain medieval. And that seemed to be more interesting than you would think it would be. It turned out to actually be more irritating and more productive… It's a Pierre Bourdieu thing, right? Where you cannot deal with the power of the World Cup and karaoke. Both of these things I love, but in the exhibition space, being relegated to that role of being the young person who's into football seemed annoying. To be medieval seemed like a good perspective.

I like the idea of annoyance and irritation as a mode of artistic practice. That's nicely contrary. Annoy your audience!

I think it was a great work. I give a lot of credit to Angela for that work. I think it was phenomenal.

As the last thing, and it would be wrong not to speak about it, we're going to have to talk about your collaborations with New Order, which is also your final track. Do you want to tell me how that came about? What you found interesting about it, and how it led to your musical output?

I don't really know the full details, because there obviously had been discussions about doing something. Manchester wanted to honour New Order, in whatever way.

This was for the Manchester International Festival?

Exactly. I think Dave Haslam was involved at some level, the DJ, on a curatorial level and a few other people. Mark Beasley, who worked for Creative Time and then went to the Hirshhorn in Washington, was involved. I think they were thinking about how could you – it's hardly a new idea – how you could combine visual arts and a band? And I think when it came round to me – actually, you know what happened? I went with Mark to see New Order play at the Rockefeller Center in New York, and Mark had gastric flu or something, so was basically projectile vomiting everywhere.

Sexy.

He left because I think he might have died otherwise. It was really brutal. I stayed. I'd last seen them about five years earlier. While I was there, I thought, I really want to do this. But what I want to do more is communicate to them that I think the idea of diluting the music with lots of people, may not be the right idea. I don't mind what happens, but I want to get the message across really clearly – a bit like you must have sometimes. It's a very hard thing to do, someone's doing a show and you need to tell them, "You know what? Don't do this. Whatever you do, do not do this. And that's all I've got for you". That was my message. Do not do like 12 artists, one per track. Just don't do it. But I'm available, if you want to talk more about any of that. I believe that's what led to them saying, "Would you like to come and meet us in Manchester and talk about what we can do, because in fact, Bernard has an idea that is a bit more focused than this and maybe you could do it together". So, I went to see them on the train, and I was incredibly impressed by a number of things. First, they were all there and just waiting. There was a table and bits of paper. We just started working straightaway. And we never really stopped after that. What's interesting, for you or for me, is when you encounter people who are from a parallel universe. It's not the same. It's a much more abusive world, the music world, it's much more hierarchical, it's more complicated. There are weird rules. They were incredibly horizontal. They just wanted to, work and I wanted to work. It meant all the things that you've heard about or read about or seen in documentaries are all true. The good bits. And it was possible to just work. That's what happened. For me, it's fascinating, but again, I just wanted to make it good. I wanted to do concerts that made sense. You learn something, you learn that it's very powerful. It reminded me why I didn't become a musician, because it's really hard work and it is dangerous. Because one of my intentions or one of my desires was to break people, a bit like a comedian will talk about killing the audience or killing people. I remember walking around the site – because I had the sneaky ways around the stage – and looking out in Manchester one night, and half the people were crying and I thought, "wow, this is powerful, and dangerous and weird". I wonder if we can do that again in Turin and in Vienna. And we could. And it was to do with the way Bernard and Steven primarily, but not just alone, made the set list, and what I did visually, all came together. You took people to a certain point and then you broke them. That's something to have witnessed and been involved in structurally in life. Also, something to then walk away from and shut the door again.

Powerful. Why did you choose this specific track? How am I supposed to pronounce this track? It's 'Your Silent Face' from the live album... Sigma...

Well, no. It's the sum of New Order, 12 musicians and Liam Gillick at Manchester International Festival 2017.

Okay. It's written numerically '-∑ (No,12k,Lg,17Mif)'. Excuse my ignorance. I'm not going to even try to say that. This is 'Your Silent Face'. Why Silent Face? Why this specific one?

I just think it's one of the most extraordinary bittersweet, positive, negative, love you, hate you songs ever written. It's musically so simple and so complex and to witness it being rehearsed and played by 12 young musicians but also watching basically the core of the band with Phil and Tom as well, their ability and their extraordinary struggle. They never stopped struggling to be able to play things in a weird way. There's a constant difficulty in the songs that's deceptive and fascinating and has a kind of endurance and I identify with it, which is the result of... in a sense an untrained background that you refuse to be limited by. Ideologically, artistically and conceptually.

Thank you firstly. We're going to play this and thank you very much Liam Gillick for coming in.

Thank you very much.

P. Staff

11.12.19

You're listening to Rough Version on NTS, and my guest this month is Patrick Staff. Patrick is an incredible artist who studied in London and is currently based in Los Angeles. They have shown at MAK in Los Angeles, New Museum, Chisenhale, Tate Modern, Tate Liverpool. Currently they have a huge show at the Serpentine. I could keep listing things here.

It feels a bit shameful when you say it like…

No, it's incredible! It's like every single big institution in the world! Which is just great. Let's talk about the moment when you seemed to break through. It was the Tom of Finland project. I feel like so many people are much more aware of the foundation after your work. Do you want to tell me about how that first came about? What interested you about Tom of Finland?

Oh my God. I almost felt like, it's quite bad to admit, that I'm not that interested in Tom of Finland. I was in LA in 2012. I had a tiny show at a project space called Montavista Projects. One of my best friends, Candice Lin, who lives in LA, and has always been like my guide to the city, said, "you should really go visit the Tom of Finland Foundation". Up until that point, my work had really been a lot about communes, commonalities and moments of sociality that emerged in resistance to capitalism, or emerged as a counterpoint to industrialization, usually in Western Europe. Anarchist movements, dance movements, whatever. Inevitably, it was archive-y and Candice recommended that I visit the foundation and I assumed that it would be a regular archive. I just got a kick out the idea of going to like an erotic art archive. I hadn't really seen something like that before. What ended up transpiring is that it's essentially a commune. It's a regular, big, old house in Echo Park. I had this really crazy visit there and that was 2012… A lot of stuff was going on in my own life. A lot of stuff was going on in relation to my feelings about gender and whether or not I was going to transition. I maybe had a slightly complicated relationship. Not romantic, but a complicated relationship with an older gay male artist…

It's a very specific representation of homoerotic desire. It's someone's obsession, in a way.

I guess I was reckoning with whether or not I was going to transition and going through some dis-identification from gay male subjectivity. So, I really went to the heart of the hat. Went to the Tom of Finland, like mecca of a certain image of gay white masculinity and that ended up becoming a really long, really involved project. I'd been interested in it and trying to figure out working with them for a while before eventually having a studio visit with Polly [Staple] from Chisenhale. She really kick started that project and it ended up being a show in Chisenhale in 2015, that then toured a whole bunch of places. I suppose that was a moment of wider recognition.

Looking at your film work in particular. I'm really interested in like how your approach to editing or using changing materials. I love 'Weed Killer'. it's an incredible film. I haven't seen the new one that's at Serpentine at the moment, which is your current show. Do you want to tell me a little bit about how your approach to film is changing?

Yeah, yeah. I don't really consider myself a filmmaker… I did the associate artist program at LUX. I also felt like I have a slightly complex relationship to moving image film versus video. The mediums and histories at least of moving image in the UK. For me, it was maybe a couple of different things. Prior to making 'The Foundation', the video that was at the Chisenhale, I had been making videos, but in a relationship to immediacy. I just had cheap crappy cameras that I could just pick up, was making a lot of performance work and making a lot of improvised work. It was about that speed of producing images. The show at Chisenhale was a very conscious shift. I think for them wanting to give me the commission to make a bigger moving image work, but also maybe me being like, "Okay, I'm going to do the thing, a big video installation". But my interest has always been in appropriation and approaching art making from the position of being almost virus-like. When I was at Goldsmiths, I just read Kathy Acker and photocopied stuff. That was my practice. I was really into the new narrative movement, like Chris Kraus' 'Native Agents' series at Semiotext(e). All of that stuff. Kathy Acker, Dodie Bellamy, Cookie Mueller, and all of that was about taking a first-person perspective and flipping it with your own identity. It was a lot of stealing and photocopying and appropriating and vandalizing and that's always been how I've thought about my practice. So, when it came to filmmaking, it's a ripe medium. We all see so much moving image all the time, that I felt like it was easy for me to go in and inhabit the shell of filmmaking and use it to do something else. 'The Foundation', then a video like 'Weed Killer' to then the new work at the Serpentine – 'The Foundation' is maybe the most that's like a 'film' film. Since then, they've got like more and more shredded up and cracked open to the point now where the work at the Serpentine, the new video. I don't know. I shot very little of the footage in it. It's more maybe about like the manipulation of image and sound than it is about filmmaking, per se.

I want to play one of your tracks. Let's play a song. What do you want to start with?

Oh my God. I felt like I sent them to you in a really particular order. But now I don't know.

The first one we have is 'Chant I, Making of Cyborg' by Kenji Kawai.

Yeah, let's just start.

Let's begin on that great one. This is from the soundtrack from 'Ghost in the Shell'. Do you want to tell me when you first heard it, and what your relationship to this track is?

I suppose I like a lot of experimental music that was coming out of Japan in that time period. Also, before then. Actually, like a lot of those films like 'Ghost in the Shell' and 'Akira' and stuff like that were picking up on that legacy of concrete music, experimental type music in Japan from the late '60s, '70s, '80s whatever. This is in that lineage, but the video at the Serpentine has detuned Gregorian chanting and so it felt like this track was particularly apt.

Nice. This is Kenji Kawai.

—

Let's talk about the subject you haven't discussed much. Let's talk about music in your work. How have you incorporated music in what you do? That can be in your performances and also everything else. How do you feel like music is influencing and incorporated in what you do?

I like started playing in bands when I was 17.

What kind of bands?

Bad punk bands normally. Weirdo, weirdo punk. That was when I was 17. Actually, the whole time I was at art school, I was way more preoccupied with playing in bands, touring, being involved in zines and putting on shows, putting on punk shows whatever. Probably right up until like 2013, or something. So, for me, playing in bands was almost a more formative experience than art school… And it's always been a natural process to have music be a big part of my practice. Before we started recording, I was slightly griping to you that I feel that the soundtrack to my shows is always so integral, and no one ever asks me about it. That's my little chip on my shoulder.

That's why we're here. It's a compliment to the work that there's so much other content to discuss. But I think that the music's obviously relevant. That's one of the first things that always strikes me more than anything.

It's maybe easiest with the video works. There are always very prominent soundtracks. I also have quite an appetite for culture – highbrow, lowbrow, whatever. I watch a lot. I listen to a lot. I listened to music constantly. From the most trashy to deep, deep cuts. I really love all of that shit. It's like very pleasurable Each of the videos has these very distinct soundtracks. I think they tend to be a reflection of what I'm listening to at the time, but that gets put through the process of becoming useful for the work, somehow. 'The Foundation' features a lot of percussion that's prominent in theatre – particularly Japanese theatre, but also classical Italian theatre. But then it features all of these stolen porn music soundtracks that I got out of the archive at the Tom house. These slow house, porno tracks. Then for 'Weed Killer', I worked with a saxophone player and was really into trying to get him to break the instrument. We would record together, and I would always be saying "blow too hard" or "hold a note until you can't, until the instrument can't contain it anymore". We recorded a lot of his breathing. A lot of the soundtrack is him playing but you also hear a lot of these sounds. I was really into pushing things through the body, pushing things through one body and out of another like the body of the instrument. Then it also has this acapella Masters at Work lip sync moment. A video that I made called 'Bathing', that was for the Hammer Museum is almost entirely silent, apart from a 2 second jungle break beat like explosion. It's really me being a magpie a lot of the time. This new film at the Serpentine. There's Gregorian chanting that I've detuned or pitched up and sped up and slowed down. There's one of my old punk bands, but it's reversed and slowed down. So, you hear that. Then a lot of me playing on synthesizers. My boyfriend is really into making little oscillators and things like that. I'll play with those.

It's an incredible variety. Another one the tropes that I've noticed is also the use of dance has emerged in a lot of ways. Not always necessarily with music. But the idea of a physical body in movement. Do you want to tell me a bit what your take on dancers is? Is that a very similar approach? That magpie approach to choreography, but I feel there is also something narrative-led in terms of your use of dance somehow.

I got into dance because I was into performance. I realized that I really liked the discipline. I started to take ballet, Cunningham and modern classes in the evening and realized that the strictness of it really appealed to me. So hard. A level perversity of really enjoying the discipline. That again, became a slight fixation in the same way as I was saying before. Taking certain histories of dance and misusing them, misreading them, performing things wrong. And that being a way of really trying to get my head around how knowledge would circulate amongst a group of people. How commonality or associativity could be embodied these days. I mean, these days, I suppose I approach it much more bio-politically, pharmaceutically. Maybe becoming more comfortable with foregrounding my own body as it relates to my trans identity. As it relates to pain or illness or things that are more difficult. But I would like it if dance ends up working its way in somewhere. Or at least just thinking about exhibition making as a choreographic exercise, rather than one of arranging objects in space.

Let's play another track and then I want to talk a little bit more about that biomedical illness related stuff. I find it really fascinating. The next track we have is Patty Waters, 'Hush Little Baby'. What's this track?

Patty Waters is just one of my all-time heroes. I forget what year it is, her… maybe '60s, late '60s LP 'College Tours'. I'm just beyond. I'm kind of obsessed with extended vocalization anything like John LaBarbera, Meredith Monk, John Lee, and Patti Waters, and particularly this record 'College Tours'. I don't know. It's like pure effect. It's insane. I love it.

This is Patty Waters. 'Hush Little Baby'.

—

I want to talk a little bit about the political motivation in what you do – particularly how a lot of the motivation between your work seems to be highlighting social structures and how they inherently are repressive or violent or about control in some way. Do you want to tell me a little bit about where that political motivation is coming from? And what you find interesting about looking at it through metaphor, rather than necessarily always through an obvious narrative?

It's obviously always difficult to summarize your own politics. I think I, on the one hand, very much come from a background in punk DIY, which in itself feels inherently leftist, very Marxist to certain degrees. That, though nascent formulations was really important to me in terms of being at art school. Understanding a practice, beginning to formulate one's approach to making work and being in the world. Also, my family are Northern. Me and my brother were the only ones that grew up in the South.

Where are they from?

Sunderland. Newcastle.

I've been to Sunderland. It's hardcore up there.

Yeah. And being brought up by a very left wing, Northern, working class, single parent – that informs a hell of a lot. And then always being drawn to trans politics, gender theory, feminist stuff. That maybe autodidactic self-made library way of the things that you read and the things you consume – to try and understand or make sense of the incredibly fucked up society that we live in.

There's a lot of pathos in what you do, though. You really, insert yourself. It's not just political work, I think part of the reason why it's successful. It's also quite emotional. You're seeing a human being, the everyday person or a queer body or trans body or people who have been marginalized are affected by those structures.

Yeah. I have a very like Piscean approach to these things. There are very few boundaries to it, and I find it very hard to not let everything bleed into everything else. And, partly it's like everything, all of these politics get channelled through a body, through my body, through a trans body. And there's always this reciprocal relationship to how much is yours, how much you get to hold on to, and how much you are at the mercy of the social structures around you. The material culture that you live in. And the many intersecting intricacies of your own being in the world. In a way I can try to talk about that in the frame of biopolitics, as much as I might try and just talk about love or suffering or physical pain. The way it gets articulated in the work is maybe just my own approach to it, which is that it's very hard to remain logical all the time. It's very hard to remain objective all the time. Sometimes things just feel stronger than I am able to objectively articulate.

Do you want to tell me a bit about the architecture. In the Serpentine show, but also in other shows, there has been architectural interventions. A lot of things were liquid, in particular drips and pipes and fountains. Do you want to tell me about how that started and what you like about messing up space?

Again, I think it completely comes from choreography and thinking about performance. I did the associate artist program at LUX which was run by Ian Wright over a course of seven or eight years, which had a huge effect on and how I approach making work… Ian would talk about the cinema as the theatre, as a proscenium. That moving image is live. We're not just repeating images. That each time is a live encounter, and that theatre or live performance in itself might also resemble film or the moving image. The collapsing of temporalities or temperament. I really took that on when it came to exhibition making and deconstructing spaces or just bending them slightly to my will. I always felt like it was a way to quickly access people… I think like a lot of the time the way I use sound, or the way that the images work, or the way that I edit or make these architectural interventions for lack of a better word, is I'm just trying to get inside your body… Is this floor soft? Or is it hard? Are you cold or is it warm? What is being in the same room as continuously running water? Or flashing images or sound that is so bass heavy that it literally makes you feel woozy? How can I always get into the room with you? We're all implicated in this thing that is happening in this room right now. Whether we like it or not. You and I right now are sat opposite each other, breathing the same air and we kind of have to deal with that. And sometimes it's easy. This is not a hard situation to deal with. Sometimes going to a gallery is a very hard experience to navigate and especially – you listed off these institutions at the top of the interview and I'm reckoning with that. There's a reckoning to be made with working with somewhere like the Tate or the Serpentine, that have these very complicated histories that you are instrumentalised by.

> *It's very interesting thinking of the Serpentine issues of that, connected to – there's lots of issues around that at the moment particularly. Let's play another track. I had to get the next one we have in your ordered list, because let's stick to the order. 'Part Four' by the House Boys Choir.*

I don't think it's the final but it's one of the last projects by Sleazy from Throbbing Gristle. Coil, who is, I guess a big influence both in terms of having like a multi hyphenate project. A great goth queer identity but also… what's the word. The vocabulary of sound

I suppose that I gravitate towards comes maybe from things like Throbbing Gristle, Television, Coil, and then this later work of Sleazy which is really, really trippy and spiritual. I guess all of the tracks I've sent you have a degree of spiritualism to them… This is Sleazy in Thailand filming these crazy rituals and then bending and manipulating the sound from them.

This is 'So Free It Knows No End' by Threshold Houseboys Choir.

—

Let's get back to the current show at the moment. Do you want to tell me a little bit about your approach to lighting because I think that's what's really interesting? A lot of Chiaroscuro. In the Serpentine show this is crazy yellow-y lit. But even in the Hammer Museum show there was also a lot of use of light.

All of them. All of them tend to be very site specific. Most exhibition spaces are really paying a lot of attention to the light even if most of the time it's meant to feel flat or neutral. In the case of the Serpentine – there's a lot of different things going on, but one of the things that was interesting about that space is that originally before the Serpentine had it before Zaha [Hadid] got involved. Historically, it was a gunpowder storage magazine. The galleries are still referred to as the 'powder rooms'. What was unusual about this one is that it was in the middle of the city. Normally they would be outside of the city centre as a weapons cache for the military. But this one was in the centre of Hyde Park. I assume, because of its proximity to Buckingham Palace and Westminster. It was actually a store of gunpowder in the case of rioting, or any civil unrest within London. This landed gentry, royal part of the city had a stash of weapons to hand which perversely, for me, felt somehow like yet another layer to the loadedness of the Serpentine and showing at the Serpentine, which was something I felt like I really had to work through emotionally to try and figure out my relationship to showing with this institution. What's really interesting about it is that the architecture of the building was designed so that if the gunpowder was to ever alight and explode, the explosion would go upwards rather than outwards so the whole ceiling was designed weakly. It's weaker than the walls and that became this really early motif, I suppose. Of wanting to think about the show working vertically rather than horizontally. The ceiling became really important. The floor became really important. Like you mentioned before, there's this network of pipes that runs all around the ceiling. But then all of the skylights, I opened them up, but covered them in these really acrid, toxic yellow, piss yellow gels. Then rehung all the lighting to also have this sort of toxic piss vibe to it. The floor then is all newly installed mirrored flooring, so it really stretches. It widens that gap in the building, but it also has this insane bouncing light feeling about it. The priority of museum staff – everyone was joking, that it's not very Instagram friendly. It makes everyone look pretty pallid.

Urine coloured?

Exactly. You look really drawn in that space.

It's not the first time that you've highlighted the inherent violence. There are other pieces where you've done photograms of knives. What interests you about references to violence without making work that is obviously necessary... Life is pretty violent but...

I think often the unintelligent answer to the question is "Don't we all feel like things are very violent all the time?" I feel in close proximity to so many types of violence so frequently, that it feels hard not to gesture towards it. I don't know. It just feels it's so present in our lives. Maybe there's also a certain ambivalence that I have towards the violence. In the Serpentine show, there are very violent images shown in the video but at least in the way that I feel that it's being presented you're not necessarily being asked to react to these images of violence in the way that it's often used.

That manipulation that's so inherent in how images play. Sontag's 'Regarding the Pain of Others' is the dream book on the subject.

Right. Exactly. The whole Serpentine show I think features these incredibly violent images, but with quite a not neutral, but almost an underplayed… it's almost like you feel like you're sat in your living room and there's just this fucking evil monster in the corner of the room. And maybe that is just a reflection of my inner world.

You are living in America.

I live a lot in America, yeah.

But I think it is this global sense of discomfort.

Yeah, completely. It's funny. I also did the press preview and walked a bunch of journalists around the show and then went and sat down to do an interview with a friend of mine who's a writer, who's a trans woman. And really quickly, I was like, "this show is really about dysphoria". And she was like, "Yeah, I could tell". But I had no point that it occurred to me to say that in the press preview, but in an intimate conversation with someone else that there is like a commonality with or a shared lived experience that relates to one's identity or body we could immediately hit on this shared feeling. I think for me, there's often a fusion with gendered violence. Often like the relationship between violence and desire, violence either towards the body or done by your own body that can be morally ambiguous. Sometimes, I don't know, sometimes people will comment to me… "It's kind of violent, but sexy. I don't really know where I land with it". Which I guess again, "Yeah, me either".

To finish, we have to play my favourite track. Which is the Masters At Work. Why did you choose this for the lip sync scene? Is it Jamie Crew who was doing the performance?

We actually think maybe it was Jamie, who first even played me that song. Jamie is like a very old, very close friend of mine. We didn't grow up together. But I've at least known Jamie since I was a teenager.

When they're doing it, she's doing it, the fact that the audience ignores her, is almost nonresponsive really, relates to the fact that there's such an emotional, vocal work.

Yeah, yeah. I knew that I wanted to have this scene of someone singing in a bar, lip synching in a bar, where they're largely being ignored. And that it would be this highly emotional scene. So much of that video is Deborah, the actor, recounting this monologue about chemotherapy really intensely. Almost directly to the camera. The frame is cut in on her face, almost the whole way through. And you're dealing with one particular register of emotion, one particular style of bearing witness, so to speak. It feels like an interview. It could almost be that she's talking directly to you. I wanted to flip it and I wanted to redirect that emotion at some point. So suddenly, instead, we're dealing with a singer in a bar, who is singing "I'm so in love with you. It's tearing me up inside". What at once could seem devotional, when sung to this bar of people who are completely ignoring her, reroutes it, and it becomes totally internal. It's like this thing is oozing out of her and she can't like take it anymore. Again, it just felt like a way of looking at or articulating something about the way that really intense emotion, declarations of suffering or love, can move amongst a group of people but it doesn't always feel good.

On that note, this is 'To Be In Love', the acapella version by Masters at Work featuring India. Thank you so much, Patrick coming in.

Thank you for having me.

Fiona Banner

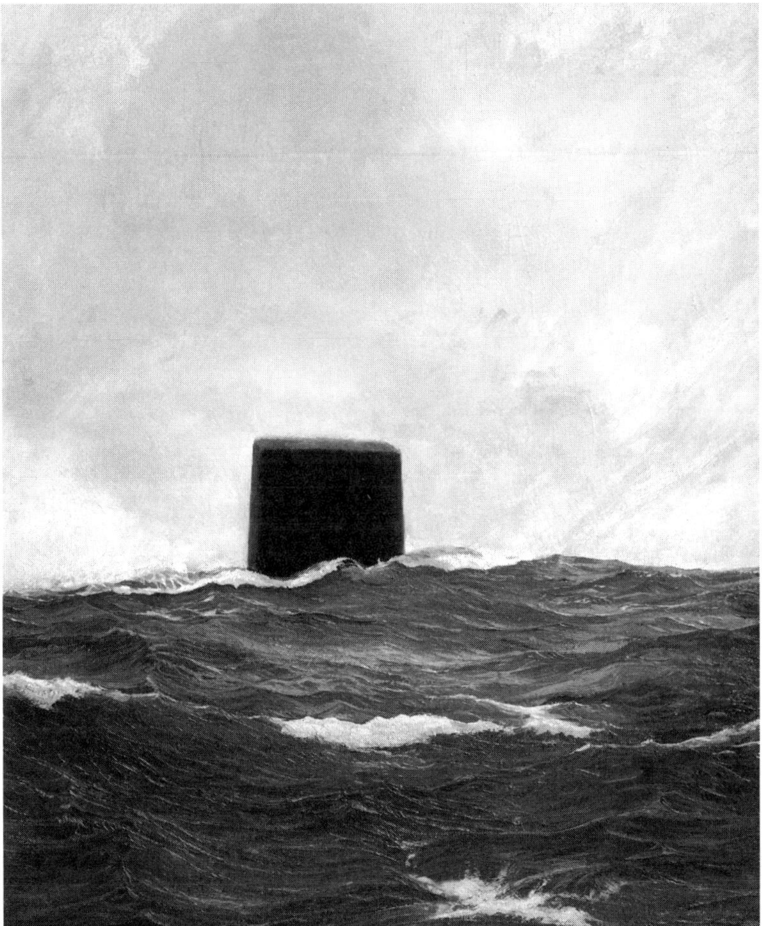

Font, Slipstream, 2019.

16.01.20

I'm Francesca Gavin and you're listening to Rough Version on NTS. My guest this month is Fiona Banner aka The Vanity Press. She's a British artist who was once shortlisted for the Turner prize, and has had major shows at Tate Britain, Hayward and MoMA in New York. She's best known for a variety of work, including installation, sculpture, drawing and books, all of which unpick our relationship to politics, language and the written word. Fiona, thank you very much for coming in. I'm going to ask you the most obvious question to begin with. You've changed your artistic name to Fiona Banner aka The Vanity Press. I wanted you to tell me what that is about.

As you know, Francesca, publishing has always been a really big part of what I do. That stemmed from my making of books, which was a way really to parcel and distribute my artwork, which is quite verbal, so found a fitting place in books. Some 20 years ago, I started a small press called The Vanity Press, which was a title that's grown on me. It came about because I was talking to somebody about my frustrations late one night in a bar. About not being able to pull together the right enthusiasm for publishing a book, which I really wanted to make happen at the time. And I said, "Oh, fuck it, I'm going to just publish it myself". And he said, "Well, you couldn't possibly do that, that would be vanity publishing". So, I went home, and this phrase rolled around in my mind. I started thinking, actually, all art is a form of vanity publishing and that's what I love about it. Then The Vanity Press came into being, and I published lots and lots of different work through it. Some take the form of mainstream sort of familiar publications, some of which is really experimental. Then I thought, actually, it is what I do. So that's when I changed my name. Not only from Fiona Banner, who was making the more on-off sculptural works, and then The Vanity Press, which was doing the publishing stuff. It is all one anyway. Fiona Banner aka The Vanity Press seemed to fit. Plus, a lot of people make my work with me. When I'm publishing a book, I work sometimes with a designer. I work with printers. There are all sorts of levels of collaboration along the way. And introducing the name, The Vanity Press is some acknowledgement of that.

It's almost like a band name in a way… Also, it's a thing that a lot of artists don't do, which is credit. The people who actually make the fact that their name is almost like a branded concept. There's so much more that goes into the making of an artwork beyond a single individual. We're not living the days of an artist alone in a garret painting and having his ears cut off anymore. That's a retro cliché. It's pretty interesting the idea of something more collaborative or collective.

It is a retro cliché, but it's also one that's alive and kicking and has deep associations with the uniqueness of artwork the autonomy of artwork, the value of artwork, particularly regarding painting as an art form. It's something that is incredibly hard to move away from in today's money. I mean it is part and parcel of how the haute capitalism of the art world works.

Haute capitalism. Nice. Like couture – very glamorous. Coming off of the obvious book format in your work, the most obvious motif in your work, or one of the most obvious is your fascination with punctuation. Full stops, periods, dashes, all the yummy things that go in between language. Do you want to tell me about… and I know that obviously whatever the process and meaning of that is varied and can change so much in your work and sculptures and paintings and print work in like such variety of ways. But let's start with what do you like about punctuation? What draws you to it?

I like that it's nothing. It is the stuff between language. It's the sort of breath or pause or sometimes conundrum made manifest in language. I first started fascinating on the full stop when I'd finished one of my early publications, 'The Nam', and I thought… What is the nature of this last full stop? Is it any different from the full stops that punctuate this entire book? And that book was already a slightly odd, breathy manual in that it didn't have any paragraphs or chapters in it. It was a bit like a marathon of a physical act that book, as something to read. I was alive to the issue of punctuation and so on, at that point. I'd done a long audiobook version of the text which was…

You reading everything?

Yeah. Just 22 hours reading that I did back in my flat. I could have done with the set-up that we've got here actually, then. And I also, by error, magnified a page of that book, really out of proportion. It was in the early days of desktop publishing. The full stop came out. The book was typeset in Helvetica. And I realised that the Helvetica full stop is this big block. It's like a big square, and that fascinated me. I just got into the idea that these anti-characters could become actually quite big characters and big players and started to discuss the pause and dilemmas and malaise in my own work. Where was I going to move on to? What was coming next through an investigation of actually doing nothing, aka, being stuck, aka how do you actually deal with that punctuation in your own practice? Whatever your creative endeavour or approach is, in fact, it's more punctuated by not knowing where to go than knowing where to go. Or more punctuated by pause and consideration than action.

I want to play a track. Let's start with one of your tunes. Let's start with this first one, which I hadn't heard before, which might be me. Let's begin with 'Dance Your Life Away' by audiobooks. Who are audiobooks and what does this track mean to you?

audiobooks are a duet or duo – Evangeline Ling who is an artist who I think just left Goldsmiths, and David Wrench who is some 20, 30 years her senior, who is a brilliant sound mixer and editor and spoken word maestro. They joined together and make this music called audiobooks. Let's hear it.

This is 'Dance Your Life Away' by audiobooks.

—

That was audiobooks. Going back to that concept of punctuation and lettering, can we start with the sculptural awareness. It's once you become aware of this awareness of the pause; you've made a lot of full stops in public spaces. Huge giant ones that almost look like bombs. What do you like about making something, almost an abstract concept, into a really physical thing?

I suppose contemplating an abstract moment, or a pause, or a breakdown of language is natural to me, because I'm involved with language as something that can't always perform as you want it to do. That became my investigation, to begin with. I thought using language as a liberation from making pictures and then I realised of course it has its own corners and shadows and problem areas, precipices.

It's really aesthetic in a way, some of your approach I mean. It's not the only way you've done it, but there is an aesthetic nature to font.

Are you referring to my font?

No, just in general.

I designed a font called 'font', that's why I ask.

Did you really? What does your font look like, 'font'?

It looks like a strange, primitive bastard of all the fonts I've ever worked with, which is essentially how it was made, but it looks rather eccentric. It might have been written with the left hand by a Neanderthal but it's also a sort of fabulously impure font, which is what I like about it.

A dirty font called font. Nice.

But to get back to your question, it's a hollowing out of language or the misuses of language. What today is referred to as a post-truth, weaponisation of language or the obtuse simplification of language in today's political rhetoric – that has made me return to the full stop. Because it ends up being like a hole or an absent – content in absentia. I guess if you take the font as being a courier for communication, it's about an inability to communicate, or a space beyond where communication is possible. Being aghast at reality potentially.

Let's talk about the paintings in your last show because I loved them. They were incredibly beautiful. Do you want to describe it? There were seascapes, where once there might have been a boat, that's been replaced by punctuation. Do you want to tell me a little bit about how you started working on this? Because it was quite a shock for me seeing you working with painting. How did that come about?

Painting isn't a medium that I thought I would return to.

Did you study painting?

I did some 30 years ago. And for all sorts of reasons to do with a disenfranchisement with that image and inability to sort of edit a picture, I left it and started working with language. But the pictures in my show 'Period' are found paintings, seascapes, which nearly always are of massive boats. For some reason, you need a boat as an excuse to wrap a seascape around. I found that really fascinating. I started seeing these things in junk shops, and so on, because I spent quite a lot of time on the south coast working. I bought some and took them home and then started painting over them. It coincided with a time when I was trying to make an installation of full stops in the water outside the De La Warr Pavilion in Bexhill and that ended up not being possible. I was frustrated by the impossibility of that. I ended up making helium-filled inflatables and putting them up in the sky instead. It's almost as a way of creating a sort of retrospective reality, the way I've made those paintings.

And then things started happening on the south coast, which involved the Channel. I always thought that the Channel between us and mainland Europe as a very contentious strip of water. The Channel is in a conduit and a connector, but also as a border. As a barrier as something that is actually hard to cross. During that time, I was involved with some, on two or three occasions, refugees coming in on boats at the end of exceptionally long, precarious journeys from across the continent. That also was an extremely visceral experience, gauging the reaction from a lot of the people on the beach and my reaction being very different. And, of course, Brexit and the Channel being a metaphor for our separation. A reality and a metaphor and really thinking about us as an island drifting off into another place and how that somehow seems associated with this endless circular impasse of language and circular discussion, and the political meltdown all contributed to me making these paintings of full stops drowning, stuck, drifting, too close, too far away. But an abstract empty language but also painted in this strange, unctuous, seductive bodily goo called oil paints, which somehow we can lose or move away from, or move on from in as a sort of system and suggestion of posterity and importance and value in art. I also found myself digressing into thoughts around oil, what that is, just the very sort of substance of oil. What that means to us in our world, also a very contentious substance that is so linked to our own downfall but also is a natural and ancient element. I got really involved in all of those things plus making these paintings that were of a sort of parallel, dual or for all I know multi authorship, which had been started by somebody else and then moved, finished by me.

They're incredibly beautiful. There's a lot of complex issues around all of this because obviously the blackness representing oil is a different kind of oil than you're necessarily using in oil paint... Also, the scale was amazing. Some of them were as big as a matchbox, and some of them were huge, mantlepiece sized. It's really interesting – that variety. I love the idea of the inability to communicate being a beautiful metaphor for our current political situation, and we're adrift in this country – recording this in the UK.

Yeah. I think making those paintings was a sort of meditation on that. And another interesting thing is that while you're making paintings, you can do other things. You can listen to the news feeds. You can be involved in this ongoing malaise.

Do you listen to music in your studio?

I actually listen to all forms of spoken word radio.

Interesting. Let's play another track. I want to play the Simon and Garfunkel, 'Silent Night/Seven o'clock News'. Why this one? When did you first hear it?

I first heard this, I think it came out in 1966 and I heard it when I was quite young. When my dad used to play chess with a friend, and they would endlessly play Simon and Garfunkel. I didn't really know what to make of it. Then one time this piece came on that had a spoken word track over the top of it and what I liked about it was that I was completely confused. It sounds like a mistake to begin with. But, of course, the totally plaintive sweet harmony of Simon and Garfunkel with Vietnam-era early day Nixon news report over the top completely busts that. It really is a left ear, right ear kind of situation and years later I started working with that track. I thought it also somehow speaks of today. I mean pre-Watergate Nixon, a time of massive crisis in confidence.

This is 'Silent Night/Seven o'clock News' by Simon and Garfunkel.

—

Coming out of that, obviously, Vietnam for a long period, but also war and conflict in a wider sense emerged in different projects you've done. I suppose in a wider sense, the political, I guess, has emerged as an undercurrent in what you do. It's a huge question. But what has interested you about the in like exploring ideas around conflict? Or even like the machinations of conflict, like giant airplanes and bombers and things that you feel like tanks. There's a lot of those things in your work.

The Vietnam conflict was on the telly when I was growing up. That was one of the early media, possibly the first media war. That got embedded and then later when I saw Magnum photography, and the Vietnam movies, it all came out and I realised that I'd sort of willingly become strangely indoctrinated by the Hollywood Nam films. That fascinated me, so it set me off on an investigation, I suppose for want of a better word, about how fiction and politics meld. And what is propaganda and how we are willingly seduced by fictional slash entertainment, retellings of the world that we live in.

Do you have a favourite Vietnam movie? I have a favourite one, 'Deerhunter', which is more like an aftermath.

It's quite sentimental, but quite amazing. My favourite's probably 'Full Metal Jacket'. Kubrick.

You can't go wrong with Kubrick. You and 2 Live Crew sampled that...

I was enlivened to, or became super aware of, the gender element of war. How war stories are heroicised. All of those propagandist elements of how we discuss conflict, and then also started looking at military hardware. Interested in how we display and celebrate this gear that apparently we hate. We are turned on by it at the same time. That one thing led to another.

I want to finish off by talking about your performance works, and I'm playing a track from one of them. Do you want to tell me how you use performance in what you do?

It just occurred to me that performance is part of making art. The act of showing is performative, is theatrical and very deliberate. Taking stuff out of a quiet, private, making, unknown scenario and pushing this idea of finished work together and creating a theatre around it. Then I started making some publication work that was performance. One, for instance, is that I registered myself as an ISBN Number. I saw that as a sort of ongoing, performance piece. That's a joke, but also very serious or also a joke.

Can you be scanned? How much do you cost?

Exactly. The letters come in from the British Library asking for copies.

Amazing. Can I have a copy of you?

I did make a book that documented all my ISBN work, so I gave them that, but then performance became a more active gesture. The piece that we're about to listen to is a soundtrack from 'S/S19 The Walk', which was a sort of piece of Haiku theatre that melded a military display with a catwalk show with a publication. I used models to display fonts and inflatable full stops and did a voiceover live in the space. It also incorporated elements from an earlier performance that I'd done with the musician and writer Viv Albertine, which was a reimagining of the 1966 pop song 'Snoopy versus the Red Baron'. It has all of that rolled into it.

Where did you do the performance?

It was at Kentish Town forum with DRAF last year.

Cool. Okay, well, this is 'S/S19 The Walk' by Fiona Banner, aka the vanity Press.

—

Just to finish off, let's talk a little bit about the things you give away. I was really interested in the idea of having materials like your press release for your last exhibition. It was really an artwork that reiterated the whole concept. Basically, writing out everything supersized on a giant note paper pad that people could take away, with the word 'period' in capitals. What do you find interesting about that form of dissemination?

I suppose there's a formality around press releases and a certain language that is deployed, which in many ways takes you further away from the spirit of the work rather usually, than close to it.

They're usually awful. I've even written them. Honestly, it's a total formula. I've actually taught people in Vienna, how to write the whole entire artist statement thing, because it's such a cliché.

I think it is. I wanted to make something of that because it's an interesting moment in publishing, even though it's sort of trite and digressional in quite tedious ways. That's why I made a sculptural stack out of the press releases. Instead of using traditional punctuation, wrote it out. The word 'period' and 'comma' appears with more emphasis actually, than the verbal content of the press release. Again, I suppose it talks about sense and nonsense.

I'm going to play your last track to finish off, so do you want to tell me, this is a Van Morrison live tune.

Van Morrison, 'Saint Dominic's Preview'. It's a live version of it. I listen to this track when I'm abroad, and I'm walking along to get openings. There's something about it that speaks of that moment. As far as I understand from Van's point of view, he's travelling in San Francisco on tour, feeling homesick. The condition of being homesick is really weird because it's a sort of magnification of home. There's a paradox in it because you lust for it, because it isn't there but then when you're there, home is something quite mundane, which you long to be liberated from often. But it's also a song about the troubles in Belfast. My family is from Belfast, and they moved across the water to Liverpool. The whole shipbuilding culture of Belfast, all the many references in this song, I think it makes it really brilliant. Also, there's a line where it says "the record company has paid out for the wine" so there's a sort of take on the strange machinations between the artist and the system or the company, the gallerist. All of these alienating forces actually coalesce to become an incredible moment which in Van's cases delivering a song like this at a gig.

Brilliantly put. Fiona firstly thank you very much for coming in. This is 'Saint Dominic's Preview (Live)' by Van Morrison.

Larry Achiampong

14.02.20

Hi, it's Francesca Gavin and you're listening to Rough Version on NTS. My guest this month is Larry Achiampong, who is a London-bred artist, I should say. Who won this year's Paul Hamlin prize and was nominated for the Jarman award. He sometimes teaches photography MA at the RCA, which blew me away, but he has done a variety of work, ranging from everything from flags to installations on the tube, to sound and performance work, and has a bit of a thing for video games!

Yes, I do. Yes, I still do!

Which I'm sure I'll get on with. So, thank you for coming in.

No, thank you, Francesca.

Let's start with how you work with performance. I haven't actually seen your performance; I know your film work more. Do you want to tell me a bit about how you've approached sound and performance in what you do?

Sure, absolutely… There are a range of projects and works where I approach the use of the body, or even the use of sound in a performative manner in a range of ways. At the moment, there have been a series of performances, perhaps over the last couple of years, in which I've performed audio tracks, which I've created or composed. Either using things like the MPC 1000 or composing tracks with a range of synthesizers and other instruments from the ground up. Some of those sounds have been then chopped up even more intricately, and then played with vocal testimonies, that perhaps connect historically, socially, or politically to the moment that we're in. So, it's quite involved. Sometimes there are collaborative elements in which I invite people to work with sounds or visuals. I've invited the likes of Nephertiti Oboshie Schandorf who is also my producer. She works with me on my films, and then also Shiraz Bayjoo, who's also an artist. They are quite involved setups, and it's an additional way for me to bring to life the audio works that I create, which of course, in their own right, are their own individual pieces.

I'm really curious. How do you approach composition? You use a lot of sampling?

Yeah, absolutely. Composition, for me, it really ranges… What's at the heart of all of production for me is the use of the MPC 1000. That connects with my love of hip hop and house and beat driven music. Just the ability to try and time travel with that machine really is the fun thing for me. But I guess over the last say 7 to 10 years I have become more and more interested in working with synthesizers. Things Dave Smith instruments, Prophet Rift to the Mopho. These machines that have a pulse. You turn them on, over time they heat up, and when that happens the sound changes. They are machines that, as far as I'm concerned, are alive. The way I create sounds separately from sampling is very much like a jamming session. I don't write loads of things down. I might make a couple of notes of things but it's really just feeling my way into the groove, feeling my way into the moment and just thinking about what kinds of textures I want at that point in time.

Even though you haven't brought any hip hop in, I was really interested that at some point, you went on a trip to the States, partly because you were interested in looking at the heritage and relationship between places that Nas came out of. Tell me a little bit about the influence of that on your work.

Absolutely. Hip hop has been such a large influence for me, specifically, through my brother who's four years older than me. He introduced me to hip hop, and he picked out Nas, who was probably one of the first hip hop artists whose albums I listened to. The sound of his album 'Illmatic' for me is the sound of New York. The first track I think is 'The Genesis'. You hear the trains running through Queensbridge. You hear a sample from 'Wild Style', the popular hip hop film, and it just gives you a feel and a taste for an environment. I'd been so excited to make that pilgrimage, listening to stuff like that. Listening to the likes of A Tribe Called Quest. To actually go to the place where it all began. So, in 2009, 2010 I travelled over to the United States. I went to New York. You could say I did my own personal residency. I was there for around 3 months. I just spent a lot of time walking or taking the trains, never really cabs, but just loads of walking or taking trains or maybe buses, and meeting people. Just kind of building a relationship with an environment that has been, I guess, so important to me due to the popular culture that I've absorbed over the years.

That seems a very natural segue into your first track, which is Tracy Chapman 'Fast Car'. Do you want to tell me why you chose this?

Totally. It's quite emotional, as well… Tracy Chapman's debut album was one that my mum would play amongst other things, but the reason why I've chosen this track actually is my first child Sinai, who is now 11 years old, was delivered to this track. There were two other tracks that were playing at the time when the doctors were delivering him: 'From this Moment' by Shania Twain and 'What a Wonderful World' by Louis Armstrong. Just thinking back to that moment… It was quite traumatic actually under the circumstances, but it was so beautiful for those particular tracks to be playing and to be hearing that. It was such a vulnerable but also special moment, I've been very careful in picking these tracks, because a lot of them are about nostalgia for me.

How lovely. Well, this is Tracy Chapman 'Fast Car'.

—

When I think of your work, the first works that I really saw were a graphic piece where you were using archive photography. You were placing these really stylized, Afro faces on top of them. Do you want to tell me about that work? What interests you in a wider sense about the archive?

Absolutely, absolutely. The archive in an ongoing sense is central to the work that I produce. Whether that's talking about histories or physically embedding them within the works. The series that you're talking about, the Glyph series, involves the use of iconography that is connected to the history of the golliwog, or minstrel shows. Stereotypically and racially charged imagery that portrays Black people within a negative light. I guess my first run in with this type of imagery was with the Robertsons golliwog images on the jars. The Robertsons brand of marmalade and jam is still around. But as a child sitting at the breakfast table, when mother would make toast, I'd see these tokens. I didn't quite understand what they meant, but they felt for me like something was wrong, and it didn't make me happy. Over the years, I did the research. I found out that the CEO of the brand had actually been inspired by the American minstrel shows in the United States pre-World War I. They then took that inspiration back to the UK and decided they needed to create a mascot. Out of that comes the Robertsons golly. You can find all this stuff online – from illustrations through to Nursery Rhymes through to theatrical productions, The likes of the BBC even had their own production show. It's essentially racism normalized. It's very structured. With this series of works, the Glyph series, I am essentially taking imagery from my family's photo album, whether that's Polaroids, 35 mm or manual photography. I'm scanning them at high resolution and I'm covering them with these motifs which I call 'the cloud face' which is a kind of visualized depiction that relates very directly or closely to the Robertsons golly, but the face has these black circles with red lips. There are no eyes, so I'm hinting at this idea of being dehumanized or being made to feel non-human.

Do you want to tell me about how your Ghanaian heritage influenced some of the motifs? Obviously, that was directly referencing some imagery. Do you feel like it's influenced what you're doing in a wider sense?

Oh massively. My mum and dad at a time when they were together and my dad, when I lived with him for a bit, they always instilled within us values and traditions from our Ashanti heritage. In some respects, it was confusing at times, which is why I made a film about my experience of going to church… The mixture of the effects of colonization via Christian imperialism, but there was always a very strong point which my mum would talk about. She would tell stories about Santoor, who was the queen mother to the Ansanti, King of the Akan people. She would talk a lot about rebellion and standing up for your rights and that kind of thing. I'd say, a lot of that kind of criticality for me was embedded into my persona as a kid growing up in East London, which is very different, I think, from East London now. It was very rough. I came from a low, working-class background. We experienced a lot of poverty. Then I spent time living in Dagenham, as a young Black man. That stuff gets really rough, especially, when you consider the time that I lived there with my dad, which was around the time of 9/11. Living in these environments in which tensions are high, I look back with pride and gratitude for not just being given that knowledge of where I come from, but also that knowledge of self, of pride, which I think is important.

> *I want to play one of your tracks that references that in one way, which is the Christie Azumha and the Uppers International. Do you want to tell me about where you first heard this, and why you chose it?*

So, this track is one of a good few albums that my mum and dad brought over from Ghana. They mainly had a highlife collection of music. As a kid I didn't like these tracks to begin with. Actually, there was something about the high frequencies that I didn't really appreciate. But over time, when my mum would play these tracks, whether she was cooking or cleaning… just hearing her sing and listening to the songs, I just fell in love with the polyrhythms. To be honest with you, it is quite difficult to choose a track because there's just so many that are really good from Alhaji K. Frimpong through to the African Brothers International Band, but I think the beauty of Christie Azumah's voice is that it's unique. I don't feel like I've heard a voice like it, within the realms of highlife or other forms of music. I think she has a sound that really commands and drives the band forward.

> *Well, I can't stop listening to it. This is 'Din Ya Sugri' Christie Azumah and the Uppers International.*
>
> —
>
> *When I think about your work, Larry, one of the most obvious things to me is your love for computer games! Partly from your collaborations with David Blandy, but in a wider sense. I come from a computer game background!*

Oh yeah, I had no idea!

> *Yeah, I used to review computer games like Rockstar. I actually stopped at some point. It's not good for your sex life.*

But on that point, do you want to tell me a little bit about... That's such a racist space. The representation of characters and avatars. I'm just really curious about how you engaged with all of that?

It's prejudiced on all levels: racist, sexist, homophobic. But here's the interesting thing about the communities that drive the video game scene. You have the developers and then the companies, but then you have the communities of people. Even then, of course, there's certain aspects of toxicity, I think, like in most environments, but... we're talking about regular folk who have all kinds of jobs or do all kinds of things within their day... Nowadays, you know, there are online communities for video games. People use various social media platforms to play or to connect, or to arrange happenings and events, some of which I go to. But going back to this conversation around prejudice, and even representation or perhaps the lack thereof, I definitely had an issue with that as a kid. I used to play games like 'Street Fighter' and 'Super Street Fighter' especially and look at like the representation of Blackness within that. The 'DJ' who is from Jamaica and has a really big smile and all of these silly stereotypical references to Jamaica or the West Indies. You get tired of that kind of thing. I'd say in more recent years, there have been video games in which there are more characters who are opening and challenging the boundaries... But there's still a lot to be done. Rockstar, which you mentioned, for example, and Grand Theft Auto. You know that game, that's one of the biggest selling games of all time. As far as stereotypes go, you name it, it's got it. And I think it comes to the point where the creators of these art forms have to be answerable to some of the things that they continue to propagate, because I think there's space for criticality within video games. It's the largest money-making medium on the planet. That's what Hollywood executives and these companies are thinking about – what sells, rather than thinking about what is the conversation that we're having here as a result of what we're putting out.

The work that you made with David Blandy, in particular, was it an interactive game per se, where you're inserting yourself or was it more video based?

It was more video based. It was interactive for us. In fact, we used and hacked the 'Grand Theft Auto 5' video game engine to create part of the 'Finding Fanon' series in which our avatars were searching for lost plays, or even the ghost of Fanon. Through what we refer to as the 'intersection', a digital virtualized space or landscape. We spent time going online and connecting with one another, building our characters up and walking across these vistas filming and capturing that. I guess, you end up spending time scrutinizing the actual media itself. If I'm honest with you the 'Grand Theft Auto' series isn't really one of my favourite series of games. I'd say the very first or even the second games, which were top-down points of view, and they were not 3D, they were much more enjoyable. They had a very pickup and play arcade sensibility about them. You still had a great soundtrack with all the radio stations, but it managed to do something with certain histories of culture related to gangster films, that I think the 3D versions of the games miss out a little bit. If I'm honest with you, with the newer games, my favourite things about them have been the radio stations, because…

The radio is good.

Yeah. They say more than what the game is doing itself.

Let's play your 'Donkey Kong' track after this, which was very filmic. The music involved in computer games is so important, but do you want to tell me a little bit about this specific one?

Absolutely. It's a track from 'Donkey Kong Country 2: Diddy Kong's Quest', and it's made by a composer called David Wise who composed pretty much all of the Donkey Kong Country series of soundtracks and then was brought back for, I believe, 'Donkey Kong Tropical Freeze', a game which my son plays actually. This track, he plays and sings and listens to… It is weird. We're really similar in that respect. He loves to listen to soundtracks, and we talk about the sounds and things. But the thing that I always loved about these soundtracks and soundtracks from video games in general – going from the eight-bit era all the way to now, where you have complex arrangements from orchestras – is that the capabilities that a lot of composers and musicians were able to push with the limits of technology that they had. Nowadays we have literally gigabytes of data that we can use within new versions of MPC's or Ableton or software in general but back then they only had a megabyte or 2, if that, to create complete soundtracks! And what you get out of those soundtracks is just incredible. I don't have a word for it, but it's certainly amazing.

Well, this is David Wise 'Stickerbrush Symphony'.

—

Coming out of that relationship with technology, do you want to tell me a bit about your take on Afrofuturism? Because I think that's definitely something that's feeding into a lot of what you do.

.

Oh, gosh. I've been talking to a lot of people about this lately. Here's the thing for me. I'm inspired by creators, artists who are fine with the term Afrofuturism – the likes of John Akomfrah and Smoking Dogs and so on. But personally, I have an issue with the word itself. Even the futurist aspect because the word futurism relates to…

Really fascist!

Took it right out of it. I've always had a problem with that. In fact, I've coined my own term through the creation of my own works in practice, which I call 'Sanko Time', which brings together the word 'Sankofa', which is a tree word from the Ghanaian language, one of many, which means to go back and to retrieve it or take what has been lost. Thinking about time as something that is not linear but is perhaps even cyclical. You're going back and forward in order to consider what the future might be. Again, another issue with futurism is that it doesn't really consider the past. The past is obsolete. The past is the older version. Even today, when I think about software, I have an issue with that, because sometimes, there's older software that's better than the newer updates or firm wares. There's certainly inspiration for me from the likes of Octavia Butler, and so on. But I'd say that I align my thinking with Nnedi Okorafor. She considers the term which she has created herself Africa-futurism which again, is not something that I personally subscribe to. I think words and where they are derived from have connotations. They have birth places. It's important to think about that, but there's certainly an African centralized set of themes that are coming through the work. But I wouldn't say it's one of the words that I would apply with my work. I think the way that people are able to connect with or identify things certainly understand that, but as far as my practice goes, I'd say 'Sanko time' is certainly what drives it.

It's a really fair point. I mean, when you think about the references. It's very much coming from a particular moment in time – Juan Atkins or Sun Ra. What's interesting about that heritage, even if we rename it, is these ideas around myth and this creation of alternative realities. Do you want to talk a little bit about what appeals to you about this narrative as alternative narratives?

Absolutely. I think what's really special about the opportunity to work with fiction is the chance to not only question histories or raise histories but be able to imagine new possibilities. And you can only do that through creating dreams or ideas of what you hope for or ideas of what we're afraid of… The use of science fiction to a degree is where all of these things become. A very important place for me to experiment because it's thinking about the unknown, possibility. Unknown ideas and with that, what kind of potential do we have as a result. It's very much like the commission that I created on the underground, for example, the pan African flags for the Relic Travellers Alliance, the re-mixing of a very popular British but also worldwide icon, in the form of the logo, the roundel. Taking colours that relate with British Imperialism. And then just switching things up a little, thinking about pan-African colours, thinking about conversations around the diaspora. Thinking about that the experience of African people from an international perspective, not simply just one that just locates itself in the continent. The ability to consider fiction, in relation to being critical, I think without that, there's not much that I can do with my work. It's very important for me.

I love the fact that when you're addressing things like the tube sign, or flags, or even your own face, which was plastered all over Somerset House – I love the idea that you're inserting yourself into things that are totally normalized and making us become aware of what they're actually referencing, which I think is really important, quite politically motivated. Would you say there's a political motivation?

Certainly, most certainly. It's just to agitate conversation. One of the things that I'm very open and aware of as an artist, as a practitioner, is you have ideas, you bring them to the table, a space, whether that's indoors or outdoors, you give that over to whoever is going to happen across that. There are aspects of control that drive the practice, but I'm very open as to how that gets interpreted. What's really been beautiful about this project with London underground is just seeing how people have been posting online, especially on Instagram and have been taking ownership of that for themselves. For me, it's creating the gesture, and then allowing people to actually own that. I think that's the exciting thing in the work.

It's time for a final track from a film I still haven't seen yet. Which is from 'Queen and Slim'. Is the whole soundtrack by Devonté Hynes?

There's the soundtrack with a range of different eyes, different tracks. It's a really beautiful film but it's very hard as well. There are some creative decisions that the director did that I don't know I personally agree with. When we talk about this idea of functioning in the context of the difficulty of trying to exist as a young Black person, whether that's in the United States or the UK. When it comes to seeing something within the context of cinema, for example, sometimes you want a happy ending. There's not a lot of happy endings around at the moment, are there?

There really aren't.

Going to the film, watching the film, without trying to spoil things, I had a feeling that things wouldn't end so well. The thing that really hit me is why can't we create things in our terms that allow us, as Black people to prosper, without it being this thing of torture again, within the context of a space that has strong connections with reality.

It can be something that we hope for or dream of, but that being said, I still think it's an incredible film. Devonté Hynes creates an evolving soundtrack with beautiful textures, with both the use of synthesizers and woodwind instruments. This track 'Hair' is at a point in the film which is a transition for the characters Queen and Slim. It's quite a tearjerker and is really beautiful. There's this point of ascension with their characters at this point.

Larry, thank you so much for coming in. This is Devonté Hynes 'Hair'.

Marguerite Humeau

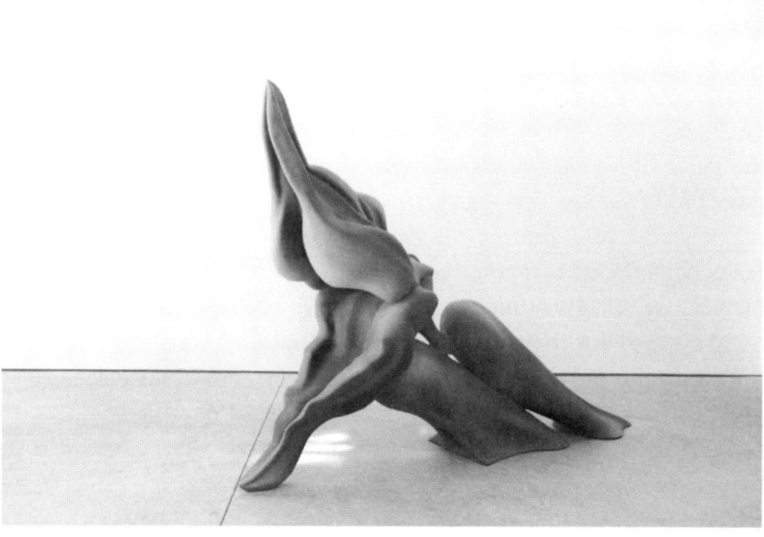

The Prayer, A marine mammal invoking higher spirits, 2019.

23.03.20

Hi, I'm Francesca Gavin and you're listening to Rough Version on NTS. My guest this month is Marguerite Humeau. She's an RCA graduate who is French. Who has been based in London for over a decade. She's had solo shows at Tate Britain, Palais de Tokyo, and was included in Manifesta11 in Zurich in 2016. Marguerite, thank you so much for coming in.

Thank you so much for inviting me.

Let's start by talking about sound in your work. In particular, how you use it in installation. Do you want to tell me how you started doing that? How you use it and what you do?

Yeah, sure. Maybe I can talk quickly about my first project. It was about prehistoric creatures. It was my graduation project from when I was studying at the Royal College of Art. I had this idea of trying to resuscitate the sound of prehistoric animals by reconstructing the vocal tracks. I thought that it would be fairly easy I would talk to biologists, and they would give me the scans or something.

No one knows what a dinosaur looked like, let alone what they sound like. Is that true?

Yeah. I mean really no one really knows. I've been talking to the 'Jurassic Park' advisor at the time. Basically, in scientific terms there's a lot of guesswork you can do but you can just go as far as you're allowed… That's where my task started. I thought, "Okay, if this data is not available, I'm going have to reproduce it or gather all these bits of information together". Coming from all different fields, not only science. Because clearly science didn't have this data, or not enough for me to do this reconstruction. I took two different people who are directly or indirectly connected with sound and with vocal cords and with prehistoric animals. I ended up creating these sculptures that are all one-to-one scale, reproductions of the lungs, vocal cords, the larynx, nasal and mouth cavities of these creatures. I injected compressed air inside of them to get these vocal cords to vibrate. So, for the first time, I could hear and everyone around me could hear, the sound of other mammals. 'Walking Whale' and

'Terminator Pig', which is the nickname that scientists gave to this. This wild boar, pre-historic boar.

Terminator pig.

'Terminator pig' or 'hell pig', depending on sensitivities. So, that's how I started. And then I worked also with an engineer. I was interested in this idea of re-evolution. Trying to re-engineer the origins. So, we basically trained each creature. Each creature was connected to a program that was activating or deactivating the air compressor, the valves. We trained them, each of them, to listen to each other. They would start with just a very limited number of sounds they could make. And as the show was progressing, they would hear each other, listen to each other, trying to copy each other. Therefore, their language would get more and more complex.

That was an AI project? Like a sound AI.

Yeah. Quite basic AI but yeah.

We'll talk about the ideas around fiction separately. What interests you in particular about – it's not music, another form of sound. You've used music and other elements, I think. Do you want to tell me a little bit because it's quite unusual to explore sound in such a physical sense?

Yeah, sure. The next project was the reconstruction of Cleopatra's voice and getting her to sing in all the languages that she used to speak, that are all extinct today. I would say it's an exploration of sound and language at the same time. I guess it comes from early research on how the voice is the direct link to the soul, direct expression of the soul. And how it's been connected to – how communication technologies and disembodied voices have usually been connected to the supernatural. There's this amazing book, 'Haunted Media' by Jeffrey Sconce. He talks a lot about how the invention of the telegraph was at the origin of celestial telegraphy, which was basically an occult communication technology. Using real technologies that then inspired occult practices. With telephone. There's a thing about what happens when a voice is disconnected from the body and what kind of collective imaginary it can trigger. I guess the sound for me so far, it's been more research on the voice rather than the sound itself. Using synthetic voices, artificial voices and then more recently recording natural voices. I'm trying to push them to the limits of their possibilities of the body. What happens when you have to get outside of your body, outside of your physical abilities to become something else – maybe to get into trance or to mutate. I guess it's research on the voice and its connection to the supernatural and maybe how also with contemporary technologies, it seems sometimes that we have to deal with a lot of beings that are not quite alive, not quite dead. That are maybe somewhere in between – living dead of different sorts.

That ghostliness is quite good leading on to your first track that you've chosen which is quite a weird, eerie song. Want to tell me a little bit about the Jean-François Laporte?

He's a Canadian, French-Canadian sound musician, sound researcher. I met him very early in my research. He's been doing this album that is music recorded in extraordinary places. This track has been recorded in an abandoned cargo ship… For another track he went to a place where how do you call… with loads of fridges, in the frozen food industry, something like that. He basically spends the night there and created this track that is just recordings of different parts of the fridges' technology. It becomes really abstract. I've seen him playing live and from very mundane setups, he just manages to launch us somewhere into the universe. That's why I chose it.

I'm going to probably start a little in because the beginning is so silent. You can barely hear, but it's amazing. This is Jean-Francoise Laporte, 'Dans Le Ventre Du Dragon'.

—

Let's talk a little bit about fiction in your work. A lot of your work is about almost like these – I would say it's like a fiction based in some sense of reality. It's like science fiction past. It's almost fictional archaeology in some sense. What do you like about that idea of narrative?

I think it comes from a need to understand our place in the universe. It seems that the planet is on fire – it's literally on fire. We're maybe going to an end, or it feels like we're coming to an end if we don't do anything about it. I guess it's also a moment when us as humans and humankind is realizing that we're not the centre of the universe. That there are other beings evolving in our equal really close ecosystems. So that eventually we might just be like a blast of wind, when you compare our story to the much bigger story of life in the universe. I guess in my projects, I'm trying to recreate this feeling that we are, that it's something very temporary. Things appear and might fade away very quickly. I guess the aesthetics is mixing ideas of aesthetics connected to the future or to an idea of projection into the future. At the same time, using primal shapes or sounds or voices that are connected to our history and that have been used repeatedly in the history of humankind. I don't think that really answers your question.

It's a good answer. Actually, I want to go on because you've given me so many tracks I want to play another one. I feel like Charles Trenet 'La Mer' is interesting continuation of this if we're going to talk about the fire. This is the Frenchest thing anyone's ever brought in. Do you want to tell me about when you first heard this classic French track?

Yeah. It's really classic. It's a track that my grandfather used to sing to us when we were young. And my mum as well and my dad. I really like the naivety of this track which sounds really, just sometimes I feel a bit nostalgic… not nostalgic but I'm French and in London, so when I need a bit of Frenchness I listen to Trenet.

What is really interesting about this track if we're going think in the context of like your ecological discussion, maybe that nostalgia is also a little bit of nostalgia but have a different relationship to nature. Do you know what I mean, that would be a nice take?

Yeah, that's true because in the track he's basically describing the sea and how it's dancing and the waves. There's something really charming about it. Sometimes I wonder if we will be able to see the sea in the same way in the future. Maybe the sea would still be here but how about glaciers or even snow. I was in Toronto last week; I saw snow and I were thinking I haven't seen snow for so many years. I think the last time it snowed in London was maybe ten years ago maybe seven, eight let's say. I don't know, but we used to have snow in France every winter when I was a kid. It's a nice song, nicely connected to our topics.

This is 'La Mer' by Charles Trenet.

—

Let's go back to the ideas of aesthetics in your work. You have a lot of fluidity of forms and use a lot of 3D printing and materials that are like glass – is it fiberglass? I'm really interested in your approach to the aesthetic and fluidity. Do you want to tell me how that developed and how that relates to your ideas of this science past future?

Yes. Originally, I started this first project when I was at the Royal College of Art. I was in a design department. It's funny using these forms. I mean I was in the Interaction department, in the next room was the department of car design. Somehow it was part of the aesthetics of what I was surrounded by. It was not intentional at the beginning. Somehow it was but not as much as now. Also, the techniques that I developed. It's the same for my tutors. The only way to produce an object of this sort was to use a computer program, and to make it in 3D, and then to 3D print it to a smaller scale to see how it will look like and then using CNC machines. Basically, I was following what they thought we should use when you're producing a piece of design. Not really thinking about it as a statement because at the time I was not describing myself as a sculptor or an artist. I was a designer. I was recreating prehistoric creatures and just using the same tools as my classmates and my tutors and other designers. I think it's only after, in the next two years that followed, that I started to understand what I was doing and how it connected to my practice. How the shapes that I wanted to create, I wanted them to feel like ghosts, coming from a different space or time. From the deep past or your deep future. I wanted them to feel like although they were really material because they are large sculptures. But at the same time completely material. I asked the model makers I was working with to remove any trace of the human hand. I wanted them to look like mirage or like sugar. Almost like you would touch it, it would just start to fade away.

You started working on new materials that have this fleshiness to them.

Yes, that's a bit more recent. I've been doing a few series of sculptures that were the scale of like really bright white. Connecting this sculpture to the idea of screens, ghosts, ghostly appearances, but also to the screen. I wanted them to be also surfaces of projection somehow. Not physical projections, but fictional projections or psychological projections. And then, as my work progressed, I thought I wanted to dig a bit more into this idea of artificial life. How I could eventually talk a bit more about those beings I was recreating in the material in which they were made of. We developed this skin last year. There is basically a material made of many, many different layers of translucent, slightly translucent coloured layers. That altogether create the skin that has depth, and that creates this weird sensation, when you move around the sculptures, it feels like their skin is almost moving or that the colour is shifting as you move, you turn around them.

Can we talk a little bit before you play your next track about research, because research seems really fundamental. You have a lot of not only book research, but you actually approach a lot of first-hand accounts, experts in what you do. What do you like about that process? And how does that influence the results?

It's a very exciting process because I get to meet people who spend their life researching on topics that I didn't even know existed. I guess what I like or what I'm interested in is trying to understand what are the unofficial forms of knowledge that haven't made our way to your visual knowledge. The main source of visual knowledge is science in our society, but I feel they're all other forms of knowledge that are not scientific, but that are as valid. That's why I'm talking to sometimes conspiracy theorists or shaman. People who are studying the brain in alternative ways to scientific ways. I'm talking to a lot of people who themselves or maybe somewhere in between. Scientists who don't really work in science anymore and are exploring other possibilities. I guess it's a way but in my work in general, which is all about recreating ghosts of history. People or beings or creatures, or any kind of living thing that hasn't been part of the official written history, I'm trying to bring them back to the surface or make them visible. In a way, it's the same in my research. It's about making visible things that have always been here but have never been understood. Or made as valid as the official sources.

> *Let's play our next track. Let's play Angel Bat David 'Impepho'. Can you tell me why you chose this track?*

Yes. I'm a jazz addict. I discovered her recently and she's a clarinetist. I read her interview in the Guardian last year, and I was really intrigued. She was talking about her being a Black woman playing clarinet. She was describing herself as a rare… I don't know, example? I started listen to her to her music. She's playing a lot of free jazz. And it's, I just really liked this. I guess it connects to what we just talked about also. How this woman suddenly starts to appear and to shine, be part of the of the official history of jazz, which is really exciting.

> *This is Angel Bat David 'Impepho'.*
>
> —
>
> *Let's talk a little bit about context. You're probably best known for doing installations where you're really taking over a space and you're also beginning more and more to work in public space with outdoor sculptures. Do you want to tell me what you like about both aspects and how you're approaching them differently?*

I started working a lot indoors, working on different museum shows, and I think it's different working outdoor and working indoors. It is two different things. How can I explain that…? Maybe for an indoor project. There are different kinds. There are the white cubes and then the spaces that have more particularities. I guess sometimes it's nice for my work, when it's in a more sterile environment, I know I can push certain things that are quite specific. Then when the context is more particular, I'm always including it in the work. So, the work always make sense with the space and the history of this space, the architecture or the way people interact with it. I can take my work to maybe more unexpected places. The same happens when I work outdoors. For example, when I did the piece for Chateau de Versailles. Obviously, it has this really grand and also heavy history. It has a lot of sculptures, original sculptures in the gardens. There was no way to not acknowledge that and make sure that the work would respond to that. I guess for different moments. Each space or each context I respond to in different ways.

I remember in your Tate Britain installation, the acid yellow, that you created a space. You made it not feel like a big giant Victorian building, but it was very futuristic. It was a really specific sense of colour that united the space and transformed quite dramatically.

Yeah. When I visited the space, I thought it makes me feel, there's something quite religious in the echo of the height of the ceiling. Because I was already thinking about Cleopatra's voice, how it would resonate within the space. Because this show, I originally I did it in Berlin in 2015. The Tate show was a recreation of this experience, two years later. To me, it was somewhere between a temple or a religious sacred space and a lab, a scientific lab. The Tate is a space that is already, has always been quite sacred, I felt. It was about how would I recreate this lab element. Also, I was thinking about Indiana Jones all these kind of quest adventures when they come next to the treasure. There's always this glow. I don't know. I feel like it's an impression!

Like the Holy Grail. That's always got this special glow around.

That glow you could feel from miles away. I thought I would like to recreate that inside the Tate. It happened with the colour on the walls, and also the voice of Cleopatra that you could hear even before you would enter the space.

We're going to finish with actually two tracks because you've given me two to choose from. So, we're going to play Nina

Simone and Omar Souleyman. Do you want to tell me why you chose these two?

Nina Simone because I think she's the greatest jazz singer of all time.

That's a good enough reason!

And Omar Souleyman because he's been supporting, without knowing, a lot of my late nights in the studio.

Do you listen to a lot of music in the studio?

Yes, we do.

Okay, this Nina Simone, 'I Wish I knew How to be Free' and Omar Souleyman, 'Warni Warni' and thank you very much for coming in.

Thank you so much.

Paul McDevitt

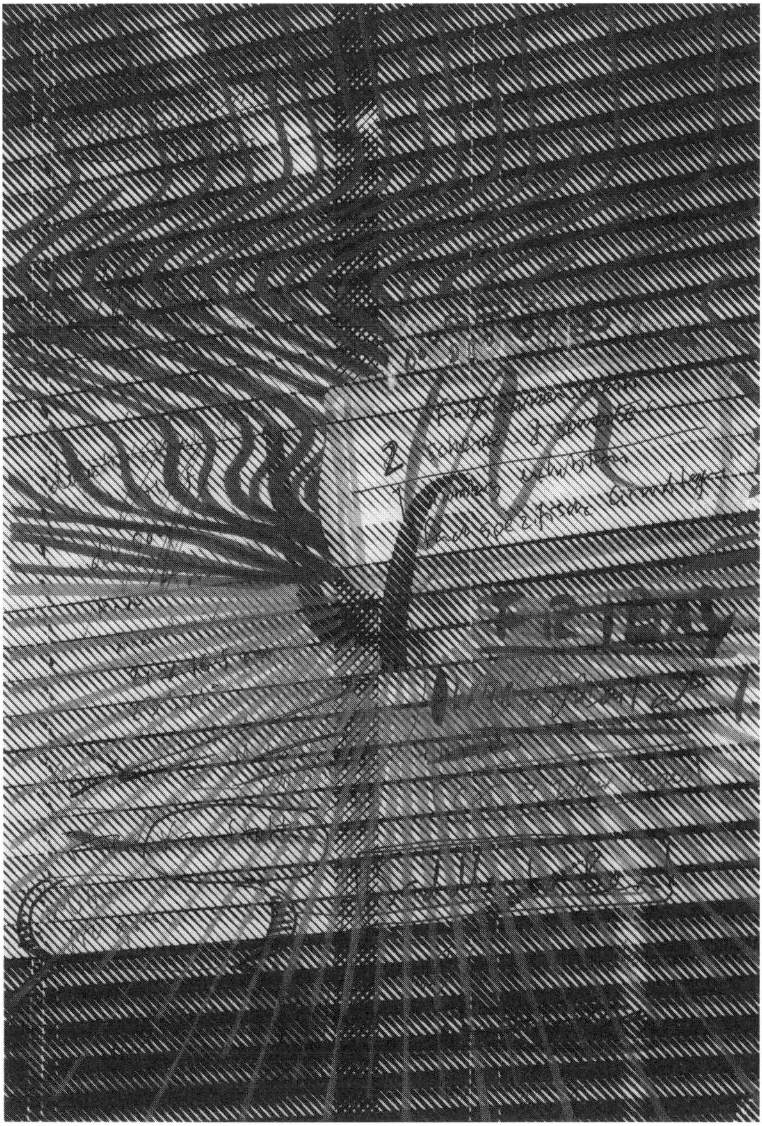

Notes to Self: 15 June 2021, 2021.

24.04.20

Hi, I'm Francesca Gavin, and you're listening to Rough Version on NTS. My guest this month is Paul McDevitt. He's a British artist based in Berlin. He does everything from painting to drawing, sculpture to book projects. He's got an amazing project space in Prenzlauer Berg called Farbvision, and also does a record label called Infinite Greyscale. Thank you very much for coming in, virtually. Let's start talking about your own practice, because you do a variety of different things. But I think it's a really interesting point, seeing how your own practice is grounded in quite a variety of different mediums like drawing, painting, collage and printing. I just wanted you to tell me a little bit about what you like about the breadth of that expression.

I suppose it just feels natural to me to always have some variety so that you don't get stuck in one place. You don't end up having any kind of signature work or significant style. I think this is what I always wanted to avoid. It's not easy to work on one thing day in day out. It's nice to be able to make a change. I think, for me, that worked as a way to work through the whole day. If I get tired or restless with one thing, I can start working on something different. I developed a few strategies over the years to help me do that. One of which is working with other artists.

Collaboration is a huge part of what you do. You worked for a long period of time with Cornelius Quabeck, and you have a record label together. Do you want to tell me a little bit about how that collaboration happened? Also, how that has emerged in music form?

I think it all began from a desire to have a little less certainty and bit more surprise and risk in our practices, so we started making drawings together. They were very spontaneous and loose, and you were always giving over control to the other artist. We made hundreds of them and showed them over the years. That slowly developed into making books and from the books, we slowly began to make records. What was just a way to put books of our drawings out there and have them distributed, eventually became a proper record label.

Can you tell me about the kind of stuff that you've been putting out? Because there is a real synergy between how you're using art in relationship to the aesthetics of what you do as well.

First, I'll describe the format. Up until now, there has always been 10-inch discs. The reason being that we did all the cover art on a risograph printer that I have, that could print A3, which is not big enough for a 12-inch record. We made these 10-inch coloured vinyl records with audio on one side, usually one long piece. Then the B side was a screenprint. The idea was to make it somewhere between an artist edition and a piece of audio art – so it was half a print, half a record.

How long has it been going? Quite a few years now?

The production slowed down a little, as there's so many special editions. But for a while we were making two a year. Now it's more like one a year. I think we're just about to do the 14th record. So, I don't know what that is… eight years or something.

Something like that. Well, let's start by playing one of the tracks that you've put out. Which one do you want to begin with?

Let's go straight in with some percussion. Let's go for Gajek 'Micromanic'.

Do you want to tell me a little about the track?

Sure. Matti Gajek was not someone we knew before. He was an associate of some friends of ours, the band Mouse on Mars. But we knew his music from releases on Monkey Town, the big Berlin label. I suppose, this is a percussive epic. A lot of the pieces we put out there are single pieces. They were meant to be a big statement, rather than individual songs. I think the duration is 12 minutes. Pieces of that length tend to have a narrative arc with lots of different ideas put into one long piece. In many ways, it is a journey. It has different sections. It starts off in a very tentative way with small steps. And that morphs into a kind of chattering electronic birdsong, which gives way to a hammering baseline, which becomes more and more intense, until eventually it crumbles and dissolves. We won't play the whole thing right now, but it's very influenced by krautrock with a very complex and varied narrative throughout.

> *Well, from birdsong to bassline. This is 'Micromaniac' by Gajek.*
>
> —
>
> *When I think about your work Paul, I often think about a durational guy in a studio. The first stuff I knew of yours was drawings. You'd be literally drawing constantly over 24 hours or over a set period of time.*

It sounds ridiculous when you put it to me, but yeah, I still do that.

> *Do you want to tell me a little bit about what you like about the durational side of it? The idea that you're literally stuck with you, a pile of paper and drawing instruments? What do you like about this almost painful, Sisyphus-like approach to making work?*

It's sounds ridiculous when you put it that way. It probably is. But I like the uncertainty and that you don't know where it's going to end up. You can only rely on your own imagination. You're not really referring to much outside stimuli. It's all about making a lot of different images over a period of time, so when unedited it reveals all of the moments of inspiration and desperation, and the ups and downs. It's about capturing a moment of time, which I suppose is what drawing can do when it's successful, by revealing everything that went into the making. There is nowhere to hide in the drawn line. So, that's where those pieces came from. Now they involve more photography, but that's still what they are.

> *There's also something comic or cartoon influenced in them. They are quite accessible and playful.*

That's my brain, I suppose. Maybe you reveal yourself in a way with these works, and the teenager or whatever you were into in your younger years comes out. You realize you haven't changed that much. Perhaps that's where the comics come from, and some of the gags.

Were you reading a lot of comics when you were younger? In some of your paintings, for example, elements of Mickey Mouse seep out...

I love comics. They're like the ultimate Modernist art form. They tick all the boxes. They are industrially reproducible, they deal with repetition, the simple essence of a form. I love them. I think they're great. They're an international language. They don't need text. I keep coming back to them in various ways.

I think we should play another track. Shall we do the Stara Rzeka?

Yes, the name is Polish. It means 'old river', which is the name of the artist. It's also the name of this record and the name of the village where he comes from. I think it's important that all of these things intertwine with him, his music and this piece.

And the name of the track?

It's called 'Stara Rzeka', as well. It's the same name.

Wonderful. I'm not going to try and pronounce it again, but here it is.

—

Tell me a little bit about your project space in Berlin.

Farbvision. We had just moved into a ground floor former printing workshop in central Berlin. The idea was to have the front few rooms as a studio, and we'd live in the back. When we took down the walls at the front, where there used to be a reception for the printing company, we found these incredible hundred-year-old decorative tiles. At once, the room was something special, too special not to have it open to the public in some way. We knew it should be a project space. It's on the street. It had toilets underneath, so you could close down the rest of the studio and just have this independent space when needs be. It was easy to do, and it still is.

It's a beautiful space that has incredible tiling in it, you're right. You've done quite a variety of different kinds of shows there. What do you like about the curatorial side of things and how that is connected to what you do as an artist?

It's great to work with different artists. There is only so much we can do as individuals. We all have our limits. To be able to work with somebody who makes work that you admire but couldn't possibly do yourself. I think that sort of scratches an itch… Plus, it's about communication. A lot of what you do as an artist is solitary and to work with someone else is always a pleasure. Talking about ideas, you reach a solution much, much quicker when there's more than one of you.

You do a lot of risograph prints with the artists that you show. They're really accessible in terms of pricing. Do you do that with every artist?

Since I started teaching a year ago, I stopped making them and gave the machine to my students to use.

Very nice of you!

Up until that point, it had been an idea to make artworks that were basically made by an artist for other artists to buy. We priced them very cheaply. They were not about the market or galleries; they were just meant to be something that friends of mine could buy without distress. They could afford a spontaneous purchase. Also, it was a way to have a record of the exhibitions after they were gone, a kind of visual archive.

Your studio is behind the space. How does that relationship work?

Right now, it's fantastic because everything is under one roof. It takes a bit of discipline to learn when to not do something else, when you should be working in the studio and not being distracted by the project space. But it is fine, it works great. It's good to have everything together. We do the printing for the record covers downstairs in the cellar.

Do you listen to a lot of music when you are working?

Yeah, it's one of the best things about being an artist, that you can really ingest so much sound and keep up with what's new.

Does it shift or influence what you're making in some way?

No, I don't think so. Sometimes, if I have to concentrate, I turn it off. But otherwise, there's so much of what I do that is close to manual labour, I suppose. And there is a lot of repetition, so that's perfect for listening to music.

Well let's play another track which I'm sure you've listened to in your studio. Let's go for... you've chosen so many things which are difficult to pronounce. Ghédalia Tazartès with 'Repas Froid' which is cold meal in French.

He's a French artist in his 70s. I first came across him through a record label called PAN, which is run by a musician called Bill Kouligas. PAN was a big influence on our label, because they had this very eclectic range of sound art, noise and things at the beginning. Now they're much more electronic music based. But the first four releases by them had a screen-printed PVC sleeve. There were very beautiful layers of imagery. They were really gorgeous objects. When we started the label, I actually had lunch with Bill and got a lot of advice from him on how to do it. We had no idea what we were doing in terms of music rights, or producing a vinyl record... That was a big part of putting our record label together. I love this release. It's a really long form track. I think it's 18 minutes. This is one of the two tracks on the record side of vinyl. It's a collage of different elements, field recordings, music contracts, chants, rhythm, poetry, sound loops. He really has this nomadic way of jumping from one style to another and I think that's what's exciting about it. It's about the uncertainty. You don't know where it's going. You've got no sense how long it's going to last and it's exciting. It's like listening to radio in a strange radio station in a country you have never been to before. There is something exotic and unfamiliar and exhilarating about it.

Nice. This is 'Repas Froids' by Ghédalia Tazartès.

—

One of the things that I always really think of in relationship to your work, particularly your paintings and sculptures, is the influence of Modernism. Henry Moore or Mondrian, those big male 20th century icons. Tell me how that influence emerged? Part of it, I assume, is because you grew up in Harrogate or near Harrogate?

Leeds.

Leeds. Excuse me. That's terrible.

Harrogate was for Sunday afternoon visits. The male thing was not intentional. But the Henry Moore influence was because I grew up in Leeds. His work is very much part of the landscape of the city and the county. Before I knew what modernism or contemporary art, whatever any of that was, I already knew what his work looked like. Because of that early exposure to the work, it never really had any meaning for me. It always had this interesting openness or meaninglessness to it… I don't really know where to place Moore in the canon of 20th century art. I don't know where he fits in, in terms of other movements and other artists. That openness meant he was someone I could play with and project onto. Like a good piece of music, sometimes you can project how you feel into it, and it can become a reflection of who you are or what you're feeling. With Moore, I used this openness, I suppose. The Mondrian thing was a bit different. That was connected to the comic books and was a way to use the breaking of the picture plane into different rectangles and forms into a grid. Thinking about it like a comic book page, I suppose, with different panels and giving it a durational aspect, as a way of telling a story or narrative. That's why I used his works a lot as a way to tell a story.

Another one of the aspects of your work I really think about, or at least one of my favourite series that you do, is the way you write all your to-do lists on an A4 piece of paper, and then reuse this as the inspiration for very different drawings. Almost somewhere between a drawing and a painting. I don't even know how to describe it. I love the layering within what you do. Do you want to talk a little bit about that series?

Yeah. I'm doing one now, as I'm sitting here talking to you. I've got the pad of paper here with a couple of notes about our appointment. They are a way to break a deadlock or to get out of a rut – a writer's block, artist block, whatever you want to call it. I have this pad of paper, which is full of fairly mundane notes and scribbles. Of course, you fill that out every day or two. I just tear them off the pad and keep them. Some years ago, I started working over them again, when I was stuck with bigger projects. They are A4. It's an easy scale to work with at a desk. If they don't work out, it's not heartbreaking to throw them in the bin, unlike something you might spend weeks on… It's a way to loosen up and to find a voice or to find ideas again. When you're working, that's when ideas come. Not when you're staring at a computer or a blank piece of paper. They're also like a collaboration with an earlier version of me. You have all these notes, which are no longer pertinent. There's always something to respond to whether it's the content of the text or the forms of the scrolls and the shapes. There's already something there to respond to. It's an easy way to start working and then they go somewhere new each time.

When I think of your paintings there's also that sense of layering, almost a trompe l'oeil sense of depth. You'll see the replication of a brush stroke on a canvas with things underneath that make you aware of the layers within things.

That probably comes through from a place of deep uncertainty, in terms of painting. I always found painting to be incredibly challenging. I never really felt like I was part of the language of painting. I think years ago, I started referencing painting as a sort of graphic gesture, rather than it being about the paint itself. That's how the works somehow became intertwined between painting, drawing and print, often with the replications of painted gestures, different scales or repeated forms.

Well, we're going to finish with your last track, which is equally unpronounceable, which is 'Uskallan' by Paavoharju.

I think that's pretty close. I mean, I've never had to say it out loud. They are a Finnish collective and 'Uskallan' means idea. Beyond that, I don't know anything about the band. The lyrics – I have no idea what they're saying, which is why this track is very special to me. It was recorded, I believe, on a camcorder microphone, so it's really lo-fi. They were a musical collective of ascetic Christians who were living in a squat in Finland, about 10 years ago. It is a very lo-fi, homemade sound, which I love, but also, they have incredible pop sensibilities, with soaring choruses. As I was trying to say before, it reflects how I feel at a time. Sometimes It can sound astonishingly uplifting, at other times crushingly melancholic, and I love that. I love not knowing what it says. I love the openness. This song is eternally open for me. I think it's just beautiful. I love the way it begins with a baby and ends with a baby crying. It is a magical piece.

Thank you very much for coming in. And stay well in Berlin.

Thank you very much Francesca.

Rhea Dillon

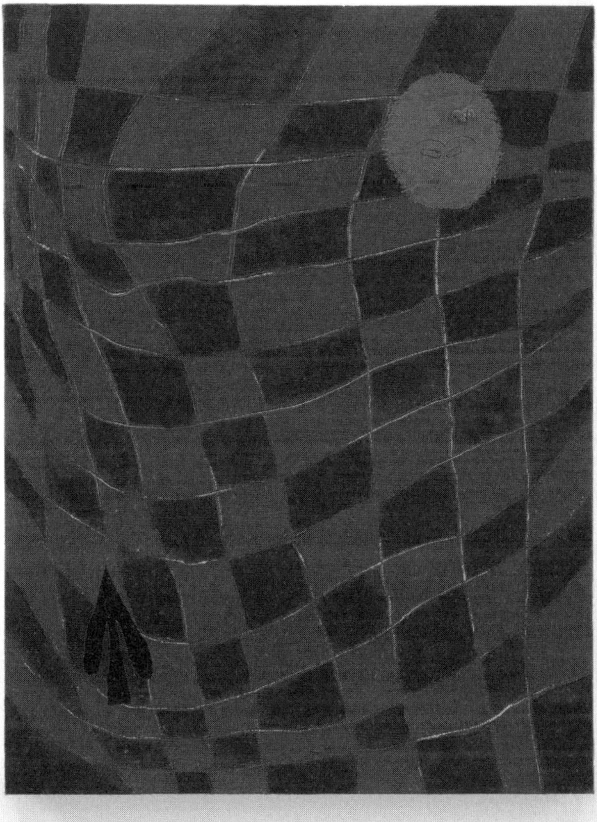

Icarus! Icarus! Icarus!, 2020.

28.05.20

Hi. You're listening to Rough Version on NTS, and my guest this month is Rhea Dillon. She graduated from Central Saint Martins in 2019 and had an incredible career, considering how early in her career that is. She's shown with Liz Johnson Artur, Red Hook Labs, Aperture Gallery, Yinka Shonibare's space in London with everything from film to photography, but also, she works with poetry and text, and increasingly experimenting with mixed media. Rhea, thank you very much for coming in.

Thank you for having me. That was a great introduction.

Let's start talking about medium. Do you want to tell me what appeals about that breadth of medium that you're working with at the moment?

Yeah, sure. I think I've always had, I guess, a multidisciplinary approach in my mind. Allowing what I guess necessarily comes out of it, or what has been shown. I think there's this odd space of what's been shown and what exists for the artists. My favourite thing to go and see is retrospectives and that amazing breadth... They obviously are just exploring and expanding in so many different places, because it's just about getting whatever is going on in your mind into a reality. I've always sketched, for example, and people are like "You draw?" I'm like, "Yeah". I'd storyboard an idea if it was for a film, or I'd sketch it to explain to another person, because I like working in groups and things like that. I think I've always really loved seeing that massive breadth of where the ideas that started inside this brain. And the work then goes on from there.

Let's begin talking about what you got best known for in the beginning, which is your film work, and particularly the way you approached film is something much more a two-dimensional passive experience. You would work with multiple screens, and you incorporated the element of fragrance and scent into what you do. Do you want to tell me a little bit about what you liked about taking film work and making it something four dimensional?

I think cinema and film and video – I have a distinction between them, which gets really weird. I just distinguish video as video art. And that's the first stage. It could be the looping process or even gifs as video. Then film is this second stage, where it can become its own narrative, but it's not necessarily into narration. It's more, the work of, say, John Akomfrah, people like that. Where it's in the gallery space. Cinema is where it becomes almost commercialized and it's about the greater audience. So, for me, film and video art is a really exciting place to explore how you can really exist within or outside of the frame. That is both on the audience side and as the director or the artist – or whatever word you want to have for the person in control. Scent is really, really fascinating to me, because we obviously use our senses all the time, but scent is the one that's seen as a dud. I guess I have an attraction to anything that's seen like this off the cuff or the queer of the senses. It's the sense that is intrinsically linked to memory. Thinking about the diaspora and thinking about how we've been taken from lands and made to travel to lands. I think a lot about what we could physically bring essentially with us on those journeys. Obviously, voice and song, when thinking of the spirituals and thus transforming into blues and jazz, and so on and so forth. But also, your sense of smell, your sense of belonging, a sense of being able to tell a story through even just food as well. I think smell is a really impeccable and incredibly, actually, simple way to invigorate the senses and just be able to tell a story. That piece that I did was dual screen, and that had a scent by Byredo. That was really cool.

> *It's really interesting how we become much more aware of our senses at this particular moment in time that we forgot about. I become very conscious of touch at this period of time, which feels to be almost muted at the moment. I'm very aware of like the idea that we have become so much focused on the idea of sight and sound that it's really interesting to consider something beyond that.*

Yeah. During this COVID-19 period, the symptoms of it being that lots of people felt they were becoming anosmic and didn't have a sense of smell. It's this forgotten sense, but it's actually really intrinsic to how we move and how we operate. Obviously, they're all connected, but we forget that we actually use our sense of smell in unison with so many of the other senses. We don't necessarily feel that we're using it as much, but the sense of smell really determines what you're tasting. Same with awareness around you. Just thinking in a more worldly sense of this is a human being coming into a space, how do they interact normally? How could I work with those means of perception, and then transfer that into the artworks that I'm making? Not just the singular screen that a painting or video can be, but how can it be multi or maximized, I guess.

> *Can I ask you a little bit about how you approach sound and music and soundtracks like you've collaborated on that before? I know you work with someone who's worked with the Theaster Gates and Khalil Joseph in past film projects, which is amazing. Do you want to tell me a little bit about what interests you about the oral element in your work?*

Yeah, I love sound. I'm so obsessed. I think that there's a distinction between sound and music. I always have an incredibly fond association with music. I grew up in a house that always has music playing, whether that's like as a deterrent to thieves or just as the means of filling the house with voices and song all the time. Sound I think is like where things get a little obsessive for me and geeky perhaps. Sound is just this incredible means of telling a story without having to have word or this linear or narrative means. The sound can really disturb a visual in a way that I think if you're quite in tune with how that can be manipulated, you can really create some incredible visual work. Even those people that we talked about, James (William Blades) is my friend and collaborator who's worked with the two of those incredible artists. I think they both really work with sound to amplify in this double conscious way. I think that's why I'm really obsessed with sound and working with James he really understands that and loves it too. I work best working with people who are equally as obsessive as I am! I want to record sound that I know on the tube and he's like "wicked here's my recorder!" Run around and come back. I like getting involved in it too.

Well, it seems like a fair moment to start talking about one of your tracks. Should we talk about 'Conversations with Angels' and why you chose this?

Yeah, I love this track because it's actually featuring another really incredible musician/composer called Chino Amobi and its pronounced Dedekind Cut. He's from California… This song I sent to my friend recently and she was really enamoured with it because I think it's healing in its tonality. That's this track.

This is 'Conversation With Angels' by Dedekind Cut featuring DJ Shadow and Chino Amobi.

—

I want to talk a little bit more about what you touched on earlier. About your interest in the element of movement as part of diasporic experience and historical movement. Do you want to tell me about how that emerges in what you do?

I think probably movement is the one concrete, or one of the concrete things, that it can expose itself in all the different mediums that I like to shed myself into. Movement to me, it's just really intrinsic to how Blackness is told, and how Blackness is experienced. The very literal movement of the bodies from their removal from their home place or their motherland to Jamaica, which is what my heritage is. I'm lucky enough again, as part of the Diaspora, to know where I'm from, in that sense. And then again, with the Windrush generation, which is what my grandparents would have been part of. Again, that movement there and then coming effectively down from Liverpool to London. There just is intrinsically a movement here. Then you think of the movement of Black bodies in terms of being sold. Then the movement in terms of dancing and entertainment and songs and movement on our vocal cords. I think it's just really thinking of how we effectively have created a culture that is known throughout the whole world today. It comes from a movement of our bodies. I'm interested in taking those histories and creating it. Not necessarily changing it but narrating it through, I guess, the modern space that we're in now…

Another thing that you've really done is also refocus attention from a British Black experience rather than say, a more represented African-American experience. What was important for you about making work that has touched on that British context?

I think that was especially with 'The Name I Call Myself', which was exhibited last year for my final university project. You're at that culmination of your degree. "What would I like to really focus on here?" It's almost a blockbuster moment. I was like, let me actually go back to the stories that have been told about our histories. Every book I was picking up was like "born and raised in Harlem". And I think it's really important how well documented that period in time is – the Harlem Renaissance. The only names that I came across in terms of the Black British perspective would be Stuart Hall and that was pretty much it. And even then books were hard for me to find. This was from, this was literally next door to his archive, which, unfortunately was closed in my final year of uni. Which probably would have helped things greater, but there was only an ephemera archive that was at Chelsea College of Art. I was going through that, and I would type in the names, as we do, on Google to find more, and they just never had any trace of themselves. And that's part of an ongoing project that I really want to work on… It's not giving them a history because they have a history, a history is so rich, but give them a platform to show that history off. Actually, I have a friend who's in Detroit, he's doing the same with all the incredible artists there that have almost been lost to documentation, not being at the forefront of people's minds. I'm really obsessed with the archive in that way. Making sure that they get their time – whether that's posthumously or whilst they're living now. That's why I was interested in trying to tell a story from a Black British perspective. I ask the mundane questions to friends and family. "What's the first thing you think of when you think of Black Britain and cinema?" Oftentimes, it would be things that are telling a narrative from a stereotypical front that's like gang culture, or unfortunately knife crime or things like that. I think there deserves to be more stories told. There are other incredible filmmakers who have seen that same narrative and have tried to break that and do their work. The two greats for me would be John Akomfrah and Isaac Julian. They actually founded their groups in the same year, which is crazy. Collectives.

Since back then to now there's this space – perhaps not even the resources to do so. Perhaps the obsession I have with all these different mediums is because our story just deserves to be told in a multitude of different ways. And that could just be really beautiful.

We're going to go onto another track now. I think we should play your J Dilla track, 'Stop'. I know you had a difficulty choosing which J Dilla to choose. Why this one?

J Dilla is a god obviously. But I think right now, this song is quite pertinent to how we should be approaching life. The lyrics that the woman is singing goes "stop and think about what you're doing". This pause of COVID has given a lot of people the means to just sit back and think about how they feel within their bodies and think about how they'd want to then move forward post this time. Perhaps, in a better thought through way.

This is 'Stop' by J Dilla.

—

That was J Dilla with 'Stop'. I've been looking at a lot of the works you've done, and it seems to be like your process is very research led. Do you want to tell me a little bit about what you like about that process and how that functions for you?

Like I was saying, I'm really obsessed with the archive, and I guess the archive is made up of all the stories that have been told or haven't been told. And we're constantly in this state of flux of rediscovering new ways of thinking or new ways of telling those stories. Working with abstraction or expressionism as well, people would assume that doesn't lend itself to that because it's more like a free flowing, state of consciousness, but I think we're always learning from people before and from people around us right now. I have so many people who inspire me who are my current friends. I'm really privileged to know them. With the research I'm just always trying to learn more about our histories and how I can navigate and be, I guess, in a new state of mind right now.

Let's talk a bit about the new work, because it's really beautiful. How are you approaching these layered collage pieces and abstract paint work and newspaper clippings? Do you want to tell me how you're approaching making those kinds of pieces? Are they largely works on paper?

There's a mix of paper and some works on canvas and some works on board. I work with whatever I can get with the state that I'm in right now.... I guess photography and film are both really great mediums because it allows you to work with a team of people. I remember I was always better at team sports at school, because I almost tried harder because I knew I had other people to not let down you know. I was very much wanting this family element when I was playing... I played a lot of sports. And I'm an only child. It's the thing I was kitted off to. When I came to graduating, so much like comes into that transition that you're not always... I don't think that anyone's fully prepared for. There's just a lot to think about. How you would like to move in the world and think about the ways in which you've been telling stories and could explore that greater, or make a new path, for example. I think I'd been doing a lot of stuff that was with groups and I wanted to just sit with myself for a bit. I actually painted a lot. That actually got me into St Martin's, which is really funny when people are like "Oh you paint, now?" I was thinking about the Black experience and what Black is and what Black ain't and what you have to perhaps present when you're being within the white walls of fear. I was just really bored with this energy that has to go into always being the Blackest person – the blacker the berry narrative. So, looking to the abstract expressionists. It's funny because I think the use of the word abstract within a Black context absorbs itself because – I describe in this analogy of a train. Basically, with Blackness you are on this linear course within society because you're seeing this lesser or this person that has to do extra, to do you know the basics. I describe as to come on and off the train. It's an innate abstract course being Black. To me it's like we're the Expressionists of this diasporic time. Like Jack Whitten. Mary Lovelace O'Neal. I think they were the true radicals in the sense that they weren't always having to present themselves through a money discussion... I think it's just about doing whatever you want. But there is this kind of conversation – an identity politic comes into it. When you are Black, there's this added thing. I'll be described as the Black artist, or I'll be described as the queer artist. Sometimes I just want to be the artist. I think I've been obsessed with abstractions since

I was really small, like when I first saw Pollock's work, probably just at galleries like school trips. But I'd never necessarily seen people like me doing it. And like me is, obviously, within the identity politics that I was describing. I was really being quite radical and not wanting to follow orders ever. I think it just is really natural to just have a means of expression. Through that I found that incredible group of artists who were just killing it, and even getting rejected by their Black communities because they felt they weren't Black enough. This again, this Black is, Black ain't discussion.

Or as you phrase it, the rules of representation and the idea of how you're supposed to be in terms of in any aspects of things. Maybe at this moment when we're seeing this wave of really incredibly talented Black filmmakers. That it makes sense. They're like, "Oh, you're another one in that pigeonhole". It's amazing that even this early in your career, you're saying "No, I want to have the breadth of expression".

I hate the box! I think about being someone who can tick boxes just with my own identity politics for a lot of institutions or whatever. I just am so disgusted by the box. Fuck it. Can you swear on this?

Yeah. I think we can. We just did! Who cares. Let's play another track by someone who also does not fit in boxes. Let's play your Outkast track. 'God Interlude'. Love this. Why? Why this Outkast?

Outkast. I mean, there's never a reason not to include those two geniuses. I really love the interlude. I think the interlude is an incredible place of expression. I have a playlist that's just full of interludes. They're just so funny. They're just so incredible. I think the interlude is just a point of access, where the artists can actually oftentimes say what they really wanted to say, because they obviously have to fit within this two-to-three minute spectrum of making music that can then be sold. But the interlude is this incredible moment within the album where they get to tell their stories often. 'God'. He's like talking to God, and he recognises that God is a woman and I and obviously I fuck with that. So, this is 'God (Interlude)'.

So, here's Outkast.

—

There's a phrase that you've used to do quite a few times in terms of past interviews, which is the idea of 'humane Afrofuturism'. I will say that I'm really trying to resist using the word Afrofuturism, after speaking to Larry Achiampong, his understandable statement that futurism was essentially intertwined with fascism. So, we have to come up with different words, which is cool. Nonetheless, let's talk about humane Afrofuturism. Do you want to describe what you mean by the phrasing?

Afrofuturism, when you break down the description, is the advancement of Blackness through science fiction. I'm all about escapism, and the need for that to navigate better or more sanely in the world. And equally love Sun Ra but I guess as Larry has said there's a new language that's needed. There's a new conversation that's needed. And I think, taking it back to its intrinsics, when you're thinking about the advancement of Blackness, it should just be in the everyday. In the humane perception and reception of Black people. I don't want to be seen as an alien because that further alienates myself from the everyday. I guess I talked about it, in a talk for a magazine. I was saying, how being (as many people are) a lover of Kerry James Marshall's work. What do we learn about actuality? We're looking at these visuals of everyday life and we're quite obsessed with the mundane acceptance that's in his frame. That to me is a conversation of humane Afrofuturism. That to me is a plight of just wanting us to be humans. Wanting us to be treated as equals. And being someone that works with film sometimes people are like, "oh you're an Afrofuturist". No, just because I use a lens and am Black doesn't mean I'm an Afrofuturist. I think it's been this word that has been taken over and used even for perhaps intellectual Blackness, which is just even worse. I think this humane Afrofuturism really centres the conversation on allowing Blackness to be. It goes into that radical conversation of just taking away this representation of yourself or your identity, again, when you're making art, and just making art.

That's what I love about Kerry's work. I remember when I first saw it. He was also reinventing the lexicon of art history, and reinserting representation into every single genre possible – from still life to nudes, to pastoral landscapes to history painting, That's why his work is so powerful. It's such a shift between historical perception and reality. More Kerry James Marshall!

He's looking at the mastery of art and the mastery of that conversation. Who are the masters? I think it's such an interesting conversation because we do have to take it away from being the European masters. Because the European masters were learning from the African masters, but the Africans weren't allowed to be masters in the conversation. Because it's about who told the story, and who's been telling the stories of history. Who actually has been able to help take pen to paper. That's what he's breaking down. What he's reintroducing. I'm sure if we had the artefacts or if they had the means to archive properly, their work from that time, we would see. It's quite an obvious narrative when you actually study it for even a second. Obviously, the most mundane of that conversation is Picasso's paintings and Cubism. I think that's what humane Afrofuturism is. It's just a way of working with the word. The word that people are used to, but actually, I guess, not abstracting it, but refracting the conversation. Just in a slightly different angle.

We're at the time to play your last track, which is Nina Simone, who I think is the most popular artist that's ever been on my show. People love a bit of Nina Simone. You've chosen one I've never played before. Do you want to tell me why you chose this track in particular?

Nina… Nina is just one of these incredible people who is so defined in her voice and she's an incredible poet. She's an incredible performer. This recording was when she came to Europe back in the day. She has a means about her and this incredible energy that I just see so much or hope to see so much of myself in, how she presents her work. You can tell that she loves music so much in the interviews that you're watching. She's just a badass mother. I remember just crying when I first heard it because it's just such a retelling of all these different narratives within Blackness. That's the same with 'The Name I Call Myself', it was a video piece that was focused on what it means to be within the Black community and almost be part of a problem or part of a narrative that isn't always told. 'Four Women' is my mother track.

Okay, Rhea thank you very, very much for coming in. This is Nina Simone doing 'Four Women' live in '68.

Marianna Simnett

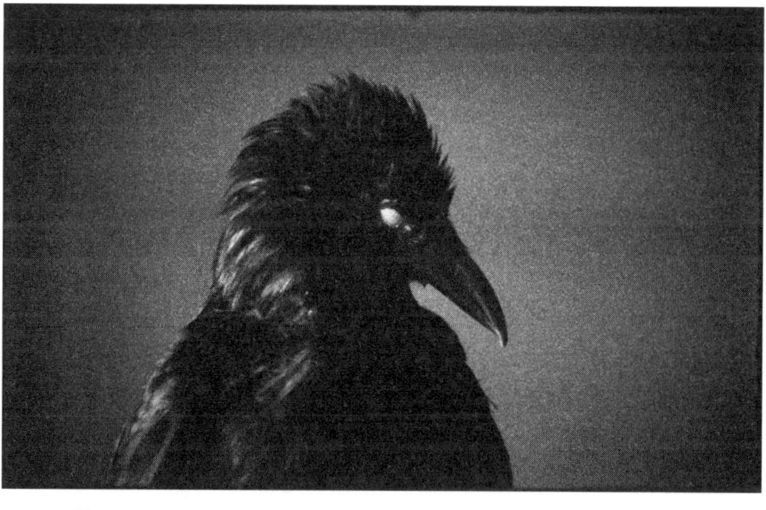

The Bird Game, 2019.

01.07.20

Hi, I'm Francesca Gavin and you're listening to Rough Version on NTS. My guest this month is Marianna Simnett. She completed her BA in Nottingham and her MA at the Slade. She is best known for working with video and film installation, but she also does things with performance and drawing. Her work explores ideas around sexuality, innocence, animals, kind of Gothic-ness. And she also has a great online television project called 'Home Cooking' at the moment, which emerged during COVID. She's exhibited everywhere from the Kunsthalle Zurich to MMK, to the Zabludowicz Collection. Firstly, Marianna, thank you very much for coming on the show.

Thank you, Francesca, for having me.

I want to dive straight into talking about your last film, which is 'The Bird Game', because I think it brings together a lot of the themes within your work. Particularly, let's talk about the fairy tale element to what you do, and this relationship between the weird, disturbing aspect of folk tales, fairy tales and narrative. Do you want to tell me about how you started working with that, and what the appeal was?

I've always been fascinated by fairy tales because of myth. Myth because it goes into deep time. For me, it seems to transcend the contemporary moment and speak universally to many, many people. Fairy tales are super important to me in the way that you can toy with them and subvert them. They have this foundation. They twist and turn and mutate with time. One of the stories that was really key in 'The Bird Game' was 'Sleeping Beauty'. It pivots on lots of different retellings of it. The original was by Giambattista Basile, and had the princess, 'Sleeping Beauty', marry her rapist who slept with her whilst asleep in the forest. All these troubling narratives come to the fore in these Disney-fied versions. There was also Robert Coover, who did a book ['Briar Rose'] based on 'Sleeping Beauty', about what was going on in Sleeping Beauty's head while she was asleep for so many hundreds of years. I took the character of Prince Philip – I say 'I' but it was co-written with Charlie Fox. I took the character of Prince Philip and killed him off at the start. The very figure that is supposed to be the redeeming one. The one who saves the princess is the one that gets punished for approaching, by Crow. So, fairy tales, for me, are a way to play mischief with these patriarchal forms or traditional story plots that I'm trying to battle with or twist and distort in some way and show some alternative.

> *I was really into fairy tales when I was younger, typically because of this American TV series called 'Fairy Tale Theater', which you can find online. Which is really dark, from Shelley Duvall. What's really interesting about looking at them is that they were often perpetuated to reinforce social taboos, or from social structures. Because you're coming at it from a very contemporary perspective, it's almost more about a feminist or post-feminist positioning. Would you agree? Or are you more interested in more universal narratives? The whole point of view?*

Definitely coming from a very queer perspective, I suppose, where gender and social norms are thrown out of the window, and they allow for all possibilities to emerge. Also, the appearance of non-human characters. In another work the temperature takes on a spiritual role. The weather becomes as much of a part, as the human or the animal, or even a medical instrument could become a character. I use fairy tales to flip the hierarchies between objects, things, people, animals, and so on. To interrogate social norms, or the way that people are put into boxes and classified as one thing or another.

> *Let's talk about animals for a minute, which is the thing that a lot of people, I mean, I just think of you doing a talk at Engadin, wearing a giant bird on your head. Animals are often anthropomorphised in your work, or you are positioning them in different ways. I'm assuming you're vegan, actually.*

Really?

> *Yeah. Do you want to tell me what you like about rethinking how we as human beings relate to the animal world?*

Actually, I've got a film that I just made called 'Tito's Dog' where I dress up as a German shepherd. That is the latest piece I made during lockdown. It's about Tito, the former president of Yugoslavia's dog, who sacrificed his own life when he was being hit by shrapnel. To talk more specifically about the birds, I wasn't massively into ornithology as a kid. More recently, I started to look at sleep in relation to birds, particularly with 'The Bird Game', and the way that birds have this incredible ability to stay awake. Unlike humans, I think the longest flight that's ever been recorded is 10 months without stopping, ever. Sleeping, eating, mating, everything in the air. And that fascinated me. I started working with ornithologists to obtain some of their sleep wave recordings. They gave me the data and then I've been working with musician Coreless to turn that data into music. We've been working with the inside of bird brains to try to enter into these different ways of listening. That's something coming up that actually got cancelled due to the current situation, but it's still in progress. It's not only that the animal is a symbol or a metaphor, but it's also working with sleep patterns and behaviours of animals and recordings of them. I also kept two pigeons for a long time, studying them and making friends with them. Making kin with them, I guess, and really being a carer of these birds that were living in my home. I'm going on and on. Now you've opened the box.

Did you name your pigeons? Do they have names?

Yeah, they're called Winona and Scissors.

Obvious referencing there.

Exactly and named with Charlie Fox. We named them together. Scissors was more snappy and aggressive than Winona, who was very sultry with these black circles around her eyes. Scissors had a slightly more silvery edge to his colour. We called them appropriately.

On that note, we're just going to have a pause, and I want to play one of your tracks, because you have a lovely variety. Shall we start with Oliver Coates?

Yeah.

Do you want to tell me why you chose this track?

'Tommib Help Buss'.

Thank you for pronouncing that.

That title – so this is a track that for me keeps mutating because the original is actually by Squarepusher, which was released in 2004. I discovered that the title came actually from Aphex Twin, because he was helping Tom Jenkinson with another track, and named the project Tommy. It's got this weird Aphex space naming. Anyway, I got deeply into Ollie's work. And I was listening to his incredible album called 'Towards The Blessed Islands'. It was around the time I was making 'The Needle & The Larynx', or just before I made it, which is a piece in which I lowered the pitch of my voice using Botox. I didn't know if my voice was going to come back, so I started to archive it in preparation, so I could electronically sample it in future.

Wow.

Every day I'd do these voice recordings. I'd start with just the alphabet. It was a pragmatic approach to the archiving of voice. I'd start with the alphabet, and then words, and then useful short phrases. Which ended up quite abstract, like "pink and blue" or "Fuck all of you who say girls must be high and boys must be low". Or "The gullet becomes a dead and motionless tube". Just these snippets. Ollie's track got so embroiled in all of this process that I had no choice left but to ask him if I could use the track in my piece, and he said yes. We had to clear it with Warp and Tom Jenkinson, which we did, and then I wrote the next track for 'The Needle & The Larynx' with Lucinda Chua, another brilliant musician… In 'The Needle & The Larynx' there's lots of different music that blends together and Ollie's track blends into Henry Purcell's 'March for the Funeral of Queen Mary', when we're talking about the mass deaths of botulism. I co-wrote the track with Lucinda and that picks up Ollie's. I guess they're both cellists so it's a very different type of sounding song, but I was thinking of the cello as this mutating throat, and the vocal cords being plucked and distorted in this eerie but comforting melody.

Okay, this is Oliver Coates' 'Tommib Help Buss'.

—

That was Oliver Coates. Let's talk a little bit about the use of your own body. Or your feelings about bodies in general. The idea of dissection or cutting up of the body or these medical references – that's been another one of the themes in your work. What do you find interesting about bodiliness?

One of my earliest memories is getting a black pen and dissecting my body from my forehead to my toes, and across and up my arms. I would draw these black lines. It was an alienating experience for me, I think I was about six or seven. I just remember looking in the mirror and acknowledging that I was going to be doing some strange things in the world in the future.

How prophetic.

It was the moment where I was like, "okay, I'm not going to be friends with those people at school". I just knew something. It was just a feeling. And it was related to dissection. It was related very much to the cutting up and re-composition of the body. I think it comes from a very deeply unsettled state in me where I feel uncomfortable with the idea of unity and cohesion, and rigid types of identity or the binary naming of things. The cutting of the body is for me a way of taking away the visible sack of flesh that we are and reconstituting it into a way that feels more habitable.

A lot of fairy tale references are also quite horror film. They're quite gore-ish.

Yeah, and there's always this exchange– you barter with the body. It's like a pound of flesh. It can be a type of currency. It used to be in old law but also in fairy tales, that you cut off the finger in exchange for something else. It's got this very vivid, visceral way of talking about language, as well. All of the stories again and again, that I reference in some of my earlier films had the sacrificial, self-mutilating acts of women. Who would cut off parts of their face in the name of virtue. The cutting of the body was aligned with this sense of agency – a fucked up kind of agency where you're gaining virtue by completely destroying yourself.

I want to talk a little bit also about children. When I first saw your work, I came in the middle of a video installation, and there was a little girl. I always felt like it was a stand-in for you somehow. But the children obviously seem very intertwined with a lot of the narrative approach you do. Do you want to tell me about how you use children in particular?

Children don't do what they're told. They can be nasty, too. I think I try to dispel this idea of innocence in children. I think Dennis Potter was a really amazing, amazing influence, who would talk about the cruelty of children in his amazing TV film called 'Blue Remembered Hills', where he has adults playing children. A brilliant fable about how nasty things can really get when you're a kid. I think I try to build worlds, and the reason I often drawn to film is because it is almost rubbing against reality. Unlike a piece of paper, or a picture frame, the frame is borderless. When you're making a film, you're having conversations. You're constructing scenarios. You're having a bird fly through a magic castle… You can't stop some of the real life entering the frame. I love the way that children interrupt my plan, and that they take charge in a way and if I've done my job correctly, I've made a world that they want to exist in where normal rules don't apply. And then to play out that in the most imaginative way possible for that beautiful moment of time.

Let's play another track. Let's play your DMX track. Do you want to tell me why you chose this one and when you first heard it?

DMX 'Slippin' is a Sisyphean tale. It's DMX pushing his boulder up the hill, and he keeps slipping. It keeps slipping and he keeps pushing it up. I first heard this song when I was about 12 or 13. I'd just moved on to my dad's houseboat after a heavy custody case, and we won the case. But the winning didn't feel much like winning. And there was this great big, empty void, mixed with guilt and freedom and water all around me. I remember the CD. It had DMX covered in blood on the album, 'Flesh of My Flesh, Blood of My Blood'. I'd lick the plastic CD. I remember it so, so well. In fact, he might have prophesied 'Blood In My Milk', the title of my future installation. I love the way he barks like a dog. He's also more animal, more dog, than human, I think. I also love the soothing ghost lady that sings under his barking. She says, "I've got your back" as he's slipping and as he's saying he can't get up she's saying, "I've got your back". It's so restorative and needed. It transports me back to a place of anger and love and guilt that I still carry today. He used that track to get him out of a tax evasion sentence in court. The lawyer played the track and instead of five years, he got a one-year prison sentence because they were like "Look, he's a reformed man. This is the story of his life". So, there we go.

This is DMX, 'Slippin'.

—

I want to talk a little bit about how you use sound in your work. Let's start with 'The Bird Game'. I loved the dance scene in it – where you have their fairy tale outfits, blindfolded, dancing to quite heavy, gritty, noise bass. Also thinking about how you used it in 'Faint With My Light', which is a light installation. It's echoing the sound of your own breathing. What do you like about sound as an element within the installation-side of what you do?

So, there's sound and then there's music, and then there's the convergence. That whole soundtrack was composed by Ollie Coates, as well. I love how my collaborators drift in and out of different projects. The sound in 'Faint With Light' is the work. The sound is this. It's about the unconscious sound of the body. When I'm fainting, there's this eruption of noise that is emitted from my body at the moment of fainting. Just to describe the piece, it's basically for back-to-back recordings of me making myself faint by hyperventilating. And as I fall unconscious, there's this, I guess, repression or suppression of air, that gets let out of my body, that I've been containing. Which is a part of the process of how you make yourself faint – which is compressing air in quite an extreme way. Anyway, it howls from the deepest part of you and it's this. It's beautiful. It's like a horse having an orgasm.

That's a visual...

Yeah, it's completely untamed. Completely untamed. It's without any manners, or anything that we've been taught. I love noises that take off that filter that we've been so trained to obey. The noise, the sound – well, I mean sound everywhere. For many projects, I worked with Lucinda Chua, and we thought very anatomically often, because my work was so related to the body. In 'Blood', we have the turbinate bones and the bony sounds represented by these kids playing xylophones. And in 'The Needle & The Larynx', it's these very woozy hypnotic cello, like a slowing down of the body. Like the pace was just unbearably slow with this sense of Botox paralysing my body, and also the viewer. In 'The Bird Game', totally different. The way Ollie – we would send each other tracks and references, but he didn't look at the film before he wrote the music because he didn't want to Mickey Mouse the image. Everything was done in dialogue – a lot of the artists that I love, it clashes in this sort of deranged way, where it almost shouldn't go together. But somehow it does. We were sending tracks from 'The Shining', 'The Caretaker', lots of distortion, lots of ugliness mixed with this very Baroque classical cello, industrial dirty grunge. Yuck yuckness. But with this princess quality at the same time.

I think it's a really good time to play another track. Let's play AFX 'Every Day'. Do you want to tell me about why you chose this one?

This song makes me so happy. It's like some circadian rhythm thing – just the perfect glove or Cinderella slipper. Whenever I listen to it, it feels just like absolute perfection. I love the weird child-lady who reminds me a bit of David Lynch's lady in the radiator from 'Eraserhead', who is saying the lyrics "Get me another tie. Give me another shirt. Give me another woollen". I think I thought she was saying, "because heavens piling over me". But actually, I looked it up, and she's saying, "because I have things piling over me'. But I imagine if it's heaven. That she's sort of transcendent near this death space, dying of boredom, like some '50s repressed housewife having a party in her mind as she fetches her husband's woollens. She's just brilliant. I listen to this one when I start feeling sorry for myself in the studio after long periods of extreme isolation and sleep deprivation towards the end of the project and it gives me a final kick to get me through.

Okay, let's give us all the kick. This is AFX 'Every Day'.

—

This is quite a funny question. But would you agree that there's sexual aspect in your work? I'm thinking it's quite a distorted, strange idea of what sexuality is. I'm thinking about cows or udders, or like this moment of childhood sexuality where it's present, but it shouldn't be, but it is. Because that's part of children's existence. I'm just curious to see if you feel like that's an undercurrent in what you do, or is that just me with my dirty head?

No, you filthy rotten… No, I think it is. I think it keeps returning. I think it is the return of the repressed probably. I think it's something that I need more language for and deal with it in my work all the time. Through these varying symbols with the udder becoming – like trying to make sense of these symbolic phalluses, and milk producers and different ways of thinking around identity. I still don't have the answer. I still feel so uncomfortable within my own identity and sexuality. And the only solace is that loads of other people do too. And that language can change. It's starting to. It's becoming much, much easier today to verbalise or… I don't know, just have something to be able to attach yourself to. Because I haven't been able to for a long time and then you go through your life thinking you're a woman and then you get subjected to things and certain gazes and certain violating acts and personal stories, I shan't go into here, but it's still an issue for me. I think it's really liberating to be able to construct a world that doesn't involve these endings where the prince marries the princess.

You also work in a lot of other mediums – watercolour, but you also work with performance. I've never seen any of your performance work. I'm really curious about how you adapt your language and approach to narrative in that kind of space.

Yeah. I've done several, but some are adaptations of other works. One I did at the Serpentine. But most recently, it's a ventriloquist act with a crow. That performance where I wear a bird on top of my head is a continuing one. The title comes from Kurt Cobain's journals and I'm going to say the whole title in full, which is 'Birds Scream At The Top Of Their Lungs In Horrified Hellish Rage Every Morning At Daybreak To Warn Us All Of The Truth, But Sadly We Don't Speak Bird'. And that is my attempt to listen, and not necessarily to conquer, meaning, but to listen to the screams of birds. And I play the flute. I play the character of the bird a bit like Prokofiev's 'Peter And The Wolf', where all the instruments play different characters. I'm starting to use instruments. There's this dead bird on top of my head, and I don't want to put words in its mouth, because that would be to anthropomorphise it too much. So, I either play samples, or I play music as the bird's voice, and then I have my own as a different character. I split myself off into these different roles and tell stories.

As a finishing question, do you structure your narrative a lot, because there is real emphasis of the borders between pure fantasy and what might be semi-reality? I'm just curious about how you put narrative together. Is it very scripted?

Yeah, it tends to be scripted, with big chunks of improvised sections left in. Because I love the wilderness, and I love things to not go to plan, but I'm a planner. It's like holding all those contradictions up at the same time. I've learned how to embrace the fear and to contest, almost to ensure that fear is guiding, is governing the whole project. Fear of not fear. Like everything's hanging on tenterhooks. The whole thing could come crashing down, and it's that risk of things not working. But that stops it from being stale and boring and rigid, that there are these moments where things could change. And then obviously working with collaborators like farmers or surgeons or roboticists or engineers – people that gives it that every day. I love that in the same way as like an AFX song. It's taken from off the cuff, everyday language that's not overly performed or dramatized. I love those. I love the surgeons soothing patter at the bed. The bedside patter. I love that as a texture. And I embrace all of these, and heighten all of these parts of the everyday, as well as telling the grandmaster fairy tale narrative at the same time.

We are going to play your last track. Firstly, I'd like to say it's been amazing having birdsong playing behind you through all of this it feels so apt. Tweeting birds in the background. Your last track is SOPHIE 'Is It Cold In The Water?' Do you want to just say why you chose this?

I love this song. SOPHIE is the first musician for about a decade to fully wake me up and break the mould of predictable, symmetrical pop music. And she has definitely helped me to embrace the clashing contradictory parts of myself. Somehow to synthesise these fighting components of my identity or sexuality, that previously I would think were wrong, or bad, or not normal, or I felt somehow that I should be hiding. Now I just don't care. SOPHIE doesn't really sample other people's music, so all the sounds and textures are totally created from scratch, and they send me into such vivid places in my mind. Her Water reminds me of glittering metal tiaras with square teeth that bite. SOPHIE believes vocals are so frosty and cold, and they engulf and sue the jaggedness of the water. SOPHIE does a similar thing to the ghost lady and DMX's 'Slippin' track. I couldn't find the name of the female vocalist in DMX's track; I don't think she's credited. If someone listening could tell me, because I've looked everywhere. SOPHIE's someone who's fallen so far into the abyss that she's never coming out, and that is the most beautiful place I can think of to inhabit.

This is SOPHIE 'Is it Cold In The Water?' and Marianna, thank you very much for coming on.

Thank you very much.

Scott Treleaven

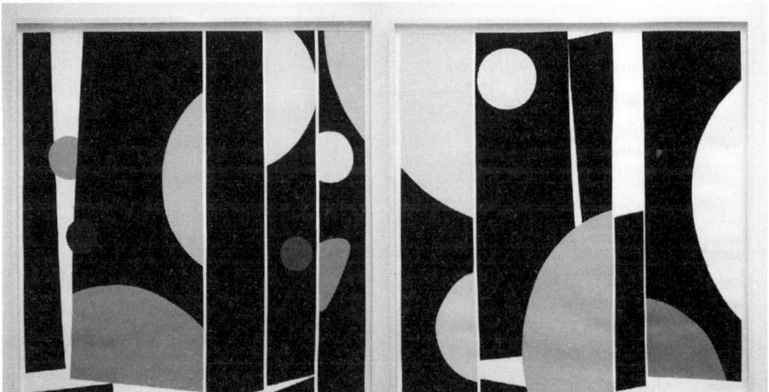

I Put it You, That Time Has Come Again, 2018.

30.07.20

Hi, you're listening to Rough Version and my guest this month is Scott Treleaven, who's a Canadian artist based in Toronto. He used to spend his time halfway between Toronto and Paris. He's shown at the Palais de Tokyo, KunstWerke in Berlin. He's done a lot of projects with AA Bronson and Genesis P-Orridge. And he's represented by Cooper Cole. How are you, Scott?

I'm good. It's so nice to be talking to you.

You too. You've got such a varied practice. Let's talk a little bit about your beginning. You originally came out of a film practice, I think, if that's correct. Do you want to tell me a bit about how you made that move from film into other media?

It's even more peripatetic than that. If we go further back, my background is actually in theatre and performance, which is where I imagined that I was going to go. And then that changed to film. And then filmmaking led to making a documentary about the nascent queer-core scene in North America in 1996. While I was doing the film and interacting with all these zine makers and musicians and sort of fantastic anarchic characters, I started doing the zine as a way of keeping up with the ideas and sort of responding to things that I was experiencing. And also, to encapsulate some of the ideas that I felt weren't being expressed popularly. The zine was very collage dense. That Jamie Reid punk rock approach to collage. So, a lot of collisions of imagery, and it was very confrontational and scary looking. Then eventually, the collages superseded that. And superseded filmmaking as well and I made a film about the experience of making the zine.

It's called 'The Salivation Army'.

Yeah. So, the zine was called 'This is The Salivation Army'. Salivation was a nebulous, hazy concept, where salivation was based on sense-derived experience, centring people back in their body, so to speak. At that moment, my practice bifurcated where the film kind of went off, like a child embarrassed to be seen with its parent and has its own life and continues to be shown, at least once a month, somewhere in the world. It's kind of crazy. That was 2001. The zine left this more surreptitious legacy of collages and artwork that people began to look for, increasingly. I was still making art, just because it's something that I've always done even since I was a little kid. People started to look specifically for the artworks and then people approached me. Curators and collectors approached me about wanting to buy them or show them. So, it was something I was already doing quite naturally, and preferred to filmmaking. It took over. During that time, as well, I was also painting, but I wasn't raised with connection to art museums. I wasn't being taken to art museums as a kid. A lot of the people I learned about art from were either people who stood on the periphery or the margins of the art world looking in or were never going to be accepted. Or were people that were out right hostile towards it, looking at it as a vulgar horse bedding scenario where rich oligarchs, and their lickspittle, pitted artists against each other and created a whole marketplace around something that's supposed to be sacred.

That's a beautiful description of the artworld, can I say!

It was really funny. It's this perception of what the gallery was and what the museum was. Which is not entirely inaccurate but over time, as cinemas closed down and as bookstores vanished and record stores faded away, the gallery, I began to realize, was the remaining repository for unplanned for communal experience. Where people actually paused or suspended their normal modes of behaviour to stop in front of things and genuinely look at them, and often together. That, I realized, that's always been exciting for me.

Looking at your zine work, for example, it's always felt like a moment of activism within your approach to culture. The intersection between activism and subculture, really.

It's funny, the situation where – well it's not funny – I mean it's odd the situation that we're in right now with the pandemics raging through the world. The increase call to action and awareness around racialized peoples, the climate collapse and everything else. All this stuff was very much being spoken about in the culture that I was consuming, or the subcultures that I was consuming, and I was much, much younger. Even as a kid. All the music I listened to; the refrain was "This is coming. This is coming. It's going to happen. Everything's going to collapse. These things are unsustainable. The centre cannot hold". And so, to make any gesture in an artwork that was less than heroic, or less than acknowledging those facts seemed, I don't know, either irresponsible, or churlish, or just adding to the problem. I don't really care about entertainment, and I don't really care about distracting people. My trajectory – I started out as straight-edge because a lot of the people were taking drugs at the time that I was coming of age, were looking to distract themselves. To drop out, to evade whatever situation or life they were in. And I didn't understand the idea of further anaesthetizing yourself when you're already under the deep sleep hypnosis spell. It was only later when I began to read things by different authors, like Terence McKenna or something like that, where I realized like "Oh, these are tools for actually gaining a stronger awareness of where one is at and one's relationship to the world and other people".

> *On that moment, where the psychedelic and the esoteric meet, I think we should play your first track, which is the Alice Coltrane. It seemed fitting! Do you want to tell me why you chose this one in particular?*

Alice Coltrane Turiyasangitananda, the Sanskrit name she also added to her name. I love this track so much because there's a joy and an ecstasy that it telegraphs so beautifully. I remember the first time I heard it. There are just certain experiences you have with certain artworks, and I include, obviously, sound and music in description when I say artwork. They just make you stop. Everything just suspends for that moment. You're just caught up in this communication from another person. Even though it's based on the chant, "Brahma guru, Krishna guru", repetitively, you fall into it. There's this great meshing of gospel and Hindu and European arrangements. But there's also this early electronic sound to it. After her husband John Coltrane died, Alice Coltrane was so bereaved that, apparently, she could barely speak or eat. Her children tried to get her interested in music again. She is this incredible harpist, but she just didn't want to touch her instruments. So, they brought her a synthesizer thinking that maybe this would trigger something in her. And when she started playing with a synthesizer, she started looking at these ecstatic sounds that could be made with it. In this track, you must forget how outdated the noise sounds compared to how we understand synthesizers today and just listen to it purely for the tone and what that must feel like to have created that sound at that time, and in the context. This song is this incredible synthetic mashup of all these different spiritual influences and it just takes you where you want to go.

> *Okay. So, this is 'Rama Guru' by Alice Coltrane.*
>
> —
>
> *Looking at your work, Scott, another one of the things that has come to the fore is how you've often met and at times even collaborated with some of your influences. I'm thinking of people like AA Bronson and Genesis. Do you want to tell me a little bit about what attracted you and how those collaborations work and manifested?*

Going back a little further, I was in school studying film. I was at York University, studying screenwriting, and it fast tracked me to the second year. So, I skipped the first year and was plunged into this screenwriting class and I realized pretty quickly – it was baffling to me because I always thought I wanted to make films. But I realized that I'm actually not attracted to filmmaking. I'm more fascinated by the way that film illustrates our relationship to reality. How we can speak to each other about the oddity of being alive through various media. Film does something very peculiar in the way that it arranges time. The way that edits make us create causal connections where there actually aren't any. The way it creates a sense-surround that we plunge ourselves into and just accept even though our eye is being guided, our ears being guided, our narrative expectations are being fulfilled. So, I dropped out of university. I moved to London for a year and literally starved. I was so broke. I was living in this horrible bedsit in south of Lewisham in Hither Green. It was so cold at night. There was a little sink in the bedsit and the water would actually freeze overnight. That's how cold the room got. And one morning I was walking through Soho being like I can't live like this. This is not sustainable. If this is part of the artist's life, I have to at some point think about my self-preservation, but I didn't know what to do. I thought I was going to save up some money and go into the London International Film School and maybe just make experimental films. That day, I literally bumped into Derek Jarman. This is I guess, in '92. I literally bumped into him. He had been going blind from the AZT he was taking, and I went, "Oh my God, you're one of my heroes. I don't want to talk to you about filmmaking, though, I just want to talk to you about this book that I'm reading of yours called 'Modern Nature'", which is still one of my favourite books of all time. It's sublime. It's like the Alice Coltrane track. It's something that freezes you in your stead and makes you want to re-examine the world or embrace it more fully. I spent the day with him as he went around to get his groceries and he was incredibly generous and really, really kind. He read me the riot act where he said, "Listen, don't stay here in London". This is Thatcher's London, where the buildings looked healthy, and the people looked like they're dying. He said "get out of here, go back to Canada. Don't study film, just ditch any idea of making films, because the way that films are going to be consumed, and the way they're going to be made is not the way that you want". And he said, "I know that. I can tell from speaking to you, this is not the kind of world you want to be involved in, so learn to be an artist instead". So, he sent me home and it turned out to be the best advice anyone's ever given me. Then years later, I met Genesis at a conference in New York. And we bonded over both having known Derek, and the astonishing insight and incredible artist that he was. Gen had been a huge formative influence on me, as well. I dismissed – not dismissed – but I didn't like Psychic TV in its earlier incarnations, and I didn't like Throbbing Gristle because they flirted with basically fascistic imagery. There are certain types of imagery, and there's certain types of thinking that I don't think you can just pause it without explaining your stance or your reason for doing it.

The transgression for the sake of transgression is a little bit...

It just doesn't wash with me because these ideas are poisonous. And I really, really do believe that certain ideas have – people have been talking about mimetic culture for much longer than we've had memes. But we realize that they're infectious they get under people's skin. They get into people's psyches. The amount of conspiracy theories flying around right now is crazy and ideas have consequences. Without you bandying about fascist imagery and not openly critiquing it at the same time seemed irresponsible to me. I could tell what side TG was on and I knew what side Genesis was on. But I still thought it was repugnant and irresponsible. Then after I'd moved back to Canada, after having met Derek that one time, the whole trajectory of Psychic TV changed, and they became more connected to hippie and Acid House, and everyone was taking ecstasy. They wanted to telegraph a more joyful, more liberating position. And that turned me on, not so much because I wanted to sign up to the Temple of Psychic Youth, Gen's cult for lack of a better word, but because I am always fascinated by narratives where people make it through the dark patch and emerge on the other side.

Let's play the Psychic TV song that you chose. It just seems so apt. Do you want to tell me about why this song in particular?

'I.C. Water' was written for Ian Curtis by Gen. Ian was a big fan of Throbbing Gristle and had corresponded with Gen and they spoke regularly on the phone the night that Ian killed himself. The legend has it the Gen spoke to him and was worried that he was going to kill himself. And Gen felt guilty for not having done more to try and save him. How much of this is rock and roll mythology and how much of it is true sometimes is very hard to know. It was very hard to pry out of Genesis. But nonetheless, Gen was so broken up by it she wrote this beautiful lyric, and it's probably some of the best things she ever wrote. It's probably one of my favourite songs of all time. It morphed in this expansive, heart-breaking but incredibly catchy and jumping tune.

Let's play it! This is Psychic TV 'I.C. Water'.

—

That was Psychic TV. Let's talk a little bit about some of the work that you're making now, because coming from this very narrative, very subcultural background, your work has really developed into something that's very abstract. Or focuses a lot on abstraction. I'm thinking about your first works on paper, but now it's really developed into paintings. I want you to tell me a little bit about how that fits into what you make.

Because I come from a background of zine culture and this subcultural, teeth gnashing activism and I like all of the looks of this heavy-handed aggressive stuff, sooner or later, it occurred to me that people tend to make assumptions about these things. Or tend to shut down when they're confronted with them, myself included. So, I started to think about other ways to communicate with people and communicate certain ideas. But I guess the line is all the way through. I'm interested in psychedelic culture, occult influences, popular culture, magic and mysticism. You can't really continue to play around with these things without them affecting you. But the position that I'm coming to and from is not as a believer or an adherent, so much as I'm fascinated by the language – visual, auditory, spoken – that people use to explain transcendent experiences to one another. The kind of language that people use, regardless of what their background is, what their cultural bias is. I'm interested in the language of ecstasy that usually exists on the periphery of whatever the mainstream is. If you're talking about the periphery of Islam, it would be Sufi culture. If you're talking about the mystic stream that runs through Buddhism, we'd be talking about Tibetan Buddhism. If we were talking about the place that I grew up, which is the '80s in North America, there was the whole Satanic Panic and this fear of the Other and the great, ugly Other. If I had probably grown up in the '60s or the '50s, it would have been communism. But for me growing up, it was witchcraft and occultism and magic. And as a young, queer kid, I realized pretty quickly that the mainstream, seeing the way that the AIDS crisis was handled, basically would have been quite content if hundreds of thousands of people just died in abject misery. Very early on, I got the message that mainstream society, the intolerant faction of it, was not your friend. That the people that enabled it were the people that did nothing and unfortunately, they were legion. And so, I started to look for other avenues of expression, other ideas, other things that seemed inclusive. Things that seemed radical. Things that seemed more embracing. Paradoxically, these things that were supposed to be horrible and frightening, tended to have a component that was, actually, more compassionate, more generous. I would find this kind of sweetness in these expressions. Witchcraft, as far as we know, is a fairly contemporary creation, you know. It's based on bad, bad archaeological evidence, and even worse anthropological studies. But the great thing is, it's completely protean because it's completely made up. You had it start as a conservative, "We will create the ultimate British religion" thing, had it shuffled over to the west coast of America, and had it come back with the feminist attributes of it completely enhanced, and the voice of liberation was now at the fore of it. And it morphed into something really beautiful. Watching these trajectories, this to me seemed important and exciting. Where people can talk about, or to each other in a way that was one spirit addressing another. But over time, the language of mysticism, the language of occultism, the language of spirituality and religion has been so denigrated, and so reduced to either ad copy or something that people snicker over. I mean, remember, for the longest time, people would use the term 'poetic' as this withering epithet when they would look at an artwork? I thought, God, what a situation to be in where "this is poetry, or something that's poetic", is used as a derisive term. So, I started thinking more and more about how people telegraph these ideas of beauty and transcendence to one another without language. And of course, that led me to look more at the origins of abstraction. Before Clement Greenberg saddled us with the idea that abstraction means nothing, the initial flight from expressionism to abstraction was sincere inquiries into the nature of consciousness, into shared experience of all living beings and into the nature of psychedelic experience, I guess is what we would call it now.

> *On that note, it seems like a good moment to play your Éliane Radigue track because it seems to be an audio expression of a lot of the same kind of thoughts. Do you want to tell me a little bit about how that expands for you? And we can come back to the painting after?*

Yeah, of course. Radigue's work is so fascinating. She's born in 1932, and she's one of the pioneers of electronic music. She was very hands on. If you hear a drone that lasts for an hour and it modulates within that hour, she was sitting there, doing the processing. Sitting there for an hour with a series of stopwatches, with the patches on this old synthesizer, creating these tones and having transcendence in real time. She studied Tibetan Buddhism, and she stopped making music for a number of years while she was doing it until the Lama that she was studying under encouraged her to go back to it. One of the things she created was a sort of musical version of the songs of Milarepa. Milarepa was an 11th century Tibetan yogi, who repeatedly achieved extremely high levels of transcendence and left this liturgy. You've got this incredible drone that she's making. You have the chants of a Lama – Lama Kunga Rinpoche – who's still around. He's born in 1935. He has a temple on the west coast. So, it's him chanting in Tibetan. Then you have Robert Ashley, the video artist and contemporary opera, writing polymath delivering this deadpan translation of the Milarepa text… You ask yourself – how do you communicate these ideas that are pretty heavy in a way that people want to listen to? And I think this does a really gorgeous job. People will definitely want to take time with this. The track is 18 minutes long. I think we're going to play like five minutes, but I would encourage people to listen to the full cycle. I play it when I'm painting. It's usually the background to my day, or something like this.

This is Éliane Radigue 'Les Chants to Milarepa: Elimination of Desires'.

—

That was Éliane Radigue. Let's go back to the painting. You were talking about how your interest in abstraction came out of an interest in, let's say, the psychedelic and the spiritual in different ways. Do you want to tell me a little bit about how that emerges in terms of how your version of abstraction is existing? Which is often very much these very vibrant colours against dark backgrounds, or even UV colours. These jewel-like colours you're using now. Do you want to tell me, just continue, talking a bit about that?

The funny thing is, coming from where I come from, making films and making zines and doing photography and making collages and stuff like that – painting seems like something that one would leave behind with all its other technology. But the more I thought about it, the more I liked the way that people interacted with paintings. The way that I interact with the process of painting is there's a lot of silence involved! There is silence involved. The paintings don't speak. It's a slower experience. It's a slow experience. It really taps into something in the viewer that I think is fascinating. It requires space. It requires time. You're not being led anywhere that you don't want to go. Films have a beginning, middle and an end. That's the nature of their trajectory. It's the only way we can understand filmmaking. It runs linearly. The same with a piece of music; the same with reading text. The fact that painting stands outside of that idea of time is really intriguing to me. Initially, I started with a much more expressionistic approach to it. I'd always loved people like Joan Mitchell and Louise Fishman, these more expressionist gestures on the canvas. The more I got into that, the more I realized, there's this other component that I really liked, which is hard edge painting. Someone like Ellsworth Kelly or something like that. Or the great lesbian and master Agnes Martin. It's only now that she's unimpeachable, and curators are less stuffy that they embrace her and her fullness. I went into the hard-edge stuff for a little while as well. Then I took a year off to just see if I could kind of merge these two opposing but two different veins that I have in my work. A lot of it involves painting works, that were flat on the ground, adding a lot of water and a lot of primers and things like that, and just letting the mineral exuberance that's latent in the paint perform itself a little bit. My desire to make a painting or to make an artwork would slowly get picked away at by the way that the paint wanted to behave. Then it became this more collaborative experience, where the paint would do something that would fascinate me. Then I would respond to it, and it situated me back almost in the stream of reality, where you're just dealing with a stream of contingencies all the time, and you're responding to them, and you're shaping them in ways that make sense to you. But ultimately, all that you're in control of is the way that you respond to these things.

> *Just to finish there, because we're running out of time, I'm going to say let's play your final track, which is Grumbling Fur (which Mark Titchner also played). I think he's a Grumbling Fur fan. So, your last track, which is Grumbling Fur, why this one, 'Dancing Light'?*

This came out in 2013, on an album called 'Glynnaestra'. I had actually been a little disillusioned with the way music had been going for a while, so I wasn't listening to any new bands. I couldn't find any that I liked. I didn't see that music was progressive or interesting or held the same kind of delight for me that it used to. I attribute a lot of that to maybe getting old or grumpy! But then a friend of mine sent me this album. It's funny. He used to work in a record store when I was a teenager and would always palm off things to me being like "Oh take this home, listen to this", and turn me on to a lot of great bands. So out of the blue, I hadn't heard from him for years, he's like, "you have to listen to this album". And it was incredible. Talking a little earlier about the language of the occult and psychedelic and everything; these are ecologies that if they're really dealing with the numinous, they should be growing beyond their fairly limited range of signs and palettes and things like that. Here was genuinely new and exciting psychedelic pop in a way that I'd never heard before. I met Daniel O'Sullivan, who's one half of the duo last year. He's just as real and as fascinating as I could hope for. The voice behind it seemed really authentic and it turns out, it's absolutely true. I think Grumbling Fur is easily one of my favourite bands since I heard that. They've moved to the top position. Tying it back to like the Alice Coltrane. It's sheer delight, sheer joy.

Well, here's some sheer joy. We've got 'Dancing Light' by Grumbling Fur and thank you so much for coming in Scott.

It was a pleasure. Thank you for having me.

Otobong Nkanga

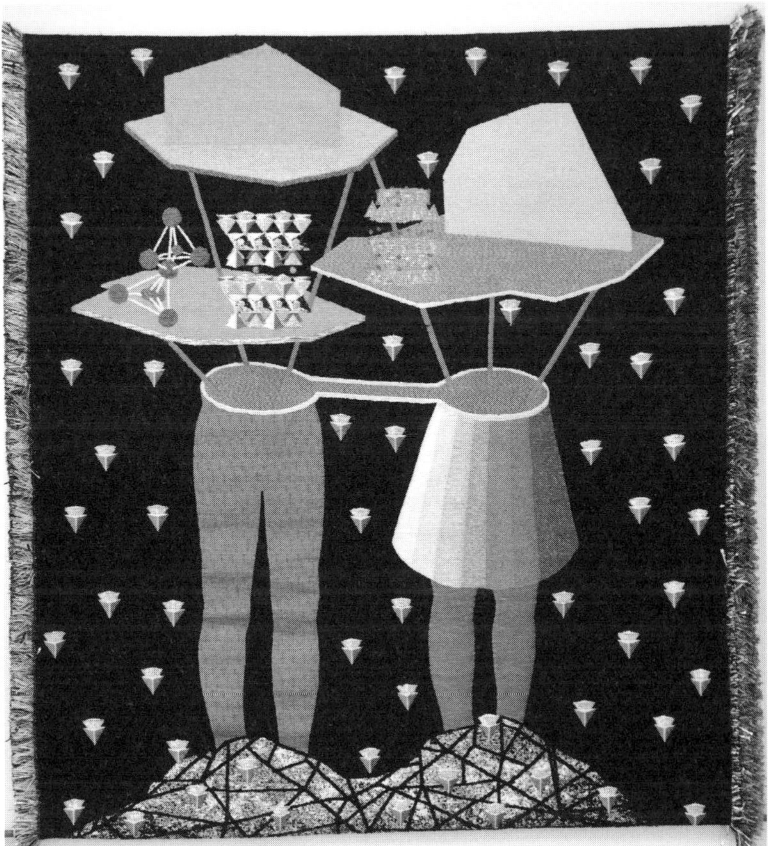

In Pursuit of Bling: The Transformation, 2014.

23.08.20

Hi, you're listening to Rough Version and my guest this month is Otobong Nkanga, an artist born in Nigeria and based in Antwerp, who is becoming one of the most exciting artists getting recognition at this moment. Her current exhibition, 'There is No Such Thing as Solid Ground', is on show a Gropius Berlin, where she was artists in residence. This follows exhibitions at the MCA Chicago, Tate St Ives, MIMA and a stand out presentation at the last Venice Biennale curated by Ralph Rugoff. She shown at Documenta, at the Sharjah biennial and was the winner of the first Lise Wilhelmsen Art Award. Otobong, thank you very much for taking the time to chat to me.

Thank you very much, Francesca. It's a real pleasure to be here.

Super cool. Let's talk about the breadth of what you do. Because there's a stylistic link in your work but you work with sculpture, with painting, with drawing, with performance, with writing. Do you want to tell me a little bit about what holds all that breadth of medium together?

There are many connections with the work. I'm very much interested in architecture, and working through ways of thinking about support systems, support structures. But also, I'm very much interested in materials. I think one of the things that really connects the work together, it's that quest and thirst for understanding how materials work and function. Where they are coming from, the places of extractions, and what it means in different contexts and in different worlds. In that sense, the work even before thinking of a material, already start thinking what its implications are in the world, and how it affects different places, how it enhances different places. I think the work stems from multiple kinds of interrogations, of personal interrogations, but also linked with my autobiography from my childhood. How certain things appear to me and how those things then connect to my histories and other people's histories.

You trained in Nigeria; did you always want to be an artist? How did that process work for you?

I studied in Nigeria, definitely. And also, in Paris and in Amsterdam. But from childhood, I've always enjoyed drawing. I've always enjoyed watching things like manga. I've always been interested in creative aspects of that we see around us. But for me, it was very clear, well, not always very clear. At one point in time, I was hesitating between studying architecture or being an artist. And my mother was like, "you could do architecture, you can do anything in art". It's easier to just do art. You have to follow your passion. And my true passion was actually making and creating works and having the freedom to express things. I felt with architecture, there are too many rules. With art, you can create your rules.

If you look at a lot of the imagery that you're representing, there seems to be a real investigation between the relationship between the environment and nature and humanity. I want to know what are like your feelings – the questions or conclusions that are coming out of that examination. Because it seems to be quite fundamental.

I think it's very fundamental because in a way, I think one of the things I've been really interested in looking at has been that connection of the body with the environment and the landscape that we live in. The idea that we dominate, and we take over, is for me very sad to see. Because in a way, we are the same as the materials or the minerals that are on this planet. We are connected to the animals. We are connected to trees. All these are interconnected elements that make us exist and without those elements we cannot exist on this planet. So, the way we treat it, the way we behave, the way we work with this thing and our gifts that are connected to our bodies is quite destructive. When we look at the way we have used up – we haven't changed the systems that should be helping to keep us alive. And that for me is very important to understand. That we are totally interconnected with every single element – the air, the wind, the soil. And once we start destroying that we destroy ourselves.

Before we go on, I'm going to get you to play a track. Do you want to start with your Ibeji track. Do you want to tell me about your relationship to the song and why you chose it?

I chose this song because I love the voices of the Ibeyi. Ibeyi here is written in a different way than the Yoruba would write it. Ibeji, if we would say it from the Yoruba context, the Nigerian-Yoruba context, means twins. They are two girls that are singing, and they are twins. Oya is very much linked to the Yoruba mythology. Oya is a powerful woman that is connected to Shango, who is the god of thunder and both of them together become powerful forces. Lightning and thunder working together to become a force. For me, the song is extremely beautiful, and I also love the video that they made, which is about trees. When I'm working, it's one of those songs that calms me down. Their voices are very soothing, but it also brings me back to thinking about this force of nature – the lightning, thunder, Oya, the powerful woman. This is why I chose this song because I just love it and it's from my own nation, my own history.

This is Ibeyi 'Oya'.

—

Going back to that relationship you have with examining ideas around soil and air and water, it seems to come out quite a lot in narrative work. It seems to be this ongoing story, that your works inhabits somehow. Do you feel it's an all-encompassing world? Is there a connection for you? Or is it more abstract than that?

I don't think it's abstract at all. I think it's very much linked to things that I have experienced. Things that I've seen in different places, around soil, around the air we breathe. If we're in different parts of the world, we start realizing that some places are more breathable than others. Some places, the soil is totally destroyed, that crops cannot come out of there. You then realize that in some places, the water is totally polluted. That even the fish cannot have a life in there. And the people that live on those landscapes and those places cannot generate the kind of resources they need to generate. You realize that their health is also in danger. That their kids cannot have a long life and already start life in a non-favourable place. So, when you start understanding that there are some other places that the air is very clean, that the water is great – that it's not equal. In the way that places have extractions, places that have been prodded, have to deal with the residues and the remains that are not favourable for their lifestyle or for their health. For me, it's not something abstract. It's not something that is not happening – it's happening. And we're seeing it happening more and more.

That depiction also seems very much to have a political motivation in particular, highlighting the legacy of colonialization on the landscape. There seems to be something quite strong about that happening in the work.

There is an aspect of environmental racism in a way. There is an aspect that is very much linked to colonization and what that does to places. Not only the places that have been colonized, but the places that have benefited from that colonization. In a way, we are all embedded in these histories of colonization, and we have to find ways in which one has to survive. One has to move forward with this. Ways of regeneration and ways of care and ways of repair. I think that at this point in time, the world is actually having – it's a manifestation of the non-care that has been taking place for centuries. That non-care, we see it today is expanding in different places, is affecting people's lives and affecting groups of people. That legacy from colonialism on different parts of the world, we're seeing it manifesting in the environmental crisis. We cannot dissociate human racism to environmental racism. It's all interconnected. For me, it's important to understand it. I think also as a Black woman on this planet, it's also important to understand one's position and to understand how to deal with these kinds of issues in the world. How to open up spaces that can allow for other people – like me – to be able to navigate the world and believe that they can navigate the world without having to go through those kinds of issues that we're having now.

I'm looking to play another track, let's talk about 'Saa Magni'. Tell me why you chose this piece.

I chose Oumou Sangaré 'Saa Magni' because she's someone that I've always loved the voice. She is a griot, so someone that carries this history, the oral history that has been given from generation to generation. She's one of those women that carry that weight of history. But this song I chose because it's a song that talks about death in a way. It's a song that is quite a sad song, but the way she transmits it or the way she puts it out is very emotional. It's one of those songs that I've listened to to be able to cleanse my eyes. It allows me to cry a bit and allows me to pour out certain feelings. You need songs like that to be able to trigger and cleanse the eyes and cleanse the feelings or the emotions that you have. There are certain songs that have that power, and the song of Oumou Sangaré does it.

Cleansing your eyes is one of the best phrases I think I've ever heard. That's an amazing concept. This is Oumou Sangaré and 'Saa Magni'.

—

You also incorporate sound and performance and music in different elements. Do you want to tell me about how you yourself have used that medium in what you do?

The sound situations – I enjoy word making sound. I don't make them that often because I normally go into the studio and record. For example, the sound works that I've done so far, which is 'Wetin You Go Do?', one of the sound pieces that is also showing in Gropius Bau 'Wetin You Go Do? Oya Na'. I recorded the sound in 2015. I went into the studio there were about eight mics around my throat, my hands. Around my mouth. Just trying to get sounds from different parts of the body. I was in the studio for 18 hours – well three days, six hours each day – and just went through recording non-stop. The way of recording it's very much a performative fit. It's six hours intensely working from the voice, the sound from the throat, from the chest, making volumes in the mouth. Of course, having different topics that I'm thinking about and accumulating and layering with the voice. As a kid, we did a lot of voice work, without me realizing that we were doing it. In our family, my mother with my sisters, we would sing, and we would have our voices. My sister would maybe sing soprano. I'd have an alto. My mother would sing another voice. We would have these polyphonic voices going on. That has followed me over time. I've always enjoyed working with my voice. I sing a lot of times, but it's different singing in your shower, than making a work. Not just singing for pleasure, but has to have the emotions, the content, the issues that you're dwelling with. But how can the voice transmit of that? That is the way that I work and twist and search with the voice. How can I bring out the emotions I'm looking for? And how can that be transmitted to the public that listens to it. There are many things that I feel that I can still go on working with the voice, with sound, with elements. Because I think those are one of the most powerful elements that pierce through the pores of our skin and can actually shift and heal at the same time. It's one of those powerful tools that goes beyond borders, that can actually melt a hard soul, but can also harden the heart. It has such a power that is not tangible. You can't hold it, it flows. I feel that is something that is extremely powerful to think through as an artwork.

> *The documentation I've seen of your performance work, it also seems again, to be using the body in a similar way. Enacting the movements of something, but what you're actually doing is more unclear. It feels like you're trying to communicate the actions of something.*

I wouldn't generalize on all the performances I've done. But there are some performances that are very much linked to thinking through gesture and what that means if you clap, if you lift your hands, if you clamp something, or if you grab something. It means something. How you do that expresses what you want to say. If you repeat it 10 times the same way, what does that mean? I think it's really looking at what do the gestures we do tell us of what that person or what that place – what it does to a place. They're not just coming from an emotional place, but they're coming from reading how the body works. If we think of the training a politician will have in relation to how to use their hands, to be able to talk to a public, they don't just use their hands anyhow. They actually go through a training to teach them how to be confident. How to stand in front of someone and have a certain posture that reflects emotions or that reflects I am with you. All those gestures are interesting to look at. When you bring it within a performance and you break it down, and you expand on ways of moving. I think the way of reading plus emotion plus the intellect, work together to understand that that gesture could mean certain things, at a certain time, in a certain culture.

I'm going to say it's perfect time for us to talk about another one of your tracks. Let's play 'Mahlalela', which is incredible track on Motown, which really surprised me. Do you want to tell me a little bit about why you chose this piece?

Letta Mbulu. I just love the way she goes "ahhhhhhhhhhhh"! That for me, it just pierces through your skin. It's a good way to just start the song and then it begins. I tried finding out what the song means, and there is no way to understand or to even know what the song is about. I've been trying to find out what is 'Mahlalela'. But she has been such a powerful figure. And I think she was also one of the, she was the one that sang in one of Michael Jackson's songs… Was it 'Liberian Girl'? I'm not sure. She's just one of those figures that you don't really see but she's really behind the scenes working. Hugh Masekela is just an amazing artist. I just found that this duo together and the song itself, just the starting of the song just gets me going. It pierces. It wakes me up in the morning bang, and I can start working. All the women I have chosen are just powerful women – with their voices, with the sounds, with the way they transmit emotions or the way they wake you up.

This will definitely wake you up! Letta Mbulu and Hugh Masekela with 'Mahlalela'.

—

Looking at your work there seemed – and this could be my misinterpretation – there felt like there was almost like a sci-fi utopian element in what you're doing. Would you agree in terms of the aesthetic? That that's an influence? Or is that just my interpretation of your aesthetics?

It might be yours. There are many aesthetics that I'm interested in. For me, sometimes a lot of things that are going on on this planet seem like science fiction. Just the other day, we had the explosion in Beirut. I looked at that it almost looked like I'm watching a film. It doesn't look real. Can this really be real? There are some things that are coming from a place that when you're thinking, you're looking at it, the way you're also designing or putting things together goes beyond the place of a realistic world, or what you're seeing in reality. But sometimes you have to put certain things together, to be able to make one thing beyond their own space. To be able to think farther than just this planet. That aspect of materials – I think the bending and the using and the twisting of the material – might be able to bring out something that is not what we will normally look at or want to look at. But I think that already the world we are living in has that thing or that structure sometimes. The kind of aesthetics and results of things that are happening that makes me think that this is not from this world. This is not a place. This is not happening. And maybe that transmits in the work. But there are many kinds of aesthetic. I deal with also soils, making soap, oils, making a foundation. There are different kinds of aesthetics. And not just one I'm not interested in just one, I'm interested in all.

Do you want to tell me about like the process of your work? Is there a lot of research involved before you begin making a thing? Do you have a clear idea from the start on how you approaching stuff? Or is it all very site specific?

Yeah, it's all. Just everything! There's work. There's research. There's work coming from emotional spaces. I feel something I make it. There's the works that comes from stories I've heard. There are works that are linked with autobiographical stories. There are works that are coming out, because there are few people together that I'm working with that have ideas that we work together and create things. I don't have one way of working. I'm not interested in one way of working. I'm interested in multiple ways of working. I'm interested in being still excited about my work that I wake up in the morning. I'm like, "Oh, I don't know how to do this, how can I go about it? How can I work in this way or that way?" I think that's the richness that this world offers. Also, what people offer. There are some things that need research and there are some things that you need to just vomit out into the world because it's necessary and there is that urgency. There are some things that have to be a bit more latent, you have to be a bit more dormant in it and take time, to think through and breathe it and eat it, and then it comes out slowly. There are some things it's just, you just make them. I like that idea that it shouldn't be one process or one methodology. But there are many methodologies.

It comes out in incredible ways, and I recommend everyone look at your work. We're going to finish on your last track which has a lovely name – grateful. Do you want to tell me why you chose Asa?

I chose Asa because all the women I chose, I chose them for their voices. They have to touch me in a way, but I also love this song because it's about being grateful for things. It's about being happy grateful for the things that you have, the things that have come your way. She sings also in Yoruba and it's just nice to also have another kind of language within the work. It's not just English language, but you also have a language that rhymes, that has a beauty to it, that flows amazingly. I love the way she writes. I love the content of her writing and the songs that she makes and it's very soothing. At the end of the day, the gratefulness of being alive of being you know of being here, of having people that care, people that work with you. And no matter how hard things are that it's still possible to wake up in the morning. It's still possible to do things and still have good health and that is something I'm always grateful for.

A beautiful way to end. Thank you so much for coming in. This is Asa 'Grateful' and thank you everyone for your time.

Thank you so much. It's really a pleasure to see you.

Trevor Paglen

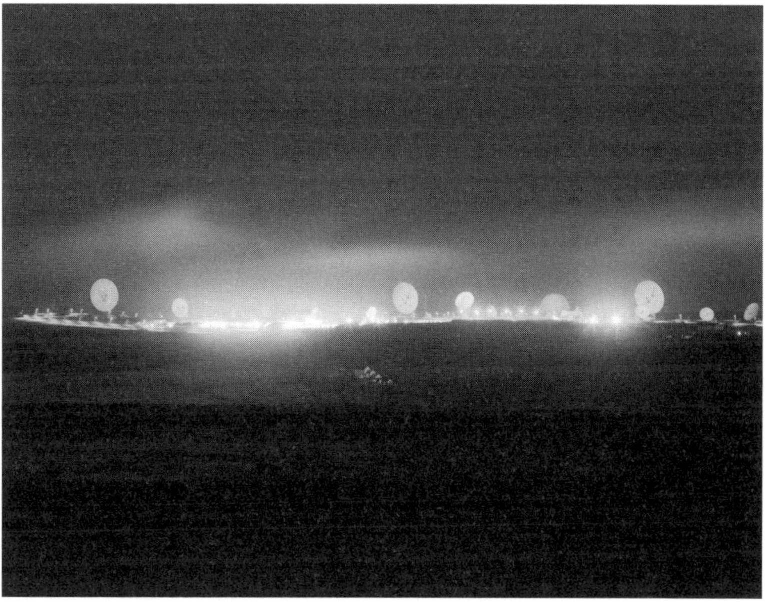

NSA/GCHQ Surveillance Base, Bude, Cornwall, UK

23.09.20

Hi. I'm Francesca Gavin and you're listening to Rough Version on NTS. My guest this month is Trevor Paglen. He's an American artist based between New York and Berlin, best known for photographic and digital projects that aim to make the invisible visible. He has done big projects with Fondazione Prada, Vienna Secession and Protocinema in Istanbul, working with everything from drone warfare to code names, military surveillance and the wires that go under the Atlantic Ocean that carry the internet. Firstly, thank you so much for taking the time to chat to me from Berlin.

Thank you so much for having me.

Let's start with talking about your current work, because I think in the past couple of projects, you've been taking it, if nothing else, into a different aesthetic direction. It's becoming very much about looking at the natural world from, let's say, a technological point of view. Do you want to tell me why you were interested in focusing on things like landscape, in a wider way?

I think in general, if we're hopelessly and ridiculously simplistic, and we think about basic orientations of an image as being a portrait or a landscape, I think I've always been much more drawn towards the landscape tradition. In terms of, very broadly thinking about our environment, and thinking very broadly about how we in effect, create our environment, and are in turn created by the ways in which we've created our environment. So, what are those feedback loops between us and our kind of material, and cultural surroundings? And I guess, in a very broad sense, you can think about that as having to do something with landscape. I think in the more recent works, and concerns, I've been thinking a lot about the automation of vision – things like computer vision systems, machine learning systems, artificial intelligence systems. Thinking about what sorts of technologies that we build to look at and interpret the world for us, and what kinds of forms of seeing and what forms of interpretation are built into autonomous seeing machines or vision systems. We all know that vision is never neutral. That seeing is never neutral. We always bring our own cultural assumptions to the way that we see the world. We bring our own physiological aspects. My eyes literally work differently than your eyes. Seeing is highly situated. But what does it mean when we build machines that are – purport to be much more universal, that purport to be objective? Then build those machines into infrastructures that affect people's lives.

I mean what's also interesting, in that idea of machine perception, is when you're in some of the ways – it's coming out, it feels innocuous. We're looking at trees and leaves or clouds – things that you would think of as maybe harmless in some way. I think your work emphasizes that there might be something – there's an undercurrent of something going on beyond what we see visually as human beings when it comes to ideas of machine perception. There's some kind of conflict there.

Yeah, yeah, absolutely. I mean when we look at how computer vision systems or AI systems work, the logics of seeing just even formally, how they work is really different than how humans see, I think. That's really interesting as a place to start to try to unpack that. I'm trying to think of a good way to phrase this. So very broadly, you can think about the fact that when you build a computer vision system, where you build a machine learning system, or an AI system, your goal isn't actually to look at images. Even though that technically, can be what's going on. Your goal is to make money or to make policing more efficient. There's some kind of political or economic goal that you're using that system for. The form of seeing that's built into the system is going to be inflected by those goals. And so, there's really deep cultural stuff that's in and really deep power relationships that are built into what we might otherwise think of as being relatively neutral mathematical or kind of technological systems. They're anything but that when you actually open them up and start looking at what's going on inside them.

Looking at your work for the past decade, what's really one of the undercurrents through it all seems to be a desire to reveal what is invisible, or to expose what truth is, or question that in some way. Would you agree?

I think that it – the goal – is to learn how to see our surroundings and learn how to see the operations, or things that are around us that shape who we are. And I think that that's not necessarily as simple as revealing something that's invisible, so much as it is trying to learn how to see the contemporary moment that you're in. And that's often hard to do, because it's not necessarily obvious, what is around you. It's not necessarily obvious, how, where to direct one's attention or how to notice things that may or may not be significant.

> *I'm going to start by playing one of your tracks, now. Let's play the Eric Satie. Do you want to tell me why you chose this one in particular?*

Yeah, so Eric Satie. Obviously, the latest work that I've been doing has been under quarantine. I've been really grounded, as it were, in my studio in New York for months and months on end without really seeing anybody, or really interacting with people. I guess it started feeling like the world's longest like business-class flight! Just going on and on and on. I was thinking a lot about the Satie piece, because if you actually play the entirety of the piece, it can take huge amounts of time. It's a really, really, really long piece of music because it's just this endless loop that goes and goes. And although the music is a loop, it's really hard to follow. And people who perform it describe playing it as not really being able to memorise it and just play it as that you'd have to continually read it and keep playing it that way. Because the tonality of it is so, it's a little bit alien to our ears. I guess that's, for me, that felt like a kind of a metaphor for quarantine.

> *Okay. This is Erik Satie's 'Vexations'.*
>
> —
>
> *Looking at your process. I'm really curious. How does it work? Do you come up with an idea? What's that process between idea and realization? There seems to be a lot of research that goes into your projects.*

Yeah. All of the work that I do is, tends to be very research-based. The process usually is, I look at something; I look at it again; I look at it again; I look at it again. I try to see it from as many angles as I can, and in as much detail as I can. At some point, the subject I'm looking at, starts to kind of tell me what it wants to be. That sounds mystical, it's anything but mystical. I think you just, you look at a topic to the point where you start finding moments in it, that stand in for larger ideas. Almost like trying to find metaphors or allegories that are imminent in the material that you're looking at. And then just trying to grow it from there. But there's an enormous amount of experimentation that goes on, in addition to research. There's a huge amount of research that goes on, but also just a huge amount of experimentation. Just thousands and thousands of failed artworks!

> *Most of your work is obviously photographic, though you've done some other installation-based projects and more interactive pieces and things using technology. What interests you about that medium? Why do you think it's apt for the realisation of what you do?*

I think photography is the obviously… a form of machine-assisted seeing. That to me is just interesting as a place to start, in terms of thinking about what is the relationship that we have to a particular technology. What forms of faith do we want to have in the technology? What forms of artifice do we know are built into that technology? And so, I guess for me, photography has a very distilled set of questions about what it means to look at something. What it means to reproduce something. What it means to say that something is there. Right? And it's, obviously, these questions are present in many other media. But for me, there's a clarity of working with photography in terms of really being able to make a concise point.

> *I want to play another one of your tracks, and actually might play a couple from this, which is the Hildegard von Bingen 'Ordo Virtutum'. Do you want to tell me about where you first heard this, and why you chose it?*

I think I first heard this when I was an undergraduate at Berkeley, I actually studied like comparative religion, and I also studied music composition. This sounds strange, maybe. Hildegard von Bingen is obviously somebody that's going to show up in both of those contexts.

I think, I guess this year with the latest body of work, which is called 'Bloom', I've been thinking a lot about – and maybe even less thinking than feeling the real fragility that this moment of time has made so present? Especially in the United States. The fragility of life, the fragility of political institutions, the fragility of even basic ideas like democracy, the fragility of a society that is founded on really violent forms of inequality. I guess for me, in terms of thinking about what it means to make work in a context like that, had me going back to really much older forms of art making. There is a kind of fragility that I find in that music. And, obviously, a kind of grace. I can't give you like a one-to-one relationship – why this music now? It's much more of a feeling and much more of a part of the moment in time that somehow seems to feel relevant now.

> *This is Hildegard von Bingen 'Ordo Virtutum'.*
>
> —
>
> *Since you studied musical composition at university, do you think technically, or in any other way, that's influenced your process of art making? I find that a really interesting relationship.*

I think that it has actually completely informed my way of thinking about art. I go back constantly to devices that are used in music and constantly trying to translate those into the visual work that I do. Either formally or conceptually, and I don't know why that is. I think it is because, relative to visual art, music has a highly articulated formal language that allows you to do stuff with the medium. In visual art, we don't have anything like that. I think we have a very robust theoretical apparatus, but we don't – and I don't think it can exist, that we would have a formal language to talk about visual art, or to inform the way that we make visual art that's anything like what exists in music.

> *I just find that a really fascinating relationship to what you're making. I mean, your work seems to also be playing around ideas of structures, in some way, so there's obviously like a connection there somehow.*

Absolutely. I think there's a connection there and I think there's an overall affect as well, which I think when I was writing a lot of music,

I was playing a lot with timbre and tones, and a lot of field recordings. Thinking about how do recordings of the world become musical and vice versa. These very blurry boundaries between what music can be and what just our surroundings can be, and what and how do different places sound different from each other? How do different kinds of music sound different from each other? What forms of perception, really, are enabled by different forms of music. For me that feels very related to, certainly the way I think about art.

> *On a completely different note, I'm thinking about when you first gained wider recognition, it came out of some projects that were reflecting an interest in the military in America. I wanted to know, firstly, where that initially came from, for you?*

I grew up in the military. That was an environment that was not at all alien to me. It was something I was very comfortable being around, and I was very conscious of. I think when you grow up in the military, you're very conscious of the fact that the United States does not end at the borders. That there's hundreds or thousands of military bases around the world. You grow up in an environment where that's very present. You're around people that are being deployed in Korea, or deployed in the Middle East, deployed all over. It's very much a part of your psychic understanding of the world and of the US' footprint in it. In particular, the work that I was doing grew out of, work that I was doing in the 1990s around prisons. I was thinking a lot about prisons as being a really foundational part of how the US had been, was being restructured, in the aftermath, really, of the civil rights movement. Thinking about those institutions. When this war on terror business started, the signature institution of that is a prison, right? Guantanamo Bay. Then, of course, in relation to that the CIA was running a network of secret prisons around the world. I just started thinking about these relationships between incarceration, secrecy, new forms of colonialism, violence. That was just something I was just trying to learn how to see, as best as I could. Quite literally. In order to try to look at that, you obviously look at colonial histories and histories of, race, but you also have to look at military histories. If we're talking about secrecy, in a formal sense, you have to go back and look at things like the creation of the atomic bomb. You have to look at nuclear histories.

You have to look at weird things like Area 51. Histories of secret weapons, technology development. All of these things inform each other, actually, and I think that for me in the in the 2000s that was so fundamental to the ways in which society was being organised.

My favourite rumour about you that I also emerged, that I'm sure you found funny, was that you were in the military yourself? In the Secret Service, I think it was? Which I find fascinating that you come from criticism and then getting, as your research perhaps is so good, you are accused of being part of the thing you're criticizing.

Obviously, I don't work for the military or intelligence agencies, but I think that when you research anything, you become a part of it. I think you have to. I don't mean formally that you're part of the military or the intelligence community, but you have to talk to people. You have to immerse yourself in something in order to try to understand it. I don't think you can stand outside of something and look in and that's not just me, I mean, that's the basic theory of social science these days.

Let's play another track. Let's play the Holly Herndon 'Eternal'. How did you discover Holly's music?

I discovered Holly's music from her album before. I had, when I was working on the 'Citizenfour' film, I was working with Laura Poitras, and a lot on her work on the NSA. I had made a film that was kind of like a trailer that would open before 'Citizenfour'. It was a very simple film, where it was just flying around the GCHQ headquarters in a helicopter and just doing these loops around it looking down. I was trying to figure out how to do the soundtrack for it. Holly had done a piece of music that was also inspired by that same moment and thinking about surveillance, and thinking about the ways in which the state, aided by technologies like the internet, was able to peer, more and more, into the intimate parts of our everyday lives. She did a piece of music called 'Home' that was about that. I was thinking about her music in relation to this short film that I was working on. We ended up becoming friends. She's an artist – we think in very parallel ways. Her latest album was thinking a lot about artificial intelligence, and what are these blurry boundaries between humans and technologies. I did a little bit of work on her music videos for the new album. I guess what she was trying to do with the new album is just with many things, but she's trying to find joy, and trying to find community. The newer album is an ensemble of singers, which is the exact opposite of what most electronic musicians would do in this era. It would put together a bunch of people in real life and sing. There's just something really inspiring and beautiful that I found in that. She's trying to work with technology, but really it's also trying to find joy and collaboration with other people and connection with other people in the work.

This is Holly Herndon, 'Eternal'.

—

I have a few more questions. Last year, you did a collaborative project with Prada, that expanded far beyond the confines of the art world. It became a huge, almost exposé of how facial recognition works. I'm really curious to know about your feelings. I mean, obviously, the motivation of the project seems very much in tune with all of your other work. But were you surprised with the level of the two-dimensionality of the way machines interpret individuals? Were there things that shocked you about that whole experience?

The exhibition was a collaboration with my friend, Kate Crawford, who is a researcher studying social implications of AI, and technology more generally. We did an exhibition that was called 'Training Humans'. What it was doing was an exhibition that looked at the photographs and images that machine learning systems are built on. So, if you're building a machine learning system, and you want it to be able to recognise different kinds of objects, or what have you. You build what are called training libraries – huge databases of images that you use to essentially teach that computers vision system, how to differentiate between one thing and another. We were just looking at those images, because to me these were really interesting images. They were, literally images that were parts of technical infrastructures. And in many cases, they were never even meant for humans to look at. They're created in labs purely for machines. It's weird when you look at them. There's one piece that I made as a part of that, which is called 'ImageNet Roulette'. It was a piece that was looking at the most widely used of these training sets, which is called ImageNet, that was created at Stanford in 2009. This is a massive, massive database of images. It's about 14 million images organised into over 20,000 categories. About two and a half thousand of those categories are different kinds of people. They would have a category, for example, like 'Scuba Diver' and there would be a bunch of pictures of scuba divers. There'd be a category like 'Cheerleader' or 'Boy Scout' and pictures of cheerleaders and boy scouts, but they would also have horrible categories in there. I think what they essentially did was import a dictionary and then took all the nouns. Then created databases of images that were supposed to be representative of all those nouns. There are nouns in the English language that are horribly racist, horribly misogynistic, horribly cruel and ableist. All of that was in this database. I don't think people in the computer science field actually ever even bothered looking at this stuff. I think the assumption was, "well, this stuff is in the dictionary, and we want to accurately represent real life. And that's how you do it". I think anybody who doesn't have that technical background or that way of thinking will say, "No, no, no, no, no. That is a guaranteed recipe for reproducing terrible politics".

> *It's nineteenth century thinking as well – or even earlier. When dictionaries began to be formed, you're reflecting a lot older and a lot more limited point of view.*

Exactly, exactly. So, I just built a web application, out of this, that could upload your picture, and it would classify you based on the categories and images in this data set – that is, again, the most widely used one in artificial intelligence. And horrible things start happening. I said, this is going to do racist stuff. This is going to do misogynistic stuff. This is going to do terrible stuff. That is the point. I'm trying to build a system that will give you feedback about how it's classifying you, because in many contexts, we are being classified by machine learning systems, but we're given no feedback whatsoever about what those classifications are. That caused a huge, I guess, scandal? I don't know; however, you ever want to describe it. I mean, it was very influential project.

It's amazing to see how it exposed, in such an immediate way to such a broad audience, how appalling technology is functioning. Obviously, this is the same stuff that's happening in Google searches and the way we access all of the internet. That's what seems to be so interesting about all of your work... Technology in general has such a Utopian language around it. Like it lives in the sky, it's superhuman, it's not wires underneath the Atlantic Ocean. It's this positive power for good. A lot of your projects, and in that one in particular, really highlighted how it's actually quite wrong and evil. I think that's something that shifted in general. We've become a lot more aware as a wider audience to be critical towards technology in our lives.

Yeah, I think that's absolutely right. That we should be very careful about whcrc wc put our faith.

That's a beautiful way of phrasing it. I'm going to leave that as your last sentence. Let's finish with the Steve Reich. 'Europe – During The War' from 'Different Trains'. Tell me why 'Different Trains' interested you – it seems to be an interesting conceptual album.

'Different Trains' is a piece by Steve Reich. That was written for the Kronos Quartet. And I've had a collaboration with the Kronos Quartet for a number of years at this point, called 'Sight Machine'. Where the Kronos Quartet performs and I built an installation around them, that is essentially watching the performance through the eyes of different computer visions and AI systems. There's a projection behind them that is showing how these different machines are interpreting the performance as they're doing it. The conclusion of that performance is the first movement of Steve Reich's 'Different Trains'. 'Different Trains' is a piece of music, which is about basically the development and the expansion of trains. Thc first movement is about the promise. The promise of progress that the trains represented. The promise of connection that the trains represented. The promise of being able to make the world a smaller place. You can probably already see that there's some similarities between that language and the language of technology. Of the internet, of social media platforms, etc. That the first movement is all about that promise, and all about that sense of progress and the sense of the creation of a better world. And we end the performance there, at the end of the first movement. The second movement, which we don't play, is about the '30s and '40s. And the way that trains – it's about the Holocaust. It's about the ways in which this technology become a part of the facilitation of absolutely unimaginable crimes against humanity. I guess that's what's left hanging, I guess, in terms of the performance. Is thinking about how easily technology can be used to do unspeakable things.

Very frightening. Steve Reich, 'Europe During The War', from 'Different Trains', and Trevor, thank you so much for taking the time to chat.

Thank you so much. I really appreciate it. It's been great to talk to you.

Prem Sahib

30.10.20

Hi, I'm Francesca Gavin and this is Rough Version on NTS. My guest this month is Prem Sahib, the London-based artist works with a broad selection of media, from sculpture and installation to painting and performance. Club culture, in particular, queer club culture, is one of the central influences on his work, as well as wider interest in identity and public and private space. He's represented by Southard Reid and has exhibited at the Hayward, Lorcan O'Neill and the Gwangju biennial. Prem, thank you very much for taking the time to chat to me today.

Thank you for having me.

When I first started seeing your work, it was really clear that club culture was a huge influence on what you were doing. Do you want to tell me precisely what your club background was before you were making art? Or was it at the same time? Do those two things intersect?

I guess my relationship to club culture goes way back. I grew up in the suburbs of London. And as a queer person, it was important for me to find my community as well as find a space to express myself. That's kind of what led me to clubbing. Coming to London meant I had access to lots of different scenes. I had a lot of fun discovering myself and going out a lot and getting dressed up. The usual I guess… Probably, the first gay club, big gay club I went to was Heaven. But between and before that, I'm just remembering getting my dad to weld me an outfit for Torture Garden. It was for me to go to a fancy-dress party and having to carry this big metal harness with like six-inch nails in a binbag, all the way to Brixton. All sorts of places. I was a little metaller to begin with. Then, I moved around a lot and moved through lots of different clubs and enjoyed, going out partying quite a bit. I guess in terms of my work, club cultures definitely fit into that in a way. But I also think, my work encompasses a lot of other spaces. Not just club ones.

I remember seeing these boxes you were making that had the sound of bass inside of them, and this almost sweaty drip over window. It's in between. It evoked a lot of the physical relationship to a club without a club being present.

Exactly. I'd be making these paintings, which have since evolved a lot over time. At the point that you might have seen them, they were these anodised sheets of metal, aluminium. I used resin to paint droplets on to, which looked as though they were condensation on a window or the sweaty walls of a club. Then I'd interrupt those compositions with abstracted bodily marks. I would add many things. I was making lots of posters at the time. I think one actually, I remember you liking. Lots of different references to club histories and club spaces, both finding yourself in clubs and being alienated in clubs, as well.

> *Actually, that's a thing no one talks about. The not belonging as much as the belonging. Feeling on your own in these weird spaces. But also, maybe there's something good about that alienation.*

Yeah. I've been exploring it a little bit more recently, as I've started to think more about my identity in a way. Thinking about how I've navigated those spaces as a person of colour. I've looked more in recent years, more critically at some of the politics of exclusion that exists in some ways. For instance, things like gender expression are policed or regulated. Where desire is often bound up with ideas around whiteness, or proximity to it. I'm thinking about the types of bodies that are venerated or give an agency in their spaces and who they're seemingly designed for.

> *Interesting. Well, this seems like a really good moment to play your first track. I think we should be playing the Barbara Mason, if you want to tell me about when you first heard this and why you chose her.*

I chose it because I liked Barbara Mason. I first heard the song when, I think, a friend of mine, an older friend, who was a DJ, gave me a copy of 'Paris Is Burning' on a VHS tape. It was like before the internet, so I was really blown away by the documentary. This song was playing quite a tragic part of the film, where Venus Xtravaganza's death is announced, and she is playing this song from her boombox. She sits on the piers, and I just remember her being so seductive and the wind blowing through her hair. Then I later came to use the song in its instrumental version as part of a playlist for some screenings that I was doing.

> *This is Barbara Mason, 'Another Man', the 12-inch instrumental.*
>
> —
>
> *That was Barbara Mason. I think we should talk about your most recent shows. You did something quite incredible with it, which was a three-part show and each of the manifestations were different. The first, very literally incorporating a performance in this installation space, another incorporating a lot of archive imagery and video work and third section had sculptural objects in it. Do you want to explain why you decided to do a triptych exhibition?*

It was really exhausting. It sounded like a very good idea before I began realizing that means three installs and making a lot of work. It was a combination of everything I really felt like I had to say at that time. I didn't want to feel limited by the conventions of occupying a space or an exhibition format. I chose to present it over three episodes or three chapters, which also required something different from the viewer. That meant they came back to the space and discovered a different kind of positionality each time. Although each three parts were conceived in a way that didn't meant it wasn't contingent on having to see all of them. They were exhibitions in their own right, but they fed into one another. The overarching title was 'Descent', which I was thinking about as a movement through time and space, as well as lineage. There was some reference to me thinking through my own heritage, as well. The first part was a massive installation called 'People Come and Go'. It was a replica of a men-only cruising club in the neighbourhood in Warren Street. I rebuilt this one particular interior section, which meant that when you entered the gallery, it was quite radically transformed. You were transported down a really narrow corridor until you got to this tunnel-like structure with these saloon doors. It was basically like creating a parallel space for the one that existed, but one that existed allowed for all sorts of access. Then there was a performance that took place, depending on when you'd come. You may see a body slumped on this plinth within the tunnel space. The performer was always a white male performer. It was a way to talk about a certain demographic, I guess, in those spaces and to position a really highly orchestrated image.

> *I went and saw it when it had the guy in there. What was amazing about the way you approached it, it felt like it wasn't an exhibition. I just stumbled into a really weird and slightly uncomfortable space for someone passed out. It was an artwork that didn't feel like an artwork.*

Yeah. I think a lot of people were surprised by the gallery having vanished in a way. Some people were excited. But then some people were nervous about that. It showed how people approach that image of this guy. If the person wasn't there, there was still detritus that pointed to it being a space that had been occupied. The whole purpose of me remaking this space, which is not something I tend to do in my work, was to try and talk about it outside of its usual space in a way. So that we can afford a view that wasn't myopic. I've been reading this one particular quote by a scholar called Marilyn Frye, which is an analogy to a bird in a cage and its relationship to structural racism. It talks about how if you're really close to the cage, you might think that the bird is free to sort of fly around the bars. It's not until you step outside of that, that you see the interlocking structure that keeps something in place. There was really this idea of getting out of yourself and experiencing an image. That I might experience one of these places outside the original.

> *The second part of the exhibition seemed to be the most autobiographical in a way. It seemed to be drawing on the street you grew up on, I think in Southall. Is that correct?*

The second part was called 'Cul-de-Sac' and it was similarly to the first – a sort of dead end. Like that installation, there was nowhere to go apart from the way back that you came in. 'Cul-de-Sac' was a video that I shot with a drone on the street I grew up on. Again, it was about transcending a familiar space. The drone moved up and down the cul-de-sac, almost quite sexually, actually. And then eventually, rose up high. You saw everything from above. Actually, the cul-de-sac looks quite phallic from above. The soundtrack to that video work was a collection of audio recordings I've made over the years. They consisted of everything from club recordings that I've made, to drunken arguments with my boyfriend, to being on an aeroplane. All sorts. Me sleep talking. About slipping in and out of consciousness and getting out of the body.

You were also including some really interesting archival material from the activist work your uncle was doing, which is also really fascinating.

My father passed away in 2018. And I became more intrigued about his experience as a young person coming into this country. In speaking to my uncle, he gave me all this archival material. I had very little idea of him. I knew that he was involved in some sort of social work, but I didn't realize the extent of his activism. He gave me this material just because I was interested, and I couldn't not share it. It became a contextual and historical device in combination with the video. It spoke a lot about the area, through newspaper clippings, and through letters that he'd written to challenge mainstream narratives about Asian youth in that area, which were very conflated coverage about gun culture. I viewed it in relation to things like to broader societal issues, such as racism, economic hardship and housing. I just felt like it was really important material to share. It was both our experiences of the same place in a way. Then I made the archive digital so that people could also take it away by scanning a QR code, which, obviously, today seems so familiar but it meant that that archive could exist outside of the gallery space as well.

Before we finish off talking about the third section of the show. We're going to play some of that audio from 'Cul-de-Sac'. Do you just want to finish off by saying how the third part works, which is also very different in terms of how we were approaching an exhibition?

That was more of an object response to the first two parts, I guess. It was called 'Man Dog'. It also included a recording, which I made in an online chat room. It's quite complicated to talk about. It's this guy who was kind of homophobic even though he was identifying as gay, a racist rant or hate speech. He also makes these really sad admissions about his own loneliness and ends up speaking a lot about dogs, weirdly. The sentiment of that part of the exhibition was really to do with being confined in a domestic space. Talking about ideas around companionship and loneliness and submission and power. It was more of an object response to the other two parts. It had some still lives on the floor. This recording was played through an obsidian mirror. Obsidian is a material that I've been working with recently, which is actually volcanic glass. I was interested in how it's produced under immense heat and pressure. And when polished up that is a bit reminiscent of communication devices like a cracked iPhone or something. I used a sound exciter to play his audio through that mirror.

Let's play the soundtrack section. Which section are we going to hear? Is this from section two, 'Cul-de-Sac'?

This is the soundtrack to 'Cul-de-Sac'.

Brilliant. Okay.

—

Coming back to a little bit about your process, do you want to tell me about how that works for you? Does it come as an idea of responding to location or something you read? How does an idea come together?

My process is quite studio-based, I would say. I like working across quite a few different things at a time. I have some things that I can really get in a groove with, like the painting which can also be quite meditative and evolves naturally through its making. But then there are other ideas that maybe require more research or collaboration and working with other people. In terms of my sculptural work, I often begin making the cuts and it's through various fabrication that they develop. Each thing is different really. I see myself as someone who works with sculpture primarily, but I don't feel bound to like one particular way of making.

Do you listen to music in your studio? Is it a quiet place?

It really depends. It really depends on what I'm doing. I would be lying if I didn't have Beyoncé on sometimes!

Hey. I have no judgment. Let's play another track – the Arthur Russell. Why did you choose this one in particular?

I love Arthur Russell. I love how diverse his work is and the range of emotions he incorporates... I was coming across his output under different pseudonyms and then realizing he was hidden behind it. There was Loose Joints and Dinosaur L and Killer Whale. I just loved all the different ways in which he was expressing himself through these different identities and projects. This particular track, I really like thinking about as moving through adversity and how you can do it. He manages to carve out the space in a very classic Arthur Russell way, which is both dreamy and intimate and hopeful. There's a timelessness about his music that, 40 years later sounds so contemporary.

This is Arthur Russell, 'This Is How We Walk On The Moon'.

—

That was Arthur Russell. You DJ and have a club night. Tell me about Anal House Meltdown and how that started.

Anal House Meltdown is a club night that I co-run with George Henry Longley and Eddie Peake. It began in 2011, I think.

I remember when it started.

That's crazy. It started really casually, and it continues that way. It was always about fun and creating a welcoming environment for people. Then also using that club environment for things like performances and exhibitions. The first one began with Eddie and I doing a performance called 'Darkroom', which had like about 20 performers in pitch darkness. We made sure of that and awkwardly making people that were there for a party endure our 15-minute performance or something. Then we ended up doing more performances and these poster exhibitions in the context of a club space. It began at Vogue Fabrics, every couple of months, or three or four times a year, for a few years. Then we started moving around. We did parties in New

York and Sao Paolo, and then for one of my friends in Stromboli – literally on an active volcano.

Many people who don't know, the Fiorucci Trust every year invites different artists to do a performance music art week. It seems incredible. Was it you who had been invited?

I think that particular edition, I had been invited. I did a bunch of other things. But one of the things was to do Anal House Meltdown and there's a club there that's a natural amphitheatre. It's a really amazing location. We just threw a party. The last time we did one was back in 2018, in Vauxhall. It was also the weekend of an installation I had in Vauxhall Park, and it happened to be Pride weekend. It felt like quite an epic one. It was something like 12 hours. We had Lauren Flax play, Total Freedom, Proscenium, Soda Planes. Geoffrey Hinton and Princess Julia, both of whom I like. London clubbing legends. It was a really fun one. It just feels such a long time ago now. We're doing some of the things that are related to the community that maybe came to our club nights, but not so much as a party. There's this pop-up shop called X Trade, which I'm co-organizing with George Henry Longley and Jared Davis. We're working with lots of people on that. It's an artist-run artist-led shop. There'll be a small program of events to keep an eye out for, some readings and screenings. Maybe even an online party but essentially, it's a pop-up shop to support artists and makers during this time and to raise some money for charity. Phyllida Reid is kindly letting us use Charing Cross Road, so it'll be the first week of December.

That's amazing. Something to look forward to, which is always nice. Wow, that's a great thing to be doing. Let's play another track because I think actually this is going be your last track, but it feels apt which is the AHMD 'Death Drive'. Is this something that you play on?

This is a track that we made in 2015 with the help of Tim Golden. It emerged out of studio sessions we had, recording lots of samples and using our voices. There are some references to the original 'Darkroom' performance I mentioned which is the beginning, the intro of the track.

We wanted it to be – I don't know we spoke about maybe making a club banger but then we decided that we wanted it to be something much longer. An odyssey in a way. Something that moved through varying emotions and crescendos and feelings like a real soundscape. Some parts of it remind me – I've just been clocking some sad moments after a high. It's a long 13-minute track, I think.

We may cut a little bit but we'll try. This is AHMD 'Death Drive'.

—

Just to finish off. One thing that seems to be a running theme in your work is the awareness of architecture in some way. I'm thinking of that work you did during Pride, near Vauxhall, which is part of that extended, public sculptural thing that's happening all around everywhere. I've forgotten its name… terrible.

Art Night.

Do you want to tell me, what interests you about the architectural? Your take on it has always been on sub-cultural architectural space.

I mentioned that it's not just clubbing spaces that I've referenced in the work. I've also brought in domestic space and other types of public and private space. Things like saunas and bath houses and cruising sites, usually from a biographical starting point, but to do with, I guess, the structures that we inhabit that shape that sense of self. I think that's where my interest in architecture comes from. Thinking about the material culture that we make, and how that consequently makes us as subjects, offer space. The one in Vauxhall, in particular, was referencing. The labyrinth-like structures found in cruising clubs. Architectures that are designed, interiors designed purposely for people to lose themselves in and escape societal constraints. I had always been making a lot of work about my experiences of those spaces. But it wasn't till some of them closed in 2016 and I managed to get in and document some of those spaces that I thought a little bit more pointedly about those structures. Some of the closure of those spaces goes in tandem with the way in which the city is changing. I think it was something like a 58% decrease in LGBT+ venues from

2006 to 2017. There's a lot of market-led development and gentrification which led to those closures. Off areas becoming prime real estate. People not being able to afford rents and excessive amounts of luxury housing rather than affordable housing being built. The project at Vauxhall was me trying to think about some of those things. I've built maze-like structure that was modelled on the floorplan for one bedroom, luxury apartments in that area. Kind of bringing it down to ground level, and having it appear in a social space very quickly. It was in Vauxhall Park. Thinking about the sanitized narratives that developers want from space and how I could allude to some of those things.

> *There's also this idea of the erotic or pleasurable being a form of resistance in the places that you're talking about. Because it's true. It's been a huge transformation. It's almost like a controlling of pleasure...*

Yeah, for sure.

> *We'll probably, that's going to do me nicely. Thank you so much for taking the time to chat. I'm very excited about the forthcoming pop-up project shopping experience. Thank you very much.*

Thanks so much. Speak to you soon. Bye bye.

Tenant of Culture

27.11.20

Hi, you're listening to Francesca Gavin, and this is Rough Version on NTS. My guest this month is Tenant of Culture, who is an artist originally from Holland, but living in the UK. Who is represented by Soft Opening, and just won the inaugural Camden Art Centre Emerging Artist Prize with Frieze Art Fair, and has exhibited internationally in Brussels, Zurich, Berlin, and the Fondation Cartier in Paris. Hello. Can I call you your real name? Am I allowed to call you by your real name, or do you like people knowing you by Tenant of Culture?

Yes, definitely. Only Tenant, for you!

So, this is Hendrickje Schimmel. It's the obvious first thing: where did the name come from? I've said this before, I always thought it sounded like you're a collective, but you're a single individual. What do you find interesting working like that?

I think the collective part of it is still an option for me, like I'm not too attached to it being me in the practice. The name is derived from the writing of Michel de Certeau – the book called 'The Practice of Everyday Life'. I came across this as I was trying to formulate a position for myself, that was interdisciplinary between art and fashion, because I have a fashion background. I didn't feel that it resonated with my methodology of work to call my practice my name and put the emphasis on the individual producer. I came across this. He writes about the tenant, and he uses this as a wider allegory in his book for describing renting within a larger pre-existing structure. This really interested me because also my use of materials is recycling existing materials. To position myself more as a transient and then as an owner, in the life of my materials was something that attracted me to this. As well, it relates to me as a play on the traditional fashion house – like Maison Valentino, or Maison Margiela. Fashion houses always referenced this kind of classical structure of in-house production. And I thought it would be funny to do a play on that by calling myself a tenant as if I was renting within that pre-existing structure.

Coming from that fashion training – but very, very much in an art context. Obviously there's some kind of critique about the world or the industry connected to fashion – a love affair and critique. Do you want to tell me, what are some of those feelings about that relationship?

That's interesting. I think it is very, very much a big love and a big critique of fashion because my very first interest was fashion and I never really wanted to do anything else. And while studying it, and learning more about the intricacies of the industry, I fell out of love with it. Because of its ambiguous production methods and its strange moral codes and ethics. I really think this is still something that I'm actively pursuing in my practice, To unite those two again, but it's kind of impossible. I think now it's more a dialectical position that I take between this love and hate, which makes it an interesting thing for me to critique because I don't come from this… how do you call it? I come from an imminent position in the fashion industry. It's not like a critique from the exterior position, which is important to me. Because I think if you have a fondness for something the critique will always be more nuanced and more interesting. The things that I look at are also always things – I work a lot around the idea of trends and the trends that I work with are also things that I am attracted to myself. It's not like something that I look at and am like "Oh, this is so bad". I need to have a connection to it as well.

What are some of the trends that you're looking at now that you're attracted to?

At the moment, I've just done a long research project on the chore coat, which is a workwear jacket. It is very simple jacket, actually. The pattern of it informs a lot of styles that we wear today. It's a very straightforward jacket with four flat pockets on the front, which originates from the old agricultural worker of France. You see it a lot now in the urban middle class creative atmosphere where there's a lot of people wearing these bright blue workers' jackets. I'm really interested in it because it communicates a sense of humbleness and groundedness. But simultaneously, it does the opposite because it's also the appropriation of the labour classes. That is always something that interests me in a trend – when it has a two-fold character.

Class seems to be something that also comes through a lot when you're looking at the information that clothing is saying and projecting. OK. Let's play your first track. Let's play Gabber Eleganza and HDMIRROR. When did you first hear this and why did you use it?

This is a recent track. I think it came out earlier this year. The reason I chose it is because I was interested in this post rave culture and the reappreciation of gabber. Gabber Eleganza is a pioneer in this wave. He really archives the original Dutch gabber aesthetics and music and repurposes and recontextualizes that. I was really interested in gabber reemerging in music and fashion recently because I'm from the Netherlands. I grew up really submerged in this culture because I was born in the early '90s. This is when that was really the main subculture in the Netherlands. I think it might even be the only subculture that ever came from the Netherlands. Sorry if I just offended people! What I find specifically interesting about gabber is that it first created an anti-fashion. So, when there would be gabber parties in the city I grew up in, there would be this influx in the city and people wearing brightly coloured tracksuits and almost futuristic sportswear and Nike Air Max and shaved heads. It was so intimidating but super exciting at the same time. This was before I even had an awareness of the music because I was quite young – I wasn't exactly rave age yet.

Age 10, no!

I observed it from the periphery which is maybe why I'm still quite intrigued by it. It reemerged and I always find it interesting when aesthetical culture and musical culture reemerges because I also see this as… These images from the past demand reevaluation in light of the present. I think within this song that is really well done which is it's recontextualized, so it sounds very current, but it really has those sounds of gabber culture, a bit of happy hardcore, the euphoric sounds, the tearing drums. That's the reason.

Well, okay, this is Gabber Eleganza & HDMIRROR with 'Frozen Dopamina'.

—

That track actually makes me think about something else that comes up in your work, which is this idea around rebellion and the subcultural in general. What do you find interesting about looking at things, or trends, or just items of clothing, or material that seems to talk about the idea of rebellion?

What I find most interesting is the detournements of value that garments go through. For example, a simple jacket such as the worker jacket and how that goes from the original context of being a hard-wearing labourers' jacket to something that is worn by the creative middle class, and then it goes back to being critiqued and maybe discarded altogether, and then reemerges. I'm really interested in these detournements. For example, with gabber, where the tracksuit all of a sudden gained a lot of status, whereas before it was regarded as the dress of the lower classes, but then they amplified it and really made it into something that everyone would wear. Everyone wanted one of those tracksuits. And then afterwards, for a while, you were embarrassed to have worn it for a while. Then it comes back into style. I'm really interested in those waves of something being the newest thing to the oldest thing. And, of course, how simple garments can suddenly be reemployed in a sort of 'anti-fashion'.

Let's talk about your materials because they're amazing. Firstly, do you want to give a list of the kind of stuff that you're using to make your sculpture? Increasingly, wall pieces too. Where are you getting your stuff from and what are you using?

All my stuff is garments and accessories and shoes and bags from the secondary market. The secondary market, I understand, as being everything that is not new. I find them on eBay in charity shops. Sometimes it's already discarded. Sometimes I get donations. That is my main sourcing process. That it's secondhand. What is interesting about that is that you get a lot of extras because there's signs of usage and there's the original decisions of the designer who designed the piece, and how its produced. All this information I extract when I deconstruct a garment. It's a very interesting process to work with secondhand materials because you can't just go into a shop and say, "Oh, can I have like 15 meters of cotton" and that's what you work with. I think a large part of my work is looking for materials. I think that takes about 70% of the time – sourcing the material and deconstructing new material. For me, that is a really interesting method of working because it takes away a bit of my autonomy. I have to deal with certain consequences that come with working with pre-existing materials.

What's also so interesting is the way you use all these second-hand clothes. You're using bits that people really would see as dirty, decaying, really worn out. Bits of the rubber, the roping, a lot of the parts of the garment that people really wouldn't necessarily – that have lost their function somehow. What do you like about the dirt?

Well, I think there's a lot of aspects to utilizing those things in garments. I think, first and foremost, they are signs that it has been utilized by something. The narrative that comes with staining and creasing and ripping and the untold stories that unfold when you start to examine the garments. The dirtier it is, the more story there is in the garment. There's also an element of it – I work with garments that are quite insignificant in a historical context. I work a lot with the idea surrounding institutional archives; where and how do we determine; what is good enough to save from being thrown away, and what to preserve. I usually use pieces that are in some kind of state of decomposition already. Which also has to do with the idea that we are obsessed with newness, and especially in fashion. Newness is the method of driving things forward. I'm more interested in the material consequences of this eternal quest for newness. That things are slightly decomposing or dirty adds to this idea. But on the other hand, I also find it quite interesting that sometimes – where is the line between when stains add to the value of a garment and decrease from the value of a garment? For example, ripped jeans are actually something that is very desirable. Or intentionally faded or stained garments that are artificially created can also add to the value of it. I find it on both sides of the spectrum, I find interesting connotations.

Let's play another track. I want to play the Lawfandah, because if nothing else it's a nice contrast to the gabber! Do you want to tell me about why you chose this one and when you first heard her?

This is also a new track, I think. It's from her album 'The Fifth Season' which came out in September. I've been following her work, because it's really incredible and it doesn't sound like anything I've heard before. She's an Egyptian-Iranian artist and musician. 'The Fifth Season' is an album that was inspired by N.K Jemisin's 'Broken Earth' trilogy. The name of the album is one of the books and a subtitle for that book is 'Every Age Must Come to an End', which I found very topical. I really think this whole album captures a certain fatality and other worldliness which really articulates the sensibility of the strange moment that we live in. This track specifically is an adaptation of Glenn Copeland's 'Don't Despair', which is really great track as well.

OK, this is Lafwandah doing 'Don't Despair'.

—

Another thing that I've been noticing increasingly in some of the work that obviously helped you get you the Camden Art Centre Prize is you really seem to be addressing a relationship to sculptural art history. Like the idea of the foot of Samothrace and linking that to disused ugly trainers and bits of rubber. Do you want to tell me about what you like about that art historical referencing?

I always try to accomplish a sense of inter temporality in my pieces. There's a lot of references to history, but not necessarily in a linear way. I think it's interesting to sample elements of historical imagery and maybe also significant in art history. For example, the petrified foot in the shoe sculptures references Greek sculpture in an obvious way. But I find that quite interesting to then juxtapose that with very contemporary imagery. As I said, when we were talking about the gabber, I see the using of images from the past in the light of the present as an interesting opportunity to reexamine those images in my work.

A lot of your work is playful in terms of rethinking how to display. You're using clothes, but the body is often absent. These plaster feet – or whatever material you're using – is probably the first time we've seen a body part. Most of the time your objects are somehow hanging. Do you want to tell me a bit about what you like about messing about with display?

Display is always derived from retail display. I look a lot at shop displays. For research, I go to like Regent Street or Oxford Circus, for example, and just roam the shops and look at the kind of atmosphere that shops create to intensify your shopping experience. Also, the thematic display methods. For example, if you would have a more industrial looking collection, then the display would be scaffolding. I find it interesting, because it has this placelessness in the shops that I want to convey in my own display as well, because fashion has this way of alienating you from a context while feeding you elements or references of origin. I use a lot of railing and plinths that you would normally see more in the retail environment. Also, some elements that have a persuasive, luxurious vibe and then I combine them with the more traditional art display. The funny thing is that at the moment, there's a crossover between those two because the shop references the white cube now. They've exchanged strategies, which is interesting.

I think historically they always have. And by the way, as a curator that's a curator's dream. I've never thought about going around like Bond Street and looking at their display. Great idea.

I just love shopping.

And now you can make it your work! Very smart. I also noticed that really recently, you've also been using textiles to make wall pieces, so making a painting out of old jeans. That's an interesting new direction. Is that a new direction for you because I hadn't seen those pieces before.

In the very beginning I was doing that quite a lot, pressing things into a flat surface. I even had things stretched at that point, but I don't stretch things now. Sometimes it can even put more emphasis on the garment to flatten it out. I find it sometimes interesting to reduce it down to this very simple shape and let the textiles really come to the fore and do the talking, and all the references that are already embedded within the fibers that I use. Sometimes it can really emphasize, what I'm trying to say, to not necessarily refashion it into a garment. But it's an exchange. I think both works well together. Both forms.

Let's play another track. Let's play The Fall. So why this Fall track?

Yeah, the cover of the Sister Sledge disco classic. I find it interesting how they reworked a disco song into their own significant style. It's just a really fun song, I think. My boyfriend plays along with The Fall at home so I'm very familiar with it and this is just one of my favourites.

This is 'Lost in Music', caught in a trance. Sorry I'm going to fall into Karaoke! This is The Fall's version of 'Lost in Music'.

—

Let's talk about your studio. I've been to your studio. It's in a disused commercial space. It's filled with material. How do you find the studio impacts your process, and how you make work and decide on creating things?

That's my old studio unfortunately. Now I have a studio that is in a disused office building. It's a floor in an office building in Marylebone so it's in an interesting space. That was kind of funny; that was a disused shop. I think my practice is very studio based. I have a lot of stuff, as you've seen. Anyone who's been to my studio comes in and is a bit like, "Oh, whoa. It's so cluttered". I think the way everything is scattered over every surface is also how I refind materials. Just by literally digging through all the piles and cutting out zippers or labels and refashioning those into pieces. I call it 'lateral orientation' because it's all scattered over the floor. Everything that goes in a box in a cupboard I just never think of again. So, I have to have this kind of tactile experience of digging through the piles of clothes to find this one element that's going to complete the piece.

It's very much like collage.

It is.

Except what your collaging is not paper. It's just a different medium.

Yeah, it's completely like collage.

Yeah, completely. And do you listen to music when you're in your studio? Is there an aural equivalent of chaos?

I go through periods of listening to music in my studio intensely, listening to it all the time, and periods that are completely quiet. It's weird, where I can't have any extra sounds or influences whilst I'm working. When I listen to music in my studio, it would normally be a bit ambient, for example, or not too overpowering because everything in my head is already quite loud and present.

I'm going say, that very obviously leads us on to our last track. Which is The KLF 'Chill Out'. Is this one of those things that you're listening to in that sense?

Definitely, yeah. It's a conceptual ambient house album. It's not a track. It's like a 45-minute composition that resembles a road trip through rural America. But it's recorded in their basement in Stockwell, without them having visited the places they reference in the sonic experience. I found it really interesting how they tap into this collective memory of America that we all have through the media that we consume. It's a patchwork of repurposed sounds, which relates to my practice as well. Like repurposing samples of Elvis and Fleetwood Mac and interweaving it with cowbells, and car horns and trains. Yeah. It's just a beautiful long piece of music.

We're not going to play all of it. We're going to play about six or seven minutes. And this is The KLF 'Chill Out' and thank you so much Tenant of Culture, aka Hendrickje Schimmel.

Thank you so much for having me.

Philippe Parreno

21.12.20

Hi, you're listening to Rough Version on NTS, and my guest this month is Phillipe Parreno. He's a French artist who arguably reinvented how exhibitions function. He's had major solo shows at Gropius Bau in Berlin, the Museo Jumex in Mexico City. He took over the Tate Turbine Hall in 2016 and was the first artist to be given carte blanche at the Palais de Tokyo in Paris and that's where you are now, Phillipe, I think?

Yep. I'm in Paris

Wonderful. Let's talk about your relationship to music in a wider sense, because looking at your approaches to exhibition making, it seems to be really influential in the structure of what you do.

It was probably during that show that I worked for the first time with a soundtrack, classically. When I started to do my shows, I needed to have a timecode, in order to hang the events and to produce some sort of synchronicity between events. At the time, classically, it is silent music. It's sort of a soundtrack that we can hear. At the Palais de Tokyo, for the first time, I'd made the set of flex time codes audible, by selecting a piece of music played by Mikhail Rudy, called 'Petrushka'. A piece of music that he plays, which is quite unique. It is played with two hands which is quite complex to play. I put that as my time code in order to hang the events on it. That was really the first time that I worked with music directly.

What was so amazing about seeing that show was also the way that you used sound and particularly these disembodied pianos to make us move throughout the entire building. It was helped move the viewer through the space.

Exactly because you will hear them. You will hear something that will catch your attention and then you walk through. Because the building is quite big, you will walk through it and be attracted by some music or some sound you hear from a distance. Then you realize that what you are hearing in the background will activate something that you can see, right where you are, where you are standing. I started to work with this – the synchronicities… That piece of music was always played as a new loop. That was the first time when where it was clearly musical.

> *Obviously, we should play that piece of music right now. How did you first discover the piece, 'Petrushka'?*

It was really the pianist, Mikhail Rudy, with whom I worked at the Palais de Tokyo for the first time but then at the Armory – when I did a short demo at Armory, in New York. He was playing live for the entire duration of the show. It was quite stunning that he accepted to do that. I was introduced to Mikhail Rudy by Alex Poots, who at the time was the director of the Manchester what you call…

> *The International Festival.*

The International Festival exactly. I was working with him on a piece called 'Postman Time' together with Hans Ulrich Obrist. I was looking for a musician to work with for the Palais de Tokyo and he introduced me to Mikhail Rudy. We will play 'Petrushka', which seems to be quite in tune with what I wanted to do at the Palais. Conceiving the show as a large automaton and 'Petrushka' is indeed for the story of an automaton.

> *This is Mikhail Rudy playing 'Petrushka'.*
>
> —
>
> *I'm thinking about your work in a wider sense. I'm thinking about the Gropius Bau show – the way blinds would move up and down, or sound come into the space, or the way the exhibition somehow moved. That seems almost musical to me. Do you want to tell me a little bit of what interested you about thinking about it as a whole, rather than a bunch of individual pieces?*

That's something that I've been working on for a while. An exhibition is not only a display of a singular object but can be by itself in a waveform. Since the beginning, this was something I was always intrigued by… Partly because it was at a time when I was producing films and screening those films in galleries or museums. At the time, you had videotapes. You had to play the piece and then have time for the piece to be re-winded. I started to have this thing where the room will be switched on and then you wait for the tape to be re-wound and then turned off again and the film will be screened. For the work to appear stochastic – will be there and then not there, by sequences. I was interested in this idea, by the notion that work can appear but also disappear. I wrote a text at the time called 'Postman Time', trying to get around the weird notion of who is in control of what. Who is in control of that time – the time of the appearance of the work and the time, of course, of its disappearance. If you do a painting, the painting will be hung and therefore exist. It is hung on a time code, and then it will disappear. But then that disappearance will not be controlled by the artist – but by the museum or institution that decides to show the work. I was intrigued by that. The notion of producing a form but also the disappearance of a form. The Gropius Bau was in a way an iteration of this idea that things will come and disappear and produce those moments. Gropius Bau was not hung on the musical score like it was in Palais de Tokyo. It was a bit like the Tate. It was directly plugged within a colony of yeasts that will live and die and therefore produce those events in the space. The timecode was not music, but it was an organism, that could and will grow and then die.

I remember coming across another piece that you did, which was a CD with a video work on it. When you played it once you couldn't actually play it again.

Yeah, yeah, it was a DVD, that will fade away, right?

Which is a really fascinating concept of something not able to survive, something totally ephemeral.

Yeah, it was a piece I think I did the first time in a gallery where people will come, I can't remember what the film was… People will see the film. They will either decide to see the film in a gallery or just take a DVD and watch it at home. And that DVD will be self-erased, after you watch it once. It's always something that I think about this production and disappearance of form and space.

Let's talk about your approach to sound and video. Obviously, some of your best-known works are film pieces. Do you want to tell me a bit about your thinking around soundtracks?

I talked about time code. I was highly influenced by that invention. Time code was created by Jean-Pierre Beauviala in Grenoble, where I grew up. It was a way to synchronize sound and images with a camera. I was always fascinated by this idea that, a bit like spectral being. It was something that you can see, but then through that creature that you will see only in between things that it seems to be synchronized, right? I think more and more involves terms in a way. That a creature or its form, whatever you call it, will exist between both momentum. That's how I approach music.

In terms of 'Zidane', how did you end up working with Mogwai? What was your thinking behind that?

Mogwai. I approached them for that film. The film on Zidane was what you call a challenge. How do you sustain attention when you watch for an hour and a half a face? Because it was a portrait. It was really on his face for an hour and a half. So how do you carry that attention? When there are no events to follow? So, you engage into a sort of non-authoritarian process. When you look at something, then you can drift at what you are looking at. Douglas Gordon, with whom I did the film, we thought that we needed to have some form of support to help – not to help but to carry that drift. You watch a film, but you will be okay to drift out of the film. And music, especially the music of Mogwai, was a good way to do so.

Let's play one of the tracks from that, which is Mogwai's 'Black Spider', from the soundtrack to 'Zidane: 21st century'. Why did you like this particular piece?

Because it's a piece that opened the film. I don't know. I felt really emotional when I listened to it for the first time.

Okay. This is Mogwai 'Black Spider'.

—

Let's talk about the ghostly figure, which seems to be something recurring in what you do. Whether it's a disembodied instrument playing on its own, or just the concept of something ghostly. Do you want to tell me about what you find interesting about those figures or concepts?

The ghost – how can I put it – ghost for me is another way to say form. I guess that's the way I always think about it. A form is a ghost. In a way, a form is an attempt to incarnate some ideas, and to make it public. There's a beautiful equation that was written by Marcel Duchamp, that says "a guest + a host = a ghost". I always find it fascinating. Meaning that you need both. You need to be invited, so to speak. This idea that you are invited to witness an appearance in a way. Art, when you enter into an exhibition, you're already invited in a way to attend that phenomenon. The spectral idea of a form was always interesting to me. There's a lot of dimensions to it. The fact that ghosts were, for the first time, described as such by monks that copied the Bible. The fact that you read, or you copy, or that you read before, this idea of an idea can reappear, this idea of a ghost reading… Something seems to be quite accurate about that idea and still resonates today.

I think it's really interesting with the work that you used AI and film where it's almost recreating a sound. We're watching an AI recreate the sound. Do you want to tell us a little bit about how that functioned?

We talked about videotape in gallery shows in the '90s. In that case, it was a film called 'Anywhen', that I was playing in a gallery'. I think it was played for the first time in New York at Barbara Gladstone Gallery. The piece was played, the film played, and then when the film ended an AI started to try to re-compose or re-memorize a sound that was re-played. So, you had a moment when you see the film and then a moment when the computer – where the AI – was trying to remember what was played. Until the end of the show where it started to get it right. It was also this idea to have an on and off. A moment when something is played and then something being remembered.

Let's play another one of your tracks. Let's do the Yussef Dayes and Alfa Mists. Why did you choose this one?

I discovered that recently and really liked the vibes of it. I thought it was a really beautiful piece of contemporary jazz, played by some young guys from London. I know I played it quite a lot for no reason, just because I like it.

Good. It's a really good track. This is Yussef Dayes and Alfa Mists 'Love is the Message'.

—

Let's talk about collaboration, which seems something quite fundamental to a lot of your projects. You've worked with numerous different artists. You mentioned Douglas, but also Liam Gillick. What do you like about collaboration?

For many years I was only working with collaborations. I start to work with Pierre Hughye back in the day, when I was at school. I always thought collaborations were a way for me to produce a form. I needed a conversation. To work I needed to exchange with somebody. I was in need of language and to share language. To produce, to find a grammar that was essential to me. I could not conceive of doing something without being engaged in a conversation. It was a time when we had a lot of ideas, and some will be realized, and some were not being realized. It was okay, because it was a straight definition of what's real. If you talk to somebody about certain ideas, and if I'm not wrong, then that person still has the idea in their head, right. That idea is in a way a little bit real because we share it. It doesn't have to be in my head only. It's like shared by somebody other than me. There's a bit of that notion too. And then I carried on because it was a way to go faster, to explore, to be less shy and try things out. I always used it. The last one where I did the mega collaboration that I mentioned before, was when I worked with Hans Ulrich Obrist on a show based around time on stage. Where we invite artists to produce a moment of time next to each other. It was a time-based exhibition. That was last big collaborative work that they did. After that, partly because I was sick, I started to become more alone and by myself. I started to develop some obsessions that I had. It became more subjective in a way. At that time, I needed to co-produce my reality, so to speak. I see those moments and phases. But recently I've been interested again by this process of collaboration and collaborative practice. But maybe for different reasons than before.

Are you doing something with ARCA at the moment?

Yeah. Before it was this need to produce a grammar in common, but also this idea I had an issue with authorship. Being an author was problematic to me. It has to be a negotiation in a way, that was one of the reasons. But today is different because I need the other to do something that I can do. ARCA, I contacted when I worked this commission at MoMA. MoMA was reopening last year. I was working on this automaton – this weird object composed of different elements. Because it was a commission and the piece was supposed to be there for a while in the lobby of the MoMA, I was intrigued by this idea that people will come in and… be exposed. By movement, by sound, a form would be perceived, but without being really clear because it's a lobby. It's an open work. The piece will be there and not there and be moved some of the time. I was thinking automaton could be sensitive to air conditions, to pollution, to things that we humans don't really pay attention to. I was working on this creature, I called it. I contacted ARCA and we work together on this sound and soundtrack and music. In a way ARCA gave the voice to the creature. She introduced me to this company in England called Bronze, who does granular sounds. The soundtrack that ARCA developed started to become alive and, and will be changing all the time, fed by the weather and by the different conditions that the piece will perceive around. In fact, she even gave the title of the work – which is called 'Echo'. It was for her to name a piece of that work out of the nymph that was doomed and only able to echo what she hears or perceives. That was the last work that I did.

Listen, let's play the ARCA track you've brought which I will probably mispronounce which is 'Mequetrefe'.

Yeah, it's part of a track on the last album that she released a couple of months ago.

This is ARCA 'Mequetrefe'.

—

Let's talk about another aspect of your work that comes up a lot, which is this your relationship to nature and often decaying nature which is quite fascinating. Do you want to say what you find interesting about ideas around authorship, when you're literally placing the authorship of something in natural form. Or the depiction of black gardens?

The relationship to all the yeasts or all these living organisms or living forces or the garden that I produced was again this – I'm tempted to call this exhibition more a manifestation because I think it's a better word than exhibition. There is still something about displaying, which I find is sometimes a bit annoying. Manifestation is something nice because as we said, you have a plateau, where things will occur. You mention the black garden, the black garden was a bit like the piece that I did before, in Thailand with Francois Roche the architect, where I was interested in producing a film, which will produce its own reality. In the case of the piece that I did in Thailand, it was an architecture designed by Francois Roche, that will then produce a film. But the film will also produce the architecture. It was sort of like a two-headed beast, with the film and its reality that will survive the film. The garden was the same idea. I built a black garden in Portugal, and I shot the film. It was a set, but then the set survived the film and still exists. So, there's an object and there's a subject. The subject may survive its object. Both exist in a way. The garden exists itself and the film exists by itself.

It seems like a good moment to talk about the Edgar Varese track, 'Desert'. Do you want to say why you chose this one?

Edgar Varese 'Desert' was a piece that I used for a film a long time ago called 'El Sueño de una Cosa'. It was a short one-minute-long film that I did that was released inside cinemas all over Sweden, a campaign. It was indeed like a campaign because it was released before the screening of a feature film. There are commercials. That one-minute film was presented within the commercials before the feature films in Sweden. It was like a switch like a dream of a thing. It was this idea that a one-minute film is surrounded by a commercial but there was nothing to sell and nothing to buy. There's no subject, no object just a moment of drift and dream. That soundtrack of Varese was on that one minute. I always like Varese because he was the most contemporary musician. He invented so many notions of the drop of strings and the use of drums. This idea to produce something in sync with the world. All this reflection and text was quite crucial for me.

This is Edgar Varese 'Desert'.

—

Looking at that thing where you're relating to film structure, it makes me think of your marquee works which are amazing. Essentially, where you're creating these flashing sculptural objects that resemble the entranceway to old theatres, and cinemas. Can you tell me about where that concept came from and what you find interesting about it, in relationship to performance?

I always played with labels at the beginning. One of the first large exhibitions I did at the Museum of Modern Art, I use labels which would be flashing with the light, so they will be catching your attention. The marquee is an extension of that as it's a place where normally you see the name of the object or film. The name has been erased and there only remains that thing that catches your attention. I thought it would be interesting to use an object as a marker of time and sound. I started to twist that thing a bit and then use it like you produce a synthesizer. The electricity and go through the marquee and produce its own soundtrack. When I did a show at the Armory, I put them all together and they produce a large symphony of some sort. What Mallarmé called 'YX', which was a word that was invented because it sounded great. For a marque is something that sounds good. It occupies a place in private or public collections, on walls and doors where normally you don't see any art. And when they come together to produce something else. They produce some of a symphony or polyphony and I was interested by that aspect – of a recollection of object producing something more than the assemblage of all the objects together.

Let's play probably your final track. Let's play the Mac Miller 'Small Worlds'. You want to tell me where you came across this?

It's also a bit like the first one before that. It's something that I like. That I discovered with my son which makes me really happy. I really like that song.

It seems like a very nice thing to listen to. This is Mac Miller 'Small Worlds' and thank you very much Philippe for taking the time.

Thank you so much.

Sebastian Jefford

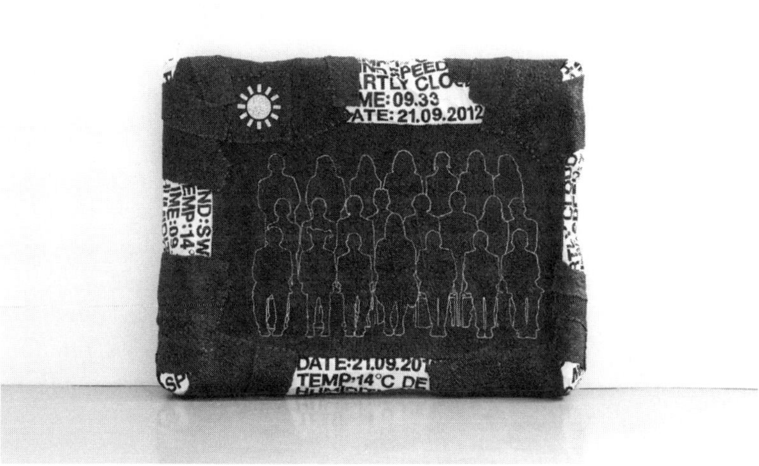

Whatever the weather, the sun always shined on Friday mornings, 2022.

29.01.21

Hi. You're listening to Rough Version on NTS, and my guest this month is Sebastian Jefford. He's a British artist and graduate of the Royal Academy who works with everything from sculpture to video, writing to drawing. He's exhibited in New Contemporaries and Hauser and Wirth Somerset and has currently escaped the UK for Berlin. How are you?

I'm good. I'm good. I'm just sitting in my flat looking at the snow come down.

Oh, yeah. It's all fluffy. It's fluffy. I think the most obvious thing to talk about first, when looking at your work, is the puffiness. You make a lot of puffy objects. I wanted to know how that develops? What was your thinking behind that roundness?

I suppose, aside from other things, I'm pretty preoccupied with thinking about images. As in image culture. How basically, almost all the information that we send to each other back and forth, receive on a daily basis, is usually, these days, in the form of images. I'm always interested in trying to find new ways of thinking about images that aren't necessarily just through using an image or, for example, painting, or anything like that. I think, for a long time, I was trying to articulate something. And it took me a while to realize that the best way to articulate this kind of physicality of the image was through using sculpture. I was always very interested in this idea of the image as something that has a life of its own. Something that inflates and deflates.

Like a balloon.

Like a balloon, yeah. I mean, it sounds ridiculous, but a metaphor that I always use when I was making these works was this idea that an image, the viral image, for example, gets inflated to the point of capacity and then it bursts. Then it lies on the streets, until it's picked up by someone else who patches up the hole and re-inflates it. Because I'm always thinking about redundancy, reused images, and this idea of the reconstructed, I suppose.

You can see when you're looking at a lot of your objects. They feel very handmade. You're really aware of your engagement with it. They look like you've sewn bits of plaster or something together. They look a bit tacked-on somehow.

I deliberately make them to almost look like they're made of a clay-like material, something that feels very dense. But in actual fact, they are made of this very light foam and then painted. They're actually tacked together by jacket fasteners, like on a garment. I'm interested in this idea that they sit between painting, sculpture, a garment or some kind of covering. That idea of covering something like a skin, or a veneer or something. They often have these nostalgic images or narratives. I'm interested in this idea of being quite overly simplified or overly binary. Tired ideas or something tattered.

Let's play a track because you've brought in some good ones, and I think it's a good entryway. Let's play the Oneohtrix Point Never. Why did you choose this one?

I've been a fan of his for a really long time. And I really like the way that every album he makes has its own concept. There is almost something similar to prog rock with him, for me. That every album is like a concept album. But when this album came out, initially I felt really disappointed and hated it. Now I'm obsessed with it. I did a full-on U-turn.

Which is all good. Do you listen to stuff in your studio, as a soundtrack to your making?

Yeah. My making is very, very repetitive. That's just the nature of it. But repetition is something that I'm interested in. Repetition is this process of deformation. A bit like the way if you repeat a word in your mouth, if you repeat a word again and again, its form and its meaning, when you say it with your mouth, become quite unrecognisable. Almost breaks down.

Don't think about the word 'which' too much otherwise it comes really fat and strange.

Exactly. Exactly. And I guess that comes back to that idea of the puffiness of the sculptures. As you said, becomes really fat. I'm aware of its physicality.

Well, here's a fattish track. This is 'Lost But Never Alone' by Oneohtrix Point Never.

—

Let's get back to thinking about another thing that I think really comes across is an awareness of architecture. Sometimes you've made things that resemble buildings somehow and you're often playing around with the architecture and space. Where did that start coming from? What are your thoughts about space?

There have been moments when I've done more interventions in the space. For example, building a roof that goes around the perimeter of a very low-ceilinged room. That was actually a reference that came from a Pieter Breughel painting. I've also made these works that are more, they literally are like architectural models. They're made in clear Perspex. For most people, it's like one of the horrible things about Perspex, but I quite like it because it really makes it wear time on its sleeve. Basically, Perspex because of the way it interacts with static in the air, attracts dust. It's quite fragile to scratches, and that sort of thing. But these architectural models were a direct reference to the Palace of Knossos, which is an archaeological site in Crete. In the 1910s, it was basically this piece of land that, in this quite classic British-colonial way, this aristocrat called Arthur Evans, just bought the land, and decided that he was going to do an archaeological dig on it.

Oh, my favourite. The British ones who mess it up and destroy everything.

He gets top marks for this because he actually built directly onto the original remains of the Minoan civilization with concrete. And it's still there today. I've never been, but it looks quite surreal. All his findings of this civilization that were very peace-loving, came out to be false in the 1980s when they found that the civilization there actually practiced human sacrifice, and were very war-like. I quite like this. Well, I don't like it, but I'm interested in this idea that he used the remains of another civilization to project his own political and historical desires onto, in this quite problematic way.

That's also a great metaphor for what art history or contemporary art does in some way.

Exactly. A lot of the objects that he had his restoration team make are now in museums all around the world, and they're apparently completely bogus.

That's even weirder. Like you're not happy with real history, so you make up your own fake history.

Exactly. Yeah.

Wild. Let's play another track, because I fancy it. Let's play the Mica Levi and Oliver Coates, who's an artist. When did you first hear this track?

I think it was probably 2016. Probably when the record first came out, really. Don't have much to say about it. It speaks for itself. It's just a great one.

I'm going to say it's 'Xhill Stepping' by Mica Levi and Oliver Coates.

Yeah, I don't have any idea how you're supposed to say it.

Zil? 'Xhill Stepping' by Mica Levi and Oliver Coates.

—

Another thing that I've seen in some of your exhibitions is your love and awareness of keys. Do you want to tell me about the key, and why you have made them so large? They're just great. Tell me about your keys.

I just was walking along the street one day, and I found a key on the floor. It seems to do this strange thing with scale, where you feel like you've found literally the key to someone's life, in a way. If you found their house, you could walk in and be immersed in their world, but at the same time, it makes the city or wherever you are, all of a sudden seem completely enormous. Because the idea that you could ever possibly find the right door just becomes ridiculous. There's this interesting relationship to scale with the key that I wanted to play with. Also, it has a relationship to sculpture. The key is one of the last analogue pieces of technology that's carved in quite sculptural way.

Yeah, literally ground into a shape. In the context of your work, a lot of your stuff seems to reference domestic spaces somehow. Things that look like windows with curtains. Things that almost look like radiators somehow. There seems to be something about the interior of places.

The windows, they do have this sense of interiority. I guess I was thinking of it less in a psychological way, but more in response to what seemed to be a very prevalent narrative in the UK, which is this idea of a rose-tinted past where everything was better. When children played on village greens. This idea of a toxic nostalgia which over the past few years just seems to be becoming more and more visible…

We believed, at some point. The propaganda became real. Because it was propaganda. Even then that wasn't even reality. Basically Brexit.

Yeah, literally. The absurdity of feeling angry about this kind of stuff resulted in making tiny little curtain windows.

You want tell me about how you approach colour. Because the colour that's quite acid. You'll use crazy yellows or weird pastel turquoise or this orangey red. How did colour come into it for you?

I'm always drawn to colours that you get on safety signage. It's quite interesting you said these acidic yellows. These colours are almost designed to catch your attention or be deliberately repellent somehow. A lot of my techniques are hobbyist in a way. I use this hobby hobbyist technique of dry brushing. We basically get a brush that's very dry and brush it over the surface and it brings out the texture. I do that on these bright colours to give it this sense of being quite knackered, or scuffed, or tired, or even oily. I quite like that contrast between toxic colours and time impacted upon them.

> *Old toxicity. On that note let's play another one of your tracks. Let's play Sun Ra. We had a few Sun Ra's in the past, why this one?*

I've obviously known about Sun Ra, but only recently I've started listening to him. This one has just been on repeat in the studio recently.

> *Well perfect studio listening. This is 'When There Is No Sun' by Sun Ra.*
>
> —
>
> *I want to talk about your curatorial project, Moss – which is moss.org.uk – and has included a lot of people that have been on past shows. Do you want to tell me a little bit about what the project is and what you're asking artists to do in it?*

Moss is basically a very bare-bones website that has a list of artists, and each artist has compiled a list of their top 10 favourite YouTube videos. I always say to people, you can either keep it really simple, and it can be your top favourite songs ever or you could use it to construct a narrative. One thing I always say to people is I like this idea of using the playlist almost as a way into the artist's work. I feel like artists, their music tastes in some way comes out in their work.

> *I agree with you, clearly. You've got people like Mark Leckey and Larry Achiampong, and then lots of younger artists like Nicholas Cheveldave and Lewis Teague Wright, who was your first show and also a long running NTS resident.*

Yeah. Fervent Moon.

> *Love a bit of Fervent Moon. And it's also almost feels like their lists are curatorial somehow. It's really amazing, the breadth*

of stuff that you're getting out of them. Do you have favourite shows on here?

I can't say. That's too difficult.

The Sung Tieu one was just brilliant for me.

I agree. That was probably one of my favourites actually.

She has a really fascinating selection of music, outside what you'd expect.

Exactly. I mean, just part of the motivation for starting it was, just trying to beat the bloody Spotify algorithm, because it just recommends you the same stuff all the time. And it's just this wanting to hear what other people are listening to, at the end of the day.

I recommend listening to this way more than I recommend listening to Spotify. It's a really fascinating selection. Also, there is something really great about the fact that your website literally is a bunch of names. It's incredibly low-fi, for someone whose work is very image-led or aesthetic. It's really interesting that your curatorial stuff is almost dry.

I just want the focus to be on the list, on the playlist.

I definitely recommend it, moss.org.uk. Just a last thing, do you want to tell me a little bit about your process? I know that you've done drawings, I remember, I saw you selling some of those earlier during the Artist Support Pledge. Do you want to tell me a little bit about how things move from an idea into a realisation. Do you do a lot of research? Or is it much more things you stumble across?

Well, it's a bit of both, really… I'll be like reading and researching about, as I mentioned earlier, I am directly referencing but then they might not be immediately apparent. It's funny actually, artists always have these strange tangents of research, but I was researching about pottage, which is this medieval gelatinous soup that was basically it would be kept on the stove for days at a time. And people would add ingredients, depending on what was available, or what they wanted. The dish would essentially change over time. As different flavours breakdown, the top would taste different to the bottom. But essentially, it's this process of these ingredients almost fermenting together. And it really just resonated with me in terms of thinking about how I make work really. It is a process of fermentation in a way.

> *Nice, and the fact that your work is textured, it almost could look a little bit like it's fermented and grown. It feels a little bit tactile. You've now explained Pease Pottage to me, which I always wondered what it was, and now I understand. Apart from being somewhere in Sussex, I think. We're going to play your last track, which is 'Terpsichore'. Do you want to tell me about this particular track from 'Terpsichore'?*

I don't really know much about old music, but I just stumbled upon it. I can't remember where I found out about it. But there was this musicologist called David… He did a series on the, on the BBC in the '70s, where he was exploring old music and they would reconstruct old instruments and play the old music. And this is an old instrument called rackets. But I really like it because it almost sounds like cluster or like a really nasty synthesizer… It just found its way into a new video I'm making, so it's been on my mind.

> *Do you want to tell me a little bit more about the video work? How is that emerging? Because I've seen other ones of your videos, and it seems to be playing a lot around time. Very much from a London context. It was shot on the top of a London bus. Do you want to tell me about the new video work?*

Yeah, it's kind of an extension of that video that you would have seen in Gianni Manhattan. I was riding the DLR, this time around the docklands because there's one route where it's amazing because you go past the Emirates cable car and the Millennium Dome. But then in front of that, you have just all these waste disposal sites. This quite amazing contrast. I'm not sure where it's going at the moment, but it's a landscape video. And I'm trying to combine it with that track.

Which is quite medieval.

Yeah. But it seems to just say a lot about the UK in some way. It's so English, you know?

This is a 1974 digital remastering by Michael Praetorius and the early music concert with London of the Courante from 'Dances From Terpsichore'. And before we play that, I'm just going to say thank you so much for, Sebastian, as I should probably call you, officially, for coming in. If people want to see more of your work, go look at Gianni Manhattan Gallery, based in Vienna. You can see some of the great stuff that you're making and thank you so much.

Thanks for having me, pleasure.

Tanoa Sasraku

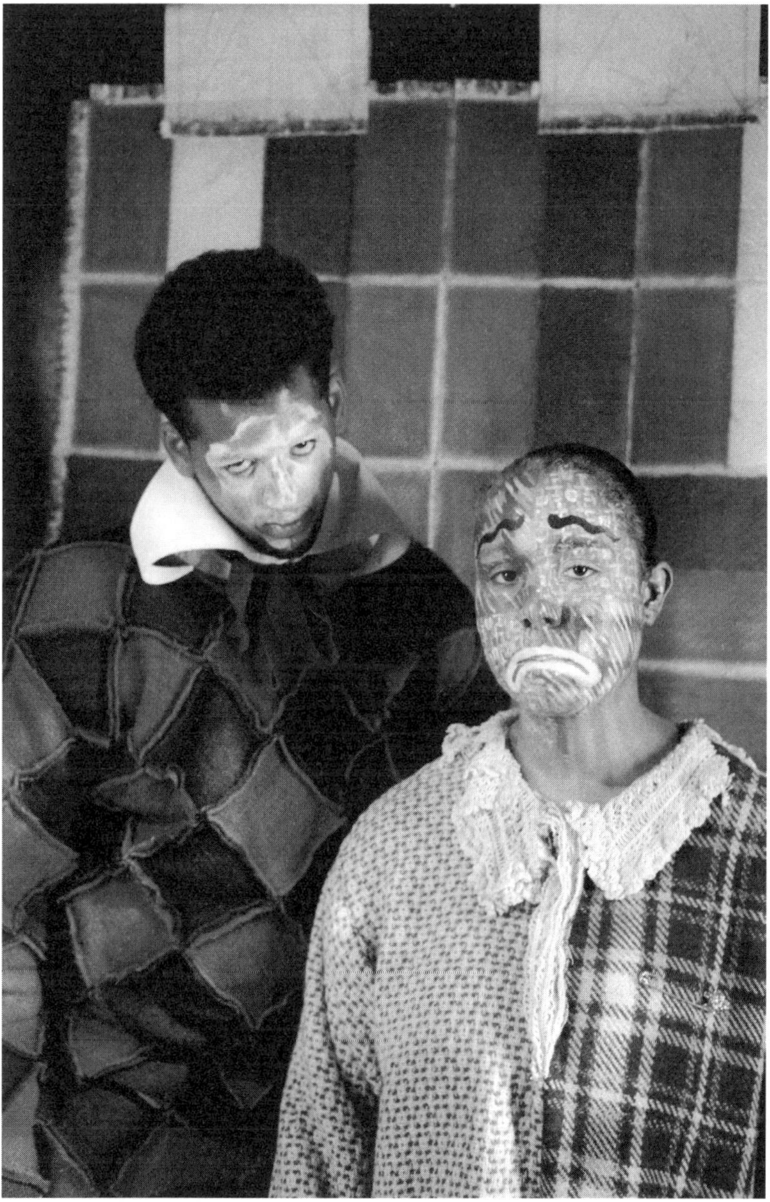

O' Pierrot, 2019.

26.02.21

Hello, I'm Francesca Gavin and you're listening to Rough Version on NTS. My guest this month is Tanoa Sasraku. A London based graduate from Goldsmiths, who's about to start at the Royal Academy. She was the winner of the 2021 Arts Foundation Futures Award, and works with film, flags, fabric, and drama. Tanoa, how are you?

I'm very well, thank you. Yeah, it's great to be on here. This is kind of like my Desert Island Discs dreams for me come true.

It's exciting for me too. I want to start at the beginning because most of the work that people have probably seen out there, or that you've gained recognition for, is film. And I want to know what appealed to you about that medium, and why?

I really had to re approach my practice, when I got to my final year at Goldsmiths. I was feeling a bit fraudulent because I'd been working in installation with bought and found objects for a while. I was just feeling totally dissatisfied with my practice. And I guess at Goldsmiths you're taught primarily how to think differently, how to break down your thought process rather than traditional art making skills. But I really wanted to turn back to something craft-based, where I could really use my hands in my final year. And I was lucky enough, sticking with that decision I was making, to have Rosalind Nashashibi as my final year tutor, who is obviously a very acclaimed artist, moving image maker and painter. I'd seen her film 'Jack Straw's Castle' at Lux, which is this beautiful 16mm documentation of gay men cruising in Hampstead Heath.

I grew up near to Jack Straws Castle, so I know.

No way? Oh, cool. I had just never seen light translated that way. I guess it was my introduction to analogue film via seeing her works. I just wanted to give it a go and try documenting these sculptures I was making out of paper, these flags. I bought myself a super eight camera and started going out onto the moors in Devon. It was just a bit of an experimentation, to be honest, in documenting sculptures in the landscape.

What's so interesting as well is – looking at the two films I've seen of your work – is that it's got this really nice, almost lo-fi texture. There's a real sense of the physicality of film. This aesthetic, which is so different from the film we're so used to doing on, let's say, digital media, or phones, even high-definition TV.

Yeah, particularly in 'O' Pierrot'. I really wanted to use a film stock that would replicate the fabrics in the costumes. All the costumes are made from wool. I'd been looking a lot at tartan, as well as looking back at mud cloth that my dad used to work with. He was a couture designer in the '90s. I just felt like capturing those costumes and those characters on analogue film would provide this painterly, sort of frayed quality that was really important to the essence coming out of the characters as well. They're all quite frayed. 8mm just worked perfectly for that.

I'm going to go into 'O' Pierrot' in more detail because it's such an amazing film. Before I do that, looking at the wider aspect of your work with that 'O' Craw Baby', another film, which is very much erecting a flag by yourself in the middle of windy, rural British landscape. I think both of those films seem to have an underlying criticality of British expectation; shall we say that? Or an idea of what Britishness is. Would you say that that's the thing that connects those two pieces?

Definitely. I've been thinking a lot about the sort of shadow of colonialism that I grew up under in rural England. I grew up in a seaside city. Plymouth is a port city but mostly it feels rural, in terms of the mentality of the people there and the lack of diversity of faces that you're seeing. My happiest times were spent in the rural landscape when I would just get away from the city and go to the moors and just spend – I mean, it would have been weeks in total over my teenage years. Just trekking and camping and understanding the landscape, but it was a complicated experience because its simultaneously lonely and very harsh, but also profound in its brutality, as well.

'O' Craw Baby' really got across a lot of those sensations. This emptiness. Maybe it was a poetic representation of the isolation perhaps that you experienced?

Yeah, definitely, I would say so. I had kind of been dreaming of escaping the Southwest for so long and then I finally ended up in London, and then decided that I wanted to really try and confront the loneliness and isolation I felt as a teenager very strongly. It's also just helped me to rebuild a bit of a relationship with my hometown, because it can be easy to just walk away and not come back at all. But I do want to also try and show maybe other biracial kids, gay kids down there – anyone who feels marginalized, growing up in that part of the country – that your story matters. That you can capture your home and use it as a metaphor for a lot of intense emotions you may have experienced growing up there.

> *Well on that note, before we go on to talk more, let's play your first track. This is the first time I've ever played Madonna 'Drowned World/Substitute for Love' on the show. Do you want to tell me when you first heard this and why it resonates with you?*

When I was two, my family essentially broke apart and my mum took me back to Plymouth in Devon with one of my older brothers and this album. She must have bought soon after we returned home – she just used to play it on loop. I remember standing and staring at this album cover as a kid and this blond, blue-eyed women on the cover just matched my mom completely in my mind and I think for a while I thought Madonna was my mum. When I hear her voice on this incredible album it just makes me feel like I'm hearing the voice of my mother, so that's why I picked this track.

> *From the most lovely, emotional reference to Madonna ever this is 'Drowned World/Substitute for Love' by Madonna.*
>
> —
>
> *One of the recurring things in your work has been flags and you've got an interesting relationship to them. They almost feel like characters or like narrative objects in what you do. I've read that they also reference Ghanaian protest flags. Do you want to tell me a little bit about how they developed and what you're making them out of?*

These flags reference, I guess it's the biggest link to my paternal heritage via my late father, who was Ghanaian. We're Fanti. Most people who have Ghanaian heritage originate from one of the nine major tribes. The Fanti used to reside typically on the Cape Coast in southern Ghana, what was known as the Gold Coast during the colonial era. When the British decided to colonise this part of Ghana to basically steal the gold from the area, the Ghanaians used to create these incredible flags, which would tell through these naive motifs and visual metaphors, and taunts and proverbs, would tell the story of the mechanisation of their people, and the story of colonialism. I just couldn't believe I didn't know about them until three or so years ago. I decided to take that structure of using tokens and symbols to tell my own story of growing up in Britain and this tug between my heritage being both Ghanaian and British and what that means. I'd started learning to draw again in my final year at Goldsmiths, on newsprint. Working with stencilling ink-jet prints. Really like basic classroom techniques and was really enjoying how ink locks into the fibres of newsprint. In a way that it sits on top of most other cheap papers. I wanted to find a way to make these drawings and works on paper more robust. I turned to a sewing machine and just started experimenting with appliqué and paper, stitching like 20 layers of paper together using these Japanese bookbinding techniques to draw these panels together and ended up with these really – what I think – are really unique, robust, ceremonial objects made out of classroom materials.

They are amazing. The textural side of that is also really fascinating. The fact that you're using newspaper to make anything is also really interesting. Because also, if nothing else, that says something about the perpetuation of knowledge. The flag is a character, the Union Jack within 'O' Pierrot' as well. Union Jack is really this horrific trickster, lying version of what the union jack is. I found it very interesting. What did you like about the idea of making the flag as a person somehow? I mean, apart from the fact that obviously, whenever that flag was created – I'm assuming the 18th century – it was the personification of nations.

I guess I was really interested in how we relate to colour and how colour combinations and the interaction of colour can rouse these very specific feelings in us. I was looking at artists Joseph Albers, Annie Albers and reading some of their books. When you get red, white and blue pushed together in that way, I feel like as a British person, me specifically who'd been looking at these Asafo flags, which always had the union jack in the top left-hand corner, watching over these interactions that are happening within the frame of the flag. It was like the flag is totally a character and it dictates a lot of, I guess patriotism and nationalism in that way. That it can incite very specific behaviour. When it's football season and the St. George's Cross is being painted on people's bodies and brandished out of windows it has quite an intense effect, that motif. I wanted to create – you'll notice that the red, white and blue in that flag and then the harlequins costume are all very muted. It's almost like dried blood and faded blue and incorporating the peephole into the flag allows the harlequin to both be the flag and then pull it away from himself revealing his matching jersey. I like that a character, the sinister character, could step out of the union jack, and then taunt the protagonist and then merge back into it as part of the scenery.

Just to describe the way 'O' Pierrot' functions, it is essentially – this is how I would describe it – a horror, fantasy, silent film that's doing a metaphorical description of colonialism. With you dressed up as the Pierrot character, but it is a very different take from the traditional commedia dell'arte. It's closer to taking the format of a silent movie and then doing a really twisted version of it. Obviously, that was part of the intention using that format?

I had been watching a lot of surrealist avant-garde films like – I always cite these three, but they are the ones which really struck me. '*8 ½*' by Fellini, '*Orphée*' by John Cocteau, and suddenly the third one's escaped my mind…

There's a Maya Deren 'Meshes of the Afternoon' vibe in there too.

Yeah. I think when you see dream sequences or nightmare sequences conveyed silently or with certain sounds, certain folie way louder than you would expect, and maybe a stare that lingers a bit too long… I just feel like dreams and nightmares are the ultimate visual moving image inspiration. I just really wanted to try and capture that on 8mm. I think working with a low budget and super limited means was the most exciting way to try and depict something that's so surreal, and so intense and believable when you're in it. When you're asleep.

The texts that you're interspersing between quite terrifying imagery and a very original take on what you're doing. Where did that come from because it's sort of in rhyming verse? Some of it seems to be this awful, pseudo-minstrel language, other parts of it feels very almost Dutch. I was curious how you put together the poetry of it.

The main stanzas and dialogue that the harlequin rants down the lens at the viewer, and by proxy at Pierrot, are just intersplicing of – I slightly edited some of the verses – but lifted from a minstrel era song called 'Jump Jim Crow', which was the minstrel protagonist of Jim Crow's – it's supposed to be his kind of anthem or whatever. This gross stumped speech, caricatured poem, if you can call it that. And then the other part is really, is actually lesser-known passages from the National Anthem, the British National Anthem, which have been, I guess, put out of use because they're pretty sinister.

Wow. That's amazing.

So that was from the, I guess the early 1900s. That's what people would have been singing at the Jubilee or at the football or whatever.

They're quite clearly about like, "we're not going to do any work while you do it, we're just going to dance while you essentially do stuff for us". I mean, it's quite horrific. Before we talk more about the film, I think we should play another track. I think we should play aptly 'Danse Macabre' by Camille Saint-Saëns. Tell me about this track. I mean, it's quite beautifully familiar. Where did you first hear it?

Myself and my partner Kirsty Black worked on 'O' Pierrot' together and she composed the score and the sound design using live instruments. While I would be trekking down from North London to Goldsmith's library to try and edit the footage, she would be at home in Southgate where we were staying together, composing the sound design and the score. I was looking for something sort of rhythmically to edit the footage to, and she suggested that this Sisyphean, rolling, undulating structure of 'Danse Macabre' would work perfectly for it. So that's what I edited 'O' Pierrot' to, so that's why I've chosen it.

Oh amazing. It's referencing it, but not what we actually hear. I love that. Well, this is Camille Saint-Saëns 'Danse Macabre' performed by Leopold Stokowski and the National Philharmonic Orchestra.

—

That was 'Danse Macabre'. Let's talk about the choreography that's within your work, like the use of bodies, I mean, there's even dance sequences but also even not. In 'O' Pierrot' your movements are a choreographed idea you're stomping out. It's almost like running in a loop, these same choreographies but then they all slightly twist into weirder and weirder versions.

In 'O' Pierrot' I took, or at least referenced a lot of the gesture from Kenneth Anger's film 'Rabbit's Moon', which was my first introduction into the Pierrot narrative. I was writing about that film for my dissertation at Goldsmiths. This kind of repetitive action of the reaching upwards and the shielding of one's eyes and then this one gesture that I found so moving, this begging gesture, while Pierrot's kind of looking down their navel at the object of their desire. I really wanted to pay homage to that film. Then in tandem Harlequin Jack's gestures, my friend Kaivalya Brewerton is a dancer and a movement choreographer, and she worked with Mickey, who was the amazing actor that played the Harlequin. Yeah, he was fantastic. He was the first person that sent me an audition tape for it and just nailed it instantly. And he's got such long limbs, he's huge. Kaivalya just really got him to utilize the extent of his limbs and to take on this flamboyant, perverse leering, physicality. That was exciting. I would just train with him in a studio space, and we would just dance together to different tracks that Kaivalya would choose and really get to know each other's way of moving so it made it supernatural, when we were actually shooting on set.

> *I feel really weird about talking about the makeup, but the makeups interesting because you're doing an almost minstrel makeup, but it's also like a flag minstrel makeup. It really exaggerates everyone's facial expressions in a really unnerving way. Do you want to tell me a little bit about – obviously, in 'O Crawl Baby' or your other work it's very much – it's so natural compared to how stylized things are in the second film.*

I guess with the clown's mouth that I'm wearing as 'O' Pierrot', and every time an emotion from my character switches, the mouth flips in inverse. It's either arching upwards or arching downwards. I was thinking at the time about this assumption of sometimes a lack of complexity that I feel a lot of white people assume about Black people and how we relate to trauma and pain and anger and melancholy, particularly. I feel like there isn't much of a depiction of the complexity of melancholy that Black people experience which, of course, is just as wide ranging as all of that which is depicted in music, particularly from white bands and artists. I wanted to do a little satirical nod to that assumption of stock, emotional responses in my makeup. Then with the harlequin's makeup, I guess I wanted him performing white face because his character is this tragic, vulnerable villain, who has been aspiring to whiteness for so long, and proximity to whiteness, that it's just consumed him. And he in turn is trying to encourage Pierrot to strive for her white potential, being a biracial figure. It was really exciting being able to have Olivia, my makeup artist apply painstakingly, this scalloped white face paint every morning and then just having Mickey dragging it off his face with his black gloves. It kind of sticking everywhere and the messiness of what it is to constantly be striving for something that you will never attain was exciting to depict through the makeup.

> *It comes across well. Let's talk a bit about the costumes. I know you've mentioned earlier that your father was a fashion designer, and you made all the costumes within the piece. Do you want to tell me in a wider sense, how the experience*

of having your father doing that kind of creative visual work influenced what you do?

I didn't grow up around my dad, but when I did start going to Ghana in sort of my early teens, I would exclusively be plonked down in the studio and watch him pattern cutting and stitching and interacting with his assistants all day and dressing models and doing fittings. I definitely got a sense of the gesture and approach to creating silhouettes that he applied. He was the sort of person, in the style of McQueen, who could just look at someone's body and just draw the pattern for a garment. I'd like to think that with me starting to learn how to sew with the flags, that something of my dad was coming out of me in that way. I was based at Academy Costumes, which is an amazing costumier in South London from June until September 2019 and just immersed myself in the workshop there. Working with all the patterns that they had in stock working with makers and just learning on the job basically how to create every single type of silhouette and bulge and shape that would be in both character's costumes. It was again a series of experimentations and learning on the job, with a lot of guidance from friends and other makers.

Let's play another track. Let's play your Faithless track. Why this one? And when did you first hear it?

Faithless is one of my favourite bands just as a disclaimer. When I was a kid, obviously growing up in Plymouth, my mum would take me to London quite a lot because all my family pretty much live in London and have grown up in London. I remember being six years old, just hearing whenever we'd be walking around the streets – like muffled from cars – hearing a lot of these big trance, floor-filler anthems. Particularly, I think 'Insomnia' was the first track I heard, naturally, and it really stuck with me. I've been listening to them consistently since I was a child. So, 'Drifting Away' is one of my favourite Faithless tracks.

This is 'Drifting Away' by Faithless.

—

Can I ask you what you're working on now? Because

you're about to go into the RA I believe, which is great. Congratulations. You've also just won an award, as you enter the RA, which is a very unusual situation to be in. I'm curious about how you see your work developing because, yeah, I'm just curious where you're taking it.

I'm in a bit of a tug within myself because of the way that lockdown is just extending. I feel like I'm running out of time, before I get there and get to the RA. And need to really focus on my studio practice, to still fulfil my filmmaking ambitions, outside of a studio context. Lockdown has been great for me in terms of my practice. I've gone back to drawing and been really developing. I've gotten really into a lot of Neo-geometric artists, people like Peter Schiff, particularly. I've totally fallen in love with his work and been working with textile structures like tartan and mud cloths, and kente, creating lots of stencils. Working with quality of light and quality of colour a lot more in these gestural, geometric works. I've got this exciting opportunity coming up at the Chelsea Sorting Office in West London, which is a huge, huge space. It's this double-layered hanger where I've got the opportunity to do a solo show. I've been working on all this work to fill and augment this space from my bedroom, from my tiny bedroom, so it's been a strange experience trying to wrestle with that. I think my studio practice is going in quite an exciting direction in that way because of that juxtaposition of scale that I've been forced into. But in my moving image works, myself, and Kirsty, who worked on the music in 'O' Pierrot' have been developing the treatment for a new horror fantasy, queer retelling of the Selkie folklore, which is a Scottish folklore of these shapeshifting seals. And this Greek tragedy unfolds. It will allow me to home in on my experience growing up by the sea, rather than just growing up in rural England, but my relationship to the sea, as a biracial person, as a gay person. That prize money is partially going towards developing that film, but we'll just have to see the timelines are so unpredictable.

Time does no longer exist in any form whatsoever! It's interesting that you're still going to, and I'm really pleased, because it's just incredibly memorable, that your take on surreal, fantasy, horror is going to be developed in a new direction. One argues that's probably one of the most interesting tropes in contemporary cinema that's really happening, let's say post-Get Out, which I think had such a huge effect. But your work feels very much more to have a Cocteau avant-garde heritage to it. It's really re-conditioning how the avant-garde is positioned and the role of Blackness within that. And what you as a director are allowed to be creating, like Black surrealism is something that's not necessarily been explored.

Exactly. I think it was the realisation of that when I started, investigating into cinema and the historical canon a bit more, that I wanted to almost retroactively fill that space that's been left in the canon, but do it in a contemporary way. And I just love folklore. I think there haven't been enough Black or brown characters in contemporary iterations of traditional folklore. It's exciting to be able to work with this material.

Amazing. We're going to play your last track. It's very timely. Do you want to tell me why you chose 'Is It Cold in The Water?' by SOPHIE?

I think a lot of people in the queer community have been listening to this song, particularly, since SOPHIE's untimely passing a few weeks ago. But this question 'Is It Cold in The Water?' really struck me when writing and rereading this story that we've written about this protagonist that falls in love with this shape shifting seal, who's from the water and the seal is luring and convincing the protagonist to end her life and enter the water so they can be together forever and find love in the depths. I just feel like the protagonist would be asking – this would be the first question – that she would ask to her mythical lover. It's just a beautiful track.

It's amazing. Well, thank you very much Tanoa for coming in and doing the show.

Thanks so much for having me. It's been great.

Tai Shani

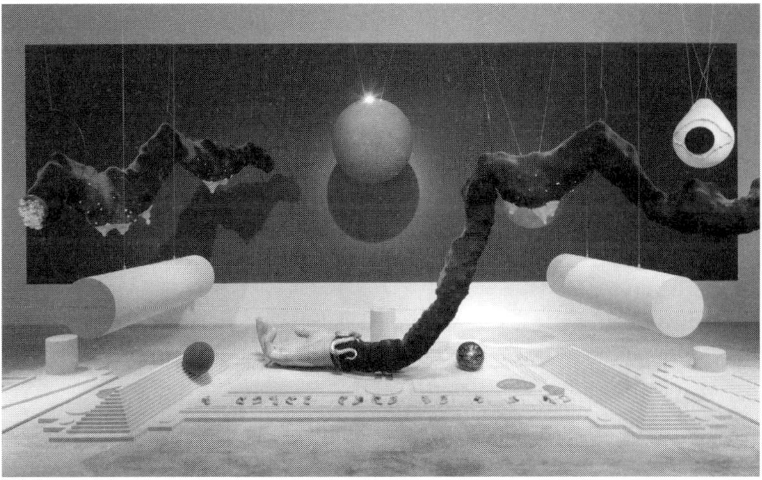

DC Semiramis, 2019.

25.03.21

Hi, you're listening to Rough Version on NTS, and my guest this month is Tai Shani. She's the co-winner of the 2019 Turner prize. She works with performance, installation, photography, video; has exhibited at Glasgow International, The Tetley and her book Our Fatal Magic is published by Strange Attractor Press. How are you Tai?

Very well. Thank you for inviting me on your show.

It's so my pleasure. Let's talk about the breadth of what holds your work together. I'm really interested in what you think the underlying thing is for you. Is it narrative? What is it that holds the breadth of media together?

That's a good question. I think it's more affect than narrative, although the narratives obviously produce affects. I think there's certain tonal qualities that I've been attracted to and intrigued by. Often actually, they emanate from music, weirdly, or cinema. So, I'd say the kind of pull of reference for me is more music and cinema, than visual art. Often there are certain tonal qualities that I want to find a way to interpret into narrative, or into objects, or different kinds of artefacts, I guess. But it's often trying to find a way to, or a mode of translation for a quality, that I feel touched by in music. And then that obviously refracts into different lenses, like a political lens, and an aesthetic visual language. But I think that the thing that holds it together is strangely, an atmosphere and maybe a form of speculative or utopian thinking.

Just coming back to the music thing. I'm curious, is it specific music pieces? Or is it more genre, or a particular artist? Or is it just the atmosphere of the tracks? I'm curious to see how it's held together for you.

It can be something really, really tiny. Like one small segment of a track with how it relates to the light quality outside. It's these moments that feel very loaded in terms of feeling and are very profound, and there's no real reason for that, apart from the, I guess, engagement with what you're listening to. It's often very fleeting, that's the thing.

It's not really a process of looking at a full track, ever. It's often a moment, an ecstatic moment, or a moment of pure joy, or also the opposite. A moment where you feel very moved or very low or succumb to something. So, it's often these kinds of qualities that don't last very long, even in a song. It could be a few bars from one, an intro to a song, or something like that, it's quite random. I don't often have a handle on when it's going to happen, or how. It's not even that I necessarily refer back to it specifically. But they're just these moments that are very intense. I think intensity is probably the affect that binds my work. It's a mode of attention and a place that your subjectivity is maybe slightly different than it normally is in the everyday. I think those are the kinds of things that I try to achieve in the work.

> *You brought up the concept of utopia, and I find that interesting. Do you want to tell me a bit about what your idea of something utopic is? What is your utopia and how are you manifesting that in a performance work, for example, or a VR piece?*

I think I slightly backtracked when I said the word utopic, because I think it's something that offers a solution, and I don't have that. I don't think that there is a destination, in that way. I guess the closest thing that I could see as an ideal world would be an egalitarian, anarcho-communist world, where people self-governed but in a completely equitable, ethical way. So those are the very broad types of politics that underpin the work. But then you work back from where you are. I think with the project 'DC Productions', I was very much looking through a feminist lens and where I felt I was positioned socially when I began the project. It changed over time. A lot of conversations happened in those years during the project, and a lot of interesting ideas became more central to feminist thinking. And I think that's a good thing. I think that a shift from the – I don't know, maybe this interest in inscribing feminized experiences into culture, which is very much where I began the project, shifted towards thinking of a more intersectional kind of position. This was something that I feel was really an important part of making work over a long duration, as well as an opportunity to shift your position through engaging with your own work and other people through it. But I'm not sure any more about what I feel in terms of art as activism, if that makes sense. I think I've been quite vocal about how… I'm not sure that some of the paradoxes of the art world can really sustain the political radicality of some of the ideas. I think that there are ways to think about activism in a different way – for me anyway. I feel like I want the work to think about the politics of the world and I want it to contribute, but also I am an artist predominantly. That's completely what I do.

Politics is something I was going to bring up because if nothing else, you've also written quite vocally about how you feel the art world is moving towards the right or the far right. One could argue by extension that it ain't just the art world! It's generally like the political world full stop. But I find that interesting because when you look at your work, part of what's engaging about it is it doesn't feel so… Your take on activism is very playful and satirical and fun to look at and engage with. It's more welcoming than a lot of let's say, more politically active activist work.

I think that we should also reserve the right to have multiple ways of using our visibility and our platforms and our voices and they don't have to all coalesce as one thing. I think you can be an incredibly political abstract painter. Do you see what I mean? I think you can do these things. I think you can have the politics of a citizen and be an artist. I don't think that they are necessarily exclusionary of each other, so I think that that's also something that I'm coming to terms with a little bit more. As you say I am interested in the visual elaborateness that maybe isn't read directly as activism. I'm sure there's lots of problematic things about my practice. I use a lot of materials that aren't great in it, big things, and there's lots of questions around the sustainability of it. I think that you can advocate for things in different ways they don't all have to be through the work. I've been very fortunate that I have gained a little bit of visibility and I'm trying to use that in other ways that aren't necessarily directly through the work, as well.

Before we go on, let's pick one of your tracks. Let's start with – I'm going to mispronounce it because I always do on the show – Holger Czukay. Do you want to tell me a bit about why you chose the track?

I chose tracks that are a little bit of markers in time for me. I grew up in a very hedonistic environment. My dad used to DJ at parties in Goa and he loved Can and Holger Czukay. We travelled a lot in India, and there was always music around me. My dad very, very, very strongly believed in the poetics of music and the transformative powers of music. It was always something in our lives. I remember, when I was about 11, my dad took me to buy me one of these systems that have like a LP player, a record player, two tapes and a CD thing – like a little tower. It was important to him that music would be present in my life. I think he really encouraged me to be exploratory. I remembered this music. I hadn't heard it for years, and then I was living in a flat share in Dalston, and someone played it. And it was like this total arrow into my heart of really being thrown back there. I couldn't believe I was hearing this. Memories can be so fleeting and ungraspable and strange and mutating. Suddenly, this piece of reality from my childhood was present in this warehouse in Dalston. And it was very powerful for me. So, I chose this song, because it was a family favourite, really.

> *Bloody good taste your dad had too. This is Holger Czukay 'Fragrance (Ode to Perfume)'.*
>
> —
>
> *Let's talk a little bit about your background because it's so refreshing to me coming across people who have, let's say, very nonconformist experiences, and how that emerges in making work that's outside of the structure you're supposed to be like. I know that you struggled for a long time. Like you didn't get accepted to Goldsmiths multiple times. But before that, probably after Goa – or maybe before Goa – you were growing up in a commune in Israel? Do you want to tell me a little bit about the freedoms that you grew up with, and how you think they made you a different kind of artist?*

It's difficult to say because in Goa there were lots of casualties. Not everyone came out unscathed. It's difficult to imagine, but in the context of Goa, my parents were quite conservative compared to some of the other parents that had very radical and not safe practices around drugs and kids. I think my parents did want me to have a choice. They wanted me to be able to make a choice. I'm sure they wanted me to be unconventional. It was so central to how they lived their lives. But I think they definitely wanted me to not be put into that position, without being able to choose so myself. I didn't go to school until I was 10, which is quite late. And then I was thrown into the Western school system. That was a bit of… a huge wakeup call actually. I was very, very, very behind and ashamed. Very ashamed of not being able to follow. We were so different and strange. My parents were polyamorous, and I lived with my dad and his wife and my mum. So, two wives basically. It was very difficult to explain these things, so I had an on and off relationship with unconventionality. There were moments that I absolutely was so profoundly intimidated by convention, that there was nothing in the world that I wanted more than to be conventional, really. Both in the way I looked, and in our lives, and the things I aspired to. I think it's a strange mix of this push and pull between the two things. Its only through maybe through maturity that I was able to – the thing is that ultimately, when the establishment said "no" to me I did have these resources to draw on that made me want to continue. But I think it's also disingenuous, and I have tried in the past to make it very clear that growing up in a bohemian artistic family has incredible privileges in the art world. That I was able to become an artist because of them, because I was educated. My parents knew about interesting books and films and art. So, I did get an education. I wasn't coming completely from a different milieu, if that makes sense. So, I did have that privilege of coming in with some knowledge and some kind of capital. Unconventionality has its own capital, particularly in the art world.

> *I've read that you've curated something at The Horse Hospital. For me, coming from a straight art historical background, I found that space – which, by the way, I think we should all be supporting to continue – an interesting location, seriously. As an art space that connected to a really wide variety of people who would not feel comfortable going into white cube galleries or even museums. It was weird. Do you want to tell me about how you first got involved with them?*

When I came to London I was very, very naïve. It was 2001. I've told this story loads of times, but I basically just went door knocking on galleries, with some photographs of my work. I was a little bit I think defeated and someone said, "Oh, you should really go there, they're very open". And I went there, and it was the first place that said, "Why don't you come in?". When I called, they said, come in, like, "come and show it to me". It wasn't like, "Oh, send it in a self-addressed envelope, blah, blah, blah". It was like, "come and show me". I went with my VHS, and I showed them these three films that I'd made of children in the forest with punk songs. One was a Dead Boys song called 'I Want to Be a Dead Boy'. And the other one was a Misfit song called 'Mummy I Want to Go Out and Kill Tonight'. They liked the subcultural element of what I was doing. I'd been a fashion photographer before, so I think the visual language was also a little bit borrowed, maybe from that late '90s, grungy-type aesthetic. They were just incredibly welcoming. It was the first place like that, and I showed my work there a few times. It's one of these places that you can get involved in. You know what I mean? So, I started hanging out there. I was working for Shush at the time, the sex shop. I was making dildos for them, and I got a call. Roger from The Horse Hospital said that Heather was leaving – I'd already had a solo show there actually – but Heather was leaving who worked in the clothing archive, and if I wanted to take the job. I was working in a café, making dildos and I was also an usher at the Rio Cinema at the same time. He offered me a job in a place that I really wanted to work, and I was like, "Yeah, definitely". I went to work full-time there and then James Hollands, who was a curator at the time left. Roger was struggling to find someone. It's a very specific thing The Horse Hospital. It isn't a normal art space, and you have to not only have knowledge of counterculture and subcultures, but you have to be interested in that stuff. It's not just enough to know. It was difficult to find someone who was able to do it for the money – it wasn't very well paid – and was interested in the thing. I slowly started to just help with the gallery just to keep it running until he found someone, and eventually it became a full-time thing, and I was there for 12 years. And there were some amazing things. We did a program called 'Cults, Communes and Collectives', and we brought some incredible things. We brought the Unarius Academy of Science, which is a kind of positivist UFO cult in America. We bought lots of their costumes because they make – they're an outsider film practice, so we brought the films and their costumes. They came and did workshops. I mean, it was an incredible year of celebration of this genealogy that The Horse Hospital is very much a part of.

This seems like an appropriate moment to play your Mandy song, since it's also by children, by the Langley Schools Music Project. Do you want to tell me about why you chose this track?

This predates The Horse Hospital a little bit. I was working at the Cafe at Ray's Jazz in Foyles, if that makes sense. It was a real musical education for me to work there, because I often parasite on other people's musical taste. I've often discovered, I think everyone does, through partners through friends, that kind of thing. But this was really like an eye opener, because I'd never really ventured into that… I mean, it was predominantly jazz, but that's a very broad term so lots of things also got played there. I formed a folk band with one of the people that worked there. I remember hearing one of these songs played while I was working and just being like, "Oh my god". I spent so much money, but we had a discount on CDs from Rays Jazz. I first heard Ethiopian jazz there. Things where you're just suddenly like, "What is that? What are you playing?" And it was amazing to be like, "Oh, it's this", and then you could just take that home and listen to it. But it was a turning point for me in many ways, and I felt like that period was a departure from something and then entering something else. When I first arrived in London, I had so many awful jobs you wouldn't believe. Like really horrible situations. I think working at Rays Jazz was the first time I felt like I was part of something that I was interested in, even if it was really tangentially. I was making coffees, but I was making coffees in a space where really good music was being played. And that gave me a lot.

Ray's Jazz shop was so amazing. But even before that, before it was at Foyles, when it was in Covent Garden. I mean, I spent a lot of money on vinyl there. I miss that shop. No one talks about that shop. You're the only person that's ever mentioned it. But also, unconventional jobs, making dildos is definitely high up there. Anyways, this is 'Mandy' by the Langley Schools Music Project.

—

Let's go back to the work that you're making now. Do you want to tell me a little bit about how you approach installation and your approach to sculptural objects, and how those things come together?

I came out of performance. My installation work and my sculpture work definitely comes out of performance. I think that it was a process where I was making a lot of sets more temporary, quite bish, bash, bosh made sets for performances. And slowly, slowly, I started becoming more interested in what these objects were. It's difficult to put into words, but I think it's almost like gaining confidence and becoming more experimental. I started by doing very straight up things like a chair with something or something quite simple like that. And then I did this installation for the 'MIRRORCITY' show, and that was the first time, really, that I felt I exercised something that was beyond the temporariness of putting together a kind of setting. That was basically a mixture of props and whatever happened to be there. This was much more considered. I created an environment. There was something really powerful about that for me. And it worked really well for me. I was really happy with it. I think I've had these moments where something has fallen into place and that was definitely one of those. After that, it became something I wanted to continue doing and also I became more object-orientated in how I was thinking of these environments. Let's say things became less and less functional, and became more and more objects, really. I started thinking about them as like: Why is this a prop or not? Or why is this a set and not a sculpture? What makes that difference? And some of it is to do with how you make it, the care you put into it. How you think of it as autonomously away from any activation, let's say. I think it was a slow process. I think that visual things that I'm really, really obsessed with are always between figurative and abstract. If you think about an installation, that is somewhere between a performative space, a site and an installation. It also has an inherent figurativity embedded within that. There's the absence – not necessarily the absence of a person – but there's this suggestion that these things could exist in a slightly different way. I think that was what really started me thinking about sculpture in a more serious – not that it wasn't serious before – but in a more specific way. Then I was really fortunate to be invited to Wysing to do a residency there and it was, I've said this before, but it was again, one of these moments, where things fall into place. Where I had six weeks, and I was very focused. It was all I did really, make this installation that was a collaboration with Florence Peake called 'Andromedan Sad Girl'. It was like revelatory to myself, of what I wanted to pursue.

I'm going to play another track with you now. I'm going play to the Maxwell Sterling 'Tenderness' because I really liked it. Do you want to tell me about when you first heard this, and why you chose it?

I chose it because Max and I have been collaborating for a long time together. We met at Wysing, so it is quite a good segue as well. Max did an incredible soundtrack for a virtual reality play I did but also my forthcoming project called 'The Neon Hieroglyph', which launches at the end of the month. It's a nine-part film and Max has done one of the most beautiful soundtracks I've heard ever. We began collaborating, in quite an easy way. I asked him for a track, I think, for a film I made. Something he had lying around. But there's something about, again, this tonal register that I was talking about before. It's really one of the joys of my life, working with Maxwell. I have to say, it really, really is. It makes me feel so lucky when I hear the sketches he sends through and they're always in response to this body of work. I feel really grateful, you know? Sorry I sound so effusive, but it's true. It's really like an incredible thing finding someone like that.

It's really cute. This is Maxwell Sterling 'Tenderness'.

—

Looking at your work, it's interesting, a couple of different narrative formats come up. That's either things like science fiction, or let's say ancient Greek tragedy. You're almost a weird pop lyrical midpoint between those two things. What do you like about those structures?

OK. I think in Greek myth and Greek tragedy, Greek poetry, Greek theatre – there is this blueprint of Western civilization. These are stories that we retell all the time. They are archetypes that get reinvented.

There is something mind-blowing to me about that. That they sustain themselves somehow, these stories. 'Antigone' is a story that is as relevant today about state violence as it ever was. It's a story that gets reinvented all the time. Well, it doesn't even need reinvention. It gets adapted all the time. To me, there's something really compelling about that. But also, I like the idea of a pagan world where the gods are amongst us. I really like that idea. Because I think that music does that as well. It makes you feel like you're guided by voices, somehow. That you're there with something that's much bigger than yourself. To me, even thinking about the idea of the muses as these kinds of entities. Obviously, I try and think about these things in a more abstracted form, in a kind of an animist form almost like these gods are these energetic fields that live amongst us. I'm interested in what it would feel like or what a reality, where that is the reality, would have been like. To be so at the whim of these forces and feel so beleaguered or pulled up by them must have been quite an amazing thing. Also, the subversiveness of the stories. They're violent. They're weird. There are so many hybrids and so many strange creatures. So many poetic images that are really enduring and I don't think that they ever will not be. There's something like an essence there that I find captivating. And science fiction is both – it's funny the word science fiction because it implies that it's not a serious idea, but I think that speculative fiction is a way of casting a net also into darkness and it is a way of almost doing an abracadabra. "Abracadabra": it comes to be. These words create. I think there's something about that. That you can project an image or project a kind of system into the future and it can be drawn into our own time somehow. I think it's really incredible in that way; the unlimitedness of it. It's been such an important form for feminist writing. Various political movements have really engaged with the potentials of science fiction because what is science fiction but writing the future?

Well, on that beautiful note, I'm probably going to say that we're going to have to play the next track. But I want to play the Mackenzie because I'm into the techno vibe. Do you want to tell me about when you heard this and what it connects to for you?

I'm really, really interested in subcultures. I feel very fortunate that I have known other lives apart from being an artist. That I didn't do my kindergarten, school, BA, MA and then thrown into the world. I've had cultural experiences outside of art. And one of the most formative ones was probably rave culture in Belgium when I was a teenager. This is one of the tracks that was very popular when I very first started. I started going to clubs because we had a neighbour who was 18, who took me out when I was 12 to clubs. I mean I have a lot of criticism about rave culture by the way. I don't think it was like a nadir of freedom. I think that there was a lot of misogyny, sexism, violence in it as well and I experienced a lot of that myself. I think maybe for straight men it was but I'm not sure of that as the ultimate cultural artefact that we should try and return to…

There was a lot of drugs. There's a dark underbelly that people try and avoid talking about. I think what is interesting is that for a new generation it was their moment of dissent. I think in a weird way, it's now a generation of punk or something like that.

Yeah, totally. It was excessive, and it was wonderful. And you did end up talking to people and spending like a few days and going out with people. It was very free in many ways as well, but there were obviously people that were predatory, blah, blah, blah. But there was something incredible and that feeling of hearing a song that you really wanted to hear come on, when you're three Es in or something like that, it's an incredible experience. And these are intensities that I've carried with me through my life, I hope.

I want to make sure we play it, so this is Mackenzie 'Higher in The Sky'.

—

To squeeze in our last track, simply because you had such great choices, why did you choose 'Ostia (The Death of Pasolini)' by Coil?

Their ethos is something I'm interested in. It's a gesamtkunstwerk. It's this idea of various forms. They were very interested in the visuals of their work and costumes and writing in culture. I think that's something that has been slightly lost, this atomization between disciplines. It's something I've always been interested in – musicians that create worlds. World-making is the core of what I'm interested in, and Coil were very much like that. They had this incredible sensibility that permeated everything they did, and they were very radical and experimental in their choices. And I really love the music as well, obviously, but there's something more than the music. It's not just the music.

> *This is your last record. Thank you so much Tai for your energy and choices. This is Coil 'Ostia'.*

Paul Mpagi Sepuya

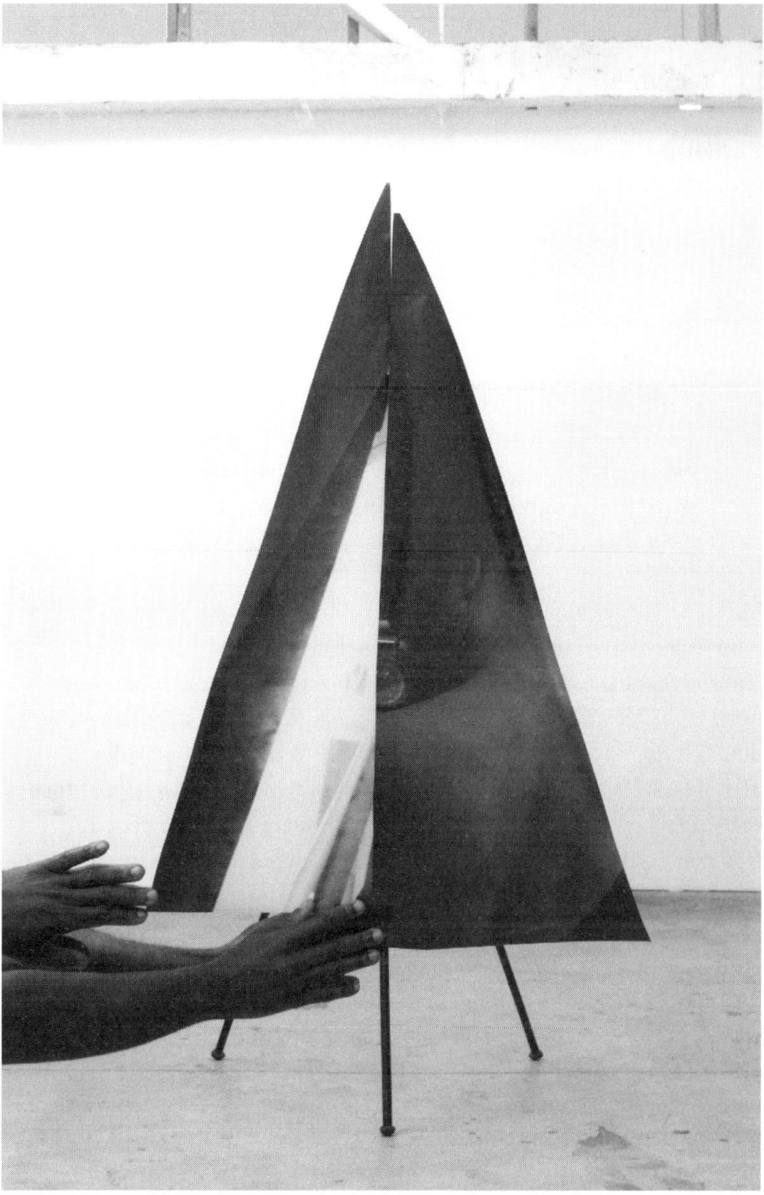

Mirror Study, 2018.

30.04.21

Hi, you're listening to Rough Version on NTS. My guest this month is Paul Mpagi Sepuya, who studied at NYU and UCLA. He's exhibited at MoMA in New York, Barbican in London, was part of the Whitney Biennial, shows with Document in Chicago and has even done a residency in one of my favourite spaces, Studio Museum in Harlem. And you're very kindly speaking to us at the moment from Los Angeles. How are you today?

I'm doing well. It's morning here. Everything is another sunny day. Everything is blooming.

California forever!

It's been a great place to have spent his last quarantine year.

Completely. Well, on that note, let's just dive straight in and start talking about your work. I'm going to say that one of the things that really fascinates me about your work is your placement within it. When did you first start using yourself? And your role as an artist inside your photographic imagery?

Since the very beginning. The very beginning of taking pictures. I think sometimes the taking pictures is before I would think of having realized that I was an artist or making projects. But I think ever since I picked up a camera, to make images of people, it was always in relation to trying to ask questions about myself. When I was an undergrad, I took lots of pictures of people. I didn't think they were portraits. I had no real ongoing relationship or interest to those people. But afterwards, around like 2005, when I started making the first work that I considered portraits, which was really asking people that I was close to, or wanting to get to know, or reconnecting with, to sit in front of my camera, I quickly realized that I had to be a part of the work as well. That I had to photograph myself alongside them at times, and also just my own self-portraits to be inserted within that project. So that goes back to the first bodies of work from 2005 to 7, then I think you're probably also asking just about like the current work? The mirror portrait? All of these things?

You as an artist are embedded in your work, looking at us as a viewer. It is really interesting twist on how we look at photographic imagery. It's usually photographer, subject, viewer, looking through the photographer's eyes, but you are playing around and turning all of that upside down somehow.

Yeah, yeah. So, with the mirrors, being included in those – the mirrors were less about making pictures of myself. In end of 2014, maybe early 2015, when I started working on those, when I came back to Los Angeles, they were a surface that I could organise this type of outtakes, fragmented material, bits of images. It was a surface I could organise that on. Set the camera in front of, perpendicular to the mirror and make a new photograph. That would help make an image that held the fragments in the type of composition but also in relation to each other, which would provide a kind of meaning. I guess I have to make a little detour on that but because with the initial portraits, I thought I had that faith in photography that making portraits when you use the camera in a precise technical way – it gives you a clear document to clear record. So, making a portrait of people can be your affixing meaning of how or what a relationship is or whatever. But quickly realizing that within the social space, the ways in which portraiture is within an economy of images and how it moves at speeds faster than people, the work became about everything around the production. The complications around the production of portraiture. Anyways, 10 years later, when I'm using the mirrors, I wanted to return to that initial desire for the photograph to make sense of things to be able to fix meaning. That's why the photograph could hold these things that were temporarily arranged on these surfaces and then I could let that material go aside. Or I could put it away, archive it. So back to your question about me being in the images. It was always important that I wasn't just making Photoshop layer collages, like brain scans and stuff. That I was physically doing it because I wanted to be physically incorporated into the image while I was making it. Because the image only comes together through the viewfinder, looking down through the Mamiya RZ for those original ones or through eventually the digital back, so that even if in the final image, I decided to walk away and set the camera on a timer to make the photo, that in the making I was always in the image. And any resulting thing came after. Does that make sense? That's why that show at Foam Amsterdam was called 'Double Enclosure'. Cause I thought of this thing, there's a double enclosure of myself within the work – in the making and then possibly in the final image or not. But still, there's the traces and stuff. That's the second part. And then it's also moved on. With the darkroom project that's come after that. On the one hand there's the playful element of composition. And arranging the images with the bodies. Using the double meaning of darkroom, but also just using my body and the black velvets and the camera as all black materials and surfaces and things that can reveal the traces and touch and smudges some things on the mirror surface. You can't see any of that when the space that's reflected in the mirror is white. But black material makes the surface of the mirror visible. So that's now how the body comes in. Everything is cumulative.

As a metaphor, that's incredible. I might add for the idea of Blackness, revealing it, the complexity, and let's say flaws within how things have worked out. That's quite beautiful – how to turn something quite physical into something more poetic at the same time. Because there is something very emotional within your work there. I read a gorgeous quote that you had that photography cannot exist without queerness and Blackness, which I thought was quite amazing take on medium. Do you want to explain a little bit what you were thinking when you said that, if you remember?

I've always been very ambivalent on representation being the end goal. I don't know, a political goal. I've never really been 100% on board with the idea that image, that beautiful images of Black or queer people is the thing that makes work interesting. I don't know this is going to be really – I'm going to get myself in trouble saying things like this. Because that's so tied to consumption. And we can get to this later, but I'm very much interested in acknowledging and trying to complicate ideas of presentation, consumption, mutual objectification versus outside objectification. So, I've always wanted to think about what if you remove an identifiable subject from the work what structurally, in the aspect of photography can make the work hold on to a queer or Black position, subject position… I was so disconnected from photo history when I was a younger student because in an interesting way desire is totally removed from talking about why certain pictures were made. I came back to this thinking about Henry Fox Talbot and all those photographs of the Bust of Metropolis, which if you are reading queer literature, you recognise, you understand it. You walk into someone's foyer and there's this object. It's the way that you're like, well, this person is queer. Okay. Everyone talks about these images, but why did this person take all of these photographs of this object? I'm thinking photography is putting desire towards a productive means of practice. So, you have to talk about the development of photography – all of the social, political, technical things. But also, that it's so tied to desire and queerness. I think as a way to get to that space, because it's not structured around social roles, like marriage. Maybe now it is. But I think about queer desire, as this point, where it all meets is both erotic but also collaborative. It's intellectual but also totally platonic. It's like family. It's all of those things. And so being able to talk about the unstable or hard to define nature of queer desire at the beginnings of photography seems really important… We'd have to be making pictures pre liberation for us to acknowledge this thing. And the same thing with like Blackness. So, in thinking about, I guess, that metaphor that I was talking about, of the type of trace, latent information on the surfaces of this glass, that requires a reversal of the hierarchy, a presumed hierarchy of light, clarity, white, as the ideal space for viewing. You have to enter; you actually have to go to the dark room. The space under the dark cloth is the beginning of photography, but it's also the space where queer, marginalized, social space has been. You think about these historically Black social spaces, but that having to privilege that position makes visible a whole, beautiful wealth of depth, of touch, and trace and records of presence. It's really thinking, these darkroom images, these images are not about defining any Black political position or social condition, but really emphasizing the impossibility of separating out Blackness as a material and Blackness as a subject position from looking and making visible types of information and images. It's complicated. Maybe one way to sum that up is I'm really interested in being able to insert work into photo scholarship or curatorial exhibitions etc. That are not about photography telling us about Black life or this is photography about queer liberation, but how can this work be? How can you go from here, going forward? That we will have exhibitions on just the history of the apparatus itself that necessarily have to include queer and Black photographs in them, regardless. There's this show at the Getty, which is such a complicated place because they just keep getting themselves into trouble. I don't know if you follow a lot of just the conversations happening around museums and stuff. It's very conservative place but their photography department is the one place where interesting things are happening. I was really excited to have work in an exhibition that was just on the history of the camera itself and to be centered in that. That you can no longer think about just the apparatus without its use.

Before we go on, I think we're going to play a song. Let's start with your Yola track. When did you first hear it? What do you like about this song?

Oh my god, I mean, she's amazing. I do not know the time of day or when exactly it was it must have been early or mid 2019. I was just scrolling through I think like the LA NPR stations, maybe it was KCRW or KPCC, some music program. And I heard this voice, and I was like, this sounds like a country song. That is a Black voice. That is an amazing Black woman singing the song. And I think maybe a little, I can't remember, before or after Lil Nas X doing everything, upsetting the country cannon. But there was just something that, I was just so drawn to her voice. It's one of the few times when I got out of the car. I went to the radio stations website, because now they will post the playlist and I looked up and then I got the album. It must have been in, probably the fall of 2019. I was driving to San Diego twice a week because I was beginning this faculty position there. I think the reason why I pulled the song up – I spent so many hours listening to this album from beginning to end. She just takes you through everything. I listened to a few interviews with her, and I don't know. It's just such a beautiful, beautiful album. I don't know what else to say. I never know what to talk about with music.

It's great. This is 'Ride Out In the Country' by Yola whose work I didn't know before.

—

That was Yola 'Ride Out In the Country'. We talked a lot about the fact that there's a staging element to your process. I'm really curious is it very intuitive? How do you compose those images? Is there a lot of preparation? Does the idea come first, or is it much more improvised in front of your viewfinder?

There's a lot of improvisation. But I think it's also important to say that 95 to 99% of my time spent in the studio making pictures is just me by myself. I have a part time studio manager there. I usually try to stay a little bit later on into the evenings. I just have time. I'm looking around. I'm thinking through things. I'm playing around. I'm often moving things around, and I'm shooting a lot of bad pictures, a lot of outtakes and things. But a few things will hit and then there might be an idea for a starting point. Eventually, I'll start a conversation with a friend and we're planning something, and I was like, "Oh, yeah, I'll come by and make some pictures". And I might have an idea. I'd like to use this type of fabric and its position will be here in relation to the camera and then relation to the subjects or figures, and then we just take it from there. Overall, it's the best when it's just very easy going and it just plays off of just the dynamics. I sometimes describe it as – a compositional idea comes from something that I observed at a party that weekend before or thinking back to various arrangements of people in spaces and it all is coming from that. I've never sketched out a composition and then made that. They all happen in time. Same thing with the mirror studies. The ones that look like collages. But they're material taped and otherwise held onto the surface of the mirror. That's also very much improvised…

Like objects and the human form. It seems interchangeable in a lot of ways… What do you like about the inclusion and let's say the concealment of the naked human body? Because there is skin and legs and arms and bodies within what you do but it's not like always nothings obvious. A lot of times things are intertwined and you have to really read the image to try to work out what's involved.

Yeah. I'm weaving all of these elements of skin and touch and fabric and reflection. A lot of those are just really fun. I maybe feel a little guilty thinking, just for myself, that some of those ones are not as deep. But they allow me to do – I had to think about how fragmentation worked in a way. Thinking about the scale of the elements that I use. Thinking about a responsibility to, an accountability towards the cutting or the tearing. That it's not just left to some other impersonal device. I wanted it to be my hand involved in it. There is a lot of careful thinking in there. But I just think they're just really beautiful and I just enjoy making them. They also helped me work through a lot of fragments that come from outtakes, test prints, etc. It's like my way of recycling material before I let it go and making it to another image. But the conceit there is concealing, and all of these things that are happening. But all of that work exists. So, in the context of the full portraits, the full body is present somewhere. That may not often make it into exhibitions. But it's something that I am really thinking about in terms of the overall collection of the work. Also, these ideas of indexing and mapping out the relationships between the portrait work and the studio-based work. Work that is more fragmented or collage etc., That there's a continuity between them.

I'm going to play another one of your tracks. Let's play the Annie Lennox, which I hadn't heard for years. When did you first hear this? Probably when you were little, I'm assuming.

So, Annie Lennox. It's funny because the Eurythmics is one of those bands that I have one of the earliest memories of hearing as a child in the car sitting in the backseat of my parents' car. Songs from Savage playing or something. The Eurythmics, Smokey Robinson and Tina Turner are like my earliest. And Michael Jackson. The earliest things I remember are these. Annie Lennox has been this obsession of mine since – I can't even think of how long. There was this moment I want to say maybe around, when did YouTube come? Like finally arrive? 2005? 6?

That late, yeah. Maybe a little bit earlier...

Maybe it was a little bit earlier. So, to get to 'Little Bird', because 'Little Bird' I feel like is the culmination of an entire series of performances and persona that Annie Lennox has developed since the Eurythmics through her solo career. When YouTube came around, and suddenly there was this accessibility for watching videos, I was like, "oh, wow". This singer that I was really into when I was a teenager. I was this weird teenager in Southern California who was really into the Eurythmics in the '90s. But anyways, I started watching all the videos in chronology and became obsessed with how she developed these characters like the housewife, the drag queen, the butch character, the character that crosses gender. Maybe this has something to do with my obsession with Virginia Woolf, as well. I was really into watching all of the Annie Lennox videos. Then when Lady Gaga came out, and everyone is really into her. "She performs characters so well". I was like, no. I've made all my friends who are into Lady Gaga, sit them down and watch all of the Annie Lennox videos. So, the reason why I picked 'Little Bird' is it's a great song, but I like the way she's this ring master who brings out her previous music video personas from 'Sweet Dreams' to 'Walking on Broken Glass' to the woman from Beethoven. I love to listen to the David Bowie performance with the Freddie Mercury Tribute Concert – all of these. She brings them back some in drag, some not. And she's like this ringleader performing them. I think it's such a fun video, and she's also seven months pregnant with Tali Lennox in that video, if you notice. I actually have a whole crazy obsession with Annie Lennox. She was the only celebrity that I followed on Facebook, when I was on Facebook years ago. It was very strange and Christian Holstad, and I would always just send each other like Annie Lennox clips back and forth.

> *I actually think I should play it back-to-back, that and one of your other tracks you've chosen is David Bowie. In a way they're quite an interesting pairing… Do you want to tell me why you chose 'Word on a Wing' by Bowie? Bowie I never know how to say that.*

Bowie. I've never thought of Bowie. I like that. 'Word on a Wing' is one of the most beautiful songs I think I've ever heard in my entire life. That entire album 'Station to Station'. In that way that maybe this connects all of the people that I've mentioned. That Yola album from beginning to end just takes you there. The whole story, this whole arc of love and loss and escape and then just like passion and everything. Annie Lennox, I think does that in both with the music but also visually pulling you across but that album 'Station to Station' and 'Word on a Wing' is just so heartbreaking because isn't that one that's made after his recovery and this dark period?

Berlin period, isn't it?

Berlin, right? And it's just like total surrender. It's just a total surrender. I feel even though I've never personally faced anything like addiction and dependence in that way, I think there's a way in which any artist can relate to processing an experience through making work sometimes. I just always imagined following and listening to that song or that album the work that comes through that music might even proceed even knowing what was even done. I feel like that song casts a spell and then it takes a while to figure it out. Anyways, it's just so beautiful.

So, this is Annie Lennox 'Little Bird' followed by David Bowie 'Word on a Wing'.

—

I'm going to talk about something that happened this year. Your work – part of what makes it interesting is the fact that it isn't political in an obvious way. But you also did quite an incredible fundraising work this year with your prints. I want you to talk a little bit about that process. And I think it was particularly as BLM exploded, but how that affected the work you were making at the time.

I've never made an image or made a series of work directly through some kind of metaphor or through direct representation, responding to an event that's happening. But I think we can. We'll probably be able to look back. I think it might be interesting to look back and see a correlation between work that was made during the Bush years, then the Obama years and then the Trump years. There's going to be that, but I was thinking more I didn't want to make up work for a while at the beginning of quarantine. I really resisted this media around visual artists to be making quarantine work. So that was one thing that I was thinking of. Resisting that. But also, when something urgent as needing to raise, wanting to raise funding for causes, like bail funds, to support people who are on the front lines protesting to be able to support the most radical political candidates – all of these things, mutual aid. I wanted to do something that was direct. There's also this way in which every organization is always asking for something, but artists don't get anything out of it. I didn't want to be doing fundraisers through other people. I've still said yes to a few things but I'm trying to narrow that down. So, what I ended up coming up with was this idea of the solidarity print as a gift. I talked with the galleries, and we figured out that in order to be able to administer it, because what I wanted to do – it was important that it was not selling. There were a lot of artists fundraisers for things. Like "we're selling something and then donating the proceeds". This was not that. It was here are lists of local Black Lives Matter chapters, bail funds, mutual aid for queer, trans people etc. And we promoted it by saying you make a donation of at least $250 to one of these organizations or split it amongst them, as a minimum. We wanted to reach out. We asked collectors, so to speak, to give more. It was like… an honour system. There was one for students, queer students and students of colour on $40 minimum but send the receipt for your donation and we will send you as a gift this print. Because it was really important that it be a gift. That it not be a shopping experience and that each donor had to actually go to the organization and support them directly, hopefully starting some kind of relationship with them. I know a few people said that they were actually thankful for being introduced to certain organizations and they became recurring or sustaining donors. It was really interesting. When it first launched, we kept rolling our eyes at the end laughing to ourselves that collectors who would be emailing the studio, or the galleries being "is this going to come with a signed certificate of authenticity? What is the value of this thing?" At first, I was just like, "oh god people" but then I thought about it. Okay. So, we decided that the work was not signed. It was an open edition as long as the fundraiser was going, but that it came with a statement that said this work is given as a gift for having shared the receipt of supporting specific organizations. And the value of the work is only the value of the donation that you made.

Give two grand then it's worth two grand.

Yeah, but it's also just trying to like separate it from, to forefront the ridiculousness of trying to tie the work itself to some kind of value.

And then because there were some things that happened last summer and fall around museums and places trying to exhibit – using a lot of artists fundraisers at ways of cheaply collecting and exhibiting work, rather than going through the longer processes of curatorial conversations and acquisitions. Like this happened at the Whitney.

Yeah, I remember that.

I was aware that things like this might happen. There's no total work around. But we also made it clear that if anyone is ever going to show this work, that it needs to be exhibited with the statement and with the receipt of the donation to the organization. So that it could not be separated into just this little print on the wall and recontextualize that it always is going to be, this is the image. This is the organization that was supported and here's the statement. We did three rounds of those. I don't have the numbers in front of me, but I want to say we raised over $300,000 for organizations.

I love the play on receipts with the idea – like show me the receipts from people say. There's something quite humourous about that. You're kind of demanding people to put their – actually actively engage into things that they often just talk about and to prove that relationship.

Exactly.

We're actually at the moment to play your last track now. But we're going to play two because I love 'Innervisions', the Stevie Wonder album. We're going to pick 'Golden Lady' and 'Don't You Worry 'Bout a Thing'. Tell me, as a giant Stevie Wonder fan, about your feelings about Stevie.

I don't like tear up very easily, but I will tell you, a Stevie Wonder album can make me misty, make me cry. 'Golden Lady' I'm always just saying the song is just so beautiful. I just picked like beautiful songs. But that's one of those songs that I think I could listen to on repeat and not get tired of it. He's musing that she's going to take him there. That song just takes me there.

The albums got such a variety of different approaches...

Yeah. That album is from '72, right? It's like before all the synthesizer stuff. It's an in between album from maybe the earlier Stevie Wonder albums to the more experimental ones. 'Don't You Worry 'Bout a Thing'. If you're having a bad day, just put that song on. I think I actually listened to that song a lot at moments when I was just really down years ago. It's funny because that album is one that I haven't been listening to as much lately. I think some of the later Stevie Wonder albums have come up. But maybe in my last years in New York, like 2012 to 2014, I listened to that album to get by. I feel like I had that song 'Don't You Worry 'Bout a Thing' on repeat on the little boombox in my kitchen, you know?

It's a great opportunity to remind everyone they should listen to 'Innervisions' as an album. This is 'Golden Lady' and 'Don't You Worry 'Bout a Thing'. And thank you so much, Paul, for taking the time to talk about your work.

Thank you. Thank you for having me.

Rachel Maclean

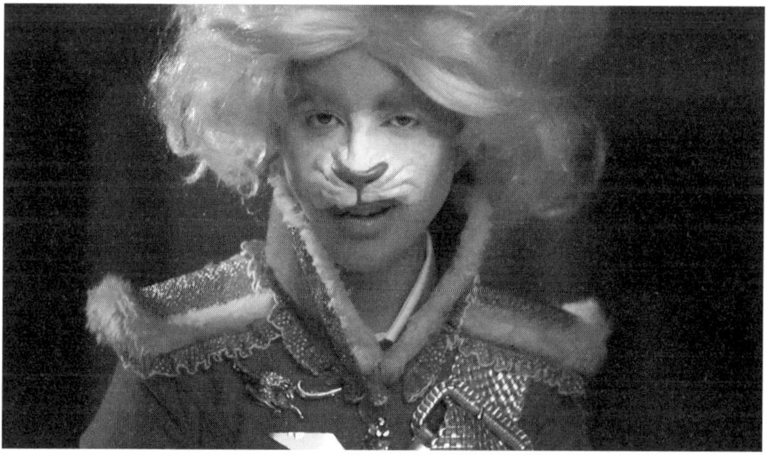

The Lion and The Unicorn, 2012.

28.05.21

You're listening to Rough Version on NTS and my guest this month is Rachel Maclean. She's an incredible artist who originally worked with herself and found video footage to create incredible installations and film works using a lot of pink and prosthetics. She represented Scotland in the Venice Biennale in 2017 and has exhibited at the National Gallery in London, Tate Britain, National Gallery of Australia and various TV commissions for BBC and Channel Four. Based in Glasgow, she's just opened her first public sculpture at Jupiter Artland. So, Rachel, thank you so much for coming in. How are you?

Thank you for the invitation. I'm good. Cheers.

Let's just dive in and start talking about your work. I suppose the first thing I noticed about your work, which has expanded is the use of yourself within it. Do you want to tell us about how you started and why you started using yourself almost as the main protagonist-material in what you do?

I think it started at art college, exploring that whole idea of performance art and using yourself and using your body. And very quickly, started making wee videos and dressing up. Realizing that it wasn't any idea of my authentic self I was interested in, it was more the potential to become different people. That immediately just became something that seemed fun, and there seemed a lot of mileage in it. So really, since then, I've been exploring that idea in different formats.

What's amazing about it is how you can make yourself into such a variety of different characters. Are you using a lot of prosthetics? It's incredible how malleable your face is!

I think there's an oddness to film in that you can do so much. There's so much illusion that you can create just through film in and of itself. And then on top of that, I mime either actors' voices or I find audio. I take other voices and use prosthetic makeup. It is this kind of illusionary transformation.

One of the other things that's really central to what you do seems to be kind of playing with quite established narratives. Things like fairy tales, or the Tower of Babel, or Pinocchio. What do you like about those kinds of references?

I think for me, I'm interested in using references that are not too niche. Things that are very familiar to people. They're already not just in the Zeitgeist, but also something that exists in different forms and different cultures. I think fairytales are interesting because they're recognizable, but they're also very malleable. They're persistent but they don't often persist and have the same meanings. They are these stories that you can take, and you can very easily change the perspective on them or change the meaning.

Let's play a track. I want to play your Björk track, because I've always loved this one. Do you want to tell me about when you first heard it, and why you chose it?

I think I first heard this when I was quite young, maybe about 14, 15 and it was amazing. I think it's the first time I'd heard anything this weird and that I connected with to quite this degree. I love Björk and I guess I can't say anything about how great she is that many other people haven't said already. She's just totally unique. She's just been doing her own thing for a very long time. I love this track.

This is 'Jóga' by Björk.

—

In your work – definitely a lot more in the beginning but again this is shifting – you've used a lot of pop music as audio. Do you want to talk about some of the tracks you've used and what you like about that pop-ness?

I usually in my work try to have a specific reference point for the music, so it doesn't tend to just be music that I like at the time. It's something that's evocative of a certain genre. I guess in some of my work, there's almost like musical theatre reference points. Sometimes very specifically a Disney movie style musical theatre song. I've worked with various composers. Finn Anderson, Julian Corrie and

Scott Twynholme have worked with me, to almost take a genre and then do something a little bit weird with it.

> *Musicals are a really specific thing because you do play on the musical idea, but they're way darker than the surface of your material implies – the pinkness.*

A lot of my films have that classic musical theatre thing, that "I want" song when the character at the beginning says what they want, and they say it in a song format. I'm interested in desire, and I guess how that's filtered through culture and how it's so integral to our experience of consumerism. I wanted to satirize that genre a little bit and satirize this idea of, I guess, aspirational culture, or the whole sense of what you want and then the achievement of it.

> *Actually, thinking about some of that satire, it also seems to be a criticality towards technology and our relationship to it, as well. You've used a lot of fake social media, and that seems to be commenting on our relationship with that, too.*

Yeah, I use a lot of emojis. And I'm quite interested in how cuteness is a big part of our relationship with technology and the internet and emojis being these. I don't know. It's almost like they signify the way that we've managed to reduce an understanding of emotion to these very simplified ideas of happy, sad, angry. And then the extent to which that is now being able to be used by AI and algorithms to sell things to us based on what our emotion is imagined to be. I did a workshop recently in film, where they were able to pick up using AI technology on the emotion that was in a film just based off of facial tracking or facial reading of film posters. I'm fascinated and scared of the sense in which our understanding of our emotional selves is being reduced in this way.

> *Let's play another track. Let's play the Dorian Electra – you suggested a couple of theirs. Do you want to tell me about your relationship to that music?*

I discovered them I think maybe about a couple of years ago and their music is brilliant and just the whole visual that goes with it is so imaginative and totally spot on. And I think the sense of humour in their work is great. Just this satirical eye for things. I think if anybody out there has not seen their work before then I would definitely look them up.

This is 'Gentleman' by Dorian Electra.

—

I want to talk about your current project that's just opened for Jupiter Artland. Do you want to describe what the project is?

The project is the first public sculpture that I've made, and it's in Jupiter Artland, which is a sculpture park. You arrive at the work through a forest… And you see paving stones that look like heart emojis, and you follow them until you arrive at this building, which is called Mimi's Store. It looks like this candy-coloured shop in the middle of a forest. You enter and inside, the shop stocks Mimi dolls. Then there's a film at the back, which features the same character, Mimi. It's this fairytale, almost Hansel and Gretel experience of discovering this candy-coloured building in the middle of a forest.

Amazing. What did you like about taking your language and aesthetic and making it into an installation that exists like that? It must be quite surreal, almost like your films are coming to life in some way.

It was a challenge in some ways, because I guess public sculpture isn't conventionally, or sculpture parks, don't conventionally have video. Partly it was thinking of a way that you could incorporate video into that format. It's been great fun. I've always wanted to make a work that feels this complete and feels this expanded. I've worked a lot on the details, so I hope if you come, that you can pick up on so many different things that I've added into the experience.

Let's talk a little bit about process. Are you very studio based? Does it always come with an idea or is it more site specific? How do you conceive ideas?

It usually depends. A lot of commissions comes with a very specific context. A specific physical context, but also a political context. I've made works that are very specific, like my film, 'The Lion and the Unicorn' was a commission. I was asked to make a work about the upcoming referendum and Scottish independence. I was asked to make it specifically in this historic house in the Scottish Borders Traquair house. So that was a very specific commission, but I loved it. Because I make very maximal work, you need to put limitations on yourself, because you can really just keep adding. Although I've also made works – I'm working on a feature film script just now and because feature films are just an incredibly long process, you really can't tie your idea to a context because that context might be gone by the time you get to make it. So that's much more like thinking of an idea that's really going to endure and you're still going to be interested in potentially like seven to ten years later, when you get to make it.

> *I assume for a future film it won't just be you acting every single character!*

No, I hope not. I'd like to work with actors and do something that feels I guess more in the feature film genre.

> *Exciting! Let's play another track. I want to play one that you've used coming off of that Scottish referencing which is the Kenneth McKellar version of 'Skye Boat Song'. Which I thought was a hilarious addition but also really fascinating. Do you want to tell me how you used this in your work and what you like about the track?*

This was in my film 'The Lion and the Unicorn' which I just mentioned. It was about or related to the run up to the first independence referendum – I realize there's not been a second one yet – so, the independence referendum in Scotland. The song is about – it's a romantic song about when Bonnie Prince Charlie fled the Battle of Culloden and then got taken over the sea on a boat. It's tied into this idea of romantic nationalism and the history of romantic nationalism. What I was trying to do with the film was play that off – I guess a more pragmatic political debate that was going on at the time and almost question the relationship that we have with that conception of national identity.

Well, this is Kenneth McKellar's 'Skye Boat Song'.

—

Let's talk about the politics in your work in general. You've also done incredible computer games. I remember a shoot 'em up that was Brexit related, which was terrifying and totally spot on at the same time. What do you like about incorporating politics into what you do?

I think usually the way that I use politics, like in that work, I don't want it to be too didactic or too on the nose. I want it to be something that feels like it's slightly open to interpretation. With that piece, the VR piece, I wanted you to really feel something. I think that VR is good, and that it's such an immediate medium. That the minute you put the headset on you can feel emotions that would take quite a long time to build and film. So, you arrive in this empty, dark semi apocalyptic place that feels a bit like London maybe, or at least a British city. But all the buildings are oversized tourist tat. Like Big Ben teapots, and London bus key rings. I think you are, or at least my intention is, you immediately feel that sense of being on a street on your own. Then these characters, these stereotypes of privileged city dwellers, turn up and start to try and elicit money from you. After a while, it develops into almost a first-person shooter zombie, shoot 'em up situation. My feeling is that, or my hope is that you leave with a sense of you just killed a lot of people and was that you that did that? Was that baked into the narrative? Or did you somehow will that to happen? You get a sense of your own complicity in the narrative somehow. I wanted to filter politics through a feeling of complicity, maybe.

I ended up feeling really weird after watching it because a VR shoot 'em up in itself is also really physical, you're like really physically engaged in what you do… Do you want to talk a little bit about the context of your work? Now you're working in an outdoor space but a lot of times that I've seen your pieces it's been in not necessarily white cube kind of spaces, but actually more historic buildings. For example, the Venice Biennale, where you did Scotland in Venice with an incredible looping giant Pinocchio, rags to riches to rags story and then obviously, the National Gallery. What do you find interesting about showing something that's almost hyper pop, and semi futuristic in these kinds of old spaces?

I think it's interesting because there's so much there already. I think with history, there's a sense of… there's always been a popular history that's partly in our imagination that you can play off or play with as an artist. I'm not really at all interested in that idea of the imagined neutrality of the white cube. Or the sense that you can take your work and place it in isolation, because I just think that is impossible. I think it's much more interesting to put it within a context that already carries a lot of meaning, and then see how you can play off that. I think… I'm interested in initially creating a sense of comfort or familiarity, so you understand the way a certain space is coded or how you're supposed to behave. There's a sense that you can settle into that. And then that allows me to start throwing things at you that are weird or unsettling, or not quite what you expected. I guess we find that in Venice, where I showed 'Spite Your Face' in a deconsecrated church. People walk in a very, really respectful [way], they didn't talk as much as they normally would. There was a sense that the church just made them behave in a way that they wouldn't do in a gallery, which was kind of fun to play with.

Also at the same time, it also felt like your visual references, this kind of opulence that you were depicting, was a really interesting contrast to the Baroqueness of Venice. These crazy churches with Tintorettos in them, and ridiculous stucco cupids everywhere. It seemed to be touching on that at the same time, too.

Definitely. I quite like the over-the-top-ness. My work is always intended to feel like a little bit too much. I want that to be something that verges on being a little bit uncomfortable. It's not just Baroque beauty. It's almost pushing that a little bit too far. Nothing is ever real, so it's not real gold. Obviously it is not genuinely Baroque. It's always the much more fake plastic version of that.

Just before we finish can I ask you like what other influences or inspirations you have at the moment beyond music? What other stuff plays into inspiring what you do?

I guess I've been watching film and TV. I love that series recently, the one with Billie Piper – 'I Hate Suzy'. I thought it was really brilliant and it gave me a lot of ideas. I guess because I'm trying to move a wee bit more into script writing and feature film, it just felt like the most beautifully written program that touched on a lot of things that I never really thought about before but did so in a way that didn't… it was smart and engaging. I think that program is brilliant and so is Lucy Prebble who wrote it, and Billie Piper also I think are talented.

> *That's my first Billie Piper reference ever on the show. Let's finish up with playing your last track, which is The Knife. Why this track?*

I just love The Knife. It's just so dark and I love the way that she doesn't play the game with you. I guess how you're intended to behave is like a female pop star or a female musician, where she often disguises her appearance or makes herself intentionally ugly. I went to see – it's not The Knife, I guess, but a Fever Ray concert and she was wearing odd aging prosthetics. I love that almost denial of what you're expected to be and turning it around or inverting it and the music is brilliant.

> *This is 'Silent Shout' by The Knife. And thank you very much Rachel for your time.*

Thank you so much.

Bedwyr Williams

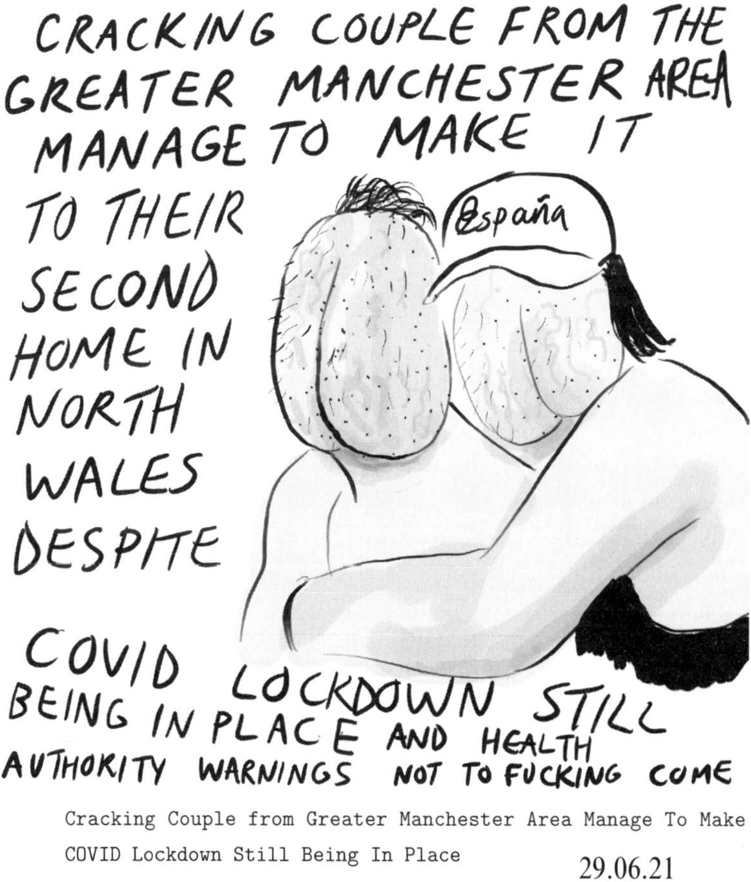

Cracking Couple from Greater Manchester Area Manage To Make It To Their Second Home In North Wales Despite COVID Lockdown Still Being In Place

29.06.21

You're listening to Rough Version on NTS, and my guest this month is Bedwyr Williams. The Welsh artist is a former Paul Hamlyn award winner and represented Wales at the Venice Biennale in 2013. He's exhibited the Barbican, Southward Reid gallery and is currently on show at Southwark Park Gallery in London until July 11. From video to installation to drawings, his work is intelligent, critical of the art world and politics and people, in general, and very, very funny. Bedwyr Williams, thank you very much for coming in. Let's talk about like one of the biggest motifs I think in like the breadth of your work, which is humour, and a really weird dark humour. What do you like about using that in what you do?

I mean one thing that pisses me off is there was an exhibition in South London gallery that I was in about humour, and then all kind of Twitter grumps, were like, "Oh, no, another exhibition about humour". But nobody says anything when there's a boring, sad exhibition or a boring worthy exhibition. For me, I don't think of myself as somebody who's trying to be funny, like an annoying British person on holiday. It's just my shtick. It's just how I do it. It's not like I think I should put humour in a certain work. It's just that's my style, you know? Some people play snooker with weird expressions on their face. That's just how I do it. The wiff of my thing, that's what it's like. Sorry, that sounds like a bit of a grumpy answer...

I loved it, bring on the grump. It's good.

I grew up kind of sheltered in a chapel-going family with a Welsh name in an English speaking area, a Welsh speaker. It's a boy named Sue situation where you just get the piss ripped out of you, consistently, continuously. I knew I wasn't thick, but I didn't think I was a genius either. But at a certain point, I started getting good at taking the piss back, because you figure out what you're about, don't you a little bit and what you like. I guess that's partly why, it's related to the music I've chosen for today. Why I've chosen it. Whilst I was a misfit, then I think I find myself being a misfit now. Because this is a programme where artists choose like clever music, isn't it? Like rare things, and I love music. I listen to it in the car, but that's private. What

I like, what gets me off or whatever. So, I just have chosen tunes that irritate me, on a primeval level, almost.

Let's begin with one of those. Let's do the Haysi Fantayzee track, which is definitely the first time I've ever played one of them. When did you first hear this, and what do you like about 'Shiny Shiny'?

I actually really hate the song 'Shiny Shiny'. My parents had an old Dansette, and they didn't have any popular music. They grew up going to young farmers events and stuff. Their records were Welsh, middle of the road, light end music. Shepherds that sang. There's like a tradition of Welsh, semi-religious, but also a bit folky music. Quite a big explosive scene in the '60s, but boring, some of it – most of it. And that's what they had. The only record that was exciting for us was there was one where the shepherd was singing, and he'd whistle for a bit in the middle, and I was excited about that. When I started watching like Swap Shop, Tiswas and stuff like that and bands would come on, there'd be like a guy in leather trousers or something. I'd just be like "what do I do for three minutes while this is on?" and because they put adult bands on children's TV. So, you'd have like Thompson Twins or something, but irrelevant to an eight-year-old. Here's no nothing for me to hook up with them with, so I'd just like do something else and then when the music was over I'd come back. But I remember like playing in the hallway of my parents' house hearing that hook from – it's not a hook I don't even know what a hook is – but the repeated thing in that 'Shiny Shiny' song. So, she repeats shiny shiny – I'm not gonna do it but all of these tracks I've chosen are songs that have like an irritating almost jig to them, that's nothing to do with the words, do you see what I mean? So that irritates me almost like a horrible birdsong in a nightmare or something like that. It's not like this is a shit song, it's more like it's irritating to the point it's plugging into my mainframe and fucking me up you know. I mean, that's overstating it a little bit with Haysi Fantayzee. The name Haysi Fantayzee as well is really.

It's painful. It hurts.

It's painful. I watched the 'Top Of The Pops' video before sending you the name and there's something about the shit 'Top Of The Pops' thing – and also knowing now all the Jimmy Savile stuff and things. It just looks like the private parties of millionaires you know when their daughters do horrible shit with other people's horrible kids. There's something about… I don't get excited by music in the same way that I used to. That makes me sad. When I was 16 going to see Welsh bands in barn dances and stuff, loved that. And the Manchester thing and then Aphex Twin and things like that I really got into, but there's some point in the millennium I think where music became this really worthy thing. And the way they talk about it. Like Jo Wiley on the radio, how she talks about music makes me not want to like music. It's worthy. Noel Gallagher, in my Instagram feed, him. Like a man that should be coming round to give you an estimate, giving his opinion about stuff. Horrible. I didn't sign up for any of this, do you know what I mean?

Okay, on that note, this is Haysi Fantayzee 'Shiny Shiny'.

—

Let's talk about your drawings, which also emerged initially on Instagram. At first, wow, they were incredibly on point and really addressed to the art world. Do you want to tell me about when you started wanting to depict the awful aspects of both the art world and social media around you?

I had this weird moment where I had the show in 2016 at the Barbican, at the Curve, and a week after the show went up my mother died, after being ill for four years. And then I was in 'Artist Monthly', a week after that. A few months later, the gallery I was with went under. I split up from my long-term partner. Also, there was a sense that like white men needed to like step back for a while, which is perfectly right, isn't it? So, I kind of anticipated that there was going to be a bit of a lull, for a while. I didn't just anticipate it, it just washed over me like a big fart smelling realization, you know. And good, in a way. I mean, tough. Even though you totally concur with making the art scene more diverse, you're still an artist trying to live – not like doing it in between. So, I'm lucky, I teach, and I love that. And I just thought I want to just do something that is like totally me, without a gallery allowing it all. You see what I mean? It's not an opportunity, it's just Instagram. I'd like noticed this thing that the Instagram community had become like a real love-in, or a lovey-in. I quite liked that the art world used to be quite acid and unpleasant. I mean bits. I didn't like it when they were unpleasant about me, but it used to be a bit more fighty, or a bit sarky, or something. When people started saying "that show was beautifully curated" and "stunning" and "love this" and I just thought there's something not gen about this. Because I know, in the back channels of social media, with your art friends, you hear who's the fucker. People tell you the mean shit. You have this kind of an icing where everyone's being nice and liking the pictures of a fucking artists' kids that you will never meet is disgusting. I mean horrible. So, it's related to this. I mean, this is gross, that I've made tote bags but this, isn't it. 'There's solidarity in insincerity'. That's art Instagram. A lot of people have moved away from the platform now I think but at that moment about 2017 it was peaking a little bit.

> *Apart from the fact that you really know the characters that you're drawing and describing, I think everyone following you felt that in themselves. I mean I felt it in me, and particularly the comments that you would write, almost as fake comments. Making the way people comment on social media satirical – wow it was almost viscerally spot on the language people use.*

I mean my big worry was, for a person from North Wales from a non-arty family, no bohemians in my family, no one. No one. I've done all right, you know, I've done all right, but neither have summitted the proper peaks of being an artist. My worry is that I'm taking the piss of base camp you know. I'm not invited to holidays with Italian curators in their villas and stuff so when people say, "ah it's really spot on what you make fun of". I sometimes think yeah, but other people think "he doesn't really know" you know. "He's guessing a lot of this" or something.

> *But it also seem to develop throughout COVID and become more wider I would say, vitriol, well-directed vitriol, at a lot of stuff happening in Wales and the second homebuyers coming out there and these Brexit dickheads. What did you like about*

shifting there? It just seemed to be you expressing yourself and how you felt about it.

It was a bit like trying out like a machine gun, and realizing that it works quite well and then just spraying the people in the car park behind you, as well. I think what I realized was that I get some weirdos that message me privately saying that I'm anti-English or something like that, but basically, all it is, is I'm just pushing back a little bit. When Jeremy Clarkson makes fun of Welsh people on TV, there isn't the equivalent Welsh person on the same panel to tell him to go and fuck himself, ever. It's always, you have to just take the blows and it's that. It's not a thin skin thing, it's just that we never have a right to reply, you know. And I figured I've got a point here about the second home thing and the breaking the COVID thing that, if I can just air it without being a twat, then it's worth doing. It's pushback. I'm aware that we're a completely anachronistic out of touch, ancient nation, but it can't all be, you know, the people in Fat Face having their way? It can't all be that. That's bullshit. I'm not just going to be a shepherd in the corner of the shot while they're on their jet skis, I have to have some kind of – I'm allowed to defend myself. No.

Depicting them as giant ballsacks I think does that.

I love how unreasonable that is as well!

It feels really good fit… The series emerged on Instagram, but you're doing an exhibition of the work now and I've seen other shows where you've done them. Where they're quite intimate as well. What do you like about, like you always wanted to keep them small to reflect where they came from?

There's this French sketch paper called Sennelier, well it's not, Sennelier's the name of the brand, but it's called Le Maxi. And they're square – so perfect for Instagram. Because I was living with my father for most of the last four years, I was drawing in bed a lot or in an armchair, so that worked. The first thing I did in lockdown was buy an iPad and that took things to another level. I could just draw pubes and stuff like that really well, and layer them and all those stupid like hair effects on procreate that you don't really need are great for doing big, second home-owning testicles.

I think it's a good point to play another track, which is War 'Low Rider', which I think we all know from shitty ads. Do you want to tell me about where you heard this, and how this annoys you?

It's the melody again. The melody, it sounds like it's trying to tell you something, but it's nothing to do with the song. It's a question like "meh meh meh meh meh meh meh, meh meh meh meh", and then it goes "meh meh meh meh meh"... It's just ridiculous, it's like something from the Muppet Show or something. Then the voice says "low rider" – like it's meaningless, you know? I just think like when I'm in a shop and something like that's playing, and then I see like a really old person. And I think what the fuck did they do to deserve having this, blasting while they're shopping, do you know what I mean? It's such an encroachment. It's also like at the moment, there's a lot of that monotone rapping – like my kids like it. Like "mmm, mmm, mmm mmm". Like the fuck is that? Why is that when I'm buying trousers? Like it's obviously niche and my kids like it. Then I say all these songs sound the same. And they say no they don't. They do. I don't even know what genre that is, but it's like "mmmrmrmmrmrmrm" like a guy just rapping in a monotone, horrible.

OK. Well on that note, this is War, 'Low Rider'.

—

I want to talk about some of your other work. I want to talk about 'ECHT' which is a film I am obsessed with. Which I first saw I think when you showed it in Venice, when you did Wales in Venice, which seemed to be very prophetic, even though it was surreal as hell, about describing the Brexit landscape we're in. Do you want to tell me, do you want to describe the film a little bit and your thinking?

So actually, that was in GI festival that I showed that film.

Oh yeah, In Glasgow. I saw it there.

Weirdly, not that I want to be going on about Jeremy Clarkson again, but 'ECHT' was – I'm not saying that I predicted Brexit, but there was a moment where British people started buying four-wheel drive cars more than ever before. And also, those Barber quilted jackets. To begin with like artsy people were wearing that like ironically I think – those like weird gamekeeper jackets, but then men with like tight tapered jeans started wearing them with flat caps and stuff. And this weird cunt-turned-gamekeeper thing that started happening really spread across the UK. Like watching Peaky Blinders and stuff like that. I think it's like the whole country became Guy Ritchie or something like that, and a bit racist – not saying that he's racist or anything. But like, bigoted, like the crap bits of being British. I mean not the good, diverse melting pot. What I thought was a country as well that used to even though they did awful things would be able to challenge itself. That there was like a healthy – I used to like to think that there was a healthy satire scene in this country, and that people would always fight back that we would never let things pass. And I just saw that slightly being eroded a little bit. It was when something about Clarkson making fun of Mexican people and the way that people would defend him and also there was that footballer that was accused of raping a woman and how young lads defended him. I just felt like, the hell is going on, you know? Or maybe it's just becoming clear that we're an unpleasant country. That's what it was. When the guy got kind of found, or like the case against him was dropped. The guy said to Jessica Ennis, who had asked for her name to be taken off the stadium where this guy was playing football, they said, you need to apologise to him, and started haranguing her. I just thought like, what kind of bullshit is this? Where young lads in tracky bottoms are haranguing Olympians on Twitter? What a load of shit. I was like – I'm not saying that all of this was funnelled into that film, but it was just that general sense of entitlement that British people were like really rolling in and I didn't… I just wanted to make a work of somehow about that selfishness.

What was so great about it is also, the way that you do that isn't like worthy. It's really satirical. It's like JG Ballard on crack, mixed with strange ass comedy like these narratives of this sort of post-apocalyptic future which basically did predict

Brexit in a way, or the landscape of Brexit in the media somehow. You couldn't help but watch it, be disgusted and drawn towards this Clockwork Orange-like madness in it.

Yeah, it was weird because some kind of PhD-type writer wrote something like, I was making fun of working-class people. And I was really offended by that because the whole deal of the thing was, that it was bullies taking over. Didn't matter what class you were. And the reason everybody was in tracksuits was because that was the cheapest – I figured if people had taken all the good stuff what would be leftover. Whenever you see somewhere where there's been a natural disaster, that's what they dump on those people. There's loads of old sportswear. I was really offended by that, because, you know, why would I do that as well? It wasn't the point I was making. It was about bullies. It was about the guy in your street with the muscles who like lords it over you a little bit or doesn't go over to the side in his car. That's what Britain has become. It's the country that doesn't go to the side in its car it's just – it's like bad driving. The country's being badly driven.

I would agree with you on that one!

OK since I've been going on about Welsh independence and so on my Instagram that's not to say, there's a lot of great things about being British that I like. It's not that I hate Britain. It's not that at all. It's culturally amazing – the history, the literature, the music. All that stuff is great – well not all of it, but a lot of it is great. I could just sense that we were coming to an unpleasant point. As somebody said on Twitter a few weeks ago that, was Britpop maybe to blame, somewhere. That's a really interesting point or they were going to try and figure out if it was to blame. I can't remember who said it, but it was like… this is, sorry to go off on a tangent…

No go for it.

How do you go from the Stone Roses and the Happy Mondays to Oasis, do you see what I mean? You have a scene in Manchester and the dance rave techno acid house, all that stuff that is quite it felt progressive, right, or like something that's going somewhere? Eventually it didn't really go anywhere but it could have been the step to. Oasis is like going back to primary school isn't it or something, or to the reading group in primary school. It's not a progression is it?

I would also say that I agree that it's almost really the people that loved Oasis and the way they loved that band was kind of pre-empting those dickheads wearing Barbour jackets.

Yeah, and the Union Jack cushions and stuff like that.

Yeah that particular clichéd idea of Britishness, maybe.

I mean you know I remember going to Glastonbury and seeing Oasis play on one of the stages like just before or as they became famous or something. I guess I quite liked the contrast between them and the grow your own clothes people in the audience, but whatever that was didn't develop into anything interesting, do you know what I mean. It was like a long Dad fart; you know that is still in my Instagram feed now.

I'm going to play another song. I'm not going to play all of it because these are getting, really painful. So, we're going to play the Black Eyed Peas. Tell me about your feelings about this track.

I don't know much about the Black Eyed Peas but I remember seeing a video where the guys are looking at the woman twerking, or something like that like. She's in like one of those weird netball skirts that's for showing your bum. They're looking and even maybe rapping about her bum – I can't remember what they're doing. But it's this song because they repeat the word good. Because they say "tonight's gonna be a good good night". I hate that – that's like fingernails on a blackboard. A good good night. A good good. What the hell is a good good, I hate that… that lyric annoys me, but that song is like a kind of mental torture for me, like me trying to buy clothes for my children and that coming on – I want to go back into the car.

Well, we might be doing that to people listening right now. I mean, I'm feeling uncomfortable even playing it, but here we are. A segment of Black Eyed Peas 'I Got A Feeling'.

—

I want to talk a little bit about narrative in what you do. I saw the Barbican show and its weird stuffed goat. This is the thing I remember the most, there suddenly being a horned goat in like the office space, really mental. I really like the way that exhibition and the other films I've seen you do, play around with stories. What do you like about that kind of narrative stuff?

I'm not going to pretend that I listen to the Goon Show or something like that, but my dad did like it. And I loved Monty Python and Spike Milligan. Anything where like people would like go on flights of fancy like that. One of my favourite – I remember my parents bought me a Panasonic cassette player for Christmas. Not with any music on it, obviously, because they didn't listen to music but what they bought me was 'Wind in the Willows' double cassette read out by Kenneth Williams. I absolutely loved Kenneth Williams as a child. Just him, the way that he spoke and stuff like that, the intonation… There's something about a narrator's voice reading things out that gives me tingles a little bit. I'm quite into audiobooks where – not every book translates well into an audio book – but ones that almost make it sound like you're listening to a radio play are great. I think as well growing up in Wales going to Welsh schools, a lot of the Welsh language curriculum is reading like myths and stuff like that from the Mabinogion and I find that – I think more and more about that now as an adult. How – not that I'm into myth like there's this big esoteric thing at the moment like all artists are like wizards and stuff like that, but I am the legend rather than the magic if you know what I mean. If I think about like an example from the Mabinogion, where there's a wedding in Ireland where the Irish wedding guests cut off the ears of the Welsh horses and the lips or the other way round, I can't remember. I don't know where that story came from but it's so alive in your head as a kid, when you read that. In a way, I like writing, but I'm not quite bright enough to write just for its own sake. But the thing that's a shame. I always think, or for me anyway, what I struggle with is, even though I try to read like clever writing – the ones that just like put narrative to one side, or they try to fuck around with the 20th century model of the novel. I still like stories. If there's no story, it doesn't even have to be a long, Sherlock Holmes-type story. It's just if it's nothing, then I'm just like

ah for f-gods sake. I'm a bit of a thicky like that with writing – I just like good stories. I like good stories in the pub.
So, I've used the bard as a character in a couple of works, and in Wales the poet is a big important character, contemporary poets and so on. What they've done is they've kept alive what the poets did, which was write poems in strict rhyme and meter. I'm rubbish with poetry but for my part I think that the bard also had a role that wasn't just about the method, it was also what they did. They travelled around telling stories in strict rhyme and meter, but it wasn't like a poem about a curry in a biro or something, because contemporary poets try to be a bit I like "ooooh". I like that the poets used to go around from court to court telling stories. I mean I don't know enough about this but that's what I've read about it. I like that thing of using the artwork to tell a story. Sorry, I've just repeated that in different ways four times, so it doesn't mean anything. Doesn't mean any more if I say it like that.

> *You did a good job! I like the way you do it, it's almost like you'll have an idea and you'll build it into another even crazier idea. You let things get to their most extreme, but really left field in the approach you're like chewing gum, or mosaic tiles or the goat or whatever that is.*

I think that is just lack of writing skill to be honest. I just like write things in chunks and then can't think of a good way to segue, so I just… I don't know I've thought a lot about how there's a way that – and this is twatty in a way and I'm not making any kind of comparison – but one of my favourite things about The Fall was the way Mark E. Smith would like phrase things. He could just turn a thing on the 360 like that, just by – I just, there's something about a person's voice, even if it's with music or whatever, just telling even if it is a sentence telling a story or something like that. I mean I like The Fall, but I'm not like a knob that's ruined his life, listening to everything, but there's… He will say a man goes to something. Blah blah blah is there to see him. That just seems to be such a natural thing to do? You're telling, this is what's happening or something.

> *Okay, to finish off, Oh my god. I'm going to play an excerpt, not the full track, Taylor Swift, 'Shake it Off'. Do you want to*

tell me why you chose an even worse song than the Black Eyed Peas, if that was possible.

Yeah, so this is like this is irritating, all the way through I think, so the song starts with these kind of weird honks, like ducks or something. It's like a little tune of a honky duck kind of sound. But later on, it's when she repeats herself. So, it's similar to the shiny shiny thing. So, she says, "shame, shame" or something like that. And I don't know why she's repeating it, it's not related to the song. It doesn't make any sense to repeat that bit. I'm not casting any judgment on the production of it or her or anything that. That sound of her saying like "shame shame shame". Like that is so fucking irritating, do you know what I mean? That could make me crash, it's so irritating.

Well, I'll be sure to play that section. Thank you so much Bedwyr for taking the time to chat. That was the funniest Rough Version I've ever done.

Ah, that's good.

Dominique Gonzalez-Foerster

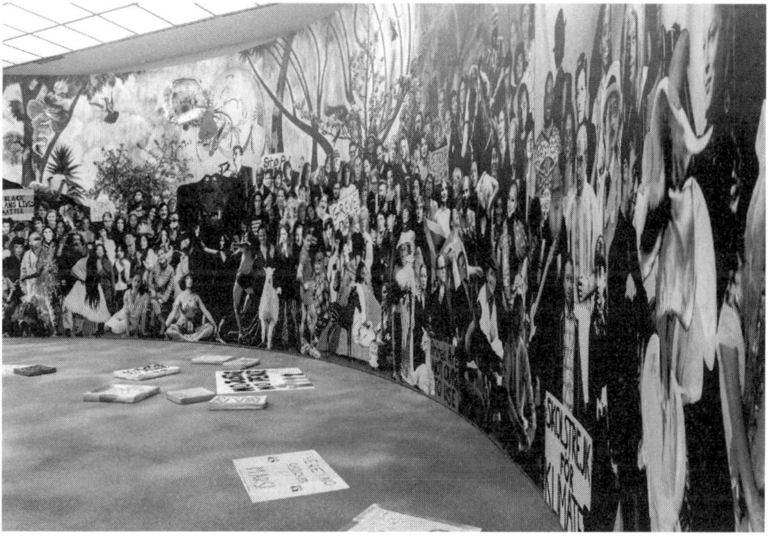

Volcanic Excursion (A Vision), 2021.

30.07.21

Hi. I'm Francesca Gavin and you're listening to Rough Version on NTS. My guest this month is the French artist Dominique Gonzalez-Foerster. She is best known for work that pulls apart the experience of space and her magical take on installation, video, mise-en-scene and photography. Her influences range from science fiction to politics to architecture, and she's had solo shows at Centre Pompidou, Dia Foundation, Kunsthalle Zurich, Musee D'Art Moderne de Paris, Reina Sofia, Guggenheim and Tate Modern, which is incredibly huge. She's currently on show at the Vienna Secession. Well firstly, Dominique, thank you very much for speaking to me today. Let's begin with talking about your current exhibition at the Secession in Vienna. Do you want to tell me about how you got the idea to create this supersized diorama collage work?

Okay. I will try to rewind into the moment. I wanted to when I was working on the exhibition, I wanted something that would— I wanted to imagine to plan something that would be as close as possible to… That will be faithful to the most intense moment I experienced in 2020. I had different thoughts. I wanted it to be kind of an audience-based exhibition or project, which for me means that since exhibition is the medium here. It's like a concert. It doesn't work without the audience, basically. It's totally part. There are many ways to think about that. I had a first plan, but it was somehow smashed by sanitary issues. So, I had to rethink it all. Then I started thinking about the intense 2020 moments. This huge contrast I experienced between the very lonely solitary trapped moments at home, and when we went out in the street in June 2020, several times in France on different occasions. These moments where suddenly, we existed as a 'we' in a collective urban space. This is something that is very urban. It was probably a great thing last year, or even this year. When you can be like in the countryside and far from you know… But it's also an interesting thing in an urban environment that you can somehow experience this human landscape of resistance, desire, protests and joining together. This is less likely to happen, let's say, in the countryside. Although, as a child I experienced, my parents took me to this very big protest. It was in the '70s. When the militaries were planning to buy a whole portion of land, and there was a huge resistance… It was a new generation of *agriculteurs* we say in France.

Agriculture, it's the same in English.

Agricultures, like real rurals. I think that the military didn't expect this resistance. Then it was soon joined by anti-nuclear, anti-racists, feminists, and it became really one of the most intense fights in the '70s in France. Finally, the military left and didn't get the land and it's still now a place of resistance. This is just to say an example of a non-urban fight. Location for a protest, but what I somehow – what came back in my mind, in my dreams as a kind of vision – was this year, and these moments of joining and being together in this space and generating a new space. I felt this really, this was saving me. Saving us from all this isolation and so step by step the crowd grew in my head. It started with friends, inspirers… I wanted to include Typhoeus, the father of the gorgons which is on Klimt's 'Beethoven Frieze'. Then I remembered the big Diego Rivera mural, 'Saturday Alameda in this Mexican Park [Dream of a Sunday Afternoon in Alameda Central Park]', which became the model, the structure for this and somehow the landscape. So, it's a giant collage, but it's also it's a very emotional landscape… Some protagonists appear several times. It doesn't have this sterile way when you have these big murals with famous men or figures, or where you have this scientist, No, it's much more emotional than that. So, some friends reappear. My daughter is there several times. It's a trans-feminist and trans-historical protest because some figures appear from the past. And it's still in progress, because I think I will work on a larger version for next year for the Serpentine in London. It has humans and non-humans, and by non-humans. I also mean even extra-terrestrials. I don't like to call them aliens so much. It's a giant, very open group. I would say, everyone has his own emotional landscape when it comes to inspiration and friends and what keeps you alive. This is mine. You can come and say, "but this person who's very important is not there", but I would say, well then do your own. This is mine. But it's also, one more thing. It's also a place where I feel completely part of it… I appear in it as many selves, not just embodying different characters. It's also a kind of symbiotic feeling somehow. Like a way of being connected to two different beings, characters.

What's interesting among all those kinds of trans, queer, feminist, anti-racist, cultural revolutionaries is lots of people who self-invented themselves.

Yes. Yes.

Which is an ongoing thing in your work. I wanted to know what you like about those characters, that create themselves somehow?

I think this is somehow the essence of art. Whether it's visual, acting, music. I think the possibility to have your own narrative and to reinvent yourself, whether it's in a non-binary way, whether it's changing your name, whether it's changing your work. All that, I think to me is very connected to I would say art as an open medium beyond usual classifications, such like painting, sculpture. I think it even works in this incredible reinvention, goes also through appropriation of new medias. I love to think of the Castiglione, the Contessa from the late 19th century who was doing all this photographic work and at the beginning of photography. I think there is a line going from her to Lola Montez and Cassati but then reaching Claude Cahun and reaching Cindy Sherman, Ana Mendieta and so many artists who either use photography, film, video. But even performance as a new medium, or stage or just the stage. Being this or using the idea of being a medium. Medium in the sense of producing a séance. And gaining a lot of freedom as opposed to academic or an artistic field that would be ruled by standards. I see, I really see very strong connections. I mean, you might not believe that when I say that… I feel connected. In the past I didn't feel connected. In the 19th century my main [inspirations] are Lola Montez and Ludwig II, and Castiglione because I think they also experimented with new mediums. Whether it's photography or narrative space or stage. I think Lola Montez was really, had a very similar impact as Madonna in the 19th century. I really love all these figures of invention and reinvention of all possible selves.

Also, what's interesting is the way that you present this work and again is something that seems to come out in pieces is the idea of the stage. Somehow it feels like – I mean you're surrounded by all these figures. Us as a viewer are within it but you often seem to play around with mise-en-scene, the setting. What do you find interesting about the stage with or without performance?

I've been exploring in the past 30 years. I've been exploring a lot of relations to exhibition, display, stage. There is always an issue of stage. Whether it's stage or film. There is always a way you have to bring things in and things out and edit. There is a notion of dramaexplore. This is where it's a bit linked to all these late 19th century inventions in that case is this diorama, diaromatic stage I would say. When I said 'diorama' I mean a structure device where you connect two dimensions with three dimensions. Except here, I think. I've worked on some dioramas which were housing books instead of endangered species. Here what I find exciting is that as a viewer, you can totally be part of this diorama structure which is usually also set in a way that it's not – that it excludes you but that you can enter it. You have to watch it from outside which also makes it very powerful. Because usually it's also a stage that you can't mess. You can't disturb it. You're confronted to it but there it's the opposite. I think it only works if you jump in or if you sit inside.

Let's play a track which I think is one of the people featured in the diorama. Do you want to talk about the Arto Lindsay track?

Arto is a friend since almost 20 years. We met the first time in Bahia, Salvador… Arto has been staging parades, aside from his great musical work. Since so long he's been also doing some great, more visual but also I would say total art moments and these parades. He's staged some in New York and Venice and Frankfurt. Really amazing moments where he has all these different groups. I remember the one in Frankfurt was involving the philosophers and there is of course, there's a strong influence coming from the Rio Carnival or even all carnivals. There's also an amazing carnival in Bahia. Arto has a really, has a very open way to think about music. He can do a fantastic concert. I was very happy to start my own humble contribution to some stage, live music with him in a great place in Paris, Silencio. It's a small club which was designed by David Lynch some years ago and Arto is terrific. My favourite guitarist in the world but also a very open artist.

Well, this is Arto Lindsay 'Seu Pai'.

—

Actually, let's talk about your own music. Why you started making it and how you've incorporated that into the rest of your work?

I don't come from a family of musicians, and I didn't learn an instrument as a child, but I was always very much into music. Twenty years ago, a French singer, and you might not know him, because it's more like a French phenomenon, Christoph, you might know? About Alain Bashung? Maybe not. Anyway, they are really great French singers and musicians, and I was lucky to work with both in the early 2000s, on their concert tours. To work on the visual part. I've spent a lot of time touring with them and watching the rehearsals. I think at this time, there was no – I mean I couldn't even imagine that one day I would be brave enough to sing, but I think it grew deep inside. Slowly step by step. A few years ago, one friend asked me to write a song – Saâdane Afif. He's doing this collection of songs by friends, artists and they become part of his work and exhibitions. So, I started to write a song. Then I asked a friend, Perez – he's also a great French singer-musician, too – if we could try something. It became very, I don't know, it was very natural somehow. I think because maybe I spent all this time listening and watching and being fascinated by musicians, I also felt I had to try. So Exotourisme is small – I mean, we're only two… I'm exploring a kind of replicant persona. I'm not going on stage as a sincere Dominique. It's a replicant, and she has some issues with different things. The songs, some have a very '80s flavour and some… I'm basically an experimental artist. I've done architectural projects, I've done films. This is what defines me… I can't repeat and rehearse so much but we try. We also worked with The Vinyl Factory in London and made some vinyl and started to do some concerts. Then like so many we were hit by the possibility to… but it's taking shape again. It was a bit sleepy but it's like a volcano it will spit lava again.

Nice. We're going to play 'Pangea Innamorata'. Do you want to tell me how Paul B. Preciado got involved or how you drew from that?

So, Paul. I met Paul more than three years ago and I was already a big reader. I think 'Testo Junkie' is one of the most important books in the last decade. To me it's very important that a philosopher is also so experimental and also so involved in visual arts. Then when I saw that his 'Parliament Of Bodies' document is an incredible setting and for sure, the volcanic excursion owes a lot to his 'Parliament of Bodies'. When we met, the conversation went on many levels, many different projects. We also discussed an opera… and then I asked him to write a song. I think 'Pangea Innamorata' is one of my favourite songs.

This is Exotourisme with 'Pangea Innamorata'.

—

I want to talk about another aspect of your work, I know you showed this at 180 Strand. The idea of the ghostly, or the apparition, that magical figure, Do you want to tell me about what you like about playing with that kind of figure?

I think what I was touching a bit on before is the idea. There is a really great book about that. How some women in the late 19th century decided to become – you also say mediums in English? I think at that time, to have a different type of life. You could be, there were possibilities to be an actress or… These mediums some went into what they call automatic writing or Georgina Houghton into exploring painting. But I think they gained through this setting and frame of the spiritual or mediumistic practice. You gain a lot of freedom. It's a kind of paradox but I think that this… I don't think I can, I wouldn't define myself as a mystical person, but I find a lot of freedom in this, let's say, blurry zone between. It's has also something non-binary. Between the living and the non-living and everything in between. Whether it's ghosts or what I called apparitions. I often say that these apparitions, these different characters – I don't even want to use the word perform – but I always feel I enter a kind of trance and they find a door and they enter. It sounds weird but I think now with this sort of volcanic excursion for me belongs more to that. The visions… I see it as a giant freedom like I don't know how much you know of Hilma Af Klint as a painter? Recently, her work – hidden work [that] she kept hidden because it was so far from the academic standards – is now surfacing. And one can see that by accepting another, a different context, a different vocabulary or different process or by putting the work in another area, there is another type of freedom… It might all sound a bit strange, but that's how I would define it.

I want to play another one of your tracks, let's play the Perez track. Do you want to talk a little bit about Perez?

Perez is the co. Exotourisme is our place. It's where we meet, in terms of music and art. Perez is, I think, a great singer and great musician. He's also composed some great film music. We have a very fast way to do things which I find great. We don't need to rehearse so much, and it comes very easy. This song. So, Perez is also I think a bit similar to Arto. He has also a strong attraction to visual arts. He himself I think sings in very visual ways… I'm not talking about synaesthesia, now. More like he's also been to – he's seen a lot of exhibitions, visual art. So, it makes it easier to discuss things and also he's very open to the fact that I'm not, that I haven't – I started singing when I was 52 or 53 it's a bit strange but it means also I want to say that to everyone it means you can start any time. There is no limit to trying things. This song 'Cerveau' means brain. It is really about how souls and emotions, and things are circulating inside, and I like this song very much.

Well, this is Perez 'Cerveau'.

—

When I think about your work that I've seen, a lot of stuff that I was really fascinated by it's also very immersive and almost science fiction. You're in sound and light and you're using such a variety of different media in what you do. What do you like about that space to create?

I think this is what I'm sensitive to, you know. For me when I look at – I like some paintings and images but what affects me is to be surrounded by something. I've always felt that for me a space – maybe this is something that is connected to some kind of neuro atypical or typical thing, I don't know – but I need to be surrounded by art to feel something. If I'm in front of a small painting… my eyes are drifting to the ground or the ceiling. I like to be enclosed in an environment. I also like to I read a lot of, I still read a lot of science fiction. I love to discover. I'm always curious what is the art of the future. I always like to imagine what is art in the future and will there be a moment when there will be an artwork that I can't identify. That I can't even experience as an artwork because I don't have the antennas for that. But I'm always very excited in this again blurry zone between what is art and what is not and if it stops somewhere. I'm delighted when people question, is it really still art. I don't know if you've seen images from the Turbine Hall experience 'TH2058' but that was this giant shelter in 2008 with these sculptures which were growing and all these bunk beds. I think it was another vision I had which, for some people, it was almost too much like but now some also realized that it was… I think I'm more interested in exploring the future in terms of what art can be, but I'm also constantly navigating on a long timeline, and collaging different elements in a kind of Walter Benjamin way. Again, it's a lot of experiments, but I found out that the one-to-one scale or the human scale, which implies that things are real size, is my place. It's my beach.

On that lovely note we are going to play your last song, which is Melissa Laveaux. Do you want to tell me why you chose this one?

Melissa I met in one of Paul Preciado's seminars in Paris, at the Pompidou in October 2020. I mean, it started in March 2020, and then there was a second part in October 2020. Paul did this great seminar at the Pompidou which was also a very important moment in that year. Melissa was there to sing, and I think she lives in Paris, and wow, she's a fantastic singer, and also an incredible I think, storyteller. Her way of combining music, thinking – yeah, she's great.

This is Melissa Laveaux 'Kouzen', and thank you so much Dominique for your time.

My pleasure. It has been a great moment with you.

Madelynn Green

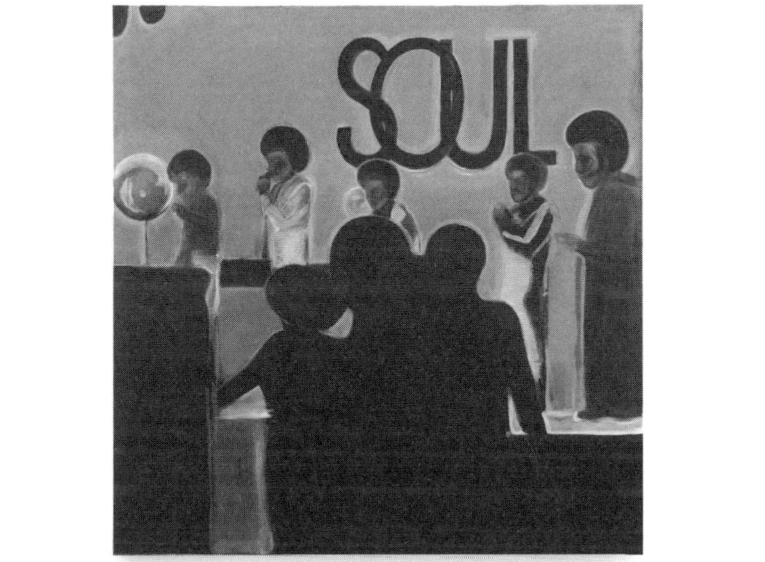

Devotion,2020.

27.08.21

Hi, I'm Francesca Gavin and you're listening to Rough Version on NTS. My guest this month is Madelynn Green. Born in Milwaukee, she's a painter based in London, currently a teaching Fellow at the Slade. She's exhibited at Almine Rech, VO Curations, and is in the UK Government Art Collection. Currently, her first London solo show is running until September the ninth at Taymour Grahne Projects. Madelynn, thank you so much for taking the time to talk to me. Let's start at the beginning. Why painting? Why did you choose painting as a medium?

Thanks a lot for having me. It's great to speak with you. I think painting for me has come automatically. I've been painting since I was a child, drawing and painting. It feels like an instinct. When I first went to art school, I got my Master's at Central Saint Martins in London, I tried to do other mediums. I tried sculpture; I tried video, and it just didn't work. Painting is where I feel at home. I think with painting, you get the chance to create images that are subjective instead of objective. Images you get in pictures or video. You get a chance to create images that are crazy and radical and weird and from perspectives that you wouldn't normally get. I think in the spaces with painting, you can create anything you want. And I think there's so much possibility when it comes to painting. You can never run out of ideas. You can never run out of colours. You can never run out of subjects. Painting is where I feel most comfortable. I also find it really comforting to paint, the act of painting is fun for me. I think that makes the work of being an artist really enjoyable.

Let's talk a bit about your process. Do you always draw from photographic imagery? Do you plan out compositions? How does the process work for you?

I think I began mostly working from images, like photographs. Then I moved on to film stills. When I was in high school in America, I had a business where I would work with (not exactly work with) – other high schoolers would ask me to draw pictures of them and their friends or their family. They would give me $20 to do that. I started drawing and painting through working with images. That stuck with me, because I think images have this unique visual language. You can tell the time based on how the image looks – if it's blurry, or if it has a halo around the head it's from early 2000s. It's from the 1990s. I think there are interesting properties that come with images that can be transformed or reimagined in painting. Recently I've started working more with imagination. I've seen so many images, so many movies, so many videos. I think I have enough. I guess we all have enough material to work with to create our own images. I've been doing sketches and thinking about ways to make my paintings more imaginative, and thinking about crowds, as ways of imagining painting. I would say it's about 50/50. I really don't box myself in, if I want to work from an image, I'll work from the image. If I want to imagine something, if I want to do a combination of the two, which I often do. I'll do that as well.

Before we play your first track, can I ask you about some of the films you've been influenced by? Are you interested in their narratives, or is it more about the aesthetic?

It's definitely the aesthetic and the cinematography. I am obsessed with thriller movies and horror films. I feel like they do such a good job of building suspense, just based on camera angles. They use a lot of mirrors. I saw this film the other day, it was dark. They filmed the reflection of someone from a pool of blood. I thought, "wow, that would be a great painting". I don't know if that means that I'm sick and twisted. I just think those genres of films are designed to create suspense and a sense of intrigue and mystery. Those specific genres are interesting to me. I just re-watched 'Midsummer' yesterday, and I was looking at the cinematography of that film and how bright it was. The colours were so vibrant. So, it's not really a specific film. It's just mostly the genres that I'm interested in and how they use camera angles to tell stories.

Let's play your first track. I want to play D'Angelo, because I'm probably the biggest D'Angelo fan you'll ever meet. Have every single, every album. Tell me about your relationship to 'Brown Sugar', and why you chose it.

Oh my god. I think that might be one of my favourite songs ever. I think it's nostalgic because I was born in 1993. I think that song came out in like 1997, so I was four years old. I know I always heard it in the car with my parents or on the radio. It has this nostalgic feeling. When I hear it, it transports me back to my childhood but as I've grown older, I've been able to appreciate D'Angelo and his artistry a little more. To me that song is just like the definition of the sublime, and a perfect song. I mean, his voice, the instrumentation, the video that comes with the song is really nice, too. When I listen to that song it feels, it's so perfect. I think that perfection in the notion of sublime is something I'm interested in, when it comes to art and how those concepts transfer over to painting, or art making. That's the philosophical explanation for why I like it, but I just think it's a great song to dance to, and it puts me in a good mood.

That's a very good reason. This is 'Brown Sugar'.

—

One of the other things that's a regular motif in your work, you mentioned it briefly, is the crowd scenes. Often, they're a diverse selection of people having pleasurable moments. Either at clubs, or on the beach. Do you want to talk a bit about what you like about that grouping, and the idea of community that you're representing?

I think that subject is something I found my way into while I was doing my MFA at CSM. I was trying to think why am I interested in this. Sometimes you like something, but you don't really know why you like it. I did a crowd painting, I was like, "wow, this was really fun". All the different perspectives, genders, races and ages together. There's a sense of a radical gathering of people that necessarily wouldn't gather. I was thinking from a personal perspective. I have a twin. I feel like my whole engagement with the world has been in a group. I even had trouble seeing myself as an individual as a kid, because I thought it's me and my sister, me and my twin. I think my experience as a person has been shaped by being in a group and in relationships with others. I've also experienced not being seen as an individual, because I have a twin. I think that's just my own perspective, as someone who goes through the world as part of the group or part of a unit. It makes me really curious about the relationships between people and how different people interact with each other.

When I make those paintings. I feel like I'm trying to create a dialogue between everyone. So, the person that's in the upper right-hand corner, are they thinking about the person in the lower left-hand corner? What about the person in the middle versus the person on the side? I try to create these secret interactions in those paintings, and it's really fun, because when you make it, when you look at it, you can learn so much just based on the interactions between the people. There are also unlimited permutations of crowds you can create. It's really open-ended. There's lots of opportunity to imagine different crowd settings.

Let's talk a little bit about your representation of music. You've done some amazing 'Soul Train' paintings and performance paintings. Tell me about those pieces and why you started doing them.

I think that's another thing that steals from my own experience. As a kid, I grew up with my great grandparents watching 'Soul Train' and seeing bell bottoms and afros. The bright set with all the lights and people dancing. I thought the aesthetic of it was really nostalgic and beautiful. I hate to be that person that says there were no phones, but there were no phones. People were having a good time. It was a very natural, organic setting, which I guess I feel a little nostalgia for, even though I wasn't there. It comes down to the aesthetic of it, the nostalgia, because, the colours are bright, the clothes are interesting, people are beautiful and stylish. I felt that wasn't represented in art the way I'd like it to be. The artist Tschabalala Self did a series about 'Soul Train' recently. But beyond that I hadn't seen this cultural phenomenon represented in contemporary art in any way. I wanted to bring that image out of obscurity. Because we've all seen the images of 'Soul Train', we all know what it looks like, but I haven't really seen it represented in a painterly language. So that was what I was interested in doing. I hope to make more of those, because they're really fun to make. I think people really feel a connection to them.

In a way, you're elevating the subject matter a lot by making it into a painting. There's something about that medium, the focus that goes into it.

Yes, it's really historical. It puts it into our history.

Let's play another track. Let's play Souls of Mischief. Since I'm enjoying your '90s references. Why did you choose '93 'Til Infinity'?

I just love that song. I can't think of a deep explanation. I just love that song. I was born in 1993, so I consider it one of my anthems. It feels like a song that I relate to because I was born in that year and the video for that song is super cool. It was filmed in Yosemite National Park in America. I've never seen a rap video filmed in that great outdoors. It's really beautiful. The video's really nice and I love the '90s in terms of music, especially rap music. I listen to a lot of rap in the studio. With all my tracks I try to like do a mix of genres so there's house, there's rap, there's R&B. I find rap music really inspiring. This song is just speaking about living right and who doesn't want that? Who doesn't want this motivational song playing in your ear while you're working. I just love the song. I had a hard time picking which rap song to choose, because I listen to a lot, but it's one of my favourites.

This is Souls of Mischief, '93 'Til Infinity'.

—

With some of the imagery that you're representing, and the characters and figures that you're giving weight to, there seems to be an element of politics in terms of what's driving you. Do you want to tell me what you find interesting about the relationship between representation, politics and art?

I think art is a great opportunity to get narratives that have been underrepresented to the forefront, and images. People that have been underrepresented to the forefront. It's one of the central aims in my practice. I think that, as artists, we all have some sort of responsibility. Not all artists believe this, that we have some sort of responsibility, but I do. As image-makers, we don't have to change the world, but we have to make some sort of commentary on the world around us. I think, as a Black woman, I see the world around me and I don't necessarily see the things represented in mass culture, or in my experience represented in mass culture or mass media. I see my practice as a chance to fill those gaps. I don't see that as the exclusive aim of my practice, I don't sit in the studio, thinking I must show these people who I am. I just make what I want to make, and that's it. But I find the act of doing what you want to do quite radical in itself and not having to cater to some sort of diversity quota. I think of my own background. I did my BA in Political Science. Then I shifted into art. I'm naturally interested in politics. I have always been interested in policy and social causes and stuff like that. I did even work in politics for a bit. After I graduated uni, I worked in New York City for the city government for a year, which was a good experience, but it was quite administrative. That's why I wanted to go more into art. With art, you can do some of the same things you do working in an office in politics, but you get to speak to people more directly. You get to speak to people through images. I guess my first introduction to art was through photography, specifically new photography, documentary photography. My great grandmother had these photography books that I would go through as a kid. I was just really inspired by images of the civil rights movement, of protests all over the world, of wars, and I saw art as a chance to bring narratives and current events to the forefront. I see them as inextricably linked. I think art and politics will always have a relationship, whether we want it to or no.

Coming from the American Midwest and now living in the UK. There's quite a different cultural context in London. It's very different from the Midwest. What do you find interesting about those contrasts, and do you think they're feeding into what you're doing somehow?

Oh, my goodness, it's been such a culture shock living in London. You wouldn't think there would be such a big one, because when I moved here, I thought, they speak English. It's fine. It will be cool. It was, in the beginning, but then subtle differences started to settle in. The main ones, I think, have been social. I think Americans are very friendly. I thought that was just normal. I didn't realize that it was weird to speak to a stranger or smile at a stranger until I moved here and realized people will think you are a psychopath if you talk to them and if you smile. I've gotten to that point, too, because I've lived here for four years so if someone smiles at me, I'll be like, "what's wrong?"

And it's sad. I don't want to be that way. Normally back home, I'll just smile back at someone if they smile at me. So, that's been an adjustment and I feel like that has really affected my work. Because it's almost like you're a fish out of water. When you're in the water, when you're in the Midwest, everything seems fine. I lived in New York. Everything seems fine in New York. But then once you get out, you get this bird's eye view of everything. You realize, this is where I'm coming from. Now I fully understand it, because I have this other experience to contrast it with. I feel moving to London helped me to understand myself more. And see some problems with America, obviously, but also see some problems with this country, too. It's been a great way to get this enriching, cultural experience, where you get to understand where you come from isn't the only place on Earth. There are other places, and other things to learn from, other art histories. Living here, I get so much information about art history, from a European perspective, and from a British perspective. I think that's really helped me, and my perspective definitely isn't singular. It's had its challenges, but I think overall, it's really helped me understand myself, and I think that is one of the keys to being an artist – introspection.

Let's play another track. Let's play Floorplan. Why did you choose this?

Oh my god. I love that song. I was playing it before I sent it to you, and I was dancing. I love that song so much. It's a house song, but it's also a gospel song, because it has an Aretha Franklin sample in it. I love the original song, 'Never Grow Old' by Aretha Franklin, because it's just really inspiring. I listen to a lot of gospel music in the studio. Really inspiring, uplifting, positive music. What more can you ask for? I love the crescendo of the beat of that song, when it starts off slow but then it explodes into this screaming ecstasy. I love it so much. That song really energizes me in the studio, and I love listening to Floorplan, Robert Hood and Aretha Franklin. I find them really great people to listen to in my studio.

This is Floorplan, 'Never Grow Old'.

—

I want to ask you a couple more things that are very much

painting-based. Firstly, do you want to tell me what draws you to the scale of your work? How big are your paintings and why are you working on that scale?

I started out working on a smaller scale, but once I got into art school, you get your own studio space, you don't have to work in your bedroom. You can explode the scale that you work at. I had great tutors that said "Madelynn, just make really big paintings". I said, "Okay, I'll try". I was really lucky when I was in my MFA, because I got this bursary to help me pay for materials. It's not cheap to paint. Big paintings cost money, big canvases cost money. I was able to afford these big stretchers and canvases. I found that I enjoyed working at that scale, because it's this full-body scale. I'm five foot six inches tall. I'm 165 centimetres. I'm pretty much the same size as a lot of the canvases that I'm making, or I'm smaller. I feel like I have to attack it with my arms, my legs and my whole body. I get to stand on ladders, stand on chairs. It feels like a full-body experience. I like the idea of not just making a painting with your mind, but with your body. I think the experience of looking at a large painting can be really visceral and physical. I'm thinking of someone like Mark Rothko, who made giant paintings. When you stand in front of them you feel insignificant, and I like that feeling of being dwarfed by this sublime painting, this sublime work of art. I think scale is an opportunity to really communicate with people, because I think people are drawn into things that are larger than life… It's a way to bring images out of obscurity. It's so big you can't miss it. At the same time, I love giant canvases, but I also love tiny ones, because they almost feel like a joke. You have to walk up really close to them and you get a sense of intimacy with those types of work. I tend to do a lot of portraits on that scale. I think they are really powerful because they invite you in. I'm of two opinions. I love large, big canvases, and tiny ones.

Your style is quite stylized. Sometime features seem to almost fuzz away, or haze away. Other times, I feel like you're trying to give more depth to what people look like. I'm just curious about clarity or haze.

That's something I think a lot about when I paint, the decision about what do you show, what do you conceal. What information do I want the viewer to know? What don't I want them to know? I think faces tend to be the most important aspect of a person if I'm painting a person, I don't really care about hands. I tend to make them look like flippers or be very inconsiderate of the person's hands. I don't really bother about them, because I just think that information isn't necessary. If I wanted you to look at the hand, then I would make it really clear. I think you can use the paintbrush as a tool, almost like Photoshop, where you're blurring out things that don't matter, or that I don't want you to care about. Then making things clear that I think are important. One of my favourite artists, Noah Davis, has a style that I'm really inspired by. He would render faces really stylistically, too. When you render it softly, I think it gets to the emotional qualities of the figure. I think the eyes capture emotion, lips capture emotion, and the way you depict those, the way you depict the body can make you understand the feelings behind that figure. I think how you render them is a way to explore emotions and characters.

Let's finish by playing your last track which is Michelle Weeks & Voices 2. When did you first hear this? And what do you like about this track?

A couple years ago, I found it on YouTube. I'm a big YouTube user. That's where I find a lot of music. I just love the fact that there's a similar build-up in this song too, where it starts off mellow, then goes into this screaming and yelling and the beat gets really powerful. It's really inspiring. It has a similar gospel message to never grow old. I love this song. It gives me a lot of energy in the studio and the voices are really incredible. I just love them. I'm inspired by their music, because I think that they do something so sublime and so perfect with their voices and their talent. How can I do something similar in the work that I'm making. So that's why I love that song.

That's brilliant. Thank you so much for your time, Madelynn. This is Michelle Weeks & Voices 2 doing 'Can You See the Light (Kings of Tomorrow remix)'. And thank you so much.

Thanks.

Paul Purgas

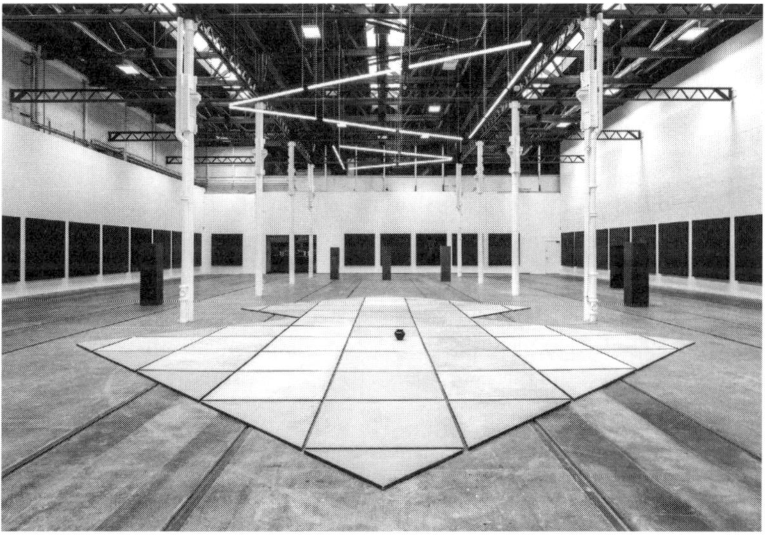

30.09.21

Hi, I'm Francesca Gavin and you're listening to Rough Version on NTS. My guest this month is Paul Purgas, a London based artist and musician, curator and broadcaster who works with sound installation, performance, and is also known as one half of Emptyset. He's done projects for Serpentine, Camden Arts Centre, is a resident at Somerset House Studios, and currently has a solo show on display in Glasgow at Tramway. Hello, Paul.

Hey, Fran, thanks for having me.

So, you're one of the most unusual people I've had on here. Because most of time, I really have people who are coming from a straight visual art background. But what I find really interesting about what you do is its breadth. Do you want to tell me about your background – how you started from an architectural space. I knew you first in the curatorial space. How did you start doing what you do?

I guess it started after finishing college, and not really having any plan, or any kind of vision for my life or where that journey was going to take me or what it would be. My mum was basically saying she would kick me out of home unless I went to university. I didn't really have any options. I had to go and study something. I guess that that sense of coming from an Indian family, even if it was not necessarily strict, meant I had to have some kind of vocation, some kind of strategy, whether it was being an accountant, or a doctor, a solicitor or something like that. I guess I chose architecture because it resonated within my family. I felt that my parents could tell people that Paul is going to be an architect, so I could make that fly, right? And then I was just running, fixated on electronic music, I guess, throughout my teens. I was lucky enough to go to the University of Westminster, 'cause I didn't really know what architecture was all about. I knew I wasn't going to go to art school. My strategy was to do something creative in some form. I was lucky enough to get to the University of Westminster at a time when people like Cedric Price and David Greene from Archigram were teaching, they were quite visionary and into psychedelic periods of reimagining the built environment, as well as ideas of cybernetic systems design. I guess it was very much in the spirit of the late

'60s and '70s, when a lot of different art forms were converging into a unified cultural experiment. I went to architecture school, and I guess I realized that all the people that I was interested in, never really built anything. Cedric Price did build the Aviary at London Zoo, which is a masterpiece. I guess that set me off on a certain path. Then I went to the Royal College of Art and studied Design there. And I guess, after having done all that, I realized that all of my friends in architecture practices had become CAD monkeys. They were shackled, designing handrails for toilets, a Norman Foster fraternity. That was their destiny. I was still listening to music all the time. I was going to Berlin and meeting a lot of amazing musicians. I didn't know if I wanted to become one of these cogs in the wheel of an architecture firm. So, I quit London, and moved back to Bristol. Amazingly, I managed to get a curatorial post at Arnolfini where I learned a lot more and expanded my knowledge beyond music and design. I was thinking about art history, the history of visual art and its relationship to all these other spheres. At the same time, I started making music as Emptyset. I guess, I had been on a journey of curiosity. The history of art and the history of cultural production across the 20th century was what really inspired me. People like David Tudor, and the Fluxus spirit, or people that connected the dots between these different art forms in a way that was probably quite natural in that moment. But as the arts became more specialized, or more industrialized, it's become more of a personal politic to think about what are the spaces in which work can exist? How we can reimagine that cultural landscape? I guess I've just tried to find a way to make something, to the best of my ability, to make a practice, which feels coherent, but at the same time, not have too much reverence for the existing infrastructures. And to not think that an art gallery is more important than a nightclub... Everything is different. Everything sits within an ecosystem of ideas. And we can gain value and experience these things in very different ways. There is no hierarchy. I think that's probably the journey that I've been on and will probably continue to follow.

> *That late '60s, early '70s period is my happy place, culturally, too, because it's such an interesting mesh of things. I'm really interested to know how that influenced the kind of music you were making, and continue to make, which is obviously very*

much emerging from techno and electronica, a minimalist background. Do you see this as a relationship between what you're making and have made aurally, and those other cultural ideas? How do you feel that is feeding into your music?

Well, actually I think one of the great benefits of going to the Royal College of Art when I did was that there was a film historian guy called Alan Rees who was digging into the histories of structural materialist film and video. He was showing lots of films by Brakhage, and Liz Rhodes. I think it was Liz Rhodes particularly who lit a fire in my mind. I saw films like 'Dresden Dynamo' for the first time. But at the same time, listening to a lot of music that's come from the Anglo-American and European minimalist electronic traditions. Whilst also starting to get a clearer understanding, I think Fluxus, once again, was super useful at connecting the dots. Of thinking through these languages that were very resourceful. People working with what they've got. I think a lot of that moved very closely to language of materiality, just by its very nature. That slightly DIY sensibility. I guess, like a lot of the artists I was interested in, were trying to communicate and express ourselves through different material forms, conditions restrictions. Whether that be European modernism and minimal electronics, or even actually, when we're thinking about the traditions of modernism in India, that resourcefulness. Resourcefulness has been a kind of anchor that I found super interesting, like a maximalist potential of expression, through a very, very refined sense of forms or source materials. I just find that a fascinating methodology.

I'm going to say this is like a really good time to play Jeff Mills, because we're thinking of someone who is emerging from Detroit, who is also really representing that transatlantic sound. Do you want to tell me why you chose this specific track and when you first heard it?

I can talk about Jeff Mills with so much passion. The reason I went to architecture school was because I was obsessed with Jeff Mills as a teenager, and Jeff Mills went to architecture school. So, I thought, well, if Jeff can do it, then I should probably do it. I first met Jeff, in a record shop in Bristol in the late '90s. He was DJing to launch a mix CD, 'Live at the Liquid Room in Tokyo'. And he turned up in HMV when I was a teenager. As a South Asian man, growing up in the UK, it was very difficult to find like a cultural identity that I could connect to. Bristol was very much in the Bristol sound, the trip hop, drum'n'bass thing. I could understand it, but somehow it didn't resonate with my being. I couldn't act the bad man, that was my problem. I always struggled with that routine. But to turn up at HMV in Bristol and see a Black man with three turntables playing this incredible, futuristic electronic music, blow all the speakers. He signed this CD for me. What we're about to listen to is the first track in the opening of that CD, from the live in Tokyo mix. I listened to that incessantly in my bedroom in Weston-super-Mare in my early teens. It shaped so much about how I think about the world. That's why it's an honour to play this record.

> *We're going to play it. By the ways I used to follow Jeff Mills around clubs all around the country about that period, and I cannot believe he played HMV! This is Jeff Mills, 'Utopia'.*
>
> —
>
> *We've touched on it briefly, but let's go into more detail about your work and the influence of your South Asian heritage on what you're doing now. You've uncovered the incredible history of electronic sound and Indian modernism – a pet project in recent years, do you want to tell me a little bit about it? Firstly, tell me how you started working with it, and how it's feeding into what you're doing?*

It started originally by me getting wind of this Moog synthesizer that was taken to India in the late '60s by David Tudor. Whilst I was working at Arnolfini, I became really interested in experiments in art and technology, the foundational projects set up by Billy Cleaver, Robert Rauschenberg and Robert Whitman, that connected the dots between the art, industry, and utopian futurism. I was already quite fascinated by their work. Then to find out this link that E.A.T. was plugged into India, and was taking this moog synthesizer over there, that blew my mind. I was just fascinated. It was such a strange tale, that I just felt like I had all these air miles from playing live shows of Emptyset, I'm just gonna blow them on flying out to this design school in India.

I'm going to find this synthesizer. And in a classic quest tale, the synthesizer itself is a massive MacGuffin. It was like the fool's gold that I was trying to find that was always outside of my reach. But what I did find was in the library of the National Institute of Design, which is essentially India's Bauhaus. It was an incredibly radical, design school set up in the '60s that was part of the industrialization of India. It was a visionary space with this whole holistic pedagogy around it. In the archives of the National Institute of Design, I found this box of tapes. That box had a collection of electronic compositions by five composers that no one had heard of or paid any attention to. In the school, there was a functioning electronic music studio making this incredible experimental music across the late '60s and early '70s. It was an amazing discovery. I was always approaching not from the position of an academic or researcher. Just being an electronic musician, practitioner of the South Asian diaspora, trying to find some kind of context for what I was doing. I realized, after the fact, the whole journey had been quite a beautiful one to discover – to feel I was in continuum. The beautiful thing is that I was inspired to try… I knew certain Bollywood producers were working with electronics, but this was a legit, avant-garde tradition, operating within that peak moment. And it's been beautiful to uncover that, but also to see it meant something for many other people, not only in the South Asian diaspora, but also within India itself. People feeling it's given them an anchoring and a sense of likewise feeling they're part of a continuum. That what they're doing has a context. I think that's been quite amazing.

> *I want to talk a bit about how that's emerged in the exhibition you have coming up in Glasgow. You seem to have taken a lot of that heritage and transformed it into something that's very much part of your own practice. Do you want to describe how the Tramway show functions?*

Yeah. When I discovered the tapes and things, I think there was something self-evident about that there was this archive of audio, but it sat very much at the centre of a wheel that encapsulated everything from spiritual philosophies, radical pedagogies, and exploratory methods of modernist design and ancient geometries. What became quite fascinating was the sense the tapes articulated. There was a sensibility of what was happening in India at that moment. And I guess, a lot of the frictions in the story. The complexities of the relationship between Western and Indian modernism. How money and power were manoeuvring their way through that region. The story is a beautiful flourishing within a certain, dreamy window of time in India. There's likewise a kind of complexity in terms of how money is moving around and how America is manoeuvring to use design as a language, in order to initiate soft power – the infusion of Western capitalism into India. There's so much spinning around. One of the aspects that gave the whole archive a science fiction angle, is the Sarabhai family that funded this electronic music studio. The daughter, Gita Sarabhai, was composing this electronic music whilst the same time her brother, Vikram Sarabhai, was setting up the Indian Space Program. So once again it has this amazing mirroring within the history of electronic music of futurism, science fiction, imagined futures. There is so much at play, that I felt the Glasgow show at Tramway was an opportunity to try and extrapolate all these threads of the story and find a way to take all the disparate premises of Indian modernism that were fractured and try to unify them into a singular statement. That would start to mirror this sense that… The sound work exists once again, as a central kind of axiom of the show, but there are these supporting methodologies, whether that be architectural systems, colour systems from Gujarati textiles and fabrics. Anthropomorphic systems, which I became super, super interested in. The ways of defining design around the South Asian body and the idea to reclaim that space from the West. Also, there was this floor work that is a central component of the show, by an architect called Aditya Prakas. It's an amazing system that was used in the theatre in Chandigarh. The way it operates it mirrors another system that was used at the National Institute of Design, where a number of squares with gaps. It was a system devised to seamlessly integrate infrastructure into the architecture, enabling all the cabling to run seamlessly through this floor. I use the same system from Aditya Prakash as the central visual element of the exhibition. There's also this beautiful fact I discovered through the research for the exhibition that prior to going to Chandigarh, Aditya Prakash studied at Glasgow School of Art. Literally before he got head hunted. It's one of those things you circumstantially discover and go wow, this gives the whole show within that context, a beautiful reading. Especially in the

Scottish Rennie Mackintosh heritage, in ways that have been quite surprising. I guess the show all in all, has been a way to locate that sound archive, within a container in which there's an infusion of all the semiotics of colour, of material, of form, of structure, of anthropometrics. So that actually, it feels like the perfect location for it to be presented. I think that's what I was hoping for. I feel that the show has managed to achieve that in a way that I've been really happy with.

I want to ask you more questions about it. But first, can you play on some of the audio that comes from the exhibition. Can you explain what we're listening to?

This is actually one of the pieces – the audio for Tramway is divided into three elements – one is field recordings and environmental sounds, one element that's more speeches and lectures that occurred at the National Institute of Design and a central composition in the space of which we're about to play is a part of that section. I guess this was an interesting challenge in terms of navigating the archive because it's about 30 hours worth of audio. A lot of it fell within a Radiophonic tradition, tape experiments and things that we're often quite familiar with from those different archives, like from the BBC Radiophonic. I guess the difficult thing or the trick for me in the show was trying to create the sense of slippage through time. How do you take an archive like that from that moment? There's always a kind of subjectivity in terms of your relationship to it. How do you let's say use certain contemporary sensibilities to build something up, that feels like it can speak to an audience in the present, without people feeling "Oh, this is like archival tape recordings", or "this is a familiar language"? Part of it became a process of collaging 30 hours of audio together into something that has this quite slippery sense of time. Very much in the tradition of electronic music. The thing that I really, really love is often you're like, "is this from now? Or is this from like the 1960s?" I guess I was once again in a slightly manipulative like science fiction-ish framing of time. I've very much navigated the sound archive with that sensibility of how do you make something that sits to an audience now. Obviously, it is echoing and operating within the past, but it can feel like it can potentially have a presence in this moment also.

Brilliant. Okay. Well, this is a segment of that music.

—

Looking at this amazing body of research and how it's manifesting in different ways and knowing you. I'm really curious to see, is there a political motivation behind doing this work for you? In an anti-colonialist way? Because it's impossible to do this work without having some very positive, I think, elements of exchange involved.

This is the thing I'd be trying to move on that razor's edge… Like meeting the last surviving composer of the National Institute of Design, Jinraj Joshipura. And realizing how amazing let's say this moment of the '60s, '70s was in India. But likewise, when we zoom out, we're seeing a lot of Machiavellian or devious operations at play. Whether it be like MoMAs project, 1950s exhibition 'Design Today in America and Europe', which is very much this colonizing sense of bringing design and Western sensibility into India within that moment. Post that, everything's like being funded by the Ford Foundation, which is an outpost of the CIA at that time, right?

An alternative to the European avant-garde was American abstract expressionism.

Totally right. It's a fascinating moment to unpack the 20th century, because we tend to think about that postable window with a lot of dreamy idealism. But, specifically in India, it's an interesting theatre, because you're seeing as the British leave, it's where the other soft power mechanisms start to come in. Russia was doing it more through technology, telecommunications, satellites and let's say the space race, but America's strategy was very much one of cultural colonizing South Asia. I guess, I've been trying to explore and celebrate the achievements that were done and made within that window of time, but not be in adoration or blind to the entirety of what was going on with the picture. I think it's important for us to start thinking, with more level heads about how cultures operated across the 20th century.

After chatting to Larry Achiampong, I'm trying to avoid the phrase Afrofuturism, but you're really creating and presenting a kind of Indo-futurism. There's something Utopic in the same way when you're looking at those kinds of ideas by extension.

The way that I've approached it, certain possibilities never unraveled themselves in South Asia. Let's say, due to economic circumstances or practicality. Things that echo in my own life, actually. I came from a culture where I couldn't go to art school. That wasn't really part of the game plan. I feel like I enjoy this process of excavating these histories and creating, once again, these quite slippery timelines and reimagining a possibility. I guess there's a certain fictive playfulness and manipulation of time that I'm really interested in. How do you respond to these echoes of history, but find a sensibility and a language to pull them into the present, and make them speak and give them a life that doesn't feel arcane and doesn't feel like it's embedded in the baggage of history? That's the space that I'm interested in exploring at the moment. I guess thinking about people like Jin Raj. He was offered this scholarship by the Rockefeller Foundation, by David Tudor in the '60s, but he wasn't allowed to go to New York to become this potentially, visionary composer, because the practicalities of India never allowed that to happen. I believe that there were so many voices and so many stories that never came to life. That actually it feels like a responsibility to look into that window of time and to shed light on it. It's a future that never happened. It's a timeline that never completed itself. I guess my politic is very much a personal sense of responsibility to look into that world and actually redraw those timelines of modernism. The presumption that the power and knowledge flowed from the west to the east. The project that I'm working on next is actually a BBC Radio documentary about the life of Jiddu Krishnamurti, and the school that he set up called Brockwood Park in Hampshire. They are teaching this holistic program of education and is still teaching that today. I guess one of the things, the premises of that whole project to me is to deconstruct or dismantle this idea of the influx of South Asian culture and ideas and identity as being a post war phenomenon into Europe. I'm very much interested in Rabindranath Tagore's infusion into British modernism in like the 1920s and the 1910s. To try and redraw that timeline to actually rethink what was modernism? What was defining the avant-garde? One of the things that still blows my mind is in the foundation of the Bauhaus, they're writing letters to

Rabindranath Tagore in response to his like eco-conscious University Santiniketan, which was set up in the 1860s. They're asking him about the foundations of a holistic University. We're presented modernism as a kind of blank canvas but actually it's much more murky. It's much more blurry than that. I think it's that my politic is actually unraveling the pluralities in the timeline.

I want to play another track. I want to play the Laurie Spiegel one. Do you want to tell me about this track?

As a fan of late 20th century, minimal electronic music, it's interesting because so much exists within that canon. Terry Riley, Philip Glass, Reich and, and everything but actually, 'The Expanding Universe' by Laurie Spiegel is about two hours of music that she recorded between 1974 and 1977, when she was part of Bell Labs. One of the tracks – this is a beautiful fact – one of the tracks from 'The Expanding Universe' is actually on the golden disc they sent out on Voyager into space. And we think about the canon of all this music, but actually 'The Expanding Universe' is the record I keep coming back to. I think that Laurie Spiegel is such a visionary. She's in her mid-70s now. Still living in Tribeca. Still making work. It's people like that, that I just find super, super inspiring. Hopefully, Spiegel will be identified as one of the most important figures in Western electronic music in the 20th century.

This is a segment of Laurie Speigel's 'Patchworks'.

—

I know that you've also been working on some music stuff with the filmmaker and artist and ex-Rough Version guest Imran Perretta. I'm curious to and have a question around narrative and what you do. Obviously, he's coming from a more filmic background. But even within you as a musician, how that idea of narrative seems to fit into things structurally or conceptually.

I think working with Imran is… We've known each other for a couple of years. And we ended up sharing a studio together at Somerset House in London. I think eventually, just to the anecdotal sharing of life, your experiences, and your knowledge starts to blur together. Imran obviously, he's coming from this experimental film, language background, artist film. But at the same time, a music lover. We both had this sense where we both grew up DJing. That was our education… I guess starting to work together at first is a process of figuring out and marrying together your language, aesthetics, principles. But I think, as we're evolving, it definitely is stepping into this more narrative space. Thinking about ourselves as both, I guess, children of the diaspora. Trying to find some kind of anchor point or relationship or connection to our histories as characters, entities, beings, within the West. I guess that's sonically, visually, performatively. That's starting to become a driver in terms of what we're doing. There is a sense, at some point, it will be more explicitly within that narrative sensibility. But at the moment we're storytelling through what we're doing but in a very playful way. In a way that is actually one of the joys about making music, especially collaboratively. It sits within a great tradition of people making sound together… What I enjoy about working with him – it's constantly a space of learning for both of us. We both have very different practices, but we get to work together and learn about music. Learn about our histories and ancestries and origins and do research together and speak to people. Work with vocalists and dancers and things like that. We were chatting recently about this. This shared practice allows us a space – it's a very free union for us where you can just do things that we probably wouldn't do with our own individual practices. There's a magic to it in that way, for sure.

We want to be playing that obviously, because it hasn't been released yet, and I look forward to it. I just want to play your last track, which is Test Dept. Do you want to tell us about why you chose this?

Actually, I've become slightly fixated by Test Dept and the whole history of Industrial music, specifically in South London. That's my new little pet research project. It's like suddenly discovering the Nettleton Road down the back of like the Sainsbury's that I go to, at New Cross Gate, that was this house where like Test Dept were based. Actually, in a former synagogue just across the street, which I think now is a Jehovah's Witness church. There was this whole DIY industrial music scene in South London. Test Dept in Nettleton Road, Nocturnal Emissions in Camberwell, and another scene up in Oval where like bands like SPK and that Chris and Cosey, we're hanging out and stuff. You realize the whole of South London had this beautiful history of Industrial music. Very much operating in this moment of resistance to Thatcherite politics, and the beginnings of the erosion of Commonwealth and public space and support and welfare within the UK. I guess like a lot of those musicians operating in that moment. Music in this very DIY, once again, materialist sense of just banging bits of metal from a scrap yard in Deptford. Using that as like a palette for making music. Much in the tradition of improvised music, the Scratch Orchestra, punk, whatever. You have that sense that you don't need to go to music school. You don't need to go to the Conservatoire. You can just get some fucking metal and you can express yourself, right? I guess that sits within my ideas of anti-hierarchical centres of knowledge and production. I just think that Test Dept to me have done so many amazing projects, very much in this kind of anti-Tory reclaiming human dignity, actually. Has been a central premise of Industrial music. Embedded in the provocative language, there is a sense of liberation from a lot of the tyranny that I think like the Tories have brought to Britain, specifically across the '80s. That echoes into the present. I'd encourage anyone to start excavating that history of Industrial music. Its politic is kind of under acknowledged, I think.

> *This is Test Dept, 'Total State Chain'. And thank you so much, Paul, for chatting to me and coming in.*

Great. Thank you so much Fran.

Metahaven

28.10.21

Hi, you're listening to Rough Version on NTS. My guest this month is Daniel van der Velden from Metahaven or half of Metahaven with Vinca Kruk. Metahaven are an incredible duo/ collective who are working with film, theory, writing, graphics, textile works, books and a variety of different media. They have exhibited in places like the ICA and Stedelijk in Amsterdam. Daniel, thank you very much for chatting to me today.

Thanks so much, Francesca. Great to be here.

I want to start by talking about the way that you've used music in your work, because I think that's something that's not necessarily focused on. You've worked with a lot of music in different ways. Firstly, with your film pieces, can you tell me about what your approach to music is?

Our first video works – that we consider a serious video work – was done as music videos. Those were music videos we did around 2014 – 2015. Very much coming out of our own strand of experimental graphic design, at the time. One thing that we felt strongly about in our work in that period was that our graphic work really came alive when responding to music. I think that music has this function of a trigger for us. It's not just a trigger in the sense of what can you do visually? How can you react? But it's really about an interaction between image and sound. Moreover, I also think that these disciplines of visual art and music are not as distinct as we treat the sensory regimes of vision and sound. I think they're very connected and that they are, in some ways, on the path of moving into a single discipline. A single time-based discipline. I think that music is almost too wide a concept to use. I think we can talk about various music. We can talk about the general realm of sound. Then within that we can talk about music, the different types. Music always, inherently, responds to the emotion of the moment. There's always something very, very much of the moment in music. Something to do with temporality that is performative and engaging in ways that images alone are not necessarily. Images can – when they have a time base or a time code – invoke certain feelings. That's something that we're really interested in. Next to that, we're also really interested in a notion of collaboration. The idea that a score, or a way that sound responds to image or image responds to sound, is not a one-way street. It is not something that comes off an assembly line in which there's a fixed order of what parts get produced first but is very much something that takes on the notion of interaction, which focuses on the relationship with the musicians and with composers. For us the aspect of a relationship also really precedes the idea of the availability of music. I think that in streaming culture, the presupposition of availability is something that's very difficult for artists to relate to. Because you are available on the conditions of the streaming platform and not of your own conditions or conditions that you co-created. And I think collaboration is one of the ways in which we love to think about music coming together rather than, let's say, the music being available and ordering it. I think in our work, music and image have a highly entangled position.

> *To illustrate that let's play the track from 'Information Skies'. Just to pre-empt, you gave me a very long list of music and I chose four tracks from your choices. Can you tell me a little bit about this specific track from M.E.S.H.?*

What we're going to listen to is a track by M.E.S.H. which originally was called 'The Black Pill'. It's music that he created using very sophisticated sampling techniques of acoustic instruments. 'Information Skies' is a film from 2016, that engaged with a neo-medieval virtual reality. M.E.S.H.'s work at the time, really embodies that neo-medieval sense that was enfolding us at that time. The music really captures the way in which the film was made. It was made in the Black Forest in Germany, and it has that really dark, textured vibe of an under-lit forest in which seemingly spring, autumn and summer are coinciding into the same seasonal mood. We felt that this track in particular, which is a version of an earlier track he did, is something that really interacted with what the film was going to be.

> *This is a track, as you say adapting 'Black Pill' by M.E.S.H. for 'Information Skies'.*
>
> —
>
> *Daniel, looking at the way that you use music in your film,*

I think there's something really interesting about the way that you approach speed or tempo. There's seems to be a relationship across your film work. A slowing down, that is intertwined with how you use sound. Would you agree? Are you interested in playing around with those ideas of speed?

Yeah, very much so. We're interested in slowing down. The notion of slowing down has been interpreted in the digital age as a sort of Zen therapy against the way in which we've accommodated digital regimes into our lives. But we think that there's more to it. We don't think this is a retreat from the digital. We think that the accommodation of digital regimes is so profound that we, in a certain sense, leave the temporal experience that's associated with constant updates and constant, let's say distraction or the constant punctuation of time, with the notion of the feed that we have. We're becoming so used to that. We've digested it and what that produces is a condition in which time and slowness are possibilities that are really about generosity towards and with viewers. Meaning that when we share a real time in which nothing happens, which is not punctuated by the notion of the update, or the notion of the feed, there's something that we can gain there. That we do not necessarily get all the time in our everyday lives, but that nevertheless reminds us of what life can be and how our lives could be. So, that's not to deny the notion of speed or the notion of constant urgency, but it's to articulate a possibility in which time is not the only way in which we articulate that possibility. Other things, other thoughts, other feelings are slightly more possible. Not just music, but sound plays a role. That's almost as important as the image. That's more or less how we see that notion of time. To add one more thing, when you talk about film work, you always talk about sharing a certain piece of linear time with somebody. You never talk about that in the art world. You talk about portions of a film. You can also potentially talk about the film but seen twice. You can talk about other temporal possibilities that are coming into view when you're not bound to a movie theatre as the context for seeing the film. I think that whilst the digital, or the coming of digital film or video, may initially have been associated with something called 'post-cinema', which is much more about speed, or it's about mayhem, things like that. It is also like a slowed down version of that. That's highly interesting to us.

Another aspect I really love, and it's a bit of a sidestep, is how you address past, present and future. A lot of your work seems to exist in a near future and a semi-science fiction, other space. I'm thinking in your most recent film, but just in general, the concept of how we're addressing our relationship to what tense we're existing in.

Yes. There's the way in which films can have circularity to them or cyclic units within the linear structure that film up to now still is. We love the notion of more circular or recursive patterns. There's a way in which films are also not stories necessarily, but evolving patterns. At the level, when you're not engaging with the story or when you're not engaging with narrative, you're engaging with patterns. Not necessarily abstract patterns. These can be figurative or real or bodily or other lived patterns, but they're not necessarily stories. The notion of the near future – I see what you mean with that. There's a well-documented problem that we have in our day and age which is picturing the future, picturing a better future. There's a lot of writing and a lot of talking and a lot of making that has been done about that. That has given rise, I think, to something that you could call the genre of the near future dystopia. The genre in which there is a vaguely foreboding near future in which certain ideas that we have about the way in which techno capitalism and the environment and other currents have developed, are becoming more articulated. And this genre is also associated with certain camera work, certain visual moods, that are in turn made possible with what has happened to digital cinema, technically, since the 2010s roughly. There is a vague current that runs from, let's say, Scandinavian crime series in the 2010s to 'Game of Thrones' in 2019, purely based on what cameras do. And at the same time, there's a current that runs from Tarkovskian cinema from the '70s and '80s to 'Blade Runner' remakes in the late 2010s. There are still those currents that are about accommodating a certain sense of sci-fi. But we are really interested in breaking through the notion of the dystopia that's associated with that and really trying to think about, ultimately, a more desirable or hopeful embodiment of the notion of futurity. Taking into account that future is always an abstract proposition if you don't render it concrete through some sort of lived experience. Whilst I think we would agree with what you're saying about this notion of the near future, I also think that we need to set it apart from the notion of speculating or even predicting futures that nobody can really predict. It is the very notion of the unpredictability and in a certain sense, the indeterminacy of time that film is a medium to really deal with. It's not that it can ever solve that or give us that future that we want. It's always a coping strategy maybe, rather than a solution. If that makes sense.

> *Yes, a beautiful way of phrasing it. Let's play another track and I want to play your Mdou Moctar because I really liked it. Can you tell me about why you chose this? When did you first hear it?*

Mdou Moctar is a musician from Niger, whose genre is also known as desert rock. It's music that Vinca, the other half of Metahaven, played incessantly, just before the pandemic started. The album with this track is from 2019. I think what we love about Mdou Moctar is the embodiment of space that happens in this track, in particular, but in all of his work I think, which is articulated through the guitar. For us, it's just this really rich and amazing articulation of energy and space basically, that's taking place in his music. His music comes from a long strand of Tuareg music. And there's much more to be said about that historically and culturally. But I would say the notion of space embodied in it is something that we really love in this track of Mdou Moctar.

> *This is 'Kamane Tarhanin' by Mdou Moctar from 2019.*
> —
> *I want to talk a little bit about your approach to language, which is another really interesting thing that goes across quite a variety of your mediums. This sense of poetry and fragmented language, voiceover and different languages. Do you want to tell me what you like about experimenting with communication in that sense?*

When we started to do moving image, we worked with voiceover as a conventional device. A voiceover is the all-knowing narrator, who actually creates the brackets within which a visual timeline unfolds. I think after we did that, we encountered the singing voice in the work of Holly Herndon, who we made music videos with. And there was, of course, a huge difference between those two voices. The voiceover, in its traditional sense, affirms a placeless authority. Comes from nowhere. Literally a nowhere. Somewhere in the assumptions that we have made about how media work, there is a voice there. And it doesn't need to be an authoritarian voice in order to be an authority. The authority idea is much more based on the arbitrary arrival of this voice from nowhere, which we have to imagine is a witness or a narrator or a director or some form of participant in the story. On the other hand, the singer is somebody whose vocation is way more lyrical and less distanced from what is being described. It is one with the music and it is also one with the image. And when we started to work a bit more with voice and a bit more with actors, and the way in which actors could become people that speak with the camera and not just have their voice over an image, we became much more interested in the lyrical possibilities of the voice. To use other languages than English, to articulate thought in other languages than English and to use subtitles as a parallel exploration of a more multilingual space that can exist in film, in which we can celebrate other things than merely the meaning of a sentence or merely the meaning of an exchange of words. That's something we've articulated in a bunch of films since 2016. Something that this relates to is to do with the notion of translation. Something to do with the notion of untranslatability. No translation of another language than English into English is going to capture the full meaning of what that sentence has in its original language. There's going to be many, many mistakes. There's going to be things that don't work and things that work. This is something that is highlighting I think that the way in which films function is not and never supposed to be smooth. So, for us seeing the latest film of whoever, a famous director in English, is always about the idea that everyone supposedly speaks that language, and that meaning can arrive in a smooth way into the minds of the ones who are viewing it. This is itself premised on a relatively limited idea of what the world can be. So henceforth, our interest in poetry from other languages than English and other cultures than the Anglo-American context, brought us in touch with the originals of these poems. Also, with the translations that these poems have had and with the thoughts that the translators have had. The notion of translation being part of what we do is something that has enriched the way in which we know, or we experience language as something that can be felt or sensed rather than just understood. There's one more thing I wanted to add to that. If, for example, in the latest film that we did 'Chaos Theory', there is a dialogue taking place between two protagonists. They're not really in dialogue, but they're sort of in an exchange. One of them speaks Hungarian, and the other speaks English. What's interesting for us is how that misunderstanding does not happen because they're acting on a premise that is not about them both speaking the same language or the same language group. But there's a bond between these two protagonists that's on another level and that actually creates the sense of understanding that these two characters have in the film, even though they don't speak the same language.

I'm going to take a sidestep into one of your other tracks, which is actually an extended collaboration. I'm talking about the Holly Childs and Gediminas Žygus album 'Hydrangea', for which you did the graphics. Do you want to tell me about that collaboration and why you chose in particular this track by them?

We have known Holly Childs and Gediminas Žygus for a good while already and collaborated here in Amsterdam at the Sandburg Institute. At some point, I think it was during the pandemic, Holly and Gediminas approached us, and asked whether we wanted to do graphic design for their album, which had been in the works for two years or so, that was released in 2020, called 'Hydrangea'. That album is a collection of the music from Gediminas who is a Lithuanian composer. It's their music, combined with poetry by Holly Childs, an Australian poet and writer, who has also been in the cohort of 'The New Normal' at Strelka Institute in Moscow, in which we're also involved. There is this sense in which there's this spoken word art or performative text. It's almost an audio book, combined with an experimental electronic album. When I talked earlier about the notion that film and music and audio becoming one discipline, I think that this album, 'Hydrangea', is one example of that. It's one example of how we see cinematic experiences evolve into media where there's no image. In this case, it's really music and words. We were interested in not just a design effort but really the effort of embodying those slow moves towards a more unitary understanding of time-based media. We've also done a few lyric videos, single covers and also their most recent album, which just came out, which exists only digitally. There's a physical album for 'Hydrangea' but there's only a digital album for its follow up, 'Gnarled Roots'. This was also a little bit of a trade because this was the pandemic and for most people the economic models that we use were coming to a standstill and we needed to do something different. We needed to basically do a kind of transaction here, where Gediminas composed a score for 'Chaos Theory' that we are exceedingly happy about. It was really not just the commissioning of a score, but the evolution of a much larger dialogue that had taken place across maybe two years or so, becoming embodied in a score and from our side becoming embodied in a bunch of record covers and lyric videos.

This is Holly Childs and Gediminas Žygus 'A Circle, A Spiral' from 2020.

—

I'm just going to ask you one final question that leads on from that track, which is about your approach to graphics, which is what I knew you as first emerging from, as a medium or discipline. I'm really interested in how you feel your approach to graphics is evolving because in the latest film, for example, there's some really interesting takes on shape and round circles. Obviously in your installations you use a lot of graphic elements. Perhaps, it's an aesthetic question. How are you incorporating the graphic in different ways in your most recent work?

I think that to understand your question there is, when we talk about graphic design or graphics, for example, we talk about a distinct branch of the visual arts that is involved, often commissioned, in the making of visual communication involving a variety of various media and also graphic shapes. And that's technically what graphic design is. But at the same time, of course, graphic design is connected to visual art in many more ways that are, let's say intrinsically methodological, rather than to do with the teleology or goal of whether it should be an artwork or something that's commissioned, or anything in between.

And for us, it's quite important that there's no real difference between the two. Something that can be done for somebody else, or with somebody else, is done with the same energy and the same type of commitment or interests our mind, as something that we do purely as our own research, or something that we publish on our own account, or something that we create on our own account. I think that one important development for us has been that we think about graphics, or shapes, or form in a much more live and imperfect way than the computer invites us to do. For example, the creation of textile work, as we've done it since a few years, involving weaving and embroidery, on the one hand, and let's say cinema or film images, on the other hand, have in common two things. One, is the notion of texture, which is rather than purely an image or purely an image as a smooth thing that's continuous and elegant. There's always an encoding of the image in a texture, whether that's digital film, or whether that's actually a textile piece. And on the other hand, there's the notion of that the thing itself is never completely as you wanted or expected it. You could design this all you wanted, but it never comes about quite as you planned it into an image. That is something that we're really interested in; the fact that there's this tension, or this type of differentiality between intent and outcome. That then needs to be handled, managed, narrated, stretched or compressed to fit with the contour of the expectation, but sometimes can also change the expectation altogether. The notion of rendering into material or rendering into materiality, that's something that's really, I think, a development from the idea of design as something that is very, very smooth. There's clearly not that. Working with, for example, people, actors, in the context of filming, is something that is inherently not about getting the shapes in the right position and getting things organised on a computer screen. It's about mutual interest and a form of relationality becoming something you can see as an image. That is, for us, really interesting to work on and work with. Yes, we're coming from the legacy of graphic design, but we're taking that legacy into fields where design does not have the last word.

To finish off, we're going to play your last track. This is DeForrest Brown Jr. from the album 'Black Nationalist Sonic Weaponry'. Can you tell me why you chose this?

We're very big fans of DeForrest Brown Jr.'s work, 'His Speaker Music'. We met him in 2019 at Unsound Festival in Poland. We're interested in the forcefulness with which DeForrest Brown Jr. uses music as an educational tool, at the same time as an evocative tool, at the same time as a tool for poetry. We have a really hard time to use our work to educate people or to use didactics that's something we're not really good at. I think that DeForrest Brown Jr. is really good at that. You've chosen from the tracks that we've given you, a lot of these tracks, are tracks without rhythm or without beats or without pulse. It had been much more about melodies or moods. With this track, by DeForrest Brown Jr., we're going back into the notion of pulse. We're going also into what is to be understood as a radical reflection on the history and legacy of techno music and its origins. From that perspective, we really admire what he's doing. That's why this was also in our list of most loved music we wanted to play with you.

Firstly, thank you so much Daniel for your time and for coming in. This is DeForrest Brown Jr. The track is 'Of Our Spiritual Strivings' featuring Syanide from 'Black Nationalist Sonic Weaponry'.

Gaika

18.11.21

Hi, you're listening to Rough Version on NTS and my guest this month is Gaika. Gaika is London based and best known as a musician, but also works with a variety of other media, from installation to curation to collaborative projects to writing. I'm bringing him on here in connection to a large collaborative project that he's put together called 'Channel B' at the ICA. How are you?

Okay, I'm awake somehow, after a long night in the studio.

I'm going to start at the beginning, because I remember when the 'Nine Nights' thing started emerging during the pandemic, as a online performance-based platform. Do you want to tell me a little bit about the motivation behind it?

I think we were just a little traumatized from the pandemic, as everybody was. But I think, particularly for me and GLOR1A, we lost a few people. We just felt it seemed that it was another normalized mode of dying for Black people. We just felt like we wanted to do something. And I think more than wanting to just do something, we felt what we actually do with our lives, with our work, with our creativity, with our talent or power – that doesn't really benefit the community that we come from. It doesn't. The music industry isn't really set up to reward the artists full stop. Especially if they're Black. So, we just started thinking, "okay, what can we do?" What we can do is set some sort of example. That's the beginning. Let's try and actually start a conversation about where does the spoils of winning in music – where did the money go? What does it get spent on? There were a lot of live streams that were raising money. I think we were really one of the first ones, because it was something that we had been planning to do, just in terms of trying to perform anyway. I think someone had a venue and we just thought, "Look, we've got to go and do this". It wasn't just about raising money for charity, but also paying people to come and perform in the pandemic. Rather than telling them it's for exposure. Just to try to change the expectation around what you have to do as a up and coming artist. Change expectation around, a show being just about the biggest stars getting paid all of this money. There's no sense of community or collective thought. It's just each man for himself. I found that really weird in my own career as a musician. You are just this entity. Separation from everyone else seems to be encouraged, or competition seems to be encouraged. I don't think it's effective or efficient. With all that in mind, we started Nine Nights as a platform to, I guess, showcase – showcase is the right word. To support Black talent, particularly around alternative or avant-garde electronic music, but not limited to that. Maybe with a more of a focus in that area, because we felt we're those sort of artists, and we've failed to be represented by what already exists.

It is interesting the way that's developed. That was like 18 months ago. Now you're fusing that very much into a three-dimensional space, activated by performances, but with a lot of audio-visual installations by you, by other artists. You are archiving a lot of the performances and stuff coming out of this project. What did you find interesting about making something that was very initially music-led and spillover into something that's in an art context?

That just mirrors my practice. I believe that you've got to do it for yourself. I feel like I can't make a change that's inauthentic to what my life actually is. My practices has really moved towards fine art or towards multi-disciplinary practice for some years now. Part of what we are trying to achieve is to create ecosystems that allow Black artists to self-define. I've been variously told "I thought you were a musician that did fine art, but that I found out that you were a fine artist who did music, and therefore, that's a problem", right? All of these things are creating nonsensical divisions, I think. I think they're really acutely applied to Black people, because there's an expectation of what we shouldn't be doing. And where we shouldn't be doing it. I've always tried to try to push that boundary. So, it was like a natural progression, really. I wasn't going to be like, "Okay, this is my art practice and I'm here doing this. This is some separate thing, that's somewhere else". It's not really helpful.

I remember the first installation I saw you do was 'System' with Somerset House. It was a really amazing fusion of politics, sculptural objects and moving image, stuff from carnival and plants. I'm really curious, do you want to tell me a little bit about the thinking about that, and how you feel your approach to installation is changing?

It's changing. My approach is changing, because I'm doing more of it. Because I'm getting more confident with it. And because I am more concerned with aesthetics than I was then. I mean, I'm still generally led by function over aesthetics in what I do, because it is more authentic for me. In 'System', I felt like Carnival was this representation of immigration. I felt like I wanted to make something that also represented immigration, but from a slightly different perspective. When you go to the Caribbean, there is this phenomenon of all these empty houses where people have, where returnees leave, and they died before they finished them. Then their children don't want to finish them. They don't want to go back. They don't want to go because they've never been to that place. You have all this concrete in a jungle, half done, kind of rotting away. I'm fascinated by those houses. At the same time, I see this, the sound system, as this symbol of power, physically symbol of power. They are physically big. They're physically imposing. They're physically heavy. I guess, in my head, they are two mystery objects – one attracts people, and one is a symbol of people that have been repelled. So, what happens when you put one inside the other or you join them together. And in terms of the technology and politics, those other two things, facets of my own life. I think 'System' was very much like, this is who I am in totality. Let's just put it all in one place. As times progressed, I felt more confident to be more nuanced than then. It's still a learning process. It's still a learning curve. I like the learning. I like to teach myself to think. I'm kind of developing a visual or architectural language. I'm happy to do that in public rather than go away and do some studied research and then come back with an answer. I think for me the point is that it's like you see it. You see the machinations, you see the function, you see the learning and progress, if any has been made.

Let's play one of your tracks. I want to play one of the ones that are influences. Do you want to tell me about the John Glacier track?

I have just heard his voice. I saw him at Corsica [Studios] last week, and I just thought this is something that I think is really good. And I think he's really symbolic of what's interesting about London at the moment.

This is 'Senseless' by John Glacier.

—

Let's talk about the London thing. How do you feel about London as a city and how growing up there has influenced what you're making creatively?

I think I'm in a kind of dysfunctional relationship with the city. I love it but I don't love it. And I think a lot of my work is about that tension. Having been here consistently now, through the pandemic, for the first time in probably a decade without going in and out and stuff like that. It's just heightened that feeling of being really connected to it and to really try and physically build things here. But at the same time the British class system has never been something that's sat right with me. I've never been able to make sense of it or understand why it still exists. I think the fact that it still exists and so viscerally in London, which is such a multicultural place. It's in my face. I have to comment on it. I have to make work about it. I think if I lived somewhere else, or when I did live in other places, I was like less inclined to make work about Britishness and about British things. Because I didn't feel as pressed upon by the class system as I do in London.

I know that you come from an architectural background, and your family, but also architecture seems to be something spilling into your work in a wider sense. Do you think the gentrification and relationship in London as a city, is much a part of how we function in it? I'm just curious to see, do you think there's a connection there? And what in particular about architecture influences or interests you at the moment?

When I was in school, I nearly went to be an architect and then didn't. I think as I get older, and I'm struggling, scrabbling around to describe what my practices, and we work out what it is, I realize it is essentially just an architectural practice, actually. I guess, I've always been trying to build complete environments. Whether that be the sound of it, the look of it, the feel of it. No works feels finished when it's not been all of those things. And I guess that's part of architecture. It's been one of those strange things, where I think some people in that field identified it from the beginning. None of those people were surprised that my work is gone this way. I didn't, but I think it's more of a confidence issue or an issue with looking back at my youth and the difficulties I may have had. It's just a natural progression… I think part of that is as a response to the gentrification of London, of South London that I've witnessed. It feels like a push, it really feels like that. I go where my mum lives and stand there and see these buildings have just popped up and pushed everybody out. I guess my reaction is to try and some way counter that or make something about it, because it's just really apparent to me. I always noticed the buildings. I was looking up at them. I've always been fascinated by them and what they look like and what they feel like and what they mean. Sometimes, these things creep up on people and before they know it, the whole area has changed. Whereas for me, it's just always been super present. And my work has often been a response to that because what else is there?

It's around you the whole time! I get it. Do you want me to play one of your tracks? Do you want to tell me which one you want to play first that you brought in?

London Posse 'How's Life in London'?

Yeah, I love that tune. You're the first person to bring London Posse on the show so I'm very happy. It's very apt. Do you want to tell you about when you first heard it?

When I first heard it? I was a little kid. I was a little kid when I first heard that. I thought it was from around here and this is wild. I probably was too young to really get it. But I remember hearing it and thinking this is music that I like. I like this more than Vanilla Ice – that's all.

I think that's fair! Okay, this is London Posse 'How's Life in London'?

—

Do you want tell me a little bit about your process? How do you start? Does it come out of research or writing? Are you responding to technology? Like how does that work for you?

It starts with writing. Everything starts with writing. I write an essay or a poem or some set of notes to myself. It's nothing like collections of music or collections of scribbles or different sort of things that are not really about anything. But when I sit down and say, "what am I making these sketches about?" Or "what am I making these doodles about?" Or "what am I doing with these little fragments of writing?" I kind of collect them into something that is a body of writing. It won't be song lyrics; it will be an essay or a poem. In my head, that's the backbone. That's the foundation of the building. That's the backbone or the structure – this central text, whatever it is. A lot of the time, no one ever sees that. Then from that, I start thinking about visual things. Start thinking about images and drawings and photos, and what this world that this piece of writing sort of pertains to, actually looks like. Then when I've get my head into a sense of where it is I'm going, then I'll start to write music. And I don't think too deeply about music. I just learned it. It's like to put myself to space on it, let it flow. When I've got all of those things, and there's a structure. Is it a mystery object that's playing the music? Is it some representation of the space? Is it a building? Is it an interface or whatever? That's when the physical bit comes in. Once I've got these things hashed out, I then go back and start again, but build on that framework. I do that a few times. It's like putting plaster on to something or building a pot or something, I don't know. And just flesh it out. It doesn't always make sense. Until some point it does. Invariably, I'll refer back to my original poem and it'll be exactly what I wrote at that time. I think the writing is storing it in my subconscious, and then I just live in that space for a bit. At some point, I'm like, "Okay, I need to actually make that space, not my life". Make it a thing.

I also want to talk about the concept of 'ghetto futurism'. Two terms that I actually have an issue with, but like the way you're reclaiming both of them. The influence of technology on what you do. Do you want to explain a little bit about what the idea behind that was and how that emerges?

Which of the two terms that you find difficult?

> *Ghetto as a word, obviously. Ghettoization is complex and 'futurism' because it's so intertwined with fascism. Hence, people looking for alternative phrasings to things like "Afrofuturist" that are positivist. It's like you're using two negative terms to cancel each other out and create something positive out of it. Do you want to tell me about the idea behind it for you?*

I go through cycles of wishing I'd never said that. But then also thinking, this is exactly the reason why I said it like that. The thing for me is, I was fairly sick of people asking me about Afrofuturism. I have nothing to do with Sun Ra. Like some of his works, but that's a wholly separate thing to my connection with science and technology. Afrofuturism as it has been defined, and it's not been defined by Black people and African people in any way, is something to do with fantasy and escape. Whereas my connection with technology is just based on my actual life. It's like the opposite, the diametric opposite of fantasy or escape. It's just how I grew up and where I grew up, what I was doing, and what I studied and stuff like that. I would always be asked about Afrofuturism. I was like, is this a way of turning the political, or suggesting that the political connotations of what I might have to say is in some way a fantasy? Or is in some way, an abstract comment or an abstract notion? When, again, that's completely the opposite of what I was trying to say. And I think events over the last four years have proven that to be true, right? I just said, "no, I'm not an Afrofuturist, I'm a ghetto futurist". The ghetto side of it was like what people feel when you say that word. When in fact, all we're doing is talking about inequality. In a way, it was a bit of a poke and a play to how people might view somebody like me, because of the way I dress or way I talk. Whatever their preconceived ideas are about me, and what my work is about. It's just so funny, because people will really be mad about this. I don't really know why but they're not mad about that, about Afrofuturism. Which is a suggestion that we have some outcome that is different from being tomorrow. Having a future for us, is fantasy. Having a future for us, is science fiction. So, we've got no history, and we've got not future, so we live in the present. So, our lives are just completely transient. And we see how that operates. For me, the futurist part is if Ridley Scott gets to decide what tomorrow looks like, in an extremely racist way I'm going to comment on that. I also want to decide what my own future looks like. I don't view it as this dystopian fear, xenophobic vision. It can be whatever I want it to be. It can be whatever we want it to be. I guess, there's a side of it that is using two things that are loaded terms and trying to reclaim them. I guess, in some way connected to hip hop or whatever. I think primarily, it was because I didn't like the narrative around my work, in that time, being controlled from the outside. I wanted to put a stop to it.

I think we should definitely get to play one of your own tracks. Let's Play the 'Marchioness' one.

It is collaboration with an artist called Torkwase Dyson, a fine artist called Torkwase Dyson and Ron Trent, the house and techno legend. She's from Chicago. I've collaborated with her a couple of times, and we did part of her work, at Pace gallery, both in London and in New York. Somehow the idea to do a record came up and I wanted to do something that was about London and about the river. One of my earliest memories is losing an aunt in the Marchioness disaster.

Wow.

I think I've written about that in a few things, but it's not a well-known thing. Torkwase's work is about bodies of water and a lot about Black people's relations with water was the transatlantic slave trade. And just in general, waterways. For me, I made this situationist wander around London and went into the studio and made some music. And it came out like garage music a bit. It started making me think about my own life and history, precisely where I've come from. It just kind of flowed out. And then turns out 'Marchioness' was on the other side.

This 'Marchioness' by Gaika.

—

I'm just going to ask you a couple more questions. I want to talk about your NFT project briefly. We're talking about the reclaiming of power around production. You are minting live stream performances. Do you want to tell me about that idea and what you found interesting about that experimental space?

I've started this project with a new platform called Voice, where my approach to it was to create a live stream that use data and real time animation to generate some artwork. And then edit them into NFTs, which is something I'm doing. But in doing these experimental tests, we found that the actual streams were great. We really enjoyed doing them, and suddenly seeing the potential of real time animation or real time rendering and video and performance. And recording those live performances. I started to think, if I'm going to make that into an NFT, that can be something that other people can do. It overlays with what the Nine Nights mission is, which is to look at the economics of music. A performance seems not to live on beyond the moment. But why is that the case? It certainly doesn't live on for the artist. You either have to make yourself sick by constantly touring, or have no way of making any money, or some extra things that you may not want to do in terms of your career. What if you can actually have more ownership of the fruits of your labour. In recent days, it's been in really sharp focus, I ended up in a big debate, an argument with somebody really powerful in music. My point to him was, that I don't think owning master rights in perpetuity is the most efficient way of actually navigating relationship with an artist. Where there's a power imbalance, because you're rich and they're poor. You might make a lot of money for yourself, but the turnover is going to be high, and eventually, it's going to come back and bite you. He just couldn't see there was a validity to what I had to say.

With the structure of capitalism. You're creating this place where creative production and capitalist protests are both intertwined in the same place. And the music industry is exceptionally, very capitalist.

100%. This is a fundamental discussion, a fundamental debate, or a fundamental thing that I feel like I need to overturn. It's a labour issue. It's about paying conditions. It's about rights for the workers, when it's the musicians that are the workers. Everything that I'm doing, is really connected with this issue. It's acute when you throw race into the mix.

It's not just about that, it's about class, it's about everyone. Especially, who is working in the creative industries, where it's like, wait a minute, we don't really have any rights. This guy was saying to me about his legacy and his family and all of this stuff. Then at the same time, to a roomful of Black people, he's not a Black person, that they shouldn't want to own any – there's no point in them owning any of their works. It's like what? It's so brazen. So, for me, when it comes to the NFT thing, if the NFTs can work to just give us more ownership of what we create, then I'm all for it. Because ownership is connected to generational wealth. I'm not talking about having an excess of money, I'm talking about being able to maintain capital in the system. And that combat comes from some form of ownership. Anything that tips the balance back towards the work of someone, I'm all for.

Love it. Get a bit of socialism in there. I totally support. I haven't had a chance to do that for a while! Let's play the last track. This is an unreleased track?

Yeah. I guess it ties into what I'm talking about. This unreleased track – I don't have a name for it. It is a project that I'm doing with a young artist called CHAMBER45 or Chamber four five. He's a guy that I know through the decentralized institution that I'm trying to build. I've got studios, I've got a gallery, I use whatever money I earned to increase the facilities for those places or increase a number of those places. And try and open them up to people who want to make something interesting, and maybe don't have the support from funding bodies or record labels or whatever. My thing is that if there's no one using it, then you come in and develop your practice. Whatever reputation I've got, if you can swing off it then by all means because I'm trying to replicate this. He's just someone that I've met through doing that. He's out DJing and doing his thing he played the first Channel B and absolutely smashed it. I just feel like I can see this plan working through him and through others. This is a tune that was done for a project that we've called Cyborg. We haven't got a name for the tune yet.

Brilliant. Thank you so much for coming in. It was great.

Thank you so much.

Tony Cokes

23.12.21

Hi, you're listening to Rough Version on NTS and my guest this month is Tony Cokes, an American artist working with video and multimedia installation. He's exhibited at MoMA, the Whitney, Documenta, the Berlin Biennial and is currently on show at Felix Gaudlitz in Vienna. And thank you very much for coming in, Tony. How are you?

I'm doing well. Thank you for inviting.

I want to talk about your relationship with music to begin, because it seems to be something quite fundamental to a lot of your video work. They often have audio things; the content seems to be referring to music? Do you want to tell me about what your relationship to music is and why you like to incorporate it into your work?

That's an interesting question. I think it has multiple dimensions. I mean, personally, historically, I feel a little bit like I was raised by teenagers. The presence of popular music was an important part of my childhood. That being said, I also have come to believe over time that sound can provide additional registers that may be textual and, or visual material can't. I think it's a way of encoding certain attitudes towards history, for instance, that don't often find expression in visual culture. Those are primary reasons. I like the idea that sound can provide a supplementary layer, and maybe even a competing and contradictory one to visual or textual material.

A lot of your work – to describe it for people who don't know it – it is largely text-based pieces, against a soundtrack. That are moving very rhythmically. There's a really interesting connection or clash between the audio you're playing, and then the changes of the sentences we're seeing in front of us. There's something very rhythmic in the way that you're using text.

I think there are double rhythms and maybe even competing and contradictory rhythms. I like that idea. It's a way I think of also sometimes focusing the viewer-listener's attention. So that it's not too easy or too similar. That there's almost an implied polyrhythm in the juxtaposition of the two forms.

> *Do you want to tell me about how you choose the music you work with for different pieces. Are they always responding to the content within each different piece? Does the music come first? Or do the words come first? How does that function?*

I guess you could say that I work on them in layers, like I do most things. When I have a topic in mind, usually a specific text, or two or three texts, sometimes I combine texts to create a work, I then begin thinking about soundtrack material. Often the first thing that I decide on in a piece, besides maybe the theme and the textual materials I'm working with, is the soundtrack. When I'm doing that, I am thinking about ways that the sound can amplify or contradict the material that's in the text. In a way, you could say, the text is the first thing that I commit to, but sometimes I do change the music later, after I've begun setting the text. For instance, the other day working on this piece for the Gaudlitz show, I thought it might be interesting to insert a track that I had been thinking about the back of my mind and had listened to over last weekend. It seemed to resonate maybe specifically with the current moment. It was that kind of thing. I make a plan. I start with the sound and I'm, through repetition, mostly looking for the right timings between the text and the music. Then making small adjustments or sometimes even large ones, but usually it's mostly small. Because I usually start off with a very, very simple pattern and template about duration depending on the text. I ear and eyeball it. I don't use a really strict formula. It often takes me multiple passes through in order to get a sense of how the two things feel in relationship to one another.

> *Before we go into more detail about the content, I want to play one of your tracks. Do you want to play a track you have actually used within your work? Have any of these been in your pieces in the past?*

I think all of them at different points.

How about Joy Division, because I'm in a Joy Division mood, do you worry about 'Exercise One' and how you used it?

Yeah. That piece, it's very interesting. Maybe I should set some context that. I did a special intervention on the text. I use a coding system to remove most vowels and compress the lettering of a given text. But I found that for one of the texts that I was working with, a passage from a text by Judith Butler, the theorist, it sorts of fell apart when you took the vowels out. Maybe because of the complexity, relatively speaking of the language. It was hard to be able to glean anything from it. And so, I wound up actually just doing what I would normally do, and that is to quote the text in full more or less. Without changes, without coding. But anyway, she's describing the possibilities of mourning in, let's say, the earlier waves of COVID, last year. I wanted the musical approach to be disturbing, to be quite frank. I knew that track from years ago, I think it was for – I want to say it was a BBC – a live BBC broadcast. It was not really part of the normative regular output. But it had been released with other material, I think it was a four CD compilation. That's where I probably first found it. That was quite some time ago. It always intrigued me because it begins with a long passage of guitar feedback before it comes into focus as a tune. I've always liked it, maybe because it was different in certain ways from their output. There's something about the lyric, which seems very, I guess the best way to describe it might be from a very, very different and not positive perspective. "When you're looking at light from a strange new room". I had wanted to deploy it in some way, but this seemed to be the most appropriate context that I'd come across.

This is 'Exercise One' by Joy Division.

—

Let's talk about your text sources. I think recognised, while I'm looking at your work elements of the Situationist International, Guy Debord, pieces of Mark Fisher. Do you want to say how you sourced that and how you collage it? Because you are sometimes mixing up some of that material. How you're cutting it up is really fascinating. Where do you find it, why do you choose it and mess about with it?

Yeah, that's difficult to nail down. The story is a little bit different with each piece. I like to have even several – two, three at least – bodies of work that I'm working on simultaneously. In large measure, perhaps, to allow myself if I get stuck in one, I can look at another and work for a while. I tend to take excerpts from larger texts, most of the time. There are a few works in which a short article I've done in full, because that was enough time to, enough concentration to allow that to happen. But sometimes things get radically reconfigured. I like to make things appear simple. So, if I'm taking something, it usually has some coherence, maybe as a passage. And if I'm working, say, with multiple texts, I like to have a good feel and juxtaposition between them. Sometimes in looking through various texts, if I'm lucky I find one that combines approaches. I did a work about the use of popular music in enhanced interrogation, torture. In that case, there was a lot of newspaper articles on the subject. There was also at that time, the middle of the first decade of the 2000s, there was the beginning of a lot of academic publication on the subject. I came across one article, I think it was in 'The Nation' magazine, that was written by… I can't remember whether he was English. A humanities scholar of Arab descent, I believe, who had taken both approaches in this article. He would cite some things from newspaper reportage and position it in a certain way. Then he would talk about it in relationship to cultural and theoretical concepts. It was like the best of both worlds. It was the thing of picking the excerpts rather than having to collage the text itself. Other times, I like to juxtapose different voices or different categories of texts to keep things maybe a little more interesting than if it were just a single positionality. Sometimes, let's say very short work which the project that uses the excerpt from the Joy Division track, it was neither possible nor necessary. It was the juxtaposition between the four parts of the piece that provided that relationship. Each of them were direct quotations from a different source. The one that actually uses the Manic Street Preachers with Green Garside on vocals, was an example of a single text. In fact, that was probably the shortest text I used in that project. In that case, it was the last words of a young man who encountered with the police and dies as a result. It was one of those things where it was a really powerful text. I had read it in a few versions. It wasn't unique. It was like a number of people had transcribe these words in a social media context and I thought I'm going to do something else with these words. Powerful though they were. It occurred to me that music might be a way of giving a different register on one's reading the text. Almost from a different position rather than a person's last words. Reciting the lyric seems to imply that there's a certain complicity between the voice in the lyric, and the voice as represented in the text.

> *It seems an apt moment to play 'Between The Clock and the Bed' by Manic Street Preachers featuring Green Garside.*
>
> —
>
> *Another thing that seems to be holding all of the text choices you made together, and this is quite an obvious statement, is politics. Particularly works that seem to be, let's say, critical of capitalism, critical of fascism, racism. All those nice things! You want to tell me a little bit about the political drive behind your choices?*

I think that there are politics in almost everything that we encounter, especially in the world of culture. Maybe some might argue less so in science, although there are often sometimes political implications in science as well. I think, in the popular idea of what might constitute artistic practice. I guess, I grew up in an era where that desire and that drive to see or to underline the political was questionable or seen that way. Because I'm kind of a wilful person, it made me more interested in trying to find ways, to bring legibility to politics in multiple spheres. In everything from academic discourses to newspapers. And for me, I guess that idea, to some extent, I think I was especially as a young person influenced to some extent by the Situationists and their project in a direct way. A way of looking at the world and manifesting it differently. Not trying to conceal those political valences. In fact, trying to amplify them, if that's possible.

> *Another thing that I think is very interesting is the way you approach that material. The way you make the process of reading, which is quite an intimate internal one, external and public. The way you cut up sentences and present them in this very bold font (though you have used imagery and we can talk about 'Black Celebration' afterwards, in particular). I think there's*

something very interesting about shifting how we read or address the process of reading.

I think that is the important element. And I think it's become even more important as the pieces have become more text driven, in a certain way. I think it's almost, maybe the desire to produce new readings out of things already allegedly published and understood. It's almost as though I want there to be possibilities and spaces for differential readings, or readings from positions that are not normatively cited. Then it seemed to me that the idea of actually producing questions around readings, where they're located, who they're for, whether they are private or whether they are perhaps meant to be public, has always been an area of interest and tension for me. In fact, I recently began to have more opportunities to produce works for more general publics and not so much for just gallery-type presentation. I think it goes with that idea about trying to make reading a differential and public experience as opposed to a private one. There's something about, I think, the possibilities of reading that are engaged in a different way when it's not in a direct relationship with the viewer but has maybe even this implication that there will be, either through the scale or through the mode of presentation, that there could be a public aspect to it, as opposed to private. I don't know. I think maybe that even in itself, implies a different position with regard to what texts are for and who they're for and how they should operate in the world. I guess I've always read from a different position than many of the texts that I have encountered in my life. It's that desire to produce a different sort of reading or condition for reading that inspires me to continue doing the work that I do.

Before we play another track, I just want to talk a little bit about fonts, because it's so important. You choose a really bold, very simplified font. Are you always using the same font? Do you vary it?

Sometimes I change things. Sometimes for referential purposes, like if something were originally published in a book, I might use a similar font. Whereas if something may have circulated in a more designed or more historical… But yeah, I try to keep the fonts actually quite simple, because I'm not a designer by training, and I don't want people to get too distracted by arcane font choices. On occasion, I have done things based on particular fonts, but usually I have some backstory reason for doing it. Like the source uses this particular font. That also happens with colour, which a lot of people comment on. I have to keep it interesting. I have to keep it interesting for me, in order to continue doing the work, which sometimes is rather tedious to be honest. The process is repetitive. I run it again, and run it again and change the timings, those kinds of things. It's almost as though for me, I have to change things sometimes. I usually set a pattern and I keep doing it. And then occasionally, either something in terms of subject matter or context triggers some change.

Let's play the Skream track. Do you want to tell me when you used this and when you came across it?

That is actually for one of the current pieces in the show at Gaudlitz. Basically, how it came to us, it was that recently, sometime last year, I guess some tracks that had not been released at the time, were released as a new project, I don't even know, when this particular track was originally released. But it's a different version of the famous track 'Midnight Requestline', and I think they call it 'Requestline VIP' for this purpose. What's a good descriptor, I'm trying to think of what the genre is… More a distorted electro approach to that and it just fascinated me, because it was sort of familiar, and on the other hand, it was completely different. It really struck me. It was like encountering something you claim to know, from a very different perspective. I was even fascinated by the fact that he had done it as opposed to someone else remixing. And it's something also that I was called upon to do a one-off, that I've now incorporated into regular talks. Where I thought – and this is a question that comes up rather commonly – I show a set of videos or excerpts from things in a screening situation, projected large on the screen. And almost immediately afterwards, someone jumps up and asks, "How do you actually show your work?" Because this is a screening situation. And then "is that normative for you?" And actually, the answer is something more complicated. Often, I do arrangements of multiple work or works, at large scale as a part of my practice. Not all the time, but I've been gradually getting there over the last few years. I should do a slideshow of actually, of situations in which the work has been shown to give a specific characterization about the similarities and the differences between the ways in which works are deployed. I was asked to do this one-off talk. And I said, "Well, since I'm not going to talk during this slideshow, I need to have, again, something that will keep the viewers occupied". I'm also interested in working in installation, the possibility of reading any relationship to the body. Often, we think about reading as an activity that happens in – you sit in a corner in a comfortable chair, and you read a text or the newspaper. I'm interested in what happens if your body is activated, while you're thinking. What differences does it mean? I basically needed a track for this purpose. I actually used the track 'The Number One' by Oneohtrix Point Never, which I really liked, and hadn't gotten a chance to use. And it was the mandate for me anyway. It was picked to use in a future project. So now I've done one of those two. It started, as this one-off thing. And now, I have to take the opportunity to use it. The context, I would say is the works that I'm doing for this project have to do with the pasts – multiple pasts. I can't do them all, but the multiple pasts, and hopefully the presents and futures of clubbing, in relationship maybe to COVID as much as anything else. I've been thinking a lot about, what happens to the club, and what will happen to the club as a useful possibility and social possibility. It just seemed totally appropriate. Since the older texts, the more historical texts I use, don't really explicitly refer to Skream's practice, but I like the idea that there's a stretch that one might have to make. That's often the way I approach soundtracks generally. I tell people I don't do period of soundtracks. I know what a kind of desire for accuracy or representational legibility would do. And I try to do something else. Because it's almost like I, again, want to expand the notions and possibilities for what soundtracks can do. It's interesting to me to take something, for instance, that's very contemporary, when you're doing a quote unquote, "historical" subject. Maybe because I'm not so sure the differences that we all often like to ascribe to the historical are accurate in a way. Which is I think one of the things that maybe fascinates me about Mark Fisher's work. The sense that the past is not really resolved. It's only deferred in a way. The problems remain. The language is coded differently, but the essential questions are still there.

Let's play 'Requestline VIP' by Skream.

—

Just to finish off I want to talk about music as a topic within your work. I recognised lines from 'Ghosts in my Life' the Michael Jackson, Mark Fisher text and 'The Morrissey Problem' was another work. The current work seems to also be addressing music as content directly. What do you find interesting about making it not only incorporated in your approach, but also part of the topic that you're addressing?

I think I reached the point where, I think it was probably in the late 1990s, early 2000s, where I was involved for two or three years in a music project. Even though I don't consider myself a musician. It was a kind of offshoot of a long standing, visual and media collaboration I was involved in. And I felt because of music had been important, you could even say, constitutive part of my practice, that it might be interesting to take this detour not only into music, but also maybe as a way of thinking about how music operates. What it does both socially and culturally. That was, I think, the beginning of it. I made a few very short essays about the then state of contemporary music. Things like Bedouin practices as opposed to large scale studio and or live material. It was really interesting to take it on as a topic. Because I myself, at that point, sort of wondered why it was so important, or what its qualities and uses might be. That was the beginning of it. I did a series of works that were like always, for me. I was working on other projects, too. I wrote like the short essays, I want to say in 1997, they didn't get produced for a couple of years. I produced a couple of tests and then shelved them. Then after my involvement in the music, collaboration dissolved, strangely enough, I decided I wanted to actually do most of the essay material and incorporate practices from a variety of mostly people I know, who were thinking about some of the same things. I decided not to limit it to the thing that I had just been involved in. It was really, really productive for me. It's a subject that I've returned to, from time to time. I'm a music fan. I'm thinking about, what is it about music and how it might function in different contexts and either historical or in imagining futures, which also, I think resonates with Mark Fisher's work to a certain extent.

That seems quite an apt moment to play your last track. Do you want to tell me about 'I Need Your Love' by Hackney Polo Club and when you used that?

That is actually the opening track of this new work. In some ways, I think the reason I chose to use it was because it was both familiar and uncontemporary. Is it acid house? Is it garage? Is it house and garage?? Why hadn't I heard it, even though it was produced in 2015? Those kinds of questions are often things that inform my interest in a track. Since this was about histories, I basically on principal use two texts and go back and forth between them in this project. One is a book called 'Discographies' by Jeremy Gilbert and Ewan Pearson which sets up a history and you could argue political themes in acid house. The passage that I borrowed from that book. I thought, "well, here's the acid house, but it's not. It's from a different period". So, a short history meets its child or its progeny or something, which is a kind of juxtaposition. The other text is a book by Rainald Goetz called 'Rave'. You've probably encountered it before. I guess recently translated into English.

By Fitzcarraldo.

It was a text that I'd heard about, but I don't read German well enough to have gotten through it. I thought, "two versions of the '90s from two different locations". One tried I think to capture the experience, and the other trying to contextualize what it meant. And it just intrigued me to go back and forth between those. There's a third channel also that actually gets into some selected ways to deal with the current or recent COVID situation. Clubbing now and what are its desires and its uses. The one thing that it actually did point out to me, working on this project, is that there's more material that one could I think productively work with and think about. So, I think there will be a sequel, but it'll probably take a couple of years for me to get to it. More time to gather material and sift through it.

Thank you so much. This is 'I Need Your Love' by Hackney Polo Club and thank you Tony Cokes for coming in.

Thank you.

Appendix 1: Song Titles

Adam Pendleton
Alicia Hall Moran + Jason Moran - Two Wings
Albert Ayler - Old Man River
Silver Harps - I Am Saved

Alex Da Corte
Janet Jackson - You
Erykah Badu - I Want You
The Breeders - Too Alive
Donna Summer - I Feel Love

Appau Jnr Yiadom-Boakye
Art Blakey and the Jazz Messengers - Caravan
Novelist - 1 Sec (instrumental)
MF Doom - One Beer
Depths of Love - I Just Can't Find a Love

Aria Dean
Young Thug - Me or Us
The Birthday Party - Release the Bats
New Boys - FM$
Modest Mouse - Teeth Like God's Shoeshine

Bedwyr Williams
Haysi Fantayzee - Shiny Shiny
War - Low Rider
The Black Eyed Peas - I Gotta Feeling
Taylor Swift - Shake It Off

Celia Hempton
Ryoji Ikeda - Data.Microhelix
Celia Hempton - Untitled (rehearsal)
Pantera - Mouth for War
Slits - Instant Hit

Dominique Gonzalez-Foerster
Arto Lindsay - Sue Pai
Extourisme - Pangea Innamorata
Perez - Cerveau
Melissa Laveaux - Kouzen

Dozie Kanu
Smerz - Oh My My
Fela Kuti - Colonial Mentality
Koopsta Knicca - Smoking On A J.
Jay-Z - Imaginary Players

Eric N. Mack
Lil' Kim - Queen Bitch Pt. 2
Patti Smith - Easter
Junkyard Band - Sardines
Azealia Banks - Anna Wintour

Fiona Banner
audio.books - Dance your Life Away
Simon & Garfunkel - Silent Night/7 O' clock News
Fiona Banner aka The Vanity Press - SS19/The Walk
Van Morrison - Saint Dominic's Preview (live)

Florence Peake
Igor Stravinsky - Le Sacre du Printemps, IV. Spring Rounds
Igor Stravinsky - Le Sacre du Printemps, XI. Glorification of the Chosen One
The Internet ft. KAYTRANADA - Girl
Maxwell Sterling - Andromeda Sadgirl
Beatrice Dillon - Curl

Franziska Lantz
Franziska Lantz - Es Go
Franziska Lantz - Salute
Drexciya - Lake Haze
Caustic Window - Garden Of Linmiri

Georgina Starr
CCMC - THEDA
Krzysztof Penderecki - Je' t'aime Je t'aime
Georgina Starr - Before Le Cerveau Affamé
Scott Walker - Farmer in the City

Graham Little
A-ha - There's Never a Forever Thing
Orla - Stork
György Ligeti - Glissandi
Sparks - My Other Voice

Hannah Perry
Hannah Perry and OKZharp - Untitled and unreleased track
Mica Levi and Hannah Perry
Erykah Badu - Ye Yo (live)

Haroon Mirza
Haroon Mirza - Untitled tracks from soundtrack to ããã

Imran Perretta
Charanjit Singh - Raga Bhairav
AMRA - Heema
Japan - Ghosts
Trim - Confidence Boost (Harmonimix)

Jeremy Deller
Melodeon Steel Band - The Man Who Sold The World
Jeremy Deller and Jonnie Wilkes - unreleased
Jeremy Deller and Acid Brass - What Time is Love?

Jeremy Shaw
Santo & Johnny - Sleep Walk
Circlesquare - 7 minutes
Freur - Doot Doot
There in Spirit - Dipsomania (unfinished)
Exocet - Demon Seed
Louis Armstrong - What a Wonderful World

Katharina Grosse
Steve Reich Mallet Quartet - 1 Fast
Steve Reich Mallet Quartet - 2 Slow
Katharina Grosse and Stefan Schneider - Stromung
The Jimi Hendrix Experience - If Six was Nine

Kaye Donachie
Janis Joplin - Piece of my Heart
Prince - Sometimes It Rains in April
Justin Timberlake - Cry Me A River

Larry Achiampong
Tracy Chapman - Fast Car
Christie Azumah and The Uppers International - Din Ya Sugri
David Wise - Stickerbrush Symphony
Devonté Hynes - Hair

Lawrence Lek
Lawrence Lek - In My Prime
Liquid - Sweet Harmony
Lawrence Lek - Dive (Heart Sutra)
This Mortal Coil - Song to the Siren

Liam Gillick
Neu! - Hallogallo
Augustus Pablo - King Tubby meets the Rockers Uptown
Workshop - The House of Marvick
∑(No,12k,Lg,17Mif) (New Order and Liam Gillick) - Your Silent Face

Liz Johnson Artur
Shut Up and Dance feat. Nicolette - Single Minded People
Gregory Isaacs - Night Nurse (live)
Sun Ra - Space is the Place
Larry B - I Gotta Pick Myself Up

Madelynn Green
D'Angelo - Brown Sugar
Souls of Mischief - '93 Til Infinity
Floorplan - Never Grow Old
Michelle Weeks & Voices 2 - Can U See The Light (Kings Of Tomorrow remix)

Marguerite Humeau
Jean-François Laporte - Dans Le Ventre Du Dragon
Charles Trenet - La Mer
Angel Bat Dawid - Impepho
Nina Simone - I Wish I Knew How It Would Feel to Be Free
Omar Souleyman - Warni Warni

Marianna Simnett
Oliver Coates - Tommib Help Buss
DMX - Slippin'
AFX - Every Day
SOPHIE - Is It Cold In the Water

Mark Leckey
Acen - Trip II the Moon (Part 2)
Jeremih - All the Time
Jonathan Richman and The Modern Lover - Roadrunner
Cobra Killer - Six Secs

Mark Titchner
Grumbling Fur - The Ballad of Roy Batty
Oxbow - Ecce Homo
Nurse With Wound - Soliloquy for Lilith 1

Martine Syms
The Shirelles - Dedicated to the One I Love
The Shangri-La's - Remember (Walking in the Sand)
Wendy Rene - After Laughter
Charlotte Dada - Don't Let Me Down

Metahaven
M.E.S.H. - Untitled
Mdou Moctar - Kamane Tarhanin
Holly Childs & Gediminas Žygus - A Circle, A Spiral
DeForrest Brown, Jr. - Black Nationalist Sonic Weaponry

Michael Landy
English Baroque Soloists, John Eliot Gardiner, Stephen Varco - Purcell: King Arthur, Z. 628, Act 3: 'What power art thou'
The Wolfe Tones - The Men Behind the Wire
David Bowie - Space Oddity

Mike Nelson
Crosby, Stills, Nash and Young - Almost Cut My Hair
The Fall - Rebellious Jukebox
Love - I'm Down
Shirley Collins and Davey Graham - Hares on the Mountain

Oscar Tuazon & Gardar Eide Einarsson
Gucci Mane - I Can't
Pusha T Feat. Jill Scott - Sunshine
Pet Shop Boys feat. Dusty Springfield - What Have I Done To Deserve This
Little Feat - Willin' (live)

Otobong Nkanga
Ibeyi - Oya
Oumou Sangare - Saa Magni
Letta Mbulu and Hugh Masekela - Mahlalela
Asa - Grateful

P. Staff
Kenji Kawai - M01 Chant 1, Making Of Cyborg
Patty Waters - Hush Little Baby With Ba Ha Bad
The Threshold HouseBoys Choir - So Free It Knows No End
MAW feat. India - To Be In Love (acapella)

Paul Maheke
Mihasu - Walking Hand in Hand in the Rain
Nina Simone - Along Again Naturally
Nkisi - Can You See Me
Michelle Gurevich - Party Girl

Paul McDevitt
Gajek - Micromaniac
Starka Rzeka - Starka Rzeka
Ghédalia Tazartès - Repas Froid
Paavoharju - Uskallan

Paul Mpagi Sepuya
Yola - Ride Out In the Country
Annie Lennox - Little Bird
David Bowie - Word on a Wing
Stevie Wonder - Golden Lady
Stevie Wonder - Don't Your Worry 'Bout A Thing

Paul Noble
Denim - Job Centre
Daddy Hole - Theme
Daddy Hole - Outro
Paul Noble and Laetitia Sadier - Dot to Dot
Charles Dodge - Speech Song 3

Paul Purgas
Jeff Mills - Utopia
Paul Purgas - We Found Our Own Reality
Laurie Spiegel - Patchworks
Test Department - Total State Machine

Philippe Parreno
Mikhail Rudy - Petrushka
Mogwai - Black Spider
Yussef Dayes & Alfa Mist - Love is the Message
ARCA - Mequetrefe
Edgar Varese - Desert
Mac Miller - Small Worlds

Prem Sahib
Barbara Mason - Another Man (instrumental)
Prem Sahib - Cul-de-Sac
Arthur Russell - This Is How We Walk On The Moon
AHMD - Death Drive

Rachel Maclean
Björk - Jóga
Dorian Electra - Gentleman
Kenneth McKellar - Skye Boat Song
The Knife - Silent Shout

Rhea Dillon
Dedekind Cut ft. DJ Shadow & Chino Amobi - Conversations with Angels
J Dilla - Stop
Outkast - God (interlude)
Nina Simone - Women (live)

Rhys Coren
Haircut 100 - Evil Smokestacking Baby
Sylvester - Over And Over
Love International - Airport of Love
Queen - Cool Cat

Scott King
Alan Vega - Love Cry
William Byrd - Agnus Dei - Mass for 5 voices
The Deviants - You've Got to Hold On
Supremes - Back in My Arms Again

Scott Treleavan
Alice Coltrane Turiyasangitananda - Rama Guru
Psychic TV - I.C. Water
Élaine Radigue - Les Chants De Milarepa: Elimination Of Desires
Grumbling Fur - Dancing Light

Sebastian Jefford
Oneohtrix Point Never - Lost But Never Alone
Mica Levi and Oliver Coates - Xhill Stepping
Sun Ra - When There Is No Sun
Courante M. M. Wüstrow - Dances from 'Terpsichore'

Seb Patane
Seb Patane - Abdomen
Fog School - The Fog
Dj Taye - We're Thru
The Ecstasy of Saint Theresa - Sooper Kosmos (Love stepping in Disco Inferno remix)

Steven Claydon
Cabaret Voltaire - Big Funk
Add N to (X) - Buckminster Fuller
Shut Up and Dance/Blackman - Bastards (remix)
2UP - Microcosmos

Tai Shani
Holger Czukay - Fragrance (Ode to Perfume)
Mandy - The Langley Schools Music Project
Maxwell Sterling - Tenderness
The Mackenzie - Higher in the Sky
Coil - Ostia (The Death of Pasolini)

Tanoa Sasraku
Madonna - Drowned World/Substitute for Love
Camille Saint-Saëns (Performed by the Leopold Stokowski, National Philharmonic Orchestra) - Danse Macabre
Faithless - Drifting Away
SOPHIE - Is It Cold in The Water?

Tenant of Culture
Gabber Eleganza & HDMIRROR - Frozen Dopamina
Lawfandah - Don't Dispair
The Fall - Lost in Music
The KLF - Chill Out

Trevor Paglen
Eric Satie - Vexations
Dietburg Spohr & Ensemble Belcanto - Hildegard von Bingen: Ordo Virtutum
Holly Herndon - Eternal
Steve Reich - Europe: During the War

Wolfgang Tillmans
Wolfgang Tillmans - Device Control
Wolfgang Tillmans - Fast Lane
Mr Fingers - Can You Feel It

Appendix 2: Images

Alex Da Corte
TRUE LIFE
2013
Archival pigment print
37.5 × 30 in
Courtesy of the artist.

Appau Junior Boakye-Yiadom
Carmine Lake
2015
C-type Print
Courtesy of the artist.

Bedwyr Williams
Cracking Couple from Greater Manchester Area Manage To Make It To Their Second Home In North Wales Despite COVID Lockdown Still Being In Place

Celia Hempton
Quebec, Canada, 29th September 2015
2015
Oil on wood panel 20x25cm

Dominique Gonzalez-Foerster
Volcanic Excursion (A Vision)
2021
Installation view
Courtsey of the artist.

Dozie Kanu
RIMOWA Shell Stool
2018
Hand carved marble, Rimowa suitcase component
46 × 38 × 33 cm
Image courtesy of Rui Wu.

Fiona Banner Aka The Vanity Press
Font, Slipstream
2019
Oil on found painting
51.5 × 41 cm

Florence Peake
Rite
2018
Dancers Iris Chan and Katye Coe.
Photo by Anne Tetzlaff

Franziska Lantz
gateway (THAMES)
2016
Metal, bones, string

Georgina Starr
Quarantaine
2020
Film, 43 mins
Photo by Amy Gwatkin.
Courtesy the artist, Film Video Umbrella, Glasgow International, Leeds Art Gallery & Art Fund.

Graham Little
Untitled (Drawing Room)
2017
Gouache on paper
62.2 × 50.4 cm, image size
92.5 × 78.5 cm, framed
Courtesy of the artist and Alison Jacques, London

Haroon Mirza
Stone Circle
2018
Courtesy of the artist and Ballroom Marfa.

Imran Perretta
The Destructors
2019
Film still
Courtesy of the artist.

Jeremy Deller
Bless This Acid House
2022
Screen print on aluminium
63.5 × 87.5 × 0.4 cm
Courtesy of the Artist and The Modern Institute/ Toby Webster Ltd., Glasgow
Photo by Patrick Jameson

Kaye Donachie
The eclipse that settled
2018
Oil on linen
55.5 × 40.5 cm
Courtesy of the artist and Maureen Paley, London.

Lawrence Lek
AIDOL
2019
CGI 4K Video, 83mins
Film Still
Courtesy of the artist and Sadie Coles HQ.

Liam Gillick
Cadence!
2021
Courtesy of the artist and Maureen Paley, London.

Madelynn Green
Devotion
2020
210 × 210 cm
Courtesy of the artist.

Marguerite Humeau
The Prayer, A marine mammal invoking higher spirits
Exhibition view, Clearing Brussels
2019
Polystyrene, polyurethane resin, fiberglass, steel skeleton
295 × 100 × 204 cm
Photo by Eden Krsmanovic
Courtesy of the artist and C L E A R I N G New York/Brussels.

Marianna Simnett
The Bird Game
2019
Digital video still.
Courtesy of the artist.

Martine Syms
Installation View, Incense Sweaters & Ice,
Graham Foundation, September 26, 2018 - January 12, 2019
Photo by Nathan Keay
Courtesy of the artist and Bridget Donahue, NYC.

Mark Titchner
The world isn't working (ND)
2017
Courtesy the artist.

Michael Landy
Saint Jerome Beats His Breast
2012
Collage, ink on paper
77 × 57cm
Courtesy of the artist and Thomas Dane.

Mike Nelson
To the Memory of H.P. Lovecraft
1999-2008
Installation view from Psycho Buildings: Artists Take on Architecture at Hayward Gallery, 2008.
Photo by Stephen White.
Courtesy the artist and Hayward Gallery, London.

Oscar Tuazon & Gardar Eide Einarsson
The Pig Will Eat Its Children
2012
C-print on aluminium
154 × 119 cm
Courtesy of the artists and Maureen Paley, London.

Otobong Nkanga
In Pursuit of Bling: The Transformation
2014
Tapestry - Woven textile
Viscose, wool, mohair and bio cotton
182 × 180 cm

Paul Maheke, Nkisi & Ariel Efraim Ashbel
Sènsa
2019
Performance part of Meetings on Art, La Biennale di Venezia - Biennale Arte 2019
Photo by Marco Franceschin
Courtesy Delfina Foundation and Arts Council England.

Paul McDevitt
Notes to Self: 15 June 2021
2021
Pen and pencil on paper
30 × 21cm

Paul Mpagi Sepuya
Mirror Study
2018
34 × 51 inches
Image courtesy of the artist, DOCUMENT, Chicago, and Vielmetter Los Angeles.

Paul Noble
The Cleaner
2022
Pencil on paper
64cm × 48cm
Courtesy of the artist.

Paul Purgas
Courtesy of the artist.

Rachel Maclean
The Lion and The Unicorn
2012
Digital video still.
Commissioned by The Edinburgh Printmakers for Year of Creative Scotland.

Rhea Dillon
Icarus! Icarus! Icarus!
2020
Oil and acrylic on canvas

Rhys Coren
A Stella
2021
spray paint, acrylic and pencil on board
50cm × 50cm

Scott King
Suicide 'American Supreme' cover
2022
Art Direction by Scott King
Photo by Jonathan de Villiers

Scott Treleaven
I Put it You, That Time Has Come Again
2018
Gouache, acrylic and collage on paper
diptych, each panel 41.5 × 40.5"

Seb Patane
The Three Crooks
2019
Ballpoint pen, acrylic, collage and enamel on printed paper
29 × 20 cm

Sebastian Jefford
Whatever the weather, the sun always shined on Friday mornings
2022
Polyurethane foam, acrylic, plastic snap fasteners, styrofoam, polypropylene fabric, paint marker, cardboard, wood
190 × 147 × 22 cm

Steven Claydon
The Graven in Tandem
2012
Thermalite, Formica, polyurethane foam, ceramic, parcel tape
132.0 × 64.0 × 60.0 cm
Couresy of the artist and Sadie Coles HQ, London.

Tai Shani
DC Semiramis
2019
Installation
Turner Prize 2019 at Turner Contemporary.
Photo by David Levene

Tanoa Sasraku
O' Pierrot
2019
Photo by Lewis Brander.
Courtesy of the artist.

Trevor Paglen
NSA/GCHQ Surveillance Base, Bude, Cornwall, UK
2015
Courtesy of the artist.

Wolfgang Tillmans
Outside Planet, view
1992
Courtesy of the artist

Thanks to Femi Adeyemi for agreeing to the show in 2016. Rough Version producer Paola Laforgia, as well as Josh Farmer, Rory Bowens, Fergus McDonald, Flo Dill and all at NTS.

Additional thanks to Amanda Burzic, Anna Corrigan, Ari Nielsson, Charlotte Ponzio, Isabelle Bucklow, Jessica Wrigglesworth, Paola Gavin and all the artists and their studios.

Rough Version
The NTS interviews with Francesca Gavin, 2016-2021

First edition, 2022

www.francescagavin.com

These are transcriptions of the first five years of Rough Version on NTS Radio, created between 2016 and 2021. The archive and ongoing episodes of Rough Version are audible online at www.nts.live.

NTS

Edited by Francesca Gavin & Hans Munk
Designed by Hans Munk

Printed by Tallinn Book Printers
Set in Times and CMU Typewriter

Published by At Last Books
www.atlastbooks.com

ISBN: 978-87-972616-2-0